Nation and Family

THE SWEDISH EXPERIMENT IN

DEMOCRATIC FAMILY AND POPULATION POLICY

BY

ALVA MYRDAL

THE M.I.T. PRESS

MASSACHUSETTS INSTITUTE OF TECHNOLOGY

CAMBRIDGE, MASSACHUSETTS, AND LONDON, ENGLAND

Original Edition © 1941, by Harper & Brothers

Foreword by Daniel P. Moynihan and
Preface to Paperback Edition by Alva Myrdal © 1968, by
The Massachusetts Institute of Technology

First M.I.T. Press Paperback Edition, March 1968

Library of Congress catalog card number: 68-16727
Printed in the United States of America

NATION AND FAMILY

FOREWORD TO THE
PAPERBACK EDITION

Some three decades ago the Carnegie Corporation, with its singular and persisting sense of what matters, brought Alva and Gunnar Myrdal to the United States to undertake enquiries into two areas of social policy destined to assume a pervasive importance for American life during the years that followed. Gunnar Myrdal, and his associates, began the studies of the position of the Negro in the United States which produced, in 1944, the now classic work *An American Dilemma*. Alva Myrdal addressed herself to what was then called the issue of "population policy," and in 1941 published her no less distinguished volume *Nation and Family*.

For a period it would have seemed as though history had sidetracked both efforts. The 1940's were a time of intense preoccupation with foreign affairs, to the near exclusion of other matters. In the 1950's there was a general retreat from too intense an involvement with social issues of any kind, certainly ones so clearly marked "Danger" as those of family and race. Even had such matters eventually gained a place on the public agenda by virtue of their inherent and unavoidable relevance, it could well have been supposed that books written in the remote past of economic depression and political isolation would either have been forgotten or dismissed. But nothing of the sort has happened. Both books have lived, and increasingly their influence on events can be seen at work. This has, of course, been most conspicuously so in the case of *An American Dilemma,* and the reasons for this are clear enough. No study before or since has so carefully assembled and organized the facts of race relations and Negro life in America. Neither has any related those facts to the *values* of American society, so as to predict which way events would move. It will be recalled that Gunnar Myrdal had declared that the near stalemate in race relations that had persisted for two generations after the national compromise of the 1870's, which brought an end to the reconstruction period, was itself coming to an end. A period of considerable forward movement for Negroes was about to begin. This was so, Myrdal had argued, because the position accorded to the Negro American in reality was so far removed from that to which he was entitled under the terms of "The American Creed" that eventually the larger society would be forced by its own awareness of the contradiction to alter the reality in the direction of the ideal. Now, a generation later, with many such advances securely embedded in legislation and public policy, it is perhaps difficult to grasp the audacity of Myrdal's assertion — in the midst of the Marxist 1940's — of his belief in the sincerity of bourgeois morality. But he said it, and events have proved him correct. That this progress has come about largely through the intervention of brilliant Negro strategies, abetted by the pervasive influence of television, does not alter the plain fact that in the end the nation acted not because it was prudent to do so, or even necessary, but, as President Kennedy said, because it was right.

Because *An American Dilemma* has been almost continuously in print, and has been available in paperback through most of the 1960's, Myrdal's thesis and its essential soundness have been rather constantly in view, and readily acknowledged. The experience of *Nation and Family,* out of print in hardcover since 1945 and only now, for the first time, available in paperback, has been significantly different. It has had almost an underground life, having been directed to a subject that may have been on the hidden agenda of American politics, but has certainly not been much in view. *An American Dilemma* was addressed to a problem that any moderately informed citizen knew was there, even if he had no notion as to how it might be solved, or indeed had no desire that it should be solved. *Nation and Family,* by contrast, sought to elucidate problems concerning government family programs, an area of social policy few persons deemed even to exist. Perhaps, especially, political liberals of the kind who have been most concerned with issues of racial equality have, in the United States, been more or less traditionally averse to the points of view put forth in *Nation and Family.* Indeed, the general statement might be made that the more anxious a given person might be to see government involved with social questions generally, the more vigorously he would likely oppose the very notion of "government interfering with family life." Moreover, although "written in the United States with American problems in mind," the book takes as its case in point the problem of a declining birth rate in Sweden and the apparent imminence of depopulation, that is, the very opposite to the circumstances of the "population explosion" that has come to be a pressing issue in postwar America. As it happens, however, these difficulties constitute the essential strength of the book and give to it a potential influence today as great as or greater than that of *An American Dilemma* itself.

The theme of *Nation and Family* is that in the nature of modern industrial society no government, however firm might be its wish, can avoid having policies that profoundly influence family relationships. This is not to be avoided. The only option is whether these will be purposeful, intended policies or whether they will be residual, derivative, in a sense concealed ones. This is a conclusion drawn not from books but, if you will, from nature. In the early 1930's, the Myrdals became concerned about the seemingly imminent decline of the Swedish population and put forth a program to counter this trend in their book *Kris i befolkningsfragan,* published in 1934. From that work, and from her subsequent study, Alva Myrdal developed the two general propositions that inform and shape the argument of *Nation and Family.* The first is that a family policy (or population policy as the term then was) "can be nothing less than a social policy at large." Such a policy is not so much the subject of one social program as an object of all such programs. The second is that "constructive social engineering" requires a knowledge of values as well as of facts. Facts indeed are to be seen in the light of values. This latter point is at the heart of Myrdalian analysis: social values are neither to be assumed nor merely declared. They are a fully equal cognitive category in their own right, subject to the same processes of enquiry and verification as the "facts" themselves, and altogether as important. Gunnar Myrdal's entire hypothesis as to the future of white-Negro relations in the United States rested on his analysis and assessment of the dominant American values relating to issues of liberty and social equality. By the same process he and Alva Myrdal had earlier developed what they judged would be a viable family policy for Sweden. The first questions to be answered concerned such matters as how the Swedes felt about one another, about children, about government. Thereafter came program proposals. Thus they reasoned that a *sine qua non* of any such policy would be that it provide "all the freedom for the individual that is compatible with social orderliness." But also, given the Swedish concern for comfort and "nice things," there could be no question of sacrificing the standard of living for the joy of having more babies. Further, in that Swedes place considerable store on keeping the range of living standards in a fairly narrow band, so that few persons are dramatically better or worse off than the generality of folk, a family policy must promote equality. Finally, and only with these other values laid down, it was to be said that the Swedes placed an "undeniably positive valuation on children, family, and marriage," happily to the point even of being prepared to reproduce themselves given a reasonable opportunity to do so.

In structure *Nation and Family* is divided in two parts. The first, "Problems and Principles," sets forth the argument for an open and conscious family policy in the United States and elaborates the principles that might underlie any such policy anywhere. There does not exist in the literature a more careful and lucid exposition of the subject than in this superb feat of pure intellection. The second part, "Provisions in Sweden," describes the policies that had evolved by then in Sweden. It would be hard to find a more persuasive application of a set of principles to a set of circumstances. Precisely because these circumstances were in so many ways different from those now faced by the United States, Part II becomes, in effect, an exercise in problem solving, a brilliant exposition of what must be known and considered if a viable family policy is to be developed for a given time and place, and all the more instructive because the American reader is not required to yield emotional as well as logical consent as the process works itself out.

The reasonableness and clarity of Alva Myrdal's writing ought not to lead anyone to suppose that it was an exercise in pure dispassion, prompted by nothing greater than a distaste for administrative untidiness. It was a work born of a crisis in Sweden — the most primitive and fundamental of crises, that of survival of the race — and almost certainly urged on by a premonition of the crisis that was to come, has come, in the United States.

Following World War I, the net reproduction rate in Sweden, defined as the number of girls that will be born to a thousand newborn girls, had fallen below the roughly 1.1 ratio required to maintain a population, and it even dropped below 0.75 during the 1930's. In 1935 a Population Commission was established to propose measures to reverse the trend. A wide-ranging program of government services for children and parents was begun, and with it came the world-wide reputation of Sweden as the prototypical welfare state. In the 1940's, a second wave of family programs, this time including cash children's allowances (Alva Myrdal has consistently argued for payments in kind) rounded out the system, which indeed became the most comprehensive and carefully thought out family program of any in the industrial democracies. And it worked. Not, to be sure, as dramatically as its enthusiasts might have forecast; but to expect government programs to bring about any very great change in human behavior in a comparatively short time is merely to evince a limited understanding of what government programs can do.

During World War II, the net reproduction rate once more rose above one thousand, momentarily peaked, and then settled down at a point just below that required to keep the population from diminishing in the long run, but quite enough to maintain a steady if small increase for the time being. Marriage seems to have become a bit more popular; although it is hardly to be thought that any very great number of couples were swept away with a passion to reproduce. The average age of persons in Sweden entering their first marriage remains high (in 1962 it was 26.8 years for bridegrooms and 23.8 for brides) and fully 20 per cent of those reaching adulthood never marry at all. The number of divorces per 100,000 population has more than doubled since the 1930's, but almost all the rise took place during World War II, and the rate has been more or less unchanged since 1950. The ratio of illegitimate births has risen somewhat (to 12.24 per cent in 1962), but in urban areas the ratio has actually been declining. (Urban ratios have always been considerably greater than those of the countryside. As the population has become more urban, the over-all ratio has accordingly increased, even though the urban ratio has actually been dropping.) And with all this Sweden has remained one of the freest societies in the world, with one of the highest standards of living and very possibly the largest degree of social equality of any nation on earth. In Sweden welfare works. If the Swedes do in fact shoot *themselves* rather more often than Americans do, it must be pointed out that they shoot *each other* hardly at all, a fact even President Eisenhower came eventually to see. If they drink a bit more than may be good for them, it is after all their money, and it must be acknowledged that assuredly it is their climate. Let there be no mistake: the welfare state in Sweden, with its incomparable array of public services, combined with a passionate concern for individual liberty and personality, is one of the rare achievements of human history. In very considerable measure it derives from, consists of, the principles and programs that evolved under the rubric of a population and family policy, and in that measure the policy must also be judged an extraordinary success.

Clearly Sweden undertook such a policy with singular advantages. There are few nations, perhaps none, in which the *"premises of knowledge"* and *"premises of valuations,"* to use Alva Myrdal's terms, could be so satisfactorily established as in Sweden. It is a small country, with excellent social statistics. (Typically, the work of the Population Commission established in 1935 began with a special, mid-decennial census.) The population is homogeneous to a fault, seemingly with a widely shared value system (as reflected by the comparative ease with which Swedes organize themselves into nationwide bodies of consumers, workers, political party members, and such like). Probably, also, the existence of an official state religion helps considerably. Just as it has been noted that it is the monarchies of Europe that provide the setting for the most stable democracies, it may also be that the existence of a nominal national creed in essentially secular nations such as Sweden and England gives a presumption of legitimacy to government actions with respect to minor children (as, for example, in adoption practices) that a congeries of warring tribes such as inhabit North American can never know, indeed can only dimly imagine. Modern Sweden has been, moreover, a surpassingly prudent and competent society. It was last at war in the age of Napoleon, and even before that had learned to eschew the fantasies of power, messianic and demonic alike, that continue to possess other nations of the world.

It is at least worth speculating that a further element contributing to the stability and progress of Swedish society has been the success with which academic intellectuals — of whom the Myrdals are a world-renowned example — have developed a role for themselves in the affairs of state. The essence of this success seems to reside in the distinction between superior knowledge and superior wisdom. Possessing the former with respect to many issues, they have been careful not to claim the latter, and as a result seem to have found a more willing audience than some of their more ambitious colleagues to the west. Alva Myrdal writes: "The leaders both in the social sciences and in politics have imbibed the teaching that facts make up the world of theory but that besides knowledge of facts explicit value premises are needed for rational practical action."

But all this adds up only to the fact that Sweden had the potential for formulating and adopting the kind of population and family policy that did come to pass. The essential point is that it did adopt one, having first of all conceived the possibility of and the need for such a policy. Herein lies the essential difference between the state of affairs in Sweden as against the United States and the essence of the message that Alva Myrdal addressed to an American nation which was not listening a quarter century ago. *A nation without a conscious family policy leaves to chance and mischance an area of social reality of the utmost importance, which in consequence will be exposed to the untrammeled and frequently thoroughly undesirable impact of policies arising in other areas.* Only now, with many opportunities missed, and in particular with a generation of Negro slum youth already sacrificed with neither dignity nor purpose, do we begin to realize that Alva Myrdal was right.

How is it that in modern industrial states, fully alive to the advantages and necessities of more or less comprehensive national policies directed to issues such as employment, education, health, housing, transportation, agriculture, the idea of a family policy seems so difficult to conceive, much less to develop? It came late, after all, even to Sweden.

Myrdal herself suggests that something of a cycle is at work. Social reform policies, she argues, can be thought of as passing through three stages: a paternalistic conservative era, when curing the worst ills is enough; a liberal era, when safeguarding against inequalities through the pooling of risks is enough; and a social democratic era, when the prevention of ills is attempted. Certainly something of this sort can be seen in the evolution of public health policies, an immensely significant but little explored area of political life. Such a pattern will also be found in the movement of employment policies from sporadic relief programs, through risk-sharing stages, such as unemployment insurance and workmen's compensation, and finally on to the comprehensive manpower programs which, in countries such as Sweden, maintain a highly productive work force at minimal levels of unemployment. In a sense this is an evolution from nineteenth to twentieth century programs, a development spurred as much by changing patterns of what *can* be done as by evolving notions of what ought to be.

In the area of family policy, however, the grip of the nineteenth century has hardly weakened. The most important effect of this heritage has been to locate the subject of family at precisely the wrong end of the liberal-conservative spectrum that emerged in the course of the industrial revolution. Laissez-faire liberalism was concerned to liberate not just the individual entrepreneur from the shackles of state control but, by extension, all individuals from the interference of all institutions. Even as this tradition subtly transformed itself into the present-day concern to use the powers of the state to ease the impact on individuals of the more gross hazards of life, the concept of family as a potentially restraining influence, and the judgment that the state had, in any event, no business getting involved with it, somehow persisted. This judgment was if anything confirmed by the opposite course of events on the continent of Europe, where the concept of active government concern with family life became ineradicably associated with political despotism and clerical conservatism, the classic enemies of nineteenth century liberalism. In truth, the first deliberate government policies directed toward family life arose in connection with the desire of some nations to ensure a sufficient supply of soldiers, and from the outset such policies were concerned not so much with families per se but rather with *familles nombreuses*. This pronatalist conservative cast was disastrously confirmed by the zeal that the Roman Catholic church exhibited for the subject both then and since. The nineteenth century Church, especially in its Papal pronouncements, had an honorable record of resisting the excesses of liberal economics so far as they affected the life of the common workman. The Church insisted, for example, that wages had to be set in relation to the needs of a man's family rather than through the impersonal mechanism of the market. Catholic social doctrine argued, then and now, that the family was the basic unit of society, and that nothing — neither the freedom of enterprise, nor the power of the state, nor the fortunes of political parties — nothing was so important. However, the prelates did this in the company of, and often in the name of, some of the most decayed and forlorn aristocracies ever to adorn a declining cause. As a result, Catholic social thought with respect to family life became inextricably involved with the political ambitions of Catholic powers and of the Church itself. Anxiety about Catholicism has been a potent influence in American politics; not so great as concern about race but of the same order. (One recalls the passage in F. Scott Fitzgerald's notebooks: "When I was young, the boys on my street [in St. Paul] still thought that Catholics drilled in the cellar every

night with the idea of making Pius the Ninth autocrat of this republic.")
Catholic opposition to birth-control programs came to be seen as part of a
policy designed to breed Catholic political majorities, and many of the attitudes derived from the anti-Popery era have lived on despite the disappear-
ance of their *raison d'être*. An American liberal of the present moment who
raises the subject of family stability as a social issue will almost automatically
be subjected to a loyalty oath on the subject of family planning. Indeed, when
the Americans for Democratic Action took up the subject of family life at
their 1966 convention, a resolution emerged which, in its entirety, declared
ADA to be in favor of enlightened legislation in the field of "abortion, birth
control, and divorce."

Indeed, profamilial attitudes became so identified with political conservatism that when those most eminent of Victorians, the Bolsheviki, came to
power in Russia, many had in mind to dissolve family life altogether. As if to
confirm their judgments as to the political cast of profamilial policies, as
Russia became increasingly a reactionary state it began to impose an ever
more rigid moralism in family matters. Even in twentieth century Sweden,
the subject was a difficult one to raise or at least to disentangle from the inane
discussions of birth control. A touch of Marxism (or Benthamism) will do
no harm here: the plain fact is that the industrial system had little room for
such concerns. Alva Myrdal writes:

The state and the individual were always the two poles of interest. Social and
political controversy was occupied with the question of the interrelationship of
these two social entities. Whether the issues be stated as democracy versus authoritarianism, individualism versus collectivism, or competition versus cooperation,
the dualism was unvaried — state and individual. What distribution of power and
responsibility should there be between those two? That there might be still another
competing center of attention — namely, the family — was mostly lost sight of.
Similarly, the family was strangely neglected in education and in literature. There
was, it is true, outward respect for the family with a whole system of verbal generalities, taboos, and moralities; but it remained outward only. The content of education was devoid of any attempt to disseminate knowledge which would prepare
for better functioning of the intimate relationships within the family. The family
was exalted in literature in the form of idyls; but in the idyls there was the essential falsity of Puritanism. Neither the problems nor the values of the family were
treated with such respectful honesty as might enhance its competitive value.

In such circumstances it takes a widely perceived emergency to change the
course of events. The interest of society in a stable, functioning family life is
fundamental. But if that interest is not perceived as such, matters can deteriorate considerably before any great number of persons takes heed. Family
matters, in other words, are not a subject for which there is a well-established

alarm system that alerts the larger society to dangers as they arise. Something truly alarming has to happen. For Sweden it was the prospect of depopulation, a trend that had developed gradually but that was accelerated by the world depression in the 1930's. Thus a situation arose which affected everyone and of which few could be unaware. When the specter of depopulation disappeared, as it did in the 1940's, social thought had been geared in the direction of constructing a viable system of social policy for the family; and thereafter it went forward on its own momentum.

While it can be argued with force and substance that a family crisis of considerable seriousness has developed in the United States today, it is of course not at all like that which occurred in Sweden. It is a crisis that affects only a minority of the population — and for the most part a minority set apart by distinctions of race and class — and it occurs at a time of great prosperity for the majority. The American problem is not one of a general trend but of conflicting ones. But this only enhances Alva Myrdal's argument that matters of such enormous consequence must not be left to chance.

The essential fact about family stability (contrary to a good deal of folklore) is that as individuals become more prosperous, in the sense of having greater incomes, their marriages become more stable. For this reason (and because of improvements in health and medical care) the number of intact marriages in the United States is rising and is likely to continue to do so. For blue-collar workers, the gap between take-home pay and the income required to maintain a generally accepted standard of living is wider than is generally acknowledged, but the prospects that this situation will improve through the over-all movements of the economy are reasonable enough.

While the United States, to be sure, is facing a serious population question, it is one of growth not decline. (In 1967 the number of Americans crossed the 200 million mark and was rising at a rate of 2.3 million per year.) It is, moreover, the growth of *wanted* babies born into middle-class families fully conversant with contraceptive techniques, and in fact employing them, that seems to be causing the great upsurge. Obviously the varieties of pronatalist policies developed in Sweden and elsewhere will not respond very much to this kind of problem. But, again, there is every reason to suppose that the American middle class will be able to perceive its interest in keeping the size of the population within limits and, further, has enough arithmetic to comprehend that a 1 per cent annual growth rate will lead to surprisingly unattractive results in amazingly short order.

These facts argue against the likelihood of the United States taking up the notion of a national family policy with any seriousness or sense of urgency. There is, however, another set of facts that could lead in this direction, and this is the problem that might be described as one of social control and social development among the American poor — of whom there are an enormous number and among whom there seems to be a rising level of individual and group violence.

Gunnar Myrdal has given a name to this group: the American "underclass." Similar groups have existed elsewhere in the industrial world, but one by one they seem largely to have disappeared; while the United States alone continues to live with the problem of teeming, turbulent slums and increasingly violent cities. That Negro Americans are those most conspicuously involved in the violence serves only to conceal the likely extent of the problem. Unquestionably the best indicators of the growth of this class are to be found in the statistics of welfare dependency in the great cities of the nation, and these indicators are anything but reassuring. In New York, the greatest of our cities, the number of persons on welfare each month is about to cross the 800,000 mark, having risen 40 per cent in the preceding eighteen months. Of these, half a million are children, for the most part supported by the Federal Aid to Families of Dependent Children program. In an age of large numbers these may not seem especially alarming quantities until viewed as proportions. At the 800,000 mark, 10 per cent of the over-all population and 20 per cent of the youth of the city will be on welfare. It is a situation utterly without precedent in American experience. All that can be said is that the public does not understand it and does not like it. But a very great deal more understanding will be required before there is any prospect that the public will find a way to do something about it.

The first question to be asked is whether the rise of family instability in the nation's cities at this time is not somehow connected with the United States' failure to adopt a comprehensive family policy somewhere in the course of the past generation, thereby keeping the subject of family welfare constantly before the eyes of policy makers and administrators. This is not a question that can be answered to any great satisfaction, but the plain probability is that this is so. In good liberal tradition, America has more or less consistently sought to solve the problems of poverty through the labor market, an effort Alva Myrdal declared in 1940 could not succeed, and which in the United States has certainly not done so. Thus, in the third quarter of 1967, the unemployment rate for nonwhite men 20 years old and over fell to 4 per cent. This came about after eighty months of unbroken economic expansion, associated with the beginnings of a vigorous federal manpower policy in the early period and a war in Asia toward the end. By any standards the expansion was a triumph of social engineering, and presumedly should have been accompanied by immense outward signs of inward progress within the Negro community. But that is hardly the way to describe the summer of 1967. Nor can it account for the fact that from June 1966 to June

1967 the number of recipients of AFDC payments in the nation rose 11.3 per cent and the total cost of the program increased 22.7 per cent. The social challenge before the nation is clearly greater than that of merely providing income for individuals. It is that of providing individuals with a place in society, with stable expectations about themselves and others, and with the power to love and to create and to control the impulses to hatred and destruction which are part of any human personality. At its most crude, the question of family policy for the United States might be reduced to that of providing stability for the Negro slums. In its true dimension, however, the issue becomes one of providing not just the rudiments of physical well-being for children (and parents) but also of providing the conditions of early life which produce emotionally stable personalities. Neither social nor medical science can guarantee that this will happen, given this or that set of circumstances. But the conditions under which it is most likely *not* to happen are increasingly well known and involve issues that go to making up a family policy. Thus the question can be rephrased: If the United States had followed the Swedish (or the British, or the Dutch, or the Danish) example in the 1940's, would the child Lee Harvey Oswald have grown to be the adult the nation came to know?

It would be wrong to have too great expectations. Again, ironies abound. The very strength of the traditions of liberal democracy in America work counter to any serious enquiry into the problems of family welfare. It is a subject that is simply out of the main stream. At the time the poverty program was being formulated, I had occasion to comment on the subject in terms that need hardly be changed, Head Start and a dozen similar efforts notwithstanding.

We are different from most industrial democracies with which we otherwise share many characteristics. We are, as Nathan Glazer noted, implacably individualistic. We stand for God and Country, even for Yale. But to stand for family as well is a matter for newly migrated Italians or middle-class Irish Catholics whom the dictates of conscience have burdened with nine children and left, therefore, with no alternative.

Two American scholars, Nathan E. Cohen and Maurice F. Connery, have in fact identified precisely those most American of ideals — democracy, individualism, and humanitarianism — as those which most interfere with the development of a formal family policy in the nation.[1] Each in its own way seems to militate against accepting the subject as a legitimate one, and the interactions between them are notably negative in this respect. Thus the tradition of individualism leaves no explanation for failure save that which lies in the individual himself. But the tradition of humanitarianism, with its

---

[1] Nathan E. Cohen and Maurice F. Connery, "Government Policy and the Family," *Journal of Marriage and the Family*, Vol. 29, No. 1 (February 1967).

sympathy for the underdog, resists any effort to stigmatize the poor, or whom-
ever, as failures. As a result, those who would most hope to see something
done for the poor are frequently the very ones who most vigorously resist
any public acknowledgment that their families might have special problems,
might even be unsuccessful. The careful work of men such as William J.
Goode and E. Franklin Frazier, demonstrating that the impact of industrialization and urbanization has marked differential qualities as between different social classes, and is especially cruel to the poor and unskilled, goes all
but unheeded. Lee Rainwater has termed this "protecting the good name of
the poor," and it can assume a ferocity of formidable proportions. Thus the
problem of illegitimacy, which is manifestly a growing one in the United
States, is hardly discussed at all for the simple fact that it is a phenomenon,
for the greater part, of the lower class. (Half the firstborn nonwhite children
in the United States are illegitimate, in some urban areas half of *all* nonwhite
children.) It is all very well for the moribund bureaucracy of the Children's
Bureau of the Department of Health, Education, and Welfare to point out
that better-off (and white) women tend to have their foetus aborted. The
fact remains that the poor children are born, need help, and will not get it if
it is denied that they even exist. Nonetheless, the pattern persists. Cohen
and Connery describe it as "a schism in our thought in which some processes
of our society are perceived as subject to understanding and control and
others subject only to some vague, unknowable dynamics to which we can
only hope to respond." Not, that is, to anticipate and provide for in advance.

But there is hope for change. The riots of 1967 and the preceding years
have manifestly impressed upon the minds of an increasing number of public
officials and private persons alike the fact that family instability, through the
socialization of young persons, can lead more or less directly to social instability. There is not as yet a great deal of public discussion of the subject, but
the issue is very much on the private agendas of those persons concerned with
the future course of social policy in the United States. What remains, essentially, is for Negro leaders to withdraw their veto on public discussion of the
matter, and there are increasing signs that this too will occur. And when it
does, the question is likely to be raised in quite a new atmosphere of openness
on such issues. The United States is clearly entering a period of intense reexamination of its social policies in general. So many things have been tried
of late, and so few seem to have worked. But one clear fact emerges: the
United States is paying a great price for having failed, or refused, to accept
the subject of family as a legitimate object of social policy. Significantly, an
Anglo-American conference on public welfare services, meeting at Ditchley
Park in England in November 1967, pointedly concluded that for the United
States "there is an immediate and critical need for concentrated attention on

this problem of family stability." Old certainties are crumbling; a time for new departures is at hand.

Obviously not immediately at hand. War in Asia has preoccupied the energies and used up the resources of the national government. But this will come to an end, and when it does it will be possible to return once more to domestic concerns. By that time our economy is likely, if anything, to be even more productive than at present; and it is possible also to hope that we shall have acquired a considerably more mature awareness that we cannot simply let matters at home or abroad develop day by day with no very great understanding or concern as to where tiny increments of policy can lead. If the summer of 1967 — in the jungles of Vietnam and of the American cities — has taught us anything, it is to think harder than we have done about where we are drifting. In the area of social policy this requires that the subject of family welfare be raised and taken seriously by any political leader or party that wishes to be taken seriously in return.

Cohen and Connery have suggested the alternatives:

Paradoxically, as we stand at a moment in our history when the elimination of poverty, the control of human suffering, and the release of individual and collective potentials lie within our grasp, we falter in defining our national purposes or the kind of society we seek to create. An address to these issues that ignores the unique institutional role of the family in American society or that neglects its psychological or social meaning to individual development can only lead to failure to achieve the promise of our time.

It was with something of the same tone, and in the same spirit, that Alva Myrdal wrote the introduction to *Nation and Family* in Stockholm at the end of the summer of 1940, as the lights were going out once again in Europe. She hoped that the United States might be spared the World War, that in the 1940's we would "fulfill in grander style the achievements of the 1930's in Sweden." We did not, and now once again the lights are dimmed in our own country. But this too will pass; and now, therefore, is the time to consider not only the wasted opportunities of the 1940's but the promise of the 1970's.

Cambridge, Massachusetts   Daniel P. Moynihan
December 1967

PREFACE TO THE
PAPERBACK EDITION

To an author it is certainly most gratifying that a book which has not been available in the market for many long years will now see a new day and hopefully reach a wider circle of readers.

A sense of apprehension, however, also becomes part of the author's reaction. Have events and developments subsequent to the first publication of the book made its presentation of facts, theories, and programs outmoded?

Evidently, the statistics ought to have been brought up to date, if I had had time to edit a revision. But, as can also be gleaned from the short review of later developments given in Mr. Moynihan's foreword, there would have been no reason to change the "message" of the book.

Perhaps, however, I should, if writing the book anew today, have slightly re-emphasized certain aspects of the "message." For one, I should now reduce any semblance I might have to a "pronatalist" approach; the fact that population trends in Sweden during the 1920's and 1930's *if unchecked* pointed in the direction of depopulation was a temporary thing, serving to dramatize the message of our work on formulating a social family policy but not in reality directing that policy to any greater inclination to breed children.

The main framework for a positive family policy was, is, and must be that society will shoulder responsibility for the security of the preproductive age group — the children — as well as for the postproductive one, the aged. It remains the greatest mystery to me that this insight has not yet dawned on this great country, even now when the United States is beginning to take seriously its duties toward the aging population. The parallel is so apparent between the prevalent insecurity of these two groups, who are outside of the category of individual income earners. Yes, I would go even further in advocating a still more imaginative social policy system for the young, because they belong to the preproductive groups and thus expenditures for safeguarding them can legitimately claim to be social *investment*.

I would advocate just as adamantly as in the original book (and even in its 1934 precursor, written together with my husband) that as much as is possible income transfers between adults with and without children should be *in kind* rather than *in cash* when they are to pertain to the whole child population. This argument seems even to be strengthened nowadays, when the average family income is at a so much higher level. Cash benefits, however large and consequently difficult to squeeze from the taxpayers, will tend to be marginal, perhaps often used not to equalize basic consumption "before and after children" but to pay for the extra baby and for teenage consumption, the latter a profitable new development in commercialism. The other option is to provide directly, and thus also in a "classless" way, for children's dental care, for their medical care, for their school meals, for their tuition (the very word "tuition fees" hardly exists any more in Sweden). Thus, the quality of the new generation can be and must be safeguarded by society, thereby safeguarding its own future.

Finally, one word relating more to the sociological and psychological aspect of family structures. Today I would find occasion to warn even more strongly against "improvident parenthood." Children should in practice never be born without being planned, being positively desired; sex education should see to that. But I would go further and ask young partners really to think twice and then decide whether the coming of the first child cannot be somewhat postponed. If people want to marry young, and so establish an entity away from their parental environment, it is an individual choice. Young marriage, taken per se, should only increase the chances of two partners to develop together and so both enrich their personalities and stabilize their marriage. But I believe they owe it to society, and to themselves, to grow up, to get their education, and to mature as personalities before they choose to bend their lives to a nursery level. This judgment of mine perhaps takes on something of a sermonizing tone because I know that it is the young women who sacrifice more of their development possibilities if they start a family when too young, very often when they themselves are but teenagers. With increased longevity before us, there need be no such undue haste.

New York   Alva Myrdal
December 1967

PREFACE

As I sign the preface of this essay on efforts and plans for preventive social policy in peaceful and democratic Sweden, devastating totalitarian war is ravaging the Old World and threatening the New. We fear the end of an historic epoch during which humanitarian ideals, despite slips and setbacks, have been steadily making this world a more decent place in which to live. The proponents of other creeds are victoriously exploiting the results of science and technology to conquer the earth and reshape Western civilization. Sweden is in the midst of the danger zone. Sword and fire have ravaged the small and equally peaceful countries surrounding Sweden; she herself is isolated and pressed although still outwardly intact. Our spirits are low.

It may be that before this book is published our form of free and independent democratic government in the far North will have perished. This book, begun and in the main written in time of peace and in a spirit of assurance, would then come to stand as an epitaph of a defunct society. Even if that should be the immediate fate of our Scandinavian democracy, this essay will have been worth writing. Our house may be burned, but this will not prove that there were basic faults in its construction. The plan will still be worth studying.

Oppressors of civic freedom must always attempt to exterminate even the vestiges of the accomplished deeds and the animating ideals of democracy. They must depreciate what they are obliterating. Their miserable subjects must, if possible, be led to believe that democracy has been inefficient and corrupt and has collapsed as a result of its inherent defects. A huge falsification of history must be contrived by skilled experts of delusion. If fatality should smite the Northern democracies, this book will be one of the testimonies of how we were laboring, planning, and dreaming in the fields of population, family, and social reform while we were still free and independent.

If, on the other hand, the present calamity is resolved in such a way that freedom and progress again have a chance in Europe, we will have to take up our work where we left it. Such an end of this war, even more than that of the earlier one, will present a challenge to democracy, again reasserted, to fulfill its social obligation. Political freedom and formal equality will not be enough; real democracy, social and economic democracy, will be exacted. The success of construction and reconstruction to be undertaken then is largely dependent on how we plan now and how the public becomes educated for the tasks that lie ahead.

Europe will be impoverished. The fiscal structures of belligerent and nonbelligerent countries alike will seem bankrupt when measured by traditional norms of financial solvency. The rich will have seen their wealth taxed away. The masses will be hungry. When the structure of war-time economy breaks down, the dislocations of normal exchange and commerce will be left as enormous maladjustments. The demobilized millions will crave employment and security. Both courage and wisdom will be required to preserve orderly freedom and to avoid social chaos. These circumstances, however, will not prevent the undertaking of social reforms; on the contrary, they will force reforms whether we want them or not. Nothing short of a social revolution, and perhaps also of an economic one, will then suffice. And the major question is whether we shall have enough humanitarian zeal, calm reason, and cooperative will to carry out huge social programs and at the same time preserve social peace, i.e., to meet the needs of the hour without jeopardizing anew democracy itself.

Among all the other social and economic problems of that reconstruction period, the one centering around the family institution and the quantity and quality of population will gradually assume a dominant position. The prime of the adult male population in the belligerent nations will again have been decimated. At the same time a crisis of reproduction, previously foreshadowed in the tendency toward precipitous decline in fertility, may be brought about by a birth strike of potential parents reacting to abysmal times. And as soon as the economic machinery has been repaired in a provisionary way so that international exchange is again functioning and the masses of workers are given employment and bread, a new interest will attach to productive investment in a nation's chief economic asset: children and their health and capabilities.

This, then, is the theme of the book: that social reforms in their relation to the problems of family and population will of necessity receive more attention than ever before. As a framework for the presentation, the setting of the problems in modern Sweden has been utilized. So recently has a fairly comprehensive program been formulated and partly tested out there that it would seem irrational to let it be submerged in oblivion because a war goes on in the world.

The comments on specific endeavors in Sweden refer to developments up to the summer of 1939. Few references are made to what has happened since then. In so far as accounts are given of plans and programs, these represent developments which were anticipated and desired before the catastrophic events of the fall of 1939. The main body of this book on Swedish family welfare was written in the United States with American problems in mind. If the United States is comparatively spared in this war as in the earlier one, she will have a greater opportunity and a greater responsibility than ever before to help shape the trend of democratic progress in the future. We nurture the hope that the 1940's in the United States will fulfill in grander style the achievements of the 1930's in Sweden.

This book is written anew for the public in English-speaking countries. It is, however, at the same time to be considered as a substitute for an English version of the *Kris i befolkningsfrågan*, Stockholm, 1934, by the present author in collaboration with Dr. Gunnar Myrdal, Professor of Political Economy and Public Finance at Stockholm University. In preparing the earlier book, the latter author assumed responsibility for the demographic and economic aspects and the present writer for the treatment of social policy. This new book also contains a digest of the 17 reports prepared by the Swedish Population Commission, 1935–1938. It is hoped that it will be clear in the text when the author speaks in a personal capacity only, when the consensus of Swedish opinion is voiced, and when the authority of Swedish royal committees or public agencies is involved.

To the Carnegie Corporation of New York the author is deeply grateful for a generous grant, facilitating the time-consuming and extensive collection and checking of the data. For encouraging the undertaking and advising in planning the work the author is in the happy position of being able to thank some of the best experts and friends: Mr. Frederick Osborn, Dr. Earl Engle, Dr. Dorothy Swaine Thomas, Dr. Frank Lorimer and Dr. Gunnar Myrdal.

Dr. Ellen Winston has done most of the editing, sharing the responsibility with Dr. Richard Sterner, formerly of the Swedish Social Board, who has himself contributed so much to some of the reform programs described in this book.

ALVA MYRDAL

Stockholm, August 31, 1940

CONTENTS

CONTENTS

LIST OF TABLES

LIST OF TABLES

LIST OF FIGURES

LIST OF FIGURES

PART I

PROBLEMS AND PRINCIPLES

CHAPTER I

POPULATION, THE FAMILY, AND SOCIAL REFORM

T HIS is a study of social policy in its relation to family and population. According to the traditional philosophical usage of terms, this book is "practical" or "political" and not simply "theoretical" or "factual." It endeavors to investigate planned social action in the field of population in terms of goals and means.

The author believes that social planning should be a rational procedure based on factual knowledge and pursued by means of logical analysis. She insists, moreover, that the immensity and intensity of today's social problems and the vast scope of today's social actions are challenges to social science to proceed more courageously — to advance from merely recording facts and analyzing causal relations to constructing rational plans for purposive changes.

It is true that planning of necessity implies the future and that the elements of prognosis inherent in a program can never be exposed to the ultimate empirical check before they have already become history. It is also true that social engineering will never allow the specialization reached in fact-finding research. A program will always have to be founded on a much more comprehensive range of insights into many fields than is necessary in most of the simpler scientific crafts. But the greater difficulties involved are no excuse for avoiding the task of attempting to formulate programs in the practical sphere of rational social planning.

The principal difficulty in constructive social engineering is, however, the need of value premises to supplement knowledge of facts. One of the chief reasons for the underdeveloped state of the allied social science field today is the approach toward dealing with values. An established tendency to drive values underground, to make the analysis appear scientific by omitting certain basic assumptions from the discussion, has too often emasculated the social sciences as agencies for rationality in social and political life. To be truly rational, it is necessary to accept the obvious principle that a social program, like a practical judgment, is a conclusion based upon premises of values as well as upon facts.

We can then proceed by selecting and stating explicitly our values relating to means as well as to goals. By applying this system of relevant value premises to the system of ascertained facts, we can construct social programs which *per se* are just as rational as any social theory. This is, in short, the theory of cognition in this essay in social policy.

POPULATION POLICY

It is a general thesis of this book that a population policy can be nothing less than a social policy at large. This does not mean, however, that the population problem is so diffuse that it is unlikely to appear on the political scene as a population problem proper. On the contrary, the expected trends in population are such as to arouse sooner or later a very lively public concern. The population problem will be brought into the political foreground. It will, the author believes, in the near future become the dominating political issue. The very fact of its wide ramifications will intensify, rather than neutralize, public interest. It will be felt to condition the life of the individual just as it determines the welfare of nations. It touches sex life and the institution of the family as well as national production, distribution, and consumption. Population is becoming and must become still more the subject of political discussion everywhere — in the folk-parliaments of street, workshop, and family circle as well as in the parliaments of states and in the conferences of economists, sociologists, and biologists.

When that happens it is of the greatest importance that it be made common knowledge that the population problem concerns the very foundation of the social structure and that a problem of such giant dimensions calls for nothing less than complete social redirection. If practical social science is not on the watch, there is a palpable danger that population policy will be irrationally narrowed down and forced into remedial quackery. The very phrase "population policy" connotes to the lay mind — and, alas, sometimes also to the population expert — nothing more than one contrivance or another for controlling migration or for encouraging childbearing. To avoid this political short circuit there must be wide realization of the inadequacy of such an approach. A population program must work itself into the whole fabric of social life and must interpenetrate and be interpenetrated by all other measures of social change. The population crisis must, if we are to react rationally, make us rethink all social objectives and programs.

THE NEO-MALTHUSIAN ISSUE

From this point of view recent population discussion has only had the character of forebodings. There have been various schools of opinion, but most of the discussion has lacked proper integration and perspective. There have been active controversies, but they have, in the main, turned around isolated points. Because the broader problems have not been defined, the arguments have usually not met. In most cases the alignment in these controversies has been determined by reactions to birth control. This has been attacked or defended with an amazing lack of insight into its deeper causes and further effects, such as the dynamics of the family institution itself, the economics of the nation, the dichotomy of quantity and quality in population, and the interplay of education and economic reforms in induced social change.

It is unnecessary to anticipate in this introductory chapter the discussion of the criteria of judgment to be utilized and the doctrines of policy to be developed in later chapters. But it may be stated at the very beginning that in writing this book it has not been possible to side either with the conservative denunciation of birth control as immoral and as contrary to national interest or with the radical belief that birth control will solve practically all social problems if only pushed far enough. The one opinion stresses quantity only; the other does not care about quantity at all but has some concern for population quality. Neither school has been able to broaden its view enough to comprehend the social dynamics which are much more responsible for the spread of birth control than doctrines and propaganda. Still less has either school caught the idea that influencing the whole structure of modern social life may be the only effective way of controlling the development of the family institution, including the factor of procreation.

This statement of the old birth control issue may be oversimplified, but it gives roughly the limited boundaries within which opposing attitudes have been confined. The conservative school — with its impersonal and harsh view of the family — can count on few adherents in a democracy. The denunciation of birth control as contrary to morals and religion is weakened by the statistically established fact of its almost universal spread. Under the influence of democratic doctrine the individual is too cognizant of his own identity and interests to forfeit the right to serve his own welfare in what touches him so intimately as the size of his family. The radical school, too, must revise its premises. The gospel of birth control has already been adopted to such an extent that rapid depopulation is threatening. The effects of depopulation are problematic, but propaganda against overpopulation is in any case rather out of date. The most important point, however, is that our social difficulties are far from a solution in spite of the increasing prevalence of small families. The family still has its very serious problems, some of which have increased in intensity, and the welfare of children is not safeguarded. All this points to the conclusion that reform must go deeper and develop on a broader front than Neo-Malthusianism. There is nothing quite so sterile as a radicalism which has outlived itself.

This new attack does not find such easy solutions as either of the two earlier doctrines. The conservatives had, in fact, nothing else to propose than exhortations to the individual to do his duty and fulfill his fate and in addition, perhaps, the offering of small honorary grants. These inducements did not work. The approach of the radicals, which consisted of exhortations to the individual to adjust the size of his family to social malformations, did not materially readjust the malformations but led in the direction of extinguishing the human content of society. It is certainly more rational and more promising for the future, though much more difficult, to remake society so that it fits the children rather than to abolish the children in order to fit society. Some new orientation, which honestly accepts voluntary parenthood and birth control without idealizing extreme family limitation, is more than a compromise between the two opposing views. It represents a synthesis, which is necessary in the present phase of development. It has, in fact, been necessary since the World War and would have been historically most appropriate at that time. For many reasons, including the state of confusion as to the true dimensions of the population problem, there has been a delay which is proving all too costly.

THE MALADJUSTED FAMILY

The population crisis is only the external aspect of what is really a crisis in the family as an institution. So deep-rooted and fixed a system of human relations as the family has necessarily lacked the plasticity to adapt itself to the fundamental and pervasive economic changes of the last century. The family even in its modern structure has its moorings in a preindustrial agrarian society. One after another these moorings have been lost.

Considering the major functions of the family in turn,[1] the need for readjustment everywhere becomes glaring. Most fundamental is the change in the *economic* function. The family was once the main unit of economic production, independent and self-sustaining in a sense now largely forgotten. Today the economic unit tends to comprise the whole national economy. The productive capacity of the individual operating in a vast market becomes the basis for computing income. The chances of eventually getting a higher family income and of attaining greater security in old age by having more children are now much smaller than in the earlier economy. The productive work of children begins at a later age and seldom has any direct connection with the family economy. Changes in the economic structure of society weaken the family as an institution. Unproductive age groups

[1] Based, with modifications, on analyses of family functions by Professor William F. Ogburn.

have no assured place in the new economic order of individualistic money-making in nation-wide competitive markets. In the family economy of old the two less productive periods at the beginning and at the end of life did carry some undefined but material income rights; and persons in each period had a claim to be housed and fed according to their needs.

Since we cannot, and do not want to, revert to an agrarian or patriarchal order, some collectivistic devices must be instituted in the larger national household to substitute for the relative security enjoyed in the family household of old. In Western societies the philosophy is gradually gaining ground that it is a social responsibility to guarantee the maintenance of human beings even during periods when they are not productive. But in all systems of social security the periods of illness, unemployment, and old age tend to be provided for long before there is any recognition of the need of providing for the period of unproductive childhood. This might seem surprising since it is not only a humanitarian measure to house children well, feed them correctly, and keep them healthy and strong, but it is also a profitable national investment in order to secure their optimal productivity in the future. This neglect can be justified only from the viewpoint of extreme Neo-Malthusian individualism: childhood is a condition that can be prevented by the expedient of not bearing children, while the other conditions of need are more unavoidable. This is the logic of the position that the individual family has unconditional responsibility for its own children. Conservative moralists should recognize that this doctrine requires Neo-Malthusianism as its logical premise. A broader social philosophy is needed for the sound readjustment of the family within the framework of industrial society.

The *protective* function of the family likewise plays a declining role. Hospitalization, institutionalization, and social security measures are taking the place of family care for the old and sick. This tends, on the one hand, to alleviate the crisis in the family as an institution and, on the other hand, to decrease the value to the individual of marriage and childbearing.

In the *educative* function of the family similar changes have occurred. Training for a varied vocational and civic life must be obtained in more professional and specialized forms than can be provided in the individual family. Educational institutions have taken over many family functions but require new forms of collaboration which in turn call for new social relations.

Some of the same comments would apply also to the changes in the *recreational* function of the family. Outmoded forms of family recreation have often, however, been replaced by new ones. Though it is probably false to conclude that this function of the family has decreasing importance, the changes in form require continued readjustments of family patterns and of society's surroundings for the family.

Even the *sexual* function of the family which gives the sanctioned frame for love relations is challenged by new developments. A multitude of disturbing factors are at work. Birth control, for example, has loosened the absolute relationship between sex and procreation and thereby destroyed one of the natural constraints to continuity in sexual relations. The *biological* function of prolonging the existence of a people through new generations has been most visibly affected by recent changes. The crisis in the family culminates in the decrease in family size. The change in fertility under way represents nothing less than a revolution. And revolution should not go unnoticed and uncontrolled.

The only function that would seem to have lost nothing in the process of change is the *affectional* one, as the family situation continues to provide the opportunity for supreme intimacy. In order that this function of deepest personal value may be left intact, however, we must apply our ingenuity to the challenge of a rearrangement of the external conditions surrounding the family. Whatever the cost may be in comparison with the illusory comfort of relying on traditions and habits, this challenge must be met.

In retrospect it is difficult to understand how the fate of the family under the impact of the industrial system should have passed almost without notice during the nineteenth century. The state and the individual were always the two poles of interest. Social and political controversy was occupied with the question of the interrelationship of these two social entities. Whether the issues be stated as democracy versus authoritarianism, individualism versus collectivism, or competition versus cooperation, the dualism was unvaried — state and individual. What distribution of power and responsibility should there be between those two? That there might be still another competing center of attention — namely, the family — was mostly lost sight of. Similarly, the family was strangely neglected in education and in literature. There was, it is true, outward respect for the family with a whole system of verbal generalities, taboos, and moralities; but it remained outward only. The content of education was devoid of any attempt to disseminate knowledge which would prepare for better functioning of the intimate relationship within the family. The family was exalted in literature in the form of idyls; but in the idyls there was the essential falsity of Puritanism. Neither the problems nor the values of the family were treated with such respectful honesty as might enhance its competitive value.

The task of our generation is to reintegrate the family in the larger society. The family should not be gradually sterilized through birth control carried to its extreme. Neither should the family be absorbed through an indiscriminate collectivization of all its functions into a deindividualized and amorphous communism. Utilizing our knowledge and our common sense we should reconsider in a realistic and cautious manner the division of functions between the family household and the national household and induce such changes in this division as may best preserve the fundamental values of our cultural heritage in a period of structural economic and social changes. Our social reforms should aim at conserving, not uprooting, but they will have to be truly radical in scope because the primary changes have been so significant. This reform activity will, as it is getting under way, mark a new epoch in social policy. It started centuries ago as charity, which developed into private philanthropy and public poor relief. Labor legislation was introduced much later to stamp out exploitation on the labor market. Recently our strivings have been to regularize and liberalize society's aid to the aged, the sick, and other needy groups by huge schemes for social security. Even in countries where this system of social policy is most adequate, it is still only ameliorative or symptomatic in character. Truly preventive or prophylactic policy must concern the family and the children. The family reforms will thus introduce national profit and investment motives in addition to the motives of democratic justice and humanitarian sympathy. They will lift social policy to the level of social planning.

Why Sweden?

The family crisis represents the microcosmic view of what under the macrocosmic aspect stands out as the population problem. Under the influence of very similar causes it is becoming a burning issue in the entire Western world. Some countries are, however, several decades in the van of the development. Sweden not only has the lowest crude birth rate among the countries of the world but also in terms of net reproduction rates Sweden's position remains at the bottom of the roster (Table 1). There is thus a material reason why Sweden should be the country first to voice concern about the situation. It still has to be explained, however, why Sweden is here presented as having any particularly worth-while contribution to make to population policy. Why did no other country take the lead in formulating a population program for democracy?

The first country in modern times to experience severe reduction in family size was France. A reminder of that fact is that birth control in earlier generations was commonly referred to as the French system. Family limitation in France has had some peculiar characteristics. It started in the rural districts rather than the urban and kept, even when reaching other classes of society, the character of prudence in a landowning class attempting to avoid too great division of the paternal legacy. The fall of the birth rate caused anxiety very early. Total population in France was growing at a much slower rate than in other countries (increasing only from 26,800,000 in 1800 to 37,700,000 in 1880 and to 38,600,000 in 1900, while Germany dur-

NATION AND FAMILY

TABLE 1. — COMPARISON OF NET REPRODUCTION RATES IN
SELECTED COUNTRIES, 1931–1938

COUNTRY	1931	1935	1936	1937	1938
Austria	(1931–1932) 0.714	0.64			
Belgium			0.831		
Czechoslovakia	0.939				
Denmark	(1931–1935) 0.932			0.947	
England and Wales	0.81	0.764	0 773	0.782	
Finland		0 956			
France	(1928–1933) 0.905	0.866	0.88	0.87	
Holland	1.28	1.145	1.140	1.119	
Ireland				(1935–1937) 1.162	
Italy	1.209			1.128	
Norway		0.831	0.783	0.786	
Poland	1.25	(1934) 1.11			
Portugal	1.334				
Sweden		0.729		0.756	
Switzerland					0.789
Canada	1.319			0.947	
U. S. A.	(1930) 1.078	0.969			
Japan	(1930) 1.571				
Australia			(1935–1936) 0.956	0.989	
New Zealand			0.949	1.001	1.022

Source: League of Nations, *Statistical Yearbook.* For more complete data on Sweden see Chapter II.

ing the same period was increasing from 25,000,000 to 45,200,000 and 56,400,-
000, respectively). Also, quite early this trend called into being a number
of social measures. Nevertheless, France has not been able to formulate,
and still less to export, a democratic population policy. Both in philosophy
and in practice the difficulty hampering French population and family policy
was, and is, that France has never been able to reconcile birth control and
a positive interest in population. The population interest has remained
isolated, and it has opposed birth control as such in vain. It became chiefly
identified as a movement for *familles nombreuses.* Even the new *Code de
Famille* enacted in 1939 aims only at continuing to encourage family size
through cash bonuses, a venture in vivid contrast to the Swedish scheme as
will be discussed later. Population interest in France has been dominated
from beginning to end by clerical influence. Socially, population striving
has been aligned with political conservatism. It thus never became sufficiently social-minded to care rationally for the economic fate of the
large families it encouraged. No group in France was able to bring together
and synthesize into a coherent system of thought the ideals of rational
birth control, maintenance of population, social reform, and family readjustment. Hence France was unable to assume leadership in presenting to
the world a truly democratic population program.

Germany also lost this opportunity, but for other reasons. The pattern of family limitation began rather late in Germany, but it spread all the faster when once begun. About 1930 the problem was intelligently discussed among the Germans, always alert to self-analysis. There existed all the prerequisites for a democratic population *Magna Charta*: a strong and widely endorsed movement for birth control, a rational treatment of social ills through social reform, and the dawn of the idea that social policy had to be reconsidered in the light of the findings of demographic science. But the years required for unifying these factors into a program and for national education for its acceptance were not given to democratic Germany. The intellectual excursions into the field of social policy remained superficial. In the regime that has followed, specific distributive measures have been enacted, but two distinct features mar this program. The goals are phrased in terms of nationalistic expansion, and a rational and honest foundation in birth control is absent. Thus a population program of constructive readjustment to modern society is not given by German leadership, which may be natural enough in a country where freedom of science and public discussion is barred and where the people have no intelligent voice. It is pathetic to read German writings on population during the last decade and to talk personally to the experts themselves. One senses the Procrusteanization of the German soul.

England might have been expected to develop the new democratic population program. In that country there is a long tradition in the population field stemming from Malthus's classic essay. The birth control movement was early intellectualized, although in a doctrine which remained rather sterile in its approach to family problems. Up to the last decades of the nineteenth century, England may also be said to have been in the lead in social reform policy, particularly in labor legislation. Later the English Labor party showed much interest in reforms which are of importance from the family viewpoint. Still, England never came as near as even Weimar Germany to visualizing an integrated family reform policy. The strong impact of individualism in English social philosophy may have been to some extent responsible, as family values have never been stressed in English public life. Economic stagnation, financial strain, and unemployment after the World War too exclusively absorbed social and political thinking. The international situation grew more and more tense and forebodings of war dominated the English mind long before the outbreak of the new catastrophe. It is in any event difficult to avoid the impression that England in the interval between the two world wars did not have available much courage and vision in the field of social philosophy, particularly as regards population and family.

The United States is in still a different position. In spite of the heritage of an equally ardent economic and political individualism, the family has remained central in the thoughts of a people drawing its most cherished traditions from pioneers. The strong impact in America of Low-Church religiosity in early days and later of Catholicism has tended to conserve these ideals. It is no accident that American sociology has to an unusually high degree centered around family instead of social class. But the United States has until lately had a very high fertility rate. Only recently has it dropped below the level of a balanced aggregate reproduction. Up to the last decade the United States has also been a region of immigration, and it still feels the pressure of foreign masses wanting to move in. Any concern for replenishing the population has seemed gratuitous to the ordinary mind during the prolonged depression of the 1930's, while millions were unemployed and it was doubtful whether the productive apparatus ever would be able to make use of them. The economic stagnation has absorbed all social interests and undoubtedly has also distracted them from a long-range point of view. An integrated program for a population policy could, therefore, be less expected to emerge in the United States than in some other countries. The very basis of such a policy must be a fairly well-developed curative system in the form of social security, and such a program is only now being carried into effect.

It may finally be asked why Soviet Russia in its extensive social experimentation did not give the world a population program. But there the whole situation is different. No population decline is impending. On the contrary, there is in Russia a reproduction surplus of a magnitude nowadays unknown in Western society. If Russian statistics are accurate, fertility has actually been increasing. The family program that Soviet Russia inaugurated in an earlier stage had some features making it offensive to our culture, especially the systematic undermining of inherited family values. Later Russia sharply revised her radical attitudes. This is indicated most clearly in the new abortion legislation. Undoubtedly Russia has greatly assisted in the revival of interest in problems relating to family and child welfare, but anything like a complete family program adapted to democratic population planning has not been developed.

Such a task has been attempted in Sweden. To understand why this has been possible, certain preconditions in the social and political situation of that country have to be recalled. Sweden is no land of perfection. Some of the favorable publicity recently bestowed on the country has been exaggerated. The descriptive parts of the chapters to follow will show deficiencies in many important respects, but there is a palpable excuse for these tales of Sweden as a social paradise. The Scandinavian countries, and particularly Sweden, have by an historical accident been given a most advantageous set of prerequisites for a bold experiment in social democracy. Consequently, these countries will have to give an account as to whether they have envisioned a democracy that really works for its citizens. In this book such an account will be attempted in the limited area of social legislation. It must, however, be seen against the general background of the cultural and political possibilities for developing purposive social schemes, so that some summary remarks on the cultural milieu may therefore be ventured.

Sweden has had fixed boundaries for 125 years. No question can ever again arise about land we want to gain. Thus Sweden is free from the special strain of imperialistic ambitions. The position of a small power is accepted by the ordinary Swede without inferiority feelings. For a thousand years the Swedes, like other Scandinavians, were bellicose in the extreme. Sweden was herself never conquered; the wars were, in the main, carried on abroad. In the seventeenth century Sweden was a Great Power embracing Finland, the Baltic countries, and important parts of Germany, and at times even some colonies. But among the Swedes that history is past and buried. While the memories of it are cherished, they do not create a present urge toward imperialistic ambitions.

The long and continuous peace has had important effects on the psychology of the people. Patterns of normality and lawfulness have gradually been firmly fixed. Killing other human beings is considered simply not good form. The homicide rate is extremely low. Even the state does not take the lives of its enemies. The last execution of a criminal occurred in 1910 after having become more and more rare before that time. (Only 15 executions have occurred since 1865.) In 1921 capital punishment disappeared from the statutes. Brutality and violence are gradually being stamped out like other contagious social diseases.

Particularly important in explaining the psychology of the 1930's during which social policy made its most rapid advances is the fact that an extreme trust in national security was to be discerned in Scandinavia while all the rest of Europe lived in a state of war scare. The people simply did not believe in the possibility of a revival of violence. The danger of a new war was not realistically presented and actually had little impact upon attitudes and life. Personal and national tasks were undertaken as if Sweden were absolutely secure in her peace and independence. Subjectively, at least, peace and stability in external relations existed to a degree one could scarcely dream of realizing for the world at large.

Internally, a great number of the usual causes of struggle and friction in other countries have not been present. Sweden has had no problem of minorities. The 6,500 Lapps, because of their nomadic life and their wanderings across national boundaries, fall somewhat outside the ordinary structure of Swedish society, but all doors are kept open for them. When settling and seeking assimilation, the usual social privileges are extended to them. In the far North there are also some 34,000 Finnish-speaking people, but there was never any urge either to enforce their total assimilation or to keep them out of the Swedish communion. The ordinary Swede has felt a corresponding indifference toward the Swedish minority in Finland. The Jewish population, which is separated in the census only with regard to religion, amounts to only some 6,700 individuals in spite of the fact that Sweden was one of the first countries (in 1782) to grant Jews considerable freedom. As Sweden has no traditions of active anti-Semitism, the Jews have been integrated in society with no special interest attached to their extraction or religion. The Norwegians were until 1905 bound to Sweden in a union under the Swedish king. When they broke away in that year, the Swedes resisted the temptation to retain them by violence. This afterwards created an exceedingly warm feeling between these racially and culturally related nations and pride in having been able to settle so serious a dispute without resort to arms.

Neither have there been regional differences to divide the nation. Culturally, the regional differences were originally great. The semifeudal southern provinces, taken from Denmark in one of the early imperialistic wars, had little in common with the mining and farming districts in the middle of the country, the forest regions in the north, or the fishing districts on the west coast. But the incorporation of all regions with their different cultural traditions and economic interests into one unified society of mutual responsibility has been the ideal for a long time. The modern democratic measures to equalize local taxation and employ the resources of the state to fight local substandard conditions are following old patterns of government and administration. Not regionalism but rather equalization has been and is the goal.

An important role in this historical process of cultural equalization has been played by the state's persistent endeavors in the field of education. Public education was made compulsory a hundred years ago and the educational system centralized with the same minimum requirements applied in all regions. Higher education has never been a monopoly of the upper classes, but social mobility has been encouraged by tax-supported, practically free secondary schools, universities, and professional schools. It is true that despite the cheapness of higher education it has not been utilized so widely by all social groups as in the New World, and this is felt to be an urgent problem for reform. In recent decades adult education has won a place for itself in addition to the ordinary school system. It was not superimposed from above but grew from the needs of the people themselves and was governed by their own organizations. For all these, and perhaps other, reasons the reading public in Sweden is unusually large. Political issues are discussed by wider masses and with more social knowledge than in most other countries. Adult education has always been a group instead of an individual matter; and its goal has been group rather than individual advancement. It has been sponsored by the great civic organizations in which the modern Swedish mass movements have found their institutional form — the labor movement, the cooperative movement, the women's movement, the temperance movement, and others — and it has always been closely connected with their public activities. These mass movements have given content to the political democracy which was gradually achieved. The last income and sex limitations with respect to the franchise were abolished during the period 1918–1921.

Even though the landless and poorer strata of society were excluded for centuries from political participation, democracy has its roots in pre-Christian times. In the early course of Swedish history the farmers took large political responsibility. At crucial times they drove foreign usurpers out of the country and preserved national liberty. In cooperation with the farmers the king at times overcame the germinating tendencies toward feudalism. Together with Norway and Iceland, Sweden is in contrast to all the rest of Europe a country where the farmers have always been free and where feudalism never developed as more than a threat. A parliament with four estates — nobility, clergy, burghers, and farmers — emerged some five hundred years ago out of the earlier provincial meetings. The farmers constituted the estate with the largest electoral basis (Table 2).

TABLE 2. — ESTATES AND CLASSES IN SWEDEN ACCORDING TO
OCCUPATION STATISTICS IN EARLY CENSUS REPORTS

Estates and Classes	1805	1830	1855
	Per cent distribution		
Total	100.00	100.00	100.00
Nobility	0.39	0.36	0.32
Clergy	0.63	0.49	0.42
Others belonging to the two higher estates .	2.88	2.44	2.18
Burghers	2.71	2.30	2.24
Farmers	72.90	75.10	65.35
Foreigners and Israelites	—	0.07	0.05
All others	20.49	19.24	29.44

Source: Wohlin, Nils, "Den jordbruksidkande befolkningen i Sverige," *Emigrationsutredningen*, Vol. IX, 1909.

At least since 1632 the government has been bound by a written constitution, the basic principle of which is that the right to levy taxes on the people belongs to the people's own representatives. In 1864 the four estates were dissolved through a parliamentary reform and a two-chamber parliament was

instituted. Through various franchise limitations the lower income strata
were excluded from a voice in politics until the twentieth century, when they
gradually broke down these limitations.

The long tradition of free and lawful government gives a conservative
note also to political change in Sweden. According to the constitutional
framework, the administration proper has a unique independence and in
principle can be commanded only by changing the laws in regular order.
There have been periods of graft and corruption, but politics and administration were fundamentally reformed about a hundred years ago, i.e., in the
earliest stage of the liberalistic era, long before the present extent of state interference was envisaged. The new social state has thus inherited an honest
and reasonably efficient instrument for its endeavors to remodel the old
society.

It is inevitable in an old country that the system of social distinctions is
rather rigid. Status in the civil service and higher education mean, however, as much and sometimes more than wealth in this social stratification.
Family relations *per se* have gradually lost their significance. In Sweden
class distance is now being steadily diminished by three factors: social
mobility through education and other means has been comparatively easy;
large incomes are gradually being redistributed, so that extreme wealth and
extreme poverty are leveling out; and, finally, all social groups share the
ideology of "work that ennobles," with the result that it is practically
impossible to retain a high social status without a profession. The "gentle-
man of independent means" is foreign to the Swedish social structure.

The country has a more than fair amount of natural resources. The soil
is hard and labor-hungry, but with industry and care it yields all necessary
food. About one-third of the population is now engaged in agriculture.
The technological progress in agriculture continues, however, to keep pace
with internal migration, and soon the feeding of the nation will be
accomplished by the labor of one-fourth or even one-fifth of the available
man power. Other resources are plentiful enough to have made possible
the development of industry and commerce. Sweden has become an
important exporter of timber, paper, and iron, as well as of a great number
of the products of highly skilled industry.

The industrial progress of Sweden has been facilitated for the reason
that to a great extent Swedish export goods are either raw materials against
which foreign countries do not raise high protective walls or else products
that can climb those walls. Of even greater importance has been the
secular trend of prices in the world market since long before the World
War, resulting in a gradual rise in the prices of export goods in terms of
prices for import goods. This fact has given an added impetus to Swedish
industrialization. This must not be forgotten when explaining why all

curves of production, incomes, and level of living have continued to rise sharply even during the last decade and why Sweden has been able to cope so successfully with depression and unemployment.

Finally, the human capital is certainly not inherently any better than that of any other country, but it has lately been cared for and developed to a relatively high level of efficiency. The people are affected in their aptitudes and attitudes by the inherited national culture. They do not shun hard physical labor but rather seem unable to get along without it, as the intense gardening of townspeople indicates. Intellectually, they are said to possess a maximum of technical, but a minimum of psychological, ingenuity. Temperamentally, they may probably be said to be rather slowgoing with more emotional inhibition than spontaneity, and as a result they give an appearance of unnecessary dignity.

When in the traditional orderly society of Sweden the forces of industrialization, late but with cumulative force, started to work in the fifties and sixties of the last century and more efficaciously in the nineties, they were bound to give rise to serious maladjustments, especially in the sphere of family life. But industrialization never reduced the workers to the status of dependent proletarians. The people by this time were sufficiently mature to take things into their own hands and organize. So the mass movements became organized, and the fight for full political democracy was waged and won. Social reforms were emerging out of the democratization, and they could be carried on successfully because of the extraordinarily favorable economic trends referred to above. In terms of the possibility of developing a population program of family reforms in the early 1930's it was of decisive importance that Sweden at that time had already carried into effect a social security program which, if not perfected, was fairly advanced.

*   *

*

This inventory of extraordinarily favorable circumstances in Sweden is not presented in order to enhance the estimation of the country; quite the opposite. It is presented to explain why an advance in democratic policy could reasonably be expected. If democracy could not develop successfully in Scandinavia, given by historical chance quite exceptionally advantageous conditions, it will probably not work anywhere else. This should be remembered throughout the book, as it is difficult to avoid the semblance of patriotic pride when writing of one's own country. The knowledge that some people in some countries will accept only idealized truths about Scandinavia and the knowledge also that other people, both abroad and at home, will be watching only for exaggerations and embellishments has made the wording of this book as personally difficult as the subject is dear to the author's heart. Out of sheer objectivity it has been necessary to make some positive evaluations. For the same reason it has been just as necessary to keep a keen eye open for the shortcomings of the social reforms described in succeeding chapters.

CHAPTER II

POPULATION TRENDS AND OPINIONS

S WEDISH population trends prior to 1750 were not of such a nature as to lead to general awareness of a population problem. There were some periods of growth, as in the sixteenth century, and some periods of decline through plague, famine, and war. But the movements of the population pendulum induced by these causes were always narrower than those caused by imperialistic adventures, which brought about sometimes a gain, sometimes a loss, of whole provinces. Then came such an increase of population that a problem of major social import was bound to arise. From 1750, and more markedly from 1800, the total population grew considerably "with the onset of peace, vaccine and potatoes" as the national poet Tegnér has well said. It increased from 1¾ million in 1750 to 2⅓ million in 1800, to 3½ million in 1850, to 5 million in 1900, and to 6 million in 1925. To show how these millions were assimilated is to reveal the dramatic shift in Swedish social structure.

Theoretical speculation could have foretold the first result: intensified pressure on the means of subsistence. Farm homesteads could not be perpetually partitioned; handicraft establishments were relatively closed by guild rules; mercantile occupations did not yet offer opportunities for numerous enterprises; and industry was not yet organized for mass production. In a word, Sweden of the early nineteenth century may be used as an example of the Malthusian menace of pauperization. It is true that comparisons as to welfare and level of living among the masses of people are difficult to make between distant periods of time just as between different countries. Reliable authorities [*156* and *157*] [1] generally agree, however, that in comparison not only with later decades but also with earlier ones this first half of the last century was a period of acute poverty. The main impact upon social stratification was an increase in nonpropertied classes in agriculture.

[1] Numerals in brackets refer to items in the bibliography.

The structure of Swedish society from the Viking period through the Middle Ages and during the centuries as a Great Power had been supported chiefly on a broad basis of operators of small and medium-sized farms, independent owners of their own land. The nobility, the clergy, and the urban burghers made up the three upper estates; the peasants made up the fourth and largest. Below these politically recognized estates there was always a stratum of landless workers in agriculture and of persons engaged in the few industrial pursuits, but it had never grown to large proportions (Table 2). With the rapid growth in population from the eighteenth century onward, however, rural proletarians on the fringe of the stable, patriarchal, agrarian society surviving from older days increased importantly. While the population in the independent farmer group has been estimated to have grown from 1,053,000 in 1775 to 1,396,000 in 1870, the increase in the "loose" rural population during the same period was from 549,000 to 1,288,000. [219] Homeless bands began to rove the country; poor relief costs grew apace; and social thought became feverishly occupied with this new problem. The only social reforms at that early time purposely calculated to deal with the problem were in the realm of poor relief administration.

The economic changes involved in the Swedish agrarian revolution which had its beginning at that time did, however, open some new avenues for the growing numbers. Without such changes the pressure on the level of living would have been more serious than it actually was. Through laws on enclosure and inheritance, the farming land under the open-field system was parceled out, breaking up the village system and scattering the farm families on individual homesteads. Colonization and an increase in the arable land area followed. Thus, within the farm-owning population itself a certain readjustment was effected and a certain population increase absorbed. But for the growing masses of the poor this reform did not suffice. Occasionally it even aggravated their plight, as cotters and squatters who earlier could have made a meager living in a hut on the forest common lost this possibility when the village common was divided up among the individual farm owners.

Punitive regulations of a mercantilistic type were at first practically the only remedy utilized to meet the rising social difficulties. Conservative spokesmen, who saw nothing evil but rather an advantage in the increase of poor people if only they became productive, called upon the authorities to enforce old regulations of domicile whereby the individual had to be definitely attached somewhere either by homestead ownership or by a labor contract (*laga försvar*). If not, he was liable to custody in a workhouse or to service in the army. But such attempts to regulate the labor supply in the interest of the capitalistic employer and the farmer with large holdings were not sufficient. The national economy was not expanding, and the pressure of population grew more and more intolerable. It coincided, however, with the dawn of liberalism and the maturing of social and humanitarian ideas. During the 1830's and 1840's a number of reform proposals were presented; the public discussions in parliament and among provincial authorities reflected the growing concern. The Poor Law Commission of 1837–1839 was finally instructed to institute some change and integrate the piecemeal reforms by which the community had taken on more and more of the poor relief costs. The resulting poor law of 1847 marked the end of a period in which begging and charitable alms were supposed to provide solutions for the problems of poverty.

The decades between 1830 and 1850 mark the climax of this period of economic pressure and rural proletarianization. As a matter of fact, the aggregate income level seems to have been maintained during the whole period. But the gains had chiefly accrued to the propertied classes while the losses had been borne by the poor. No appreciable rise in real wages occurred before the middle of the century. The industries, crafts, and trades continued to stagnate. Medieval guild regulations and manufacturing privileges hampering economic life still resisted the liberal ideas. Little living space was thus opened for the new tides of human beings. The cities continued to house only a tenth of the population (1800 — 9.8 per cent; 1850 — 10.1 per cent). Agriculture continued to account for the same major part of the population in 1850 as in 1750 (1750 — 79.8 per cent; 1850 — 77.9 per cent). It may thus be surmised that up to the middle of the last century little was achieved economically to meet the problem of population increase and little attention was given to stemming the tide of population increase except by warnings against improvident marriages, particularly in the landless class.

EMIGRATION, INDUSTRIALIZATION, AND FAMILY LIMITATION

After the middle of the century and more particularly from the 1860's onward, a new era in Swedish social history emerged. Sweden entered its dynamic phase. Population increase continued, but now at least three avenues of adjustment were opened. Emigration took one part of the overflow; industrialization took another and still greater part. Considerably later family limitation gradually began to be practiced, stemming population growth at its very source.

Emigration, chiefly to the United States, became important during the 1860's (Table 3). In the period 1880–1910 it drained out of the country a number equal to half of the natural increase. At about the same time that emigration became important, industry began to employ increasing numbers. This resulted in greater internal migration with the migrants absorbed in industry and commerce. At all times internal mobility between occupations and places far exceeded foreign migration. Agricultural pursuits constantly lost in relative proportions, and from about 1880 they lost in absolute numbers as well. The agricultural population constituted 72.4 per cent of the total in 1870 as compared with 62.1 per cent in 1890, 48.8 per cent in 1910, and 39.4 per cent in 1930.

The first industry to experience an upswing was the lumber plants, which began to expand in the 1850's. Soon afterwards the ironworks also started to expand. Both industries were responding to the increased demands for Swedish exports which arose at that time. Gradually other branches of production became industrialized. Factories sprang up utilizing the speedily developing machine techniques. Through parliamentary acts of 1846 and 1864 the guild system was dissolved, rural commerce freed, and restrictive regulations on industry relaxed. Perhaps the most significant industrial activity illustrative of the swiftly changing times was railroad building, which reached its peak in 1875–1880.

The changes in the occupational structure of the Swedish people also shifted the people to other districts and other types of living. There was an exodus from rural to urban communities, supplementing and competing with emigration and productive of equally as important sociological changes. In 1900, 21.5 per cent of the population lived in cities. By 1935, 34.2 per cent of the population was urban. Not only did cities increase; they also became more and more urbanized. The mode of living in cities had previously been of a pseudoagrarian character. Home production of both clothing and minor home furnishings was traditionally important. The art of housekeeping relied upon food storage rather than food purchases. What now developed was a sudden turn of the dominant pattern in the opposite direction: the diffusion of urban modes of living to rural communities. A considerable part of Swedish industry was, and is still, located in rural districts which were being urbanized. Also, the farmers came increasingly under the influence of urbanized civilization. The mores and psychology of the people were being transformed. Not enclosed, self-sufficient stability but dynamic expansion became the ruling principle of the social order. From the point of view of the sociology of the family nothing could be more important than this transition from self-dependent farming and clan-family production to the collectivistic integration of individuals which is typical of an industrial economy.

Through these simultaneous changes of migration and industrialization, a new equilibrium between growing masses and increased opportunities was reached. Before the century ended, however, another force was at work, tending to halt the marked expansion in population itself. The rate of natural increase, i.e., the excess of births over deaths, in population

TABLE 3. — GENERAL SURVEY OF VITAL STATISTICS IN SWEDEN, 1751-1939

PERIOD[a]	POPULATION	MARRIED PER 1,000 POPULATION	BIRTHS PER 1,000 POPULATION	ILLEGITIMATE BIRTHS PER 100 CHILDREN BORN	DEATHS PER 1,000 POPULATION	DEATHS DURING FIRST YEAR PER 100 CHILDREN BORN ALIVE	EMIGRANTS PER 1,000 POPULATION	INCREASE IN POPULATION	
								EXCESS OF BIRTHS OVER DEATHS (Per Cent)	TOTAL INCREASE (EMIGRATION AND IMMIGRATION INCLUDED) (Per Cent)
1751-1760	1,862,347	8.99	35.67	2.37	27.24	20.46		8.43	7.76
1761-1770	1,982,355	8.52	34.17	2.55	27.57	21.61		6.60	5.92
1771-1780	2,043,290	8.49	33.01	2.94	28.87	20.18		4.14	3.71
1781-1790	2,138,000	7.88	31.95	3.89	27.92	19.99		4.03	3.22
1791-1800	2,282,896	8.55	33.31	5.02	25.35	19.61		7.96	6.99
1801-1810	2,400,349	8.27	30.86	6.14	28.23	19.87		2.63	2.04
1811-1820	2,477,506	8.73	33.31	6.78	25.79	18.34		7.52	7.60
1821-1830	2,751,330	8.32	34.63	6.63	23.63	16.73		11.00	11.02
1831-1840	3,013,772	7.14	31.47	6.72	22.78	16.68		8.69	8.32
1841-1850	3,306,269	7.27	31.10	8.64	20.59	15.32		10.51	10.39
1851-1860	3,642,321	7.61	32.79	9.05	21.69	14.60	0.46	11.10	10.36
1861-1870	4,079,233	6.54	31.40	9.57	20.16	13.89	3.00	11.24	7.57
1871-1880	4,386,953	6.81	30.48	10.36	18.27	12.99	3.43	12.21	9.05
1881-1890	4,673,225	6.26	29.06	10.22	16.94	11.05	8.05	12.12	4.69
1891-1900	4,931,944	5.94	27.14	10.87	16.36	10.16	5.00	10.78	7.13
1901-1910	5,310,120	6.00	25.77	12.72	14.89	8.45	4.85	10.88	7.27
1911-1920	5,713,967	6.26	22.11	15.01	14.29	6.93	2.07	7.82	6.69
1921-1930	6,044,818	6.49	17.51	15.38	12.07	5.88	2.13	5.44	3.93
1931	6,152,319	6.97	14.80	16.31	12.54	5.66	0.48	2.26	3.29
1932	6,176,405	6.75	14.54	15.96	11.57	5.07	0.34	2.97	4.52
1933	6,200,905	7.00	13.71	15.49	11.23	4.95	0.39	2.48	3.42
1934	6,222,328	7.73	13.68	14.45	11.24	4.72	0.39	2.44	3.46
1935	6,241,791	8.22	13.76	14.22	11.67	4.59	0.39	2.09	2.79
1936	6,258,697	8.51	14.21	13.37	11.96	4.34	0.38	2.25	2.62
1937	6,275,805	8.67	14.33	12.94	11.99	4.52	0.36	2.34	2.85
1938	6,297,468	9.01	14.85	12.15	11.52	4.12	0.33	3.33	4.06
1939	6,335,759	9.51	15.31	12.25	11.50	3.87	0.57	3.87	4.93

[a] Data for 1751-1930 are computed as annual averages by 10-year periods.

Source: Statistical Yearbook of Sweden: 1940 (*Statistisk Årsbok*).

Note: Sweden has highly reliable and well-organized vital statistics consecutively since 1749. As they rest on continuous and compulsory registration of the people, there are practically no errors of enumeration. Only in the case of emigration may figures underestimate the actual exodus, as emigration was not always intentional and thus definitely reported.

gradually slowed down. Having reached its peak with an annual increase of over 12 per cent in the period 1871–1890, it fell to below 8 per cent in 1911–1920, 5.4 per cent in 1921–1930, and about 2.5 per cent in the first half of the 1930's (Table 3). A future could be foreseen in which the traditional increase would turn into a definite decrease of population.

THE DYNAMICS OF POPULATION GROWTH

The interrelationship between population expansion and economic expansion is not known. Neither can the experience of Sweden be offered as an explanation. During its first period (1750–1850) population increase appeared, as has already been pointed out, to be coupled with the risk of pauperization. During its second period (from 1850) population expansion appeared simultaneously with economic expansion and a rapid rise in real earnings and level of living. What is cause and what is effect or what is merely coincidence cannot be surmised. It may, however, be pointed out that the greatest increase in standard of living and family welfare did not occur during the period of greatest demographic expansion but in the period from 1910 onward when economic expansion was continuing at full speed while individual foresight had begun to limit population expansion.

The upward swing in the demographic pendulum had not been brought about by any deliberate and planned social action. The decisive factor in causing the population increase so typical of the last century was reduced mortality rather than increased births.

Since 1814 no war has killed off young men entering the reproductive age period. Also, the most disastrous cause of death next to war, famine, has been gradually conquered. Hygienic conditions in general began slowly to be improved, although probably not noticeably so until the country entered the period of economic expansion. When that happened, the incidence of illness declined. Infant mortality in particular was checked, decreasing from around 20 per cent in 1800 to 10 per cent in 1900 and to less than 4 per cent in 1939. With so many more of the children surviving, average family size increased and a saving of prospective parents occurred. The death rate continued to fall during the same period but its beneficial effect on population growth was partly offset by emigration and by a falling birth rate. From the middle to the end of the century the marriage rate also fell and then began slowly to rise.

Some of these factors retain their dramatic importance for formulating the problems of the present and the future. But some have gradually lost their significance. Thus emigration has practically ceased. In the 1930's immigration into Sweden, and particularly remigration from the United States, was more important than emigration. No marked change is to be foreseen in mortality conditions, except that the infant mortality rate still leaves room for some improvement. The expectation of advances in health and longevity is statistically offset by the fact that as the proportion of old people increases a higher death rate follows.

The strategic factor now and in the future is fertility. In the 1880's the birth rate started its downward trend, although it did not gain much impetus before the turn of the century (Table 3). After 1910 this decrease became the outstanding feature of the whole demographic development, at present wrought with catastrophic significance.

This situation is most definitely mirrored in figures of the so-called net reproductivity. Expressing a population's ability to reproduce itself as the number of girls which 1,000 newborn girls may be expected to bear during

TABLE 4. — NET REPRODUCTION RATES IN SWEDEN, 1925–1937

YEAR	NET REPRODUCTION RATES BASED ON MORTALITY STATISTICS FOR THE FOLLOWING PERIODS:			
	1921–1925	1926–1930	1921–1930	1931–1935
1925	0.958			
1926	0.914			
1927	0.867			
1928	0.858			
1929	0.802	0.809		
1930	0.828	0.834		
1931		0.777		
1932		0.761	0.758	
1933		0.709	0.706	0.729
1934			0.703	0.726
1935				0.723
1936				0.749
1937				0.754

Source: Population Changes (*Befolkningsrörelsen*).

their lifetime (assuming constant fertility and mortality conditions), it has been calculated that up to 1910 that figure remained around 1,500 in Sweden. For 1911–1915 it was around 1,300. It continued to decline and in 1925 fell below the net reproduction limit of 1,000. In 1930 it was calculated as 828, and during most of the 1930's it fluctuated between 725 and 750 (Table 4). This means that at present only three-fourths enough births are occurring to sustain the population in the long run.

POPULATION DISCUSSIONS

The problems of population have thus greatly changed in their import during recent times. So have opinions on population questions. Only on three or four occasions can the population discussion be said to have aroused such interest among the whole people that it transformed general thinking and became of significance for political action. The earlier, sporadic, and largely academic discussions of population problems in Sweden are therefore disregarded here. The first time population problems became of general concern was in the 1880's when the birth control propaganda was started. That the fall in the birth rate began almost simultaneously must be noted, but no direct causal relationship is postulated. The second time population problems came into the foreground was around the turn of the century, when emigration became a problem, weighing heavily on the national mind. A broad public investigation was started, and colonization and homeownership movements encouraged. Here there was the remarkable coincidence that emigration became a source of worry at a time of rapid increase in population and that the problem of emigration had already lost its practical importance when the conscious planning for its solution began. A third occasion was when a conservative counterattack upon birth control propaganda succeeded in gaining national attention. This resulted in the so-called anticontraceptive law of 1910, which ironically enough was followed by the unmistakable spread of family limitation. The nation was again aroused about population problems in the 1930's, when the impending decline was realized. To continue the chronicle of historical irony it may be noted that when the readiness to launch a program of family security was reaching its climax, the problem had already taken another coloring because of the new World War surrounding the country.

The story of the first intellectual approach to the problem of population policy is a fascinating one, both as personal history and as a cultural document. It was made by a man who could combine high scientific theorization in the fields of demography and economics with the ardor of an evangelist for birth control. His name was Knut Wicksell. Later he became an economist of world-wide fame, but first he was a crusader against Victorian public hypocrisy in the small university town of Upsala.

As a rosy-cheeked young student, Wicksell appeared in 1880 at a youth meeting of the Temperance Lodge "Army of Hope" and gave a public lecture on "The Causes of Human Misery." [211] He asserted that poverty was the ultimate cause of all moral ills — of the vices of intemperance and prostitution, the late marriages and the double standard. With Malthus he believed that poverty arose from the perpetual pressure of population increase on the means of subsistence. He set forth the common Neo-Malthusian conclusion that in the long run nothing but voluntary family limitation could lay the foundation for a happier society. Wicksell considered no place too elevated for preaching these precepts, not even the pulpit. He appealed to the doctors to give advice on contraceptives to poor people without regard for prejudices. He advocated the forming of societies, the members of which should make a vow never to have more than two or at the most three children.

Wicksell's lecture came as a bombshell. All the bourgeoisie raged. The national culture had for a long time been becoming increasingly narrow and isolated. The newspapers rang with eloquent outcries. A professor of philosophy accused Wicksell of turning "marriage itself into prostitution." He talked of "new Baal worship by the servants of lust." A professor of economics dwelt on the danger of informing the contented poor of their misfortunes. The clergy were even more outraged. Doctors hastened to oppose the dangerous issue. The local medical society, embracing the professors of the medical school, issued a declaration that it considered "the use of contraceptive measures unworthy of the medical calling." It solemnly pronounced further that its "holy duty was to protect every function in the animal life and not least the one where creation is revealing itself in man, thus constituting the deepest mystery in the medical field," and that even if the woman's health was in danger medical art could recommend only abstinence and would not recommend means that would "open the doors for vice itself." The now somewhat humorous phrasing cannot conceal the sincerity of the attack.

A flow of pamphlet literature followed this declaration. Wicksell was reprimanded by the university authorities, who issued a warning to the young student as a preliminary to expulsion. But Wicksell continued his crusade. He devoted some years to touring the country with his message, given, it must be stressed, in a sober, learned, statistical, not to say boring, form. He continued despite a hostility so great that he was publicly denounced as an "apostle of promiscuity." But he also continued his economic and legal studies, finally becoming professor of economics at the State University at Lund in 1904. Despite his propaganda and despite even a term in prison, on the accusation of blasphemy rather than of obscenity, he thus obtained one of the most distinguished posts in the secure Swedish civil service. This must be said in order to show that even if the cultural atmosphere was far from advanced, academic justice was swayed only by scientific considerations. This also helps one to understand why despite outcries birth control propaganda started to gain popular response within the Swedish nation on its rational merits.

In his fight for birth control and in his economic thinking, Wicksell never went so far as to visualize a system of reform in the social order. In the spirit of the liberal era to which he belonged, he stopped with the demand that the wrongs be righted by individuals. Birth control information was spreading and family limitation beginning to be discussed. Partly because of the prestige of such a proponent as Wicksell, who was a great scholar, and partly because of the awakening social thinking of the labor groups, the cause advanced on a comparatively smooth path to endorsement by various progressive groups. But even 50 years after Wicksell's first appearance the verbalized public opinion of newspapers, church, Riksdag, and public speeches had not sanctioned birth control as a normal practice.

Several setbacks were encountered on the road to enlightenment. The first decade of the present century was marked by nationalistic concern about the people's future and reactionary concern about its morals. It is probably correct to interpret the discussion about the danger of emigration and the danger of birth control under one and the same head. In both cases the actual trend which was dreaded was one of diminishing population or even a slowing down of previous population increase. The evaluation favoring certain remedies was colored by a romantically conservative conception of the "naturalness" of the large family and the rural home. The emigration discussion resulted in a remarkable set of investigations (*Emigrationsutredningen,* 1907-1913), which produced a wealth of information about social conditions in Sweden. In the field of practical reforms the information collected greatly encouraged the movement toward homeownership. A lively discussion about religious and sexual morals took place at the same time. Wicksell's propaganda continued. Great authors like Strindberg influenced thinking in a parallel direction, and Ellen Key's messages about the supreme rights of real love were added to the discussion. The conservatives also assembled their forces, with the consequence that at the opening of this century Sweden witnessed its final public discussion on religious dogmas, looked upon in later decades as "the time when the devil was abolished."

In that same stream of moral interests must be seen the "decency" campaign against birth control, which resulted in the so-called anticontraceptive law of 1910, to which reference has previously been made. Effective from 1911, this law against the dissemination of information about birth control, and particularly the accompanying publicity, probably did more than anything else to familiarize the public with the existence of contraceptives.

Popular thinking develops at a dangerously slow pace. Wicksell had tried to draw attention to the impending flood of population when presenting his program of family limitation. His facts were true in 1880. But when his message, after much resistance, began to be more generally accepted in 1920 and 1930, the facts were no longer the same. Birth control practices had become fixed. Already in 1923 Sweden had a lower birth rate than France and thus the lowest in the world, only yielding that place after a decade to Austria (1934).

Suddenly quite a new problem faced the people. Within the lifetime of a single generation this fundamental problem of life and death of the nation had totally changed its import. The story of the 1880's had to reverse itself. It now became as necessary for advocates who wanted society to adjust to the family to teach and preach in the face of calumny as it once was for Wicksell and his followers in order to liberate the individual from reproductive slavery.

The trend toward an impending decline in actual population, following the decline in the birth rate, began to be realized by both experts and laymen around 1930. The situation with regard to public opinion was highly explosive. Progressive groups were still committed to the simple ideas of the birth control movement, which were still adequate so far as the need for individual enlightenment went but which were no longer adequate in socio-economic philosophy. No overpopulation now threatened, but just the contrary. The more conservative groups were still nervously engaged in trying by incantation to turn population trends upward.

In the fall of 1934 the attention of experts, politicians, and the educated public was once more drawn to the population question, when a work *Crisis in the Population Question* [*168*] was published and widely read. It first served to bring to general attention the fact not only that a decline in total population was impending but also that such a decline was destined to take the form of an incessant and self-perpetuating liquidation of the people. Next it succeeded in making people realize that the practical problem of averting that fate involved social reforms creating a new foundation for the institution of the family. The scheme of social reforms outlined was well in line with the reforms for social security and increased welfare launched by the dominant political party, the Social Democrats, and so immediately entered the domain of practical politics. When it was finally stressed that honest discussion of sex and family and intelligent planning of childbearing must be made the foundations for any public population policy, elements from what had been widely divergent sets of ideals became merged.

This merging inevitably led all political parties and ideological groups to take a vital part in the ensuing discussion of a population program for Sweden. Still more important was the fact that adult education and the widespread habit of active participation in democratic issues had made practically the whole general public competent to take part in such discussions. A concerted effort to give the whole people a background of factual knowledge on this question followed. The radio carried a year-long series of lectures and debates on the subject of population. Study groups were formed all over the country, the leaders of which were informed by a correspondence course from the national broadcasting company. The Workers' Educational Association issued a study manual. Books and pamphlets appeared in ever larger editions. Every newspaper and magazine carried article after article on the subject, together with — not least important — jokes, letters to the editor, and so forth. Ridicule in stage reviews and elsewhere, following the old pattern of classifying all connotations of sexual and family life as indecent, was tried as an evasion mechanism by many, but this only helped to keep the discussion alive. The population question was news for a long time, but it was news with an impetus to study, to social deliberation, to political action.

It cannot be denied that it is more difficult to face squarely problems of population which may touch clandestine sexual problems in people's own lives than it is to face other social questions. The discussion was far from harmonious and peaceful, but a general debate throughout the nation was obtained not only on birth control but also on the double standard of sexual morality, the disharmony between conventional standards and actual behavior, and the differences in attitudes toward sexual problems between young and old. The lancing of the boil of public dishonesty was painful, but it was lanced. In general the discussion penetrated to the roots of the problems and was pursued in most social groups with courage and rationality, with dignity and understanding of its social implications.[2]

---

[2] No complete analysis of the formation of opinion is undertaken here. For an elaboration of that fascinating theme, see Gunnar Myrdal, *Population, A Problem for Democracy*, Harvard University Press, Cambridge, 1940, Chapter V, "People's Opinions."

CHAPTER III

THE CHANGING FAMILY: MARRIAGE AND
ILLEGITIMACY

Wᴴᴱɴ approaching the task of planning a rational program for population, one must first ascertain what factors are subject to change. Two closely interrelated demographic factors appear as strategic in the general picture of present Swedish population dynamics presented in the preceding chapter, namely, the low marriage rate and the high illegitimacy rate. The marriage rate fell steadily for several generations. In recent years the fall has been checked, however, and turned into a surprising upward trend. The illegitimacy rate has, on the contrary, ceased rising and actually turned downward. Both these changeable factors appear to be strategic in the sense that they ought to be susceptible to induced forces of social policy.

Mᴀʀʀɪᴀɢᴇ Rᴀᴛᴇ

During the period 1751–1830 the Swedish marriage rate already was lower than in most countries (Table 3). This is probably to be explained as reflecting prudence among a population consisting for the most part of farmers with small and medium-sized holdings. Access to land was not easy. Division of holdings was held undesirable and was controlled, on the one hand, by the laws regulating succession and partition of land holdings and, on the other, by the practical difficulty of splitting the narrow strips held by individual households under the open-field system. When the enclosure reforms gradually broke up the village holdings and families moved to individual homesteads, colonization became easier. At the same time the marriage possibilities of the landless rural classes became still less as those classes grew in size and population pressure was intensified. This operated to keep the national marriage rate low. This tendency seems to have become stronger toward the middle of the century, the "poor decades" of 1830–1850 being marked by a decline to about seven marriages per 1,000 inhabitants. With the onset of emigration and industrialization the rate decreased still further, declining to about six per 1,000 around 1900.

TABLE 5. — FIRST MARRIAGES PER 1,000 UNMARRIED IN SAME
AGE GROUP IN SWEDEN, BY SEX, 1751–1937

Period[a]	Age in Years								
	15–19	20–24	25–29	30–34	35–39	40–44	45–49	50 and over	20–49
	Men								
1751–1760 . . .									117.7
1761–1770 . . .									109.3
1771–1780 . . .									97.2
1781–1790 . . .									83.3
1791–1800 . . .									98.5
1801–1810 . . .									94.5
1811–1820 . . .									97.4
1821–1830 . . .									101.3
1831–1840 . . .									86.9
1841–1850 . . .									77.0
1851–1860 . . .									78.0
1861–1870 . . .	0.08	42.3	104.4	106.2	72.1	48.9	26.4	6.35	70.1
1871–1880 . . .	0.12	45.3	113.2	120.2	85.1	51.0	28.9	7.53	75.2
1881–1890 . . .	0.18	45.4	104.5	101.7	71.0	43.3	25.3	6.36	69.4
1891–1900 . . .	0.25	44.5	101.3	92.6	65.9	41.8	23.7	5.96	67.0
1901–1910 . . .	0.27	42.5	100.2	88.9	60.7	37.4	21.7	5.31	64.4
1911–1920 . . .	0.26	37.1	101.5	91.5	60.7	38.1	22.4	5.68	63.2
1921–1930 . . .	0.19	33.0	95.3	94.4	62.9	37.4	20.9	5.17	60.5
1931	0.23	34.0	94.9	96.2	65.2	37.4	21.5	5.33	61.8
1932	0.18	32.7	89.9	90.4	61.1	36.6	18.4	4.90	58.7
1933	0.15	33.3	92.6	91.4	61.6	37.0	19.7	4.89	60.2
1934	0.27	35.9	100.8	101.2	68.7	38.8	20.9	5.39	66.1
1935	0.27	38.3	107.8	108.0	69.6	39.8	22.3	5.39	70.4
1936	0.29	40.4	113.0	110.3	72.2	42.2	23.3	5.32	73.6
1937	0.34	42.8	118.3	115.8	74.6	43.2	22.4	5.24	77.1

[a] Data for 1751–1930 are computed as averages by 10-year periods.

The age distribution and the sex ratio were both undergoing considerable changes during this long period because of decreased mortality and fertility and also because of emigration which drained off the young people, especially the young men. In Table 5 the number of first marriages per 1,000 unmarried is shown by sex and age for the period 1861–1937. The figures for the first decade, 1861–1870, are abnormally low, the reason being the extremely poor crops, particularly in the latter years of the decade. The figures given in the table relate only to first marriages, but there was a still more rapid decrease in remarriages. In spite of the substantial increase in divorces discussed below, which *per se* should tend to increase remarriages, the proportion of all new marriages with at least one partner having been married previously was 26 per cent in 1801–1810, 16 per cent in 1851–1860, 10 per cent in 1901–1910, and only 9 per cent in 1931–1935. This remarkable development can be only partly explained by improved health conditions and lowered mortality in the mature ages.

Patterns surviving from the agrarian culture with regard to prudence in founding a family may have been at work in keeping the marriage rate low. But it must be noted that the pressure causing this prudence should have been of decreasing force in the period when emigration began to reduce the number of young people competing for the available employ-

THE CHANGING FAMILY: MARRIAGE AND ILLEGITIMACY

TABLE 5. — FIRST MARRIAGES PER 1,000 UNMARRIED IN SAME
AGE GROUP IN SWEDEN, BY SEX, 1751–1937 *(Continued)*

Period[a]	AGE IN YEARS								
	15–19	20–24	25–29	30–34	35–39	40–44	45–49	50 and over	20–44
	Women								
1751–1760 . . .									117.4
1761–1770 . . .									111.6
1771–1780 . . .									102.9
1781–1790 . . .									89.7
1791–1800 . . .									100.7
1801–1810 . . .									96.3
1811–1820 . . .									99.7
1821–1830 . . .									110.6
1831–1840 . . .									97.8
1841–1850 . . .									86.2
1851–1860 . . .									87.1
1861–1870 . . .	8.40	65.8	98.1	83.1	53.4	29.6	14.5	—	78.6
1871–1880 . . .	8.80	70.4	104.6	83.8	53.0	30.5	15.5	—	82.9
1881–1890 . . .	9.11	66.6	95.9	71.4	43.6	24.8	14.2	2.21	76.1
1891–1900 . . .	9.33	69.8	93.5	67.5	40.2	23.6	12.1	2.02	75.0
1901–1910 . . .	10.10	73.1	92.5	62.5	34.9	19.4	10.7	1.68	74.7
1911–1920 . . .	9.53	74.1	93.7	61.3	33.4	17.9	9.7	1.72	74.3
1921–1930 . . .	9.67	72.4	94.7	61.5	32.1	17.1	9.1	1.63	73.1
1931	11.06	76.4	99.6	62.6	31.2	17.0	8.9	1.64	76.3
1932	10.69	74.5	95.2	59.9	31.2	15.4	9.0	1.52	73.6
1933	11.14	76.9	99.5	62.7	32.0	15.9	7.9	1.63	76.1
1934	12.43	84.7	111.6	69.7	36.3	16.1	8.5	1.64	84.2
1935	12.46	91.1	122.2	76.5	37.2	18.3	9.4	1.48	90.6
1936	13.13	96.7	129.1	79.7	39.7	19.5	9.3	1.55	95.6
1937	14.30	103.4	136.4	87.2	40.6	20.0	9.8	1.68	101.6

Source: Statistical Yearbook of Sweden: 1940 (*Statistisk Årsbok*).

ment possibilities in the country and when economic opportunities were
rapidly enhanced by industrialization.

SEX DISTRIBUTION

The increase in mobility during the period of industrialization led to
an exceedingly unfavorable sex ratio in different localities (Table 6). This
fact, which operates to reduce marriages, may somewhat relieve the Swedish
people from the suspicion that interest in marriage is simply underdeveloped
in the national psychology.

Notwithstanding the fact that many women move to join their husbands'
households at marriage, which may explain part of the difference in the distribution of the sexes, it seems probable that men are more stationary and
women more migratory as far as internal migration is concerned. It is certain
that men are more rural and women more urban. Both differences obviously
tend to reduce mating and marrying. If adequate data were available for
the more marriageable ages separately, this unfavorable distribution would
become still more apparent. Long-time series showing the historical development in this respect are difficult to obtain. Some inferences may be
drawn, however, from a study of migration for 1926–1930 (Table 7). It
should also be pointed out that only 50.7 per cent of the men migrating were

TABLE 6. — LOCATION AND MIGRATION OF THE SWEDISH POPULATION,
BY SEX, 1880-1930

YEAR	NUMBER OF FEMALES PER 100 MALES			
	Living in		Having moved from	
	Rural districts	Urban districts	Rural to urban districts	Urban to rural districts
1880	104	120	124	110
1890	104	119	125	110
1900	102	117	125	105
1910	101	117	127	105
1920	99	115	127	103
1930	97	117	134	102

Source: Population Commission, Report on Rural Depopulation (*Betänkande angående
"landsbygdens avfolkning"*).

TABLE 7. — INTERNAL MIGRATION IN SWEDEN, BY SEX AND AGE,
1926-1930

AGE	MEN		WOMEN	
	Migration to rural districts 1926–1930 as per cent of total rural population in 1930	Migration to urban districts 1926–1930 as per cent of total urban population in 1930	Migration to rural districts 1926–1930 as per cent of total rural population in 1930	Migration to urban districts 1926–1930 as per cent of total urban population in 1930
Total	16.1	18.3	17.9	20.8
Under 15 years .	15.8	15.6	15.6	16.0
15–19 years . .	15.5	19.1	19.1	28.3
20–24 years . .	21.6	27.9	34.8	41.2
25–29 years . .	27.3	31.6	37.3	36.9
30–34 years . .	25.7	26.5	27.9	26.8
35–39 years . .	20.3	19.8	19.9	18.9
40–44 years . .	15.9	15.2	15.1	14.4
45–49 years . .	12.6	12.2	11.9	11.9
50–64 years . .	8.7	9.1	8.3	9.3
65 years and over	5.2	7.0	5.1	6.9

Source: Population Commission, Report on Rural Depopulation (*Betänkande angående
"landsbygdens avfolkning"*).

in the age group 15–30 years, while 61.6 per cent of the women belonged to that age group.

Sweden has thus arrived at a stage where the geographical distribution of men and women is an important deterrent to marriage. Women, mostly in low social positions, are numerous in urban districts where men are scarce. At the same time women are scarce in the rural districts where the men live who could best afford to marry and who really need wives in their agrarian pursuits (Table 8). In the most favorable age group for

TABLE 8. — NUMBER OF UNMARRIED WOMEN PER 100 UNMARRIED MEN IN SWEDEN, BY AGE AND DISTRICT, 1935

AGE	TOTAL	RURAL DISTRICTS	SEMIRURAL DISTRICTS	URBAN DISTRICTS
15–19 years . .	95	87	98	108
20–24 years . .	81	62	78	110
25–29 years . .	72	52	66	105
30–34 years . .	85	60	80	130
35–39 years . .	105	74	110	161
40–44 years . .	129	91	143	200
45–49 years . .	148	107	172	216
50–54 years . .	153	112	180	218
55–59 years . .	161	116	197	236
60–64 years . .	167	118	192	266
65–69 years . .	190	130	226	312
70–74 years . .	196	136	205	349
75–79 years . .	211	146	227	402
80–84 years . .	230	162	234	488
85–89 years . .	265	193	316	486
90–94 years . .	294	224	294	531
95 years and over	493	409	900	667

Source: Population Commission, Report on Rural Depopulation (*Betänkande angående "landsbygdens avfolkning"*).

marriage, 25–29 years, there were only 52 unmarried women in rural districts in 1935 to 100 unmarried men. Not until 45 years of age do the women exceed the men in numbers.

The tendencies toward separation of prospective partners in marriage go even further than the data indicate. Many of the Swedish industries are located in semirural districts, and the most conspicuous characteristic of such districts is the predominance of a single type of production. Thus men find employment in mining districts, in the iron- and steelworks, and in the lumber and pulp districts, while women monopolize employment in the textile districts. In most of these districts normal vocational opportunities for more than one sex, whether married or not, do not exist. Thus the very structure of Swedish industry, sometimes praised because it "ruralizes the workers," would seem to be one of the factors accounting for the low marriage rate.

Even when industrial conditions do not separate the sexes geographically, the vocational structure itself may make it difficult for them to meet. The labor market, which is more and more becoming the chief determinant of the individual's social setting, rarely functions as a "marriage market." The female domestic servant is as isolated from marriageable men as the nurse or even more so. In factories where men and women are both working there is even a tendency to separate the sexes in order to avoid the unpleasant comparisons of their unequal wages. Sometimes this separation means the monopolizing of one fabrication process by one sex; sometimes it means keeping men and women at different stages of the production chain; sometimes it implies only assigning them to different workrooms. All these devices reduce their chances to meet and particularly to meet as equals and to remain near each other in such a way that marriage seems a natural and not an extraordinary outcome of their everyday contacts.

In the professions there is less separation of work, although even there tendencies toward segregation on the basis of sex appear. In publicly supported schools for older youth the mingling of young men and women has until lately been restricted. The state secondary schools (*realskola* and *gymnasium*) did not admit girls as students until 1927. Changes in normal schools for training teachers, adopted as late as 1935, did not abolish segregation. On the other hand, the universities and professional schools have been open to both sexes for over 50 years. Other grounds than the separation of the sexes accounted for the earlier barriers against women.

Segregation in both factories and schools will be defended by its proponents on grounds of decency and discipline. Sometimes there are no grounds whatsoever; it is just taken for granted. But as a result the possibilities for young men and women to meet young people of the opposite sex with whom they would have specific chances of sharing happy married lives are sharply curtailed. This point of view is, of course, altogether foreign to the older men and women who control society. Their blindness may one day become a subject of satire for the sociologist. In the course of reforming teacher training in 1935, [41] one normal school for men and one for women with university entrance qualifications were established. To have set up two coeducational schools seems to have been inconceivable. Moreover, the school for men was placed in the old university town of Upsala, where these men would always feel inferior to the university students and where girls on approximately the same cultural level are scarce among the thousands of students, while the division for women was placed in Stockholm, where there are already 1,250 women per 1,000 men and a still greater difference in the younger ages.

These examples are not selected for their curiosity value but because it has never been recognized that one of the practical problems for Sweden is the occupational structure which makes marrying difficult. Only the new tendencies toward joint recreational activities serve to counteract this segregation of the sexes. There is, however, a growing necessity for some recognition of the problem. If great hopes should be attached to any population policy, some fundamental attitudes and habits on the part of society will have to be considerably changed.

Half the Adult Population Unmarried

The prudence in marrying, which has become a pattern in Sweden, also results in a high average age at marriage. Average ages have not changed significantly since the first decade for which such statistics are available, 1861–1870. At that time the average age at marriage of men was 30.57 years and of women 27.91 years. In 1931–1935 the average ages were 30.55 years and 26.92 years, respectively. The average age at first marriage has, however, shown a slight increase for men, from 28.82 to 29.47 years, and a slight decrease for women, from 27.12 to 26.50 years. (See Fig. I.)

A long waiting period before acquiring sufficient economic security to marry has been typical among both the farming and the professional groups in Sweden. The average age at marriage is particularly high for civil servants, officers, physicians, and clergymen. Stabilizing one's income and finishing one's studies are some of the ambitions that tend to postpone marriage. As age at marriage is also comparatively high for women, it is logical to conclude that when marriage finally occurs it often joins persons who had selected each other long before. Firsthand knowledge of Swedish culture also reveals the frequency of long engagements, the conventional pattern even being to announce a betrothal years in advance of marriage. This particular matchmaking structure has two important consequences for population problems: it shortens the fertility period within marriage and thus reduces the number of children, and it increases premarital sex relations. Both these consequences should have closer attention.

The result of all these tendencies to avoid and postpone marriage obviously is to make Sweden a nation of unwed persons. In the census year of 1930 single persons accounted for 44 per cent of the total population over 15 years of age. In addition nearly 9 per cent were widowed or divorced. In 1750 the single constituted 35 per cent and the widowed or divorced 10 per cent of the total population over 15 years of age. At least 20 per cent of Swedish women reaching 50 years of age have never married, while the corresponding figure for Denmark is about 15 per cent and for France about 10 per cent. What this difference in design for living means for the whole cultural, moral, and psychological atmosphere in the different countries should not

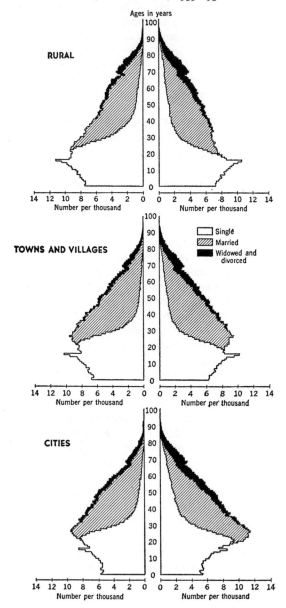

Fig. I. — Distribution of the Swedish Population by Age, Sex, and Marital Status, by Residence, 1935–1936

be overlooked. To pursue these differences in their subtle workings would, however, be to venture into deep waters.

RECENT TRENDS AND PRESENT TENDENCIES

The crude marriage rate shows an upward trend for the present century (Table 3). Until recent years, however, the rise in the marriage rate has been largely fictitious. It has resulted chiefly from changes in age distribution and sex ratio. If the number of first marriages per 1,000 unmarried men aged 20-49 years or per 1,000 unmarried women aged 20-44 years is used as a more refined measure, the apparent increase in the marriage rate is reduced considerably and for a long period entirely disappears (Table 5). The marriage rate increased for both men and women after the low point of the depression of the early thirties but the increase was much less for men than for women because of a shifting proportion between the sexes, whereby the relative number of men was becoming greater. In fact the marriage rate for young women 20-29 years of age was higher in the late thirties than at any time since 1860.

As economic considerations are paramount in contracting a marriage and as men are most often the breadwinners in the contemporary social order, which makes their attitudes decisive, the situation may be summarized by saying that up to the year 1934 no net increase in men's inclination to marry had occurred. The change in the economically favorable years after 1934 may be explained as partially due to the realization of marriage plans postponed during the previous lean years and as probably due also to the positive encouragement of family life derived from the tumultuous family discussion itself.

The prognosis for the future is along two lines. Some decrease in inclination to marry may result if through more efficient birth control fewer premarital sex relations result in pregnancies which force cover-up marriages. On the other hand, some increase is due to accrue from practically the same cause. A more reliable birth control technique will make it possible for many young couples to marry earlier as they can avoid having children. It is impossible to foresee, however, whether improved contraceptive techniques and a wider diffusion of birth control practices will tend to decrease or increase marriages. These factors with their contradictory effects are the most tangible of the forces which will influence the frequency of marriages. The economic development, war, international dangers, and changes in social attitudes and values will have their effect as well. Induced changes consciously engineered toward reshaping the economic basis for marriage and family life and toward enhancing the valuation of married life have to be superimposed upon the undirected changes.

This is not the place for detailed treatment of the role of the marriage factor in population development and population policy. In a general way it may be pointed out, however, that its importance for population quantity is derived from the fact that marriage represents an increased probability of births. If constant marital fertility is assumed, more marriages and earlier marriages mean more children. But a rise in the marriage rate and a decline in average age at marriage, which are made possible through improved contraceptive practices, make this assumption of marital fertility remaining the same highly questionable. Such changes may, in fact, increase the number of births little if at all.

DIVORCE

With life expectancy increased and age at marriage remaining approximately the same, the prospective duration of marriage itself has increased, thus making the demand on lifelong, faithful marriage quantitatively more exacting for the modern couple. This factor should obviously not be over-estimated; neither should it be as completely overlooked as it usually is. At 25 years of age the life expectancy for women in the period 1816–1840 was 37.0 years, but in 1921–1930 it was 46.4 years for the married and 44.7 years for the unmarried. An increase of nearly 10 years in marriage duration will evidently of itself somewhat increase the strain on modern marriages in comparison with those of the earlier period. Although the divorce rate after a certain point decreases with the duration of marriage, a little more than one-half of all divorces during 1931–1935 involved couples who had been married for 10 years or more. Almost one in five of the marriages broken by divorce during that period had lasted for at least 20 years.[1]

The increase in divorces in modern times usually is given another explanation, namely an economic one. It is evidently true that improved economic conditions have made many divorces possible, which otherwise would not have materialized. It is also apparent that the dependence on landownership and the unwillingness to split or mortgage landholdings were strong deterrents to divorce in the old patriarchal rural society. These deterrents have been gradually diminishing in importance as a smaller proportion of the people depends on agriculture and as agriculture itself is becoming more and more a modern business in which the personal attachment to a particular piece of land is being lost. The increased mobility in industrial society and the secularization and rationalization of ideals and mores have had effects in the same direction. Even in modern times, however, divorces are much less common in the country than in urban areas (Table 9).

Under these and other influences, which on the whole have not been very different from the forces operative in other parts of the Western world, the trend shows a gradual increase in divorce from 0.5 to 5 or 6

[1] Statistical Yearbook of Sweden: 1938 (*Statistisk Årsbok*).

TABLE 9. — DIVORCES IN SWEDEN, 1831-1939

PERIOD[a]	NUMBER OF DIVORCES	NUMBER OF DIVORCES PER 1,000 NEW MARRIAGES	NUMBER OF DIVORCES PER 100,000 POPULATION		
			Total	Rural	Urban
1831-1840	106	4.9	3.9	—	—
1841-1850	108	4.5	3.6	—	—
1851-1860	121	4.4	3.3	—	—
1861-1870	130	4.9	3.2	—	—
1871-1880	193	6.5	4.4	—	—
1881-1890	234	8.0	5.0	2.8	15.5
1891-1900	338	11.5	6.9	3.4	20.5
1901-1910	474	14.9	8.9	4.2	24.5
1911-1915	733	22.2	13.0	5.8	33.4
1916-1920	1,088	28.3	18.7	9.0	43.1
1921-1925	1,566	41.4	26.1	13.1	56.2
1926-1930	2,060	50.7	33.8	16.7	70.7
1931-1935	2,548	56.1	41.1	19.3	84.6
1936	2,848	53.5	45.5	20.7	92.2
1937	3,128	56.3	49.8	25.0	95.2
1938	3,461	61.0	54.9	28.2	102.7
1939	3,541	58.9	55.9	29.1	103.1

[a] Data for 1831–1935 are computed as averages by 5- and 10-year periods.
Source: Statistical Yearbook of Sweden: 1940 (*Statistisk Årsbok*).

per cent of new marriages. Using the measure of number of divorces per 100,000 population, comparisons may be made with other countries. These show Sweden with 46 divorces per 100,000 population in 1936 as compared with 35 in Norway, 37 in Belgium, 35 in Holland, and 10 in England, on the one hand, and 52 in France, 75 in Germany, 86 in Denmark, and 129 in the United States, on the other.

ILLEGITIMACY

The Swedish rate of illegitimacy, high in comparison with the rates of other countries and until recently steadily increasing, helps to illuminate fundamental attitudes with regard to sex and family. In the decade 1921–1930 one child in every six or seven was born outside of wedlock. At present one child in every eight is illegitimate. (See Table 10.) These figures should, however, be used with care. Part of the apparent excess of illegitimacy in Sweden as compared with other countries is undoubtedly due to more accurate statistics. The complete and continuous registration of the people prevents underenumeration of illegitimate births.[2] Moreover,

[2] Only if one widens the concept of illegitimate births to include cases in which children are the results of extramarital relations of married women may underenumeration sometimes occur.

a large proportion of the illegitimate children become legitimatized after birth by the parents marrying, while some of the children technically classified as born out of wedlock are the offspring of stable, marriagelike relations of couples who have simply omitted the marriage ceremony.[3] Such common-law marriages are called conscience marriages in the intellectual group and Stockholm marriages in the working-class group. Up to 1915 a clerical ceremony was necessary for marriage. Before this date the growing

TABLE 10. — EXTRAMARITAL FERTILITY IN SWEDEN, 1751–1937

PERIOD[a]	PER CENT OF ALL WOMEN BEARING CHILDREN	PER CENT OF UNMARRIED WOMEN IN SPECIFIED AGE GROUPS BEARING CHILDREN							
		15–19	20–24	25–29	30–34	35–39	40–44	45–49	20–44
1751–1760	2.46								1.22
1761–1770	2.64								1.27
1771–1780	3.05								1.31
1781–1790	4.04								1.59
1791–1800	5.20								2.19
1801–1810	6.37								2.44
1811–1820	7.04								2.85
1821–1830	6.87								3.26
1831–1840	6.93								3.11
1841–1850	8.83								3.34
1851–1860	9.22								3.52
1861–1870	9.69								3.71
1871–1880	10.47	0.41	3.14	4.91	4.72	3.67	1.67	0.17	3.96
1881–1890	10.33	0.51	3.17	4.33	3.93	3.03	1.45	0.16	3.68
1891–1900	10.97	0.72	3.51	4.10	3.59	2.78	1.32	0.14	3.78
1901–1910	12.84	1.07	4.04	4.16	3.39	2.52	1.18	0.12	4.12
1911–1920	15.14	1.24	4.14	3.70	2.81	2.11	0.98	0.10	3.97
1921–1930	15.50	1.25	3.37	2.54	1.80	1.31	0.61	0.06	3.05
1931	16.31	1.29	2.96	2.10	1.51	1.03	0.43	0.06	2.65
1932	15.96	1.27	2.88	2.05	1.35	0.90	0.41	0.04	2.32
1933	15.61	1.18	2.61	1.85	1.25	0.92	0.42	0.05	2.32
1934	14.48	1.15	2.46	1.63	1.17	0.84	0.39	0.03	2.16
1935	14.32	1.16	2.47	1.70	1.15	0.83	0.33	0.03	2.17
1936	13.46	1.11	2.46	1.66	1.21	0.75	0.33	0.03	2.14
1937	13.03	1.13	2.44	1.68	1.18	0.74	0.32	0.03	2.15

[a] Data for 1751–1930 are computed as annual averages by 10-year periods.

Source: Statistical Yearbook of Sweden: 1940 (*Statistisk Årsbok*).

radical opposition on social issues sometimes expressed itself in contempt for the religious vows combined with marrying. Among urban industrial workers this secularization and radicalism was sometimes supplemented by a certain disinclination toward the affectation and bourgeois display of having a special ceremony at some arbitrary date, when sexual relations and even the establishment of a common household could develop so naturally and unpretentiously. The lack of a registered ceremony is thus

[3] An effort to determine the number of such unions was made at the extra census of 1935–1936. It was found that at least 0.5 per cent (5.4 per thousand) of all single women above 15 years of age were living in a marriagelike relation where the man in the household obviously was father to her child or children also living there. [75]

not always to be interpreted as immorality. The children are, however, statistically classified as illegitimate.

In the preindustrial rural society the rate of illegitimacy was considerably lower. Rising illegitimacy is one of the most significant indices of the social changes connected with industrialization. Illegitimacy has always been much more prevalent in cities than in the country (Table 11). The leveling

TABLE 11. — ILLEGITIMACY IN RURAL AND URBAN DISTRICTS IN SWEDEN, 1821–1939

PERIOD [a]	CHILDREN BORN OUT OF WEDLOCK AS PER CENT OF TOTAL CHILDREN BORN	
	Rural	Urban
1821–1830	5.07	22.27
1831–1840	4.99	24.34
1841–1850	6.75	27.10
1851–1860	7.12	25.50
1861–1870	7.55	23.47
1871–1880	8.53	20.86
1881–1890	8.45	18.17
1891–1900	8.95	18.55
1901–1910	10.32	20.63
1911–1920	12.62	22.01
1921–1930	13.70	20.16
1931–1935	14.55	17.22
1936	13.13	13.90
1937	12.76	13.32
1938	11.81	12.84
1939	11.94	12.86

[a] Data for 1821–1935 are computed as annual averages by 5- and 10-year periods.
Source: Statistical Yearbook of Sweden: 1940 (*Statistisk Årsbok*).
Note: Some rural children tend to be registered in cities, as rural women may move to and register in cities for the purpose of secrecy. As permanent domicile then must be established, however, and as births otherwise are counted as occurring where mothers are registered, this factor ought to be fairly insignificant in Sweden.

out of this difference, effected through a rapid rise of the rate in rural districts, reflects the social and psychological changes resulting from increasing urbanization.

As marital fertility has decreased in cities, one might have expected that the group of illegitimate children would have constituted a larger and larger proportion of all children. But this is not the case. The decrease in fertility in the cities seems to have occurred in both the married group and the unmarried group. In the country, however, the more recent decline in marital fertility tends to emphasize the high rate of illegitimacy.

PATTERNS OF PREMARITAL SEX EXPERIMENTATION

Hasty conclusions about changes in sexual morality should not be drawn from the changes in illegitimacy rates in recent decades and the simultaneous although opposing changes in the marriage rate. The historical background helps to provide an explanation.

In the old agrarian society premarital sex relations may or may not have been exceptional. There was, however, a structuralized system of mores controlling the meeting and mating of the young within which sexual experimentation could occur. The preliminaries to marriage were fairly well adjusted to that type of society. Youth could be given great relative freedom in playful mating experimentation in the stable society of yore. Such experimentation could be tolerated because it was always "safe," meaning that, if sex relations were involved and if a pregnancy occurred, the male partner was practically always known and marriage followed.

Much curiosity has been aroused about the old forms of courtship in the agrarian Germanic cultures. The aristocracy and the urban merchant class even in Sweden had other, more regular, and at the same time more romantic, forms for the prelude to marriage. These later developed into the Victorian morality already referred to and also into the double standard. But it is from the nation's bulwark of small, independent farmers that the dominating habits are inherited. It is impossible here to follow the development of these patterns historically.[4] For preceding centuries it suffices to indicate the great freedom in premarital preparation, the independence in choosing the mate, and the fact that controlling authority rested with the youth group rather than with parents. All this was set off against the extreme reticence in regard to relationships between the sexes in other age groups and under other situations than the defined ones. In daily life, in work, and in church socials the patterns were designed to keep the sexes apart. Some work situations and some festivals, however, were supposed to provide for the playful intercourse of young men and women between the ages for confirmation and marriage (from about 14–15 to about 30).

Particularly interesting in this connection is the pattern of "night courting" (*frieri*). Sometimes organized groups of young men went out together "calling" the girl who was in bed in the separate "girl house," then sitting around her, joking and singing and leaving one as her bedfellow

---

[4] This whole body of courting habits in Germanic Europe is singularly unnoticed in Anglo-Saxon sociology. Even in itself it ought, however, to be at least as interesting as the overemphasized mating patterns in Polynesia. The closer cultural relation ought to make it still more interesting. It could readily become a standard illustration for college youth of freedom and self-restraint, experimentation, and gradual personalization of love relations. For an exceedingly interesting presentation see K. Rob. V. Wikman, *Die Einleitung der Ehe.* [214]

for the night. This regularized form of flirtation was accepted as a chaste form of entertainment. Shame and in some places even fines and other forms of punishment were provided by group regulations for the young man who broke one of the many rules: who went courting alone without the company of the youth guild, who came from another village, who removed other than prescribed items of clothing (never the skin apron), who lay otherwise than on top of the bedclothes the first time, who was too young or who broke the rule of sexual integrity of the girl he visited in this way. For the girl the risks were even greater, as a girl who was known to have "slept herself away" had practically forfeited her right to a suitable marriage.

Gradually two young people came to select each other regularly. Certain signs made it clear to the youth guild that they were "courting certain" (*fria visst*). Most definite of these signs was the exchange of presents, particularly spoons. The couple was now left alone more and allowed to court even in the middle of the week. Proposing and marriage developed.

The parents attempting a rational excuse in terms of the climate and the housing conditions which made the winter house rather crowded facilitated this courtship by providing separate sleeping quarters in summer for their maturing daughters. During the summer the girls were often quartered at the upland pasture ground (*shieling, fabod*), and the young men came visiting them. Also down in the village the young people used to sleep in barns, storehouses, etc., while the regular living quarters were kept for the older people and small children. Even when housing conditions did not make this exodus to separate buildings desirable, separate summer quarters for the girls were often provided. The interest of the parents in the choice of a mate was to a certain degree safeguarded by the youth guild's own rules which gave some consideration to wealth and status. The individual choice rested, however, with the young people themselves, and the youth guild was even ready to defend the lovers against the parents if necessary.

The descendants of these farm groups will probably continue to disagree as to whether this night courtship included sexual relations as a rule. There is no doubt that the initial period with changing young men was one of sexual restraint. Such training in self-control was highly valued in the old Scandinavian culture. Also a definite pattern of lying "with a girl on faith and promise" was recognized. Whatever may be said about the chastity in the majority of cases, at least two developments toward sex relations must be taken into consideration. Some girls would care less about the strict rules, thus becoming village prostitutes or semiprostitutes, and other couples, having grown to love each other or at least not to regard marrying each other as inconceivable, must also have disregarded the rules. No guess can be made as to how often this led directly to marriage or how many sex experiences with different partners a young man or woman had before marriage.

Only one thing is certain: in most cases where pregnancy occurred, marriage followed. The whole community knew with whom a young girl slept repeatedly. In most cases the parents gave tacit sanction. As a family pattern this period of free experimentation was not devastating, and rules and traditions only helped to build up this tradition by allowing it regularized forms. The secure status of the family was not affected. The bearing of children was not likely to occur outside a legalized family. Many social scientists of later ages have even been willing to subscribe to a rationale, often put forward by the wise old men of this agrarian culture, that this was a method of "testing fertility."

The Old Mores in the New Society

In the course of social development, industrialization set in. Its effects did not come primarily through a shift in mores but through increased mobility. The breaking up of the stationary life of the village or of the community of homesteads deprived the existent organization for mating and marrying of one of its primary sanctions. Sexual relations within courtship now involved risks. The migrant laborers, and foremost among them the navvies, the industrial workers, and the commercial travelers, did not have the same respect for the girls as the local men, implying either abstinence from sexual intercourse or birth control through coitus interruptus or finally marriage. And the girls did not have at their disposal the impact of the whole society to force men into marriage if relations resulted in issue. Even in the cases where the men could be reached, parents would not look on them with satisfaction unless the men possessed land.

Migration itself thus led to the virtue of daughters becoming a social problem and, consequently, a moral problem as in the more romanticized relations between the sexes among the bourgeoisie. Illegitimacy, not resulting in subsequent marriage, rose. A whole folk literature reflects the growing consciousness of the problem of chastity, desertion, and shame. Illegitimacy increased as young women also began to migrate. They were no longer daughters with a parental home which could protect their virtue, if caring much about these things, or at least protect their eventual offspring. To take in a "natural" child in the maternal grandparents' home became a fairly well-established pattern for a time in all groups but the most proud. As a result the Swedish people have remained relatively tolerant of premarital sex relations.

Traces of the old habits have continued far into recent times in spite of new social conditions. Young women move about even more than young men. There has been an unceasing flow of young women to the cities, where their anonymous life as domestic servants and in a smaller degree as factory workers and sales clerks certainly has not been conducive to maintaining a close connection between sex relations and marriage. The interesting fact is that the habit of fairly lax authoritarian inhibitions of the sex life of youth, which stemmed out of the agrarian society, persisted so long that it was paralleled by more modern patterns and thus strengthened before its ultimate decline. One of these patterns was the religious secularization of the Swedish people, diminishing the prohibitive forces of religion. Another was the rise of emancipation ideas, so that even the intellectual upper class accepted a freer outlook on sexual relations. The propaganda for birth control, the discussion of "free love" in the radical movements toward the close of the last century, the theory of Ellen Key that "passion is right" and social hypocrisy is the "sin," and the influence of psychoanalysis all became widespread before a peasant pattern had vanished. This amalgamation of different designs is offered as a tentative explanation of the apparent frequency of premarital sex relations in Sweden.

Illegitimacy as a demographic factor is undergoing considerable change. A general decrease is discernible in recent years. The percentage of unmarried women bearing children started to decline (around 1915) even before the proportion of illegitimate children did (around 1930) (Tables 10 and 11). As this latter measure of the frequency in society of illegitimacy is dependent on the general trend of fertility within marriages, the former unrelated one seems to be more useful for predicting that illegitimacy is slowly declining as a pattern affecting the unmarried women. As a matter of fact, the low proportion of only slightly over 2 per 100 unmarried women of childbearing age who had children in recent years can only be matched by going as far back as the 1790's.

There are no indications that this considerable fall in extramarital fertility is due to a decrease in extramarital sex relations. On the contrary, it is obvious to everyone familiar with the Swedish situation that the trend rather is toward greater freedom in relations between the sexes. The old-time sanction of a cover-up marriage, however, probably does not work more efficiently now than 20 to 30 years ago. If there is any change in this factor, it is rather in the other direction. The conclusion, therefore, is that the rapid decrease in extramarital fertility is a result of the spread of knowledge about more effective birth control techniques. Another observable change is that illegitimacy tends to be concentrated in the younger age groups (Table 10). This apparently means that illegitimacy is more and more directly related to ignorance. The fact may be pitiable in itself, but it would also seem to be amenable to intentional social change in the form of sex education.

The high rate of illegitimacy is not the only proof of the prevalence of premarital sex relations. A considerable proportion of births occurs so early during the marriage that conception must have preceded the marriage (Table 12). In 1931–1935, 25 per cent of all births to married women under 30 years of age took place within eight months after the marriage. Other

TABLE 12. — CHILDBEARING IN RELATION TO DURATION OF MARRIAGE IN SWEDEN, BY AGE OF WOMEN, 1937

TIME BETWEEN MARRIAGE AND CHILDBEARING	BIRTHS PER 1,000 WOMEN BY AGE IN YEARS					
	All ages	Under 20	20–24	25–34	35–44	45 and over
	All districts					
Total	1,000.0	1,000.0	1,000.0	1,000.0	1,000.0	1,000.0
Under 3 months . . .	67.1	456.2	164.3	36.3	11.7	2.4
3–5 months	81.8	331.2	198.3	54.3	14.6	4.8
6–8 months	30.8	64.0	64.0	26.3	7.5	2.4
9–11 months	46.6	47.3	80.0	46.9	14.3	—
1 year	128.2	91.3	220.1	130.7	39.1	9.7
2–4 years	253.5	10.0	249.1	317.6	120.7	29.0
5–9 years	226.4	—	24.2	307.8	237.0	72.5
10–14 years	100.8	—	—	76.6	274.2	120.8
15–19 years	52.0	—	—	3.5	232.5	265.7
20 years and over . .	12.7	—	—	—	48.2	492.7
Unknown	0.1	—	0.1	—	0.2	—
	Rural Districts Only					
Total	1,000.0	1,000.0	1,000.0	1,000.0	1,000.0	1,000.0
Under 3 months . . .	66.0	435.9	163.7	35.9	10.1	2.9
3–5 months	75.5	331.7	183.4	50.2	12.3	5.9
6–8 months	29.0	71.0	60.9	24.9	6.3	2.9
9–11 months	45.4	49.2	79.0	46.6	13.8	—
1 year	121.4	99.2	224.2	120.9	36.5	8.8
2–4 years	243.8	13.0	261.0	305.5	115.9	20.5
5–9 years	228.3	—	27.6	321.0	219.9	61.4
10–14 years	112.4	—	—	90.4	276.4	114.0
15–19 years	62.1	—	—	4.6	252.9	269.0
20 years and over . .	16.0	—	—	—	55.7	514.6
Unknown	0.1	—	0.2	—	0.2	—

Source: Population Changes (*Befolkningsrörelsen*).

than first-born children are included in this proportion. Had it been possible to base the calculation on first-born children only, the proportion would have been much greater. Somewhat more direct information is contained in the proportion of all marriages which resulted in births within eight months. This proportion was 34 per cent in 1916 and 33 per cent in 1926. In 1936 it dropped to 26 per cent.

This phenomenon is very old in Sweden. As the most recent figures show, it is rather on the decrease as is the related phenomenon of illegitimacy, but still the proportion of pregnant brides is amazingly large. The explanation is to be sought in one or the other of two possibilities: either extramarital sex relations have been entered upon without intentions of marriage but when conception has occurred the partners have decided to cover up the situation with a marriage; or a marriage is decided upon and the partners then do not see any reasons strong enough to prohibit premarital sex relations. Between these two extremes are all possible situations in which marriage has been discussed although no definite preparations made. Whatever the situation, the marriage ceremony is less valued and the absence of it is less of a taboo in Sweden than in most other countries. The historical patterns behind the present situation have already been sketched. Perhaps a warning against overemphasizing the uniqueness of the Swedish data in this respect should also be given. The same phenomenon may exist in other countries which have less complete statistics of the occurrence of pregnant brides. As there is no reason to believe that premarital sex relations are diminishing and particularly not where marriage is already decided upon, it may be concluded that the recent decrease in pregnant brides is exclusively due to contraception.

Those who wish to evaluate the facts concerning premarital relations and illegitimate childbearing in Sweden from moral points of view will, of course, have to remember that there are wide variations in extent of occurrence. Some geographical sections are different from others; some occupational and cultural groups also are different from others. The most important distinction when the moral issue is raised, however, has to be made between premarital or nonmarital liaisons and extramarital relations proper, i.e., sexual relations of married persons outside their marriage relationship. The former is an established part of the mores of the unmarried population and shows the noninclusiveness of marriage as a social institution and its lack of success in regularizing sexual relations. It is also the only type of sex relation outside marriage for which data are available. On the other hand, extramarital sex relations, which break up an already existing love partnership, must be evaluated on quite a different basis. About these liaisons, involving infidelity among married or betrothed persons, nothing specific is known. There is no reason to believe, however, that they are frequent enough to necessitate any special comments on Swedish conditions.

The frequency of sex relationships in the unmarried population should not lead to any definite conclusions about irregular relationships in the married population. It may even be that the very ideal of an exclusive, faithful, monogamic marriage causes people who do not individually want that sort of relationship, or who are not enough in love to want it with their actual sexual partner, to abstain from marrying. Thus sexual freedom in youth might lead not to more sexual license in marriage but possibly to fewer marriages.

CHAPTER IV

THE CHANGING FAMILY: PARENTHOOD

A RELATIVE disinclination toward marriage has been stated to be typical of Swedish family patterns in comparison with other countries. Limited realization of parenthood must also be stressed as typical, both in older times and, more particularly, in recent decades. In this respect dramatic changes have occurred, confronting the nation with the prospect of cumulative underreproduction. Sweden has become the prototype of a nation facing a population crisis. The marked decline in marital fertility, its causes, and the means by which it has been brought about are the theme of this chapter.

MARITAL FERTILITY

In the early 1930's the Swedish birth rate dropped to the low point of 13.7 per 1,000. In spite of the favorable mortality trend, the recent rate of childbearing is only three-fourths of that necessary if the population is ultimately to become stationary. But gross measures of births are not adequate when demographic data are used for answering questions as to how and why family patterns have changed. A somewhat better measure for depicting population changes is the fertility of married women in different age groups. On this basis it is found that the decrease in childbearing within Swedish marriages is the result of a gradual movement (Table 13). It started earlier among older women than among younger women. The change has taken place primarily within the present century.

IMMEDIATE CAUSES OF FAMILY LIMITATION

There are various opinions as to the immediate causes of the decline in fertility. One school of thought asserts that the change in marital fertility is — mainly or wholly — unintentional. The change is assumed to be due to a decrease in biological fecundity of women (decreased fecundity of marriages ascribed to causes relating to men is usually not assumed). A whole literature is devoted to supposed disturbances of female biological functions by modern life. Increased sterility has also been ascribed to an increase in abortion and

TABLE 13. — MARITAL FERTILITY IN SWEDEN, BY AGE, 1751–1937

PERIOD[a]	CHILDBEARING WOMEN PER 1,000 MARRIED WOMEN							
	15–19 years	20–24 years	25–29 years	30–34 years	35–39 years	40–44 years	45–49 years	15–44 years
1751–1760 . . .								305.7
1761–1770 . . .								291.2
1771–1780 . . .								286.3
1781–1790 . . .		458	362	305	213	116	28	276.4
1791–1800 . . .		469	396	336	228	120	28	289.7
1801–1810 . . .		456	374	307	220	117	26	276.0
1811–1820 . . .		458	376	318	235	127	26	288.9
1821–1830 . . .		460	384	324	244	137	27	295.5
1831–1840 . . .		448	368	309	237	133	24	280.2
1841–1850 . . .		456.7	370.0	316.8	245.2	136.3	23.1	288.6
1851–1860 . . .		470.4	378.0	326.8	258.2	148.1	24.5	296.4
1861–1870 . . .		457.2	376.0	320.4	258.4	152.3	24.8	289.5
1871–1880 . . .	522.6	474.1	389.2	332.7	266.3	155.4	24.6	300.9
1881–1890 . . .	508.5	446.9	373.9	321.5	255.4	145.9	22.3	291.8
1891–1900 . . .	561.2	461.9	367.2	301.9	238.2	132.6	18.2	276.1
1901–1910 . . .	619.7	452.9	349.7	277.5	211.6	112.7	14.7	258.6
1911–1920 . . .	595.5	397.9	287.5	220.0	165.9	87.0	10.7	211.5
1921–1930 . . .	588.2	331.7	220.2	158.5	113.6	56.8	7.2	155.4
1931	517.9	285.3	183.7	126.1	83.3	39.1	4.9	124.1
1932	545.7	280.2	178.6	123.9	80.6	37.5	4.2	121.0
1933	516.8	264.7	169.4	116.4	74.6	34.7	4.1	113.8
1934	559.2	266.1	166.5	117.2	74.1	33.5	4.0	113.5
1935	517.7	268.9	165.9	115.2	72.1	31.0	3.5	112.1
1936	511.7	268.4	169.1	119.2	73.0	31.1	3.7	114.5
1937	519.8	263.5	169.6	117.4	72.7	30.2	3.0	114.0

[a] Data for 1751–1930 are computed as annual averages by 10-year periods.

Source: Statistical Yearbook of Sweden: 1940 (*Statistisk Årsbok*).

venereal diseases. Sometimes a decrease in frequency of sexual intercourse within marriages, diminishing the probability of conception, has been suggested as an explanation. The pressure for time and the complexities of modern life are assumed to have weakened the drive toward and potency of coitus, particularly on the part of men. It becomes necessary to scrutinize these explanations because, if correct, a population policy would have to be developed accordingly.

The last of these factors has not been studied directly in Sweden, but some deductions can be made on the basis of general observations. It would indeed be venturesome to assume that work dissipates the energy of people to a greater extent today than in earlier times. Even if the tempo and instability of work have increased, their effects on the love life ought to be offset by more leisure time and more comfortable living conditions generally. It seems valid to dismiss the argument that quantitative change in the frequency of sexual intercourse can have caused any part of the decline in births. Even if a greater number of sexual neuroses in individual cases should appear in modern times, no one knows whether their frequency or only our awareness of them is increasing. Certainly such causes of involuntary sterility cannot explain the tremendous changes in number of children.

For much the same reasons the suggestion that the fecundity of modern women generally has been reduced may be disregarded. The work of women in general cannot be considered harder or more detrimental to child-bearing now than earlier. On the contrary, shorter hours, legal regulation of working conditions, higher wages, and improved levels of living are increasingly protecting the health of working women as well as men. When working wives have fewer children than wives who devote their entire time to homemaking, the difference can partly be explained as the result of selection, as wives without children or with few children are more likely to turn to the labor market than those with several children. For the rest it can be assumed to be due to more intensive birth control on the part of working wives (Chapter 22). Their work is not of such a different nature from home-making as to cause physiological differences.

Venereal disease may have direct effects on sterility in the case of both men and women. But Sweden is in a position to demonstrate that this cause can hardly be responsible for the decline in the birth rate, as the occurrence of syphilis has been conspicuously decreased and gonorrhea has been brought under control since 1920 (Chapter 16). Cases have been increasingly brought under treatment, and treatment has become more successful. Spontaneous abortion seems to have increased somewhat according to a survey by Wetterdal, [208] particularly as a result of previously induced abortions. On the other hand, a tendency toward decreases in spontaneous abortions might be expected as work is less hard and as births in the middle ages when health risks become greater are less frequent than formerly. Also, both abortions and sterility itself can now be more successfully treated by medical attention than ever before.

Thus there seem to be no good reasons, as far as Sweden is concerned, for looking for unintentional causes of the decrease in births. There is rather a high probability that the trends in the particular causes cited are such as to tend to increase fertility. No other plausible conclusion remains, therefore, than that the decline in births has resulted not from involuntary but from voluntary sterility. Intentional family limitation has been the immediate cause.

There are numerous indications of the increase in intentional birth control. As a matter of fact, conscious family limitation must have been practiced in earlier times, even if less frequently than today. The general low level of Swedish fertility in the preindustrial period in comparison with that of other countries would otherwise be difficult to explain. The differences in fertility in olden times between various regions would also be difficult to interpret. The desirability of restricting the new generations to such numbers as the farms could sustain would seem to have been at work just as in France where modern family limitation had its first pronounced start.

So also present-day differences in fertility between regions and social classes would seem to support no other explanation than that of voluntarily contrived infertility. The fertility figures by age in Table 13, showing how consistently the older women were the first to have fewer children, would also seem to indicate that intentional birth control and not involuntary sterility has been at work. The fact that the older women were pioneers in family limitation throws an interesting sidelight on the problem also in that it relieves the younger generations of the accusation of having been the ones to become degenerate enough to practice birth control. The simple truth obviously is that birth control has always existed; its wide extension in modern times has caused the fall in marital fertility.

The next question, then, deals with the techniques by which intensified birth control has been brought about. Because of lack of direct studies the answer cannot be given in quantitative terms. The few investigations having made use of the materials from birth control clinics and interviews have only an indicative value. Some inferences can be drawn from the data on the production and importation of contraceptives and also from the statistics on differential fertility in the several regions and social classes. The experiences of doctors and social workers have also been scrutinized. All these sources point in one specific direction, namely, that even at the present time technical contraceptives, in Sweden mostly condoms, play only a minor role in birth control. The technique most generally used, even in the urban middle classes and still more so among the broad classes of farmers and workers, is coitus interruptus. This method of birth control has thus been proved relatively effective. As knowledge of this method must be assumed to have existed as long as people have known that there is a causal relation between coitus and conception, no spread of knowledge of birth control, particularly of contraceptives, can be held responsible for the great change in fertility during the last two generations.

MOTIVES FOR FAMILY LIMITATION

With the fact of the importance of nontechnical means for family limitation in mind, it becomes obvious that the change in childbearing cannot be explained by any change in the technical feasibility of birth control. It must be explained in terms of some deeper changes in the motivation for having or not having children.

The preconditions for the family have changed and so the individual's reaction to the prospect of having a family must have changed accordingly. There is, however, another chain of causes at work: an increasing disposition to weigh rationally the motives and actions in one's own life. Even if all reasons for having or not having children remain the same, people in an industrialized as compared with a preindustrial society develop the habit of trying to interfere rationally with the course of human events, thus giving more consideration to what these reasons are. But easy as it is to point out this growing rationalism of modern times, it is difficult to classify it in precise categories.

Many people classify this growing rationalism as a moral phenomenon, meaning by this that it is immoral. But if it be considered more moral not to interfere with nature and thus direct what sexual relations may result in issue and what not, then it must be realized that giving up such habits of rational deliberation must mean giving up an inherent part of modern culture. Rationalism in the sexual sphere is not unique. It is rather related to rationalism as contrasted with superstition, rationalism as interference with nature for technical purposes, rationalism as demanding free discussion and control of government. In short, it is one of the strongest pillars of what in the present day is called civilization. Reversing the trend and turning away from rationalism will not meet with approval from the majority. Even if their verbal approval could be obtained, they would not support it in their behavior.

The search for causes for the decline in births has thus to go further in order to find such reasons for having or not having children as may serve as bases for attempts to counteract the trend toward lower birth rates. The very process of rationalization has to be studied also to give an answer to the question as to what people are becoming rational about. Still, all talk of reasons and motives must refer only to a superficial level of man's conscious reasoning. Motives are not only incomplete representatives of causes; they are also vague. Between different motives there is never the question of simple addition or subtraction; they cover, cross, and merge with each other in a much more complicated manner. Thus it is impossible to separate personal or psychological motives for fertility reduction from economic motives. They are intertwined with each other. There is a dynamic process preceding any decision about family limitation, a process in which are merged known facts, supposed facts, acknowledged goals, dreamed goals, experiences and expectations about economic pressure, material inconveniences, and social ambitions — all weighted according to some secret coefficients. These personal equations forming the new pattern of family limitation may never become accessible for direct study.

One aspect of what is thus chiefly a problem of social psychology, however, is open to study. The social sets of conditions for parenthood and their changes may be observed: the income structure in society, the employment condition for families, the labor division within families, and so forth. Also, a multitude of traditions, conventions, folkways, social patterns, habits, and generally respected ideals with regard to family life and its place in society today may be analyzed. All this appears to the individual family as an exterior frame, which exerts a certain pressure on the balance of motives for or against children. Some of these factual foundations behind the pros and cons of childbearing have been radically changed during the last dramatic century. Some have not. But even those which remain unchanged may nevertheless be evaluated differently. A good example of this kind is the amount of bodily pain and discomfort connected with childbearing. From a simple quantitative point of view such obstacles must be judged to have decreased; anesthetics and improvements in both the art and the amount of medical care have increased. Still without doubt these bodily discomforts are evaluated as a greater factor today, when the birth of children has become a matter of calculation of relative pleasure and pain, than formerly.

One more warning must be given before attempting an analysis of how motives for family limitation may have changed. It is not valid to make any study of such motives relating to childbearing in terms of general averages. All the motives which may be enumerated will in reality work very differently with different income levels, different occupational patterns, different regions, different cultural connections, and different family sizes. By way of reservation against all generalizations the last consideration should be particularly stressed. When deciding on family size motives are given totally different values according to the number already born. This is of utmost importance also for the formulation of population programs. The measures which can be effective are widely different according to whether there are some oversized families and many very small families or whether the majority of families are just marginally undersized. Because the psychological attitude toward a prospective child which will be number 1 or number 3 or number 5 is so inherently different, different measures of policy will be practical according to whether the goal is more children of the middle order or more of the higher order. This is a general reservation, impossible to incorporate duly in any presentation dealing with generalities. Particularly in any schematic discussions of motives for family limitation, the failure to mention this complication would be inexcusable.

The motives for childbearing are not to be directly scrutinized. It would be difficult to treat the question whether the drive to have children has undergone any changes in time, while it is easy to see that the arguments for not having children certainly have. When in any attempt to analyze the pros and cons the latter are chosen as the frame of reference, it is tacitly taken for granted that some desire to have children exists in mankind and that this desire has remained fairly constant. It can hardly be analyzed but has to be cloaked in some sweeping terms, such as a desire to marry, inclination to found a family, love of children and desire to have some of one's own.

As long as this positive inclination went fairly unquestioned, it need not even have been conscious. Children were being born without the "why's" being discussed. When, however, in recent times family limitation has rather become a pattern, the decision required in connection with coitus is whether to let pregnancy result or to prevent it. This fact is important. It may well be that a great number of families remain undersized because of lack of energy to realize a wish when it involves breaking the steady habit of birth control. On every single occasion the easiest way is to postpone such a decision.

The motives against childbearing are the ones to be analyzed. These deterrent motives, having become more effective and conscious than ever before, are many, but in an admittedly general and vague way they may be catalogued as follows:

Childbearing involves discomfort and pain for the female partner.

It causes drawbacks and even breaks in her work and ways of life.

It temporarily impedes a satisfactory sexual life and so, more often than is generally admitted, endangers marital fidelity and confident partnership.

It tends to reduce the mobility of the parents.

Childbearing further entails considerable increase in the family budget and lowers the level of living.

It makes the family more exposed to all sorts of economic insecurity.

It involves worries in the future about education and ability to cope with problems of so raising children that the family will not through the children be brought into conflict with social standards.

These and similar motives play on the sounding board of increased insecurity with regard to the permanency of marriage, a general pessimism about the future opportunities for children, a momentarily mounting distrust in any future on account of wars, and a temperamentally oscillating uncertainty as to whether life is, on the whole, worth living, an uncertainty which is greatly strengthened since heaven is more rarely believed than formerly to offer material rewards and compensation for evils suffered in this world.

The negative factors may all be studied more closely by following the dynamics of the different functions of the family institution. An outline was sketched in Chapter 1, emphasizing particularly the gradual loss in importance of the economic, protective, and educative functions of the family. When it is here attempted to view the interplay of motives for family limitation from the inside as a basis for psychological understanding, it seems more appropriate to discuss motives under the three headings of insecurity, discomfort, and economy. Most of the active motives for family reduction can be placed under these headings or at least most of those which are of a sufficiently general character to be studied and to be dealt with through social reforms.

The Factor of Insecurity

Little discussion is needed in order to show that the factor of insecurity plays a greater role in childbearing now than in times gone by. Only a few marginal remarks are necessary.

It must first be recognized that insecurity is a general cloak under which to rationalize a variety of unrecognized motives. All insecurity invoked as a reason for not having more than a minimum number of children may thus not have been directly instrumental in bringing about birth reduction. Particularly must one doubt whether the war risks in the Western world during the 1920's and 1930's have had the influence which has often been ascribed to them. When war really came, the situation must have become quite different; the pessimism of that time can almost never have been equaled. But two things may be referred to in order to deflate at least somewhat the importance of the earlier war risks in the reduction in births. First, the period when war would have seemed more imminent, namely, after 1933, did not show a striking decline in childbearing. Second, if the risk of having one's children killed in war was felt strongly, it should have operated to prevent the birth of even one child. But the main feature of the birth decline has been that it has occurred as a reduction in the later births. In Sweden particularly the war risks had little psychological effect. Up to the time of actual war operations in Europe the Swedish people had lived and governed their country and determined its military strength according to the philosophy that war did not concern them. It should not be denied that war risks and world insecurity may play a part in the motivation for family limitation, but it must be pointed out that this factor, more than any other perhaps, is convenient for *ex post facto* explanations for other unrecognized or unadmitted motives.

In any comparison between past and present it is necessary also to stress that the psychologically determined insecurity may have increased more than the actual dangers that are risked. Death and hunger were not less frequent or sudden in olden times. It would rather seem as if mankind's resourcefulness for meeting risks should have increased. But the attitude toward risks has changed. Passivity and complacency have decreased. The very fact that the individual is considered more directly responsible for success and failure in an individualistic, competitive, and nonreligious society than formerly makes him more inclined to seek the security he can guarantee himself. He is less willing to choose the poverty now following the birth of children than he was earlier to tolerate the poverty following dearth. The psychological nature of insecurity makes it difficult to make comparisons over periods of time and to match them with factual changes. To a certain extent a loss of the basic feeling of security has probably accompanied the process of religious secularization, which in Sweden has been carried far. To a large extent also the new insecurity is only a psychological translation of the greater mobility of modern times. Without the former stability of life in the midst of one's own clan, neighborhood, and church, the individual feels more strongly the necessity of planning life ahead and therefore also feels more strongly the impossibility of doing it in a secure way. While the risk of poverty and of an adverse fate in the future may in reality be less for the average man now than it was a hundred years ago, he fears it more because he does not know in what form it might appear. The large-scale public measures taken to guarantee social security must have decreased risks considerably. Yet the intensified discussion around these political problems may have been instrumental in increasing the fears of insecurity in the population or at least of directing people's conscious strivings toward security, which is much the same thing.

Perhaps the most important generalization to be made is that people increasingly seem to ask for more and more security and that insecurity has to be understood as an attitude, with all the rights of being whimsical and illogical. As such it has obviously been of great weight in the balance of motives against childbearing. Particularly the risks with regard to employment and income must become of great weight in any calculation of such a long-term enterprise as that of supporting children. Those risks, hovering over the working classes in the form of unemployment and over the farming and business classes in the form of losses of income and income-earning assets, are widespread in the Western countries. As long as the economic fate of children continues to be dependent upon that of their fathers, such risks will continue to play a large part in the calculations with regard to bearing children.

THE FACTOR OF DISCOMFORT

The effect of children in impeding the mobility of parents has undoubtedly increased, perhaps risen from unimportance, during the last century. This is partly a direct function of urbanism as leaving children alone involves greater danger of life and limb under modern conditions than in the past. Sociologically, however, the location of an increasing proportion of remunerative work outside the home is more important. Productive work and child-rearing no longer can take place side by side. A choice is forced on the parents. The social crisis for the family originated on the day when the father made his exodus from the home to the factory. Gone was the division of responsibility which for centuries had tied parents together and made the burden of supervision easier for both and gone was the equality in evaluation of work and status between man and woman. Children earlier experienced such an equality of father and mother while now unequality is being demonstrated to them with results that influence their own attitudes toward family and the sexes. The significance of this crisis of the family can hardly be overestimated. It is true that the inconvenience of children increases when the married woman is also considering wage-earning work outside the home. But that has had far less influence than the exodus of the father. As this phenomenon in Sweden has taken place at the time of most rapid industrialization (since 1870), it also coincides with the decline in fertility, allowing for a certain time lag.

The burden of children tends to be felt increasingly as not only working time but also leisure time is spent more and more outside the home. Recreation in older days had a different pattern. It generally took the form of rest periods interspersed in working hours. A type of accompanying manual work was often carried on in leisure hours (carving, embroidery). When such was the pattern, any lack of freedom on the part of mothers could not be complained of as anything widely different from the situation of other groups. Now working hours mean regulated and concentrated work and demands on efficiency are increasingly heightened. Leisure time is correspondingly set off as decidedly free time. Typical of the era of industrialism is the further fact that recreation is becoming more and more mobile. In the old agrarian culture only the yearly fair, the church, and some family treats called on the family to leave its abode for pleasure. Children could be taken along more easily than now. It was also considered more natural that leisure should be sacrificed if vital needs occurred, if a cow was about to calve, if the crop had to be harvested, if the bedridden old father had to be nursed, or if small children had to be looked after. Thus again, if the mother was kept immobile, that hardship was not an extraordinary one. In the large households, with even the menfolk working around the house, there were also many more persons to release her or to keep her company when "on duty."

And people's attitude toward recreation has changed. It now represents more of a craving which it takes strength to resist, and it is carried on mainly outside the home. This does not necessarily involve a reduction of common family interests; it may even be said to have increased the resources for companionship of the mates, e.g., in movies and dancing, club and civic activities. Through motoring, picnicking, and the like the family members of different generations have pleasures in common. But, in general, recreation has become specialized and thus separates the different generations. It decidedly debars small children. The whole public organization of life makes even unborn children a greater nuisance to their mothers than formerly.   Culture in its tendency for specialization and segregation thus widens the gap between the different age groups.

The demand for cultural development through participation in a group of equals also must tend to make adult women more unwilling to take the lonely part of being restricted to the child level of social life. Extra burdens are imposed by the new knowledge of child hygiene. The generalized observation may be made that infants and children participate in adult night life more rarely in Sweden than in any other country. But when young children must stay at home at night the mothers must usually remain at home with them. This deprivation of recreation has social consequences. Not only is a large part of that progress of civilization which is a national ambition dependent on sports, games, gymnastics, hiking, and outdoor life generally, which it becomes increasingly difficult for women to give up; but also successful democracy requires all adults to use part of their leisure time for their duties as citizens. Wide participation in civic duties, in adult education, and, through reading and discussion, in the ironing out of social issues is the very soil and air of a living democracy. That young parents, and again particularly the women, should give up this participation must be a cause for national anxiety.

In this enumeration of the difficulties implied in childbearing, there must be added still another. The modern attitude of fundamental inhospitality toward children is expressed in the extreme in two situations in which parents are placed in the position of suppliants, namely, in regard to landlords and domestic servants. In both cases it is true that abundant economic means might avert the unpleasant experiences. But under ordinary circumstances parents of large families, in addition to the costs of supporting children, must suffer humiliation and distress because of them. Landlords refuse to accept them as tenants; domestic servants shun them as employers. This is but a sign of the increasing bias against children in the modern social structure.

THE FACTOR OF ECONOMY

The greatest maladjustments between social structure and family needs appear in the economic field. The costs of children have risen. In a period of unsurpassed increase in general welfare, costs of children have probably mounted faster than incomes. This gives justification to the saying that children have changed from assets to liabilities. This change operates to a greater or less extent in different social groups, but none can be wholly excluded from the statement that children have become increasingly expensive. Looking backward, it becomes clear that the proverb, "Children are the poor people's wealth," is less true now than formerly. In an agrarian society children probably were a positive asset, even if it may be difficult to decide if a maximum number of children in the family really was desirable, for much depended on the size of the farm.

The trend, however, is to make this old statement that children are an asset less true. Everything that is called progress tends to bring about costs that turn the former assets into heavier and heavier liabilities. Cultural progress on the whole seems to cost most for the children. The most luxurious of all consumption in our economic system is that of children and mothers, namely, the luxury of unproductivity. For children this is not a feature of conspicuous leisure but has been directly enforced through labor legislation and compulsory schooling as common social ideals.

Child labor was one of the factors that in the old days could make children desirable. The successful campaigns against child labor have made children less desirable. This may be a cruelly honest way of stating the change that has taken place, but it is nevertheless an appropriate one. The world had earlier known nothing else but that children in proportion to their ability should pay for their consumptive rights with some productive contributions. On the farm everybody in the household took part in the work. This was particularly true of the closed, self-dependent, clan-family household that was typical of old Sweden, where feudalism, bondage, and tenancy were practically unknown. Who in the family worked and why and for whom were matters of little discrimination when all were dependent on all and all had to work as hard as ever they could. When no accounting of individual contributions and individual costs was made, income earning was an indivisible, cooperative, family undertaking. It had not even dawned upon people that anybody should be considered as "the supporter." All supported all. The weaker generations of old and young consumed more than they produced, but they were still valued parts of the productive family, as either they had given or were going to give fuller returns to the family economy at other times.

An interesting indication of how undeveloped was the very ideology of supporter and of the recent origin of the allegedly traditional duty of supporting dependents may be found in Swedish legislation. No earlier than 1853 was it explicitly stated in law that a man had the "duty to support his family," a clause that in 1920 became duly rephrased to "both husband and wife have the duty of contributing to the support of the family."

When the basis of the economic structure began to be changed from agriculture to home industry, these conditions did not change right away. In the early period of industrialism the ideology of joint income earning and manifold support and child labor within the family enterprise carried over so that often whole families came under the employment contracts. In Sweden this was particularly manifest in the textile plants of the eighteenth century, the man being assigned to a loom with his wife and so many children or domestics. Child labor, then, was no eruption of inhuman cruelty but was a fairly normal feature of an earlier economic system, overlapping into a new one.[1]

The way of progress, however, was different. A pattern of sparing the children developed. Laws were gradually enacted in attempts to better conditions for working children. The first law in Sweden directly regulating the work of minors, that of 1881, only codified rules that had long governed the thinking of responsible citizens. The Workers' Protection Act of 1912 finally made all work of young people under 18 years of age subject to strict regulations and forbade work in industry before 14 years of age or in agriculture and domestic service before 13 years of age. These being minimum ages, the general starting point for wage earning is much later, adding years of parental support for every child in comparison with former times. Obviously, also, the parents first to acknowledge the right of their children to freedom from work were the more ambitious ones. This helped to establish the fact that the culturally more alert parents — and in earlier times cultural alertness was more directly related to economic and social progress than at present — were the first to reduce their families.

Compulsory schooling worked in the same direction, hindering child labor and diminishing the economic value of children. In Sweden a law providing for compulsory schooling was enacted in 1842; and soon thereafter the law was unconditionally enforced. It has been a costly step. Pride in the extinction of illiteracy and democratic reliance on a widely read and enlightened electorate have caused society to incur great direct costs and also to sacrifice incomes from the labor of children. The children and the families have been legally forced to carry their part in this advance. An increase in the cost of children has resulted from which there is no escape. Again it is to be observed that the first to sense the necessity of schooling for their children beyond the compulsory minimum were the same groups that also by their rationalism first were ready to take measures for limiting their families.

Without aid of laws other demands have arisen that make childbearing and childrearing a considerable economic burden. Participation in modern

[1] In a decree of 1624 about the hospitals it was laid down that children without defects should not be institutionalized in hospitals but in orphan asylums and that at the age of 8 they should be apprenticed or given to domestic service. In 1718 a private person in a southern city obtained the right to utilize the children in the local asylum for his hosiery shop and this factory had the right also to take up vagrant children "to be kept regularly to Godliness and trained to hosiery looming." In 1754 a well-known economic writer, who was also a lessee of some important textile works, complained that the infants of his female spinners were taken to asylums which was thought unwise "as children of workers who from their very mother's milk have been nursed and reared for work and misery would in the asylum become pampered, weaned to more comfortable living and in the end distracted from and spoiled for factory work." A committee to the parliament of 1756 talks of "the deep rejoicing that they felt at the remarkable deftness small children — and some only five years of age — showed in wool and cotton spinning in the manufactures."

culture generally demands more expensive consideration for delicate child-hood. In earlier times a large number of children were allowed to be "called to heaven." Such waste is now avoided. But every step forward in hygiene — all the demands for improved care of babies, better nourishment, more sunshine, better housing — means that costs accumulate. Again it has been the more intelligent, culturally awake parents who first realized this duty and also reduced the number of children rather than expose them to conditions they now understood to be detrimental to health. Since the turn of the century such knowledge of child hygiene has become the possession of most social groups in Sweden. That health propaganda has succeeded is reflected in the reduction in infant mortality. But the same propaganda has demanded so much more in the way of cost, supervision, and anxiety that it has proved an unspoken but efficient warning against thoughtless and excessive childbearing.

Expenses for food, housing, fuel, clothing, medicines, and education have increased with these rising demands. Moreover, the shift to a money income basis from a closed production-consumption unit makes every new item stand out more clearly. Even if this change in economic structure does not by itself increase the cost of children, it at least makes for more conscious weighing of the costs. Urban groups and industrialized groups thus necessarily must sense the economic pressure of children more than rural and agrarian groups. Again this is a step toward rationalization. And again it appears that rational-izing the human world must mean a sharp reduction in children.

INCOME AND FAMILY LIMITATION

It has been stated repeatedly that the process of social change must have made some groups more likely than others to sense the necessity for meet-ing such change with family limitation, because their lower fertility has so often been misunderstood in social interpretations. If the widely publicized paradox that "the richer the family, the fewer the children" contained the whole truth, it would be catastrophic for any attempt to develop a popula-tion program. As the changes and conditions considered here may serve to make social action feasible, it becomes necessary to analyze that argument somewhat more closely.

The fact that income, by and large, shows some tendency to decrease as the number of minor children increases has several causes. The father of a large family is more immobile, has greater obstacles in looking for more remunerative employment, is less resistant against wage pressure, and also shows somewhat greater susceptibility to unemployment than men with fewer dependents. Some employers may hesitate to employ a man who sup-ports a large family. He would need more to maintain himself and his family, and it may be that he eats less and worries more and so works less efficiently — a vicious circle indeed. The same situation may in broad terms be true under agrarian and even professional and business conditions. The supporter of a large family cannot compete on equal terms in the race after the better farm or the more rapid advance. He cannot take as great risks and must forgo major chances. A further cause of reduction in the large family's income is the fact that the mother's contribution from paid work is smaller. All this, making for a relative status of poverty, is an effect, not a cause, of children.

The most important explanation of the apparently irrational relation between low income and large family is, however, that the very process of rationalization has spread at different speeds among the different groups. When it became crystallized as a cultural pattern, it did not appear first in the economically most depressed groups. Notwithstanding their apparent need of more careful family planning, the habit of planning first developed in other groups. It started with the better read, those with more varied contacts with people and ideas. In earlier times even more than now these circumstances were linked with greater wealth and higher social status.

A rationalized, sophisticated psychology seems to be related to the phenomenon of social changes as such. The very uprooting of individuals, the rapid shift in values, implies a rational weighing of situations and of inherited patterns which formerly have been taken for granted. It was thus only to be expected that those social groups that were most mobile and already most emancipated from the static scales of values should first start consciously to consider their childbearing. Thus, family limitation is not a function of families being richer. All the instances generally quoted of "the richer the family, the fewer the children" relate only to a transition period, when the upper social classes have temporary precedence in utilizing methods of family limitation.

It is not the differences in fertility between different social groups that need to be explained but the different time order and velocity in the acceptance of birth control by these groups. Wider and wider social groups begin consciously to weigh motives for and against childbearing. This may be partly explained by the so-called law of social gravity, according to which the lower social strata are supposed to imitate behavior that they associate with the prestige of the upper classes. Partly, however (and it is the author's impression that this is the more important in Sweden), the very difference between the classes disappears. The broad masses come into the swirl of changing conditions. They are exposed to a variegated set of values and freed from the dependence on inherited patterns and from the inertia and relatively unquestioning attitude of obedience to authority that is one concomitant of static poverty. In other words, they too become sophisticated.

The relationships among poverty, isolation, ignorance, and inertia may further be illustrated by reference to the large relief family. Extreme poverty tends to result in indifference and irresponsibility for the fate of oneself and one's family. Thus up to our time economically incapable families have lacked that self-reliance and social ambition that could induce them to restrict their families. Poverty of a static type also tends to be closely associated with an unquestioning obedience to authority and to social clichés. The so-called moral criticism of birth control voiced by public opinion tends to determine the actions of these groups more than of others or at least to serve as an excuse for inaction, just as in olden times the authority of the church taught complacency and noninterference with nature. Poverty of an earlier period was much more generally of that hopeless static type, and it failed to result in social opposition or in family limitation because of the attitude of "no-use" which nowadays characterizes only a small residuum of the population.

Neither theorists nor laymen have had the patience to outwait the period of unequal transmission of new family patterns and unequal sensitivity to changed social forces in order to note how the correlation between income and family size would work itself out in the end. Recently, however, some regions in the world have been so thoroughly permeated by the same cultural changes in the field of sex mores that they have begun to indicate a new relationship. Statistics tending to show a positive instead of a negative correlation between fertility and income have been presented for large cities in Europe and for selected groups. One of the most noted of these "new" correlations was published by Edin based on the marriage groups in Stockholm from 1920 to 1922. It shows that families tend to have children in direct rather than in inverse relation to their economic resources. [103]

After the special census in Sweden in 1935–1936, a country-wide indication of such positive correlation was apparent for the first time. Fertility showed a recurrent, though slight, tendency to be higher in the highest income group (with 10,000 crs.[2] annually or above) than in the next highest groups. As higher incomes are associated with older age groups and thus a longer duration of marriage and fertility period, the figures were corrected for age, but they continued to show this slight excess in number of children over the lower income groups. As the same slight upturn repeats itself in all series, in different social and regional groups, greater significance may be attributed to it than the relatively small numbers might seem to warrant (Fig. II).[3]

Even so, the number of children in the highest income group is far from sufficient for population replacement. It is thus apparent that stabilization of fertility is taking place on a low reproduction level. The few additional

[2] A Swedish crown (in Swedish *krona*, pl. *kronor*, abbreviated crn., pl. crs.) corresponds according to the exchange rate to about a quarter of an American dollar. Its actual purchasing power, before the rise in cost of living from the beginning of the war, should be reckoned somewhere between a third and a half of a dollar.

[3] Unknown incomes are ordinarily incomes below the tax limit of 600 crs.

"tenths of children" associated with higher family incomes as contrasted with middle-sized incomes are not proportionate to the increases in income. Thus, there still exists the problem of why even fairly good incomes do not lead to families of the size that in earlier times was considered normal or why the number of children does not increase proportionately with income.

The answer has been given in the previous section: the differential costs per child have been growing faster than general income. If it is noted that the focal point in any discussion of population and economics should be the

FIG. II. — FAMILY SIZE IN SWEDEN, BY RESIDENCE, OCCUPATION, AND INCOME

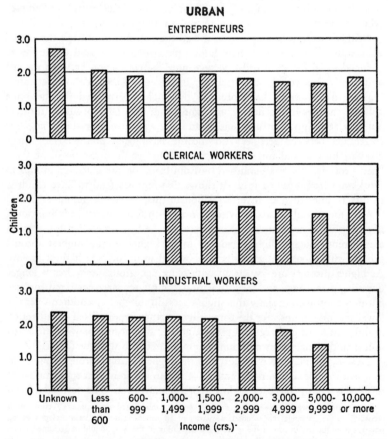

URBAN

Source: Population Commission, Report on Demographic Investigations (*Betänkande med vissa demografiska utredningar*).

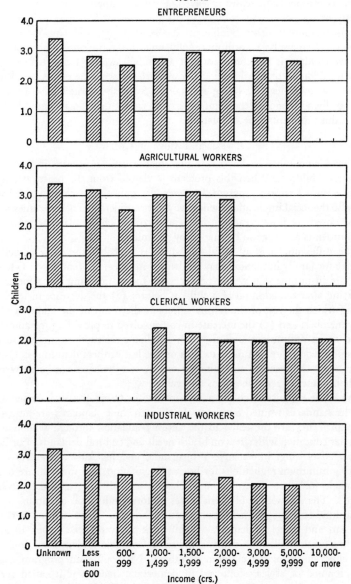

RURAL

extra costs for children, the whole apparent riddle of why children become scarce as prosperity increases is solved. Such a comparison is omnipresent. In any occupational and economic class the level of living of a family is seen in relation to other families in the same group, and equality is lost when children are born. Still more influential in the decision to have or not to have children is the comparison of a family's level of living before and after the addition of a child. In all income groups, with the exception of the highest, a lower level of living results. As Swedish statistics have proved, level of living is more dependent on size of family than on income. In the main, this represents a new situation.

The Differential Cost of Children

The dilemma has to be faced: the chief cause of poverty in modern society is children. When this problem is viewed from the practical angle of an eventual reform program, however, not only the psychological effects but also the social implications will have to be considered. Then the questions to be raised are how great the differential cost of children is and whether the burden is too large to be carried by a family.

The differential cost of children, which is probably the most powerful motive for family limitation, may be defined in three different ways: (1) the increase in income that would be necessary for maintaining the same level of living after the addition of a child as before; (2) the decrease in level of living which the rest of the family suffers as the result of the addition of a new member; and (3) the increase in cost involved in providing for an extra child at an optimum standard. Both psychological motivation and social planning tend more and more to turn on the last of these definitions. Questions about childbearing and family economy can therefore not be answered without some reference to norms and values.

What the support of children will involve in terms of cost is dependent on the standards wanted for them. In Sweden these standards are accepted as high. They are presented to the entire population through schools and popular education with stress on health needs and cultural demands. Furthermore, advertising, informative propaganda, and legislative measures containing minimum regulations for housing, sanitation, and so forth, are other channels for their dissemination. These standards are continually being raised. The knowledge of them serves to form individual ambitions as to what kind of life is wanted for prospective children. These higher standards are part and parcel of democracy itself, making every citizen even in low-income brackets likely to demand the same favorable growth conditions for his children as for the children of others. No population program could be proposed or at least followed in democratic Sweden if it called for a lowering of the generally approved standards for children.

These norms enter as a determining factor in all deliberations as to bearing a new child. They are analyzed in terms of the family's income and its previous budget setup. Rarely will a direct calculation of costs be made, but the knowledge is widespread that most family incomes are insufficient to provide children with the goods which are considered socially desirable. Statisticians, specializing in cost of living studies for families, have lately attempted to go a step farther and actually calculate the cost of a child. The minimum cost for a child in urban communities on a hygienically tolerable level of living was determined for the first 15 years of life, using budget statistics from working-class homes.[4] It called for an expenditure of about 666.67 crs. annually per child. As the most frequent family income in urban households is about 2,000 crs., it is obvious that the margin for several children is nonexistent.

This calculation was made as an experiment. More concrete and less debatable information may be derived from actual family budgets showing the difference in level of living between families with and without children and among families with varying numbers of children.

CHILDREN IN RELATION TO FAMILY SIZE AND INCOME LEVEL

Before analyzing family budget statistics, a broad perspective of the actual location of the nation's children in families of various sizes and on different income levels is needed. The increasing frequency of childlessness and the decreasing frequency of large-sized families — in fact already of 2 children and over — connotes urbanization (Table 14). Actually, 55.0 per cent of all normal families in Stockholm and 42.0 per cent of all families in Gothenburg, the second largest city, were without children under 16 years of age in 1935–1936 as against 41.8 per cent in all other cities and only 31.2 per cent in agricultural communities. While only 1.4 per cent of all normal families in Stockholm contained 4 children or more, the corresponding figures were 3.0 per cent in Gothenburg, 4.0 per cent in other cities, and 12.3 per cent in agricultural communities. These figures should not be used as representing the fertility or reproduction levels, as only children under 16 years of age are included and as a large proportion of marriages have not passed out of their productive stage. Also, the age distribution varies con-

---

[4] The calculations, which were made by Richard Sterner, were based on (a) the estimate made by the Nutritional Council of the General Medical Board as to the minimum cost for a fair food consumption, counting the child as 0.7 consumption unit and figuring a cost of 0.75 crs. daily per consumption unit; (b) the difference in rent between an apartment of 2 rooms and a kitchen and one of 3 rooms and a kitchen, 352 crs. per year according to the housing census and halved because it was estimated that two children could share a room; (c) an investigation by the Population Commission that clothing for a boy would require a minimum cost of 120 crs. annually and for a girl 100 crs.; (d) the assumption based on general budget studies that the previous three items represent not quite ⅔ of total cost of consumption. (Unpublished study.)

TABLE 14. — NORMAL FAMILIES IN SWEDEN, BY NUMBER OF CHILDREN
UNDER 16 YEARS OF AGE AND RESIDENCE, 1935–1936

NUMBER OF CHILDREN UNDER 16 YEARS OF AGE	TOTAL	RURAL DISTRICTS				URBAN DISTRICTS
		All rural communities	Agricultural communities	Mixed communities	Industrial communities	
Total . . .	100.0	100.0	100.0	100.0	100.0	100.0
0	38.0	33.8	31.2	32.3	36.5	45.0
1	29.6	28.9	25.8	27.6	31.6	30.8
2	17.3	18.5	19.4	19.1	17.6	15.3
3	8.0	9.4	11.2	10.0	7.8	5.6
4	3.7	4.7	6.0	5.5	3.4	2.1
5	1.8	2.4	3.3	2.8	1.7	0.8
6	0.9	1.3	1.6	1.5	0.8	0.3
7	0.4	0.6	0.9	0.7	0.4	0.1
8	0.2	0.3	0.4	0.3	0.1	—
9 or more . .	0.1	0.1	0.2	0.2	0.1	—

Source: Special Census, 1935–1936 (*Särskilda folkräkningen*), Part VI.

siderably among the various community groups. The data do show, however, that only slightly more than one family out of seven has 3 children or
more to support, but more than half of all children (exclusive of illegitimate
children and the children of widows, widowers, and divorced couples) are
reared in those families. The large families are found to a disproportionate
extent in rural districts which contain considerably less than two-thirds of
all families but more than three-fourths of all families with 3 or more
children.

The income data in the Swedish census materials are procured from the
income tax returns of the census years. Every person with an income of more
than 600 Swedish crs. has to declare his income annually for local and national taxation purposes.[5] In spite of the fact that income tax returns are
subject to more rigorous control than in the United States they undoubtedly
represent a serious underestimation of actual income, particularly in rural
areas where so much of the family income is in kind. Certain cost of living
items (domestic food products and housing) are also lower in rural than in
urban districts. For these reasons and also because direct relief and certain
other welfare items are not included in the income figures, the income differentials in Table 15 are somewhat exaggerated. In addition the whole level
should be moved upward in order to give a correct representation of facts.
It is impossible to state this correction in precise terms. The author, how-

[5] Failure to file an income tax return is, consequently, equal to a declaration that one's income is less than 600 crs. The unknowns have for this reason been lumped together with the
lowest income group shown in the income tables.

TABLE 15. — INCOMES OF NORMAL FAMILIES[a] IN SWEDEN,
BY RESIDENCE, 1935–1936

INCOME[b] CLASS (Crs.)	TOTAL	RURAL DISTRICTS	URBAN DISTRICTS
All families	100.0	100.0	100.0
Less than 600 or unknown	10.9	14.5	4.9
600–799	4.3	6.3	1.1
800–999	6.0	8.7	1.5
1,000–1,499	16.3	22.4	6.0
1,500–1,999	12.6	14.9	8.7
2,000–2,499	11.9	11.8	12.1
2,500–2,999	10.4	7.7	14.7
3,000–3,999	12.9	7.4	22.1
4,000–5,999	8.4	4.0	15.8
6,000–7,999	2.6	1.1	5.0
8,000 or more	3.7	1.2	8.1

[a] Marriages concluded 1900–1935.
[b] Income is defined as the sum of the husband's and the wife's incomes.

Source: Special Census, 1935–1936 (*Särskilda folkräkningen*), Part VI.

ever, would hazard a guess that the underestimation contained in aggregate figures is seldom greater than 25 per cent and seldom less than 10 per cent. In international comparisons it should be remembered furthermore that the real income of a Swedish family in all income classes, but most so in the lower ones, includes a relatively large amount of free or practically free public service.

With all these reservations Table 16 is presented to illustrate how the various family types are distributed among income classes. Over one-fifth of all normal families have incomes of less than 1,000 crs. Among families with 3 children or more an increasing proportion belongs to this low-income group as family size mounts. Thus one-third of the families with 6 children or more are within this low-income group. This tendency is explained partly by the greater frequency of large families in rural districts where incomes are lower [6] and partly by the general tendency for poor families to have the most children. More than half of all families have incomes of less than 2,000 crs. Even in the smallest families rarely do more than one-fourth of the families have an income above 3,000 crs., and the proportion is much less among large families. Table 17 gives the median incomes of families of different sizes in the various districts.

[6] The separate figures for urban and rural districts are, by the same token, in part influenced by the fact that large families are more prevalent in community groups (agricultural communities, rural-industrial communities, small cities, large cities, etc.) where incomes and living costs are lower. However, even in individual communities income usually shows some tendency to be lower in families with many children than in families with only a few children.

These data on family income indicate the differential cost of children, measured in the sacrifices in level of living enforced upon a family by the addition of another child. To express this quantitatively by dividing incomes by number of consumption units is extremely difficult without splitting the expenditure budget into its various items. As a tentative conclusion the general statement may be ventured that families with 3 children or more have to economize on an income which in relation to needs is only between one-half and two-thirds that of a childless couple.

PRESSURE OF CHILDREN ON THE FAMILY BUDGET

Until recently budget studies have paid too little attention to the factor of family dynamics. In Sweden as elsewhere such studies used to be mainly directed toward consumption on different income levels and in different

TABLE 16. — INCOMES OF NORMAL FAMILIES [a] IN SWEDEN, BY NUMBER OF CHILDREN UNDER 16 YEARS OF AGE AND RESIDENCE, 1935–1936

NUMBER OF CHILDREN UNDER 16 YEARS OF AGE	All families	PERCENT OF FAMILIES IN INCOME [b] CLASS (Crs.)										
		Less than 600 or unknown	600–799	800–999	1,000–1,499	1,500–1,999	2,000–2,499	2,500–2,999	3,000–3,999	4,000–5,999	6,000–7,999	8,000 or more
Rural Districts												
Total	100.0	14.5	6.3	8.7	22.4	14.9	11.8	7.7	7.4	4.0	1.1	1.2
0	100.0	17.5	7.7	8.9	19.4	12.8	11.1	7.6	7.9	4.6	1.2	1.3
1	100.0	11.1	6.2	9.4	22.5	15.7	12.9	8.4	7.8	3.9	1.0	1.1
2	100.0	11.7	5.5	8.7	24.6	15.6	12.2	7.9	7.4	3.8	1.3	1.3
3	100.0	13.9	5.0	8.1	26.2	16.3	11.2	7.2	6.0	3.7	1.1	1.3
4	100.0	17.1	5.1	7.4	25.1	16.1	11.4	7.2	5.6	3.3	0.8	0.9
5	100.0	19.7	4.2	7.0	26.7	18.0	9.9	6.2	5.1	2.4	0.2	0.6
6	100.0	23.3	4.4	5.5	25.4	18.1	10.3	5.6	4.7	1.8	0.4	0.5
7	100.0	26.2	4.2	5.4	21.2	18.1	11.0	5.4	4.5	2.9	0.5	0.6
8	100.0	32.9	2.6	6.5	20.6	16.2	9.1	5.6	4.4	1.5	0.3	0.3
9 or more . . .	100.0	39.3	1.8	4.9	20.9	11.0	8.6	3.7	6.7	3.1	—	—
Urban Districts												
Total	100.0	4.9	1.1	1.5	6.0	8.7	12.1	14.7	22.1	15.8	5.0	8.1
0	100.0	5.5	1.3	1.7	5.9	7.9	10.9	13.3	21.6	18.3	5.5	8.1
1	100.0	3.8	0.9	1.3	6.3	9.6	13.1	16.0	23.3	14.7	4.4	6.6
2	100.0	4.2	0.8	1.1	5.9	8.8	12.7	15.8	21.5	13.6	5.8	9.8
3	100.0	5.6	0.8	0.9	6.1	9.6	12.4	15.2	21.5	12.7	3.9	11.3
4	100.0	6.7	1.0	1.9	5.9	11.3	13.7	16.7	22.6	9.3	2.6	8.3
5	100.0	8.4	1.3	2.2	4.5	11.8	16.3	18.1	20.0	8.4	2.5	6.5
6	100.0	7.5	2.7	2.0	7.1	11.0	18.4	14.9	20.0	11.0	2.7	2.7
7	100.0	14.3	—	4.1	7.2	8.1	20.4	14.3	20.4	7.2	2.0	2.0
8	100.0	10.4	—	—	—	6.9	13.8	24.1	31.0	10.4	—	3.4
9 or more . . .	100.0	15.8	—	—	—	5.3	42.1	15.8	21.0	—	—	—

[a] Marriages concluded 1900–1935.
[b] Income is defined as the sum of the husband's and wife's incomes.

Source: Special Census, 1935–1936 (*Särskilda folkräkningen*), Part VI.

TABLE 17. — MEDIAN FAMILY[a] INCOME IN SWEDEN, BY NUMBER OF
CHILDREN UNDER 16 YEARS OF AGE AND RESIDENCE, 1935–1936

NUMBER OF CHILDREN UNDER 16 YEARS OF AGE	MEDIAN FAMILY INCOME[b] (Crs.)					
		Rural Districts				Urban Districts
	Total	All Rural Communities	Agricultural Communities	Mixed Communities	Industrial Communities	
Total . . .	1,996	1,456	1,103	1,249	2,087	3,046
0	2,148	1,411	967	1,145	2,084	3,160
1	2,072	1,526	1,115	1,262	2,119	2,970
2	1,955	1,488	1,169	1,314	2,131	3,031
3	1,751	1,439	1,200	1,321	2,023	2,980
4	1,612	1,407	1,197	1,325	1,997	2,786
5	1,474	1,358	1,171	1,283	1,818	2,655
6	1,426	1,330	1,223	1,223	1,729	2,553
7	1,411	1,338	1,128	1,339	1,833	*
8	1,279	1,196	1,121	1,135	*	*
9 or more . .	1,199	1,103	*	*	*	*

* Reliable data not available.
[a] Marriages concluded 1900–1935.
[b] Income is defined as the sum of the husband's and the wife's incomes.

Source: Special Census, 1935–1936 (*Särskilda Folkräkningen*), Part VI.

regional and social groups. The population discussion created a demand
for official statistics both for housing and for family consumption analyzed
in terms of different family types. Since then statistics have been presented
to show in more detail than formerly the budget changes following family
changes within the various income groups. Although these statistics will
be discussed at length in Part II, as they are fundamental for developing
social reforms for the family, a general picture will be given here.[7] All the
statistics refer to working-class and lower middle-class urban families. They
depict the average situations in the groups in Sweden that have to rear
most of the children. There is little doubt that in any nation nine-tenths of
the people will have to face the same practical dilemma. Are we going to
have family limitation to the extreme or children reared on substandard
levels of health and culture?

Children in a family first have some general effect on the disposing of incomes. With children a larger amount has to be spent for the basic need of
food, and cultural and recreational activities have to be curtailed (Table 18).
The distribution of taxation in Sweden tends to rectify this somewhat as

[7] For descriptions of material, definitions, and reservations as to validity see particularly
Chapter 15.

TABLE 18. — EXPENDITURES IN SWEDEN IN URBAN FAMILIES WITH CHILDREN AS PER CENT OF EXPENDITURES OF FAMILIES WITHOUT CHILDREN, 1933

(Income Class: 3,000–4,999 crs.)

EXPENDITURE ITEM	FAMILIES WITHOUT CHILDREN	FAMILIES WITH CHILDREN, THE OLDEST BEING							
		Under 7 years		7–15 years			15 years and over		
		1 child	2–3 children	1 child	2–3 children	4 children or more	1 child	2–3 children	4 children or more
Food	100	113	124	124	137	165	126	148	181
Drinks, tobacco . .	100	95	90	131	108	87	86	101	78
Housing	100	100	89	88	84	86	84	78	71
Fuel and lighting . .	100	101	110	96	101	114	102	101	106
Clothing	100	98	100	106	109	116	92	107	110
Shoes	100	122	141	141	174	206	130	158	220
Taxes	100	78	72	79	67	48	89	71	46
Home furnishings .	100	73	61	60	54	65	74	50	53
Dues to associations, clubs, etc. . . .	100	95	96	98	114	85	100	109	86
Newspapers, books, etc..	100	78	72	69	64	61	77	61	49
Bodily care, laundry .	100	90	85	90	81	81	86	77	78
Miscellaneous . . .	100	92	89	93	83	71	85	85	67

Source: Cost of Living Study, 1933 (*Levnadsvillkor och hushållsvanor i städer och industriorter omkring år 1933*).

FIG. III. — FOOD EXPENDITURES PER CONSUMPTION UNIT IN URBAN FAMILIES IN SWEDEN, BY INCOME AND NUMBER OF CHILDREN, 1933

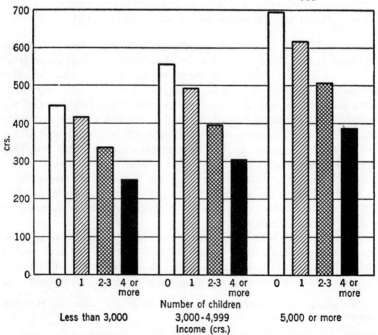

Source: Cost of Living Study, 1933 (*Levnadsvillkor och hushållsvanor i städer och industriorter omkring år 1933*).

does the right to enjoy many free services in the spheres of schooling, health, and social consumption generally. These factors have more force now than in 1933, the year the budget study referred to was made. The data refer to a fairly high income group, containing only a minority of families. They show that the pressure is not only a matter of sheer poverty, but also naturally becomes more intense in the lower income groups.

The most clearly demonstrable change is in the food percentage. So much less flexible is the need for food than for other items that food will always tend to hold its absolute cost, thus increasing the percentage of the income expended for food as other needs are left unsatisfied. This makes the food percentage one of the most reliable single indices of poverty. In the Swedish series it is easy to see that the index of poverty closely follows

FIG. IV. — OVERCROWDING IN URBAN FAMILIES IN SWEDEN, BY FAMILY SIZE

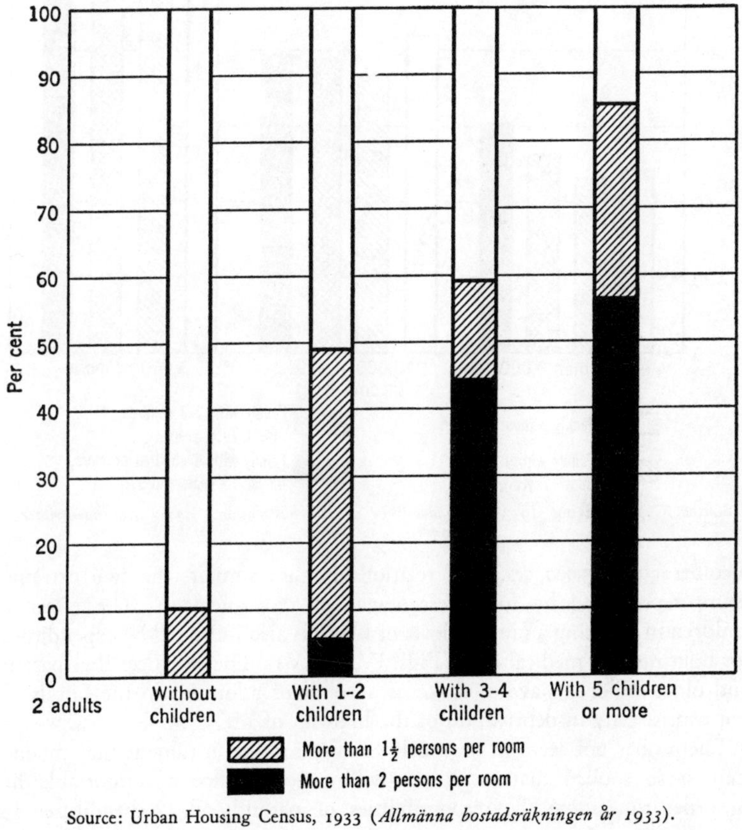

Source: Urban Housing Census, 1933 (*Allmänna bostadsräkningen år 1933*).

the appearance of children in a family. While the childless families in urban areas with less than 3,000 crs. income spent 29.7 per cent for food in 1933, families with the same income but 4 or more children had to spend 43.7 per cent (Fig. III). In the next income group the corresponding figures are 22.3 and 40.4 per cent, respectively. Also in the highest income group (with

FIG. V. — MEDICAL EXPENDITURES IN URBAN FAMILIES IN SWEDEN, BY INCOME AND FAMILY SIZE, 1933

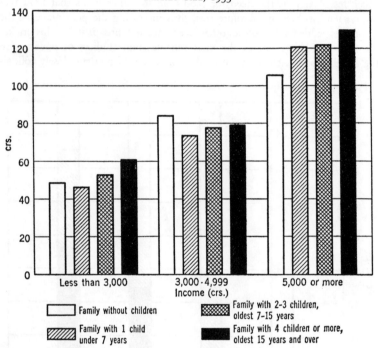

Source: Cost of Living, 1933 (*Levnadsvillkor och hushållsvanor i städer och industriorter omkring år 1933*).

incomes above 5,000 crs.) the relationships are similar, the two extremes being represented by food percentages of 16.3 and 29.2 The effect of children in reducing a family's level of living is also indicated by expenditures for housing and medical care (Figs. IV and V). The sacrifices that parents and older children have to make as a result of additions to the family do not consist only in deprivation of the luxuries of life.

There does not seem to be much validity for the argument that modern man is so spoiled that he is not willing to sacrifice a comfortable life in order to assume the responsibilities of parenthood. Expenditures for luxuries do not seem to leave much leeway for more children even if the "moral" attitude toward childbearing changes. If doubt still exists, the recreational and cultural budgets of the same families may be consulted (Figs. VI and VII). How many children could be supported in the

FIG. VI. — CULTURAL EXPENDITURES [a] IN URBAN FAMILIES IN SWEDEN, BY INCOME AND FAMILY SIZE, 1933

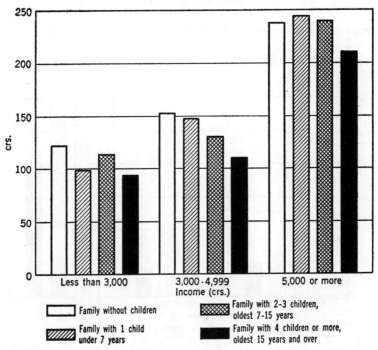

[a] Exclusive of education.

Source: Cost of Living, 1933 (*Levnadsvillkor och hushallsvanor i städer och industriorter omkring år 1933*).

childless families by curbing "luxurious" recreation? Even if the whole recreational item in the budget of the more well-to-do childless family were omitted, it would hardly pay for one child and still less for several. To provide for more children on average budgets, except in the case of some childless families, is impossible except by sacrificing the standards for health and culture that we want to set for the nation. It can be said with assurance that the ambition of the Swedish people to raise standards has not meant more motion pictures and automobiles but rather more baths and vitamins and doctors and travel and reading.

Comparing family income with family needs thus reveals the crux of the situation. Often the social conscience refuses to face the realization that there exists a real choice between children and approved standards of life. Nations allow the children who are going to be their own future generation to be born under the poorest circumstances and to live in the

FIG. VII. — RECREATIONAL EXPENDITURES IN URBAN FAMILIES IN SWEDEN, BY INCOME AND FAMILY SIZE, 1933

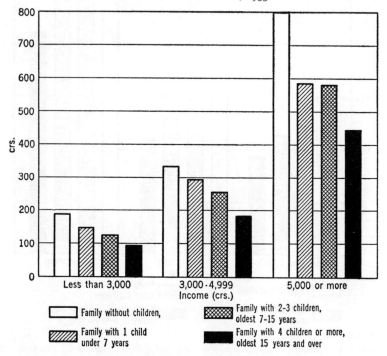

Source: Cost of Living, 1933 (*Levnadsvillkor och hushållsvanor i städer och industriorter omkring år 1933*).

most unhealthful homes and in the districts least accessible for cultural transmission and even for schooling. Still worse, they allow parents, young, normal people, to become poor on account of children. Society is organized with so little wisdom that the persons who contribute to the upkeep of the nation are dragged down into poverty, poor housing, meager nourishment, and diminished cultural and recreational life because of that very contribution. There exists no other cause of birth limitation comparable to the economic one.

CHAPTER V

FORECASTING THE FUTURE

THE Swedish people are not yet actually diminishing in numbers. The annual population returns continue to show a natural increase.

THE BALANCE OF BIRTHS AND DEATHS

Since 1930 the excess of births over deaths has been around 15,000 persons annually, with a low of 13,093 in 1935 and a high of 24,113 in 1939. The most significant point, however, is not whether children born in a year balance the number of deaths occurring in the same year but whether such a balance is secured in the long run. About such interrelations in the population mechanism, these simple data on population changes tell next to nothing.

The birth rate, calculated as the number of births per 1,000 population, was 14.4 in 1937. The death rate calculated in a similar manner was 12.0, giving a rate of natural increase for that year of 2.4 per 1,000. The middle-aged groups in the population, characterized by a high fertility and a low mortality, are, however, abnormally large as a result of the high birth rates before the World War. With corrections for age the birth rate drops to 11.8 per 1,000 while the death rate rises to 15.6. This signifies a natural decrease at a rate of 3.8 per 1,000 instead of the actual increase at the rate of 2.4 per 1,000.

The Swedish public is largely aware of the delusion of the age distribution. It has been brought home that the death rate is artificially low because of an abnormal situation in which the two age groups most susceptible to death are underrepresented: the children and the aged. As the overrepresented middle-aged groups become older, the number of deaths will increase. The recorded death rate of just above 11 per 1,000 is in reality so incredibly low that it corresponds to a far higher average length of life than modern medicine can now make possible. Thus the death rate in 1933 or even in 1939 would require an average life expectancy of nearly 74 years in a normally distributed population while the actual expectancy calculated on the mortality conditions for the period 1931–1935 is only slightly above 64 years. Likewise it is common knowledge that unless fertility increases the birth rate will drop still further in the course of time. The picture of constant decline, not only of a given reduction, has been made vivid in the public mind. The concept "net reproductivity" has been popularized and almost everyone has come to understand that retaining the present low fertility rate means the self-consuming of the potential population stock by about one-fourth in each generation. The last age group of Swedish women that has succeeded in barely replacing itself consists of persons born in 1890.

The birth rate reached its temporary low point in 1934 when it dropped to 13.7 per 1,000. Then the downward trend seemed to be checked and a gradual rise occurred. The rates for the following years were 13.8, 14.2, 14.4, 14.9, and, in 1939, 15.3. The rate of marital fertility, i.e., number of children born per 1,000 married women 15–44 years of age (Table 13), which of course is less dependent on age distribution, has shown a greater fall than the birth rate — from 300.9 in 1871–1880 to 113.5 in 1934, a decline of 62 per cent while the birth rate fell only 55 per cent. It was even lower in 1935 (112.1) than in 1934. For the two following years it amounted to 114.5 and 114.0, respectively.

As these slight increases were made public a new optimism concerning population trends became widespread. People believed that the trend had turned, even if it was understood that the road to full reproduction was fairly long. It must, however, be doubted if these figures really prove that the downward trend has been reversed. For one thing the marriage rate has been increasing slowly since the beginning of the century. From 1933 a rapid rise occurred which raised the rate from 7.0 in 1933 to 9.5 in 1939. As was pointed out in Chapter 3, this rise is partly due to changes in the age distribution. It is also partly to be explained by the strong and gradually intensified business recovery beginning in 1934. Both these causes are temporary in nature and represent no trend. The increase in marriages must have resulted in additional children and first-born children nowadays constitute a greater part of all children born than formerly. The advantageous economic conditions during these years must also have tended to increase fertility somewhat in the older marriages. Some of these extra births might be said to have been "saved up" from the earlier lean years. Thus some of the babies augmenting the birth numbers of the later years "should have been born" earlier if economic conditions had been equalized. In any case, they do not represent a change in the trend.

PROGNOSES

Several attempts have been made to calculate the future population development in Sweden. Such population prognoses are nothing else than extrapolations of previous trends. They must be based on definite assumptions as to the factors of change in the population mechanism: fertility, mortality, and external migration. They are useful in revealing the play of various quantitative interrelations in this mechanism and its sometimes astonishing results. Their value in predicting the future development of population depends upon how closely future events conform to the stated assumptions. The plausibility of these assumptions ought therefore to be discussed realistically. It should perhaps be noted that net reproductivity is in fact a sort of simple prognosis, based on the assumptions of constant fertility and mortality conditions, leaving external migration entirely out of account and not relating the analysis to the years directly ahead.

Only one of the more elaborate prognoses made for Sweden will be commented on here. It is not only the most recent one but also technically the most satisfactory one and has most directly influenced political action on the population question. Constructed for the Population Commission by the late Professor Sven Wicksell, son of the population theorist Knut Wicksell, it is based on material from the Census of 1930. [16]

This forecast takes into account the following four different hypotheses of fertility and nuptiality.

Hypothesis I: Fertility among married and unmarried women combined is extrapolated from the previous trend by separate age groups and thus is assumed to continue to fall at first, though at a decreasing rate, and then finally to become stabilized in 1985. On this assumption the gross fertility at that time will be 70 per cent of its value for the year 1933.

Hypothesis II: Fertility among married and unmarried women separately in the several age groups is assumed to remain the same as it was for those groups in 1933, while the nuptiality rate from 1936 onward is stabilized at the level of 1901–1910.

Hypothesis III: Fertility rates are assumed to be the same as in Hypothesis II, while from 1936 nuptiality is stabilized at a level raised to 125 per cent of that in Hypothesis II.

Hypothesis IV: Marital fertility is assumed to remain the same as in Hypotheses II and III, but extramarital fertility is assumed gradually to decline to 50 per cent of its height in 1933 and then become stabilized from 1956, while nuptiality is stabilized from 1936 onward at 150 per cent of the level of Hypothesis II.

In all cases the mortality rates in different age groups are assumed to remain the same as the actual rates in 1933, which are the lowest on record.

Although some of these hypotheses are quite optimistic, the total population is shown to decline in all cases (Fig. VIII). Only the turning point for the actual decrease and the rate of decrease differ. According to Hypothesis I, the actual decrease of the Swedish population would start between 1941 and 1945. According to Hypothesis IV, it would not start before 1956–

1960. The calculations are not carried beyond 1985 but at that point all four curves tend toward continued decline. The birth rate would decline from 14.1, as of 1931–1935, to 6.4, 10.5, 11.8, and 12.2 per 1,000 in 1981–1985 according to the four hypotheses, respectively. According to Hypothesis I, the depletion of population would be precipitous. The net reproduction toward which it tends would be only 53 per cent of that required to

Fig. VIII. — Swedish Population, 1900–1985, According to Four Hypotheses

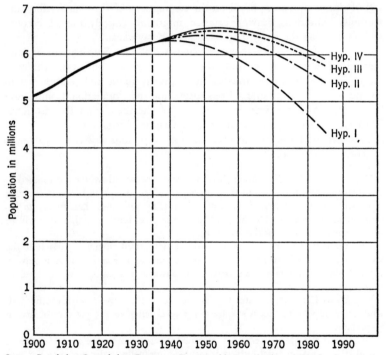

Source: Population Commission, Report on Demographic Investigations (*Betänkande med vissa demografiska utredningar*).

replace the population. That implies that if such a structure of the population as is now imminent were stabilized, nearly half the potential population would be lost with each generation. For Hypotheses II and III the net reproductivity would be 72 per cent and 80 per cent, respectively. Even the extremely optimistic assumptions of Hypothesis IV would result in a net reproduction of only 82 per cent, implying a net decrease every year of about 6 per 1,000 population as against the present increase of 2 or 3 per 1,000 population.

Wicksell's assumption in all four alternatives that emigration and immigration are not going to have any appreciable influence on the Swedish population development seems, on the whole, to be well founded. Emigration has evidently ceased to be a problem, the immigrants already outnumbering the emigrants by 1930. This immigration has consisted to a major extent of reimmigration from the United States which probably will not continue long as the Swedish emigrant stock in the United States is dying out. The other part of the immigration is made up of refugees. Sweden has reluctantly opened its doors to exiles from other European countries, having a net immigration from Germany, Austria, and Czechoslovakia of only 409 persons in 1937, 749 in 1938, 1,587 in 1939, or slightly above 2 per 10,000 inhabitants in the latter year.

Wicksell's assumption that mortality conditions will be stabilized at the actual rate of 1933 is obviously pessimistic. In all probability some advance in health and longevity will occur. It must be noted, however, that the fate of persons above the reproductive ages has only limited effect on population trends. On account of the fact that they will not contribute further to childbearing, any additional years at the end of their lives serve only to attenuate the decline in actual population numbers but not to replenish the stock from which new generations arise. The life expectancy of people in the years of parenthood is of greater importance. The mortality in those ages is, however, already low and great decreases are not possible. Whether the improvements in medical care will continue to outweigh the increase in accidental deaths is somewhat uncertain. Still the death rate in these middle groups seems to continue to decrease slightly even in recent years.

The most important changes to be expected are, however, those with regard to infant mortality as this rate is still rather high. Nearly every twenty-fifth child is lost before reaching the age of one year. The trend toward improvement there is unbroken, the rate of mortality during the first year being down to 3.9 per cent in 1939. It would seem absolutely certain that the propaganda for child care will reach ever new groups and that the improved economic conditions generally, unless undone by the wars in Europe, will ameliorate health conditions so that more infants are saved. In regard to infant mortality in particular there is opportunity for directed social change. The wide social differences with regard to infant life and death indicate that some 2,000 children a year could be saved. This would evidently create a wider basis for future parenthood and would decrease the demand on increased fertility for maintenance of the population. If Wicksell had made such an assumption, it would have increased the estimated net reproductivity proportionately. The factor is thus by no means unimportant from a quantitative point of view, although it does not change the calculation radically.

From the discussion in Chapter 3, Wicksell's Hypothesis IV concerning extramarital fertility would seem to be quite realistic. It would be surprising if under the influence of improved sex education and the accessibility of contraceptives illegitimate births should not continue their rapid fall.

The future of nuptiality was also considered in Chapter 3. As was pointed out, only the very recent rise in marriage rate represents a rise in real nuptiality frequency and its causes may be only temporary in nature. Nothing in recent figures gives much promise of a spontaneous increase in the proportion of married people in the population. Wicksell's assumptions as to nuptiality in Hypotheses III and IV would therefore seem to be overoptimistic. These two hypotheses contain an even more doubtful implicit assumption, namely, that the additional marriages would show the same fertility as the other marriages. It is curious to note how Wicksell and many other population statisticians constantly seek escape in this absolutely unwarranted assumption in order to be able to preserve an optimistic view of the population problem. It should, however, be evident that a great number of the additional marriages may take place only because birth control can keep them less fertile. The "marginal" bride and bridegroom may not be as willing to assume parenthood as the average couple. Or, to criticize the theory itself, the fertility of the increased sum of marriages could not be assumed to remain the same; changing one factor (marrying) can hardly be done without changing the other (fertility) because they are interdependent. The social patterns may encourage more marriages, but if nothing else is changed for the family — and social inaction is here an assumption — the social pattern most instrumental in increasing marriages is that of voluntary sterility.

Judging Wicksell's alternative hypotheses from what has been said so far, Hypotheses III and IV must be declared overoptimistic on account of both the explicit assumption of increased nuptiality and the implicit assumption of average fertility in these additional marriages. Hypothesis II would also seem to give results not likely to be realized because it assumes that extramarital fertility will remain unchanged. This is counterbalanced in part by Wicksell's failure to calculate the effects of the decrease in infant mortality which may reasonably be expected.

The main problem is, however, yet untouched: fertility as a whole. In Hypotheses II, III, and IV fertility is assumed to remain constant; in Hypothesis I it is assumed to fall by another 30 per cent. If an offhand choice should be made between these two alternatives, the more pessimistic one would seem to be the more plausible. It is true that fertility has risen somewhat since the calculation was made at about the lowest point of the curve. But this rise is influenced by causes of an obviously temporary character, so that it appears sounder not to assume a reversal of the earlier trend. Hypothesis I seems the most plausible also when not only the directly discernible statistical trends are taken into account but also the sociological interpretation of reasons for the tendency toward family limitation discussed in Chapter 4.

The Future of Fertility

Even without going too deeply into the psychosocial interplay of causes and reasons for birth control, a number of tendencies are perceptible in the Swedish population situation that definitely indicate a continued downward path. For one thing illegitimate children will hardly continue to be born in the same large numbers as formerly. As has already been pointed out, only the last of Wicksell's hypotheses contains any reasonable allowance for their decline, although this allowance is counterbalanced by overoptimism in other respects. The rate of decline cannot be foretold, but it must be understood that the reproduction of the Swedish people is still dependent by more than 10 per cent (1939 — 12.25 per cent) upon children born out of wedlock. If this number is declining, it means a corresponding loss in the already low birth rate. Without the illegitimate children the net reproductivity rate in Sweden would already be not much over 60 per cent.

The high rate of illegitimate childbearing also teaches another lesson. It shows how large a number of children seem to be born without their parents having intended to have them. Even if some of them when once born enjoy as much parental affection as any other children, most of them must be considered as accidents. The same holds true of many of the children conceived prior to marriage and born within the first few months after marriage. Those born within the first 8 months still constitute one-sixth of all legitimate children (1931–1935 — 17 per cent). They account for more than 10 per cent of the total number of children born. To a large extent marriages must be considered precipitated by them. This should tend to deflate expectations of a higher marriage rate in a future characterized by still more widespread birth control. If birth control measures were absolutely effective, most of these children would never have been born. It requires no great insight to conclude that if so many premarital sex relations result in unwanted pregnancies, a great number of marital sex relations must also do so. There is no way of knowing how large a proportion of children born well within marriages are "accidental." With birth control spreading and becoming more effective the question of how many children are predetermined by the parents becomes a question of great importance for the future. Would much more than one-third of all children now born have been born if rational family planning had prevailed in all groups, both in and out of marriage?

Some parallel inferences can be drawn from the wide differences with regard to fertility within the country. Such differences are now being leveled out and the leveling process is downward. The result will be a lower aggregate fertility. This holds true of poor versus rich as well as of rural versus urban generally and particularly of northern versus southern Sweden.

Nature's selection of homes for the nation's young continues to favor the economically less secure groups. Figure II, showing the average number of children born in different socio-economic groups, gave an idea how, despite the slight upturn in size of family in the highest income groups as noted in the latest census, the traditional relationship between poverty and child-bearing still holds true. It is, however, steadily weakening. Even the poor learn to behave rationally in this as in other respects. And poverty itself is being gradually conquered in a country making rapid economic progress and speeding social reform activities.

A tendency toward higher than average fertility in unfavored groups is also found with regard to occupational strata. It may be noted, however, that those placing themselves in the middle class who economically belong in the poorer section — functionaries with low incomes — seem to follow the most consistent pattern of caution in fertility. Oddly enough, the opposite extreme in the middle class, those who belong occupationally to the working class but economically reach up into higher income brackets (some urban-industrial workers), appear to follow the same pattern of extreme family limitation. The social ambitions and individual capabilities resulting in social advancement have been combined with a weak development of family inclinations. Any acquaintance with the leading groups among the Swedish working class will verify their failure to produce a new generation to succeed themselves. This very phenomenon of social advancement is part and parcel of the social mobility, generally in an upward direction, that has been characteristic of Sweden and that will, if no great interference occurs, continue to be characteristic in the future. Spread of the pattern of caution in childbearing would then be a development to anticipate. Our conclusion must be that one cannot expect an undisturbed prolongation of the present distribution of children with their excessive accumulation in the poorer families. With a decrease in such families the aggregate fertility can but decrease.

A similar trend is indicated by the fertility differences between rural and urban districts. Great local variations are blotted out in these totals.

If average marital fertility is given the value of 100, variations from 48 to 149 may be found in different cities, while the index for rural districts ranges from 67 in Danderyd, near Stockholm, to 282 in Pajala on the Finnish border. [16] In 1930–1931 the net reproductivity for rural districts was 91 per cent (76 per cent within and 15 per cent outside of marriages) but in cities it was only 58 per cent (48 per cent within and 10 per cent outside of marriages).

Isolation and more resistant traditionalism may account for only a part of the excess of rural children. The rural environment as such may in reality be better adjusted to children. Time may thus not be expected completely to obliterate the difference. Changes are, however, taking place rapidly in the country. Farming is being industrialized and made more dependent on a money income and less dependent on self-subsistence. Education is becoming standardized throughout the country and other ideological influences are becoming more and more similar. Standards of hygiene, food, and housing as well as educational and recreational desires are becoming the same in the country as among the favored city folk. At the same time the proportion of the farming population in the nation has diminished and will probably diminish further. This leads to a reiteration of the conclusion reached in the study of other fertility differentials: the future can in the main offer only a downward trend.

To sum up, differentials in fertility are unstable and likely to be wiped out but only in a downward movement. This forecast gains added weight if the general development in the country is toward economic prosperity and cultural progress but without any new social organization for families and children. It also gains added weight if not only the spread of patterns of family limitation is regarded but also the spread of artificial devices for birth control. In addition the qualitative improvement of such devices may be foreseen, making family planning more efficient.

An important proportion of the children now being born stem from relatively few of those large families which are doomed to be more and more commonly judged too large. The present distribution of children in families will be superseded by one in which the high numbers disappear and no significant change — unless it be toward still further decline — can be expected among the low numbers.

Effects of Population Change

The discussion of the basic assumptions as to the factors of change in population has thus led to the conclusion that only Wicksell's Hypothesis I seems to be fairly realistic while all the others for various reasons must be deemed much too optimistic. One important reservation, however, must be added: consideration has been given only to the forces inherent in the social and demographic trends themselves. These forces have been supposed to work uninfluenced by induced changes on the part of society, but population policy is intended to affect those tendencies by reshaping the mental, social, and economic bases for marrying, homemaking, and childbearing. The real meaning of the program is found in changes in the prognosis. Only on the basis of the very prognosis which it is the aim of the program to challenge can such a program be constructed.

The most reasonable hypothesis, number I, or any sensible variant of it, points to a continuous, rapid, and cumulative population decline. Its acceptance as probable means the denial of the popular idea that the population decline is going to be halted by itself. In the interplay of personal, social, and demographic forces regulating population development there is discernible no harmonious principle which would in the long run procure an ultimate balance of births and deaths. If such a balance is to be realized, it will have to be created by superposing on the "natural forces" a purposive social policy.

The problem of forecasting the future also involves a study of the effects of the different alternatives as to further population development. Enough has been said to make it plausible to direct the discussion exclusively to the effects of a population decline as compared with a stationary population, any population increase being entirely out of the question.

The economic effects are naturally of paramount importance.[1] The problem is definitely one of dynamics. The old static analysis, represented by the theory of the optimum population, entirely misses the point. The economic effects of population decline in a country like Sweden have little to do with the size of the population; they are mainly caused by the population changes as such. The process of population contraction will increase risks for capital investment and labor employment and accentuate all adjustment difficulties. The depressive results might be overcome by central control, and certainly the population trend is one of the factors favoring the development of state capitalism. It may be doubted, however, even by an ardent old-fashioned socialist if public administration of a nation in the process of gradual liquidation is in line with human progress.

The most obvious effect of population decline is not of this general scope; it is the change in age composition of the people, the aging of society. Using Wicksell's most optimistic and most pessimistic prognoses of future trends, the age group 65 and over may increase from the 9 per cent of the Swedish population in 1935 to 18 per cent or 24 per cent in 1985 (Table 19). The economic, social, and psychological effects of such an aging of society must be considerable. The direct economic costs of

[1] See Gunnar Myrdal, *Population, A Problem for Democracy*, Harvard University Press, Cambridge, 1940, Chapter VI, "Effects of Population Decline."

TABLE 19. — AGE STRUCTURE OF THE SWEDISH POPULATION, 1910, 1935, AND 1985

AGE	ACTUAL PER CENT DISTRIBUTION		ESTIMATED PER CENT DISTRIBUTION, 1985	
	1910	1935	Hypothesis I	Hypothesis IV
Under 20 years . . .	41	31	15	24
20–34 years	22	26	16	19
35–49 years	16	20	20	21
50–64 years	12 } 21	14 } 23	25 } 49	18 } 36
65 years and over . . .	9	9	24	18

Source: Population Commission, Report on Demographic Investigations (*Betänkande med vissa demografiska utredningar*), Vol. 24, 1938.

support and upkeep may first be examined. Here the increase of the old is offset by a decrease in the young. In order to decide whether this means a final plus or minus, the whole life span must be considered, counting productive contributions, on the one hand, and cost of maintenance, on the other, and showing the net cost of support at different ages. Such calculations do not exist. In all countries, however, the cost of supporting both the unproductive young and the old is increasing. Whether the increase in costs for the young, owing to improved health and school standards, is higher than the increase in costs for the old, with larger pensions and finer funerals, is difficult to say. It is evident, however, that the increase in the cost of supporting the growing number of aged will be felt everywhere and that in comparison the costs for children will be considered more profitable as a form of investment. While investment in human capital is unprofitable with regard to the old, the actual outlook is that the aged nevertheless are going to inherit the earth.

The number of persons to support the aged will continually decline. At the present time there are in Sweden about six persons 20–64 years of age to every person 65 years of age or older. If the trend continues there will be not quite three persons in the productive ages per person 65 and over in another 50 years. A proportionately greater share of the nation's income will be drawn upon for maintaining these old people. The problem of supporting the unproductive ages will be increased by the fact that the generation now in its prime, which in old age will exact more than any previous one, has already been preying upon the population in its days of strength.

This present generation of productive age groups will go down in history as the most ravenous of all. It has increased its spending income per consumption unit by not bearing enough children to replace itself, and at the same time by self-insurance and by social legislation it has usurped legal rights to a labor-free income in old age. The annuities then to be paid must as always be paid out of the working income of the productive people, of which the consuming old will not have provided a sufficient number. Consumption at both ends thus characterizes this generation. That is the interpretation in human terms of the abstract fact that a temporarily increased level of living can be gained by individual families at the turning point from progressive to regressive population trends. If, later on, it would be possible to increase fertility enough to attain full reproduction again, it would likewise mean temporary pressure on the level of living, as the nation then would have to support the increased relative number of children in a stationary population and at the same time the greater number of old people corresponding to a shrinking population.

The overrepresentation of the old will not only have direct economic effects. The psychological attitude of the people will be different. The whole expansionist psychology of the last half century may be lost. Old people are not the most enterprising investors or administrators. Still, they will have the power over wealth and will hold the key positions. This mastery of old people has already manifested itself, but it will grow to more oppressive importance with the increase in relative numbers of old as compared with young. In Swedish public life the institutional setup is such that old people control important positions in administration on account of the two principles of life tenure and seniority, widely applied not only in civil service, where they are actually prescribed, but also as a matter of practice everywhere else. In the business and financial field older persons already have disproportionate control as, according to the Census of 1930, persons over 50 years of age owned 69.5 per cent of all wealth and persons over 60, 43.5 per cent, although their share of the population was only 22.4 and 12.8 per cent, respectively. In private life and social situations, finally, the suggestion must be ventured that an equalization between generations has not taken place in Sweden in the same degree as in the New World. This has augmented the impact and the authority of the aged. The total cultural atmosphere must tend to become static as the old gain in importance.

Still more subtle effects may result. Old people are not the ones particularly to tackle new problems or to adjust with a minimum of friction to new situations. Yet economic and political problems are likely to become more complex. Problems are less likely to take care of themselves in a shrinking population than in an expanding one. A certain psychological discomfort may also result from the very competition between young and old. Public advantages of the one group or the other will be the subject of battles which the old are likely to win on account both of greater power and of greater numbers at the ballot. In every vocation it may be easier to enter the ranks of employed when young, because there will be fewer at the same age level, and easier to fall out when old, because there will be more of the aged. But it will certainly also be more difficult for the young to advance because the old will more completely control the career posts. The conclusion can hardly be avoided that it will become more difficult to be young in a society that is controlled by the aged. Whether it will be more enjoyable to be old than now is hard to say. Life rarely provides compensation directly but usually either expands more generally or contracts more generally.

CHAPTER VI

QUALITATIVE POPULATION CHANGES

TECHNICAL development seems to lead in the direction of greater demands on human quality. For the world in general it may be difficult to estimate whether the trend toward technical complexity, with higher demands on quality of labor, or the trend toward mass production, with relatively lower demands on quality, is the greater. For Sweden, where farming is so largely on the basis of individual landownership and where industry is so definitely organized for skilled production, there is less doubt that the dominating trend is toward increased demands on quality of labor. Compared with the situation 100 years ago before the rise of industrialization, or even 50 or 25 years ago, production now requires less and less sheer strength. Electrotechnics have provided cheaper and more efficient sources of energy than human muscles. Demands on the human participant in the productive process are concentrated increasingly on intellectual and moral capacities — vigilance, quick comprehension, technical insight, control, and imagination — or, generally speaking, intelligence and character.

The whole rhythm of life in modern society has been intensified. Standards of efficiency have been raised. This is true in all fields, but the relative differences are greater in so far as physical work rather than intellectual work is concerned. It is becoming true of agriculture as well. A person who wants to get ahead on a small farm in Sweden nowadays must be a capable person in quite another sense than a few decades ago, when a large part of the farm population could subsist by hard work along customary and primitive lines. Today, a man on a Swedish farm must have a head on his shoulders; he must make accurate calculations and keep informed concerning the outside world in many technical respects; he must be active in the work of cooperatives and other organizations in his sphere of life.

In industry the workers themselves and their powerful trade organizations have been important factors in actively promoting higher standards of efficiency. Trade-union theory, particularly as developed in Sweden, has emphasized that unionization and collective bargaining will so transform the competition among workers that instead of pressing wages downward it will lead to greater efficiency. Wages would be fixed at a high level but would thereby force employers and workers to procure maximum labor efficiency. On the whole, this theory has been successfully followed in practice.

THE PROBLEM OF THE SECOND-RATE WORKER

The steadily rising demands for efficiency which are in the spirit of the times must, however, leave a small but continuously increasing percentage of people behind as second-rate. The constantly growing standardization of labor conditions, the more highly organized capitalism of business enter- prises, and the passing of paternalism in employment increasingly deprive these unfortunate leftovers of the chance to work, even at substandard wages. So the number of the unemployable grows.

In two phases of life the development toward standardized, minimum demands on labor output has not yet been fully developed, thus leaving some leeway for individuals below par to muddle along. These are agriculture and women's work. In some backward rural districts it is still possible to get along as cotters, living in dilapidated houses, growing some simple products for food, and earning a little money income at irregular intervals. But with rationalization of agriculture and with union- ization of farm labor, the possibility of earning a living without belonging to the majority groups of employables dwindles in agriculture too. Struc- turalization in this field will mean increased demands on and advantages for the many, but at the same time it will mean the casting out of some few who are falling behind the standard demands on efficiency.

The situation is much the same among women. The pressure for efficiency standards has not yet reached women as completely as men. More women than men lead a protected existence. One field exists for women — namely, matrimony — in which success has only faint relation to work capacities and where also income is meted out not in relation to the wife's productivity but rather according to that of the husband. It is to be expected that as long as matrimony determines the ambitions of young girls to such an extent as it does today, women's strivings toward economic efficiency and vocational accomplishments will be retarded. Marriage is certainly one of the havens from competitive productivity. Domestic service, in which many women are employed, also continues to be the most un- regulated of all labor relations. Minimum wages have been neither legalized nor established through union control. Therefore, there continue to exist both exploitation and less demanding conditions of work under which handicapped individuals can live. It must not be forgotten that prostitution or semiprostitution also offers a way out for some women who fall below par in working efficiency. In all these fields the result for women is greater protection against economic competition, evidently a situation involving both good and evil. As long as such protected lives are offered women, it should not be surprising that the number of women in prison or in custody in various institutions is so much smaller than the number of men. But as for men in earlier times, conditions for women are undergoing change. As this new trend develops, it will bring increased efficiency and productivity on the part of the many women whose abilities will grow as they have more need and opportunity to use them. At the same time there will be an increasing number of women, just as there are now of men, who simply cannot be fitted into normal productive life.

The Problem of the Unemployable

Even if all individuals cast out from the highly competitive economic system could be maintained in idleness within institutions or on relief, which is not the case if the standard of living is to be raised, another solution of their problem is necessary, if we want to achieve their social adjustment and protect their self-respect. The utilization of the partly employable was introduced into the discussion in Sweden in connection with the population crisis. Subsequently measures were taken with regard to them. As a result there is a report on the problem by the Stockholm City Council, and the 1939 Yearbook of the Association for Social Work is devoted to the subject. [193] Some account of the recommendations made and actions taken should be given at this point.

The problem of finding a place in productive work for the partly unfit involves borderline mental defectives and psychopaths, the crippled, and those below par in health, as, for example, the tubercular. In all these categories there are many persons now forced to lead lives of unnecessary idleness. Similarly, some sort of transition employment should be arranged for those who, once they have suffered punishment for their antisocial conduct, find it difficult to reenter the labor market, although they may be capable workers. Such persons are ex-prisoners, tramps, alcoholics, and prostitutes. A third group within the same general framework consists of the aged, who will form a larger and larger percentage of the future population. Their ability to work could be far better utilized than at present to provide at least part payment for their support during the long period before they reach full retirement.

The prerequisite for achieving suitable employment for the partly employable is first to do away with general unemployment. Long periods of unemployment can in themselves destroy the capacity for work of even individuals who could otherwise meet the new standard of efficiency. The problem of employment has of late not seemed unsurmountable in Sweden, where the employment situation has been satisfactorily handled since 1933. As a result the more subtle problem of semiemployability can be taken up.

Assuming the general unemployment problem successfully tackled, a more active labor exchange service for these particular groups is needed. Classifying the whole group as partly employable does not do justice to the fact that many of the persons included may be able to meet the full requirements of some employment, if only the right employment is found. This group, which, if left to themselves, have small chance of retaining employment, have still smaller chance of finding new employment as intense searching for job opportunities is not to be expected of them. Active efforts to place them must therefore be demanded from the public employment agencies, which otherwise are often content to "empty the waiting room" by matching registered job opportunities with registered job seekers. A specialized public service is needed. A three-year experiment under the city authorities of Stockholm has indicated the practicability of such a scheme.

Furthermore, part-time work must be provided. Swedish social progress has only recently advanced to the point where concern for these marginal workers could gain attention. As long as both workers and employers were in the transition period of becoming organized, it was inevitable that employers should prefer to deal with labor on normal terms. Once positions are solidified and a smooth bargaining procedure is established between organized labor and organized employers, as is the case in Sweden, it becomes the task of these two groups to adjust labor conditions and agreements so as to provide employment and regulate wages in other categories than full-day work at full-rate efficiency.

Finally, types of closely supervised work must be organized for some secondary workers, particularly those of low mental abilities. Surveys of work requirements from this point of view, locating trades where placement of workers of secondary caliber is possible, and eventually securing some form of social service for job supervision of secondary workers are among the tasks that lie ahead.

Cooperation among state, employers', and workers' organizations in planning for the utilization of the partially employable is needed. The value of unused productive ability of these groups must reach tens of millions of crowns annually. Other values, human ones, are also involved, and there the urgency of the task is recognized. The pressure of international dangers, however, has forced a delay in taking concrete action on a broad scale. Unless the problem of using this marginal and submarginal man power is dealt with successfully, the number of wasted individuals will, particularly with the expected increased proportion of the aged, soon submerge the Western nations under an insupportable relief load. Also, for that human material itself which is somewhat injured bodily, mentally, or socially, the best therapy is occupational therapy.

POPULATION QUALITY

The social and technical forces which are steadily raising the standards of human efficiency represent a development entirely in line with present-day ideals of the Swedish people. We are all constantly striving, whether consciously or unconsciously, to rationalize and complicate production and all other human activities. As the increased demands on human efficiency have permeated the whole of society, the question of population quality has taken on new importance. Meanwhile, the social costs of low productivity and of care of the handicapped are steadily increasing. The population development itself is such as to lay still more stress on the social valuation of quality. When the population fails to regenerate itself, the problem of how the human material may be preserved and improved becomes urgent.

Advance along this line is strengthened by the more earnest acceptance of humanitarianism. People today simply cannot deal with economically weak and socially handicapped human beings in the same rough-handed manner as earlier. This is particularly true in countries, such as Sweden, which have developed strong democratic attitudes. The people take pride in the effort to produce a sound national stock. Even those who have to face economic sacrifices in order to make possible equality for others have much more than in earlier times identified their interests with such a conception of the public good. They feel that the country, and thus the individual, has something at stake in the quality of all.

The whole problem of quality of population is far less concrete than that of quantity. It has sometimes been postulated that the spread of family limitation during the last two generations has caused deterioration of the hereditary quality of the Swedish population stock. Birth control was first practiced in the upper classes and there is still, generally speaking, a negative correlation between fertility and social and economic status. If the upper strata in society represented a qualitatively superior population stock, the conclusion would be apparent.

A great number of reservations must be made, however, before such a conclusion can be accepted as valid. Social groups, such as income or occupational classes, are not defined with reference to the hereditary qualities of the component individuals. Any direct analogy with the simple situations in plant and animal breeding where the groups are picked with regard to the hereditary quality studied (e.g., plants bearing large peas) is therefore excluded. Plant and animal groups are biologically homogeneous; social groups are not. The essential difference is much deeper. No yardstick exists for evaluating what is good or bad in the development of human beings. In plant and animal breeding all comparisons are made on the one valuation of economic profit, while man is more than a means for production. Not science but only fluctuating life philosophies can decide whether it would be "better" to develop man as a highbred intellectual, a social family man, or an obedient instrument of authority. Hereditary worth cannot be defined scientifically; it has to be postulated according to valuations.

Even apart from this philosophical difficulty it must be remembered that factual knowledge in the field of human heredity is extremely limited. The idea that social mobility acts as a sieve, straining out the less capable, is, to say the least, a great oversimplification of social facts. How important is the effect of social inertia in keeping some of the fittest in other groups than the socially highest? To what extent have hereditary factors rather than environmental factors or mere chance been operative? What specific hereditary factors are at work? Are those personal capacities which seem to be favorable for success always socially desirable? Is the selection of the successful sometimes dependent on traits not particularly valuable in a social sense? Furthermore, in most of the arguments for the hereditary superiority of the upper income groups one-half of the parents are forgotten, the mothers. Granted for the sake of the argument that there are hereditary traits which make men succeed in economic life and that those traits are desirable, are those traits which make for economic success of women, i.e., through moneyed marriages, also socially valuable? And are they hereditary? Are they such that their intermixture with those of the fathers assures particularly desirable offspring? These suggest some of the reasons for questioning the popular belief in the greater value of the higher social classes.

Without entering further into this and other speculative problems, it can be pointed out that it has not been possible to give any empirical verification for Sweden of the *a priori* hypothesis that the higher income classes represent especially desirable genetic potentialities. Both racial and cultural homogeneity are particularly high in Sweden, and social mobility is not so directly related to financial success as in some other countries. In any case it is now generally agreed in Sweden that for the purpose of practical political population programs the vast majority of the people are of like hereditary worth. There are no such group differentials of quality as to justify special encouragement of the reproduction of one or the other of the stratified socio-economic groups.

THE SOCIAL SUBSTRATUM

Below the broad social and economic classes which constitute the bulk of the population, there exists in all countries a residuum of individuals with marked deficiencies. In order not to confuse the argument, nor to convey the idea of a social pyramid of increasing biological merit toward the top, nor grossly to misrepresent the working class — which in Sweden already in its second generation has taken on the decisive political power of ruling the country together with the farmers and has done so in a manner highly esteemed by all groups — the defectives should not be included in any of the social groups but rather be counted outside of them all. In terms of class structure the biological picture in Sweden is not pyramidal in form with this lowest group constituting the broad base. Rather the whole people form a solid block at the edge of which is a separate layer consisting of the defectives recruited from all social classes.

On the basis of all general premises the reproduction of this group must be deemed undesirable, since the offspring are under grave hereditary risks for health and intelligence. This principle must not be applied to all people of extremely low incomes but only to the limited groups of the mentally diseased and mentally deficient. The most hopeless of these are to be found in institutions, but a borderline group is left at large. Regardless of the social desirability of sterilizing these individuals, as their offspring may be judged to be undesirable, there remains a theoretical problem: Is their actual fertility such as to justify the fear that it threatens the quality of the total population?

From what has already been said it is clear that differences in fertility between income groups or between rural and urban populations should not be used for such an inference. That birth control is slower in reaching some groups has been shown to be largely, if not totally, due to a different velocity in the spread of values and behavior patterns. It is probably true, too, that during the transition period the more intellectually alert individuals in all social groups are the first to practice family limitation and practice it with greatest efficiency. This means a tendency toward negative selection in reproduction, but in itself it will not be of great importance if the transition period is not prolonged.

Those individuals, on the other hand, who are definitely undesirable as parents seem to show diversified tendencies with regard to fertility. For those in institutions the tendency must generally be toward nonfertility. The limitations of institutional life act as a deterrent to childbearing. The shunning of mentally afflicted persons in social life and as possible mates works in the same direction. Interesting differences in fertility might be expected between persons with the schizophrenic type of mental disorder, mostly requiring hospital care and characterized by lack of sociability, and those in the manic-depressive group, who move in and out of hospitals and have personalities less objectionable for social contacts. The same situation holds true for low-grade mental defectives as for schizophrenics. Their opportunities for reproduction are even less as they are institutionalized at an earlier age than the schizophrenic group. The lessened personal appeal of the great borderline groups outside of institutions ought also to serve as a protection against reproduction. It is highly probable that this is commonly the case, although in some such individuals, particularly women, lack of sexual self-control has the opposite result. Feebleminded women with an excessive reproduction rate are found in most local communities. Because of the existence of these few examples the many who cannot find a mate or found a home on account of their deficiency [1] are likely to be forgotten.

Our main conclusion is that so far as hereditary qualities are concerned population trends can scarcely be said to be effecting a progressing deterioration of the stock, and in any case such deterioration has not been proved.

ENVIRONMENTAL FACTORS

Improvements in human quality through improved environment are said to be lost with the death of the individual. On this account it has seemed tempting to many to seek more lasting results through influencing directly the genetic stock of the population, the so-called race. But in a sense it is unfair to call all environmental influences temporary. In so far as such improvement affects folkways and habits, as for example with regard to hygiene, or takes the form of provisions for child welfare or legal regulations of income distribution, the effects in a democratic, stabilized, and legalistic country like Sweden are prolonged. Theoretically speaking, these influences are not fixed as are biological ones. Their significance for social policy and population planning, however, often fails to be fully recognized because of the tendency to talk about them as of only temporary efficacy.

[1] Professor Gunnar Dahlberg of Upsala University, who studied beyond their 45th year a sample of 1,219 women having been committed at least once to a mental hospital, found the following relationships between average number of children and age at first commitment: before 20 years of age 0.05 children, 20–24 years 0.34 children, 25–29 years 0.80 children, 30–34 years 1.04 children, 35–39 years 1.39 children, 40–44 years 2.26 children 45–49 years 2.37 children, and if they had first been institutionalized above the age of 50, 2.45 children. The average number for the whole group of both married and unmarried women was 1.97 or well below the national average standardized to the same age distribution and same period (1890–1929). The general conclusion about subnormal fertility ought to be strengthened by two additional considerations: mentally afflicted women probably have a higher than average mortality rate and they probably have greater sexual chances than equally deficient men. It should be added that the marriage rate was found to be considerably below average for these women; even those committed after 45 years of age contained 34 per cent unmarried as against around 20 per cent in the general population. [*102*]

The trend toward improvement can be discerned, if environmental influences of the past and of the present are compared. All that is called progress is significant for the population. Living conditions have become more favorable to growth. The care of health is more solicitous and successful. Nutrition is more ample and adequate. Schooling has provided greater opportunities for the development of mental capacities and vocational aptitudes. A raised level of living means human quality improved to a degree hitherto unforeseen. Statistics on mortality, showing the increase in life expectancy, give one measure of such improvement. Rising curves of productivity in industry tell a similar tale. Human material is becoming better equipped in each new generation than in the preceding generation. In various sections of this book it will be pointed out that there is much room still for improvement of the environmental factors most important for further raising the quality of the Swedish nation; but it can be definitely ascertained that the trend in human quality, so far as such factors are responsible, has been and is markedly upward.

The connection between the qualitative and quantitative aspects of the population question here becomes clear. Much in the heightened level of living that has worked so favorably for the children who are born has been attained by not having so many children. This has been definitely true from the viewpoint of the individual families concerned. For a short period it has been true also from a wider social viewpoint, i.e., for the period of transition between an expanding and a contracting population when the number of children has already decreased but the aged are still relatively few. A temporary rise in the level of living in the whole nation is realized.

Even when this transitional period is passed, many individual families will face a choice between number of children and maintaining a level of living high enough for the development of healthy children. From a social point of view over a long-time period the situation will be different as increased family limitation will not raise but rather lower the aggregate level of living. There is here an acute conflict between the private and the public interest, between the direct and the indirect economic effects, between the chance of the individual family to secure its share in well-being and the necessary dependence of all families upon the cumulative result.

Each family will be able to raise its level of living by intensifying its practice of birth control. All families might, however, have to suffer a lowered level of living as a result. Harmony between the individual and the collective interest will not emerge out of the play of natural forces. The harmony will have to be created. The solution of this conflict of interests can be found only in public measures to nationalize differential child costs. Each family will then realize that the collective interest is its own interest. At the same time the level of living for children and families will be safeguarded. This is the point toward which the relationship between the qualitative and the quantitative aims in population policy is focused.

The quality differences between social groups within the present Swedish population are caused not by heredity but by environment. Quality is threatened not by racial waste but by social waste of the human material. The quality of the coming generation is threatened because as soon as children are born in numbers above a low minimum poverty results for the ordinary family. The more children there are in a family the more decidedly will poverty become their atmosphere. It will change the very volume of air they breathe, reduce the food they eat, and narrow the margin of culture available to them. In this respect grave concern must be felt about the fertility differences between social groups. When a disproportionate number of the nation's children are born of the poor, this becomes a cause of national worry, not because the poor are racially inferior but because their environment offers relatively few advantages.

The crisis pending in the field of population is one both of quantity and of quality. The circle which presents itself to prospective parents is a vicious one. Quality may be secured but only by controlling quantity. Quantity could be secured only by sacrificing quality.

CHAPTER VII

GOALS FOR A POPULATION POLICY

POPULATION has been studied far less as a problem for political action than as a problem for fact-finding research. Population policy, as well as social policy generally, does, however, require systematic thought. The Scandinavian countries have been fortunate in that they have achieved a closer collaboration between social science and politics than other countries. It is natural, therefore, to expect from them a contribution toward the clarification of the methodological problems of framing a population policy that will comply with scientific standards. The fact that academic experts are consulted on political questions under investigation and exert influence on public opinion and politics is one of the characteristics of our type of rationalistic democracy.

The distinction between truths in the theoretical sphere and recommendations in the practical sphere has on the whole been clearer in the Scandinavian countries than elsewhere. [*170* and *171*] The leaders both in the social sciences and in politics have imbibed the teaching that facts make up the world of theory but that besides knowledge of facts explicit value premises are needed for rational practical action. This critical philosophy, here oversimplified, has pervaded much popular literature and influenced adult education. Whatever its importance in the realm of thought may be, we cannot overestimate its hardening and purifying influence in intellectualizing the discussion of political action. Politics has, to a considerable degree, been brought under the control of logic and technical knowledge and so has been forced to become in essence constructive social engineering.

It has been recognized that social scientists who pretend to be able to ascertain values and prescribe social action out of pure fact-finding are just as much on the wrong track as social scientists who are so afraid of responsibility in the world of action that they hide behind an eternally insatiable "need for collecting far more detailed knowledge before practical action can be wisely planned." There is no doubt that social action is more purposeful and effective with the guidance of the experts than without it. To make their position unmistakable, scientists should distinguished clearly between the factual relations they can establish and the value judgments they will have to assume.

Two sets of premises are thus to be kept separate when discussing population policy: the *premises of knowledge* about facts and factual relations and the *premises of valuations*. The premises of facts in the population problem turn on both demographic and other social data. Various future trends are thus ascertained to be in the realm of possibility. It is these alternatives with their foreseen effects that become evaluated, marked with different coefficients of preference. In this way the goals are established. The value premises, however, become of importance not only for the goals but also for the means. When different measures are contemplated to influence the trend, these measures themselves will have to be evaluated, and human ideals and interests are again expressed. Thus the possibility exists that people who want a certain population development may not want to approve certain means for obtaining it. There is no must in the sphere of valuations.

Into people's values, as they are presented in public debate on political issues, there often enter misconceptions of facts and of their interrelations. Decline of population may, for instance, be positively evaluated because it is believed that its effect would lessen unemployment. The scientist is not on shaky ground when he reveals the false elements of knowledge in popular political thought. The positive task is, however, to establish what a man should rationally want on the ground of improved knowledge and on the assumption also of his own values. These values can vary and do vary in democratic society, but there is no need of presenting to the public a chart of all the alternatives to be inferred from all the possible sets of values. A reduction of the alternatives to be studied can be made by selecting only those values as relevant premises which seem to be held generally enough to be of political importance. It may perhaps be added that the choice of one's own values as premises, which is the same as making social propaganda, can be made in a scientifically impeccable manner if these value premises are manifestly listed and strictly adhered to. Again it must be emphasized that premises should not be hidden because that involves bias and logical confusion.

Choosing a set of value premises makes the ensuing recommendations valid for the reader only if the values are shared by him, or become shared by him, which of course is the aim of propaganda. The validity of any program of social policy is completely dependent on whether its value premises are approved. It is regrettable, therefore, that most authors do not attempt to state which value premises they have chosen. This is the practical reason why it has appeared necessary to emphasize these otherwise fairly simple principles.

To account for the general value of premises underlying the Swedish program of population policy is the tedious but necessary task of this chapter. Here they can be phrased only in vague and abstract terms. The only way to make them precise and concretely determined is to relate them directly to details of means and objectives. This is a task for the subsequent discussion of population aims and measures.

<h3 style="text-align:center">THE GENERAL VALUE MILIEU</h3>

Just as in general the Swedish people take all the freedom for the individual that is compatible with social orderliness as a condition *sine qua non* for the democracy they are living in, so freedom for the individual in relation to parenthood must be protected. Only the sanction of voluntary parenthood would fit the democratic foundations of this society.

Similarly there is a positive valuation of a high level of living. That is part of the whole social philosophy of modern industrialism. In the field of population it has shown itself in deliberate efforts to raise the standard of living by reducing family size. A population policy will also have to take account of this attitude by trying to find the means by which it will be possible for families to have children without having to accept as a result an unduly depressed level of living.

Coupled with this undeniable striving toward the elevation of living conditions, there is in a democratic country like Sweden an equally undeniable positive valuation of economic equality. The cultural homogeneity of the people is no mere fact, but it is, or rather it is increasingly becoming, a vital sense of identification with the interests of others. Equality and justice, vague as ideals always are, may probably be said to be more highly valued in the Scandinavian democracies than in any other political organization. Trends toward equalizing incomes, leveling the effects of regional advantages and disadvantages, pooling of risks, cooperating instead of profiteering — all testify to the existence of some such deep-seated evaluation. In the realm of population policy these attitudes call for increased equality of opportunity for children of different social groups and for families with or without children. The tendency to regard a concentration about the average as more desirable than a wide dispersion toward extremes carries over to social sanctions in favor of families of moderate size.

Finally, there is in the general value sphere of Swedish democracy an undeniably positive valuation of children, family, and marriage. Children are liked although such an attitude does not indicate the number wanted or the degree of willingness to overcome obstacles to their procreation. The family is regarded as a value, even if some things in the exterior form of family life may have to be changed to meet needs for adjustment.

Between some of these basic values there will in actual life be many occasions for conflict. But one judgment is unanimous, namely, that quality of children should not be sacrificed to quantity. The desire for children, both as a private attitude and still more as a political attitude, will have to yield if it is in conflict with the desire to defend standards, particularly the welfare standards of children themselves. There can be no approval, therefore, of childbearing that infringes on the welfare of the children. It should be added that in Sweden the average citizen has a rather strong belief in the usefulness of social control exercised through collective agencies, such as the state, the municipalities, and the large civic organizations. At the same time, this average citizen abhors arbitrary action. He can be said to have a legalistic bent of mind. He wants to have all public interference limited by specific laws and regulations that transfer a maximum of relations between the individual and the public bodies from the sphere of discriminatory judgment to one of fixed rights and obligations. He will insist upon this procedure even if the administration of justice sometimes becomes more rigid than a system which permits freer consideration of individual cases.

These generalizations as well as the more precise values which will be presented when confronting specific problems, goals, and means are intended to represent not an arbitrary choice by the author but the controlling values in actual Swedish policy. There is nothing sacred about these values. Some individuals or even whole nations may supersede one or all of them. The people, or at least the leaders, in totalitarian countries will obviously not subscribe to the first one of individual freedom nor the last one of legalism. Certain groups, especially intellectual sympathizers with the Russian family ideology of the 1920's, will not subscribe to the positive valuation of marriage and family, as they hold that society should be indifferent to the sex life of individuals. Many extreme individualists will refuse to attribute any political value to a rapidly declining birth rate, as they profess no concern for what happens to future generations. Ardent supporters of the doctrine of *laissez faire,* as well as of state socialism or communism, will deeply mistrust the Swedish pragmatic kind of variegated interventionism, which they will judge to be opportunistic.

The goals of population policy must be established as inferences from both the facts and the values. For practical purposes it is usually not necessary to determine those goals in an absolute sense. It is generally sufficient to fix only the direction toward which social action should be pointed. In generalized form the goals for which the Swedish population policy is striving include increased aggregate fertility, more even distribution of children in families, raised living standards for children and improved quality of the population stock, reduced illegitimacy, and more generally available birth control information.

These goals may seem contradictory. When the final policy is being determined, they will have to be weighed against one another. There is also the possibility that such an apparent contradiction may resolve itself when the social world is really conceived as manageable. The dilemma of wanting increased birth control, on the one hand, and increased fertility, on the other, will then be revealed as one which can be solved, one in which both horns can be seized. The new idea in what has here been called a democratic population program is that it does pay heed to the wants of the people, even if they seem irreconcilable. Out of disharmony a harmony has to be created by social action. Seemingly conflicting desiderata have to be reconciled if we do not want to take the easy way of stopping on either side; that was the unresolvable dilemma in which the population problem was formerly caught.

If there was doubt whether a large enough majority of the Swedish people favored maintaining the population, the reaction observable during the recent population discussion removed all uncertainty. The prospect of a cumulative population decline was definitely classified as undesirable. Knowledge about relevant facts made it clear to almost everyone that conversion of this decline into an actual increase would be entirely outside the field of possibilities. The only alternative future trends which could be considered within reason and, therefore, the only ones to be evaluated were either that of continued, accumulated decline or that of reaching a fertility level which might maintain a constant population in the long run.

In determining the goal of keeping population constant, the various social and economic effects of population decline touched upon in Chapter 5 were taken into due account and evaluated. In addition to this indirect evaluation of the population trend by means of its effects there was also a more direct evaluation. Population constancy was felt by the average citizen to be an end or a value in itself. This direct valuation, a feeling of national self-pity at the prospect of death and a pride in the collectivity of the national culture, was presented in various forms. Its common minimum basis was an attitude that "our society is too good not to be preserved." This certainly is nationalism but just as certainly it is not nationalism of a militaristic and expansionist type. The reaction may rather be intellectualized in terms like these: "It is not going to be so stimulating to work for a national culture that is under liquidation. It is not going to be so satisfying to build up a social structure which our children are not going to inherit. The risk is great that a depopulated country with rich natural resources and a wide coverage of social security will attract foreign peoples. It is practically certain that these peoples are not going to be our culturally related Scandinavian neighbors. They will constitute an overflow from larger nations, and it is then virtually inevitable that in their strong clasp our cultural heritage will be completely submerged. This we dislike."

It must be stressed, however, that this recent anxiety has been focused not on the size of the nation which should be considered as optimal but on the prospect of incessant decline with its inescapable effect in the near future of an aging society and its possible long-range result of allowing a culture and an economy to decline. Stopping this process has seemed the important thing. If stabilization of the population could be achieved at all, which would involve making up the present 25 per cent deficiency in fertility, there is reason to suppose that Sweden could adjust to various magnitudes of population. In a country with plenty of natural resources the quantity of population cannot in itself, within practically relevant limits, be conceived to have any important effects on the general welfare or the standard of living of the people. The available number of producers could work for the available number of consumers. The crucial factors of population thus are direction and rate of change rather than any optimal size.

Since the imperialistic days of the seventeenth century, the Swedish citizen has not complained because his nation is small. He has fortified his mind against the confusion of "great" and "big"; and, besides, he has increasingly felt the whole world open for his cultural and economic ambitions. There is a considerable degree of indifference in regard to all total figures of future population in Sweden. The only cause for worry is the trend toward an ever smaller nation that would be threatened with self-liquidation. In view of the contemporary psychosis of militant nationalism, this fact cannot be stressed too strongly.

Constancy thus becomes the goal of a population policy for which public opinion can be mobilized. This constancy will demand a policy because population maintenance involves in the long run not a mere *status quo* of fertility but a considerable increase. Increased fertility becomes the main desideratum.

Medium-sized Families

This goal of permanent maintenance of population can be translated into terms that show more precisely the implied demands on the fertility of the individual family. Assuming the record low mortality figures for different age groups in 1933, every woman reaching 15 years of age would during her later fertility period have to have on the average 2.21 children. [*187*] If only those marrying are supposed to have children, that would require, with the low nuptiality rate of Sweden, 2.95 children per married woman. In all marriages which last to the 50th year of the wife, 3.14 children would be necessary, allowing a margin for marriages which are dissolved earlier (no allowance being made for illegitimate childbearing). This is evidently equivalent to the popular estimate of three children to keep the next generation as numerous as the present one. This holds true even if the present rate of illegitimacy should be maintained. In those Swedish marriages in which the wife has in recent years just reached the end of her fertility period the average number of children has been around three. [74] In the younger marriages the average number of children is so small that there is doubt that a final average of even two children will be attained.

This method of considering averages is, however, an unsatisfactory one. No account has been taken of sterility; no allowance has been made for other personal variations. The question as to what percentage of marriages must be excluded from average fertility computations on account of involuntary sterility naturally arises. Taking into consideration the scanty data available about physiological sterility and spontaneous abortion and allowing a certain margin, it is estimated that 10 per cent of all marriages in Sweden will be completely childless, 7.5 per cent will have only one child and 5.0 per cent only two children owing to involuntary causes. [187] The remaining 77.5 per cent must then be divided between 3- and 4-child families, but mostly the latter (65 per cent of all families, while only 12 per cent could have as few as three children) to maintain the population at the present level. Even if nonmarital fertility should be calculated to remain on a high level, only a slight reduction in the number of children within marriages could be allowed. Now it is scarcely possible to assume that the number of small families, with none, one, or two children, can ever be kept close to the minimum. For various reasons, such as late marriages, hereditary considerations, and economic distress, some families will always remain childless or have but one or two children. The 4-child family and not the 3-child family evidently will have to be the practical minimum aimed at in all nonsterile families. [187]

In order to settle which of these or other distributions should be chosen as a goal for population policy, we must again resort to certain value premises. One of these has to do with individual values as norms for behavior. Another is concerned with the attitude as to what size of family is preferable for society as a whole. According to the first value premise, parenthood should be voluntary. Knowledge of prevailing conditions then reveals that with planned parenthood most of the very large families are not going to come into being. The only choice, then, seems to be such a distribution of families that a large majority become middle-sized rather than that many be undersized and some oversized. How does this goal conform with the natural inclination of parents? If ignorance did not operate to increase the number of children and economic difficulties work to decrease them, would it seem normal or abnormal to parents that families should cluster around the average of three or four children which is "normal" in the demographic sense of being implied in the established goal of population constancy? Here an extremely difficult conjecture is necessary in order to arrive at any generalization as to the number of children families actually want.

A desire for children has to be taken for granted, but it is not quantitatively circumscribed. The wish for offspring is no imperative craving like hunger or sex. The demand is highly elastic. A survey was made of the existing literature on the subject of marital happiness under different family constellations, of the psychological and educational situation in families of different sizes, and of position psychology in regard to the influences of family size and birth order on mental and moral development. [*158*] Only vague conclusions could be drawn from this survey. It would seem natural for the variegated desires and considerations of parents to converge on three or even four children in the family if economic conditions and educational stimulations were readapted for the family size that society wants. The 1-child situation contains certain risks and problems which are neutralized in families of a somewhat larger size. In the very large family, on the other hand, certain hardships mount. In the marginal reasoning about preferences for two or three or four children, nuances are many, and any one conclusion is difficult to draw. The additional burden and displacement of family arrangements that result from having three children instead of two, or from having the fourth child when there are already three, would not seem to be prohibitive, particularly if to the balance of motivation should be added the general appreciation that it is socially valuable to reach that average.

This social valuation on the part of individuals as citizens would seem to be not only that children should accumulate to the number needed for a constant population but also that a more general clustering around the average would be preferable. It would also seem to correspond to a basic Swedish ideal that equalization as to the number of children in itself would be a good thing. Such a democratic leveling of family size to produce more middle-sized families thus can be specified as a goal for population policy.

IMPROVED QUALITY

A basis for a consensus with regard to population policy further develops out of the concern for human quality. Improved quality of succeeding generations, and particularly improved growth conditions for children, can be fixed as a goal for the population program.

The available facts do not furnish much of a basis for attempts to encourage selective breeding by particular social groups with supposedly superior hereditary worth. In any case common valuations do not permit such a policy. As opposed to this so-called positive eugenics, negative eugenics is commonly accepted but how far interference with individual freedom should go in the interest of the quality of the offspring is a delicate problem. Here is a real conflict of values which cannot, like many others, be eliminated through induced social change. To decrease the fertility of mentally deficient people seems to be the minimum formula that will win common approval.

Similar difficulties appear in deciding how far strivings for improved environmental conditions should be carried. In Chapter 6 the conflict between qualitative and quantitative goals was revealed. Most families have to pay for an extra child with a lowered standard of living for the rest of the children. In a society giving primacy to quality rather than quantity this dilemma would block a population policy of the type here discussed, if it were not possible to reunite the two goals by social reform. When as in Sweden the primacy is definitely given to quality, there is still room for a certain indeterminateness: how small a risk for quality shall take precedence over how large a gain in quantity. Obviously the intention cannot be to follow the rule to the extreme, for example by spending the money and time to care for the health of one child that could secure a decent living for ten children.

In order to arrive at some determination of this goal of quality, the minimum is here interpreted as the desire to safeguard for all children, born and unborn, what are now average environmental conditions for children with regard to housing, food, medical attention, schooling, and so forth. Such a policy has strong moorings in our predilection for greater social justice. If the nation's resources or the social ingenuity for redistribution cannot ensure such average conditions for all children, no additional children should be sought. If, for example, the average nutrition for children can be ascertained, a national policy would set as its goal making available the average for all children. Sometimes it will seem reasonable to set the goal even higher than such a level. Thus the minimum level for infant mortality, which is technically possible as evidenced by the low rate in a favored social group, can be set as the practical goal for all groups.

Even if these attempts to state the qualitative goal in terms of definite levels are of necessity somewhat arbitrary, the general direction is not, and neither are the principles of primacy. On this basis population policy can obviously be directed toward fairly concrete social planning.

Reduced Illegitimacy

Parallel with the goals of increasing the number of children born and safeguarding their quality is that of having more births take place within marriage and fewer outside marriage. The fate of illegitimate children is so generally deplored that a mere statement of this value premise is enough to justify the goal that illegitimacy be reduced.

Closer examination reveals that generally the most tragic aspect of illegitimacy is that children are born without a home, without being parts of a loving complete family. The goal, therefore, is to reduce the number of children born out of wedlock to such an extent that they can all be assured a good home. This can be achieved by decreasing the number of illegitimate children born, by making it possible for more parents to live with their children, and by increasing the number of really good foster homes where the children are welcome. The goal would be fixed not at a certain percentage of illegitimate children nor at a certain extramarital fertility but rather would depend upon society's ability to take care of the children. This formulation of the vague values of the general public is offered as a more solid goal than any other yet advanced, difficult as it is to find a common denominator in this field of varying moral judgments.

The Principle of Voluntary Parenthood

From value premises directly avowed by the Swedish people, it follows that a population policy should not interfere with voluntary parenthood. An honest recognition of birth control and family planning is implicit in our democratic population policy. In this connection it is necessary to explain why birth control can so categorically be stated as a common value attitude, when verbalized public opinion has so often been to the contrary.

The relation between private attitudes and political attitudes is beclouded here and the fixing of the goal thus made difficult. Most individual families will reserve their private right of planning their childbearing. Birth control of some sort and with some degree of effectiveness is practiced in almost all nonsterile marriages, but many people have been unwilling to proclaim as a social value the attitude that voluntary parenthood should be sanctioned as normal for the whole people. This obvious inconsistency between private behavior and public principles was exposed in the recent population debate in Sweden. It appeared incompatible with enlightened and honest democracy to reserve birth control rights for oneself and at the same time to support a public policy denying the same rights to other citizens. Where such an attitude is not sheer hypocrisy, it implies a denial of equal rights and an attempt to preserve a kind of moral class privilege. It is impossible to maintain such a position for long in a democracy. Inevitably the individual's use of birth control practices becomes reflected in a social opinion that voluntary parenthood is the right thing for all.

In the foregoing conclusion many practical arguments are included. Not only is the assertion of individual freedom involved but also the necessity of spacing children, of sparing mothers' health, and of not transmitting hereditary taint. In addition there is the problem of not augmenting the family beyond the available means for maintaining a satisfactory level of living.

Recognition of the right to voluntary parenthood as a superior value premise related to the principles of democracy has, however, been carried beyond a mere policy of *laisser-aller*. It is definitely felt that equal rights are not wholly realized if equal opportunities are not afforded. A lag in the spread of effective knowledge of birth control should be overcome and easy access to contraceptives be secured for everyone. It is the duty of society to see to it that every man and woman reaching maturity receives reliable information about birth control and has individual advice and good technical resources available for its practice.

The premise of voluntary parenthood, which is fundamental to a democratic population policy, is of paramount importance in evaluating the means for executing such a policy. This premise excludes a number of alternative measures which would otherwise be possible. Any obstacle to providing knowledge about birth control to certain groups thus becomes indefensible. Furthermore, no force or coercion can be allowed with regard to matters of matrimony and parenthood. While this problem is one of little practical concern in its positive sense — "forced" childbearing is never proclaimed by any state — it becomes more important in the negative sense. In a democracy it would be just as inconsistent to compel people not to marry or have children. Forced celibacy for anyone who has reached the legal age for matrimony becomes an absurdity. The desire to marry and the desire to have children are felt to be fundamental human rights, which neither state nor church nor employer nor parents should interfere with. In Protestant Western society this becomes of practical significance only for women. Employers should not have the right to dictate to their employees with regard to marrying or bearing children through the exercise of discriminatory practices. It would thus be consistent with this general value premise to formulate the goal that both men and women be guaranteed freedom of choice as to family status and family size. Interference in these rights should be outlawed.

Moreover, any propaganda for families and increased families should be honest, should start from the true interest of the individual himself, and in any case should not divert him from clear thinking about his own values and motives. Exhortations to duty, to patriotic glorification, or to religious obedience are at least believed to be undemocratic in the country under study. The state should appear for what it is and voice the reasons it has as the collectivity of individuals for wanting more or fewer children; but it should not confuse the issue by donning consecrated vestments of superindividual powers. In order not to disturb the individual's democratically free choice as to marriage and parenthood, all measures intended to encourage the founding of families should be devised fundamentally to aid the family. In this connection it may be pointed out parenthetically that certain other values than those explicitly stated above may also negate one or another measure of population policy. Thus respect for merit only as the prerequisite for positions in administrative, political, and civic offices would make it impossible in Sweden to imitate the laws of some totalitarian countries, which make a certain family status or number of children a condition or an advantage for obtaining posts within the civil service.

We may draw certain practical conclusions from the value premises of individual freedom with regard to family status. People should neither be forced nor, through ignorance or otherwise, be lured into marriage or childbearing. Measures to encourage families should take the form of honest education and of attempts to remodel the social and economic foundations of the family institution.

The moral revolution which the acceptance of these principles implies is, of course, not completed. Individuals or even groups can easily be found who hesitate before some of the logical inferences from our ideals of enlightened rationalistic democracy, but responsible representative bodies have openly endorsed them. The Population Commission particularly has been commendably explicit on these points. As a result of the open fight that was waged, public opinion has also been moving rapidly. As elsewhere it has again been proved that the average man has quite a capacity for honesty and common sense even in sexual matters and that politician, administrator, writer, preacher, and teacher are likely to make a serious mistake when they underestimate the masses and assume that public opinion is not sufficiently "mature" to support their own advanced views. The era of public hypocrisy is nearing its end in Sweden.

MERGING THE GOALS

The cleavage of public opinion about birth control into two camps, with one talking only of the individual's right and need to limit childbearing and the other condemning such family limitation as immoral and ruinous for the nation, has made it difficult for people to keep two ideas in their heads at the same time, namely, that parenthood can be made voluntary and that society can remodel its very basis so that more children can still be welcomed. The illusion that society is static and therefore condemned to remain in its present dilemma between children and poverty has paralyzed intelligent thinking. By regarding society rather as a household that the citizens can operate for their common welfare, it is at once seen to be possible to join voluntary parenthood with positive population interests, to join birth control and fertility increase. Birth control means family planning; only social ignorance construes planning to mean reduction exclusively.

The harmonizing of the two goals of quality and quantity is also more feasible than it appears. Only by selecting for population policy a certain set of social reforms, however, can such a harmony of interests be achieved. These reforms should directly improve growth opportunities for children and at the same time reduce the individual's reasons for not taking on the burden of children. This consonance of population goals will require a much more detailed discussion as it is the main principle in determining the means of population policy. The two following chapters will be devoted to this task.

CHAPTER VIII

MEANS FOR A POPULATION POLICY

P OPULATION policy cannot be considered apart from the many other values and goals of society. All measures for attaining population goals must be judged not only with reference to the valuations advanced in the preceding chapter but also with reference to the whole complex of other ideals of our society. Reforms to be proposed must be fused into an organic whole. Our strivings in the population and family field are, furthermore, so fundamental that population policy becomes an intensification and redirection generally of social policy rather than a set of specific measures.

This profound readjustment of social policy may here be discussed under two main categories: educational and socio-economic reforms. These two types of forces induced to redirect the individual and society are interrelated. It would be futile, not to say undemocratic, to try through propaganda to influence the individual to have more children without offering him more appropriate social conditions for his children. Progapanda that is generous with nothing more than morals becomes unmoral in the judgment of the broad masses as it tries to increase the number of children while having no concern for their future fate. On the other hand, socioeconomic reforms in favor of families and children become just as meaningless without educational propaganda directed toward more positive family attitudes. For one thing, the citizens as a body of voters must be made more appreciative of family values in order to vote the socio-economic measures. No majority could otherwise be won, as those · with several children, to whom the favors would go, are so definitely a minority, while those bachelors and childless and child-poor families, from whom the favors must come, constitute the overwhelming majority.

Education thus is essential for the development of a new population policy. It will have one general objective, the influencing of the young through schools and of adults through other educational agencies to appreciate the population goals as laid down and to take more interest in the welfare of children. But education will also have to be used in a special sense with every specific reform requiring educational preparation. Thus changes in sex legislation or medical care for children must be accompanied by changes in sex education or hygiene education in order to become effective and truly grounded in every sector of the population. Homogeneity and harmony can be attained only by a simultaneous change in socio-economic structure and educational influences. Education like morals is not an isolated sphere in which inexpensive miracles can be worked merely by reforming individuals. Neither, for example, does wholesale transfer of slum people to housing projects lead to any fundamental social improvement if unaccompanied by education for improved personal housing habits. As was pointed out, a population program becomes nothing less than a realignment of all social policy. Discussion of the means for a population policy amounts to nothing less than a reexamination of the whole spiritual and material environment for the family and the thousand and one social measures shaping it. A general mapping of what a population policy should embrace will be given in this chapter, while the detailed proposals in their actual Swedish form will in turn be treated in a number of later chapters.

FAMILY EDUCATION

All the goals catalogued can be furthered by an appropriate redirection of education. From preschool years through university and voluntary adult studies a new stress on family problems could transform the life attitudes of all. The education for living that is an acknowledged need in Western society must have three goals: to develop the young to have individual personalities, and that has been the lodestar of all progressive education; to develop them as citizens and workers, which is more recently being discovered as a task; and to develop them as partners in human relationships and particularly family relationships. This last goal may have been recognized by pioneering educational enterprises; nothing short of its permeation through the whole educational structure will suffice. Such family education would range in its content all the way from problems of sex and the psychological relations in the family to problems of joint economy and practical work in the home as well as to problems of the relation between the family and the community.

The goals of the population program should serve as leads for this family education. Voluntary parenthood could be encouraged, making the individual rational in his planning for the future and for the well-being of his family. The bearing of children within rather than outside of marriage could be furthered by the same education, making the individual circumspect and responsible in his sexual relations. Improving the quality of children could first be safeguarded by enlightenment about hereditary risks and next be encouraged by educational propaganda for better living with regard to all phases of human welfare: housing, nutrition, bodily care, character development, and so forth. Increasing the quantity of population could finally be favored by cultivating more uninhibited responses of happiness in family relations, by fostering a more generous joy in children, by redesigning many of the mental patterns that are impeding the desire to have children. Formulating the scope and methods of such family education, applicable from nursery schools upward and including the vast movement of adult education, is the inspiring task awaiting one of the future innovators in the field of education (Chapter 11).

Birth Control Education

Family planning is the desirable, rational foundation of the whole program of Swedish population policy. Birth control thus emerges from its dubious position of being a private practice of shameful secrecy which is condemned in the conventionally verbalized public morals. It comes out of the dusk of repression. Due consideration for the goal both of making parenthood voluntary and of timing childbearing in such relation to family conditions as assures best quality will require that birth control techniques be made universally available. The first means presenting itself is again education. The ostrichlike attitude typical of the Victorian era has no other reason for continued existence than the lag of traditions and must be brought to an end by conscious effort.

This entails marked changes in public opinion. Not only is obscurantism an obstacle but also many declared advocates of the so-called birth control movement have paid their tribute to the same taboos by stressing the medical instead of the educational approach. Sex education for children in school, with general references to family planning up through adolescence, and more specific knowledge about birth control available to all young adults become the paths to a social readjustment of sex mores. Next, all laws restricting the dissemination of information about birth control should be abolished. The trade in contraceptives must be regulated to decrease prices and improve quality (Chapter 12). Birth control education, like family education generally, can be made to serve all the goals of population policy.

Undesirable Parents

Availability of birth control knowledge has been listed as a means for population policy because it is required to materialize the principle of voluntary parenthood, for use or nonuse according to the individual couple's own judgment. In some instances, however, an offspring is so undesirable that even a democratic state will want to enforce limitations of parenthood. Negative eugenics has its place as a means for population policy. The necessity of enforcing a radical elimination of extremely unfit and worthless individuals through sterilization is generally recognized. Even if their low quality should not be of hereditary character, they would as parents create too undesirable an environment for children. These two objectives, the socio-biological and the socio-pedagogical, are closely interrelated.

In trying to solve its eugenic problems society is assuming a heavy responsibility, as it is difficult not only to know when hereditary perdispositions are transmitted but also to decide what traits should be extinguished as undebatably undesirable. In a practical program of compulsory sterilization democratic consensus can probably be reached only on the assumption that it should never be resorted to except in recognized cases of serious illness and defect. If this assumption is accepted, the field for legalized compulsory sterilization becomes in reality very narrow. It may become wider, however, as science can more clearly determine the laws of inheritance. While the domain for compulsory sterilization is still limited, voluntary sterilization ought to be provided for by legislation (Chapter 12). The limits for its permission should be wide, if not entirely open for the individual's own decision. But society is not freed from its responsibility by allowing voluntary sterilization. Thousands and thousands of borderline cases exist in which the ones responsible for social action will agree on the undesirability of offspring but agree, too, on the impossibility of using such sharp-edged weapons as compulsory sterilization. In these cases the logical second-best choice is direct and active propaganda for voluntary sterilization or in any case strict birth control. These cases could be canvassed by public health authorities and recommendations made in less uncertain terms than general medical advice. Sterilizations should be carried out at public expense and contraceptive supplies should be made available free of charge. Social medicine has here a field for missionary work of great importance. In social problems like these we should take care not to rely too exclusively on laws and regulations, forgetting in the rough, mechanical sifting out of undesirable parenthood through compulsory sterilization that more flexible and considerate methods are available.

When birth control has been spoken of as a chief means for population policy, only preconceptional control through sterilization or anticonceptional devices have been envisaged. Birth control which realizes itself through terminating an already incurred pregnancy by induced abortion has no place in a population program that prides itself on rationality. It is, indeed, to be recognized as a danger that in some urban groups induced abortion is coming to be looked upon as a normal means of birth control. There are, however, cases in which some of the motives for sterilization or voluntary sterility are strong enough to indicate that, if they have not been used or have not been effective in preventing a pregnancy, an abortive operation may be preferable to the birth of a child. A detailed treatment of the whole subject of abortion will be given in Chapter 12. Here it suffices to state that there is nothing in the value premises or in the goals chosen that sanctions abortion except as an emergency measure in default of other less wasteful measures.

SAVING THE LIVES OF THOSE BORN

Decreased child mortality produces the same results as far as population goes as a corresponding increase in fertility, to say nothing of the difference in human happiness. The proportion of children now born who are lost should be reduced. Having laid down an increase in reproduction as a primary population goal, the first means sought for effecting that goal must be greater economy with the lives of the children already born. This calls for the improvement and extension of medical care to mothers and infants, improved living conditions, hygiene, and nutrition. As always, education takes its part alongside of social reform. Education in child care has already brought about decreased child morbidity and mortality; it must be extended.

There is, indeed, no reason to tolerate any other rate of child mortality in any social group than that which is the average in, say, the economically best situated fourth of the population. What that class can buy in the way of child health and child life, the community can buy for other groups (Chapters 16 and 17). Clinics for prenatal and infant health care, delivery care, hospitals for children, food supplementation, and medical supplies are concrete details in such attempts to preserve the lives of more of the children born. This will serve the population goal of increased quantity and at the same time it will also improve quality by safeguarding health.

ENCOURAGING MARRIAGES

Marrying and founding a family have lost many of their social advantages, at least for men. If bearing of children is to be increased and if it is to occur more often within marriages, however, marrying must be encouraged. Education can do its part to reveal to young people some of the personal values of marriage better than their own observations of parental life may seem to do. Delicate, indeed, is the task of education here. This educational effort to enhance the prestige of marriage in comparison with other forms of sexual relations has hitherto been expressed almost exclusively in moral appeals, picturing married life as a duty. Literary influences have worked in the same direction. Little poetry has been produced to depict those values in which a durable marriage relation can excel other sexual relations: the fullness of one's human relations without inhibitions, the unconditional support of loyalty, the exploration of mutual confidences, and the ecstasy of complete sexual intimacy. How can these values be cultivated in most marriages when people are never told about them, when church and school and parents talk about the duties and obligations of marriage but never about its joys? How can ordinary and average human beings live up to those standards of heightened sensitivity and activity which are always necessary for happiness, when even poetry does not have these values in its vision; when romanticism centers in the initial and conquering stages of love and adventure is associated only with love relations outside marriage; when marriage tends to become synonymous with chores and ridicule, with cooking and mothers-in-law rather than with the feelings of love and joy?

Education and some shifting of cultural patterns have the greatest opportunities for helping to develop esteem for marriage. Social reforms will, however, also become important (Chapter 13). They will first consist of tearing down institutional barriers to marriage. Rules about celibacy in modern society are chiefly enforced by employers and chiefly for women. Such rules have to be abolished as one direct means in the population program. Next, economic obstacles hindering marriage have to be broken down. For some higher vocations not only long years of study but also a long period of underpaid apprentice service are required. This whole system should be reformed, equalizing somewhat in the higher professions the income and security between the old and the young. Some form of community credit may further facilitate marriage for the young. Marriage loans would seem to be called for. This would undoubtedly be a means of encouraging fertility, by getting more people married and getting them married younger. Still, these measures should in no way be so developed as to bind anybody to childbearing. They may just in a general way encourage that kind of happiness that can be found in marriage.

Encouraging marriage will necessarily work toward discouraging illegitimate parenthood. Sex education will do the same. Some definite endeavors to increase foster-home facilities for children born outside of marriage as well as for other dependent children are particularly needed in Sweden. But these foster homes should not be conducted as a trade. There must be more desirable foster-home and child-placing agencies that attempt to find the right foster homes for individual children. Adoption laws must be changed to make adoption possible even by a family having children of its own. Institutions for children, when really necessary, should be improved. These strivings to guarantee to every child born something approximating a loving family of its own have a definite place among the means for population policy. They may primarily be listed as serving the two goals of bearing more children within marriages and of improving the quality of the next generation by enriching the growth conditions of children.

Relieving Insecurity

The causes of the decrease in fertility are varied, and the means to counteract it must also be varied. It is of course not necessary that every cause be counterbalanced by specific means. The remedies have to be affixed to the strategic causes, the ones we want and also are able to influence. However much the decrease in fertility may be due to increasing rationality in human life, few would be willing to try to reduce rationality. Other measures will have to be found which can be reconciled with both growing rationality and increased fertility.

There are three main tendencies working for extreme family limitation: the feeling of insecurity in modern life, particularly with regard to economic support; the cumbersomeness of children and difficulty of fitting their lives into the patterns of adult life in modern civilization, particularly in cities; and the fact that children exert a greater and greater pressure on the family economy. Can any means be found that would tend to counterbalance these tendencies?

A democracy can offer its citizens the fundamental security which is basic to any will to live on in subsequent generations, the possibility of identifying without mental reservation their own interests with the prolonged existence of their children in their culture. Optimism that society is developing in the right direction; confidence in the handling of its joint interests through a government and an administration under one's own control; pride in social development and in economic progress; the identification of individual interests not only with those of the country in general but also with those of compatriots in other social strata — these are the first prerequisites for people wanting to prolong their interest in society through their children and for awakening an enthusiasm for reforming that society for the children.

It is inherent in such a democracy that reform activities are carried out unceasingly to decrease the impact of all the major insecurities in the lives of its citizens: old age, sickness, invalidism, unemployment, and so on. Unemployment is the main factor in family insecurity. Even when the actual extent of unemployment is small and its worst effects cushioned by some system of public works and by unemployment insurance, the very risk of unemployment acts as a deterrent to childbearing. Therefore, it becomes a general precondition for making any population policy successful under modern conditions that it must be shaped within a progressive economic system operating at near productive capacity and full absorption of labor. There is necessary, too, an effective system of social security for unemployment risks (Chapter 19).

Preventing economic crises and restoring employment are not, of course, problems related particularly to population policy but they are indispensable to any such policy. As any employment program must be worked out differently in different countries and at different times, it will not be discussed here as part of the population program proper. It is interesting to note, however, that the most lively concern about population in Sweden was awakened just when unemployment was starting to recede (1934) and that most thoroughgoing reforms were enacted in the year when economic conditions reached a peak (1937).

PROTECTING WORKING MOTHERS

No family policy can fail to take into account the fact that children have become more and more cumbersome to parents and to society at large. This holds true both as to work and as to recreation. Still men's work is little hindered. When the father left the hearth to seek outside work, the imminent threat of this family crisis was not sensed. Men developed the tradition of outside work unhampered by the need to look after children long before the time when family problems, labor division, and child care became conscious problems. So well rooted has this tradition become that it has been expanded to establish also a customary right for men to have their recreational time similarly unhampered. This problem of the cumbersomeness of children is therefore no great problem for fathers until we again make marriage and even parenthood a more equal partnership, as it was in the agrarian society. For mothers, children tend to be an impediment both for work and for leisure. This situation requires some rethinking concerning institutional forms.

The modern woman's participation in work and recreational activities does not interfere with marriage but only with childbearing. Neither does marriage interfere with work, while childbearing does. The reactionary answer is to turn more of the wage-earning women into homemakers and more children will be born. This is evidently fallacious. Reducing earning capacities of those very families where the women now are rational enough to use extreme birth control in order to save their positions could hardly be expected to increase considerably the number of children. The causative factors to consider are rather the inability to earn enough money to support children and the work conditions which make onerous the rearing of children.

The first reform needed is the defense of the right to earn a living both for women in general and for married women in particular. It should be noted that, although the conflict arises only between motherhood and work, the attacks have generally been made against marriage on the part of women employees. This centering of attention on married women rather than mothers has confused the issue. It thus must first be clarified that no pretentions of protecting the family can make it reasonable to prohibit a woman from marrying.

Neither can any prohibition by legal methods or administrative practice against childbearing by working women serve to protect family interests. It becomes evident that women's demands and population policy run together and not contrary to each other. Defending the right of the working woman to marry and have children becomes a protection of, and not a threat against, family values. If society wants to encourage and not to punish family building, it will have to give men and women freedom in their efforts to have families and to support them. The forced celibacy or sterility among wage-earning women is a sign of society's incapacity to adjust itself to modern conditions. A population policy of democratic vision thus creates a new stronghold for married women's fight for their right to work. At the same time the frontier among feminist groups should be shifted in order to denote this new interlocking of individual and social interests. What is to be guarded is not so much the "married woman's right to work" as the "working woman's right to marry and have children" (Chapter 22).

Whether this protection for employment regardless of civil status should be made the object of legal reforms or only of educational persuasion will depend on many practical considerations. It would, however, seem advisable to get a general clause inscribed into Swedish laws that would make illegal any pressure on such private concerns as marriage.

Even if freedom to work were granted, mothers would still experience handicaps when trying to combine children and careers. Some of these obstacles lie deep in our civilization and it is useless to deny or minimize the conflicts: difficulty of getting leave of absence for childbearing, trouble in finding a satisfactory form of supervision for children by a substitute for the absent mother during their years of minority, disquietude over the children, and excessive proportion of one's leisure time consumed in labor for their needs. In some cases the problems ought rather to be solved by making it possible for the mothers to abstain from work and give all their energy to their families. In line with value premises already stated this ought to be particularly desirable in the case of much wage labor, where women toil for low wages although they may have numerous children who badly need their services. For these cases, typified in the charwomen, all the old reactionary moral concern about the conflict between motherhood and wage earning ought to be mobilized.

As already pointed out, the smaller the family the higher the income. Thus the greater the ability to pay for domestic work, and the more personally desired the job is, the less opposition there ought to be to women combining their work with motherhood.

Turning attention to those cases where the inclination to continue work is the fixed premise, problems, both economic and organizational, still remain. The chief economic riddle is that the cost of the disruption of work on account of pregnancy must be removed in so far as possible from the employment relation. There is no reason why employers should be asked to carry such an extra burden for some women on top of inconveniences from the discontinuity of service which can hardly be avoided. Neither is there any reason why those women who bear children should suffer from it in their function as workers. The ideal solution would obviously be to charge such extra costs for childbearing to society's account for children. Translated into practical terms, this means to provide some social insurance scheme for keeping these costs of lost labor income apart from the employment situation.

Also, in the administration of homes changes are called for in order to make children possible. For one thing equalization between the two mates in regard to parental discomfort, work, and constraint would gradually have to be brought about. Greater participation by the fathers in child care, greater willingness to take turns in awakening early in the morning and staying at home on recreational nights would certainly adjust parenthood much more easily into modern life. This claim on helpfulness by husbands should, however, not be confused with any general claim by women for greater comfort. In families with a small number of children and the mother a homemaker, the woman's burden of work is usually not any heavier than that of the breadwinner. In the case of a woman working outside the home, however, the man marrying her ought to realize that the greater economic asset he has won in her has to be paid for in some way, either by the engaging of a servant or by his sharing in the work created by homemaking. The educational counterpart of all population policies has a task to achieve here.

Relieving the Burden of Mothers

Supervision of children during a mother's absence for work is another problem that is going to demand the inventive and courageous creating of new social institutions and habits. In Sweden the problem has been somewhat simplified, or at least temporarily delayed, by the relative ease as yet in obtaining domestic servants. This facility obviously is increased when parents combine their incomes, especially as servants prefer positions in homes with working women partly because the positions involve more independence and responsibility. For the broad masses of the people the system of private servants as part-substitutes for mothers is, however, economically unattainable. It must be assumed that the supply of domestic servants at prices families with children can pay will continue to diminish.

In any case the supply could never meet the potential demand of all working mothers. There may even be some doubt that it is *per se* a favorable system. Are these servants the best educational agency that could be invented? Is their work in isolated small units sound from the point of view of production?

The question must arise of some kind of substitute for the married woman in her housekeeping function. When the marriage does not take the form where the labor of one person, the wife, is completely devoted to homemaking, the work of keeping house can either be simplified to the degree where husband and wife can share it as leisure activity or be industrialized by letting it be transferred to a collective service for several families. A joint maid for several families in an apartment house, pooling the need for service by eating in restaurants, and buying prepared or semiprepared food are types of adjustments to modern economic conditions. Little social interest is attached to how the individual solves this particular problem. Public or cooperative encouragement of housing types which make possible cooperative service probably is necessary in order to counteract the inertia in the private building industry, which continually builds homes under the illusion that practically all wives are homemakers and nothing else.

Population policy must be primarily concerned, however, with what happens to the rearing and education of children. In the absence of children home organization can be kept elastic according to the demands and desires of the persons concerned. Looking for the most favorable form of organized supervision and education of children, when the mother cannot give them full-time attention, will strengthen the demand for cooperative services, cooperative apartments, and cooperative suburban developments. Organizing one nursery and one maid for several families will then seem a sensible population measure.

The argument for the cooperative nursery is direct. The question is only whether public institutions like day nurseries and kindergartens or new cooperative housing forms should be preferred. Historically, class divisions have had a most unhappy effect on the development of such institutions. Instead of regarding them as rationally planned cooperatives for practically all income levels in contrast with private servants, exorbitantly expensive for the minority who have them and nonattainable for the majority, the need for such nurseries was recognized first in the poorest strata. Out of that need the day nursery was born. It came into existence at a time when two facts tended to degrade it as a social institution: married women's work was almost exclusively a phenomenon of the poorest classes and private servants were at the time attainable by social groups even below the top of the income scale. The drab necessity for these mothers, often with great numbers of children, to take on low-paid work resulted in what that time knew as working mothers. Out of pity for these mothers the day nursery was created. As times have changed, the day nursery itself has not changed sufficiently.

The population problem is demonstrating that cooperative care and nursery education for children during the mother's working hours cannot be thought of only as an emergency institution for the poor. The enthusiasm of both experts and the public for nursery schools and similar institutions, created for part-time educational activities of upper-class children, should indicate that the need of the future is to reorganize the day nursery into gay playrooms for children, cooperatively managed by the parents themselves and utilizing qualified personnel. Such a cooperative development to replace the old domestic service problem has here been placed in the foreground as the solution for wage-earning mothers.

Turning to the related problem of how to secure leisure time for mothers, the same preschool institutions seem to be the logical answer. The homemaking mother's need for recreation would combine harmoniously with the working mother's need of vicarious child supervision. Thus the population question raises a challenge to the whole field of public nursery education — day nurseries, nursery schools, and kindergartens — to see its problems as a whole. A nursery institution, open to all classes and open for both half-day and whole-day use, deserves community subsidy as part of a reorganized program for child care (Chapter 21). When the population future is given serious consideration, some such development will be found to be of central importance. Once again educational aspects are coupled with social ones. The nursery institution is a desirable complement to the family in education for the complexities of modern life.

DEFENDING THE PLEASURES OF YOUNG COUPLES

The adjustments which the family has to make to the cultural structure of today in order to survive as a family seem to imply insatiable demands. They include not only the needs of working time for gainfully employed mothers and the needs of part-time release for home-working mothers. They also include demands for opportunity for recreation of a general character. To put it bluntly, children are cumbersome not only during working hours but also at night and on Sundays. It must never be forgotten that recreational needs figure so largely in the comparison between the childless and the childbearing stage in a family that they weigh heavily for family reduction.

Curbing recreational interests in the early married years when the habits from the courtship period still persist is certainly no way to strengthen marriage and family and still less to stimulate fertility. Some place in the population program must probably be found for diminishing such restraint for young families. The practical problem is easier to handle if cooperative nurseries exist as they could then extend their services to cover evenings, nights, weekends, and holiday periods. Some other agencies or social devices may also be utilized for the purpose. In addition there may be supervisory visits of the nursery personnel to the homes of children, for example during the parents' night out. This could be done either by going the round to the homes of the sleeping children or by a part-time helper, preferably one affiliated with some institution like a nursery in order to get the best and most continuous selection of personnel.

The demands and needs of rural mothers are so different that none of these schemes would work for them. Here some plan has to be visualized by which such a mother could take her vacation in continuous periods when a substitute could be provided for her in the home. Traveling summer nursery schools in rural districts might also take on part of the desired functions.

This may seem a blueprint for a division of the child care that has mostly taken care of itself without public concern. What is proposed, however, is only a kind of modern substitute in a democratically operating industrial society of the good neighbor spirit of earlier times. Where neighbors or relatives still perform these vicarious functions for parents, satisfactory conditions usually prevail and should be allowed to prevail. Where they have ceased, and we have to organize for their increasing reduction, modern society should not be without devices for compensating for them. Cooperative nurseries and cooperation for child supervision could be organized for some of the routine functions of child care. The essential functions of a home, where the feelings of belonging and security are anchored, where the emotional needs for affection and confidence are satisfied, where the simple joy of being together is cultivated, will always be met by the parents themselves.

Redistributing Income According to Family Size

Impeding the bearing of children and degrading the status of parents more than any other factor in comparison with other people of the same income class is the economic sacrifice involved. Children in a family mean extra costs, as was abundantly testified in Chapter 4. Any "normal" number of children becomes an alternative in conflict with elementary needs of the ordinary family: their need of a healthful and roomy home, of a sufficient and nourishing food supply, of adequate medical care and education above the public minimum, of recreation and culture. To neutralize the motive for extreme caution in childbearing growing out of economic considerations, population policy cannot find escape in projects for a general rise in national income. Those indifferent to the need of social reconstruction deceive themselves by believing that if only people get higher incomes, children will also come.

The decisive comparison in the minds of those who contemplate the effects of children on their economic status is certainly not between poverty as it existed in earlier times and the contemporary ease of economic circumstances. The comparison generating bitterness in connection with the economic effects of family increase is that families with children become "declassed" as compared to the childless. This is a real effect, and there is no doubt that it is psychologically effective. The still more important comparison is, however, the lowering of the level of living of a family with children in comparison with its own earlier level of living. Voluntary choice of poverty for the sake of children is what young couples now are asked for. The essential connection between fertility and standard of living thus belongs to quite another category than economic status generally. It belongs to the differential costs which are added with each child. There is no wonder that the number of children is reduced as a result of the widening abyss between mounting costs and inflexible income.

Any measures undertaken in order to reduce the economic motive for family limitation must be directly concerned with that dilemma. They must abolish the growing class distinctions within the classes, which tend to make of families with children a pariah group within each social group. The available resources have to be distributed more fairly according to family size. That is the meaning of the economic revolution implied in a democratic population program. This redistribution of national wealth and income in favor of children or, as it may also be expressed, this forced transfer of greater sums to investment in the future generations may be achieved either through differentiating incomes or through leveling costs or through some combination of both methods. Chapter 9 will be devoted to a theoretical scrutiny of whether a population policy using cash allowances for children (increasing income to cover the extra costs for them) or one making available publicly supported services catering directly to children's needs is the more advantageous. Anticipating the results of this discussion we may next consider what costs of children could be reduced by public measures.

SOCIALIZING CHILDREN'S NEEDS

Reducing the cost for child support by community measures can be achieved for practically all the items in a family budget. The most immediate measures would concern the costs at childbirth: cost of delivery, cost of prenatal and postnatal care, cost of equipment for children, and sometimes reduction of mother's income. The next step would be to charge to public account that part of housing costs which is intended for children instead of subsidizing low-rent housing in general and to do the same for cost of food for children, cost of medical care, cost of clothing and of education, and so forth. Not all these costs are of a nature that would allow for or even make advisable a total transfer from the private to the public budget. What ought to be included in a general plan must, in order to achieve anything near the goal, be social reforms that cut down individual family costs for children and at the same time effect a certain class equalization among the children in our society.

The greatest gain conceivable in the realm of population quality can be reached by providing optimal environments. The central problem in preventive social reform is not concerned with some few gravely deficient individuals. It has to do with elevating the whole general standard, the capacity for health and vitality, for efficiency and happiness throughout the population. More specifically, however, efforts must be directed at that fraction, whether large or small, of the population which does not have what is publicly claimed as a decent level of living. No divining rod is needed if any society seriously wants to overcome its worst deficiencies. By following field after field of children's consumption and replenishing where lack exists, a direct cure can be applied where the worst ills are at work. Just as the reforms in distribution dictated by consideration of quantitative population goals unite harmoniously with broad ideals of equality so do such environmental enrichments, advocated as qualitative population policy, unite with simple humanitarian desires not to let children, the ones most innocent of the wrongs of the world, suffer most from these wrongs.

Perhaps the most elementary social desideratum is that children should be assured plenty of nourishing food (Chapter 15). Making this a goal, no matter what the income of the parents may be, would fit nutrition policy into a population program, shifting its emphasis to children instead of to low-income groups. The present unsatisfactory nourishment of children rests upon two intimately associated reasons: on the one hand, there is ignorance and lack of solicitude on the part of the parents, chiefly the housekeeper; and, on the other hand, there is insufficient family income. The first reason is, to be sure, not the least important one, but this does not warrant any conclusion that society is without responsibility. Instead, the call for educational propaganda in the service of population policy once more becomes concrete and definite in respect to nutritional information. Poor habits can be corrected. The ignorant can be enlightened, and the irresponsible awakened.

As far as the diet of children is concerned, however, study, instruction, and propaganda are not enough. The deterring factor in furnishing proper nourishment is so often financial in nature that any aid must be of the same character. In order really to safeguard the quality of children's diet, food must be provided. This could be done either by giving the parents financial aid to buy more food or by instituting a series of direct nutritional services for children. School meals for children are one concrete measure. A free school lunch, balanced according to certain health and dietary requirements, may to a large extent assure the children the necessary food minimum and the optimum of protective elements. The composition of this school lunch would in itself be the best sort of instruction for children and parents and could help create lasting health habits. Children below school age cannot, however, be reached in this way. Some other expedient must be found, and the best one projected on the screen of social discussion in Sweden from the beginning of the population battle is a two-price system, i.e., a discount for children generally on certain necessary foods. It should be fairly simple to administer such a price differential once a certain inertia in opinion has been overcome and once the urgent social need for it is grasped.

Higher housing standards are at least as necessary as higher nutritional standards. If houses are not healthful and homes not roomy, all attempts to raise the intellectual, moral, social, and economic standards will, to a large extent, be ineffectual. When the existing housing standards, as they have been illustrated in Chapter 4 and will be more fully treated in Chapter 14, are studied, certain crying evils stand out. Overcrowding for children is the worst of them.

Measures sought will again have to be both educational and economic in character. Through education pride and responsibility in as wise a consumption choice as possible with regard to limited resources can be developed. The needs of children can be stressed. False individualism can be made to yield in the housing field as it has already yielded in one field after another. What people with children do with their incomes should no longer be considered a matter exclusively of individual liberty. A more efficient remedy, however, will have to be economic in character, as the large number of families living in poor houses or in overcrowded dwellings is forced to do so because of economic need. So grave are the hazards, physical, psychological, and moral, of poor housing conditions that it is logical to make the part of housing which is for children and youth a public responsibility. Also, the housing policy can thus be changed from a subsidizing of low-income housing generally to a scheme for making optimal those dwellings where the nation's children have their homes (Chapter 14).

With the current conditions in Sweden in mind, where overcrowding is a much more serious problem than slum conditions, the first task is obviously to abolish the worst forms of overcrowding. This means rebuilding rather than demolition. It also means transferring the families to the best and roomiest houses, leaving those without children to seek relief first on their own initiative. They can wait; the children cannot. Children build the future society, whereas the aged according to the order of nature die. That is why the housing problem cannot be regarded as a problem of charity; it is a problem of the future quality of the people.

What must next be done to ensure higher quality of children lies within the field of medical care. Services for children are now drastically curbed for economic reasons, but the health of future generations cannot continue to depend on the economic resources of individual families. Those individual budgets which have to make room for children are by necessity already the most heavily infringed upon. To pool the health risks of children for all the nation and also to make a joint investment in the health of the next generation becomes a part of population policy.

There are many practical arguments for social health control for children. The system of privately organized medicine has not expanded very far in the field of preventive child medicine. Private pediatricians are a phenomenon of big cities. Expanding the public pediatric services thus meets no great resistance. On the contrary, the time seems to have come when it is still possible to choose whether to create a public system or to give the parents cash to pay private doctors. A country-wide system of public health care for children might also help to provide a group of doctors who could be leaders in child welfare and social betterment. Perhaps it would also relieve the medical profession of the charge of being more obstructive in programs for social welfare than any other of society's large professional groups.

Expressed in concrete terms, what is needed is a number of combined consultation and propaganda centers for child care in every district (Chapter 16). They would have to be supplemented at central points with well-equipped child clinics, staffed with specialists, open for both hospitalization and out-patient service, and connected with dentists, nurses, school doctors, and mental hygiene specialists. Their high-grade services would take care of the special and difficult cases. The immediate health work itself, however, could be decentralized to the local bureaus, linking doctor, school, and home in close cooperation. All these services would have to be available to children of all social classes free of cost, since this is a measure of population policy and not of poor relief. An outstanding feature of such a health service would have to be child guidance. The research during the last few decades in mental hygiene teaches us how much delinquency and social maladjustment, neurosis, decay and restraint of life, lack of personal efficiency and genuine unhappiness could have been prevented if deviations from normal development had been detected at an early stage and properly treated.

For such work it is not enough to have the few well-equipped child guidance clinics, here prospectively thought of as located at central points. The task is of such scope that it demands preventive influences in the everyday situations of every child in school and in the home. Various social agencies may have contributions to make here; the home and the school have to answer the call first. In both of the latter places greater psychological insight and a more delicate pedagogical touch are needed.

Educating children is, however, not only a matter of child guidance. Providing schools has long been a communal responsibility. In revising all social measures from the point of view of improving population quality, it must be asked whether the schools produce as good a product as possible. In Sweden little need be said about the distribution of school opportunities. These are already well democratized and the road forward is duly marked. Rather the more subtle influences on personality traits have to be questioned. In education there is always a wide margin of free choice as to what to call quality. What type of human being do we want to educate for the era of tomorrow? The art of education is decidedly not the same if we want our people to be submissive tools in the service of leaders or if we want courageous, mature, and independent citizens. It differs according to whether we want individualists or collectivists, an introverted and timorous population or an extroverted and enterprising one. Among all these there are choices to be made. The schools are making a fateful choice even if they fall back on tradition or on authoritative norms. In this connection the problem of quality is most difficult to determine, as the determinants themselves are variable. Some fairly general valuations would seem to indicate, however, that the schools in a democracy can improve the quality of personality in specific directions.

The school, as it generally works, still undeniably cultivates an excessive and false individualism and thwarts social attitudes. Also, in its selection of personality types the school system is still mainly favoring docile, unreflecting followers and egoistic competitors — types adjusted to epochs already passed. An "obedient egoist," that contamination of two types, would seem to be the ideal pupil in many schools even at present; but this is rarely the ideal citizen for any country. A more fitting adjustment to the ideals of the present era would be men with capacity both for individual independence, as contrasted with the submissive man of the feudal ages, and for collective cooperation, as contrasted with the competitive man of the capitalistic epoch. What is now needed is an active social idealism in which neither subordination nor superordination but rather coordination in deciding upon a democratically desirable set of attitudes should be the goal. Education purposively directed toward social responsibility, more vivid group feelings, and a greater talent for harmoniously living together would be part of a population program also with respect to the children's future life as founders of families and as parents of new generations. Thus, there is again a strong connecting link between a population policy that fosters quality of children and one that furthers increase in number of children.

Another function of the school is to cultivate quality by selecting the right students for the right types of education. Consideration of vocational aptitudes can increase the service of people and so through greater efficiency somewhat offset the effects of shrinkage in number. Social mobility has now to be organized through the avenue of schooling to a greater extent than in times past. In Sweden a marked difference is already visible between the era of expansion and the more static conditions of today. This difference will become still greater when population numbers fall off. The time of the self-made man has now, by and large, passed. Vocations, both high and low, have become more structuralized. The vast amount of labor security, connected first with the completion of trade-unionism and secondly with development of protective legislation, has had to be bought by sacrificing to a degree vocational mobility. This means that the *lehrgang,* i.e., learning period, is organized more narrowly but also with less risk through schooling and volunteer jobs leading directly to one vocation and one labor organization. Selecting the interested and able, promoting their study ambitions, paving their way through equalizing opportunities for youth from all social classes, and training them efficiently become of primary concern to society (Chapter 20).

Again there is harmony between quantitative and qualitative gains. Formulating population policy from the qualitative point of view, it is clear that it pays for society to invest in vocational guidance and vocational training. From the quantitative point of view it is just as clear that if society pays for this equalization of opportunities more children may be born because ambitions for higher education are some of the most consciously potent determinants of whether parents will have additional children.

A List of Reforms

When quantitative aims of a population policy are combined with qualitative aims in an effort to formulate a program in practical and concrete forms, one has a blueprint of what society will have to do, sooner or later, if it is to safeguard the welfare of the nation's children. The main lines are as follow:

Free delivery, free prenatal and postnatal care for all mothers; free medical care and health control for all children, including dental care, mental hygiene, and medicines.

Subvention of rent and other housing costs in relation to family size, gradually to cover costs for extra space for children in most families.

Reduction of food costs for children through a free school meal for all children and price discounts on certain foodstuffs in relation to family size.

Free education, including public school and university, vocational, and professional training, free books and materials for all children, free transportation where such is suitable, boarding homes for rural children, and stipends for full upkeep of selected students for professional studies.

Free nursery education.

Somewhat reduced costs for clothing, eventually through free availability of the more expensive and necessary garments.

Reduced costs and improved facilities for family recreation through cheap fare for families, vacation villages, etc., for families, free summer vacation camps, afternoon clubs, etc., for children and adolescents, and free vacations for mothers in various forms.

Increased security of employment for both fathers and mothers and coverage of costs for periods of lessened physical resistance.

Social responsibility for the children in all incomplete and handicapped families.

These family reforms would have little chance of being accepted if they were not rather easily harmonized with social trends already at work. All social policy in all advanced countries is moving nearer an acceptance of them by gradually covering larger and larger fields of basic human needs. The idea of equalizing the worst economic handicaps by cooperative pooling of resources has already been accepted by Western society at least tacitly and through some direct actions. The shape of the reforms is also envisaged. The social policy resulting from the acceptance of responsibility for the weak has had to bring about some intervention in the fields touched upon. Provisions have had to be made in housing, in medical care, in education. These social reforms are never at a standstill. They grow with every new budget year. What is proposed here in the name of population and family policy is only, or chiefly, that they should be aligned in a plan. A social policy equalizing income hazards and a population policy equalizing the burden of child support must be coordinated.

CHAPTER IX

IN CASH OR IN KIND

THE economic reforms necessary to compensate the family to a substantial degree for the extra burdens it shoulders by having children take on immense financial proportions. A redistribution of income on the necessary scale would involve nothing less than a nationalization of the economic responsibility for children. Bachelors, sterile families, and families with one or two children would not be allowed to evade their share in the investment for the future. The sharing of economic responsibility for children is actually implied in child welfare programs today. Far too often, however, new reforms are merely added to an old structure without a thorough weighing of what is really implied and how it can best be achieved. In the previous chapter concrete reforms were outlined as they seemed best to fit the quite concretely sensed needs, but the choice between alternative sets of means for the population ends is worthy of more careful scrutiny.

A main problem is whether society should organize all these services or just reimburse the parents. The latter would require redistribution of incomes within society in cash, utilizing either a system of general, compulsory child pensions or some more restricted system of wage allowances. The former would involve mobilizing the cooperation of the whole nation for creating public services directly for children. Which would be more effective? Which would be in greater conformity with the value premises assumed?

This is a problem involving principles, [162] the answer will have far-reaching consequences. Yet the problem has been singularly overlooked in the writings on population policy. Generally a writer on sociopractical solutions, after studies in demography, will single out one method and then forget the alternatives or simply add them as further possibilities. While anyone may present his beliefs with regard to the remedies and adjustments for any social problem, a scientific analysis of the two principal alternatives, their interrelations and respective consequences, is a prerequisite for a rational evaluation of any practical program. Such a discussion of the principles involved in social policy has never been carried through except in the Swedish population debate, although it is basic to even a modest beginning of family security policies.

FAMILY ALLOWANCES

The alternative of equalizing costs for children by income allowances in cash to their parents would immediately seem to be the simpler method. It would *prima facie* be chosen by all those who like mathematically executed social justice. Simply figure out child costs and divide them equally among all taxpayers or among all citizens according to some contributory scheme. Such a redistributional reform, in type quite similar to the simplified socialist idea of equalizing incomes by dividing evenly, has found many advocates but few practitioners.

In a modified form but to a large extent utilizing the wider population argument it has, however, often been proposed that an element of family maintenance be included in the determination of wages. Family allowances on the labor market have been widely tried. This linking of general social reforms to the labor market dominates the whole field of social policy in some countries. Old-age insurance and health insurance have sometimes been developed on this basis. Here some short circuit in thinking must be at work which involves the position that industrialism is to blame for modern economic problems, so that they have to be remedied by special measures for those connected with industry. This is understandable in so far as the ills to be alleviated through social insurance have only become visible with industrialization. In the specific problem now under observation it is true that only with growing industrialization did the burden of supporting a family of varying size tend to become fastened on one person, the father, without productive contributions from those in demand of support. Only then, moreover, did the cost of every child begin increasing to constitute a more and more oppressive burden. It is fallacious, however, to believe that the problem of dependency for maintenance operates only within the sphere of wage earning. Industrialization and urbanization are cultural patterns that have become dominant in all segments of the economic structure. Just as old age, death, and illness are not limited to industrial workers, so the risk coverage should not be so limited. In the same way it is an artificial limitation to construct social schemes of family reforms so as to take care only of the children of wage earners, while children are not provided for in the incomes of farmers, shopkeepers, and others. The whole system of family support is the crux of the problem. Sweden has successfully resisted the temptation of artificial limitation of social problems to the labor market, developing its insurance schemes for all the people and not for wage workers only. It is thus not extraordinary that Sweden should try to construct her family income scheme on some other basis than wage reforms.

A family wage is by no means a modern innovation. The living wage, or wage according to need, is so directly connected with closed and meager systems of support that it may well be said to have been most perfectly represented in slavery. A slaveowner, while, on the one hand, reducing remuneration for labor to a minimum, would, on the other hand, counting new generations as his property, have a direct interest in at least keeping dependents alive by distributing means for subsistence in direct relation to family size. Under early paternalistic conditions in Swedish industry, particularly in the ironworks in isolated districts, some of the same interests were at work as elsewhere in the earlier stages of industrialism. The employer could, under the then more static conditions, count upon the children as his future labor supply. He also found it cheaper to support them tolerably, together with the aged and the sick, than to have as the chief taxpayer in the local community to carry the burden of their public maintenance. In farming, in crafts, in the earliest manufactures, in mining, and in the rural ironworks and foundries, housing, fuel, and other necessities were in earlier times often distributed in kind and in amounts adjusted to size of family. This is the paternalistic, predemocratic tradition in Sweden which trade-unionism had to fight at its very start.

The connection between substandard wages and family allowances is clear. When the wage level is near the subsistence minimum, no other form of wages than that differentiated by increases per family member will give the large families any chance to survive at all. It is therefore no wonder that an element of the family wage is still retained in some industries today. Any international comparison will show that in most European countries this wage system, differentiated according to family size, appears in coal mining and sometimes in textiles and other depressed industries. This unmistakable relationship between dire need and maintenance meted out according to family size shows up also in poor relief. The economic association between a low level for wages and a system of family allowances might also be turned around. In this sense employers may effect payroll economies by making family allowances, thus not paying anybody more than he really "needs." The family wage is then a belly-strap which is drawn as close to the spine as possible.

This connection has been discovered by organized labor, which has consequently fought to get rid of the family wage and achieve wages fixed in relation to productive output, whether according to time or to piece rates. A setback in this fight was experienced all over Europe during and after the World War. When rising prices and the rising cost of living decreased the purchasing power of wages, demands for higher wages were made. Efforts to save expenditures caused employers to offer the necessary wage increases as additional cash allowances for family dependents instead of as general increases in wages. The weak bargaining position of the workers often forced them to accept this arrangement. The wage system always has greater inertia than the price system. A decrease in real wages had already set in, and nominal wages were lagging behind. The actual function of the family allowances was to cover the loss in real wages for both industrial workers and salaried employees only partly. After the war, when labor by experience had become more attentive to what from its point of view was totally inadequate remuneration for work and when labor had improved its bargaining position, the family wage was gradually taken out of most collective agreements. In the civil service, however, the system of family allowances has prevailed longer in most countries, undoubtedly with some relation to the fact that remuneration within these groups has not followed the same upward trend as among the working-class groups. Many governments have also openly declared that this wage form is a measure of economy. The cuts in real wages — comparatively speaking, as seen in relation to other social groups — are made less drastic by introducing this new margin of tolerance for dependents.

THE FRENCH SCHEME

Family allowances have, however, been introduced in recent times in some countries. This has not been done openly as a wage-saving device but under the pretense of social reform. It has been treated as the "ethical wage" in contrast to the "unethical" market wage. Some religious congregations had adopted this view much earlier, and among its later proponents the Catholics have always been strong. This wage ideology has thus been widely adopted by the Catholic trade unions in Central Europe in direct opposition to the majority of ordinary secular trade unions.

Before the World War individual efforts to practice this wage principle had already been made on a philanthropic basis by some employers, particularly in France. The companies utilizing this system would, however, naturally tend to attract the fathers of large families and repel the unmarried workers on whose wages the corresponding reductions would be made. Only some sort of pooling device, embracing all employers or at least all employers within the same trade, could evade this difficulty. Such mutual insurance by a group of employers originated in French industry and these *caisses de compensation* grew rapidly after the World War. All employers contribute a certain share of their payrolls to a fund from which certain family allowances are disbursed to the dependents of all employed. So widely did this system spread in postwar France — which it must be remembered did not succeed in stabilizing its monetary system before the world was on the brink of the great depression — that the organized workers soon found it impossible to withstand the development. They had to accept the system and direct their influence solely toward pressing for legal regulations and state control over the wage funds (law of 1932). The development in Belgium was similar. In Italy it was in line with the Fascist ideology. In other countries such a development has not taken place. As this industrial wage system has covered wider and wider regions, it has also, particularly in France, shown an interesting tendency to outgrow its own wage limitations. Other groups, such as farmers and the middle class, have become interested and efforts have been made in recent years to include such groups in similar funds. In so far as these efforts may succeed and the system in the future come to cover most sectors of the population, it will no longer be a wage system but a national system of pensions for children.

THE BASIC FLAW

Significantly enough, family wage funds have practically never been established by workers as cooperative schemes. As no one, at least in Sweden, nowadays believes workers incapable of managing their own affairs and influencing the labor market, this should be a reason to wonder why it has not developed if it is assumed that the scheme is to their own real interests. Instead, the representatives of labor have been consistently against family wages. They have declared it to be in the interest of the workers to defend high wages, standardized according to working time and efficiency and not allowing for any bargaining and undercutting on account of family considerations. A great majority of the wage earners do not have large families and would get little from the system. Hence individual interests have strengthened the ideological position taken. It is true that there is a similar distribution in the electorate at large, but there a man is reacting as a citizen in a nation and not as a worker in relation to a company. As a matter of fact the Swedish trade-union representatives have taken the stand that they are in favor of a general redistribution of income according to child costs, but they are against it when inserted in the wage system. In their view this latter approach would be a quack remedy, standing in the way of a thoroughgoing solution of the family problem and at the same time having unwholesome effects on the labor market.

Quite apart from the question of whether the workers are right or wrong, this means that a family wage system can be instituted only against the wishes of labor. That the administrative apparatus will be rather cumbersome and that the legal regulations will interfere with both business and employment conditions is also obvious. In Sweden employers have on the whole taken the same adverse view of the scheme. These interests and attitudes of the persons actually concerned are naturally of highest importance in a democracy when considering the practicability of the scheme.

The theoretical point, however, is that the family wage system as a solution of the problem of child maintenance is wholly inadequate. Ideologically it attempts a merger between the employers' interest in low labor costs and the national interest in child welfare. It only solves the problem, in so far as it suffices even there, of family maintenance for a limited proportion of the families, that is, for the families with incomes in the form of wages. If the problem is a general one and concerns the whole people, however, the solution has likewise to be a general one. The family problems of the small businessman, the farmer, and the independent craftsman are just as important as those of the laborer, the office employee, and the civil servant. The relative weight of the various groups may be different in different countries. In Sweden an approximate calculation based on the 1930 census material shows that independent, nonsalaried income earners account for about one-third of the men. This includes only the active earners. The proportion would be higher if those with incomes but without work (chiefly the aged) were included. No reform which aims at a redistribution of income for the benefit of children and which requires the legal force of the community but which on technical grounds leaves out the children of farmers, shopkeepers, and the whole middle class of small-scale entrepreneurs will win adoption as long as there is a reasonable alternative.

The basic flaw in the system becomes all the more serious inasmuch as the condition upon which even wage earners derive the benefits of such a redistribution of incomes according to needs is that the individual worker actually has work. No benefit, therefore, would accrue to the long-term unemployed, especially those who have lost connection with their occupations during a depression or have never properly entered an occupation. If these are to be covered, the system must be amended by some community insurance plan. Then the question of covering all workers instead of only those selected according to their position in the labor market naturally arises.

From wider angles of social policy another defect in principle is inherent in the family wage system. Redistribution will take place only within the same occupational group and, in the main, between families on the same income level as they share in the same benefit fund. Redistribution of incomes will thus occur chiefly in a horizontal direction rather than simultaneously in a vertical direction. This reveals an even more serious drawback in the family wage system when it is remembered that the average size of family is not the same in all economic groups. Since children are more frequent in the poorer strata, a leveling out of child costs, even with considerable allowances for each child, will hardly constitute a burden among the relatively well-paid teachers of civil service status, many of whom are unmarried women. On the other hand, even a radical redistribution of incomes among the farm laborers, whose poverty matches their large numbers of children, would result in very small benefits.

Such difficulties may be met by subsidies from the community or by some equalization through public tax money or through forced pooling in one main fund. The more such intervention grows, the more natural it will seem to arrange for redistribution of incomes for the whole population. This leads again to the idea of general compulsory insurance through which the equalization of income according to family size is made obligatory in the whole community and not merely in the labor market. Purely on administrative grounds such a system would be simpler, more effective, and cheaper It could be made applicable from the beginning to the entire population. In a child pension system of this kind, not only horizontal but also vertical equalization — not only between families of different size but also between income classes — could be achieved.

A General Scheme of Child Pensions

Nowhere, however, has any such scheme of direct redistribution in the whole nation been tried as anything but a social welfare measure. France has attempted some such system for assisting large families, first as a kind of poor assistance through *Assistance aux familles nombreuses* (from 1913) and then with somewhat more liberal income limits as *Encouragement National aux familles nombreuses* (since 1923). In both these schemes small allowances, low income limits for eligibility, and nonparticipation for the first few children are fixed rules for the families becoming beneficiaries. They constitute highly commendable social assistance schemes, but they do not constitute a population policy proper as they affect only the poorer strata. As a measure of general social welfare and not of population policy, New Zealand has since 1926 had the most far-reaching reform. Families below a certain weekly minimum income are entitled to an allowance of 2 shillings per week per child beginning with the third child.

If any such scheme should satisfy the goals of population policy, it would have to reach most income groups because extra costs for children occur in all social classes. Should such a scheme be blueprinted and the bonus calculated so as to cover these extra costs to a considerable extent, the expenditure would be so great that it would be seen at once that such socialistic mathematics of social justice and redistribution, even if only for children, simply do not work. In Sweden a crown a day per child under 15 years of age would cost half a billion annually or about half the normal national budget. In the United States $10 a month per child would cost nearly $4,500,-

000,000 annually. Adding these sums to taxation would be daring. People have become accustomed to think in such figures when it is a question of war and national defense but not as yet in connection with national improvements. In any case before making such proposals one must be relatively sure in advance of their effectiveness. Neither can the magnitude of the sums be concealed by levying them on payrolls or as special contributions paid by all citizens. The problems of incidence of taxation and of economic consequences in general are just the same and just as difficult whether general taxation or separate contributions are utilized. Even if only the broad masses, where such child allowances would seem most desirable, were included in the scheme, the amounts would be nearly as large, since in any nation the poor are the many and the rich are the few.

A general scheme for children's pensions is Utopian. It must be admitted, however, that while emphasis on the colossal costs is politically impressive, it is not a particularly valid argument. Whatever the method employed, children must be supported. Costs may not be considered increased if they are merely transferred from the individual family to the public as a whole. Also reforms in kind will show huge cost items on the national budget. The only crucial question becomes one of waste or economy. The two alternative principles for redistributional reforms, in cash or in kind, therefore have to be compared as to their effectiveness in relation to financial outlays. Just because both systems are costly, they must be scrutinized as choices. It would be an illusion to pretend that both lines could be followed. No budget could expand widely in two different directions for the welfare of children.

A Special Conflict

Besides this necessary choice between the two programs, which in the final instance is conditioned by the factor of fiscal economy, there is a special conflict which arises if the cash system is employed for only part of the population. Suppose, for example, that a family wage is applied to a particular group of workers, such as state and municipal employees, and that simultaneously reforms are adopted on the basis of benefits in kind for the people at large. Then an accumulation of income differentiation according to number of children accrues for the persons employed in public service. Shall a government railroad worker with many children receive both a cash subsidy and a housing subsidy? Or from the opposite viewpoint, shall an unmarried worker in public service pay heavy taxes as a citizen to finance the general family security program and pay special contributions as a worker for child subsidies to those of his fellow workers with many children?

This doubling for certain small groups of both gains and sacrifices will lead to economic and administrative difficulties and a political barrage against such social reforms. Those enamored of the family wage will have every reason to fight against a nation-wide system of services for children. Even if it may be asserted that differentiation according to family size could never develop too far, this is not politically true. The willingness on the part of the public to participate in redistributional reforms is limited at any time, and a choice of method has to take place. It may even be assumed that the more apparent the transfers of cash from the childless to the children the sooner this saturation limit will be reached.

The choice between the two systems is, therefore, open only for a short time, namely, at an early stage when society is not institutionally tied to the one or the other development. This is still the case in most countries. A revolutionary new wage method and a wide expansion of child welfare provisions are both far from being accepted by the general public. The need for making an intelligent choice and for avoiding a haphazard accumulation of measures is pressing.

Measures in Kind Cheaper

The first test in a direct comparison of the two alternatives is their relative efficiency. The effectiveness and economy of the one or the other depends upon how great an increase in real income can be attained for the one group of families by a certain burdening of the other group.

There are a number of reasons why the alternative of cash is the more expensive and the less efficient method. An element of saving or efficiency is implied in the very fact that the other alternative of offering children public services means that certain consumption items become subjected to social organization, thus realizing the economies of cooperation and large-scale enterprise. Services can also be continuous and homogeneous, fewer varieties being necessary and demand being keyed to supply. An example from the medical field will illustrate the point. In several countries an attempt is now being made to provide effective health care for mothers and children at public health centers. To make this health care truly first-rate and universally available is expensive, but any expert will admit that the same amount of money, divided among the individual families, would provide for a far lower quality of health care. Work for doctors and nurses at the health center is continuous and specialized; the functions of the personnel employed are well integrated; the waste of the empty waiting room is abolished; and so on. Finally, the bidding through advertising by all competitors selling medicines is done away with in the field of child health if free doctors prescribe free medicines on the basis of quality. Large-scale enterprises in certain sectors of children's consumption, elimination of both substandard and luxury varieties and many other variations which are only the result of lack of standardization, and substitution for the immense cost of advertising of the slight cost of educational propaganda are important social gains in a field where the waste of our competitive system is least justified, namely, in the maintenance of children.

A second advantage in a system of social services for children, if the state or the municipality is to administer directly a certain part of the desired addition to the consumption of the families instead of doling it out as cash subsidies, is the possibility of integrating social policy in the wider economic policy of the country. This further reduces costs and increases the effectiveness of the measures. Thus large parts of the new protective social policy, e.g., as directed toward nutrition, housing, and similar benefits, can be incorporated in the general production policy of the country and especially in the agricultural, unemployment, and trade cycle policy. Only a portion of the costs should then rightly be charged to the account of social policy. It should be largely a question of such arrangements as do not involve any real costs at all for society. The costs might simply imply improved utilization of existing capacities, stabilizing production, and reducing unemployment of labor, land, and capital. To inaugurate a nutritional policy for children, aimed at supplying them with more adequate food, is thus a reasonable element in the agricultural policy of creating demands for existing surplus products. Only to a small extent could cash subsidies be directed to such a use for advantages to producer and consumer and the national economy. The same situation holds true in housing. There is in every country a crying need for better housing. From our point of view housing reforms should be carried out immediately if they are to have any meaning for population policy. Subsidized housing should be so directed as first to help families with children instead of consisting just of low-rent housing projects, but the actual scope of building operations from year to year need not be rigidly determined. The program should rather be blueprinted for effectual release in depression times to relieve unemployment and improve business.

Cash Doles Lost in the Family Budget

Looking at the problem not only from the social but also from the individual angle, it is immediately evident that cash subsidies would become merged in the average family budget without special regard for children. Increasing that budget by adding cash amounts to it monthly will only enlarge the funds available by a certain percentage, probably to be so distributed as to constitute small additions to the various budget items. The money may be added to the rent but perhaps only in order to get a larger living room. It may buy somewhat better food, but all will eat it. It may even go toward the mother's hat or the father's liquor account. Part of it will be used for more movies and magazines. To keep it apart for the children and to reserve it for the intended consumption improvement would be simply unmanageable except through obnoxious police control.

This is no criticism *per se*. Expenditures for other items than the children's most necessary expenses may be judged to be too small in any low-income group. A general income redistribution may certainly be achieved through these cash doles, but that was not what this specific subsidy was intended for. It would not be possible along cash lines to emancipate just the children from the worst class inequalities. The equalization which would occur would be shared by the entire family, and it would not go very far. The earlier income and the family size would continue to determine the level of living in the family. The added child pension would move the margin somewhat upward, but it would not fundamentally change the children's lives as would the other alternative of satisfying the children's needs in kind, i.e., in some free consumption for all, such as the public school system. This would tend to liberate the children from class inequalities in the essentials of life.

Even if the household tried to increase only the children's budget, the expenditures could still never be planned as systematically as by some cooperative agency. The plasticity of needs will not be matched by plasticity of incomes. A temporarily great capital outlay for, say, dentistry will be nearly as difficult as before. The selection of the goods and services on the open market will not be the wisest. The family can never count upon having the expert consumer knowledge necessary for the most efficient marketing for children. There again some waste must necessarily occur. Neither is the private family large enough to organize the supply of necessities so as best to fit its needs. As an individual consuming unit it would continue to be powerless against the particular form in which the private market happened to offer things.

Instituting social services for the benefit of children directly already has been realized in some fields of consumption. Thus education is chiefly transferred from private budgeting. Just as a cash pension could not buy as adequate schooling, so it could not provide as adequate dental care, prenatal service, etc. No money subsidy will put families in a position on the open market to select, to obtain, and to pay for such adequate housing accommodations as the community could buy for them. They need the type of housing that the private market will never provide: roomy and at the same time cheap apartments with modern conveniences just for children. The family is always the pitfall for the principle of private enterprise. In our economic system neither industry nor business is able to provide adequate incomes for varying family sizes or to furnish at competitive prices the things which families need.

The possibility of beneficially influencing consumption patterns must also be noted. The need of such education is emphasized by all recent studies of family budgets and living conditions. If the community provides attractive, clean, functional houses for families with many children, the ambitions of other people will also be directed toward overcoming such housing deficiencies as are within the power of individual control. Free school meals would be just as good an object lesson for the younger generation if handled as part of active education as any theoretical instruction in the selection and preparation of health foods. Such educational propaganda for improved hygienic, cultural, and economical consumption habits is more than ever felt to be necessary. What people consume, especially what they select for consumption by their children, is no longer a matter of social indifference. Research does not give us any ground for believing that everything is all right as long as the family keeps the children on the minimum standard essential for the actual maintenance of life and the retention of a fair capacity for work. We now know that by raising this minimum standard in various respects, as for example in regard to diet composition and the spaciousness and quality of dwellings, we may reap tremendous profits in the health and vitality of the people. Such an increase in consumption, then, must appear not only as an individual interest but also as a general social interest.

This is advocated as a decisive argument against assistance in cash and in favor of assistance in kind. When society intervenes by placing an economic burden on other income receivers and thus compels them to participate in the support of the cost of childbearing, it is also reasonable that society shall reserve the aid for the children and shall keep control of its utilization. No injustice is thereby done to the parents, but a right is guaranteed for the children.

Cash Favors Quantity; Kind Favors Quality

The chief advantage of a system of social reforms for children rather than cash premiums to the parents is, however, the gain in quality. Cash premiums would probably more effectively promote an increase in numbers of children, at least in the short run, while social services undoubtedly have their foremost effect on the children's health, vitality, and well-being. Legislators and the people must choose which result they prefer.

The quantitative population effect of any method will naturally vary according to the amount spent, but there is a tendency for cash subsidies to have a greater quantitative effect because they are added to the general family budget and thus are not exclusively reserved for the children. This is why they may appear more attractive to the parents. To put it bluntly, the quantitative population effect the subsidies can exert depends upon the opportunity for parents to misuse them, i.e., misuse from the viewpoint of the community and of the children. Cash subsidies must, therefore, exercise the stronger quantitative population effect upon those parents who, on account of hereditary characteristics or deleterious upbringing or other circumstances of environment, are undesirable parents. They would be prepared to appropriate the entire subsidies for their own pleasure. This selective attraction would, in addition to the slight inducement to all parents on account of the monetary subsidy, be the chief instrument for increasing births. The poorest families would be the first to add to their progeny. Even among the poor, a further selection will occur as the child pension will be most attractive to the least responsible, which must perforce mean some of those with the least endowments. It may be ventured that the people most easily attracted into parenthood by economic motives are the least desirable parents for children.

If it is desired to have quantity of population at the sacrifice of quality, there is no doubt that cash benefits would be successful. The greatest population effect could actually be obtained not by repeated monthly or weekly pensions but by lump cash premiums linked with actual births. From a quantitative population point of view it would be possible to urge large maternal benefits in cash and, if everything else in child welfare is forsaken, public finances might also allow it. This would be what is sometimes called a direct population policy. And why stop there? If no taboos existed in considerations of the welfare of the children themselves, the most efficient device would, as Dr. Richard Sterner has pointed out, simply be a state lottery, giving, say, $1,000 to every tenth child or $10,000 to every hundredth child. Who doubts that there would be a race in childbearing? It would be the more successful in countries where people are fond of gambling and in social classes where cash is scarce. The idea of a lottery has not yet been grasped. In countries where fewer democratic inhibitions prevail about safeguarding the quality of children, however, the idea of rewards for long endurance at childbearing has led to the offering not only of medals and public congratulations by the "leader" but also of birth bonuses in cash or extra high birth premiums, e.g., at the birth of the seventh child.

In a truly democratic country this is not the choice, even if in this way many children could be brought into the world. Even bonuses at the birth of children become a suspicious means for population policy as they do not make provision for proper care during the children's later lives. The democratic strivings are, instead, first for the qualitative improvement of the people: every generation a healthier, happier, more able-bodied and more able-minded one. No other sort of increase than a qualitatively high-grade one is desired. From the very first the emphasis in the discussion of population policy in Sweden has been laid upon the qualitative population aims. The Population Commissions in Denmark and Sweden have also more and more consciously followed this line, which was laid down in the mandates for their work. While in countries with the political and social ethos of Germany and Italy most mention is made of stimulating fertility, the democratic North has rather viewed its task as the planning of social reforms which make it possible for ordinary people to follow their natural urge to have families. It has thus entered upon a social reorganization with much broader aims than stimulating births. From the point of view of quality, it is evident that the *in natura* approach has advantages over the cash approach with regard to fostering quality. It may well be that in the long run also the quantitative goal is best served by the redistribution of income in kind because it will imply a much more fundamental rebuilding of the very basis for family life.

THE CLASS ISSUE

The public discussion in Sweden concerning the problem of the principles in cash or in kind opened up by the arguments related above was lively enough but was ended, at least temporarily, by a decided victory for the latter principle. Not only the Population Commission but also the Committee on Women's Work and the Committee on Regulation of Salaries in Public Service came out in no uncertain terms against both family allowances and any general child pension system and for the *in natura* reforms. The labor organizations took an equally uncompromising stand and so, on the whole, did the influential women's organizations. The battle will, however, in all probability have to be waged over and over again because of the dimensions of the issue. One argument in favor of the first principle, and more specifically in favor of family allowances, is raised time and again. Reforms *in natura,* it is said, can only help the poorest strata in society; the only possibility for aiding middle-class families is a general wage system, differentiating earnings according to need of support. This argument is compelling. Even experienced experts sometimes accept it. It contains, however, several errors.

Measures of social policy have been directed chiefly toward helping the poorest strata for the reason that obviously they have needed help first. Behind the direction of reforms is a social valuation of a different and much more general scope, and it has nothing at all to do with the technical question of cash or kind. *Per se* there is no necessity for the *in natura* measures to be restricted to the most needy families. As will appear from the presentation of the concrete program in a later chapter, the Swedish Population Commission has as a matter of principle condemned income limits or any other means tests for the social services recommended. In the few cases where the Commission has not been able to follow that principle of population policy, and in the many cases where the Riksdag has inserted means tests in one form or another, the reason has been the financial costs. But, and this is the important point, fiscal considerations cannot be avoided simply by choosing the principle of cash instead of kind. Even family allowances must be paid for and therefore constitute a fiscal burden. Cash doles, in fact, cost more in that they are less effective or more expensive than reforms *in natura*.

In this context it is pertinent to consider briefly the whole problem of financing family reforms. There has been a world-wide delusion, which is still alive in the most unexpected quarters, that social insurance as distinct from other social aid is paid for by the beneficiaries so that the benefits are earned and constitute a right. The only reason for this difference in character seems to be that the pension schemes are often financed by contributions instead of on the regular tax budget and that they are handled separately by an administration of their own, which sometimes builds up a capital fund. It would, indeed, be remarkable if the character of a bonus could be changed so fundamentally by such technicalities which, furthermore, are entirely outside the individual beneficiary's own will or control. In reality the contributions are taxes among other taxes. As taxes they are regressive, burdening the poor classes out of all proportion to their incomes. In Sweden, where the system of social insurance has been expanded to cover the uncertainties of life more completely than in most other countries and where the lower income groups have a stronger voice in national politics, the principle of financing the schemes solely out of premiums paid by potential beneficiaries has gradually been dropped. Both the old-age pensions and practically all the new insurance schemes have to an increasing degree been financed on the regular budget. Funding has at the same time been limited to a minimum as it was found contrary to a sound monetary policy.

The doctrine of social insurance played its historical role in an epoch when, on the one hand, it was urgently desired to humanize poor relief and lift it to the plane of citizens' rights but when, on the other hand, the distribution of political power in society necessitated its financing by regressive taxation. In our present problem the underlying analogy to private insurance is doubly fallacious, as under a system of widespread birth control children are not true risks. The principle of nationally sharing the cost burdens for children and children's rights to decent support should not be erected behind the smoke screen of the insurance doctrine but by the people's representatives in view of national interests and ideals.

There is one reason for the insurance principle that is merely a psychological consideration. By specifying a need and having people's contributions separated for specific purposes, they get a fiction of personalization, a more palpable impression of their own participation. In undeveloped stages of social householding such a fiction may help preserve a strong feeling that people by contributions more than by taxes secure direct future benefits or actually share in the risks of life with their fellow citizens. In spite of fiscal clarity, which demands a unified budget, Sweden has therefore retained some such form of social security even when benefits have been financed entirely out of taxation. The goal in an educated democracy is, however, to get the citizens to look upon all public activity, including the fiscal budget, as a huge citizens' cooperative. On the principle of national solidarity our resources are pooled to even out risks and burdens and to raise by cumulated forces our standards of production and consumption and the material and immaterial welfare of the whole people. It should not be too difficult to defend this broader view at least in so far as the national investment in future generations is concerned.

In concluding this discussion of the principles of financing child welfare it should be pointed out that the insurance principle naturally could be employed quite independently of whether the in cash or the in kind method is chosen. In fact there is no logical reason why insurance benefits should accrue in cash and not in kind if the latter should be preferable for other reasons. Also, apart from the educational approach, the chief characteristic of the insurance principle as a financial norm is that it means regressive taxation. On this latter point the stand early taken by the present author and later with remarkable consistency by the Population Commission through all the detailed reform problems was simply that the benefits should be given to all children in the nation, independent of the income of the parents, and should be paid for by all citizens according to ability to pay taxes. In a democracy the implied norm of taxation is continuously judged and changed by the legislative body when deciding upon the tax structure of the nation.

It should not be inferred from this, however, that it is a matter of indifference from the population point of view how this tax structure is determined. For one thing, the great bulk of indirect taxation, particularly on foodstuffs and housing, is not only regressive taxation, burdening especially the poor strata of the nation, but also it generally has a tendency to burden quite particularly the families with children. It must, therefore, be part of a population policy to fight indirect taxation of this type. In most countries, including Sweden, family composition and particularly the burden of supporting children has not been taken sufficiently into account when regulating the relation between direct taxation and income. Modern studies of the relationship between level of living and number of children motivate much larger exemptions for children. As families with three or more children are so scarce, the larger families could, as has been shown in Sweden, be considerably relieved without great fiscal consequences. It is true that even in a country where direct taxation goes so far down the income scale as in Sweden such an increased differentiation according to burden of support would not mean much in the lower income strata. There the tax amounts are low and even moderate exemptions make them nonexistent for the large families. A reform would not mean much in the highest income strata either, if the exemptions were not made proportional or progressive. In the broad middle classes from the higher paid wage workers into the masses of professional people, however, it would mean a considerable change in the amount the family has to budget.

SOME RESERVATIONS

Returning to the main issue, it is recalled that the in kind method is more effective or less expensive. From the point of view of the quantity of the population, the policy of assistance in cash will, at least in the short view, work as the more powerful stimulus to procreation, but it unfortunately has its greatest effects upon the least desirable parents, who wish to confiscate for their own pleasures the contribution that is given for the children. With respect to the cumbersomeness of children it is still more evident that what is needed is a certain social reorganization, not cash subsidies. A choice of the *in natura* principle finally makes it possible to incorporate the population point of view into broad and variegated economic and social policies. This paramount question of the principle of cash or kind has been dwelt upon in some detail, as it has apparently been widely neglected in the literature on social policy. Clarification of the ultimate choices has to be obtained first. When the nonconformity of practical life is also considered, some modifications in the conclusions outlined above have to be made in order to arrive at a final determination of desiderata.

The first reservation is that only when a basic family income exists can there be any serious preference for services in kind instead of a cash subsidy. Nothing but a money income can be relied upon for furnishing the basic and continuous support for children, when institutionalization is not part of the picture. A cash pension for children without a family supporter thus seems to be an appropriate deviation from the principle reviewed above. It may be a direct pension when the supporter is permanently unable to contribute. It may be an advance or a loan when the supporter is only temporarily incapacitated. In the first instance money pensions for orphaned children and for children of invalid parents would be called for. In the case of illegitimate children or children of divorced parents the reasoning will follow similar lines. The justification for payments for their support is that such support has been settled by contract or by court decision, and thus the community will only have to guarantee that the income intended for the children does not fail. Advancing a basic minimum amount and then collecting it from the debtor parent should create a buffer against destitution for this large group of children. These pensions and advanced payments have to be paid in cash. Somewhat the same motivation will lead to assistance in cash in other cases of sudden loss of income. The question may be raised as to whether or not a "floor for the family" should be created by a more stable and honorable form of social aid than that of poor relief when imprisonment or desertion of the father or other causes deprive dependents of their maintenance. This aid could be instituted in the form of an advance or loan.

One specific case in which such lifesaving activity on the part of the community in providing income is especially necessary is when women are about to become mothers. Suicide, abortion, or desperation should not become realities because of the lack of the small amounts needed for the few months during which these women are deprived of their incomes. Some form of mothers' aid, as bonus or loan, must be made available for them, and again it has to be in cash in order to provide the income on which budgeting is based.

Grounds for cash subsidies when there is lack of basic income may be found in many more instances. Also, deference to private consumption choices through payments in cash must be considered.

In general the argument that liberty is infringed upon by too close supervision by the community does not carry weight. The beneficiaries of the communal goods, the children, have rarely had much voice in decisions about use of the family income. For that reason it is difficult to see how any "free will" or "free choice of consumption" is really encroached upon. The public services are given only in addition to the family budget. And, naturally, no force will be employed for compelling children to use the free services. By offering larger houses for the same rent when the family grows, a widening of choice is made possible. In some specific fields, however, caution must be exercised. This is particularly true when what is offered is not costly, but items in which choices occur frequently. Clothing falls in that category, and it thus seems to be difficult to subsidize in kind. Here personal taste is delicate and social prestige has become involved. Even if some class equalization in clothing, especially for children, is judged desirable, it would probably be extremely unwise to force any uniformity on families. Equalization could be · better achieved by other means. For these reasons community subsidy of clothing costs for children would probably only be made for some expensive items, such as shoes and overcoats, which at the same time are already fairly standardized for children.

In order to relieve the time of childbearing from all extra costs, it may seem desirable to give a subsidy for its incidental items. Again the problem of personal choice forbids a doctrinaire attitude. It would be cheap, perhaps extremely rational but still a bit inhuman, to provide layettes, bedding, and baby carriages for all newborn children. All these cost items, invested with so much tender care, are certainly not appropriate for communalization. A cash subsidy for an estimated fair minimum would be much more welcome. And as parents should not only be economically helped to have children but also helped to have them with joy, such considerations must be taken into account by any society which adopts a program for its families. It must never be forgotten that in such cases cash must be generously given and little controlled. The lack of control would constitute the advantage over direct services. Just because lack of control cannot be made the general rule in social finances, this is a reason for treating these occasions as exceptions. The fundamentals and the bulk of the population program have to be conceived of as direct social reforms.

THE THREE STAGES OF SOCIAL POLICY

A certain nationalization or even socialization of income is frankly advocated. Just as frankly there has been an endeavor to find a realm for it without disturbing the main economic structure. Instead of the theoretically traditional order of socialization, starting with key industries and financial institutions, it is here proposed to start from the consumption side. It is proposed to investigate how much socialization in the field of production and distribution of goods and services exclusively for children's consumption would be possible and desirable without any argument either for or against extending it to the ordinary spheres of business enterprise.

Such a reform policy would follow the path of consumers' cooperation. While nationalization from the production side is difficult, nationalization from the consumption side is easy and much better prepared for by previous developments in economic organization. Cooperation has from the beginning taken its point of departure in human needs, thus in a way representing a more truly socialistic method of reform than orthodox socialism itself. The economic strength of cooperation has likewise been that its activity was based on organized consumption and entrenched in industry only on this basis. It thus avoided practically all the risks that private business has to carry. What is needed in social policy is less interest in philosophizing about power over production, which is a complicated problem, and more interest in increasing control from the consumption side, which is a comparatively easy task for competent social engineering.

Cooperation, finally, may be the key word for this social policy in a deeper sense because it rests fundamentally on social solidarity, on pooling of resources for common aims, wider in their loyalty than just insurance of individual interest. If children shall continue to be born and if they shall be reared according to standards that our democratic culture can be proud of, the competitive and destructive society of yesterday must yield to a society of solidarity. A new era in social policy will then dawn, a century of child care and family security. It has already been said that this would imply a strengthening of the protective tendency in social policy. In fact, it would mean the transition to a whole new social philosophy, a philosophy that has

by the impact of progress itself been maturing, and maturing more quickly
in Sweden than perhaps anywhere else.

Social reform policies may be conceived of as passing through three stages:
a paternalistic conservative era, when curing the worst ills is enough; a
liberal era, when safeguarding against inequalities through pooling the risks
is enough; and a social democratic era, when preventing the ills is attempted.
The first was the period of curative social policy through private charity and
public poor relief; the second was the period of social insurance broad in
scope but yet merely symptomatic; and the third may be called the period
of protective and cooperative social policy. Some phases of all these types may
be found incidentally during each of the different epochs. The schematiza-
tion is true only on broad lines.

Per se it is nothing new that social policy is aimed at the prevention of
distress instead of merely at its cure. The curative needs will necessarily present themselves with first urgency — caring for the poor, the sick, the unemployed, the aged and invalid, the inebriate and psychopathic, criminals,
and prostitutes. Even in economically and socially less progressive epochs it
was felt that society must succor the indigent. Only when a bulwark was
built against destitution could planning for the alleviation of social ills be
conceived. Noninterference of society was the principal rule in the later
liberalistic stage but "help to help oneself" was admittedly a necessity. Pooling the risks through social insurance schemes was thought to achieve just
that end. Workmen's compensation, sickness insurance, old-age insurance,
and unemployment insurance were then conceived and enacted into law.
They were most often constructed so as to be paid for by individual contributions, i.e., the insurance illusion tended to conceal the fact that the weak
and poor themselves carry the heavier part of the burden. Such a solution
seemed to be the only one appropriate to the political situation of the late
liberal era. In Sweden this period, which covered the first twenty-five years
of the present century, had to about reach its completion before the field of
vision could be cleared for still more long-range planning.

In the new era the scope of social policy will be widened to include general
social solicitude for all human beings, not only for the indigent. This social
policy will consist of cooperation in carrying through planned changes that
are greater than the spheres of action of single individuals. This social policy
will be productive. The cost will, contrary to that of relief, take on the character of an investment, an investment in the health and efficiency of the
young. This investment in human capital may be as productive as, or more
productive than, investments in land, factories, and machinery. To the
motives of charity and of justice, already operating before, will thus be added
an economic interest. It may require a long time to balance such a national
investment budget but nevertheless the costs of social reforms must cease to

be regarded only as unproductive expenses. They are the outlays for a productive social consumption, which in time will raise the standards of the nation's efficiency and earnings. This also is basic to public finances.

The financial costs of a protective policy will in time decrease the curative costs that society now has to meet. To the extent that this protective social policy is directed toward housing, nutrition, and so forth, it may also become rationally incorporated into general economic policy, especially in the agricultural, unemployment, and business cycle policies. Production for children may in many instances take care of production surpluses and be utilized as a reservoir for public work, timed so as to stabilize the national economy. If planned with consideration of both needs and resources, a population policy might be utilized as a "production for consumption" guide. It will help the underconsumer to meet the overproducer. The underconsumers are most generally the children. Economic development toward industrialism has tended to make the children unprovided for. The historical opportunity for society to find its full scope for planning action seems to be exactly in this field of children's consumption. The financial taboos about nonintervention have to be broken; their irrationality from the point of view of a society planning for its coming population is too transparent. Even if public opinion is not ready for such a revolutionary change in attitudes, clarity of thought as to what social policy is and what it could achieve should result in at least some steps in the right direction instead of petty reforms which will be stumbling blocks in the way of the greater future reforms which are inevitable.

PART II
PROVISIONS IN SWEDEN

CHAPTER X

OFFICIAL PROGRAMS AND LEGISLATIVE ACTS

THE new and imperative problem of population and family was presented to the Swedish people in the fall of 1934 in the framework of ideas set forth in preceding chapters. It was immediately grasped and discussed as a problem with the dimensions and content of a new social policy. From the beginning the discussion took cognizance of the magnitude of the changes involved, of the many different aspects of life that had to be harmonized, and of the need for conscious planning to supersede the automatic adjustments relied upon in the past. There was enough factual knowledge about demographic trends, especially about the prospects of impending decline in population, to give reality to the question whether something needed to be done. Less complete data, but still enough to make the challenge to social action concrete, had been compiled to show the effect which childbearing, even at a level below that required for stabilizing population, had on the plane of living of those families which had the children. It became public knowledge that the poverty of many Swedish families was due primarily to the fact that there were children in those families. Consequently, poverty was selective, and it particularly affected children.

The people realized vaguely that any remedial program must be revolutionary in scope. While emotional reactions to the situation and practical suggestions for reform may have been divergent, there was national agreement that population problems must be placed at the top of society's agenda. When the Swedish Riksdag opened in January, 1935, all the political parties were ready to declare their concern.[1] The Conservatives signed a party motion, significantly the first of the year's session in both parliamentary chambers. It opens with a solemn reminder:

No sooner have the relief cares of mass unemployment become lighter as a result of business recovery, and consequently the political tension about employment remedies relaxed, than a crisis of infinitely greater scope demands an answer from the Swedish people: namely, the population question.

[1] See records of the Riksdag for 1935.

The motion goes on to describe the factual situation and then gives an interpretation of the national crisis.

Against the background of the above facts the population question appears as the most important question of our day. It is not like others, just one question among many; it is the very frame for a multitude of social problems of great urgency. With it is connected the whole problem of national economy; it affects all problems of production and distribution; upon it depends the possibility of utilizing our country's natural resources, of maintaining our culture and our national integrity. The population question is literally a question of the life of the Swedish people.

More tragic than anything is the fact that in this whole field of population policy the most profound contradictions appear between what we, on the one hand, have been willing to do, and what, on the other hand, we seem to find we can just as obviously omit doing. For the children who are permitted to come into this world, our community will provide educational institutions which are generally recognized as being of high quality. The aged, the infirm, and the dependent we care for in such a manner as to arouse the recognition of foreign observers. None is allowed to suffer from want or privation with the knowledge or consent of communal or state authorities. Medical science tries its utmost to keep alive a flickering life flame. All this seems natural and is accepted in a society with an old Christian tradition like our own. But we go further in our concern for the future: modern society not only assumes responsibility for the people's own welfare and happiness, but it also furnishes prudent advice and diligent care as to how the material resources shall best be preserved. We consult as to the best means of preventing soil wastage or utilization of other resources of nature. We try to save for posterity the living capital in our forests, so valuable for the maintenance of our people, through forestry laws which forbid excessive cutting and provide for reforestation. It is only for its own renewal that this same Swedish people fails to provide. In so far as this failure is caused by selfish motives of individuals, it shows a way of life which is in no way unique in history, but wherever it has appeared earlier, it foreboded retrogression for the people themselves and the culture which they made flourish. Here, if ever, it can truly be said that the lessons of history are frightening.

The Conservative party therefore declares its willingness to support reforms, which naturally enough bear the special coloring of its attitudes.

Furthermore, these serious questions must always be judged from the life philosophy of Christian ethics in which Swedish legal principles and social institutions are fundamentally grounded. The chances of influencing the development of the population problem through direct socio-political measures on the part of the community are undoubtedly very limited. The knowledge of this, however, should not deter us from conscientiously following any suggestions along this line. . . . The national and social ideals of the Conservative party make it our duty to cooperate with such a policy without, at the same time, surrendering our principle that the greatest social resource consists in the responsibility individuals themselves are assuming.

An inventory of possible reforms is then given which almost coincides with the ones presented by opposing ideological groups at the opening of the whole population discussion. Greater stress is, however, laid on reforms in taxation, on developing single-family homes as the solution of the housing problem, on new colonization and greater security for the farming population, and on domestic training for girls. Economic reforms, on the other hand, are less explicitly encouraged, advocacy being in inverse relationship to expense. Still, considerable advances are envisaged; for instance, in relation to maternity bonuses and delivery care. Birth control is spoken of evasively. A definite change in opinion is indicated in the treatment of married women's right to work.

It is just as apparent that this problem is not solved by more or less restrictive regulations concerning married women's right to gainful employment. It seems rather more appropriate to believe that the chief aim will be better advanced through giving self-supporting women greater security in their employment relations.

This proclamation was immediately followed by a similar one from leaders of the liberal middle party (*Folkpartiet*). The most remarkable feature of this proclamation was that the practical consequence of all this anxiety, namely, having to make an economic redistribution in favor of children, was explicitly realized.

In the discussion of the population question a series of measures has been recommended which might contribute to increasing the birth rate by decreasing the economic burden connected with the birth of children, their education and support. Such proposals are founded on the *principle of equalizing the economic costs of childbearing*. If the extra expense in the family budget entailed by childbearing can be decreased, one of the most important factors leading to family limitation would be eliminated. A systematic survey of all practical possibilities in such a direction should be undertaken. It is, in fact, a main feature of a positive population policy that the costs of childbearing, and thus also the costs for the maintenance of the population stock, should not fall entirely upon the parents but should be shared by all alike.

To effect an increase in fertility or not literally means life or death for our people. It is only necessary to imagine for a moment what continuous depopulation would mean in order to understand that we should not hesitate in the adoption of radical social reforms if there is reason to suppose that they would considerably increase fertility and contribute toward the improvement of mental and physical growth conditions for our children, so that they might become good citizens. There is considerable unanimity in this respect in all political quarters. For our part, we have wanted to declare our point of view and our willingness to cooperate for the achievement of positive results.

Substantially the same position was taken by the National party of the extreme right (*De Nationalla*), insignificant in itself, since it then had only three members in the Riksdag and now has none, but interesting because it reveals the most drastic shift. There is a declaration in favor of legal security for married women in the labor market by the same party, even by the same man, who had during the previous session of the Riksdag presented a motion in exactly the opposite direction.

In so far as a married woman is employed she considers herself in many instances prohibited from bearing children. Many times she risks losing her position because in most cases she is not irreplaceable. It has also occasionally happened that an employer has summarily dismissed an employed married woman when she became pregnant in order to avoid the inconveniences resulting from interruption of her services.

It is in our opinion both proper and possible to give recourse to legal action against these abuses. There is already a law which forbids the discharge of an employee in certain cases, namely, for military service . . . and, as far as we know, no inconveniences have been suffered from this law. A law providing for prohibition of discharging married prospective mothers would not, according to our lights, meet any obstacles in principle. . . . It is the public duty to protect and shield maternity in every possible way. It would thus be an important step for the state to provide that the married woman, who wants to assume the obligations of motherhood, should not thereby risk the destruction, perhaps complete, of her whole economic existence.

Simultaneously with these party motions came the first expression of attitude on the part of any official body. The Committee on Social Housing (on which were some of the experts who had been most influential in arousing social concern about the family and population situation) dwelt at some length on "the serious demographic status of our country" in its report published in January, 1935. [18] "It must be stressed," the report points out, "that for any population policy just the next few decades furnish the respite. We are then still going to enjoy the numbers of persons in the productive, both in an economical and in a biological sense, middle ages born during times of greater fertility. If social measures are instituted during that critical period, they might, if successful, serve to maintain the very conditions, both demographic and economic, for the continuance of such a social population policy in the future." Economic reforms to help the families with children were brought to the forefront and complete redirection of public housing schemes toward families with children was advocated.

In the Riksdag the population question received much attention. The Standing Committee unanimously supported the demand for research and planning. The Riksdag itself voted in favor of this and declared that "the Riksdag wants forcefully to stress the necessity of a positive population policy by the state." The immediate result was a request that the Cabinet appoint such a study and planning commission, and on May 17, 1935, the Population Commission was appointed.

MANDATE FOR THE POPULATION COMMISSION

As the Social Democratic Labor party was in power and as the revival of the population discussion had emanated from Social Democratic groups, there had been no necessity to demonstrate its opinion by any party motion in the Riksdag. This opinion was vigorously summed up, however, in the mandate to the Commission prepared by the Minister of Social Affairs:

No people with unimpaired energy and the will to live can observe such a tendency toward its own decline as is now obvious in this country and at the same time fail to undertake strong measures to combat the situation. First of all, measures will have to be instituted to encourage marriage, particularly in the younger age groups, and the bearing of children. Through wise diffusion of information, a feeling of responsibility for our people's future and welfare may be awakened in all social classes. But no matter how important this may be, the need of a large amount of socio-political intervention in order to create economic security and to improve the material welfare of our people must be frankly faced. It will be necessary to weigh different alternatives for attaining a state in which children will not be a pressing economic burden on the parents to the same extent as at present. These measures must, therefore, provide for decreasing the individual family expenses for rearing, educating, and supporting the children. The more favorable environmental conditions thereby achieved will contribute to the healthy growth of children and young people and lead to a better utilization of our human material.

After thus briefly outlining the main purposes which stand out for the investigation as demanded by the Riksdag, which investigation should be begun without further delay, I want to dwell upon some of the basic practical questions which must be considered for the achievement of our purposes.

Especially important from an ideological point of view is a comprehensive and truly vigorous educational campaign to clarify aims as well as means regarding the population question. It should be considered axiomatic that the sociological, eugenic, and ethical arguments for and against encouragement of child-bearing under different circumstances be duly presented. As our social conscience protests, however, that economically weak homes should not be burdened by too many children, and that the physically or mentally unfit should not be encouraged to reproduce, such matters must not be neglected in the projected program of public instruction.

The list of social family reforms is of particular interest, as it outlined the reform proposals that were to be expected from the Commission.

Among the socio-political measures which have been proposed during the recent lively debate, and which are of more immediate practicality for the maintenance of the population, quantitatively and qualitatively, it has been suggested that taxes on married persons and on large families should be alleviated. . . .

Consideration must also be given to widening the possibilities for the care and education of children during the part of the day when the mother is gainfully employed outside the home. . . . The raising of a family is now further being discouraged when, as so often happens, an employer refuses to continue the employment of a woman upon marriage or when she becomes pregnant. . . . Ways and means of furnishing public loans or subsidies for homemaking and thus for founding a family at an earlier age should also be considered. The question of furthering the same purpose through planned and organized savings and the possibility of giving increased public aid to invalid persons or to single mothers who are the chief support of minor children are obviously steps in the same direction.

In order to ameliorate the position of mothers we have first to continue along the same road the state has already entered upon through maternal welfare measures. This will mean demands for a more effective expansion of that scheme for support and at the same time increased and improved social resources for maternal as well as for infant care.

As far as the obligatory school ages are concerned, there is reason to inquire to what extent and by what means individual educational expenses can further be decreased. In this connection, the questions of furnishing free school supplies and free school meals should be given particular attention. It also seems to me important in this same connection to develop measures for providing children and young people with efficient and rational medical care, utilizing such schemes as have proved successful both in some foreign countries and in certain endeavors in our own country.

In order to secure employment for the young people, present experience teaches that occupational training is most important. . . . The public has probably not sufficiently realized this circumstance. If the necessary means for training had existed earlier, unemployment in the younger age groups could probably have been decreased more rapidly during the present upturn of economic conditions. Under such circumstances it becomes an important duty to provide opportunity for all young people in town and country to acquire definite training in order to ensure their own economic support in the future.

It is evident that a positive population policy along the lines indicated presupposes that huge public measures be undertaken in order to guarantee the general living standard of the people at a desired level, even when children increase the size of the family. As far as housing is concerned, the point of view of simultaneously guaranteeing consumption and creating employment by encouraging specific production of family houses has gained consideration from the state for some time and especially during the recent crisis. But neither should, in my opinion, the problems of food and clothing for children be neglected, highly important as they are in the family budget.

No matter how praiseworthy specific measures may be in the different fields, no practical results can be expected without comprehensive planning embracing all forms of assistance from the community to the family. Seen from this angle, the problem becomes so wide as to include the whole task of creating economic security for the adults and proper growth opportunities for the young among our people as a whole.

The Population Commission, given this mandate to investigate the problem and construct a program, was composed of nine members, the chairman being a highly placed administrator, a politician of Conservative affiliations, and a former professor of statistics. The others were a professor of economics, who was also a member of the Riksdag; a professor of statistics; a professor of hereditary biology; a woman doctor; three members of the Riksdag representing the Conservatives, Liberals, and Social Democrats, the first being a farmer, the second a newspaper editor, and the third a factory worker; and finally the leader of the Social Democratic women's organization. For each special problem a committee of experts and representatives of various organizations and interests was set up with a member of the Population Committee serving as chairman.

In Sweden the usual procedure of such committees is to prepare reforms and propose them to the government in the form of printed publications. Then the proposals are sent out to administrations and local governments and to civic agencies and interested organizations in order to get their signed opinions. In case a change in civil or criminal law is involved, a vote on the legal aspects of the proposal has to be taken by the Supreme Legislative Council, an advisory body of high-ranking lawyers. If and when the Cabinet finally wants to submit the proposal, changed or unchanged, to the Riksdag, it has to take these opinions into consideration and publicly accept or refute them. As soon as they are delivered, these opinions become official documents and are eagerly seized upon by the press, which then widely publicizes the technical arguments on both sides of the questions. The Swedish press not only treats social questions as news but also by sustained discussion, by interviewing people, and by organizing feature articles on the various subjects it serves as an educational vehicle of tremendous importance. A large reading public is alert to these discussions. The whole training of the people in adult education and their participation in civic organizations prepare them to regard questions of social and economic policy as something more than politics. Reforms are thus not only prepared through a laborious and careful administrative process but also analyzed in detail through the critical study by the press and the people. All interested organized bodies express their views. They may in a sense be called pressure groups but their pressure is regulated and exerted in the open. It is fundamentally pressure on public opinion and its ultimate appeal is to reason.

THE COMMISSION AT WORK

The first step of the new Commission was to propose an extra census, to be taken at the end of the year 1935, between the regular censuses of 1930 and 1940. The Cabinet without delay sent this proposal as its own to the Riksdag where the proposition was carried without any opposition.

The first report of the Commission was issued in the fall of 1935,[2] proposing a change in the status of married women in civil service positions so that the bearing of children would be facilitated by allowing women leave of absence with more generous pay. [1] Taking the point of view that the state should act as a model employer and thus be a leader in humanizing labor conditions, the Commission made the proposals with the hope that they would influence public attitudes and thus prepare for the time when more thoroughgoing reforms for harmonizing women's work with motherhood could be proposed.

In 1935 also a most important step was taken toward reducing the housing costs of families. It was initiated not by the Population Commission but by the Committee on Social Housing. [18] Proposals for public housing schemes for families with three or more children and state grants for rent reduction according to size of family were published at the time the Riksdag convened. As may be deduced from what has been related above about party consensus, the Riksdag was ready to act favorably. The new housing bill (1935) was the first result of the new orientation with regard to population policy.

Early in 1936, the Population Commission presented additional installments of its plan, proposing free delivery care for all women, [2] state organization of maternity and infant clinics, a maternity bonus to all women at the birth of children, and special maternity aid to destitute women as an emergency measure. [5] In the same year the Commission proposed state marriage loans combined with a system of planned voluntary saving. [4] It further elaborated a scheme for the reorganization of state and local income taxation, aiming at considerable tax exemptions for families with children. [3]

In the waves of rising and falling public sympathy which were likely to surround such a complex question as that of population, the latter scheme caused a temporary setback. Touching practically everybody in his everyday life, as direct taxation affects extremely low-income levels in Sweden, it aroused the antagonism of the bachelors and the childless people who would have to meet an increase in taxation while others were enjoying a decrease. And it should be pointed out that the bachelors and the childless are in the majority. So egotistically direct is the formation of opinion in regard to taxation that from the publicly asserted opinions one could practically determine the family status of the speaker. An unfortunate similarity to the punishment taxes levied on bachelors in dictator countries accounted for the most severe attacks by columnists, actors, and others. Even if such public ridicule helped to kill one or two of the specific proposals, it should not be

---

[2] A brief chronological survey of the reports is given here, as the treatment under separate headings of these and related proposals in the following chapters may not indicate the close integration of the various phases of the Commission's work.

inferred that it was altogether unwholesome. The treatment of population problems even in these forms of publicity, year after year, served the purpose of keeping popular interest alert to the fact that here was Public Problem No. 1.

Another such reaction occurred in connection with the extra census, which shows how varied public opinion is when the complex-ridden questions of sex and family are involved. The extra census of 1935–1936 was requested in order to secure definite answers to some specific questions rarely included in the regular census: size of family, women's work, etc. The chief novelty, however, was the proposal to send enumerators to collect the census returns, filled by every fifth household, and to amplify these written answers by oral statements. The Swedish census, inaugurated in 1749, has consisted only of a balance sheet prepared from material already in the official registers as a result of the continuous, compulsory registration that has been in force since 1686. The most violent criticism was aroused by this change in administrative detail, which provided for visits to the homes by enumerators. Accusations of "invasion of privacy," "violation of domicile," and similar affronts filled the newspapers, and it was intimated that this was Nazism, communism, or something even worse. Exactly the same results are feared in countries where the enumerators are part of the customary census system, while the inauguration of a registration is thought to imply "regimentation" and "intrusion upon civic liberty." This incident is an example of the problems associated with a thoroughgoing democracy, such as Sweden. When something happens in their social sphere, all have to take their stand and articulate their attitudes. The educative process of purging public opinion of rash sentiments by referring all issues to discussion and reason requires considerable time. New experiments are therefore likely to require more educational preparation and to result in more gradual realization than in other political systems. Such things may contribute to an understanding of why the Scandinavian countries, although so uncompromisingly on their way to quite a radical social system, proceed with such conservative caution as to methods and tempo.

In 1936–1937 the Population Commission broached a new phase of its gigantic problem, proposing a thorough revision of antiquated legislation on sexual problems. This implied considerable liberalization of laws on contraception, [7] abortion, [9] sex education, [8] and sterilization. [6] In order to lay the groundwork for family reforms by public honesty on sexual matters, occasion was taken for a comprehensive discussion of principles. The Report on the Sexual Question is to be considered as the main ideological discussion of the Commission. It stresses the necessity of universal access to birth control techniques and to sex education. Curiously enough, the atmosphere was again completely calm and sympathetic.

Soon after the publication of these new reports, the proposals contained in the previous ones were carried by the Cabinet to the Riksdag. A delay of a year is practically always to be expected as a result of the procedure described above. The proposals were all favorably accepted. Some related schemes for children's pensions and state-advanced support were also carried on the tide of public opinion. So decidedly was the social program of population policy accepted and so free from opposition were the major reforms enacted that this session has been called the "Riksdag of Mothers and Children."

In 1938 most of the previous year's proposals for sex legislation bore fruit in actual reforms enacted by the Riksdag. At the same time a new series of reports from the Commission was published. At the very beginning of the year came proposals for a social policy with regard to nutrition [10] and to clothing for children. [11] Especially in the field of nutrition a far-reaching economic program was envisaged. It involved heavy expenses, as food is such a large item in the family budget. Although the new reforms to a considerable extent implied only the transfer of already instituted subsidies to agriculture, replacing export premiums by state purchases of surplus products, they had the power again to arouse public discussion. The apparent adding of tens of millions to the expenditures for a whole series of reforms already enacted, or at least authoritatively sanctioned in the name of population policy for later enactment, caused the public once more to react unfavorably. In the adverse publicity campaign which followed, the school meal was particularly singled out for ridicule. But again the agitation died down. Moreover, the school luncheon is now partly realized in the new social ventures on which the country prides itself.

The latter part of 1938 saw the publication of various residual proposals. Two of these sought to build on reforms already provided for: legal protection for women against being dismissed when marrying or giving birth to children, legitimate or not, [12] and subsidies for nursery education. [15] They were received without great stir. There further appeared a set of more fundamental research findings about depopulation of rural areas, [13] some specific demographic studies in differential fertility, [16] and a report on the ethical implications of the population problem. [14] Then, at the end of 1938, the final report appeared, [17] embodying the working compromise at which the members of the Commission had arrived.

The unanimity of the highly varied group of Population Commission members had been considerable. In itself it testifies that here was a problem view as a national concern above politics and party quarrels, with a considerable consensus as to how it should be tackled. Differences of opinion arose only in some of the later instances, namely, in regard to the projects on nutrition, clothing, married women, and nursery education. The Conservative party representative published his different views on these topics, and in the case of the proposals with regard to married women he was supported by the representatives of the Liberal party and of the Employers' Association. The strength of the process of clarification within the voting mass through widespread public discussion and appeals to rationalism may be concluded from the fact that the people voiced no opposition to the certainly quite radical revisions of attitudes and laws concerning sexual problems. With regard to the later financially expensive proposals, however, unification of opinion was more difficult to obtain. That the radical intentions of the Population Commission in general obtained a victory over the conservatives was certainly an important turn of affairs. The explanation is not only that the people as a whole had moved in that direction but also that the radical members always carried the strategic positions simply because in the whole population discussion it was the radical side that formulated goals and programs. The conservative ideology was on the defensive and thus, when forced to reason things through at the conference table, either conceded the point or stalled in a dilemma.

The reactions of the general public to the work of the Population Commission are also interesting. Apparently there was fear on the part of the public of the large-scale changes proposed but also respect for the scope and coherence of the program and a realization that the reports constitute a storehouse from which blueprints for future reforms can be drawn.

BASIC PRINCIPLES ENDORSED BY THE COMMISSION

The general attitudes underlying the work of the Population Commission may be summarized at some length as they illuminate the factual and detailed description to follow. With respect to the interrelation of social and individual aspects of the population problem, the Commission took the following position:

The population question has been taken up for official investigation as a problem of social prominence. By so doing it is principally recognized that the changes within the sexual life of individuals, which have caused a problem to arise for society, do not concern the individuals alone in the sense that society remains indifferent as to what happens in this field. Still these conditions are of fundamental importance in the life happiness of individuals.

It is the opinion of the Population Commission that the latter consideration must be given primary weight in democratic cultures of the Western world. But at the same time it is also the opinion of the Commission that in this field social and individual interests are not antagonistic but converging. The Commission is not of the opinion that individual interests in and of themselves can be expected infallibly to lead to individually and socially satisfactory progress but believe that human attitudes and the social order could and should be so altered as to lead to individual and social harmony. The measures that should be undertaken to assure such harmony must obviously, as far as individuals are concerned, work through better instruction and education and as far as the community is concerned, through certain radically extensive changes of that society itself, particularly in its economic relations. [8]

Fixing the goal for society's interest in a population policy is, however, strictly limited by social facts themselves. Thus the possibility of an increasing population had to be discarded from the beginning.

A population increasing in the long run — even if this were considered desirable by anyone — has been assumed to be so far outside the realm of practical possibility that this alternative is not considered worthy of further discussion. [17]

The quantitative goal for the new population policy thus was formulated as follows:

The goal for Swedish population development should, according to the opinion of the Population Commission, be such a fertility as would keep population in the long run at least constant with as low mortality as possible. [17]

There are numerous reasons for choosing this goal: popular attitudes of a vague emotional character implying direct valuations, international considerations, economic advantages, and psychological implications. The Commission took account of these as follows:

Popular attitudes concerning population decline
The Commission wants to remark that this conclusion as to the quantitative goal arrived at through intellectual reflection — through a social evaluation built upon as rational a knowledge of causes and effects as possible — corresponds exactly to the immediate feeling that a citizen normally experiences when he becomes cognizant of the existing tendency in Swedish population development. This immediate attitude is founded upon the citizen's natural feeling that he is a member of a people which, unlike himself, lives through generations.

International implications
The detailed effects as to international relations are hardly possible to anticipate. . . . If Sweden is looked upon as part of a greater international body, it is evident that if the country cannot solve its own population problem, it will have decreasing possibilities of acting as an influence for peace and social culture, a role that for many reasons seems to be given us and our neighbors. . . . Looking to ourselves, it becomes just as evident that a country with a declining population will not in the long run be able to erect bars against other national groups seeking a new home or resist the pressure from more crowded countries. To a certain extent it is not desirable that such bars be erected. Immigration to our country should by and large not be considered as harmful but oftentimes rather as advantageous. Even without considering our own interests we must for the present recognize our duties to alleviate the political distress and the homelessness of

large groups. But with mass immigration imminent, there would follow certain problems which must not be concealed. The smaller our own part in the new generations becomes, the less will our culture be the dominant one.

Economic implications

Certain economic effects, dynamic in character, are apt to follow the shrinkage in population. A more regressive population development must in the somewhat longer run increase the risks of losses of investments. Also in other ways capital investments would become depressed. The result in general is to be foreseen as a slowing up of economic progress.

Basic for the still greater economic effects to appear after the present transition period, when persons in the middle-aged groups are excessive in number, will be the predominance of aged persons needing support, which characterizes a shrinking population while the predominance of young or young middle-aged persons has been typical of our society in its expansive phase.

Psychological implications

The age composition of a people, however, has also other, although much more evasive, effects. The psychological differences between the generations must show their effect not only on economic but also on political behavior and on the general atmosphere in our culture.

When passing judgment on this question it would be wrong to underevaluate the importance of the calm deliberation, the discriminating caution, and the greater practical experience which accompany aging. But already the age composition prevalent in a stationary population would give full assurance of a sufficient predominance of the age groups which possess these valuable traits in highest degree. The age composition in a declining population would on the contrary constitute a real danger that in the life of the nation there would be lacking those traits, which before all belong to youth: courage, will to sacrifice, initiative, creative imagination. [*17*]

With respect to the undesirable effects of a shrinking population as compared with a constant population there is the final point that the family itself tends to become built up in small units. All the psychologically and sociologically ascertainable relations seem to indicate that if what is commonly called family values are to persist as values, they must be related to a fairly complete family. The Population Commission asserts that three or four children in a family would lead to more harmony and happiness than is now found either in the very small or in the very large family, the assumption being that social and economic stress should not, as now, have to be regarded. Thus individual interests seem to be fairly well reconcilable with social interests in the goals for a population policy.

Constancy of population thus would best be realized in a much wider distribution of middle-sized families, the two extremes becoming less frequent. Determined more exactly in terms of individual family size this aim requires the following:

The number of childless and child-poor marriages with 1 or 2 children must be decreased from one-half of all marriages to about one-third. The majority of the remaining marriages must have not 3 but 4 children. Despite this, 5 children must be born in a small number of marriages, if the proportion of married in the adult population cannot be increased.

Through special investigations by the Population Commission it has thus been demonstrated that not only the so-called 2-child system but also a 3-child norm is irreconcilable with the aim of keeping population constant. This means in practical terms that the nonsterile family must aim at producing more than 3 children. [8]

When family size is spoken of in such rationalistic terms, it becomes evident that the Population Commission was sanctioning birth control at the same time that it was deploring its excess. The latter part of the double postulate needed no further development and was not dealt with at any great length save for the statistical calculation of distribution of children per family under different assumptions of fertility. The former position was the more difficult one to get into verbalized public opinion and so became one of the fundamental contributions of the Commission. As instances are rare in which official bodies take a clear stand in defense of revised sex attitudes, some verbatim quotations may be given:

Taking the long view, the solution of the population problem must be sought in the birth of normally large numbers of children by couples in all social classes. If it is desired to apply any scheme of public education to more positive family attitudes and at the same time to afford space to important social improvements for children . . . it is necessary that *the starting point be the principle of voluntary parenthood, conscious of responsibility for one's own and others' welfare.*

The first necessity was to bring into the open the whole complex of social questions which have long been taboo because of their connection with individual sex problems.

The Commission notes that it is particularly important that sexual problems be discussed more sincerely and from a more practical standpoint in civic discussions than has been the case up to now. It is especially true that the question as to the extent and valuation of consciously practiced birth control has not usually been discussed with the frankness and seriousness that it warrants.

The Commission feels that in the future this problem should not be avoided through evasive and generalized terms. The lack of honesty which has characterized the publicly sustained and especially the official attitude is not the least danger to the morality of our people. The Commission has seen, to be sure, particularly on the part of youth a beginning of a tendency toward greater frankness and seriousness in the discussion of this question as in the discussion of sex problems in general. But this trend toward a better state of public opinion has not yet fully percolated through the population in general. [8]

The public sanction of birth control in positive terms was one of the most urgent tasks for the Population Commission.

The level of fertility existing at present in Sweden testifies that birth control is being practiced in the vast majority of cases inside marriage and in extra-marital relations of a common-law marriage type. It is self-evident that birth control is also used in most other sex relations, such as promiscuous extramarital intercourse. In the majority of cases the method is one of prevention of conception, that being the connotation in which the term birth control is used here thus excluding abortion as a means for limitation of births.

On rationalization in sex attitudes the Commission took the following position:

The direct reason for the fall in the birth rate has been shown to be principally the more and more extensive and intensified birth control consciously practiced within the greater part of the population. The population crisis is, therefore, caused by a change on the part of the individuals themselves in their attitude toward procreation. This change is usually expressed in the following way: Sex life used to be without deliberation as to procreation, whereas at present sex life has entered the area of intellectually governed life in that intercourse is accompanied by deliberation and a decision as to whether procreation is intended or not. As far as bearing of children is concerned, sex life has become rationalized.

When this judgment is passed it ought to be emphasized, in order to avoid misunderstanding, that sex life already had been rationalized to a great extent by having individuals arrange it within a monogamic, durable, and personal union. When sexual relations in the order of marriage have been sanctioned by society, there is not only an acceptance but also an approval of and demand for some such rationalization of sex life. From a general cultural standpoint, the sexual urge may carry great possibilities of happiness for individuals, but only if it is to a certain extent exercised according to mores within the society and according to moral norms upheld by the people. Sexual impulses, totally unrestrained by volitional forces, will, on the contrary, become judged by society as hostile to life and happiness. One of the hardest problems of human life is to strike the right balance between instinct and culture. The spread of consciously practiced birth control during the last two generations as here discussed thus implies a growing rationalization of sex life only in so far as the relationship between sex intercourse and reproduction is concerned.

Notice, however, should be taken of the fact that this conception of the historical development has only relative validity. There are reasons for supposing that birth control was consciously practiced in other periods before the recent fall in the birth rate. The change is a quantitative one. Birth control as such is not new, but it is being used by more and more individuals and more and more intensively.

From the point of view of the principle involved the following consideration is important: In the olden days sex intercourse may have been just as rationally considered as far as reproduction was concerned as it is today, but in this rational process the reasons against childbearing may not have been so strong or may not have been considered so strong as to exercise an influence on fertility. During the last century, with rapidly proceeding industrialization and the migration from agricultural occupations to industrial occupations, together with urbanization generally, on the one hand, and with the general increase in the standard of living and culture and raised demands in child welfare, on the other hand, children have become less valuable in the productive process or in the household. At the same time, the costs of bringing up and educating children falling upon the individual family have been considerably increased. The basis for what was rational thus was a different one.

As far as the judging of such a rationalization of the sex life in its relation to reproduction is concerned, many viewpoints may be considered, but, according to the opinion of the Commission any one-sided view runs the danger of being superficial.

On the one hand, we have to realize that the reduced fertility up to a certain point has had consequences which must be regarded as beneficial. Large families, especially in the poorer classes, had to endure need and privation. The parents often had to neglect the care and the education of the children. Food and proper housing were often lacking. Physical and mental health of mothers and children suffered. Thus a check in infant mortality came chiefly through intentionally decreasing the number of children born. Through the conscious practice of birth control it has further become possible to space the birth of children in such a way as to promote the health and growth of the children themselves, the strength of the mother, and the welfare of the whole family. If this conscious birth control is practiced in the proper way and to the proper extent, it may be considered as veritable cultural progress for many reasons, some of which are suggested.

On the other hand, grave anxiety is found in many quarters as to whether a people which has generally placed reproduction under the reign of calculating reason can survive through the ages. In so far as we feel that a people's continued survival is of value, we must fear that birth control would be harmful and should thus be condemned as dangerous to life in its innermost sense. In our work for creating a better society in the future through wisdom, work, and sacrifice, we all count upon the survival of our nation. Otherwise our efforts, except the narrowest egotistical ones, would be wasted.

The risk is that immediate needs be considered so pressing as not to permit enough births to reproduce the living generation in the next generation. It cannot be denied that the trend now present points in exactly this direction. But the question which should be further posed is whether this consequence of the rationalization of reproduction is really necessary or whether it is not due to socially and individually faulty adjustment, which in turn may be partly due to a passing reaction . . . against earlier conditions. The extreme limitation of the birth rate which now threatens the people's very existence is, however, in the long run certainly a ground for less and not more happiness within the families, that is, if there need not be sufficient reasons for such a limitation. [8]

The Commission then discussed the need for coupling educational and economic measures in reforming society for the benefit of children.

This means that the tendency itself could be reversed if certain economic and social reforms could be instituted partly to decrease the existing reasons for extreme limitation in individual families and partly to enlighten people as to their own real interests and to give them a healthier and more positive attitude toward the family. All of our population policies strive, in the last analysis, toward measures along these two lines.

These two types of remedial means will be followed in their many ramifications. The Population Commission realized the importance of relating them not only as parallel influences working in the same direction but also as mutually insuring each other. Only economic reforms could make it defensible to encourage the morale of the middle-sized family through education, and only education could prepare the political soil for obtaining social reforms.

An important observation is the following: In the lower population strata, where young people have experienced at close quarters the effects of very large families, and where they have thought, rightly or wrongly, that attempts have been made through the anticontraceptive law and other measures with corresponding aims to keep the lower social classes in ignorance of reliable preventive methods no longer prevalent in the higher social classes, great mistrust has been entertained toward all social population policy. Only when the whole of this field has been swept clean; when the rightfulness of birth control has been openly recognized in different political, ideological, and religious quarters; when in connection therewith the reliability of the applied technique itself has been recognized as a public health concern; when all efforts to hinder sound education on this subject have been liquidated; and when the trade in contraceptives has been brought into the open will a true groundwork have been created among the young people in all social classes for a new, sincerely endorsed, positive attitude toward a population policy, which is of so vital importance for both family and people. [8]

When all of its work was concluded, the Population Commission prepared a Final Report. In order to show the spirit in which the work was carried forward the concluding passages of that report may be quoted, again utilizing the solemnly phrased generalities rather than the practical policies of which the remaining chapters will show abundant evidence.

There is probably no one who does not want the Swedish people themselves to solve their own economic and cultural problems of the future. To adopt a population policy founded upon continued and increasing immigration would be the same as giving up the fundamental assumption of our positive population policy, namely the maintenance of the Swedish people and the Swedish culture.

Not of least importance in our day is the assertion that the Swedish people have a valuable inheritance of culture to guard. We are fortunate enough to have within boundaries delimited by nature a people of favorable endowment for successful cooperation, thanks to homogeneity of language, religion, and cultural traditions. There is today in Sweden a national folk communion which cuts through the social classes and which, in spite of all remaining deficiencies, is a good foundation for the development of the future. Everybody has the feeling that it is worth while to work for our people's future. If we are allowed to work in peace in our own Swedish way, we may even accomplish something of significance for the world at large in times to come. But a sufficiently large population is one of the most important presuppositions for such an undisturbed development. Without this, sooner or later, we may have such a large immigration that unity will be endangered and the Swedish tradition broken. Anyone who knows young people will recognize that this reasoning meets with understanding. It would certainly be a great mistake to propagandize for such viewpoints in a society which could not assure parents and children work and a self-respecting subsistence. But, in so far as these are assured, it would also be just as great a mistake not to capitalize upon the viewpoints specified.

During the course of its work, the Population Commission has gained a deep understanding of the economic worries of the masses of the Swedish people and an insight into many social evils still existing in Sweden. The Commission also understands that many people seriously hesitate to bring children into the world in these disturbed and threatening times. Facing not only economic and social insecurity but also the alarming war scares constantly before them, they have a pessimistic attitude toward life in general. But in spite of this no people and no nation, today as in times past, can survive and be of service to humanity if they do not have faith in the future and in the ultimate victory of the forces for good. Neither a people nor an individual should rely upon the fatalistic belief that whatever happens is inevitable and predestined. As far as the population question is concerned, it is just as true that it is in our power to work changes as it is true that no one should fool himself that the trend will turn in a favorable direction unless such special measures are adopted. Nothing can be more foolish than such a belief and nothing more dangerous than such a comfortable optimism. It is important for our people to be conscious of the still more severe population crisis which is pending. Even if the time is not ripe as yet for the radical social reforms which soon will become required by such a crisis, social enlightenment on the population question should be pushed so that public opinion may be further informed and in order that when the decrease in population is fully under way, there may not be an atmosphere of panic with less deliberate or even desperate measures undertaken.

The Population Commission does not believe in its own competency to answer the question as to whether within our people the will to life is sufficiently strong on which to build a general educational program in order to create a really positive attitude toward the family, both on the part of the individual and in society as a basis for a policy of family welfare. This fateful question can only be answered finally in the development of society itself and of the nation during generations to come. It has, however, fallen as a duty on our generation to attempt to lead the development of Swedish population in such a direction that the answer will be in the affirmative and that the future of our people will be assured. [17]

CHAPTER XI

EDUCATIONAL PREPARATION FOR FAMILY LIFE

R EFORMING the social basis for the family first of all involves clearing the ground of the public dishonesty in all that relates to sex and marriage and parenthood. No population program could be democratic with that task left undone. Or, conversely, no population program in a democracy could be successful if it evaded these things which are fundamental for individuals and in which individuals seem to have progressed far ahead of their own social formulations.

Sex relations do not always imply love; love is not exclusively a matter of marriage; marrying is not always followed by children; begetting children does not always involve providing a home for them. The breaking up of these different phases of man-woman relationships has been remarkable in recent times, and it seems to have been particularly marked in Sweden. Much of the descriptive data given in earlier chapters showed the conditions accompanying the loss of the complete partnership idea and some of the results. Illegitimacy results from sex relations disconnected from love or marriage companionship and leads to failure in providing real homes for a large number of children. Changes in the "meeting and mating" conditions keep youth artificially isolated from a wide choice of mates. Childlessness, abortions, and oversized poor families eventuate as married people fumble in deciding what is the right family size for them. Irrationality and disintegration become the outstanding characteristics of the picture when attention is focused on the fundamentals of sex and family life.

A population policy cannot take anything but the reintegration of all dispersed elements of the complete family as a value premise for its endeavors. Therefore, in Sweden it could not aim at obtaining just more children, regardless of whether they had parental care, regardless of whether they were wanted or not, regardless of whether they were being born at the right time in the right families. That social thinking should be rational and public discussion courageous in the field of sexual problems was also one of the value premises. The educational part of such a readjusted modern family policy would then be to prepare youth for sexual, affective, and parental partnership.

Young people should not be led through ignorance into unfortunate types of experiences, especially those resulting in illegitimate births. The necessity of giving all the children of the country an honest sex education became recognized. Parallel with the demand for sex education which could diligently and frankly meet the needs of actual life was the demand that the present deflation of family values be halted. To the Swedish reformers the cornerstone of the whole program was the need for education to change the family attitude, to weight it with more positive appreciation. At the same time the practical and psychological skills required for family life had to be more fully developed. The second half of the desideratum for educational reform thus concerned a broad educational introduction to home-making and parenthood.

THE ARGUMENT FOR SEX EDUCATION

Can society help to prepare youth for a love life, marriage, and parenthood less filled with risks to themselves and society? Certainly restrictive attitudes will not prove of any help. Illegitimacy, venereal disease, restless and impersonal love affairs, unsatisfactory relationships of a tentative character, unhappy marriages where misunderstanding slowly withers love — these cannot be cured or prevented by prohibitions and moralizing. That acknowledgment has been difficult for any public body, but the Swedish Population Commission tried to make it. The Commission undertook a constructive educational approach to supersede the common one which, though unintentionally, tends to cramp the ordinary human talent for happiness. Sex education had to be taken seriously. The Population Commission proposed in its Report on the Sexual Question [8] the introduction of sex education into all public schools. Although it was intended to be included in expanded education for family life as a whole, the statements regarding the more specific sex information had to be clear and the proposals quite definite in order to prevent evasion. Among other things an examination of textbooks, particularly in biology, was undertaken. Finally, a curricular plan was presented for instruction in sex education to be introduced concentrically during all the school years of a child's life in order to fit developmental needs.

The general argument of the Commission was explicit:

In general a more wholesome attitude toward sex questions will not be created until they are discussed openly and as matter-of-fact phenomena. Such discussion does not impair the ethical seriousness with which these questions ought to be considered but, on the other hand, is a prerequisite for moral attitudes. Our whole civilization is undermined when these vital questions are debased to a plane of frivolous humor or lewd hypocrisy. Such hypocrisy is often clothed in the dress of modesty, but it does not have the spirit of modesty. True modesty shows no aversion to free and open discussion but maintains that there is a time and place for everything and that serious questions should be treated in a serious and honest way. [8]

No less definite was the Commission's explanation of the strong resistance to the teaching of sex hygiene. The Commission unhesitatingly explained that resistance as, in the main, a defense mechanism on the part of men.

The Commission cannot help observing that in the earlier development in this field women have been the ones showing the most courageous clearsightedness and not the majority of men. This is probably due to the fact that women in general have had a stronger feeling as to the importance of the problem and have also had a more practical and serious attitude toward sex life, probably because they more than men suffered from the existing order. Young men and men in general have always had at hand a certain kind of sexual instruction, such as it was; while young women were generally kept in ignorance. The Commission cannot refrain from pointing out that the real reason for opposition to the teaching of sex hygiene in the schools is to be found in the attitude of a generation of men who have grown up in an atmosphere of reticence and guilt as far as sex was concerned. Since the Parliament and other authorities consist chiefly of men, their viewpoints have prevailed, while women have not had a chance to have their opinions accepted.

The true connection should be understood between the old double standard and the difficulties that have been encountered in all attempts to create a general understanding of the need for sex education. As the old double standard gives way before enlightened opinion among the young in different classes, the attitude toward sex education is in process of being radically changed. [8]

The history of sex education justifies these opinions. Sex education has had a stony path in Sweden. Although at the end of the eighteenth century the Lutheran state clergy was already admonished by the medical authorities to inform the public about venereal diseases, any general education on sex matters did not ensue. The next step was taken a century later by the first woman doctor in Sweden, Dr. Karolina Widerström, who initiated a campaign for courses in sex hygiene in higher schools for girls and as part of adult education. Institutions of learning for women have ever since then been far in advance of other schools in regard to sex education.

Women have also been active in keeping the question to the fore up to the present time. Public proposals for sex education were presented in 1918 and 1921 in connection with the law against venereal disease. These made no headway, and the Board of Education shunted off the proposals in its delayed opinion in 1925. Women, both as individual members of the Riksdag and in organizations, were indefatigable, however, in campaigning and petitioning for such education.

The Population Commission overcame such objections as were of a more practical character. If sex education is said to be difficult because parents and teachers do not possess or do not believe they possess the necessary qualifications, the thing to do is obviously to overcome the difficulty by starting to give sex education. This difficulty will disappear in so far as the younger generation, with its essentially sounder and franker attitude toward sex, assumes the responsibilities of parenthood and teaching.

Sex Information in Families, Schools, and Adult Education

When children first begin to question how living things come into the world, they should be taught to include human procreation in the order of nature.

Information should be given simply and naturally, truthfully, unsentimentally, and in a matter-of-fact way. This is what the child expects and understands, untouched as he is by the conflicts and feelings of guilt that adults have acquired through faulty upbringing or warped life habits. [8]

Children in the first six grades should continuously be given sex education by their teachers, guided by the perception of children's needs. Biology should be specifically taught to answer the demands for enlightenment.

It is well to note that the matters touched upon should be concerned with things themselves and their relationships and not with questions of sexual morality which can have no actuality in life for children before the age of puberty if they are healthy and have not been brought up in a false way. [8]

After the age of 12 comes the period for definite sex instruction. Numerous possibilities then exist of influencing the personality development of the young in a desirable direction.

The subject matter of sex instruction should now be such that it gives complete and coherent knowledge. Already the General Board of Education has realized the necessity of including the following points for this age level in both the higher grades of the elementary school and the secondary school: human reproductive organs, egg cells and sperm cells, conception, pregnancy and development of the fetus, birth, the dependence of the child upon the mother before as well as after birth, heredity, sexual maturity, the significance of cleanliness in the care of sex organs, etc. The purpose of the instruction at this level is mainly to build up and increase factual knowledge. Hygienic considerations must now be given emphasis. Generally all the information should now be given a more practical slant. It should be directed toward the biological and psychological development of the children during puberty. It should lead gradually to the sex problems that they will have to face in life. [8]

The Board of Education had sanctioned the program thus far. It had stressed the importance of assuring that all children get a complete sex education before leaving school. For that very reason the Population Commission wanted to extend this minimum of general information into the fields of venereal disease and family limitation. It did not seem enough to talk generally about the dangers of venereal infections and their harmful effects, individually and socially. Nor did it seem enough to go only one step further and inform children that sex diseases are usually spread by loose sex relations, that abstinence from such relations is therefore the best guard against infection, that everyone who has reason to suspect that he might be infected should immediately seek medical advice, and that by law it is a criminal offense for anyone who is infected or who suspects he is infected to expose another person to the danger of infection. Practical logic demanded still another step, namely, the furnishing of the knowledge that there exist means for protection against infection. This the Population Commission proposed, supported by the General Board of Health but opposed by the Board of Education.

The reason for this position on the part of the Commission is based not only on considerations of health but also on sound pedagogy. When children go out into the world, they should know that such means of protection exist. Information received in school must be truthful also in order to gain the confidence generally of the learners and in order to present to them a consistent and realistic picture of life. [8]

The same arguments were used for the introduction into the school curriculum of some general information regarding birth control. On the one hand, it was deemed neither necessary nor desirable to give instruction in the actual techniques of contraception to children at the puberty level. On the other hand, the children must be told that birth control is consciously practiced in marriage and that this should be considered normal and natural on eugenic, medical, health, and economic grounds. While this should be preparatory information, directing their search for full knowledge at the age of actual needs, in the same preparatory way some understanding should also be created for the arguments against extreme family limitation.

During the last two generations, birth control has had such significant effects on population development and, as a consequence, on social life in general that any study of social conditions and human relationships must be superficial and distorted if silence is maintained on the subject. [8]

This moot problem being solved in favor of public honesty, sex education at still higher ages did not present any difficulties. In step with the mental development of youth, new knowledge could be added. Birth control and protection against disease could increasingly move into the foreground. Greater stress could be placed on practical personal considerations, and the hygienic and ethical behavior norms could thus gain more attention. This is the route for both higher secondary education and voluntary adult education.

How to Teach Sex

The method of teaching also has to be viewed honestly and rationally.

As in all instruction in civic morals it is particularly important that it should not be given in the form of abstract rules of conduct and particularly not in the form of isolated negative prohibitions entirely separated from life situations. Children and young people are even more impervious to such moral instruction than older people. To be sure, they can learn to rattle off such rules and prohibitions. But what good are they if they are not motivating forces? [8]

The reform of textbooks became glaringly necessary after the Commission's investigation of them. Book after book in biology was scrutinized, yielding a collection of quotations unconsciously humorous in what was omitted. The greatest skill was exercised in evading the fact that two sexes exist. Only in the vegetable world and in some few utterances regarding lower animals was any approximation to a complete explanation of procreation to be found. The situation with regard to textbooks was summed up as follows: "In this way all males with the exception of the he-perch are presented as rather purposeless creatures."

Certain requirements for textbooks were formulated in order to give a reliable skeleton even if oral presentation should be considerably more realistic and complete. For books for grade schools, the following requirements were specified:

1. In textbooks on biology the sexual nature of procreation should be presented from the outset, connected with the description of the cell.

2. Somewhat later a detailed description of the mechanism of mating and childbearing among animals and men should be included. A description of the sex organs should be given along with general anatomy. Copulation should at least be treated by telling how sperm cells impregnate egg cells "either within the body of the mother with the help of the male sex organ or outside of her body in the lower animal world."

3. Venereal diseases should be briefly treated, the illegality of their transmission stressed, the hygienic rules specified along with the general approach that they are best avoided "by young people from the beginning and through life by adhering to the idea that the only worthy form for sexual life is a personal rela-

tionship founded on love and obligated to faithfulness." (It should be noted that marriage is not mentioned; neither is the life durability of the relationship made a condition. Love is the prerequisite and faithfulness is demanded as a consequence, "as long as the relation lasts." This being the moral teaching advocated for all schools, it seems important both to demarcate how far its preaching goes above individual freedom and arbitrariness and at the same time how it tries to avoid too great a discrepancy between professed ideals and normal human behavior.)

4. Sexual hygiene should be included to the extent determined by the age level. Subjects of puberty, menopause, sterility, masturbation, venereal prophylaxis, and birth control should not be evaded.

5. In wider connections a study should then be made of the importance of marriage and of family relationships, stressing both the social and the individual aspects. The shortsightedness of extreme family limitation should be pointed out.

The textbooks for high schools should be made more detailed, working in the elements of genetics, knowledge about hormones, etc. [*18*]

Who is supposed to give sex education? This is one of the predominant problems in all practical discussions in the field. The Swedish answer was the teacher, any teacher or, rather, all teachers. In the lower grades the room teacher must answer all questions and lead on to the formation of some basically correct conceptions. At any age level the one important consideration is that no strange person should be called in to give sex talks. Routine should not be broken to give information on something which is so much a part of everybody's everyday life. Less perfect information in the general run of instruction is far better than artificial perfection. In adult education, on the other hand, and in education for later ages generally, where questions become specialized, doctors particularly should be called upon to give information reliable enough to act on. In order not to erect the very barriers that this new education should abolish, boys and girls should be kept together for the teaching, if they are already together. The Population Commission strongly stresses in all its practical recommendations that what is needed is the integration of sexual life into the general culture. Segregation of this information, however technically perfect, serves only to maintain present tensions.

A main emphasis in the Swedish approach is that the need for birth control should be universally acknowledged and that its presentation to the public should be an educational matter. To wait until the individual need is so pressing that a person visits a clinic is fundamentally ineffective. A birth control movement centering its interest in clinical treatment is irrational and ineffectual. If birth control is courageously faced as a social problem, the first necessity is to make everyone aware of it before sex relations are started. Only through educational influences can such a general realization of what is involved in sexual responsibility be achieved.

If a culture is mature enough to utilize birth control, it should disseminate information through sex education in schools and in other cultural agencies.

SLOW REALIZATION

The Population Commission had in its proposal utilized and transformed into a coherent system many suggestions derived from earlier treatments on the subject of more adequate sex education, particularly drawing upon the recommendations of the General Board of Health. Still, the proposals which were made in the Report on the Sexual Question were far more radical than earlier ones. It therefore must be remarked that the Commission went to greater lengths than can here be indicated in order to assure validity for its proposals. What it submitted to the government comprised more than platonically contemplated attitudes and general recommendations. The basis was a wealth of statistical data and detailed practical discussion, compiled in appendices. The report was prepared by a body of experts (the economist from the Commission and five medical men and women) and endorsed by the special delegation on social ethics in regard to the population question, thus securing also some endorsement from religious leaders. The Population Commission itself when unanimously accepting the report put pressure behind the proposals for educational reforms by making them a *sine qua non* for proposals to liberalize the abortion laws. These proposals and those about more specific reforms for spreading birth control advice through educational channels to adults are dealt with in the next chapter.

The definite proposals for reform action in the educational field included: (1) sex education in all schools, gradually obligatory but in the beginning not enforced on the teachers; (2) an authorized revision by the General Board of Education of curricular plans and manuals for teachers so as to give best leads for such education; (3) a revision of all textbooks so as truthfully to picture mankind as two sexes and society as vitally concerned with a rational solution of sexual problems; (4) reforms in teacher training so as to equip all graduating teachers to give sex education; and (5) special summer courses, supported by the state, for giving sex education training to teachers who feel themselves deficient for the purpose of instructing the young so that present deficiencies should not be a reason for postponement *ad infinitum*.

These proposals have met with varied success. Cabinet and the Riksdag should primarily be concerned with the first one and the last one. An endorsement of the general proposals by both these bodies has indirectly been won in motivations for free instruction courses and for changed abortion laws. Enthusiastic cooperation by the leaders in school administration has, however, been wanting, thus delaying the realization of the program. The most definite results relate to the last item in the list of proposals, namely, arranging the teacher courses in sex instruction. Having had some precursors even earlier, they were started again at public expense in 1936. The number of teachers applying has far outnumbered the places available.

Thus the path for sex education was smoothed in Sweden, although thoroughgoing changes are still wanting. In the way is administrative inertia; the will of the public is unmistakably clear.

MARITAL AND PARENTAL EDUCATION

Sex education does not comprise all the education necessary for living within family relations. It had, however, to be singled out for specific treatment and lengthy argumentation. Only by demonstrating the context of taboos of not too honorable origin, of obsolete traditions, and of the catastrophic effects of the double standard and official hypocrisy was it possible to get public opinion aroused and then clarified. The premarital and preparental education in schools, of which sex enlightenment was only the more publicized detail, needed less argumentation but will probably only still more gradually become realized. It will be fairly difficult to work into the teaching of the comparatively formalistic Swedish schools a treatment of the subtle and evasive subject of the family. In adult education certainly the time should be definitely ripe for an expansion of civic studies to include more of the factual fundamentals of the art of living in families.

Venereal diseases, increase in divorce, low nuptiality rate, high marriage age, illegitimacy, child mortality, and adverse education of children were taken as evidence of needs of preparation for family life in addition to what may be given through rational sex education. Against this background of social and personal problems of the family the Population Commission advocated family education imparting both theoretical understanding and practical guidance.

In view of these data which have been brought into sharp focus by the population crisis and which tend to show that this crisis is fundamentally a crisis in the institution of the family as such, the Population Commission holds that certain reforms on top of social reforms on the economic level are necessary, namely, greater understanding of family matters and a more positive attitude toward the family on the part of the whole population. . . .

Children should, therefore, be educated to live cooperatively and yet to maintain their independence, to be socially responsible and frankly human, to have a lively social conscience, and to be able to adjust personally without conflicts. The family is without comparison the most important form of social life for all human beings. The spiritual significance of the school and of public education would, therefore, to a large extent be revived if they adopted a wide program of what is here called education for parenthood and family life. [8]

Civics, history, social sciences, and literature should be utilized for background knowledge. A study of the historical development of the family would have to be included, so that its purposiveness could be judged. The economics of family partnership should be treated, as should child care and childhood education. Training, as given in home economics and shopwork, should be designed for the purpose of giving practical fundamentals for adult life. In home economics that would mean greater emphasis on child care. In shopwork it would mean emphasis on home furnishings, household mechanics, etc. A valuable link could be made with the movement for Swedish Modern which is spreading over the whole country the tendency to beautify homes and simplify households. The fundamentals in these fields could and should be taught to children in concrete form as early as possible in the elementary grades. As the children grow up, the factual knowledge should be increased and enriched.

The Commission wants to point out that it is an established principle of child psychology and pedagogy that the education of children is easiest if they are brought to understand the purpose of this education and thus to cooperate. In this respect children are no different from adults. Education that is comprehended is the only education that becomes positively effective. Practical instruction in family problems, and even in the problem of actually bringing up children, is in itself of positive educational value. And it should be particularly pointed out that this is no more difficult but much easier to give children than much of the technical and intellectual stuff with which their brains are overloaded at present. Family problems are already the real, everyday problems for children. [8]

All instruction on the various phases of family education should be imparted to children independent of sex. This should also be true in so far as school instruction in housekeeping, child care, and shopwork is concerned. Since school instruction in these subjects must of necessity be limited, boys and young men would in any case not get more than they can benefit from in a practical way.

If it is considered desirable as a matter of principle, which the Commission feels is the case, to strengthen the position of the family in the minds of youth and to influence their attitudes toward the family in a positive direction, then the Commission feels that boys and young men should not be excepted. Ever since the beginning of the industrial revolution, the man and father has tended to be separated from family life. This is one of the most disruptive forces in the development of the family. The Commission feels that in the modern family, and especially in the modern family in which the wife is gainfully employed at least in the early years of marriage, the man's participation in household duties is necessary for cooperative and harmonious living. Distorted attitudes and habits exist toward this in all social classes. These constitute a danger to the family as an integrated joyous cooperation. [8]

Such attitudes of indifference toward family on the part of men were not characteristic of the family partnership of the agricultural epoch. They originated in the nineteenth century transitional period of individualism. They are maintained by a faulty upbringing of boys and young men. This not only makes boys and young men less fit for and less interested in family life but also gives them a certain contempt for household tasks and thus for women's part in the world and ultimately in a half-conscious way for women themselves.

If such broad education for family life is included in the school curriculum, all instruction on love life and its spiritual and physical health belongs, of course, within the curriculum. Only then can sex education be normally integrated in the knowledge needed for life.

The important questions of venereal disease and abortion can be treated naturally and in their true perspective in this education for parenthood. This is also true of the question of birth control which can then be handled naturally from the point of view of eugenics, medicine, health, family psychology, and family economy. Its true significance for early marriage can be pointed out. And it will be possible for the young people to see some of the important relationships existing between quantity and quality of population and the welfare of the family and the nation. [8]

In this way the psychological influencing of family attitudes, which has so often been presented as the moralists' alternative to costly social reform, has instead been merged with them. The spontaneous love for children and the spontaneous drive to find a partner not only for sharing sexual experiences but also for sharing life are to be helped and cultivated, not thwarted. The Commission did not present proposals for the inclusion of parent education in adult education but expected the general stimulation to work in that direction. When the powerful agency of Swedish democracy shoulders its responsibility for the family, when courses in the family are added to those in civics in the thousands of people's high schools, study groups etc., a new era will truly have been inaugurated.

THE ROAD TO REALIZATION

The authorities concerned have reacted favorably to this whole body of recommendations for revolutionizing school instruction to serve the needs of modern life and the best interests of the family. Women's organizations have been particularly eager to push such reforms; the progressive national organizations of Swedish housewives and Swedish business and professional women deserve special mention both for their interest and for their cooperation. Adult education has been impelled to broaden programs for parental education. Some professionally interested agencies, e.g., organizations of teachers, have devoted themselves to making curriculum plans for the different school ages. As yet, however, the realization of all these plans has not occurred. Sweden is prepared but still waiting for family education to take possession of the schools. The recommendations, so heartily endorsed in such wide groups, stand as a challenge to educational reformers who have both vision and the practical touch.

In thus summarizing the situation as it has developed since the Population Commission's Report on the Sexual Question was published in 1936, one point ought to be added to the presentation of ideas already given. It is necessary to clear up the question whether all the many men and women, who are not going to become parents, will be submerged in a forced enthusiasm for family life and given unnecessary education for it. Is there a danger here of a cultural waste? The answer seems to be, at least with regard to an industrialized country such as Sweden where homemaking is not as certain as under rural conditions to fall to one sex, that minimum knowledge of home organization, cooking, household mechanics, home equipment, etc., becomes essential for everybody, if only for the art of living alone. Practical skill in these thngs will be needed by both men and women for organizing their own lives, for fulfilling tasks left undone by apartment dwelling and restaurant eating and by dependence on service industries, and for sharing more evenly in the work incurred by any form of joint living.

The more subtle teaching of family understanding serves another purpose. It helps to give clearer insight into oneself and one's own maze of motivations. Less directly it is desirable on account of the demand on the citizen for greater solidarity with all the nation's children, who are going to be the inheritors of the country. Only a more understanding attitude toward family values as such, only the allocating of a more central place to the family in the cultural structure will enable men and women as an electorate to vote any of the reforms necessary for supporting these children. Although it is difficult to compare impressions of cultural patterns offhand, it may be ventured that the Swedes need to take more spontaneous pleasure in children as children.

CHAPTER XII

PLANNING THE SIZE OF FAMILY

P REPARING youth for the most difficult problem of the adult's life, which is the proper conduct of family relationships, was thus conceived in Sweden to be an essential aim of the educational process. But what amount of rationality does society allow young people when they come to tackle the difficulties of love and sex in actual situations? How much is marriage hindered? How much could it be facilitated? What social help is available for planning wisely with regard to having or not having children?

The goals of population policy are quite clear-cut. The monogamous marriage is considered the ideal love relationship between man and woman. Marriages, and particularly marriages of young people, should be encouraged. The policy of urging that as many as possible of the existing companionate relations be transformed into marriages also runs parallel to the goals of more children and of a larger proportion of births taking place within instead of outside marriages. For this purpose it has to be made easier for young men and women to meet and select their mates and then to marry if they desire to share life and to found a complete family with children. Leaving aside the social aspects of the problem, which will be considered in subsequent chapters, marriage's first concern is one of love and sex. That the official attitude taken in the name of population policy was one that considered individual happiness above everything else was indicated by the fact that young marriages concluded with no immediate intention of procreation were openly recognized to be desirable. The marriage partners then obviously need not only sex education in general but also specific advice on effective birth control methods.

By education it was hoped to incline youth toward preference for durable, individualized love relations, to do away with the double standard, to lessen prostitution, to prevent venereal disease, to diminish irresponsible parenthood, to improve the capacity for wise selection of marriage partners, and to make marriages more harmonious and consequently diminish the causes for divorce. The danger is that educational influences directed toward the experimental sex attitudes of youth easily deteriorate into mere negative moralizing which will decrease their efficacy. So, instead of working only from the negative approach by forbidding sexual relations, all efforts should be made to enhance the competitive value of the socially and individually more valuable love and sex relations. The element of risk must also be minimized. For maturing people effective means of birth control must be made easily available, thus making marriage or marriagelike permanent love relations possible, even for those who cannot bear or rear children. The sense of guilt in seeking sexual satisfaction without intentions to procreate and the worries about unwanted pregnancies must be removed. This is a prime requisite for raising the competitive value of those relations.

That childbearing should as a general rule, and not only in the first years of marriage, be planned was also taken as one of the basic assumptions of the Swedish population program. An intelligent adjustment of the size of the family and the spacing of children in accordance with the situation of the individual family, determined by economic, psychological, and health considerations, were specifically to be encouraged. The Population Commission even went so far as to offer a kind of ideal prescription — four children to every nonsterile family. This was only a mathematical derivation from the quantitative goals set for population policy, a population kept quantitatively constant and attaining that constancy through as even a distribution as possible of middle-sized families instead of through a total made up of some families which were too large and some which were too small. Planned parenthood was to be the very foundation of the democratic population policy.

From this general postulate it became a task of the Commission to define in some detail its stand on the variegated problems of birth control and to work out its conclusions into concrete proposals concerning the repeal of anticontraceptive laws, the organization of birth control information for adults in its relation to public health, and the legal provisions for abortion and sterilization.

REFUTATION OF OLD TABOOS

The Swedish Population Commission knew full well that its rationalistic thinking on the subject of birth control clashed with moralistic ideas still held in many quarters, even if they were little related to actual behavior patterns. Therefore, the Commission considered it wise to be at some pains to anticipate criticism. By framing its anticipatory rebuttal as formulations of the eugenic, ethical, medical, psychological, and economic arguments for family limitation the Commission wanted to fortify the position of enlightened rationality against reactionary influences. As official documents on this subject are rare, it may be of interest again to quote freely from the Report on the Sexual Question:

A moralistic principle exists according to which one should absolutely refrain from artificial means of preventing conception during coitus. Every means of preventing conception, no matter what the circumstances under which it is practiced, is, according to this viewpoint, a nonpermissible interference with natural processes. This moralistic principle is questionable on three grounds.

First of all, it is not quite clear why the interruption of a natural process is necessarily an act ethically condemnable. The progress of humanity is based, on its technical side, on a steady guidance and adjustment of natural processes to interests considered vital. As ethnological studies of primitive cultures and historical experiences have perfectly well shown, all progress has steadily met with the objection that it is an interference with the natural order; that it is, therefore, immoral or contrary to religion. In so far as the advances have been established as mores, the objection has ordinarily died out until a new advance was made. Then the objection and the final acceptance repeated themselves. It has been easily observable that the objection to birth control is just in the stage of dying out and that it is considered less and less vital in ethical discussion.

The validity of the principle is also questionable on another ground. Within a marriage founded on mutual love the tendency of the partners to sex relations is also part of a natural process. Even prevention of conception through continence would then be contrary to nature and ought, therefore, in observance of the rule to be condemned. This conclusion is the more compelling, the more the ethical concept is spiritually instead of materialistically determined, thus making abstinence more and more unethical. The principle referred to above thus becomes logically absurd. [8]

A social viewpoint constitutes the third basis for criticism.

Ideas about the value of continence in marriage are usually associated with a low conception of sex life, sometimes still to be found even in our day and in our Nordic culture. Continence in marriage is therefore often further motivated as a personal sacrifice which in itself is morally valuable. This sacrifice would have positive value in showing a willingness for self-denial and a power of self-restraint which serve to develop the personality in the direction of greater unselfishness. Ordinarily no attempt is made to explain just why this virtue should be shown by those couples who for eugenic, medical, health, or economic reasons must practice birth control but not by other couples to the same extent. This flaw in the reasoning gives rise to the suspicion that it is not clear and fundamental.

It should not be contended that these virtues are not valuable in themselves. . . . They are, but according to the philosophy of today these virtues should be used in human service, that is to say, to make life richer for oneself and others, and not to make life more narrow. . . . A sacrifice cannot be good in and of itself. It must have a rational purpose. It must at least not be clearly irrational nor clearly unfortunate in its effects. Life is so miserable and unhappy for many persons in our society that it is not necessary to seek the practice of self-sacrifice, self-restraint, and unselfishness in such a negative way. Each and every one of us has opportunities to practice goodness to such an extent as to require great personal sacrifice but to do it for such an end as to make other persons' lives richer thereby. [8]

Having thus rejected the once commonly accepted idea that birth control was unethical, the Commission dwelt on its positive values in normal sexual relations.

As far as the effects of continence practiced as a birth control measure within marriage are concerned, physicians declare that such continence between happily married partners in the prime of life, sexually potent, and in daily contact with each other should be considered physiologically harmful as a general rule. It may also aggravate the risks of neuroses. But probably still more harmful than the health effects is the danger that such a procedure may lead to a narrow, thwarted, and unnatural love life and consequently to unhappy marriage and to a lack of spiritual harmony between the partners. There is no longer any difference of opinion among experts as to the fundamental importance that a healthy sex life, including normal sex relations, has for all the different psychological relations between the partners, which in turn are the very meaning of marriage and the most important basis for the institution of the family.

The Population Commission cannot itself support the position nor does it find that the majority of our people feel that birth control as such should be generally and absolutely condemned on grounds of morality. [8]

To forestall a common evasion of the issue the report made clear that health considerations are not the only justification for birth control.

The most immediate concession to a less rigid idea of birth control lies in the admission, now often made by the strongest moralists, that contraception can be defended on health grounds, that is to say, in so far as pregnancy constitutes a risk to the *life* of the mother because of the presence of some disease. This line of reasoning is generally accepted in Sweden nowadays. The next admission is that contraception is justified when pregnancy is a risk to the *health* of the mother. Even this is generally acknowledged. It is then further reasoned that a corresponding concern should be shown for the *life and health of the children.* In all these admissions there is, from a purely logical standpoint, a considerable margin of doubt as to just how great the risk can be to the life and health of the mother and children before contraceptive practices are justified. As a matter of fact the definitely prohibitive moral principle is logically surrendered in all of these concessions. [8]

After a thorough discussion of the health aspects of spacing and limiting the number of children and after stressing particularly the health value of spacing for those families which desire a large number of children, the Commission concluded:

In considering the health indications the Population Commission is of the opinion that birth control practiced partly for the purpose of preventing too large a number of children and partly for the purpose of spacing births in such a way as is desirable for the sake of the health of the mother and children is in general a natural procedure in marriages that are not sterile and in which children have already been born. [8]

In some medically determined cases sterilization, which permanently prevents conception, may be the best alternative and the same thing is true when eugenic considerations call for extreme family limitation.

Where eugenic reasons are less pronounced, such a permanent form of birth control as sterilization is not called for. In such cases it may still be desirable to prevent conception by other means. This is also true in cases where the eugenically defective mate refuses to be sterilized. If, for example, a man is a chronic alcoholic but still in possession of his legal rights and refuses to be sterilized, it should not be necessary for the woman to be sterilized in order that defective children may be avoided. It would be much better to give her the chance of practicing contraception with the aid of mechanical methods.

In weighing these eugenic considerations it is the opinion of the Population Commission that, in certain cases where inheritable defects occur and sterilization cannot or should not be resorted to, it is the moral duty of a couple to practice prevention of conception for their own sake, for the sake of society, and for the sake of the children.

It is also the opinion of the Commission that from the point of view both of the individual family and of society a strict limitation of births is so necessary that serious efforts should be made by the social agencies to induce such individuals to realize the significance of birth control. Special importance should be attached to conscientious information as to effective contraceptive techniques. [8]

When the Commission turned to the psychological motivations for family limitation, the interest rather shifted to warning the families against making such limitation extreme. In so doing it made an explicit assumption that economic and other external reasons do not determine the matter.

It must be realized that birth control properly used undoubtedly has positive value in that children are not born into a family as a result of accident or blind sexual urges without due considerations for the health of the mother and the children and thus for the physical and spiritual welfare of the family. . . .

Most inquiries into the problem of family psychology seem to confirm the idea that childless marriages and marriages with one or even two children — in the majority of cases, and especially if the children are not close together in age — are for ordinary persons not quite happy or harmonious. This is an opinion built upon everyday experience and one held a long time by sociologists, physicians, teachers, and others engaged in practical social work. . . .

Therefore, from the point of view of family psychology, birth control which is used for complete childlessness or strict limitation of number of children should be opposed. On the other hand, this same viewpoint neither advocates nor condemns a very large number of children. It must, therefore, be concluded in this connection that, unless there are strong indications to the contrary, there ought to be three or more children in a family. But the point should be emphasized that in cases where there are two children near together in age, these considerations of family psychology do not constitute such an important reason against further limitation. [8]

Birth control in the ideal normal-sized family will, of course, have to be used for spacing purposes. In this connection it is interesting to note that an optimum period of about two years between children is recommended. The Commission stressed that the best maternal age psychologically is in reality somewhat later than what may be physiologically considered the best age. For best parent age the Commission recommended the years around 25. It also admonished young couples not to have children immediately after marrying, unless the relations have been intimate earlier, as some time should be taken by the young mates to perfect their own relationship and adjust to the marriage situation before they complicate it with pregnancy and children. This amounts to a recommendation of a period of birth control at the beginning of marriage.

The Commission made extensive studies of the economic reasons for family limitation. The summary only is given.

In the majority of families in our country economic factors constitute the strongest reasons for limitation of the families to a number of children smaller than that physiologically possible. If this limitation were not carried too far, it would neither be harmful to family psychology nor constitute a threat to the quantity of population desired. The tendency to extreme limitation which now exists is, however, a real threat to the family and to the nation. In considering the economically depressed conditions under which the poorer social classes live, the Commission cannot conceal the fact that even extreme limitation is morally justified by many couples who are thus motivated by a sense of duty and responsibility to the offspring.

The Commission considers the fact that socially responsible people must so often practice extreme family limitation as a potent social dilemma. This becomes the strongest reason for prompt and energetic social reforms to equalize the burdens of supporting children and to raise the general standard of child welfare in the community. It is only in close connection with such positive reforms that the community can hold up to these families in the lower social classes the detrimental effects of extreme family limitation. But the Commission must insist that such extreme family limitation cannot be considered justified under normal conditions in well-to-do families where economic reasons are not pressing. There are, however, many intermediate cases between the extremes of real poverty and economic independence in which it is difficult to pass judgment.

In any case, in a democratic community individual freedom of action should be respected, and great hesitancy should be observed before passing condemnatory judgments. This should not, however, deter the community from seeking to counteract extremely family limitation not only by socioeconomic reforms but also by presenting data and information so as to change convictions and attitudes. [8]

Young People and the Double Standard

With birth control deemed advisable within marriage for ethical, eugenic, hygienic, psychological, economic, and sociological reasons, the Commission turned its attention to the unmarried population. As again its explicit attitude was rather unconventional in defense of modern youth and also of a certain rational discrimination between valuable and valueless cases of extramarital relations, a quotation is given.

Under social conditions now existing it often happens that two young people who have reached full emotional and physical maturity fall so deeply in love that there are no personal reasons for not entering marriage; yet their economic circumstances may be such that they do not consider themselves able to undertake the responsibility of bringing children into the world. [8]

These cases in which all the personal prerequisites for marriage are present but the economic prerequisites for childbearing are lacking comprise a large proportion of Swedish youth between the ages of 20 and 30 years.

The traditional way of meeting this situation is for the two young people to postpone the marriage until they are economically able to form a family. Morality as publicly maintained further demands that during this time they should live in sexual continence. During the nineteenth century especially this theory was promulgated. But every person with social experience knows that in many cases reality has been far different from the theoretical expectations.

In this connection it is difficult for the Population Commission not to comment on the so-called double standard of morality. This originated in the higher social classes, but during the nineteenth century it spread to the middle classes and during the latter half of the century — although to a much lesser extent — even to the farming and working classes. The double standard, as is well known, insists that sexual morality differs in the two sexes. Even within marriage, but at all events before marriage, men were permitted to have promiscuous sex connections. Women, however, or at least women who wanted to maintain their good reputations and opportunities for marriage, had to practice strict continence. During this time prostitution was widespread. In accordance with this generally tolerated double standard, the man usually entered marriage after he had had a number of loose sexual relations while the woman was expected to be a virgin. . . .

It is commonly agreed that this general conception of sexual morality, and the manner in which as a consequence marriage was entered upon, must have decreased the spiritual fullness and harmonious happiness of the mates. Lack of

economic independence of women limited in many instances their free and individual choice of mates for marriage, so that the men became in reality the
selectors. Many women came, therefore, to regard marriage more as a means of
support than as an ardently desired emotional love experience. . . .

The wives who entered marriage in this way found their interests, then much
more than now, permanently alienated from sexual relations. In certain circles
it was even considered that interest and joy in sex life was not quite proper for
a wife. Numerous confinements operated in the same direction, particularly since
the idea was long current that sexual relations during pregnancy were forbidden
on health grounds. Under such conditions the greater fertility of the marriages
must have entailed a considerable temptation of the man to be unfaithful, with
consequent disruptive effects upon the marital harmony of the mates. Pregnancy is in itself an added temptation to unfaithfulness, and this must have been
particularly great in those marriages which were preceded by loose connections
on the part of the man. The presence of widespread prostitution did nothing to
lessen the temptation.

It cannot, therefore, be denied that this double standard exercised undermining influences upon the purely personal basis of marriage. Attention has
been focused merely upon marriage and the married women. But we cannot
avoid asking the following questions. With what women, according to the
double standard, were the men permitted intercourse, and what were the effects
upon these women? It cannot be strongly enough emphasized in this connection
that women were divided into two categories: a large group of women esteemed
and honored as mothers but hardly as partners in sexual pleasures — this category
has just been discussed — and a smaller but despised group of women ruined
physically and mentally. The double standard included fallen women but not
fallen men. [8]

The present generation of youth exhibits much more judgment.

The circumstances existing in the past are without doubt still in existence
in some measure today. But in the younger generation changes have been taking
place for some time. The changes have been due to the fact that women have
won certain legal rights and that they are forcing their way into the labor market
and becoming economically independent. Prostitution also seems to have decreased. The change has been due to other factors, such as a changed philosophy
of life among younger women, their increased demands on life, and the greater
integrity and practical seriousness of the younger generation in personal problems. [8]

The democratization of the national culture has also given greater influence to the moral tradition of the farming population where the
double standard was not usually accepted (Chapter 3).

Nowadays when two young people fall in love and cannot marry for economic
reasons, in most cases this does not interfere with their entering into sex relations
with each other. These premarital relations entered into between socially equal

individuals on grounds of personal love cannot be summarily condemned for ethical reasons, according to the opinion of the Commission. Under the circumstances this is from ethical, and definitely from hygienic and social, viewpoints a better solution of a complicated human problem than was the old double standard. [8]

The necessity of birth control in these cases seems obvious to the Commission.

In considering the above problem the Population Commission has reached the opinion that birth control practiced from a sense of responsibility is of positive value by making it possible for young people who have fallen deeply in love, who are personally fit for marriage, who are at the same time physically and emotionally mature, and who have reached the age of responsibility for their actions to marry and not bear children until such a time in the future as they can do so without too great economic risk. If we want to develop earlier marriage among the country's mature young people, the Commission holds that it is of the utmost importance that full knowledge of safe and harmless contraceptive methods be made available to them. . . .

The Population Commission does not find that extramarital sexual relations have been increased because of the diffusion of contraceptive knowledge. The real reason for these relations is to be found, in the present as in the past, in the fact that people marry late and that this is determined by personal economic and general social conditions. [8]

Not all extramarital relations, however, have these stable values. The Commission was careful to discriminate.

The Population Commission must now consider what its judgment should be on these extramarital sexual relations. The Commission accepts as a norm that it is conducive both to the happiness of the individual and to the welfare of society that young people continue to form monogamic sex relations and that these continue to be legalized in the social form which as of old has been considered to be in the interest both of individuals and of society, namely, marriage. . . .

But as conditions now are, the fact must be realized that extramarital sexual relations are very widespread in our society. In judging these, it is the opinion of the Commission that a sharp difference should be made between the more or less marital sex relationships founded on affection and certain durability and loose, impersonal sexual relations.

The former kind of extramarital sex relations cannot be condemned in so far as they constitute a preparation for marriage. Such an entrance upon marital sex relations before marriage is nowadays sanctioned by wide groups in our people as it has earlier been sanctioned by our peasant population. . . . On similar grounds no condemnation could be passed on such sex relations as occur within an affection-founded partnership, when marriage for many different reasons may not be planned.

As far as loose, impersonal, and above all paid-for sexual relations are concerned, these must be condemned not only on abstract ethical grounds but also with reference to their socially disruptive effects, especially if they are entered into outside an existing permanent relation. They must furthermore be judged as unfortunate because of the health hazards they present and particularly unfortunate in comparison with the more desirable alternatives in sexual relations. . . .

In these loose, impersonal sexual relations it is especially important, in the majority of cases, that conception be prevented from all points of view, not the least with reference to possible children. Contraceptive methods should also be used in these impersonal sexual relations for the purpose of helping protect against venereal infection. [8]

LEGAL BANS REVERSED

Having thus advocated birth control within marriages as a positive blessing and outside of marriage as more desirable than lack of such control, ways and means of making contraceptive practices available to the people had to be found. A necessary first step toward consistency then became the repeal of the penal law governing the sale and advertising of contraceptives (Paragraph 13, Chapter 18 of Swedish Penal Law) and of the corresponding press law (Paragraph 3, Chapter 13, Law on Freedom of the Press), which in Sweden have the rank of constitutional law. The laws had been enacted in 1910 and 1911, forbidding the "exhibition or public showing of objects intended for unchaste use or for preventing the consequence of sexual relations, spreading or offering of these objects through notification in publications or other communications to the public."

These laws commonly referred to as the anticontraceptive laws, were directed against the spread of birth control. But soon after their passage and especially in connection with the much-valued law on venereal disease enacted in 1918, the necessity of using some devices for hindering contagion in sexual intercourse gained recognition. In fact, this argument offered a sort of pretext under which doctors and socially minded people could publicly defend the use of contraceptive means. They always had as an excuse their zeal for social hygiene. This game went on for 20 years. Public authorities even helped to disseminate some information while formally upholding the law. The Marine Administration, for instance, arranged for venereal prophylaxis on visits of its vessels in foreign ports. But because of the law, means for more effective prophylaxis could hardly be officially taught. In private motions which appeared in the Riksdag practically every year and in all pronouncements by standing committees only this argument of health prophylaxis was given as a reason for any reform of the law. Even so the reformers failed.

The same inclination to evade the chief issue beset the special committee asked in 1934 to investigate the anticontraceptive law. The General Board of Health had been requesting a legal revision, again in order to be able to strengthen the prophylaxis against venereal disease. The Committee continued to discuss this point. No one dared to say that contraceptive techniques played a far more important role in preventing pregnancy than in hindering venereal contagion. No one said that it was still more in the interest of society to regard what happened within marriages than outside them. It must be admitted that this shunning of a clear statement was somewhat more understandable than has here been indicated because of the character of the birth control propaganda. As long as that propaganda is only negative, frightening some people into not having children with atrocity stories of maternity mortality, of stillborn babies, and of the horrors of "standing room only," so long must it be understandable that the very problem of family limitation is stamped with an undesirable emotionalism. The birth control movement certainly has a large responsibility for its own opposition on account of its onesidedness. This reservation made, it is apparent that dams of traditions and taboos and words were built up as defenses against the family limitation propaganda. But it is just as true that when the problems were tackled in a lucid and basically positive way by the Population Commission the sluices were opened and a liberating stream of opinion was released.

The reasons for legal revision were summarized by the Commission.

The original purpose of the law to prevent the diffusion of information and the use of mechanical contraceptive means and to increase the birth rate has not been achieved. As a matter of fact, in so far as the law has postponed the diffusion of effective methods for birth control and for the prevention of venereal infection, the result has sometimes been the utilization of less effective or even actually harmful preventive methods. In so far as the law has hindered protection against infection in loose sexual relations, it must be assumed that it has counteracted efforts to decrease the spread of venereal diseases. The law must further be considered in part responsible for the production of abortions as a means of birth control. In general, the law, as an obstacle to the diffusion of information and to access to effective means of protection against venereal infection or conception in coitus, has been able to have any considerable effect only on young and inexperienced persons and on people in the poorer social classes or on individuals endowed with less than normal intelligence, character, and foresight for the consequences of their acts. This, of course, cannot be considered other than unfortunate from a social and individual viewpoint.

The law has in many different ways also proved an obstacle to responsible and serious social enlightenment. The law has thereby also lowered the level of public discussion and enlightenment in sex questions as well as reduced the trade in mechanical contraceptive devices. . . .

An element of hypocrisy, dangerous for the people's morals, has been created.

On the one hand, the law originates in and still has its general foundation in the judgment that birth control is not ethically justified and must be fought also because of the threatening decline of population. Yet, on the other hand, such birth control is generally sanctioned by a majority of individuals in their private lives. [7]

Repealing the law would not mean encouraging extreme family limitation.

The danger of excessive family limitation has been emphasized by the Commission not only for the public welfare but also for marital happiness and the upbringing of the children. But birth control is anyway not to be confused with such extreme limitation. In order to combat this extreme family limitation we must not do away with all birth control. What is necessary is a more responsible use in marriage of birth control which as such must be for different reasons and to a certain extent practiced and sanctioned. The preventive law is a heavy drag in any attempt to accomplish these purposes. We cannot hide the fact that it is bitterly hated by many people in the lower classes. Rightly or wrongly, it has been considered as an attempt at class legislation to limit knowledge of rational, constructive birth control methods. In turn, this resentment has checked the natural tendency of these social classes to form a healthy and appreciative attitude toward family life with children. . . .

The state, by trying to hinder all birth control, has in general lost its opportunity to propagandize through informational and educational influences against the harmfulness of that birth control which carries limitation of families to the extreme. For the reasons given the anticontraceptive law appears as a symbol of a population policy which does not have the confidence of the people and which has to a large extent created suspicion of its purpose. It has not only been ineffective in achieving its purpose but has also been actually dangerous in its effect. The law is without basis in the people's sense of justice nor can it be supported on practical grounds. [7]

The repeal of the restrictive law was proposed by the Commission. Action to bring official morals in line with actual morals was taken at the parliamentary session of 1938. The government proposed the repeal of the law, and Parliament sanctioned it with considerable calm.

The new legal regulations removed all restrictions on public discussion, in the press or public meetings, concerning birth prevention. The penalties on exhibition and sale of contraceptives were removed. Trade in contraceptives was put on the same basis as trade in other pharmaceutical supplies in order to dispel the aura of the clandestine and illicit that had surrounded it. The sale of some harmful abortifacients was prohibited; the sale of others was permitted only on a doctor's prescription. Otherwise all contraceptive goods are included in the official lists of pharmaceutical supplies with prices attached. All licensed pharmacists may sell them; other dealers must have permits from the appropriate provincial authorities. On the latter question there was considerable controversy. The Population Commission proposed making the sale of contraceptives compulsory for all pharmacists, but the legislation did not go that far. Pharmacists are free to refuse according to their convictions, and thus local prejudice may still negate a considered plan. But at least a principle has been established. Provision of contraceptives has been made legitimate. As a matter of fact official statements (1940) maintain that no province is without some licensed dealers.

COMPARISON OF EDUCATIONAL AND CLINICAL APPROACHES

After the principle was established, the next step was to make it as widely effective as possible. Here the best recourse was adult education. Through public lectures, study groups, and other adult education agencies the newly legitimized information could be given the widest diffusion. Since many of these agencies, especially the oldest public lecture associations, receive both state and local grants, they were naturally responsive to official suggestion. Some agencies, such as the Workers' Educational Association and, in particular, the National Association for Sexual Information, had already been active. Now they could expand, and the latter organization has since sponsored numerous lectures and correspondence courses.

Instruction in birth control and sexual hygiene thus takes up where the school leaves off with preparatory although incomplete knowledge. Together the two educational activities can reach the great majority of the people. It must be remembered, however, that this propaganda has never been envisaged as being of an exclusively negative character; it is not just a colossal impetus for birth control propaganda. Many old Neo-Malthusian clichés must be abandoned if the propaganda is to fit into the new scheme of population policy. The positive values of the family must always be kept in mind. The social and national aspects of the primarily individual problems of family size must be presented. Therefore, nearly all lectures and courses on sexual hygiene and birth control end with an enumeration of social measures in the interests of children and families. Particularly it must be stressed that not only the sex education but also the preparental education of the schools should be extended over the mature years. The women's organizations and the adult education agencies have already started to take up that challenge.

Making information about birth control techniques available to the public through educational vehicles is one of the outstanding characteristics of the Swedish approach. When birth control movements in different countries are compared, this approach will take on still more distinction. Looking backward at the traditions within the country, it appears that this educational approach was chosen long before it had any claims to legitimacy.

It is necessary at this point to consider the relative merits of the educational and clinical approaches to the problem. In Sweden clinics have had little success and yet birth control has been widely and effectively practiced. Only a small proportion of the population has sought or even seemed to need medical advice in sexual matters. Venereal hygiene and family limitation have been achieved through knowledge acquired otherwise. Practically, this means that most family limitation has been achieved without any specific devices whatsoever, namely, by the use of coitus interruptus, and that when a technical device has been utilized it has been the condom. Both methods place the chief responsibility on the man. This is by no means the place to discuss the final, medical evaluation of the different contraceptive methods. The point is that the traditional practices have been successful, and it is of no small value that the new, more rational approach is not attempting more of a break with common practices than necessary.

To rely in the first instance upon information obtained through general education or even conversation must sound like heresy in countries where birth control movements have exclusively advocated the clinical approach. But whatever the reasons for presenting birth control as calling for individual medical consultations, whether the fear of arousing moral opposition or the desire to win the support of the medical profession, the clinical method cannot suffice. If rational planning or parenthood is dependent on clinical visits, large sectors of the population will live and die without it. Young persons in particular will continue to find themselves at a loss. They will tend to remain ignorant and to have their first experiences by the dangerous method of trial and error.

Evaluations of different methods of birth control should always distinguish between intermediary valuable methods and ultimately valuable methods. The Swedish program is based on the recommendation that the simpler methods, condom and coitus interruptus, be made known to everybody even before sexual intercourse. Methods like the pessary, requiring clinical consultation, should find their main use in a later stage, when people are deliberately and purposively arranging their sexual relations. They cannot be relied upon in the earliest sex experiences, both for technical reasons (which may be annulled by having the doctor of the clinic artificially open the vagina by dilating the hymen) and for psychological reasons, since they must rely on deliberate preparedness and outspoken agreement between the partners. Another point to be borne in mind is that what has here been termed the educational approach to birth control implies direct or indirect recommendations of methods which put the main responsibility for precautionary measures in sexual relationships upon the man, while so-called clinical methods place that responsibility upon the woman. The former has the advantage that it elicits from men a real, responsible consideration. In Sweden that has been the result, just as other social sanctions accentuate this responsibility even in cases where the moral aspect may be weak: rigid laws about paternity, obligation to pay for support of children, and so forth. It would undoubtedly be a loss to the culture if women should altogether relieve men of this responsibility and particularly the initial responsibility. In those cases where female methods of contraception will seem preferable to the individuals in the long run, clinical services will be valuable.

Many of those who regard the different methods of contraception from a purely technical point of view may find this presentation unsatisfactory. Are not the female methods, particularly the pessary-jelly method, so indisputably more secure that it is irresponsible to recommend other methods? The Swedish Population Commission surveyed the evidence in the field, utilizing both foreign and Swedish research. Simple percentage figures for reliability were not used for final judgment as they are arrived at in inconclusive ways. Information is often derived from patients at some clinic, thus constituting a selected and not a cross-sectional group. Often patients who visit the clinic do so on account of some failure in their attempts at birth control. In the main, the Swedish Population Commission held that "the choice of preventive technique — as far as the more common, efficient, and nonharmful ones of coitus interruptus, condom, and pessary are concerned — is largely an individual problem, in which general conclusions are difficult." All of them were listed with their advantages and disadvantages.

The custom of coitus interruptus was brought to the fore. Its efficiency cannot be doubted too much, as it has been mainly responsible for the considerable lowering in the number of births. Its disadvantages may be the anxiety that nervous control will not be maintained and the lessened sexual satisfaction, particularly of the woman. The condom has as its chief advantage its accessibility, its use for simultaneously protecting against venereal disease, its suitability in cases of young and old women where the pessary is not applicable. Its disadvantage is chiefly one of price. This as well as the uncertainty about its reliability may well cease to be an argument as far as Sweden is concerned with its new public control over the sale and manufacture of contraceptives. Improved quality and lowered price will enhance the value of this technique, as most failures have been caused by poor quality or irregular utilization on account of cost. The pessary is the most reliable and, for the sexual act itself, least disturbing contraceptive. It is particularly suitable within marriages and quite particularly in relations where the man's responsibility is limited, especially for women married to alcoholics. Its disadvantages are its inconvenient access, necessitating personal fitting by someone medically trained, and the need for the woman to be active in preparation for sexual intercourse. This element of laboriousness often becomes considerably enhanced by prescriptions about the subsequent douche. It is also inapplicable to young women before their first sexual relation and to women with certain organic dislocations or with the vaginal walls relaxed after a great number of births.

Individuals should choose methods of contraception according to their own greatest satisfaction. It has not been considered to be the task of society to recommend too definitely or exclusively one method or another. It has been accepted as the duty of society, however, to ensure that the different devices, perfected as far as possible, are available. The foremost task of society is seen as the spreading of information about planned and voluntary parenthood to the whole people through educational methods.

RATIONAL CONTRACEPTIVE ADVICE A PART OF THE PUBLIC HEALTH PROGRAM

All is not done that should be done for the spread of birth control even when information about sexual matters is given throughout youth, when the press is free to discuss the medical and social factors involved, and when contraceptive devices are commercially available. All these phases are supposed to assure that minimum birth control which must be open to everybody and particularly which must be available to youth. Personal guidance in determining which are the more satisfactory methods must also be available, even if this is a secondary concern. It was without hesitation that the Swedish Population Commission resolved that such birth control consultation should be provided by the community. Only the matter of organization had to be discussed. It was resolved that in the main such consultation services should not be instituted in the form of separate birth control clinics but integrated in the general public health program.

Clinics had been tried in Sweden as in many other countries, but their importance was never great. They did not flourish as long as the contraceptive law made both doctors and the public apprehensive. The three largest cities and one small university community had succeeded, however, in starting official clinics. These were not restricted to married persons but, as both birth prevention and especially venereal disease protection were needed for the unmarried, they were open also for them. Investigating their activities, the Population Commission found a remarkable underutilization. The Commission was thus led to advocate the spreading of advice on prophylaxis and contraception through much wider and at the same time more indirect channels.

Birth control clinics seem to be chiefly of value as ideological advances in the transition period when the permissibility of this type of medical advice is questionable. They also belong to a period when contraceptive information has in large measure reached the men in the population but when some women, not attaining their partners' cooperation for contraception, find themselves helpless. As long as special clinics have to be set off for a kind of physical advice which in itself is comparatively simple and does not need specialized equipment, however, the association of family limitation with secrecy, concealment, and shame is prolonged. The fact is that few of the women who need advice will ever go to the specialized clinics. For that conclusion the Swedish experiences provide irrefutable evidence.

In order to classify birth control advice with other medical and social advice, it was proposed by the Population Commission to integrate it with all other health services, offering such advice in any of the publicly organized contacts with the medical profession. The Commission first reviewed its more general preparatory provisions.

Practical birth control information can first be given to a certain extent in the courses of general sex instruction to be undertaken within the framework of adult education. A great deal of this advice can further be given in general lectures if this is done in such a way and in such a connection that superfluous sensationalism is avoided and provided the bounds of privacy are not unnecessarily violated. The more frankness and matter-of-factness and seriousness that can be injected into sex instruction, the better will be the education of our country's youth. The more successful we are in extending the boundaries of knowledge so that distorted and negative opinions on sex questions become rare the easier it will also be to give information on actual birth control methods in the course of general sex instruction.

However, one of the most recommended methods for contraception, namely, the pessary, needs individual fitting, and a woman should have individual instruction as to its proper use. Because of this, and for many other reasons, it is desirable that individual consultations should be available in addition to general instruction. During the course of this general instruction, reference should be made to this availability. The Commission considers it obvious that this individual consultation in contraceptive technique should be given mainly by physicians but also by nurses and midwives. [8]

To execute such a program the network of maternity and child health stations was singled out (Chapter 16). Some of them were already operating and a larger number were proposed by the Commission. They were to become local centers where birth control advice could be given naturally and unostentatiously. Medical training also needed to be reformed in order to equip doctors for this kind of service.

No special legislation will probably be required before the centers and stations undertake this work. After physicians have come to realize the importance of birth control and after they have learned the necessary techniques, it is expected that they will give information and advice according to the needs of their clients. It is, therefore, necessary to rely on careful supervision by the General Board of Health to see that the reform is carried out promptly. [8]

Not only has medical training to be changed, however, but also the attitude within the profession. It is in the last instance the doctors' own fault that people have not sought their advice and that the profession has forfeited its primary place in the whole matter of birth control.

The Commission wants to point out that in the lower classes especially the idea is prevalent that one cannot ask the advice of physicians on such subjects. It is well known that physicians have to a large extent refused to give birth control advice. According to the opinion of the Commission, it is of the utmost importance that there be a basic change in the attitudes of doctors in order that healthy progress can be made in this field and in order that the public may get into the habit of turning to the doctors for advice.

Normally, initiative is to be taken by those seeking advice. Yet, it often happens that the physician himself in the course of his ordinary practice or public work finds cases in which a married couple is sorely in need of birth control advice. In the future the Commission expects the physician to take the initiative in such cases. [8]

Physicians and surgeons could not, however, be given a monopoly in this fairly simple matter of birth control advice, as that would decrease its availability. Nurses and particularly midwives should also be utilized, and in this connection it should be noted that Sweden has a profession of highly trained midwives (Chapter 17).

Such an organization should not be necessary in those larger cities where there are special sex hygiene clinics or where there are health centers as described above. In rural communities, on the other hand, such substitution may be needed, and nurses and midwives should take over the work. The Commission feels that this can be undertaken by district midwives and also by the group of district nurses whose work is primarily in rural homes and in homes in small towns, where they give advice on medical care, child care, housekeeping, and special preventive care.

The first duty of the district nurse or district midwife is to give helpful information on clinics, centers, stations, or physicians where birth control advice can be obtained. In the second place, she should herself give the necessary advice on birth control and its techniques.

If such a program is carried out, there will be available over the whole country special consultation hours by physicians for those seeking advice. In the large cities there will be special sex hygiene clinics, and in the country, centers and stations for family health as described above. The number of such centers will probably be satisfactory according to present plans. [8]

Only when this whole system of organized public health becomes equipped to give advice on matters of family limitation is there any hope of information permeating all strata of the population. And, to repeat, there is no wisdom in failure to provide such information for the least enterprising in the population and in letting them beget most of the population. If family planning is taught in its positive connection with child care and maternity health, no one will shun it. Then birth control will be regarded as what it truly is: a means for making rational the foundations of a happy family life, nothing more, but neither anything less; neither propaganda for the extinction of the human race nor whispers to be hushed up in the name of decency.

The Problem of Abortion

Planned parenthood has been recognized as the foundation for a democratic population policy in the new program for Sweden. Birth control has been socially accepted. But there should be left no doubt that by such birth control is meant only preconceptual care. Abortion has been given no place among the measures sanctioned. It is easy to draw up such an ideal scheme that abortion could be made absolutely unnecessary by forestalling all undesirable pregnancies. Sterilization would then be utilized for the permanent cases where sufficient reasons exist, contraception for the normal cases when only temporary sterility is desired. But the social dilemmas of abortion would continue to make their appearance. Unwelcome pregnancies would still occur. Some of them would be due to the fact that human beings are often unable to make rational choices and act accordingly at the moment of sexual intercourse. Others would follow from rape or other forced sex experiences. Some would result because the anticonceptual devices failed. A population policy, striving toward completeness, will always have to face these cases. The underlying rationalism of the Swedish approach makes any attempt at evasion of the problem impossible. The very fact of the existing social dilemma explains why a working compromise has been effected between opinions heretofore irreconcilable: something between the individualistic radicalism of the Russian abortion laws of the 1920's and the authoritative condemnation of abortion prevailing in many other countries.

No law in Sweden had earlier admitted the right of abortion on any grounds. On the contrary, the penal law of 1734 contained a provision that the killing of a fetus made both the woman and any assistant liable to capital punishment. Later, imprisonment was stipulated. Induced termination of a pregnancy on medical grounds was, however, tacitly admitted to be within the discretion of the medical profession. During and after the 1920's it was increasingly felt that the growing liberalism of opinion on sexual matters required some changes in this legal attitude in order that verbalized morals should more truly correspond to morals as practiced. Abortions were known to be increasing although there is no possibility of making a reliable estimate. The passiveness of the prosecutor in not bringing cases for trial was felt more and more to constitute an irrational tension between law and life.

Women's organizations adopted a formal resolution in 1933 asking reform of the abortion law. The Minister of Justice in the Labor government which had come into power in 1932 was sympathetic. He appointed a committee which in 1935 submitted a report. A heated public discussion followed. Both this report and the minister himself, who personally advocated the reform, were considered to be dangerously radical. And radical they were, as far as the legal regulations themselves were concerned. It may be, however, that radical reforms in social attitudes toward sex have a greater chance of success when they are not only tearing down prejudices but also proposing constructive alternatives. In the wave of public emotionalism the problem was referred to the Population Commission, probably largely in order to gain time and let the storm abate. In its Report on Abortion in 1937, the Commission quite generally acknowledged the existing dilemma for which society had to find a way out.

In the long run widespread abortion obviously cannot be permitted to flourish unimpeded and at the same time according to the letter of the law be labeled criminal. To keep a criminal law on the statute books which merely prevents those who are expert in performing abortion operations, namely, the surgeons, from executing them and lets a paragraph stand which is only used occasionally to constitute an example is a condition which is not worthy of a nation of justice and culture. [9]

In proposing remedies neither of the two committees so recently heard on the subject proposed full individual freedom with respect to abortions. Abortion was considered too dangerous a means of birth control to be left to the whims of a people who had not yet been given the full possibility of obtaining advice about more rational prevention of pregnancy. They considered that it should be kept under a certain control. The Population Commission therefore proceeded to evaluate the reasons for abortion under certain categories. These had been ranked by the previous committee which wanted an amendment to the law which would legalize abortions on the following grounds: humanitarian, eugenic, medical, and "social," i.e., on account of economic difficulties and social disgrace. In all cases it was assumed that only doctors should be allowed to perform the operation and that quacks should be prosecuted and penalized.

Humanitarian or ethical grounds are present when pregnancy has occured after rape or after incestuous intercourse, when the woman at the time of conception is under 15 years of age, when she is incapable of consent on account of insanity or feeblemindedness, or "when coitus has occured with gross negligence of her own liberty of action." In these cases no doubts should exist.

Neither is the permissibility of abortion to be questioned when eugenic indications make it probable that one of the parents might transmit hereditary insanity, feeblemindedness, or grave bodily disease to the child. This is only a practical corollary to the legal provisions for sterilization. These will presently be taken up for discussion. It here suffices to state that when eugenic reasons motivate an abortion, simultaneous sterilization shall be a condition *sine qua non*. There would be little logic in preventing one birth for a reason that must be valid with regard also to subsequent births.

The first committee proposed to exclude altogether from legal regulation the discretionary power of the medical profession to induce some abortions on account of health. But the Population Commission wanted this right inscribed in the legal code, partly so doctors would more clearly recognize both their right and its limitations and partly because the Commission wanted to incorporate some mixed medico-social motives as sufficient ground for abortive operations. In general that means that when social reasons are added, the medical consideration of the woman's health, physical or nervous, should be given added weight.

The chief practical use of this mixed health-social sanction is to cover the many cases of "exhausted mothers." In families where means are not abundant, where the mother has a heavy burden of work, where she may be in poor health, and where she has already had several children, the abortion of an unintended pregnancy could only be deemed just. In this as well as the eugenic case, not only an abortion but also sterilization to prevent repeated distress should be prescribed.

The Population Commission went this far without much hesitation. But the fourth category comprising the cases of purely "social" indications, concerning which the earlier committee had encountered so much criticism, was handled in a totally different way. Such abortions no doubt occur in great number. They are calculated to have been around 10,000 anually in Sweden. The reasons for these abortions, illegal as they are, consist largely of economic distress and personal despair that must be understood. On the other hand, saying that the causes of these abortions are mainly social malfunctionings does not imply that such abortions should be allowed. The conclusion to follow is rather that the social evil should be abolished. The social dilemma is unavoidably clear; either the social conditions which bring women into such a situation in life that they must desire the death of the fetus must be abolished or the legal restrictions against abortion in such cases must be abolished. The Population Commission was in a position, owing to the wide range of the family reforms it was willing to propose, to support the former course.

A legal admission of induced abortion on such grounds should mean the registering in our very laws of a declaration of incompetency on the part of society itself in dealing with manifest social evils. [9]

The specific situations in which bearing of the child could be deemed subjectively undesirable may be divided into two groups in order to test society's resources to meet them by other means than removing the fetus. Sometimes economic conditions seem to warrant such an expedient; sometimes the disgracing situation accompanying an illegitimate birth does so. As to the economic distress accompanying the birth of a child the position of the Commission was that the mother and child should be given economic aid.

In a society with the economic resources and democratic culture of present-day Sweden, it should not be needed and could not be admitted that the birth of a child shall mean socially conditioned distress or despair for its mother. [9]

It is in the hands of society itself to remove such extraordinary difficulties. With this aim, social institutions must be created that guarantee economic security for any woman bearing a child. The Population Commission listed a number of such reforms, which will be discussed in subsequent chapters. As a special effort to meet the temporary distress often caused by childbirth, an emergency fund for maternity aid was proposed (Chapter 17). Only when society is willing to shoulder a great part of the economic burden of childbearing can it be justified in preventing the mothers from avoiding childbearing through abortion. But allowing economic distress to be legalized ground for abortion among poor women, while it should still remain a crime for women in economically protected circumstances, would mean a class law in the worst sense of the word.

The Commission is quite conscious of the fact that, under the present social circumstances, such a rule could be justified on practical grounds. But the Commission is of the opinion that needy pregnant women have a claim on community support so that abortion will not be desirable or necessary either in their own interest or in the interest of the community. [9]

The disgracing situation cannot be directly reformed by the community through any special laws or agencies. But also with regard to this aspect it was apparent to the Population Commission that the reform should be directed against the Puritan condemnation of illegitimacy rather than toward the coming child.

There is no reason to sanction that sort of morality which treats with disdain those, in relation to the large number of unmarried women having sexual relations, few unmarried women who happen to become pregnant. This public contempt appears so much more unjust as the men practically always escape such a consequence of the relation leading to a pregnancy. This social disgrace attached to the unmarried mother becomes particularly inconsistent and deleterious as it can be avoided through abortion. The unmarried mother who carries on the pregnancy will have to sacrifice more for her child than other mothers. If she in our day, with the widespread possibilities of obtaining an abortion, chooses not to avoid the consequences that way, is she not more worthy of honor than of disgrace? In any case it remains a public hypocrisy, dangerous for the moral sanity of all the people, when this social condemnation among all the women who have had extramarital sex relations befalls only the ones that become pregnant and do not resort to abortion and when the boycott against these women is to a very large extent sustained by persons who themselves must be supposed to have, or to have had, extramarital sex relations. [9]

The Population Commission ended its recommendations with the practical suggestion that not only should all legal rights be extended to unmarried mothers and their children but also that persons and organizations in an official capacity should carry on a campaign for educational reevaluation of unmarried motherhood. Adult education and women's movements were singled out, together with doctors, teachers, and clergymen, to be made responsible for such a campaign.

Because of the reasons given above the Commission therefore concludes that it cannot support the proposal that abortion be permitted on grounds of dishonor. This conclusion has been reached with a lively consciousness on the part of the Commission that unmarried mothers often do meet such social boycott that the birth of a child causes the mother great distress. But the Commission has chosen to presuppose that strong efforts should be made on the part of intelligent and responsible citizens so to educate and enlighten our people that they might gain a deeper insight and a more moral and ethical concept of the worthiness of motherhood, even of that motherhood which is endured under the especially trying conditions usually accompanying childbearing outside of matrimony. [9]

The terror of contempt which the unmarried mother will have to go through often has secondary effects of an economic character. Often this mother will lose her employment. Sometimes the employers themselves create the moral dilemma as they do not allow their women employees to marry. Many abortions are known to have been induced in such situations, even among teachers, nurses, and office workers who enjoy high personal prestige. "As the Commission finds that the rule against married women's work often enforced by private employers is a grave social wrong with injurious effects both for individuals and society, a change must be effected."

If the pressure of a more enlightened opinion is not enough to bring the employers to conform, legal interference in order to protect the employees becomes necessary. (Such a law was enacted and has been in force since July 1, 1939. See Chapter 22.)

It may well be argued that even if all social causes for distress in relation to an undesired pregnancy are thus in the long run foreseen and disposed of, either by allowing abortion or, in most cases, by changing the social structure, there are still left a residual number of pregnancies undesired for purely personal reasons. To curb people's right to resort to abortion in such cases has been said to invade their personal liberty. This is true. The Swedish abortion laws today do not allow perfect freedom with regard to life or death of the fetus. Women are not given what many of their organizations demanded, "complete sovereignty over their own bodies," but neither are other operations permitted at the will of the individual. All doctors are held professionally responsible that only operations which in their judgment seem necessary or harmless should be performed. The refusal to allow perfect individual freedom in the case of abortions rests in the ultimate instance on the very fact that abortion is not harmless and thus women have to be protected against it by the medical profession and society. If it were found to be totally harmless, this argument could not be upheld.

One thing should be made perfectly clear as far as Sweden is concerned: this reluctance with regard to abortions is not motivated by any desire to bring into existence a larger number of children undesired by their parents. All other measures for the spread of birth control allow the individual parents perfect freedom to choose whether they want children or not, and the children "lost" are many times the number "saved" by the restrictions on abortions. But social demands as they now stand dictate that such a choice should be made before conception, not after it. The most direct attacks upon abortion, working to prevent undesired pregnancies, are the proposals for more general information about sexual matters and specifically about birth control. Society should not keep its young people so unenlightened that abortions among these young people need to be excused. The Commission also made it explicit that its fairly rigid attitude toward socially motivated abortions was conditional. If all measures for teaching people birth control were not thoroughly instituted, abortions should be legalized. There is no other choice.

Some further reflections on the range of this legislation are in order. If information on birth control was universal and if contraceptive methods were completely reliable, this attitude toward abortions would be entirely consistent and defensible. They, however, are not. And here, it must be admitted, one flaw in the laws and in the Commission discussion remains:

the impossibility of fulfilling through abortion a birth control measure that was perfectly planned and motivated but that failed in individual cases. It is, however, extremely difficult to see how such an exemption could be fitted into the laws. It will rather have to be relied on that doctors will take such occurrences into consideration and by more lenient interpretation of one or the other of the categories in the abortion laws include these individual cases within its domain. If contraception was planned, the woman will generally have some reason which, however slightly, resembles the indications for abortion and thus by liberal interpretation can be placed in those categories: some consideration of finances, health, and so forth. In most cases when such a liberal interpretation cannot be valid and only personal wishes to avoid a new pregnancy are invoked, parents would probably welcome even an originally unplanned child for the sake of upholding a law, for the sake of protecting the health of the mother, and for the sake simply of taking with fair complacency some of the risks that can hardly ever be eliminated from human life.

There seems to remain one chief category of undesired pregnancies in which neither health nor finances nor any other reason covered by the legal rights to abortion can be adduced and in which the situation cannot be averted by any of the social measures being made effective to reduce both the economic distress and the social disgrace of bearing a child, namely, those resulting from marital infidelity. The Swedish law makes it difficult to find an escape for these cases. The compromise of ideologies which always is responsible for the scope of a law stopped in the face of this category of pregnant cases. Alleviating their misfortune by making abortion permissible was simply not possible according to public opinion concerning right and wrong. The unfaithful sailor's wife, wanting an abortion in order to save her marriage, was played up in order to arouse public pity, but it failed to do so. It even came near to bringing failure to the whole scheme of legal revision. Although it may work cruelly for some individuals, the moral conception was that such results of marital infidelity had to be faced by the partners. That important strides could be taken toward liberalization in regard to sex morals and abortion was only made possible by the extremely radical faction sacrificing its opinions just as the extremely conservative faction did. There is no doubt that the statute ensuing from the compromise still was several degrees more liberal than a plain average would have indicated.

A law was finally passed by Parliament in 1938 to go into effect on January 1, 1939. The operating doctor and a public medical officer must prepare a joint report explaining the grounds for the induced abortion. These reports are to be filed with the General Board of Health. For abortion on eugenic grounds, formal granting of permission must be given by the Board. Such abortion must ordinarily not be undertaken without accompanying sterilization. It is further prescribed that the opinion of the prospective father must be obtained. An unmarried mother, not under a guardian and not institutionalized, may veto this. Criminal punishment still is provided if other than doctors undertake or try to induce abortion. It is also provided for doctors giving false statements to the medical authorities about their operations and for any persons whatsoever giving false statements to doctors and authorities.

During the first year the law was in effect the General Board of Health was notified of 439 abortive operations: 80 on eugenic grounds (28 cases involving risk of insanity, 35 for mental deficiency, and 17 for grave bodily disease), 5 on humanitarian grounds, and 2 because the woman undergoing a sterilization operation was found to be pregnant. The rest were on medical grounds, the most frequent being because of tuberculosis (94 cases) and neurosis (90 cases). Somatic diseases covered 130 cases and psychoses 25 cases, while 13 cases were reported as "generally weak status." Regrettably, it is impossible to trace in this material the marginal category of "exhausted mothers," on whose fate most of the curiosity of social reformers is centered.

STERILIZATION

When society is helping some parents to get better conditions for their children and is helping others to avoid the children they do not want to have, there is no wonder that society also sometimes wants to dictate that some children should not be born. Such a desire, at least in a democratic state, will only appear in connection with eugenically doubtful parentage. How strong the risk of an inferior heritage must be to warrant prohibiting parents from having children is a matter of value judgments. But the Swedish public holds that compulsory sterilization shall relieve the parents and the country of some of the least desirable children and further that voluntary sterilization shall give the parents the right to exercise some option. In those borderline cases where sterilization may seem too grave a responsibility while childbearing still appears undesirable, a forceful birth control prescription should be made.

Earlier attempts by law had been in the form of marriage restrictions. The Swedish marriage law of 1920, in force since 1921, continued the old rule prohibiting the issuing of marriage certificates by the registration office in cases of severe mental disability. But omitting the marriage ceremony is rather a magical attempt to prevent childbearing. The legislators have therefore sought a more direct way to prevent the bearing of eugenically undesirable offspring, namely, sterilization. Opinion in Sweden favoring sterilization had gradually developed during the 1920's and early thirties.

An official report on the subject was published in 1929 and another in 1933, and finally in 1934 a law providing for compulsory sterilization of some insane persons and of imbecile persons was enacted. The law was, on the whole, cautiously formulated. It has to be proved that a person suffers from a definite mental deficiency; but in addition there is the further condition of two alternatives, either that he shows disability to take proper care of children (social indication) or that his deficiency implies hereditary risks for the offspring (eugenic indication). In either case there must be legal incapacity on his part in order to make compulsory sterilization possible.

If there is reason to assume that a person liable to mental disease, mental debility, or other disturbances of mental activity will on that ground in the future be incapable of having custody of his children or that he will through his hereditary disposition transfer to his offspring mental disease or debility, sterilization may without his permission be undertaken according to this law, providing that on account of his disturbed state of mind he is permanently lacking in capacity to give valid consent to such a measure. This law is not applicable for sterilization on medical grounds.

This limitation, of course, considerably curtails the practicability of the law. Society probably has to suffer such limitations, however, rather than overrule personal liberty. The compulsion, according to the Swedish law, is further so interpreted that consent is not necessary for sterilization while direct refusal prevents it. Under no circumstances is force to be used. The eugenic reasons must be quite strong for sterilization to be warranted. The law is clearly applicable with regard to the feebleminded as the importance of hereditary factors is without grave scientific doubt in these cases and as the persons concerned as a rule lack legal capacity. The mentally diseased seem to escape the application of the law by far wider margins. Against mental disease of the schizophrenic type little can be done, as the hereditary relations are complex and partly unknown and as the predisposition is widespread among the population. The carriers of the hereditary taint may not themselves show the abnormal traits and then the whole question of forced sterilization becomes void. Sterilization of persons in the manic-depressive disease group would by itself have greater effect; but there the desirability from social viewpoints of extinguishing the manic-depressive predispositions is more debatable. The illness does not so generally and not so unequivocally make the persons valueless. Swedish eugenists have at least not wanted to take any far-reaching responsibility in that respect. It may be noted that neither criminality nor alcoholism has been considered any indication for sterilization. Sterilization has never been intended to have any punitive character.

Serving as a prevention for certain classes of repeated sexual offenses, castration is recommended as more adequate than sterilization.

The actual effects of the sterilization law may be of some interest. The number of sterilizations appears to be astonishingly low. [*124*] From January 1, 1935, when the law went into effect until January 1, 1940, only 822 persons had been sterilized. Aside from those and outside the field regulated by law, 1,271 persons had been sterilized with their own consent. Of these only 5 per cent were men. Of the total 31 per cent were sterilized on directly medical grounds (chiefly tuberculosis, heart and kidney trouble, and expected complications in pregnancy and at childbirth). In no less than 57 per cent of the female cases of voluntary sterilization induced abortion and sterilization occurred simultaneously. This obviously suggests that the abortion was the urgent need, precipitating the sterilization. Only 32 cases of exhausted mothers are separately listed among those women relieved both temporarily and permanently from undesirable childbearing.

Of those sterilized according to the law as legally incapable 80 per cent were mentally deficient and the remainder suffered from mental diseases or less clearly diagnosed mental deviations. Even if the former group preponderates, the number is small as compared with the estimated number of 30,000 feebleminded or even with the official census total of 17,511 feebleminded in 1930.

A curious discrepancy will be found when sex is taken into consideration. Although only 91 of the 822 sterilized persons were men, it must be stressed that neither feeblemindedness nor mental disease nor parental inaptitude has such a predilection for the female sex. The reason is simply that the municipal authorities who have the right of initiative for sterilization find the sexually undependable women too expensive for the public budget. This is, however, an indication that a general and truly eugenic solicitude has not yet become the force behind the procedure of sterilization in Sweden. If it were, mentally deficient men would more often be held responsible for their offspring. Figures as to number of children already borne by those sterilized demonstrate that the overprolific cases have first come to administrative attention; 56.4 per cent of the women have borne children, averaging 2.5 children. The 16 married or divorced men have a total of 68 children. Among the sterilized women the frequency of children, prior to sterilization, when age distribution is taken into consideration, is about double that in the general population. It is evident that sterilization has been undertaken far too late in the lifespan of those undesirable mothers. The exhausted mothers should have been found within the group of those voluntarily sterilized but they were practically nonexistent, which is a fact of great social importance.

Some imperfections in the law are partly responsible for its underutilization. The right of initiative is widely divided: for minors, it belongs to the one having custody; for persons under guardianship, to the guardian; for the institutionalized, to the doctor or head of the institution; for families on relief, to the poor-law authorities; and for minors under child welfare care, to the Child Welfare Board. No one person or agency has had the formal possibility of canvassing any one community in order to take stock of all the legally incapable, who are thus eligible for sterilization, although such a survey, undertaken, for instance, by the local health officer, would be a much more rational procedure for eradicating the unfit while there is time.

Reviewing the effects of this law it must be realized that its safeguards narrow its scope. Only persons seriously disabled or demented on account of mental illness or deficiently developed may become sterilized without their consent. There must, however, above that stratum exist many whose hereditary or social indications are just as poor, but who are capable of consent, perhaps of refusal. As these borderline groups are also the very ones not institutionalized, they are by far the more dangerous from the point of view of future population quality. The law, for these reasons, does not reach as far as its own motives would have sanctioned. In our day of highly accelerated social reforms the need for sterilization on social grounds gains new momentum. Generous social reforms may facilitate homemaking and childbearing more than before among the groups of less desirable as well as more desirable parents. This may not be regretted in itself as the personal happiness of these individuals and the profitable rearing of those of their children already born are not to be neglected. But the fact that community aid is accompanied by increased fertility in some groups hereditarily defective or in other respects deficient and also the fact that infant mortality among the deficient is decreasing demands some corresponding corrective.

The Population Commission assumed the task [6] of proposing certain changes in the existing law concerning compulsory sterilization. Of greatest importance was the suggestion that all public medical officers should be given an additional right of initiative in all cases and that all applications should be examined by the Board of Health. At the same time it proposed legal regulation of voluntary sterilizations of persons capable of legal consent. By such legal regulation individual freedom may in a certain sense become limited; some cases of sterilization may not be allowed. Complete individual choice will no longer exist. All reasons for the desire to become sterilized must be stated. But in the nature of things these grounds do not have to be as grave for voluntary as for compulsory sterilization.

Also, the reasons for voluntary sterilization are classified under the main headings of social or eugenic causes. As to the social reasons, it is proposed that manifest incapacity to be responsible for the care of children in the future, if founded on some deviation of mental activities, should make sterilization permissible. Such indications are to be given added weight if economic status is depressed. Thus wide limits for taking social suitability for parenthood into consideration are provided where compulsory sterilization could not follow out of regard for the individual's rights. The alternative purely eugenic reasons for voluntary sterilization include all cases of hereditary insanity, feeblemindedness, and genuine epilepsy. In the case of other forms of epilepsy, medical and social grounds may make sterilization permissible even if eugenic grounds do not. Generally the hereditary risk may be considerably smaller in such cases than is necessary in compulsory sterilization. With regard to hereditary diseases of the nervous system and bodily diseases and deformities of hereditary character, sterilization will be allowed not only when the probability of transmission is great but also when the abnormality risked is a grave one. Thus psychological factors are given a place to relieve the fear of defective offspring that sometimes obsesses a person. The same consideration, together with purely eugenic ones, explains why, according to this proposal, healthy carriers of hereditary risk may also be allowed to become sterilized. In addition it is prescribed that the presence of economic distress or unsuitability for parental duties may decrease the requirement of hereditary risks even more. On the whole the intention is obviously to create a great discriminatory margin in making permissible voluntary sterilization whenever there are good reasons for it. This proposal, which would systematize and rationalize the whole scheme of sterilization and fit it into a system of family protection and which would make for population improvement without interfering with individual rights, has as yet not been submitted to the Riksdag by the Cabinet.

Thus two means, sterilization and abortion, have been provided for by law to prevent socially undesirable parenthood. Such radical measures as actual operations cannot, however, be thought of as ideal or sufficient to solve the huge problem of persons of marginal suitability for parenthood. Birth control through contraception must become the main device. It must be resorted to as a substitute for sterilization in the wide, borderline groups where heredity is uncertain but not enough so to indicate even voluntary sterilization. It must also gradually be substituted for abortion. The considerations of poor heredity, mother's health, etc., should not need to appear as afterthoughts in so many cases. When birth control is strongly indicated but fails, abortion should be the last resort. It should never be regarded as the first resort. Also, it should never be used instead of contraceptives or instead of sterilization if the reasons for not having children are permanent.

Final Victory of the Neo–Malthusian Movement

The four new reforms in Sweden — repeal of the anticontraceptive law, effective spreading of sex education and contraceptive consultation, right to abortion in certain clearly defined cases, and a widened but controlled practice of sterilization — will mark the final victory of the Neo-Malthusian movement. That movement has served its time and will become history. It is being liquidated through success. It should be noted, however, perhaps as a memento to similar movements in other countries that are still in their militant stages, that the victory was not brought about as long as the fight was carried on only in a negative sense. The whole people were won to the support of the movement only when its negative interest in preventing the birth of some children was coupled with a positive interest in family and population.

CHAPTER XIII

ECONOMICS OF HOMEMAKING

A BOUT half the adult population of Sweden is unmarried. Of every seven children born in Sweden nearly one is born out of wedlock and more than one was conceived before marriage. Obviously there is something lacking in the institution of marriage. Plainly marriage is made too difficult, especially for the young, and plainly, too, it must be made easier for the young. The subjective difficulties, those having to do with the love relation and, in particular, the sexual relation have already been discussed and the measures taken to alleviate them described. But there is more to the problem. The conclusion cannot be avoided that in Sweden there are sociological difficulties deriving from the character of social institutions. These have to be alleviated if the population problem is to be solved.

Before proceeding with the discussion of economic impediments to homemaking it is necessary to call attention to the uneven distribution of the sexes, regionally and vocationally, which operates as an initial handicap to opportunities for mating. This, too, is economic in origin, since separation follows from conditions of earning a livelihood. A rounded population program therefore seems to call for a reorganization of occupational conditions in such a way as to distribute the sexes more evenly. This phase of the problem was taken up by the Committee on Women's Work, which reported in 1938. [22] No final program was drawn up but lines of action were determined. The belief was expressed in the report that private industry could with advantage draw on new labor supplies by locating "women's industries" in what hitherto had been "men's districts" and vice versa. The Committee saw opportunities for a reapportionment of male and female employment in rural regions, also. Generally, the traditionally rigid labor division in agriculture will have to yield when there is so much less labor available. When agricultural pursuits become more specialized and more mechanized, requiring more training and less physical strength, some agricultural work might become well adapted to women employees, e.g., driving a tractor or caring for livestock.

The effect of occupational location on marriage is brought out in some revealing statistics cited by the Committee.

As more and more marriages take place between gainfully occupied persons it was to be expected that the number of cases would increase in which positions in different regions would form an obstacle to the establishment of a common household. It was hardly to be expected, however, that this situation would prove so far-reaching as the results of an inquiry among women teachers would seem to indicate. According to this inquiry not less than 14 per cent of the married public schoolteachers and 16 per cent of the married primary schoolteachers are unable to live with their marital partners.

In addition to this type of case there are many cases in which a woman has had to give up her work because of having to move to her husband's place of residence. There are also the cases in which marriage cannot take place or must be postponed for an unreasonable length of time because both parties cannot find gainful employment in the same region.

Under these circumstances it would seem to be in the public interest that the labor market should pay more attention to family formation. In private business such considerations must be based upon personal arrangements. But much would probably be gained if this desire of married partners to find employment in the same place could be looked upon as a legitimate social need.

More particularly the Committee turned its attention to the civil service as being the field where direct interference in labor conditions is easiest. It is also the field in which such interference has most often affected adversely the interests just stressed. Definite proposals in the form of civil service statutes are, however, difficult to formulate so as not to foster favoritism. The Committee had to be satisfied with expressing the hope that in individual cases the administrative authorities would give consideration to family formation and personal happiness. At least, the Committee "expects the authorities to pay some attention to this social phenomenon and this not in a negative way." With this recommendation the issue seemed to be closed for the present, no action being taken; but an incubation period for these new ideas was inaugurated.

BUDGETING OVER THE LIFE SPAN

It has been a thesis of this book and of the whole Swedish population program that economic forces tend to develop adversely to the interests of families, if left to their own evolution. Since economic life is man-made, however, its content can be remade. The bulk of the reforms proposed as population planning in Sweden were attempts at such remaking. The changes that society can induce in its own structure in order to harmonize the needs of the families with the resources of the country may seem inadequate and ill-matched when seen in individual isolation. Taken together they attempt an adjustment between the curves of incomes and of expenditures over the life span. Most of these rectifications of family economy are dictated by the advent of children, but already at the very beginning of a marriage some survey of resources has to be made, some purposive planning undertaken for the anticipated future, and, perhaps, some public assistance mobilized.

Economic planning for the whole life span has to be given a somewhat different treatment in different social groups.

In patriarchal agriculture marriage was often long postponed if it meant breaking up the working family unit and acquiring a new farm. The dependence of the young people was great, their possibility of individual saving practically nil. Marriage could as little be an individual affair for economic reasons as for socially derived habits. It must be pointed out, however, that what was, and still is, difficult in the farm economy was the erection of an independent unit of support. On the other hand, the setting up of a home, furnishing it, etc., were relatively easy. Many things were homemade; a great proportion of them were inherited; demands were less exacting; preparation and storing of handicraft objects for the homes of children when marrying were started early. Outfitting the young has thus been a traditional obligation of the parents, economically compensated for by the young people's own work and low remuneration within the parent's home. It may thus be said that for the family unit as an integral whole, embracing two and often three generations, a certain harmony was achieved between the income curve and the expenditure curve through early work and late marriage of the young. For the individual to break out of that unit and set up a new one, however, was beset with difficulties.

As modern agriculture acquires more and more of an industrialized character, some of these difficulties in marrying disappear but others increase. Individual young persons in modern farm homes may feel freer to control their own earnings, but their leaving the family farm may seem even more disastrous than in earlier times, as children are fewer and as paid labor is more expensive. If they leave while quite young, wages for labor to substitute for them will swallow up the potential savings of the parental family ·which formerly could be used for equipping the new household. Even if they want to leave when such savings have been accumulated, they may be deterred from marrying by the fear that the old couple may face a catastrophic rise in costs of production.

On a farm the arrival of children does not, however, so definitely affect the budget curve. Still less in earlier times did it mean an aggravation of the economic situation in the family. With child labor utilized less and child hygiene demanding more, it is difficult to evaluate children as direct economic assets in farm families, although it still holds true in the agrarian groups that the most profitable period of the income curve is when children are maturing.

The economic fate of industrial families follows a somewhat different course. Its typical pattern is one of relatively high incomes in youth, similarly. Expenses at the time when the worker is young ought to be proportionately lower, as he lives alone or pays little for board and lodging if living with his parents. The margin for personal spending is therefore wide, at least wider than later. The prospect of losing this margin by marriage may serve as a deterrent to matrimony. Otherwise marrying and providing a home should not be difficult in this group. Hardship comes with the children. Expenses then mount but incomes do not. A lack of balance is thus characteristic of the income and expenditure curves when viewed over the course of the lifetime.

In the middle social groups of professional, civil service, and related workers the income curve again is different. In those groups the period of youth is economically meager. Long years of study prolong a dependence that in comparison with earlier times and other social groups seems incongruous with maturity. Employment often requires experience which is gained through additional years of volunteer service. The maximum incomes come late in middle age, far beyond the years when marriage and children first make their demands. The status of economic dependence delays marriage, and debts from the preparatory years may even constitute a drain upon the individual income far into old age. There is, it is true, a compensation for all this. What is finally achieved is a more secure position and a higher total income than in any other group. These groups are, however, definitely handicapped with regard to marriage and particularly with regard to young parenthood.

Social Adjustments to Improve the Balance of Incomes

For youth in the farming group the possibility of easier access to separate farm ownership would be a fundamental approach. Avoiding speculative increases in real estate values would thus be a gain from the population point of view. Just as evidently in the interest of youth and ultimately also of founding families would be a regulation requiring formal labor contracts for sons and daughters working in their own homes. Such a change in the economic habits of the farming family is under way in Sweden. Various organizations like the Farmers' Youth League, corresponding somewhat to the 4-H Clubs in the United States, and the Committee on Women's Work mentioned above have come out in favor of the practice. In so far as such changes to more businesslike relations are practicable they will tend to put youth in agricultural groups on the same footing with regard to marrying as industrial youth.

The low marriage rate in rural districts may have still another cause that could be somewhat neutralized by social changes of a general character. Undoubtedly the uneven distribution of the sexes, giving rural men meager chances of meeting young girls of marriageable age, plays a certain role. Public attention has been directed toward the female flight from the country, and some possible readjustments on the labor market have been discussed. In addition, reductions in the work of rural housewives to bring its proportions somewhat nearer those of urban housewives may help to make marriage seem more inviting to rural girls. A public investigation of the working life of rural housewives [42] suggested many methods of reform.

What should have been noted first is the necessity of breaking down rigid traditions of what is men's work and women's work. It leaves the women of the house with heavy work even at times when the men can enjoy seasonal leisure. In large parts of Sweden, particularly Norrland, it has become the woman's job to milk the cows, feed the animals, and clean the stables because the men are so often away on timber jobs. When the men are at home, thus adding to housework, the farmwork still falls on the women far too often. Similarly, in harvesttimes when both men and women work in the fields, men may use the dinner hour for rest but women do household work. The work in the farmhouses themselves is laborious. It is a truism that men's work has been reduced much earlier through mechanization.

In the investigation referred to, educational propaganda was given first place in the list of proposals for measures of reform. As a second measure state grants for the installation of running water, bathrooms, sewerage, and central heating were cautiously recommended. Such state grants had been available as part of the public work program to relieve unemployment during the depression. It was now proposed that they be put on a more permanent basis and included in the provision for improvement grants to rural housing, with a special staff of consultant engineers for planning. Testing and recommendation of household utensils and laborsaving devices by a state-supported institute (Institute for Rationalization of Housework) was proposed, the Institute's activities to include educational propaganda. Home demonstration agents already are engaged in many districts, but a centralized research department has been lacking. Communal laundries, which are also being rapidly developed, were next proposed with state grants covering 25 per cent of the building and equipment costs (50,000 crs. were voted in 1939 and the same amount in 1940. The first sum resulted in 15 such laundries). Finally, the rebuilding activity which was sweeping over the country with the help of public subsidies was once more given a hearty recommendation. It was further proposed that 50 model farm homes be erected in the different provinces with state funds and the help of housing consultants in order to investigate the possibilities for standardization and to serve as models for the neighborhood (4 of these were completed in 1940 in Norrland). These recommendations were motivated by the general desire to obtain equalization within the country through eliminating substandard living conditions, but they also would operate directly to make farm life more inviting to modern young women. They would have a chance to have homes which are not conspicuously primitive as compared to urban homes. The Swedish farm women have awakened late, but supported as they now are by a strong Housewives' Organization and also by public sentiment, thoroughgoing reforms can be expected. Their best ally is the eagerness to rebuild farm homes, a movement which combines the preserving of cultural traditions and the instituting of modern improvements. It may be symbolized by the name sometimes given to it, "New Homes in Old Homesteads." Thus general changes in the social setup are decidedly working to encourage marriage and to rationalize homemaking among rural youth.

In the professional middle groups particularly, the prevailing pattern under which power and income are concentrated in the older age groups will come under critical fire when social interest turns increasingly to the defense of the young and their families. More of the cost of schooling could be carried in the public budget, and thus it could be lifted from the shoulders of individuals, where at present it lies in the form of heavy debts. Reforms in that direction have been making headway in Sweden and will be reported in the chapter on education. But there is little that society can do by formal intervention to distribute earnings more equitably over the years and thus create increased opportunities for the young in this group. In the field of civil service, exploitation of the young might be diminished. In the main, however, any leveling of inequalities will have to be instituted directly in the professions, where the old will have to share with the young somewhat more equitably if family founding shall not be prohibitive for the young. These demands for equalization over the age groups may appear just as radical in some social classes as equalization between the classes, but the family values which are at stake used to have their stanchest advocates in these same groups.

All these are changes and reforms of a generally rational type which can gain support on other grounds than the interests of population. Of the same general character is another reform that industrial youth in particular will demand if they are to found families without fear. This is security as to work and income. The Population Commission realized this and made some broad recommendations from its point of view, although for obvious reasons it was unable to lay down another program on unemployment.

Unemployment and the great risk of becoming unemployed depresses a large section of our working classes. This risk is often an obstacle to any long-range life planning, and to a large extent it postpones until an uncertain time in the future the possibility of marriage. The unemployment of youth, intensified in every new crisis, deprives young people of the economic opportunity of founding a family while, at the same time, it destroys their faith, self-confidence, and interest for work and disrupts their education and development. With reference to these conditions the Commission has not desired to omit stressing the fact that, if marriages are to be promoted in the younger age groups, measures must first of all be undertaken for the purpose of assuring the young people greater economic security. The problem of unemployment must once more be considered, and in doing this the question of vocational training and vocational guidance is worthy of attention. [4]

Shifting Income Over the Life Cycle

Society can certainly even out some time inequalities by pooling resources, advancing money where incomes appear too late in the life cycle to be of real value to marriage, and enforcing some savings where incomes are high in comparison with needs in earlier years. Before such specific social aids for marriage are instituted, however, caution must be exercised. The marriage ceremony and the original homemaking should not be allowed to become so costly as to consume at the beginning means that rather should be available at the childbearing stage when greater needs, and needs in a socially much more profitable sense, occur. This applies to both community and individual means. The bourgeois tradition from the nineteenth century involved such elaborate preparations for marriage that the outright and simple desire of two young people for living together was hampered. The customs had their sociological connection with a time and a group in which the wife had to arrive well dowered, for in the comparatively leisured classes that was the best way in which she could compensate for her lifelong support. When married women now more frequently continue their employment and their earnings at least during the earlier years of marriage and to a larger extent substitute for servants, the need for dowry and elaboration has passed. Also for other reasons, and perhaps with special emphasis in Sweden, there is now a contrary tendency that might be called an attitude of sporty simplicity toward marriage. It may well be that the prestige demand for ornamentation around marriage may be checked before it works down to the rank and file of the people. The roles are changed; the matter-of-fact and self-reliant young working people are rather setting the pattern for more comfortable social groups than vice versa.

Whatever the Swedish authorities are interested in doing in order to encourage marriage among the young, it should not be interpreted as encouraging conspicuous waste at marriage or a too heavy setup of material objects for the simple task of starting a young household.

In those groups where costs for occupational preparation are not high, incomes available in the younger years seem to be sufficient for homemaking. In any case, incomes cannot be expected to increase considerably in the future. Wise budgeting would rather indicate some spread from early years to "family years." No social dictates can be enforced in this respect in a democracy, but individuals might still by some means be helped to overcome a life-cycle pattern, according to which the worker during his youth frequently, if he has work, has more cash at his command to use for personal culture or luxuries than he will ever have later in life. Planned saving would be indicated in many of those cases.

Other groups of young people do not enjoy incomes from which to save. To smooth the curves of their incomes and expenditures over life the opposite course must be taken. The means at their command must be increased at the time for homemaking and be compensated for by decreases in later years. They need cash loans for homemaking.

PLANNED SAVING

The movement for planned saving is not truly directed by the government. The state saw its role only as instigator but left it to free agreement between the public and the recognized savings institutions to organize the activities. The decentralization of power and administration from the public to semi-public agencies, more directly under the control of the citizens themselves, is a typical trend in Swedish democracy. The main political agencies frame the objectives and the civic organizations develop and administer resulting programs. Credit is also largely governed by the people themselves.

Savings institutions are organized as civic corporations (*sparbank*). First organized more than 100 years ago, there are now 476 scattered throughout the country. In 1939 their deposits amounted to 3,591 million crs., and they had 3,647,000 accounts or a number equal to more than half of the inhabitants of the country. The second main institution for popular saving is the Postal Savings Bank, which has a branch in every post office and also takes small amounts. In 1939 there were 2,719,000 accounts, a number equal to nearly half of all inhabitants, with combined deposits of 628 million crs. There are also large saving organizations attached to the consumers' cooperatives and to the housing cooperatives. All the commercial banks also receive deposits on savings accounts.

All institutions encourage savings starting at the school age. Since the 1860's children have been given higher interest or sometimes an initial nest egg in the savings banks. To these institutions and the Postal Savings Bank it only seemed logical to try to arouse interest in still better organized plans for saving in youth through savings clubs and savings contracts. When the Population Commission came along with its mandate to buttress the whole social superstructure in the interests of the family, it injected as a new note the idea that savings be for homemaking purposes. This emphasis was given by a provision that a depositor may withdraw his account or break his contract for continued saving without forfeiting the higher interest he has been getting if he does so in order to marry.

The condensed recommendations of the Population Commission on planned saving were as follows:

1. Without specific legislation and in forms as free as possible, increased facilities should be created through expansion of a system for planned saving among young people. The Postal Savings Bank and the cooperative savings banks will continue to be mainly responsible for such activity.

2. Planned saving should be restricted to persons between 15 and 30 years of age. It should be entered upon through a contract between the person saving and the savings bank.

3. In order to encourage the expansion of planned saving activities, savings banks should help to institute at places of employment, within youth organizations, and in other suitable connections savings clubs, to be administered by their own elected officers. Savings clubs should have the task in cooperation with the savings banks of organizing saving activities and of ensuring that private savers duly fulfill the contract of saving they have voluntarily entered upon.

4. The savings bank shall also outside of savings clubs encourage private citizens to undertake planned saving. For such a purpose savings plans shall be made widely available, indicating what amounts could be saved under different conditions as to time, terms, and dues.

5. When signing the savings contract both parties should carefully consider the time the savings contract shall run and the rate of saving with reference both to the amount desired as a result of the saving and the economic possibilities for fulfilling the contract. The person saving makes himself responsible in a definite way for the obligations of the savings contract.

6. The savings banks shall in the savings contract guarantee higher than average interest on such savings, provided they occur in compliance with the contract. Such higher interest may be received on a maximum sum of 3,000 crs.

7. The person saving shall have the right to make larger than contracted savings and, with the aforementioned maximum, also receive the higher interest on the excess.

8. If the person saving can demonstrate that considerable changes have occured in his economic conditions, thus necessitating a reduction in the amounts to be saved or postponement of the terms for payment or cessation of continued saving, he shall have the right to get his stipulations changed in accordance

with the new circumstances but without losing his right to the higher interest on the capital already saved.

9. The person saving has the right at any time to withdraw his deposit. If such withdrawal occurs before the time limit set in the savings contract, the higher rate of interest computed shall be changed to the ordinary rate. Only if a legitimate motive for such earlier withdrawal can be demonstrated shall the higher interest remain.

10. Marriage shall always be considered one such legitimate motive without any need for investigating circumstances. Such a motive shall also be judged to prevail where the person saving can show that he needs the money for tuition or educational costs generally, for occupational training, acquisition of his own home, starting of his own business or some similarly important purpose, or on account of illness or unemployment or distressed circumstances for the saver or a dependent relative.

11. The savings bank must issue a certificate when such is requested about the fulfillment of a savings contract. Such a certificate is to be used as proof of personal reliability when applying for loans of different kinds, and it is taken for granted that particularly at the issuing of state loans considerable importance ought to be attached to this method of demonstrating savings will and savings ability.

12. When the savings period agreed to has expired the person saving shall be eligible to start, if he so wishes, a new savings contract. The capital accumulated under the earlier period shall be considered as starting capital and the higher interest be enjoyed both on that and on the new deposits.

13. For spreading the knowledge of and the interest in planned saving both the Postal Savings Banks and the other savings banks shall together carry on propaganda in suitable forms.

14. For the first year the state shall contribute 50,000 crs. toward the cost of such propaganda. [4]

The direct participation by the state should, as can be seen from the recommendations quoted, only be in the form of monetary support for general educative propaganda to encourage contractual saving. To put such a plan into practice the main need is not to recruit individuals. The close weaving of all kinds of civic organizations into the structure of Swedish society again has to be remembered in order to understand the foundations for success of any such movement. When savings clubs are formed within these organizations — youth leagues, trade unions, temperance lodges, etc. — real force is lined up behind the attempt. The Farmers' Youth League has the honor of being the originator of such activities and more groups are following its example. For any movement to become successful in Sweden it must be adopted by the people themselves in their active mass movements. The latest reports show that planned saving is thus being securely developed among the masses.

STATE LOANS FOR HOMEMAKING

A scheme of marriage loans proper has, however, both to supplement and largely to substitute for planned saving as just described. The Population Commission followed the two ways open for dealing with the problem of budgeting for homemaking: starting the saving for the home before the young person has met a partner and actually plans the founding of a home through a savings program and shifting the saving to the years just following the marriage ceremony through a marriage loan. The traditional way had been to postpone marriage. The Population Commission held that young people could just as well be allowed to enjoy their days together when saving for their home. Such a scheme for budgeting during a young couple's first years would not only serve to check the postponement of marriage but would also favorably compete with another expedient, installment buying.

For the majority of young couples marriage is associated with certain individual initial expenses. . . . Even two young people who, because of their own savings or because of assistance from their parents, have a small starting capital may need a certain additional amount to establish a household. Such an additional amount may further be necessary if the young couple, when they get married and establish a household, also buy their own home, plan to take over a small business, buy a practice, etc., by which they plan to become economically independent. . . . Of first importance is the question whether any real subsidies should be given for the purpose or not. Such a subsidy could either be given in cash or in the form of certain rebates on commodities as direct aid in setting up a household. It could also be conceived of as lower interest rates or easier stipulations about amortization of the marriage loan. Under both alternatives any number of specific conditions could be laid down.

The Population Commission is opposed to them. Setting up a household should normally not be an occasion for calling upon resources other than one's own, although a kind of "help to self-help" which consists in spreading the obligations over a period of years could well be thought of as a community responsibility. No subsidies but only loans become the practical conclusion.

The temporary expenses connected with setting up housekeeping should normally be paid through savings during youth and through prompt payment of loans during the early years of marriage when the couple is relatively prosperous. Even if among the professionals and civil servants the income is low during this period, it would be extremely difficult to defend the payment of subsidies. However, individuals in this latter social class are, on the whole, more securely employed and better remunerated than the average individual in the other social classes. The Commission proposes marriage loans by the state on such a business basis that the borrower is duty bound to repay the loan with interest. The costs to the state will then be confined to administration, together with the risk of having to write off a certain number of loans that cannot be repaid. [4]

The Commission recommended that the loans be repaid in the first years of marriage which often are economically favorable because the wife retains her wage-earning status.

The homemaking loan ought normally to be repaid before the economically most exacting period in a family's life, that when children grow in number and years. [4]

For this purpose a state fund granting loans to young people intending to marry was proposed. No formal surety was to be asked, as the aim was to free young people from dependence on their credit rating and on their success in finding guarantors. On the other hand, the loans were to be granted only where it seemed advisable on consideration of the opportunities, personal diligence, and demonstrated ability to save of the young people themselves. The loans, up to a total of 1,300 crs., could be used for the purchase of furniture, purchase of homes, and similar expenses. The repayment of the loans would not be too long postponed as the amortization ought not to remain as a burden at the time when children can be expected to place extra demands on the family budget. In line with the aim that the process of saving for a home should only be transferred to a period just following instead of preceding marriage, a maximum period of four years was proposed.

At the parliamentary session of 1937 such a law was enacted, creating a state fund available to betrothed or recently married couples from January 1, 1938. The amortization period was extended to five years and the maximum amount to be granted lowered to 1,000 crs. In both of these respects the final outcome may be said to be less inherently true to the population ideals than the original proposals. The extension of the amortization period in particular may somewhat endanger the inclination to bear children in these young families. Four years had been thought an ample waiting period. This shorter period was also motivated by the desire not to encourage young people to invest more for homemaking purposes than they could conveniently pay off at a fairly rapid rate.

The loans are handled by the National Bank with the assistance of local commissions. The total administrative costs were estimated at only 65,000 crs. annually, these being the only costs carried on the state expense budget. The fund is accounted for on the capital investment budget. The interest asked before the outbreak of the war was $3\frac{1}{2}$ per cent (in the middle of 1940, $4\frac{1}{2}$ per cent), which was expected to cover the actual borrowing costs of the state. During the first year 7,765 loans were granted, totaling 5,700,-000 crs. The 8,225 loans made during 1939 totaled 6,487,000 crs. The payments are being made with regularity, and this has caused credit administrators to comment that young people marrying seem to be an extremely sound risk. Unfortunately the great number of young men called to the colors since the outbreak of the war has caused a setback, but this is obviously to be expected.

From all that has been said, it should appear that the Swedish marriage loans not only in form but above all in philosophy are quite different from the German ones. There is no limitation as to where to shop. No subsidy to certain dealers for either economic or political reasons is possible. The loans do not contain any element of premium for the bearing of children; no fraction of the loans is canceled when children are born. They have never been coupled with any demand that the wife cease wage-earning. In addition, the loans are to be repaid in the early years of marriage, thus reserving full resources for the time when needs of children are paramount. By giving only loans and no subsidies community funds are saved which increases the possibility of giving substantial aid in that period of family life when economic pressure is greatest on account of children.

Swedish Modern Homes

The homemaking loans have certainly not called into being but have encouraged the change in home furnishing which is sometimes called Swedish Modern and which sometimes characterizes itself as "a movement towards sanity in design." Whatever the movement is called, it is envisaged as an instrument for beautifying all Swedish homes. This movement has had a conscious aim and has been a tremendous force in Sweden since the end of the World War. It has been revolutionizing mass production for homes. Its definition is given in the following statements, which emphasize the cheapness, the aesthetic values, and the production methods.

Swedish Modern means high quality merchandise for everyday use, available for all by the utilization of modern industrial resources.

Swedish Modern means natural form and honest treatment of material.

Swedish Modern means aesthetically sound goods, resulting from the close co-operation of artist and manufacturer.

The last point is probably the formula by which all has been achieved. The cooperation is not just one between an individual artist and a manu-facturer; that is business rather than cooperation. Artistic interests combined with social interests have been organized in the Arts and Crafts Society (*Svenska Slöjdföreningen*), which has been able to change the whole attitude toward home furnishing and the whole style of such furnishings. [*200* and *110*] Plans for cooperation with manufacturers are worked out; blueprints of good furniture are even provided for small-scale manufacturers; and ex-hibitions are held to give the hallmark to good things. Those confounding Swedish Modern with just another fad in style do not understand that this is fundamentally a social movement and a claim for aesthetic purification of all goods of all styles. That the present trend is toward light wood with soft surfaces is only a dramatic contrast to the cheap imitations and excessive ornamentation that first followed mass production.

In granting homemaking loans the state obviously could not decide in what style the homes should be furnished. Again, however, that close co-operation between state and semipublic civic organizations which is the mark of Swedish democracy came into play. Already in its report on the subject the Population Commission had called on these organizations to act as advisers, to publish lists of recommended goods, etc. An advisory council has also been set up by the Arts and Crafts Society together with representatives from the organizations for employed women, youth, and housewives in a campaign to educate youth to a sense of beauty and honest cheapness. This feeling for style is extended not only to furniture, lamps, and rugs but also to every object surrounding the family from the pictures and the dinnerware to the kitchen utensils. A guidebook with detailed lists for homemaking has also been published by the Taxpayers' Association. Exhibitions are held. The initiative of the Consumers' Cooperatives department store in exhibiting complete households for different income levels is particularly commendable. If private furniture stores could be induced to play that educational role also so that no persons, even if they had the money, would overspend, something truly great would be achieved. Without having any illusion that all buying blunders committed on account of prestige ideas can be avoided, it may still be worth noticing that the trend exists in Sweden. What it means quantitatively is difficult to say. A chance glance into a young worker's home will convince anybody that the balanced art of home furnishing has spread surprisingly far.

*   *

*

The road to matrimony is being eased. Youth should enter it better prepared through prefamily education. They should be able to choose with greater insight marriage or its alternatives of different kinds and values when sexual maturity comes. They should feel more confident about their marital relations, both as to successful sexual adjustment and as to the voluntary character of parenthood through the available birth control advice. They should finally feel that their desire for homemaking is met by helpful attitudes and even economic encouragement by the community. What they thereafter make out of marriage is up to themselves. No tutoring or supervision or exhortations by the nation hamper their freedom to live as they can and want to, as partners and, eventually, as parents.

CHAPTER XIV

HOUSING FOR FAMILIES

Housing reforms are just coming into the foreground of social thinking the world over. In most countries no coherent scheme of sufficient scope really to solve the problem has as yet been formulated and adopted. Housing projects arise sometimes on a frankly experimental basis, sometimes as direct responses to local needs which can no longer be ignored. The public conscience is aroused over housing conditions in some places. In others public spending to create employment is focused on housing programs. The prophecy may be ventured, however, that housing reforms will continue in a halfhearted way as long as they are not directly linked with family welfare.

A program for population can clarify housing objectives. On the other hand, a population policy would be meaningless without housing reforms. Economic equalization between families and individuals will there find its greatest obstacle because housing costs are such an important part of the total budget costs for a family and also because housing sets the very frame of the home, which determines the life of the family. When the goal is the remaking of society for children, the strongest material resistance will always be found in the field of housing. The housing supply is of necessity the least flexible of all major items involved in social changes. A new society will for the most part always have to live in the dwellings inherited from an old one. In most Western countries today, except for some rapidly growing cities where the majority of houses are newly built, hopeless masses of drab homes are depressing evidence not of how poorly modern men have built new houses but of how ill-fitted the houses of yesterday are to modern men. The lag in housing often serves as one of the most important factors in retarding both the rise in standard of living and the adjustment of family life to the changing composition and changing work of the average family. Other consumption habits will react more quickly to new movements. We may learn to eat foods rich in vitamins and to wear suitable clothing, but in our most important modes of living we will continue to be limited by the conceptions of yesterday because the very houses determine so much of our everyday life.

From the viewpoint of the individual family there is in housing an inherent lack of flexibility that is most constricting for the family's life possibilities. There occurs in time a series of changes in family size and age composition and thus in housing needs. They range from the honeymoon period through the stage of a group of two working adults with some boisterous youngsters and later the family of grown-up children demanding much space to the final period of relative solitude of the aging. The ideal home that would lend itself to change according to these different patterns without crowding or waste has yet to be developed. Flexibility can only be achieved by more comprehensive planning than the individual can accomplish. The increased elasticity of a renting market does tend to provide for the possibility of shrinking and expanding the home frame of family life, but only densely urbanized communities can offer such mobile possibilities. Even then economic reasons ordinarily hinder renting according to need.

The difficulties are accentuated in a dynamic stage of population development. When the population has been of the expanding type and is just converted to a shrinking one, the age composition of the population and the distribution of family types as to size change drastically. In Sweden these changes are threatening to cause chaos in the housing market. The number of new marriages expected in the immediate future will create a need for a rapidly increasing number of homes for one or two decades, but the low level of births during the recent period foretells a time when total housing needs will decline. The flocking of young people into the cities is accentuating the dilemma. It can be met only by clear-sighted planning.

Developments in the housing field in Sweden will be described briefly. It must first be made clear that individual families rarely administer their own housing consumption, with the exception of those on farm homesteads. This administration, once the chief function of landlords and estate owners, has gradually been affected by public control. In the dramatic development toward more cooperative responsibility by the citizens, the final turning point is reached when family problems become dominant.

Gradual Change from Real Estate Business to Social Housing

Savings available are ordinarily not large enough for the individual family to be able to make such a long-range investment as buying a house without assistance. Housing is thus typically a form of consumption directed by some agency above or outside the family itself. Creating special credit facilities for building is one form of such suprafamily activity in the housing field, particularly in rural districts. Under such circumstances the home-owner is dependent upon private creditors, savings banks, mortgage banks, or the state. Most housing in the urban districts in Sweden is, however, furnished through the activities of private real estate investors. Then the families are dependent on landlords (Table 20).

TABLE 20.— HOMEOWNERSHIP IN SWEDEN

AREA	PER CENT OF DWELLINGS OWNED BY					
	Tenant himself	Employer	Municipality; cheap housing projects	Landlord	Estate owner [a]	Other
Rural districts, 1935–1936 [b]	63.5	11.2	—	9.3	9.6	6.4
Urban districts, 1933 [c] .	21.5 [d]	10.4	2.7	63.3	—	2.1
Stockholm,[e] 1935 . .	16.0	6.7	4.7	65.6	—	6.8

[a] Farm tenants, crofters, etc.

[b] Rural Housing Study, 1935–1936 (*Särskilda folkräkningen, 1935–1936*, Part III).

[c] Urban Housing Census, 1933 (*Allmänna bostadsräkningen år 1933*).

[d] Includes cooperative apartments.

[e] Stockholm Housing Investigation, 1935 (*Allmänna bostadsräkningen i Stockholm, 31/121 1935*). Figures for Stockholm are not directly comparable with the other studies because of differing definitions.

Recognition of the fact that the individual family is mostly unable to administer its own housing consumption on its own resources has been followed in Sweden by the slow realization that housing is preeminently a social matter rather than a field for private speculation. The shifting from private to public responsibility appears in many different forms. The most general one is the time-honored policy under which Swedish municipalities acquire large tracts of residential property. The object of such a policy is both to control real estate speculation and to safeguard rational city planning. In both respects success has been attained. Prices of real estate have been controlled. This has surely deprived speculators of their gains but not conservative investors of their profits. In some instances municipalities have yielded to the temptation of realizing speculation gains for the city by raising selling prices for building lots above their costs, but they have in any case stamped out the worst forms of land speculation and stabilized the real estate market. They have also been able to furnish land free or at greatly reduced costs for social housing projects. Housing areas are developed by private entrepreneurs and cooperative associations in accordance with some central plan.

Providing credit for homeownership may be regarded as a parallel step in the same direction. It is, indeed, interesting to see how all the different movements which aim at homeownership have been made possible only by organizing public support. Individual family interests thus become linked with community interests in contrast to private business interests. This illustrates how public control in Sweden never is control over the individual but control with and for him.

Public or cooperative support of the homeownership movement appeared first in the field of rural housing. It has there become one of the most important social enterprises. The original driving force behind it was the desire to counteract emigration. As early as 1904, a state fund was appropriated for the purpose of granting loans for the building of privately owned homes, both farm and nonfarm, outside of city limits. During the first 35 years (through 1939) the fund has helped in the erection of about 94,200 family homes, of which about 55,200 are farm homes. Municipalities, industries, and other groups have also facilitated housing developments along similar lines. These far outnumber the state projects. Other sources of building credit have encouraged the same movement. There is no doubt, however, that the state loans provided the impetus for shifting landownership from landlords to homeowners. It has been estimated that in 1935 there were about 400,000 nonfarm homes (100,000 urban and 300,000 rural) which were owned by individual families. These housed about 1,500,000 persons, or nearly one-fourth of the total population.

At the time when private enterprise wholly dominated the urban housing market, the state inaugurated (1909) the City Mortgage Bank (*Konungariket Sveriges Stadshypotekskassa*), which granted owners of urban real estate credits up to 50 per cent, and in the larger cities 60 per cent, of the property value. The state is liable only for the capital it has advanced to the bank (at present 125 million crs. in government bonds); but that, together with the rigid state control which is administered cooperatively by the borrowers, has given its bonds the character of gilt-edged securities and thus made possible an extremely low rate of interest (around 3 per cent in 1939). For these loans, which have been directly profitable not to tenants but to owners of real estate, about 1,062 million crs. had been granted in 1939.

During the early years of the present century the social aspects of housing were widely discussed, particularly in connection with the concern about emigration. The Association for Social Work (*Centralförbundet för Socialt Arbete*) was particularly active at that time. As a result of the activities a new public agency, the General Social Board, was created to direct public welfare activities. This Board immediately (1912–1914) conducted a countrywide housing census, [83] but the interest in social housing soon waned, partly because the World War caused certain temporary housing problems which to some extent made people forget about long-range programs. Hopes for improvements in the housing field became centered in the cooperative movement. Cooperative building and owning of apartment houses were considered the urban counterpart of the rural or semirural homeownership movement. The ideals were the same: individual ownership through mutual cooperation.

The cooperative housing movement dates back to the 1880's, but it grew slowly. About 100 housing societies were registered at the turn of the century, and every year thereafter a number of small, independent cooperative units of one or two houses were added to the total. During the World War the movement began to assume its present importance. The World War produced a sharp rise in rents and at the same time private building was greatly curtailed. All measures were directed toward averting these two evils. Societies were organized not only for joint ownership of old apartment houses but also for building new ones. More important than the creating of these scattered housing cooperatives, however, was the fact that in 1917 the tenants, including many who were renting from private landlords, started to organize. These Tenants Societies have become a vital organization (*Hyresgäströrelsen*), controlling unfairness, setting housing standards, and promoting reforms, laws, and educational activities in the whole field of housing. In 1923, the Tenants Savings and Building Society (*Hyresgästernas Sparkasse — och Byggnadsförening, H.S.B.*) was organized. This soon expanded into a national organization and by October 1, 1940, had built homes for about 25,500 families (for 11,500 families in Stockholm alone). The individual family has to invest 10 per cent of the total costs for its own dwelling unit (sometimes reduced to 5 per cent). This investment is often made through a savings plan. Later annuities are balanced so as to pay the cost of the dwelling unit (down to first mortgages) in 20 years. Many modern conveniences have been introduced to Swedish tenants through these apartments; lasting improvements in planning of space have been made; campaigns for better taste in furnishing and wall covering have been successfully carried out. The narrow house with sun exposure for all apartments, and often terraces for all, has been widely used. Mechanical laundry equipment has been provided. Great importance has been attached to the play rooms in the cooperative apartment houses, now the leaders in the nursery school field.

The number of new dwelling units erected is not the only measure of the success of this movement. It has had a much wider influence in lowering rentals and in improving home standards generally. The greatest contribution of all, however, is probably the ideological one of educating the tenants in a form of mild collectivism. They in turn make it clear to wider groups of people that the responsibility for housing can be assumed by the citizens themselves and that tenants can solve their own housing problems.

Aside from providing an impetus for cooperative housing, the World War with its disturbances of production and the ensuing shortage of dwellings in Sweden concentrated interest on one factor: the rent. Social action then focused on legislation with regard to credit facilities. The living conditions of the inhabitants of the houses were forgotten under a long tug of war which took place between different economic interests. The most important step taken by the state was the Rental Regulation Act of 1917 which placed all decisions about rentals, selection of tenants, security of contracts, and so forth in the hands of local commissions. The renting market was freed from this regulation by the repeal of the act in 1923, and speculation mounted. The only competitor which checked private business during the late twenties was the cooperative movement. The depression of the 1930's operated as a further check.

Another type of intervention by the state in the field of housing during the critical World War years was more concerned with encouraging private business than with helping poor tenants. In 1917, the same year that rents were limited, state grants to contractors were introduced in order to help overcome the stagnation in the building trade. Such subsidies without obligation to refund were discontinued in 1922. A state fund for secondary credit (guaranteed by second mortgages up to 75–80 per cent of the property value), organized in 1920, has been more instrumental in promoting building activities. It has been estimated that between 1917 and 1930 about 32,000 dwelling units were built with such government encouragement, constituting about 20 per cent of the urban building activities of the period. These activities were finally put on a more permanent and businesslike basis by the setting up in 1930 of a Housing Credit Fund (*Svenska Bostads Kredit Kassan*) to give credit covered by second mortgages. This institution was financed and organized in about the same manner as the previously mentioned City Mortgage Bank. The two institutions together do about the same work as the Federal Housing Administration in the United States although, from the viewpoint of financial technique, in an entirely different way. While the FHA insures loans made by other agencies, the corresponding Swedish agencies make direct loans.

In almost every country the early development of housing policies has been characterized by the fact that the bulk of the work done, even if otherwise highly significant, has been of only limited direct value to families which are most in need of improved housing conditions, i.e., those which cannot afford adequate housing even if ordinary residence construction is encouraged and costs kept within limits by means of reforms in housing finance, by rational city planning, by control of real estate speculation, and so forth. This has been true also in Sweden. The state's attention to this purely social side of housing was, up to the depression of the 1930's, even less pronounced than in some other countries. The field had, however, not been wholly neglected. It had in varying degrees and with varying success been entered by some local communities and philanthropic agencies. The necessity for doing something impressed itself upon the consciousness of the communities, as in most cases the request for poor relief was made just to cover rent. Through credit facilities, direct subsidies, and some building of their own, the Swedish municipalities encouraged low-rent housing projects for the masses of the people. These activities were, however, necessarily limited by the municipal resources and thus had often to be forsworn in communities where they were most needed. In rural districts they were compeltely lacking. No picture of these varied activities can be given here.

The whole development up to the 1930's was gradual and haphazard, being directed by governments of different political colorings and without any clearly conceived motivation. Still the tendency toward increased public responsibility and control was indubitable. The state, municipalities, and the cooperative movement were slowly penetrating the sphere of private housing enterprise. Yet these activities did not accomplish much more than the balancing of the deterioration of the housing supply, except that they probably contributed somewhat to the spectacular boom in building construction which started before the middle of the 1920's and lasted, with only one short setback during the early 1930's, up to the beginning of the current war. The major causes of this boom, however, were of quite another character: the fact that the number of families increased much more rapidly than the population; the intensive industrialization and urbanization; and internal migration. Whatever the ultimate cause, there was practically no development of real slums in the cities and modern facilities rapidly became more prevalent.

Housing Policy and Depression Cure

In the early years of the 1930's the shift in business conditions and particularly the rise in unemployment again brought the housing problem into the foreground. Building was designated as the main economic activity that could reclaim the stagnated productive forces. The political change in Sweden in 1932, resulting in a labor government which has had a long and strongly supported tenure, made it still more inevitable that building activities should be seized upon as a major device for overcoming the depression in such a way as to leave a useful residuum when the depression passed. Within the framework of the Swedish system for public works and useful spending as an antidepression measure, state activities in the housing field now took on increased proportions. In the first phase, however, these activities were concerned mainly with reemployment. A social vision that took the whole country's housing situation as motivation for policy and planning had not yet matured. This lack of a program at a time when it was so badly needed was the unavoidable result of the decline since the pre-World War period of research, information, and interest in the social aspects of the housing problem. A housing census conducted in 1912–1914 provided the best available data for 20 years. The low point in interest was reached when the material gathered in the housing census of 1928 was not even tabulated in such a way as to show how people lived in the houses and how poorly the houses fitted the people. Rents continued to be the chief interest. Research in housing was regarded mainly as an item in cost of living studies.

This decline in the social approach to housing, causing lack of a program and even of information, may be more easily understood in the light of the simultaneous prosperity in private real estate. Also, during the prosperous years preceding the great depression the cooperative housing movement engendered rather wider hopes than it was destined to fulfill. No general program for housing seemed needed. Most of the socially minded individuals, who always serve as the dynamic conscience of the people, centered their faith at that time in the social device of direct cooperation. Only "help to self-help" was thought to be needed. In the lean years of the depression the cooperative housing movement came to a realization of its inherent limitations. Then it was perceived that cooperation can solve the housing problem for the middle strata in society only. There are other groups of families too poor or too mobile or too large to be able to accumulate the initial capital and to continue the annual outlays for a cooperative apartment. It is especially true that those families which are young and have children have not had time to save for cooperative shares. Cooperative houses have harbored few children. Saving for a cooperative apartment and sometimes saving for installment buying of furniture have been found to be among the most efficient inducements to sterility.

When the state in 1933 wanted to open its purse for an immensely increased building activity, the necessity of formulating some long-range policy was immediately urged by experts associated with the government. An economist, Myrdal, and a city planning director, Åhrén, published a report, *The Housing Question as a Problem for Social Planning,* [*182*] which set forth the principles for an integrated housing program. They carried out experimentally an intensive investigation of demographic, economic, and housing data for one city, Gothenburg, and proceeded on that basis to sketch the outline of how to harmonize production plans with demand trends, how to fit them into business cycle policy, and how to coordinate housing inspection, public housing subsidies, and private and public building activity. This call for a country-wide program was answered by the nomination of a Committee on Social Housing, appointed to construct a long-time program for social housing. Simultaneously temporary activities to be started on a large scale were approved. This has been related in order to show that the thinking of the authorities in Sweden during the first years of the depression of the thirties was wiser than might be realized from a record of their activities. The consistent program first got under way in 1935.

Meanwhile, the "housing policy without a plan" that was started in 1933 as an emergency measure could without risk of mistakes undertake at least one line of attack: to improve the quality of rural dwellings. This, too, was motivated by a spending policy rather than by a housing policy. Purchasing power was to be spread throughout the country by means of small allotments for housing improvements in many different localities. Building was recognized as a key activity in such an economic situation, as it is highly labor-consuming and as the material needed encourages production within the nation. The government proposed to the Riksdag in 1933 the launching of a program for rural housing. New laws were enacted covering grants for repairing houses, a system of new construction loans for replacing substandard houses, and subsistence farm loans for small holdings for forestry workers and similar groups. These measures for rural rehabilitation have proved their value and are being continued under more favorable economic circumstances.

The improvement grants are obtainable for 80 per cent of the renovation cost (before 1939 they were obtainable for 50 per cent), but they are fixed at a maximum of 2,000 crs. per dwelling (before 1939 the limit was lower). If the houses are too dilapidated, a construction loan for a new home may be made at a low interest rate and providing for full amortization within 20 years. Sometimes the two forms of help are provided for parts of the same dwelling. This state credit for building may cover up to 80 per cent of the costs (before 1939, 70 per cent), but no maximum amount is fixed. Finally, for improvement purposes a special improvement loan has been granted since 1939. This may cover up to 80 per cent of the costs, but it is not applicable to dwellings for which either of the preceding two forms of support has been granted. This loan is interest free for 10 years but must be amortized in 20 years. In all three cases the local Board of Health is first to pass judgment on the housing quality, while the formal decision and the handling of the money rest with the Own Homes Board (*Egnahemsstyrelsen*). During the first five years (up to July, 1940) about 62,000 rural homes were built or renovated with this public support. That this is a substantial achievement is more easily understood if one considers that the corresponding number in a country of the size of the United States would be close to 1,300,000 homes. The appropriated sum amounted to 63.75 million crs., four-fifths of which was in the form of grants and the remainder in loans. The quantity of the work done and the lack of professional assistance for some of the local supervising agencies, however, made it difficult to maintain adequate standards of quality. The Rural Housing Survey made in connection with the 1935-1936 Census revealed that, although most of the houses that had been reconditioned under the program were at least fair, there were some which still were in bad shape. It is probable, however, that these conditions have since been improved.

It was mainly in regard to owner-occupied homes, which are predominant in most Swedish rural areas, that this assistance was utilized. For tenants and rural wage workers, however, the program was less useful. Partly because of that, a different method for subsidizing rural housing in the form of workers' subsistence homestead loans was introduced. These loans are free of interest and amortization for five years. Thereafter, one part of the loan, designated for the house, shall be amortized during 30 years but is interest free, while another part, corresponding to the cost of the land, shall not be amortized and only a low rate of interest paid. As these loans aim at furnishing workers in the lumber, fishing, and stonecutting trades, etc., with a small farm holding which can supplement wages with production of some living essentials, the loans are considerably larger, reaching a maximum of 7,000 crs. (earlier 6,000 crs.). The number of homes, and only the housing side is here under consideration, secured with the help of this scheme was 6,657 by the end of 1939. The cost was 38.4 million crs. Special credit has also been available since 1935 for building laborers' and tenants' homes. These loans have as yet been little utilized.

These endeavors for improving rural housing were all new. They represent a definite break with the traditional view that housing is solely an urban problem, an opinion that is no less fallacious because it is psychologically easy to explain. The concentrated mass suffering in cities makes of course a much more vivid impression than the occurrence of inadequacies in isolated rural homes.

To promote urban housing the traditional method of lending funds to private builders was followed. These possibilities were now increased to include third mortgages above the 70 per cent limit on property value on the condition that credit in the ordinary market is provided up to that limit. In 1935 a special fund was created for this purpose and somewhat later loans for the reconstruction of old houses in urban areas were inaugurated. In comparison with normal total building activities these urban measures have been of little importance.

A FAMILY HOUSING PROGRAM

When the plan for social housing was finally developed, it was centered around the needs of the family. In one stroke a new alignment of housing policy was accomplished. The scheme of subsidizing families instead of houses is, perhaps, the most important Swedish contribution to the world-wide housing problem. The various traditional objectives of urban housing policy — slum clearance, reducing overcrowding of dwellings, and decrease of rents — were coordinated under the wider aim of family protection.

The earlier measures taken, particularly in the cities, had, as previously indicated, practically all aided people who were not especially in need of public help. As a matter of fact the individuals reaping the fruits of the public endeavor often belonged to an economic middle group. This was true even in regard to many subsidized housing projects, in that the subsidies were seldom large enough to make the new possibilities available to the poorest families. This gives substance to the criticism of waste and extravagance. In a democracy a housing policy, expanded to correspond in even a modest degree to imperative social demands, simply cannot gain the wholehearted support of the average conscientious citizen, if it is not reserved for a group of families obviously needing help ahead of all others. Such a direction of housing policy not only increases its effectiveness as a social measure but is also least disturbing for private business.

The number of families in need of subsidized housing is of course tremendous. On the basis of the two housing investigations previously cited it has been estimated that around 1933–1935 something like 300,000 families or 1,500,000 persons were living in overcrowded and/or dilapidated dwelling units. Only dwelling units with more than 2 persons per room were regarded as overcrowded.[1] It should be noted, however, that not all these families were in need of subsidized housing. Many are suffering from poor housing conditions although their incomes should be high enough for obtaining more adequate living quarters. This was, according to certain estimates in the Urban Housing Census of 1933, true in regard to one-third of the urban families which were living in overcrowded dwellings.[2] These cases included particularly families with many adult or adolescent children, most of which presumably were independent income earners. It seems likely that the trouble often was that the children were more or less undependable as contributors to the common family expenses.

Even if such cases are excluded, the number of families in great need of improved housing was too large to be included in a housing program

---

[1] Children under 15 years of age were counted as half persons and kitchens as half rooms.
[2] Families with more than 800–1,050 crs. (depending on cost of living in the locality) per person unit (children counted as half units) were considered economically able to secure adequate housing.

that could be realized during the next decade. It was then necessary to classify the needs and find a group for which immediate action appeared particularly justified. The statistical analysis made the selection of such a group comparatively easy. The problem of overcrowding appeared more significant than the aspect of quality, at least as far as the cities were concerned. For reasons that will be presented subsequently, it was also from the viewpoint of economy in a long-range building program necessary to attack this problem first. Overcrowding of course affects large families primarily. Those large families in which the children are small are most often economically unable to obtain adequate housing. From the viewpoint of national health poor housing conditions have much more severe and lasting effects when they affect children of tender age than in other cases. Housing for children, therefore, represents an investment that will give profits in the future. Quantitative aspects of the population problem were also considered, and this obvious connection made the program much more popular than would otherwise have been the case. A program in which these approaches were basic emerged from the Swedish committee appointed to develop a plan for coordination in housing policy.[3]

OVERCROWDING

The first task of the committee was to reorganize housing statistics to emphasize the overcrowding. When the investigations were made public, the Swedish people had to face the fact that in this respect their housing standard was extremely low. That was somewhat of a shock. The fact had previously been concealed by seeming progress and by the nonexistence of slums of which Sweden was rightly proud. Superficially Swedish housing standards are high. Towns are on the average well planned, and the development of various areas is harmonized, with few empty lots, back yards, and other ugly spots. Parks are frequent even if small. Houses are scattered with many green stretches between them. In the larger cities rather drab streets of huge houses covering a whole block, often with back yards between them, remain from earlier times. In the new developments apartment houses are separate units, built in narrow strips (the lamella type) or as small solid houses (the "point" formation). Both types are surrounded with greenery. In the older parts of the country cities may look gray and monotonous, but they rarely take on a slum character. The amount of rebuilding in recent years contributes to that impression. About 40 per cent of all urban dwelling units have been built since the World War. In Stockholm 50 per cent of all apartments have been built since 1920; 35 per cent were built after 1929. It still remains true, however, that

---

[3] Dr. Alf Johanson, the secretary of the committee, deserves the greatest credit for the work in following out the principles of the constructive practical proposals.

modern conveniences are not found in many of the older houses and not
even in all the new ones.

When looking more closely into the houses themselves and comparing
them with those of other countries, it is obvious that the Swedish people
simply do not tolerate slums. The houses are in good repair and well kept.
The inhabitants themselves are mainly responsible for the lack of mingled
litter and laundry in the familiar pictures of slums. A solicitous, minute
care of apartments and material belongings prevents slum formation. On
the whole, the Swedish housewife would probably have to be reproached
for doing too much scouring and polishing rather than too little. The
ever-present love for flowers contributes to making the homes look gay
and inviting. The investment in home furnishings and home upkeep is
great. The modern trend toward light furniture and colorful textiles rein-
forces the impression of housing conditions which from the viewpoint of
quality are above those of most other nations. Slowly the standard of rural
housing, which had naturally changed less than the urban, owing to the
trend toward the cities, was also raised.

This cherished picture of gradual improvement was shattered by the
new investigations. Recurring to the incessant theme of this survey, the
family, the one deficiency overlooked was perhaps the most important,
namely, the lack of space. A shining exterior and a fairly good material
standard coincided with a crowding that made homes deficient for living
purposes. In urban districts no less than 50 per cent of all dwelling units
contain 2 rooms or less and 77.2 per cent 3 rooms or less (1933). In rural
districts the corresponding figures are 33.3 per cent and 58.5 per cent,
respectively. If only rooms which can be heated are counted, they are
40.9 per cent and 66.8 per cent (1936). Thus the room-and-kitchen apartment is the most typical Swedish home. It is true that overcrowding is
decreasing. This development, however, is only to a minor extent due
to any increase in the size of the dwelling units. The major cause is that
the families have become smaller. Extreme birth control also offers a
solution of the housing problem. Naturally, the housing problem as such
can continue to be solved by a reduction in the number of the young, but
few would call this rational and desirable.

Housing conditions of the families were studied in great detail in two
public investigations, both largely the work of Dr. Richard Sterner of the
Swedish Social Board. The one on urban housing (1933) was published by
the Social Board in 1936 [86] and the one on rural housing (1936) by the
Census Office in 1938. [71] Rural conditions are studied in communities
with more than half their population engaged in agriculture. All sizes of
dwelling units are covered in the rural housing survey. For urban districts
the general housing survey is supplemented by two more specialized investi-

gations: the so-called representative study, covering 45 districts selected so as to be representative, and the so-called supplementary study, covering 14 of these 45 districts by an intensive sample study of small dwelling units of 3 rooms or less. These social family studies revealed that the standard of housing, both quantitatively and qualitatively, is inversely related to size of family. The problem of overcrowding is mainly a child welfare problem as the children are the chief cause both of the overcrowding and of poverty itself.

There is an intricate relationship between the qualitative and quantitative aspects of housing. If a family at the time of its increase really wants to expand its housing space, it can most often do so only by moving to more poorly equipped dwellings. The 1933 Urban Housing Census shows that rents do not become higher when the number of minor children increases except when the family income exceeds 5,000 crs. Yet there is some slight tendency toward an increase in the size of the home when there are more children in the family (Table 21). This can only mean that quality often has to be sacrificed for space. There are also some more direct observations on the same problem. The urban dwelling units studied were classified into groups according to a number of criteria of good quality. It was found that 11.4 per cent of all the inhabitants in these dwellings belonged to the lowest quality group but that they had 13.9 per cent of all children. The opposite was true of the best group. It housed 6.9 per cent of all persons but only 5.7 per cent of the children. This verifies the statement that children generally have a lower housing standard than adults. Families

TABLE 21. — PER CENT DISTRIBUTION OF RURAL AND URBAN DWELLING UNITS IN SWEDEN, BY HOUSEHOLD TYPE[a] AND NUMBER OF ROOMS

HOUSEHOLD TYPE	ALL RURAL DWELLING UNITS	RURAL DWELLING UNITS OF			ALL URBAN DWELLING UNITS	URBAN DWELLING UNITS OF		
		2 rooms or less	3 rooms	4 rooms or more		2 rooms or less	3 rooms	4 rooms or more
Small households . . .	100.0	51.2	23.8	25.0	100.0	67.3	21.3	11.4
Middle-sized households								
Without children . .	100.0	23.5	24.2	52.3	100.0	35.3	32.1	32.6
With children . . .	100.0	42.6	30.5	26.9	100.0	57.1	30.9	12.0
Large households								
With 0–2 children . .	100.0	15.8	22.4	61.8	100.0	26.7	32.6	40.7
With 3 children or more	100.0	27.3	28.4	44.3	100.0	40.0	34.1	25.9

[a] Household types as used in the text and tables are defined as follows:
Small households — 1 adult with 0–2 small children or 2 adults without children.
Middle-sized households without children — 3–4 adults (often grown children) without small children.
Middle-sized households with children — 2 adults with 1–2 small children.
Large households with 0–2 children — 3–4 adults (often grown children, servants, etc.) with 1–2 children or 5 or more adults with 0–2 children.
Large households with 3 or more children — all households with 3 or more children.
An adult is defined as a person 15 years of age and over.

Sources: Rural Housing Study, 1935–1936 (*Särskilda folkräkningen, 1935–1936*, Part III); and Urban Housing Census, 1933 (*Allmänna bostadräkningen år 1933*).

with 3 or more children under 15 more frequently than others lived in low-grade dwelling units (Table 22). The same relation holds true in the country and in fact appears in almost every case when the material is analyzed by individual cities, rural areas, or occupational groups.

TABLE 22. — PER CENT DISTRIBUTION OF RURAL AND URBAN DWELLING UNITS IN SWEDEN, BY HOUSEHOLD TYPE[a] AND QUALITY OF HOUSING[b]

HOUSEHOLD TYPE	ALL RURAL DWELLING UNITS	RURAL DWELLING UNITS IN SPECIFIED QUALITY GROUP					ALL URBAN DWELLING UNITS	URBAN DWELLING UNITS IN SPECIFIED QUALITY GROUP		
		1	2	3	4	5–6		1	2	3–6
All households	100.0	15.1	7.0	18.6	51.4	7.9	100.0	12.1	24.7	63.2
Small households . . .	100.0	16.7	9.3	20.7	47.8	5.9	100.0	14.4	28.5	57.1
Middle-sized households										
Without children . .	100.0	12.7	6.6	18.0	54.3	8.4	100.0	8.6	19.6	71.8
With children . . .	100.0	13.5	7.4	19.6	52.8	6.7	100.0	9.9	22.5	67.6
Large households										
With 0–2 children . .	100.0	13.8	4.4	16.7	53.3	11.8	100.0	10.1	20.5	69.4
With 3 children or more	100.0	19.0	6.2	17.6	51.3	5.9	100.0	20.5	30.5	49.0

[a] For definitions of household types see Table 21.

[b] Quality group 1 is lowest and quality group 6 highest on the scale. The rural and urban groups are not comparable, although they are based on similar principles. Group 1 in the rural classification comprises dwelling units which were characterized as dilapidated by the enumerators; group 2 includes other dwellings which were lacking in at least two essential respects, e.g., having the floor directly on the ground, no water supply within 100 meters, etc.; group 3 includes dwellings which were lacking in one essential respect. Group 1 in the urban classification comprises dwelling units with at least three essential shortcomings of similar character. The urban study includes only dwelling units with 3 rooms or less.

Sources: Rural Housing Study, 1935–1936 (*Särskilda folkräkningen, 1935–1936*); and supplementary housing study conducted in 14 cities in 1935, published in Urban Housing Census, 1933 (*Allmänna bostadräkningen år 1933*).

The great deficiency in housing for families occurs, however, in regard to space. The plight of the family with small children becomes apparent from the fact that 40 per cent of all urban and 27 per cent of all rural families with 3 children or more live in dwelling units of 2 rooms or less (Table 21). This goes to show how insufficient it is, and how comparatively ineffective for arousing citizens to action, to talk in generalities of the ill-housed part of the population. Concretely, it is the children who are ill-housed. Without children the space is sufficient.

In order to judge the proper size for homes a standard norm implying a scale of valuation must be resorted to. There may be difficulty in choosing what "ought to be" or what, by common consent, can be called undesirable overcrowding. Therefore two different norms for overcrowding will be used. In both adults 15 years of age and over will be counted as one and children under 15 years as one-half. Kitchens will be counted as one-half rooms. It must be generally agreed that having more than 2 adults or more than 4 children live in every livable room is socially not desirable. Many will probably even agree with the present writer that the second norm of 1½ adults per room is also an uncomfortable one. Overcrowding would, according to this second norm, mean the presence in an ordinary two-room and kitchen apartment of 3 adults and 2 children or more, or 2 adults and 4 children or more, or 1 adult and 6 children or more.

Following the first norm of two adults or four children per room, 12.6 per cent of urban dwelling units were overcrowded. Yet they contained 28.7 per cent of all children under 15 years of age. Among urban families with 3 or more children, 47.4 per cent lived in seriously overcrowded

TABLE 23. — OVERCROWDING[a] IN SWEDEN, BY TYPE OF COMMUNITY

TYPE OF COMMUNITY	PER CENT OF DWELLING UNITS WITH MORE THAN SPECIFIED NUMBER OF PERSONS PER ROOM			PER CENT OF INHABITANTS LIVING IN DWELLING UNITS WITH MORE THAN SPECIFIED NUMBER OF PERSONS PER ROOM			PER CENT OF CHILDREN IN DWELLING UNITS WITH MORE THAN SPECIFIED NUMBER OF PERSONS PER ROOM		
	1½	2	3	1½	2	3	1½	2	3
Cities over 10,000 .	35.8	13.4	3.3	47.2	21.8	6.4	58.9	30.2	8.3
Other urban districts	31.5	11.0	2.6	43.0	18.6	5.1	53.1	25.1	6.8
All urban districts .	34.5	12.6	3.0	46.0	20.9	6.0	57.2	28.7	7.9
Rural Norrland . .	b	19.7	b	b	29.6	b	b	38.6	b
All rural districts . .	b	12.3	b	b	19.2	b	b	27.6	b

[a] A kitchen was counted as half a room and a child under 15 years of age as half a person.

[b] The definitions of overcrowding involving 1½ persons and 3 persons per room were not used in the Rural Housing Study.

Sources: Urban Housing Census, 1933 (*Allmänna bostadsräkningen år 1933*); and Rural Housing Study, 1935–1936 (*Särskilda folkräkningen, 1935–1936*, Part III).

TABLE 24. — OVERCROWDING IN SWEDEN, BY HOUSEHOLD TYPE[a]

HOUSEHOLD TYPE	PER CENT OF DWELLINGS WITH		
	More than 1½ persons per room	More than 2 persons per room	
	In urban districts	*In urban districts*	*In rural districts*
All households	34.5	12.6	12.3
Small households	7.1	0.2	—
Middle-sized households			
Without children	41.5	10.8	7.8
With children	48.9	5.4	4.7
Large households			
With 0–2 children	55.7	33.1	21.3
With 3 children or more	66.2	47.4	37.4

[a] For definitions of household types see Table 21.

Sources: Urban Housing Census, 1933 (*Allmänna bostadsräkningen år 1933*); and Rural Housing Study, 1935–1936 (*Särskilda folkräkningen, 1935–1936*, Part III).

dwellings. In the rural districts 12.3 per cent of the dwellings were over-crowded, but they contained 27.6 per cent of all children. Among large rural families 37.4 per cent lived in overcrowded dwellings (Tables 23 and 24).

Before leaving these data on overcrowding, it should be pointed out that the statistics focus a criticism on some of the newest measures of housing policy inaugurated before the family viewpoint had become predominant. The improvement grants, referred to above, had been given with attention to local needs for employment, on the one hand, and to qualitative deterio-ration of homes, on the other. No attention was given to the needs of space for varying family size. Studying some of these new homes, it was found that their rate of overcrowding was nearly twice that of rural dwellings generally (23.0 per cent as against 12.3 per cent). Although this can to some extent be explained on the ground that large families were favored in the distribution of these grants, it is nevertheless an eloquent comment on what happens when social reforms are not duly coordinated. The regula-tions for these loans have since been rewritten, however, in accordance with the realigned housing policy.

Physical and Mental Effects of Overcrowding

It may well be asked if a crowded house is a real home at all. At least it does not correspond to the romanticized picture of the old home. The Committee on Social Housing published an appendix on Housing and Health, [90] wherein the risks for physical health were treated by the Chief Physician of the Stockholm Isolation Hospital, Dr. Rolf Bergman, while the present writer investigated the psychological and moral hazards in-volved in overcrowding. After a general reservation as to the validity of all statements in the field because other detrimental factors related to poverty are practically always concomitant with the influence of deficient housing space, a summary of research was made as a basis for the conclusions of the Committee.

Children and especially children in the preschool age, together with adolescent youth, are the ones that are most threatened by the physical and psychological damages which a deteriorated or crowded home may cause. Infants are espe-cially threatened by poor ventilation, unregulated temperature, and dampness. In a recent Swedish investigation it has been shown that diseases of the respiratory organs, whooping cough, rickets, and cramps occur three times as often among children living in dwellings classified as damp as among other children. In regard to a number of infectious diseases, such as diphtheria, scarlet fever, in-fantile paralysis, and whooping cough, it has been found that the age of con-tracting the illness is lower among the strata of population which live under the most crowded conditions. From that it seems probable that children in overcrowded families run the risk of falling ill at a very early age and thus also are exposed to a risk of greater mortality. Through overcrowding, complications ensue and the care of the sick is made difficult, which further increases the death risk. The connection between tuberculosis and quality of home has been widely proved. [18]

Equally disquieting are the statements of how the children fare intellectually and morally.

The deleterious effects of deficient home conditions upon mental health, working capacity, personality development, and morals play a role not to be overlooked on account of the physical risks. It seems as if, owing to a materialistic view of public health, this important aspect of the problem "home and health" has been dangerously overlooked. An expression of that materialism is found in that all sanitary rules about minimum demands on dwellings, as enforced by the housing inspection, are one-sidedly formulated as to air space and other such conditions of a physiological character — important in themselves. Sufficient attention has never been given to the effect, for example, of privacy on the psychological well-being of individuals.

Most experienced psychiatrists, criminologists, teachers, and social workers agree that deficient and especially overcrowded homes often seriously affect development, particularly of the adolescent. Despite the impossibility of directly and exactly indicating the nature and degree of the effects of housing, owing to our incomplete knowledge of causal relationships in the field of social morals and mental hygiene, it is still indisputable that such detrimental effects do occur. They may fundamentally decrease the mental well-being and working capacity of the individual, considerably increase fatigue and irritation, spoil the possibilities of a sane and harmonious family life within the home, decrease the efficiency of educational measures, and themselves directly contribute to the origin of habits and tendencies that work for family disorganization and delinquency. [18]

This generalized opinion covers real dangers indeed if they are translated into more concrete terms. Another such summarization may be quoted.

Sleep becomes insufficient. Persons of different ages have a different time distribution over the day. The activities of the old must encroach upon the rest of the young. It is, however, impossible to demand that all interests of adults should be sacrificed for the children. The conflict has only to be listed.

Also, waking hours pass under perpetual irritation. The play spaces of small children become cramped. This is not to be accepted with indifference. Play is the indispensable outlet for children's activity. It is their form of expression and experimentation by which they develop intelligence and dexterity, imagination and observation. When play is repressed there is a direct thwarting of development. In the small dwelling units a number of prohibitions and an incessant control are often added. Every housewife's ambition to keep order must conflict with every child's demand for freedom and space for his experimenting attitude toward life. Children of school age also suffer particularly by the difficulty in doing their homework. School marks indicate what the lack of a study place of one's own and of a moderately quiet environment means. Education within the home is made more difficult. Fatigue and impatience on the part of the parents will often make educational measures poorly balanced. Sometimes prohibitions, admonitions, and punishments will be meted out in consideration of the others sharing the home; sometimes they will be neglected for similar considerations. It becomes difficult to make education efficient, and it is rarely flexible enough to be adjusted to the individuality of the child.

The adolescent young run perhaps the greatest risks of all. The lack of privacy, the impossibility of being alone or of bringing home companions will, together with the restlessness of this period of life, drive them to linger in parks, in streets, in eating places, and elsewhere. The overpopulated parental home simply makes it out of the question for them to devote their time to those more serious and worthy tasks about which they are often lectured.

Sexual experiences are precipitated in crowded homes. Incest is relatively frequent, particularly in the country and in relation to children not having beds of their own. Even if direct traumata of a sexual character are absent — seduction, homosexuality, or incest — children far too early and with far too little preparation witness the sexual life of adults. This is harmful both as it spoils the harmony in the intercourse of the adults and as it warps the development of the young. Sexual precocity is often the result and particularly a depersonalization of sex attitudes which often marks the individual for life with an incapacity to reach an individualized consummation of a love relation.

Generally the inevitable close relationship in small and great things alike, in conflicts, quarrels, and love, in singing hymns and playing cards, in dressing and cooking, in sleep and work is a strain on all. The joy in family life is difficult to sense, when privacy can never alternate with being together. Even if someone in the family suffers from "nerves," intemperance, or unsocial habits, the others cannot withdraw. Moral contagion is facilitated. All must be shared by all; everything happening is experienced by everyone. [*159*]

All current complaints of the decline of morals become to socially initiated persons only superficial as long as one disregards the primitive lack of morals caused by overcrowded housing. There are many links between housing distress and social morality. Writers on social problems and politicians, who belong to the middle class and live in comfortable apartments or suburban houses, simply refuse to grasp the evidence of statistics that the average housing for the country is so far below what they are accustomed to see. Because of that the housing question is loaded with more social explosives than perhaps any other problem. Statistics themselves become offensive. When, in 1938, the broadcasting company in Sweden, which is a state enterprise although not controlled, wanted to make these figures vivid through the impressions of a novelist visiting in the districts, his revelations caused a storm of protest. The same public reaction has been experienced by all who since the turn of the century have called attention to the housing situation. In the wake of each such storm, however, progress has been made.

Utilization of Dwellings

Up to this point only nominal figures as to number of persons living in a dwelling of given size have been cited, but the family may not always live in all the available rooms. The self-created overcrowding in a dwelling roomy enough for the family has to be considered. In studies on how the family distributes itself within the home, the Swedish housing statistics have revealed many facts of tremendous interest for the sociological understanding of family life.

It was found, for example, that in one-fifth of all dwelling units of only one room and a kitchen in the 14 cities surveyed and in nearly one-third of those in the rural districts all family members slept together in the kitchen, leaving the other room unoccupied at night. The local differences are great in this respect. In one industrial town approximately 40 per cent of the 2-room dwelling units were so used, a third of those even having 3 or more persons sleeping in the kitchen at the same time that none were in the other room.

This distribution calls for closer scrutiny of the utilization of one room and kitchen units, both in general and in particular among families with children. In the 14 cities studied only the kitchen was used as a bedroom by 20.8 per cent of the families, only the other room by 33.4 per cent, and both by 45.8 per cent. In the 2-room and kitchen units only the kitchen was used as a bedroom in 1.4 per cent of the cases, only one room in 40.7 per cent, the kitchen and one room in 16.6 per cent, the 2 rooms in 26.1 per cent, and both rooms and the kitchen in 15.2 per cent. Whatever the size of the dwelling unit, there is an obvious tendency to have one room unoccupied. And the children? Well, about three-fourths of those in dwelling units of 3 rooms or less in urban districts sleep in a room and one-fourth in a kitchen. This distribution can best be evaluated, however, when the whole family pattern is taken into consideration. This can be done for the rural districts (Table 25).

Lack of wisdom in utilizing available space and pressure of the number of persons thus combine to create an actual overcrowding that is still worse than was indicated by the nominal figures previously used. Sometimes the former dominates, as when of all large families with 3 children or more in one room and kitchen units 16.8 per cent utilize only the kitchen for sleeping. Together two phenomena, the desire of a "prestige room" and a number of children, create a crowded situation at night which ordinary figures on overcrowding only suggest. It is difficult to make judgments,

TABLE 25. — UTILIZATION OF SMALL DWELLINGS FOR SLEEPING IN
RURAL DISTRICTS IN SWEDEN, BY HOUSEHOLD TYPE,[a] 1935–1936

ROOMS USED FOR SLEEPING	ALL HOUSE-HOLDS	SMALL HOUSE-HOLDS	MIDDLE-SIZED HOUSEHOLDS		LARGE HOUSEHOLDS	
			Without children	With children	With o–2 children	With 3 children or more
	Per Cent Distribution					
1 room and kitchen:						
Total	100.0	100.0	100.0	100.0	100.0	100.0
Kitchen only	30.6	44.4	14.8	37.8	8.3	16.8
Room only	23.9	38.3	10.8	26.5	6.0	9.0
Kitchen and room . .	42.0	15.7	70.6	31.5	80.3	68.6
Other [b]	3.5	1.6	3.8	4.2	5.4	5.6
2 rooms and kitchen:						
Total	100.0	100.0	100.0	100.0	100.0	100.0
Kitchen only	8.5	16.6	3.5	11.9	2.2	4.2
1 room only	33.3	64.3	13.1	54.9	5.7	13.2
Kitchen and 1 room .	30.2	11.7	45.4	22.6	40.6	40.5
2 rooms	13.1	7.0	22.4	8.2	17.2	13.9
Kitchen and 2 rooms .	14.1	—	14.7	1.8	32.8	27.2
Other [b]	0.8	0.4	0.9	0.6	1.5	1.0

[a] For definitions of household types see Table 21.

[b] Hallways, etc. Other rooms or kitchen are also commonly used for sleeping when hallways, etc., are so used.

Source: Rural Housing Study, 1935–1936 (*Särskilda folkräkningen, 1935–1936*, Part III)

however. This lack of utilization of available rooms may be translated into terms that carry a quite different connotation. The statisticians have used the figures to illustrate the socially disadvantageous habit of having an empty room for prestige (literally fine room for *finrum*). It may also be said that these figures show the craving for a living room. Of all the families living in small apartments in the 14 cities, quite a few simply would not, even if the apartment was of minimum size, be without such an unoccupied room: 23 per cent of the small households, 24 per cent of the middle-sized households without children, 50.4 per cent of the middle-sized households with children (when children probably slept in the room with parents), 18.7 per cent of the large families with 0–2 children, and 24 per cent of all families with 3 children or more.

These figures tell a pathetic story of poor families fighting in the midst of overcrowding and in the smallest dwellings to preserve one clean and orderly room always on parade. In older families it is probably more often used only for company and in the younger families more often as a real living room. The system of a fine room has been severely criticized by social and medical experts, including the Population Commission and the Committee on Social Housing. The author is inclined to take a somewhat different position. Her first conclusion is that no housing standard that really satisfies the families can be attained unless it allows them a living room. The *finrum* should be kept intact by increasing the rest of the apartment rather than by converting it into a bedroom.

Perhaps the family will prefer to save its living room by limiting the number of beds needed. It is not permissible from a population point of view to set a lower minimum requirement on a family home than kitchen, living room, and three bedrooms, one for the parents, one for the boys, and one for the girls. The prevailing housing standard is far from meeting such a norm. Housing consumption is lagging so seriously behind other levels of living that it will require decades of work before the nation reaches a status that is even defensible according to modern hygienic standards. This is still not enough. To reach a standard such that the family would not have to sacrifice its personal atmosphere of comfort and well-being or its natural pride in the home will have to be the goal from the point of view of population. Any hope of really checking the decrease in family size will otherwise be in vain. To this standard belongs the living room. But it is true that we have yet to strive for a condition in which families are not forced to expose their children to overcrowding directly detrimental to health and personal life. In this stage perhaps the fine room will have to be fought.

The number of people sleeping in one room will naturally decrease the available supply of air. After Swedish experts had approximately fixed the minimum at 12 cubic meters of air per person, it was found that half of all the persons in families with 3 or more children, living in dwelling units of 3 rooms or less, slept in rooms or kitchens allowing less than 10 cubic meters of air per person. Again the actual overcrowding has other than directly physiological aspects. When the actual distribution of beds is examined, the average middle-class person will again refuse to believe the situation. Among the so-called normal families of 3 children or more in the small dwellings studied in 14 cities, a third of the members were found to sleep in rooms housing 5 or more people nightly (Table 26). Rural districts with their larger families and greater difficulty in heating rooms show still greater overcrowding.

Another average condition is the housing of unmarried persons of different sex in the same bedroom, a mathematically necessary consequence of some overcrowding and one not fully avoided in the more voluntary forms of overcrowding. With younger children it may be a matter of dispute how far such a sharing of bedrooms is undesirable. When it comes to ado-

TABLE 26. — SLEEPING ARRANGEMENTS IN SMALL DWELLINGS,[a] BY HOUSEHOLD TYPE,[b] IN REPRESENTATIVE URBAN DISTRICTS IN SWEDEN, 1933

HOUSEHOLD TYPE	PER CENT OF ROOMS USED AS BED-ROOMS [c]	PER CENT OF BEDROOMS WITH SPECIFIED NUMBER OF PEOPLE SLEEPING IN THEM					
		Total	1	2	3	4	5 or more
All households	74.8	100.0	37.5	35.0	18.3	6.6	2.6
Small households . . .	67.9	100.0	60.5	39.2	0.3	—	—
Middle-sized households							
Without children . .	84.2	100.0	35.7	45.7	16.8	1.8	—
With children . . .	63.3	100.0	15.9	20.8	49.5	13.8	—
Large households . . .							
With 0–2 children . .	88.5	100.0	18.5	27.9	30.7	17.2	5.7
With 3 children or more	84.4	100.0	11.2	16.5	21.3	19.2	31.8

HOUSEHOLD TYPE	PER CENT OF KITCH-ENS USED AS BEDROOMS	PER CENT OF KITCHENS WITH SPECIFIED NUMBER OF PEOPLE SLEEPING IN THEM				
		Total	1	2	3	4 or more
All households	54.3	100.0	47.9	37.6	11.1	3.4
Small households . . .	42.6	100.0	61.6	38.3	0.1	—
Middle-sized households						
Without children . .	65.2	100.0	61.2	32.7	5.5	0.6
With children . . .	46.0	100.0	22.5	31.7	37.3	8.5
Large households . . .						
With 0–2 children . .	74.1	100.0	37.4	44.4	12.8	5.4
With 3 children or more	71.9	100.0	15.7	47.8	21.7	14.8

[a] Of 3 rooms or less.
[b] For definitions of household types see Table 21.
[c] Exclusive of kitchens.

Source: Urban Housing Census, 1933 (*Allmänna bostadsräkningin år 1933*).

lescents a much wider consensus will be found. In the studies referred to only persons 12 years of age and over and unmarried are taken into consideration. About one-fifth of the adolescents and adults living in dwelling units of 3 rooms or less in 14 provincial cities spent their nights in bedrooms or kitchens in which there were unmarried persons of the opposite sex. The cases include not only brothers and sisters sharing a bedroom but also father and daughter and mother and son. Again the families with many adult members living at home stand out as the sinners, or the wronged ones, depending on the point of view.

EDUCATIONAL PROPAGANDA AND LEGAL REGULATIONS

In the program for a rational family housing policy several means have to be coordinated. There is first the need for educational propaganda to teach the families to demand better homes and to utilize better the dwellings they can get. There is further need for revision of the legal regulations about minimum housing standards. The program also calls for production plans for the whole country, furnishing a guide for private building as well as public and timing the demolition of certain dwelling types and sizes with the rebuilding of others. Over all is a subvention plan whose most unique feature is a system of subsidies applied directly to the families' rents and differentiated according to family size. A secondary aspect is the promotion of building of large-sized apartments on a nonprofit basis by granting state loans for the erection of family houses. The agency coordinating and developing all these plans was the Committee on Social Housing, working with the Population Commission and animated by the same social philosophy. From 1935 to 1938 it published three reports and also submitted other proposals to the government. It is not too much to say that it has opened a new era in Swedish housing.

Education for better housing habits cannot work against economic circumstances but it can work along with them. However great the housing plight of families has been shown to be, lack of satisfactory housing practices was also revealed. An educational reformation of the art of living in a home thus was considered to be a profitable task. Such education ought to start as early as the school age. It thus becomes an added and a concrete argument for what has been called prefamily education as advocated by the general population program. Housing plans could be used in art lessons; shopwork could give instruction in home furnishings; home care could be more appealingly taught in home economics, the hygiene of housing in health studies, and so forth. The next step would be the spread of general information through the adult education groups and through the radio, pamphlets, clubs, and other channels. All these channels have been tried, but their activities ought to be widely increased and given some support through public funds.

The most persistent sinners will always evade so subtle an influence. In order to reach them an effective public housing inspection is needed. It should be backed by laws and police force to be used as a last resort but should in its practice lay stress on advice and educational propaganda. Building inspection and advice should be available for the private builder as soon as plans are submitted, and the housing inspectors should visit the homes in their daily functioning and give advice concerning home care. Thus positive work through housing inspection should always precede more rigid measures in cases of self-imposed overcrowding and other violations of housing standards. The new legislation on housing sanitation is in the first instance directed against those individual families which live in inadequate lodgings without being forced to do so by economic pressure. In the second instance it is directed against communities which let their housing standards fall too far below national standards.

Sweden got its first housing legislation in 1906. This was followed by a new law in 1919. As in most other countries it was felt to be impossible to raise housing regulations to a desirable degree, particularly as to the utilization of a dwelling (overcrowding), because that would be in violation of individual freedom. Such freedom should include the right for individuals to live as they wished. This allowance made, nothing much could be done to improve conditions before Swedish social policy was focused on the children. Then the time-honored liberalistic arguments broke down. When the free choice was detrimental to the welfare of children, it could not continue to be respected. The children had not chosen to live so unfavorably, and the parents' right to harm children became generally disputed. Matching the economic responsibility for the raising of quality which the community is assuming for the indigent families, demands for higher housing standards would have to be enforced on the self-supporting families.

The Committee on Social Housing [19] asked for more stringent sanitary regulations concerning housing. The object was to create better safeguards for the family. By an act of the Riksdag of 1936 the local health boards and medical officers were given much greater authority to intervene in conditions formerly regarded as strictly private and also to provide a better service for housing inspection. This rescuing of the family by increasing the control over it might earlier have caused a vehement ideological battle about right to free choice, private freedom, and so on. The publication of the report did result in a rather violent attack in the press. So thoroughly was public opinion now attuned to the welfare of the children, however, that the victory was won before the struggle began. A number of minimum regulations for family housing were included in the national law in force since January 1, 1937. Further optimum regulations were proposed for local enactment.

Among the many detailed regulations and prescriptions, a couple of changes will be singled out as indicating this very transfer of ultimate responsibility from the sphere of authority of the family. A law about foster children, where the responsibility of society was indisputable, had earlier prescribed that so many persons may not be housed in one room that risk for their health arises. But in the housing sanitation regulations concerning the family's own children this risk for health was stated as "grave risk for health" in order to sanction the intervention of authorities. Now the regulation was changed so as to protect children in a family fully as much as children who already were under direct community control. Furthermore, the local health board was not only authorized to intervene but ordered to intervene and compelled to investigate cases on notification. Earlier it had only the power to prohibit the habitation of a certain house, apartment, or room on quality grounds as being unsuitable for human habitation and could take practically no measures at all against overcrowding. It was now given the right to prohibit "that more than a certain number of persons inhabit a dwelling or to forbid its use altogether for minors, permitting sometimes such an apartment to be occupied only by adults or by one single adult." It was further recommended on the initiative of the General Medical Board "that in a dwelling inhabited by a family with more than one minor child, there ought to be at least two rooms, and that it should not be allowed for a family with more than two children to be housed in such a small dwelling as that of one room and kitchen; such a family should have at least two rooms and also a kitchen, usable for living purposes."

The sanctioning of this recommended regulation by any one community logically would make the same community responsible for gradually furnishing such dwelling units to any families which cannot provide them or pay for them on the open market. The second object of the new housing legislation was to induce communities to improve their whole housing situation. The legal weapon was put into their hands. The lag in production of suitable family apartments has, however, caused the communities to use their discretion in applying these more rigid rules. Even the enforcement of the minimum rules means increased family protection. The very presence of a sanctioned desideratum, as included in the recommendations by the General Medical Board, will act as an encouragement to communities not to stay on the black list too long.

Housing inspection regulations differ somewhat between urban and rural districts. Such inspection in urban districts (of more than 5,000 inhabitants) had been left to the local boards of health since 1919. Only in about half the urban districts did the Committee on Social Housing find any efficient housing inspection. Since the beginning of 1937 considerably more rigid regulations are in force and, since such inspection is a condition for the state subsidies later to be described, there is ground for hope that not only on paper but in reality an efficient control will be exerted over urban housing conditions. A considerable increase in personnel and an improvement in their skill are expected.

The solution of the same problem for rural districts is not as far under way. According to parliamentary decision in 1935, however, the district health nurses are delegated to exert the primary housing control and give notice to the local board of health of any deficiencies, whereafter this board may delegate special building consultants to check conditions within their field and finally decide about action to be taken according to the Sanitation Law. The country-wide organization of the district nurse services can be expected to reach its completion within 10 years. The organizational mapping out of this whole field of activity is achieved; the final consummation of practical results will in this as in many other instances be reached only after years of laborious effort.

PLANNING OF HOUSING PRODUCTION

Planning is not only a predilection of social reformers. Business has no less a need of prognosis and coordinated action. In regard to housing there is the peculiar situation that building and operating houses are separate economic functions. The ones who should particularly welcome the planning are the owners of real estate, while the builders can act according to the demand of the moment. The building of a house is economically a short-term speculation while making an investment by owning it is dependent on long-run prospects. A powerful indication of the value of planning was the revelation by the Swedish Committee on Social Housing that the builders were preparing a catastrophe on the real estate market some 10 or 15 years hence through a faulty selection of dwelling sizes. They were at the same time working at full speed to hinder the general rise in housing standards. Both these adverse effects resulted because they were saturating the market with undersized dwelling units.

A total production plan, regardless of whether the building activity be private or public, needs as its foundation a family curve, giving a prognosis of how many, how large, and in what stage of life will be the families to be housed within the predictable future. Even if the size of the family is only indirectly related to ability to purchase a home and thus need not be taken into consideration by business interests, the number of households cannot in the same way be overlooked. That figure will decide the actual demand for dwelling units. The family curve, at least in measuring number of families, can be accurately drawn for the whole country and for the next two or three decades. The chief practical difficulty is to differentiate this prognosis by localities, as then different hypotheses as to internal migration have to be taken into consideration.

In terms of expected shifts in number of households, Sweden faces an extraordinary situation, owing to its population development. For the last decade the age distribution of the people has been skewed in the direction of an abnormal increase in the younger and middle-aged groups. This is the result of the prolific years before the onset of stricter family limitation.

These groups are preceded by fewer of the old who were born at a time when the population was smaller, and they are followed by fewer of the young when births have been decreasing. It is the demand of this very group that actually determines the rental market and building activity. It tends to overload the market with numerous small dwellings, desired by the many young couples in their homemaking years. The decline in the birth rate has not yet checked the building boom, as the reduction in the number of the young falls on those too young to present an active, i.e., a moneyed, housing demand. Even if the total population as calculated will begin actually to decrease in the 1940's or 1950's, this young middle-aged group and thus the number of households will continue to increase until about 1960. But the houses are now being built without cognizance of what will happen 20 years hence, when they will still be standing.

The overproduction of small dwellings will one day be felt by the private owners of real estate. An oversupply of these will exist, and the newest portion of that supply will consist of small units even when the proportion of young families within the population is no longer abnormal. On the contrary, these families which by their numbers now determine the building of houses will by that time create just as large an extra demand on larger dwelling units, particularly if we succeed in raising our extremely low standard of dwelling space. For smaller dwelling units the oversupply may be shown to reach tremendous proportions in most cities fairly independent of the hypotheses chosen as to migration and birth rate.

Looked at from the social viewpoint the prospect becomes even more grave. The oversupply of small dwelling units will keep their rent abnormally low. That is the implication of the real estate crisis. Families which otherwise would demand an increased space standard will tend to remain on the lower standard. It is often falsely reasoned that at the time when population increase slackens a rise in standard will conveniently take up the excess housing. This excess will be split up into thousands of small units. There is simply no hope of raising the general housing standard if the composition of the total housing supply is not to a greater and greater extent made up of larger units. The number of rooms in a country does not decide family fate; their arrangement in units does. It should be added that the prospect here pictured is also one of the chief reasons for a falling off of investment activity in a declining population, tending to depress business generally.[4]

The total number of dwellings built must obviously not be decreased. The increasing numbers of families must have somewhere to live during their period of maximum size. In Sweden it has been anticipated that the number

[4] See Myrdal, Gunnar, *Population, A Problem for Democracy,* Harvard University Press, Cambridge, 1940, Chapter VI, "Effects of Population Decline," especially pp. 152–160.

of households in cities will increase by approximately 40 per cent during the critical period 1935–1960. In rural districts an actual increase in number of families for a time will probably coincide with the decrease in family size and a continued exodus to cities. But preparation for the future still demands increasing the number of large instead of small dwelling units and delaying demolition activities. Private building trade and real estate business must be warned about its own dilemma between present and future and be persuaded to build more dwelling units of family size in its own best interest. Public housing interests likewise must realize that whatever activities they undertake must be restricted to amplifying the housing supply with larger units. Families with many children would thus be better housed while the smaller dwelling units which they desert would increase the supply of such units for young households or older families with fewer children or aged people. The same yardstick must be applied to slum clearance activities.

If children are gradually brought out of the slums, in Sweden mostly individual dilapidated houses, slum conditions or semislum housing will no longer be such a grave social concern. Demolition of slums can then be deferred so as not to increase the housing shortage during the short period of increasing household numbers just ahead. Such demolition, selectively directed toward the more superfluous small dwellings, ought on the contrary to be undertaken on a grand scale just after the turning point in 10 or 20 years, when normally a stagnation period in building should otherwise be expected. The replacement building program in which both private entrepreneurs and eventually public enterprises can be occupied ought to be planned for that later period. In this way continuous activity and shockproof development of the building industry over a long period of time should be guaranteed.

In this way, too, shorter business fluctuations can be guarded against. When a production plan has once been made up, it can be expanded or contracted so as to stabilize the cycles in business activity and employment. To call building a key industry is no exaggeration. In Sweden it has been calculated that the building trade normally takes between a third and a half of all capital investment. For labor it means that about one-twentieth of the total working population directly derived their living from the building industry at the end of 1935, while an equal proportion of workers in industry, transportation, and commerce was employed in procuring building materials. Already during the last economic depression this fact had been realized. When a program with vision was finally set up for housing, this same realization made it imperative that the program should be elastic so as to correspond to the need of alternate stimulation and retardation of building activity. This has a double emphasis. The family housing program thus provides the ideal public works which can be started quickly, can be distributed all over the country, can employ relatively much labor, and can use chiefly domestic goods and stimulate industrial production. Last but not least, it is not artificially created employment and leaves a result of maximum permanent utility for the nation. On the other hand, the family housing program must be constructed so as to be subservient to the aims of general economic policy.

The Urban Housing Program

A subvention plan had to be the core of the whole housing program. Subsidies or credit to builders had been tried and found ineffective. Low-rent housing projects had been tried and found not to reach the neediest groups. Thus it was decided that direct subsidies should be given only to families and only in the form of a reduction in annual housing costs. Credit toward socially valuable building purposes should be facilitated on a sound business basis. For many reasons urban and rural problems had to be attacked somewhat differently in adjusting the general principles to practical administrative rules. Urban housing was found to be by far the easier to regulate, and the solution of the clear-cut problem of urban apartment houses served later as the theoretical pattern after which the more difficult schemes for privately owned homes, farm tenants' homes, and laborers' homes were modeled.

To promote the building of family houses, for which state subsidies might be available to the families, the Committee on Social Housing proposed a scheme of state loans. [18] Those houses should neither be owned nor administered by private interests nor by the state's own agencies. Credit should therefore be available only to a community or to nonprofit corporations endorsed by the community. The interest of the community was further to be aroused by making it a condition that the community should furnish the building ground free for such family houses, thus considerably lowering the total cost. It was assumed that credit up to 50 per cent of the building costs could without difficulty be procured on the credit market, usually from the semipublic mortgage banks earlier referred to. State credit should then be available up to 95 per cent of building costs at an interest rate corresponding to the credit costs of the state (1937–1938 — 3.3 per cent; 1938–1939 — 3.25 per cent; 1939–1940 — 3.15 per cent). Only 5 per cent of the total building costs need be available in cash. For this remaining 5 per cent the community should underwrite the risk. In other words, the responsibility for management is placed upon the community, but it is assumed that in most cases the community will prefer to have the administration managed by an independent nonprofit corporation.

The houses should be specially equipped for families with children. No dwellings rented to families should be smaller than two rooms and a kitchen. The houses should not be placed in dense blocks but have open spaces between with access to playgrounds in the immediate vicinity. A playroom or cooperative nursery should preferably be provided. The direct administration of the house should be in the hands of some person with social experience, a hostess more than a manager or rent collector. These houses should have nothing of an institutional or poor relief character. They should by all means be regarded more as honorary dwellings for the families rearing the citizens of tomorrow.

The families for which the houses should directly be built would be the large families, which have in Sweden been technically defined as families with 3 or more children under 16 years of age, including foster children. The husband and wife need not be legally married. The income limit should not be set too low. The program called for a scheme to rehouse all families with 3 or more children and the poorer among them were to be given first consideration. The income maximums which must be set would be on a sliding scale in relation to family size and would further be fixed differently for each community according to its position in a certain cost of living region. In principle it should include the normal working-class family. The clientele is not limited to families on relief and not even to those near the poverty line generally. It is the group that is pressed near that line principally by the fact of having children. Certain requirements as to character and social stability of parents are to be set. It has been expressly provided, however, that the dwellings should be rented also to other tenants, but for those no rent reduction grant is made. Also families which are subsidized and then move out of the large-family category may continue to live in the house but with loss of the rent reductions. The nonexclusiveness of the family house is one attempt to avoid any segregation, such as might result if only one category of tenants was housed.

The vital part of the aid to family housing was the provision for direct economic aid through subsidizing the rent costs. The state should compensate for an annual deduction of 30 per cent from the family's rent if there are 3 children, 40 per cent if there are 4 children, and 50 per cent if there are 5 children or more.[5] This would allow the overcrowded and large families living in sordid quarters to move into adequate, well-equipped apartments without increasing their rent, just as it would approximately indemnify a family for increased living space on account of a new member.

The method of determining subsidies in relation to family size is not unknown, as it has been practiced in Belgium and France and sometimes in England. Experience has taught that such a method will meet real needs in a more flexible manner than any other. "Differentiating the rent according to family size will be more essentially a differentiation according to eco-

---

[5] These provisions were modified in 1938 so that families with 6 or 7 children get a reduction of 60 per cent and families with 8 children or more a reduction of 70 per cent.

nomic resources than a differentiation only according to income, because in the broad social groups prosperity or poverty is more nearly a function of how many there are to divide the income than of its actual size." [*18*]

In other countries, however, such subsidies have mostly been paid on building costs. The amounts have been granted for the houses and the rents reduced accordingly. What may be the new approach is that in the Swedish project, which has later been followed in Denmark and Finland, the subsidy goes so directly to the families that the total state outlay for the houses will be shifting according to the size and income of the families living in them. Rent as a conception is no longer chiefly fixed in relation to the dwelling but to the inhabitants. Such a scheme is only made possible by the close cooperation between state and municipality. Their responsibility is thus divided so that the state contributes most but the local community carries all surplus risks and all costs incurred by a less efficient management.

The question may be raised why any building program at all was included when such a seemingly simple formula had been reached for transferring the surplus housing cost of children to the community. Why not extend this scheme to all families even in old houses, letting the state pay part of all rents for families with many children? This would without doubt be what has previously been called mathematical magic for bringing about social justice, but it would probably please private landlords still more. Such a change on the demand side without a corresponding change on the supply side — as a corresponding increase of the supply cannot be made a condition — must have a revolutionary and unwholesome effect on the demand-price-supply relation. A general differentiation by public subvention of rents for all existing houses would simply give the landlords an opportunity for raising the rent for these family dwellings and possibly the general level of rents. In the end the result might be that all of the state subsidy would find its way into their pockets, letting the tenants as a group in effect pay as much as before, even if the rent were distributed in a somewhat different way.

The main argument for combining the subsidies with the promotion of public building activities is that the housing supply as a whole must be expanded through a greater number of large-sized dwellings. Procuring just rent subsidies would preserve the *status quo* with regard to the available housing facilities themselves. No guarantee would be obtained for larger dwellings being built. It would be just as difficult for families to find the nonexistent larger dwellings and it would not make such families much more welcome. One difficulty now is that children are not desired as tenants nor liked as neighbors.

In 1935 the program outlined above was submitted to the Riksdag and appropriations were duly made to be followed by others in subsequent years. It had been foreseen that about 20,000 families with some 80,000 children in

urban districts would be found living in crowded homes, having 3 children
or more, and receiving incomes under the generous limits approximately
marked. Up to the summer of 1939 nearly a third of this program had been
achieved. The utilization of the grants made available has been extremely
uneven. Some communities were eager to make use of this possibility for
raising their housing standards. Others were not. The state agency handling the administration of loans and subsidies, i.e., the State Housing Loan
Authority (*Statens Byggnadslånebyrå*), does, however, encourage community pride by publishing statements comparing the number of overcrowded
families and the number of rehoused families in each locality. An interesting
indication of Swedish civic organization is the fact that more than one-half
of all the dwelling units built have been constructed and are administered
by the Cooperative Housing Society (H.S.B.).

The quantitative achievements are not impressive so far. During the period July, 1935–June, 1940 about 6,000 dwelling units were constructed. They
represented, however, almost one-third of the total need of overcrowded
urban families with 3 children or more. The explanation as to why the
program was not nearer completion at the end of the period is simple. No
sooner had the initial hesitation on the part of many communities started
to give way than the threat of imminent war began to draw the attention
of the public in other directions and possibly also made postponement of
construction appear wise. It should also be noted that private residential
construction occurred on a large scale during these years so that arguments
could be presented for saving some of this public building activity for years
of reduced private employment.

Family houses have, nevertheless, sprung up in many places, everywhere
being built with some architectural merit. They have sunny exposures and
good, sometimes even model, playgrounds and cooperative nurseries. Practically all of them are provided with bathrooms, central heating, and hot
water. In many places they are called Sun Courts, and the definite efforts
to avoid any sign of relief or charity projects seem everywhere to have been
successful.

The effects on standards and rents for the families concerned have been
studied (1938). The increase in the number of rooms has been considerable.
An average increase in floor space of 13.8 square meters per family has
occurred. The improvement in quality cannot be as easily shown but is described as "quite fulfilling the intentions." This increase in both quality
and quantity of family homes has been obtained with a decrease in average
rent (from 527 to 510 crs. annually as an average for 26 cities studied; from
736 to 541 crs. in Stockholm).

Some overcrowding still exists in these new houses. This is partly a tran-
sitory phenomenon, as for obvious reasons the very large families would re-

ceive first concern. In the future they will not make up such a large proportion even of this child-rich group. Partly, however, this is due to some unimaginativeness on the part of local authorities, who in applying the standard rule of 2 rooms and kitchen as a minimum requirement forget to find out what the individual family will need. They have, of course, had difficulties in grasping the new program, accustomed as they are to the traditional direction of public housing as well as private toward providing small-sized dwellings for the poorer classes.

THE RURAL HOUSING PROGRAM

The housing scheme for families in urban districts having been put into successful operation, an attack was made on the parallel problem, chiefly rural, for families wanting to build or buy their own homes. The first necessary step was to align earlier forms of housing subvention for the same objectives of safeguarding the family. In the first instance the Population Commission (1935) asked for a change in directions so that family size might be decisive for the granting of the recently instituted loans and subsidies for improvement and rebuilding of homes and for the loans for workers' subsistence homesteads. A general admonition to the local authorities and the administrative center of the Own Homes Board to take the family situation under primary consideration when granting these loans was also issued. Before categorical rules could be laid down, the whole problem of increased support for owners of small homes had to be tackled. This was done by the Committee on Social Housing in its third report. [20]

Great technical difficulties existed in finding some means of so controlling the subsidies that the family should be favored but small-scale speculation by the owner prevented. The subsidies should and could obviously be given according to the annual situation of the family, but the building loans must be given such a form as to make it possible for both municipality and state to recover their grants in case of attempts at profiteering. This was achieved by setting aside a fifth of the loans to be given under ordinary conditions as state credit in the form of a rent-free loan and one where repayment should only be demanded in case of speculative selling or renting of the houses.

A kind of subvention was thus put into the original cost of procuring a home. This difference from the urban program was also justified because it seemed necessary that a home-owning family, being more irrevocably tied to its dwelling, should not lose so great a part of the subvention when the children grew out of the 16-year limit. For the same reason the period of amortization for that part of the loan which should be repaid was fixed for as short a period as 20 years. The scheme for financing the cost of the family-owned home thus is calculated from the top down: 10 per cent to be provided by the owner himself, the next 50 per cent as amortization of a state loan for 20 years, a further 20 per cent as a standing state loan, and 20 per cent as a rent-free state loan, eventually to be terminated. It was assumed that the 10 per cent to be provided by the owner ordinarily should consist of his own labor on the home project. This means that even a family without any capital resources at all can avail itself of the scheme. A large-scale experiment, which has been going on in Stockholm for several years and which has resulted in about 3,500 owned homes has proved successful. The community has offered plans and supervisors for the buildings and standardized material and entrepreneurs for specialized jobs, such as plumbing and electricity. The family, often with the children included, has worked during spare hours on its own home. The same combination of financial support, specialized skill from the community, and enthusiastic labor by the family that had proved its worth in the Stockholm experiment was now planned for the whole rural housing scheme.

As for the direct subvention according to family size, this was to be calculated, just as for families in urban rented apartments, as a certain percentage of annual costs, including amortization and interest but also cost of upkeep and fuel. If the subsidy was not greater than the annual loan annuity, it was to be retained as part payment and only the remainder had to be paid by the home owner. High requirements for size and particularly for quality and modern conveniences must be met before the building project would be validated. A bathroom and central heating were stipulated so that the standards of rural families should not lag so far behind the rest of the country as has hitherto been permitted. This may seem a somewhat complicated system, but the problem of rationally coupling ownership of home with state subsidies is in itself a difficult one.

There still remained one problem to solve. How could a family housing subvention be combined with private ownership of a house by somebody other than the inhabitant? How could the proverbially large families of farm tenants and farm laborers be subsidized without merely adding to the income of estate owners? As the two desiderata were, however, to induce these owner employers to furnish better houses and also not to discriminate against large families, a compromise was believed logical. The Committee on Social Housing attempted to work out a blueprint for such a solution. Its idea was to make available to owner-employers loans for rebuilding houses according to certain standards under conditions similar to those fixed for loans to home owners. Instead of scaled family subsidies, however, the annuity should be reduced to exactly one-half for every year a so-called large family occupied the place. This proposal was never put into effect, but in 1939 another revision of the regulations concerning loans for homes for farm laborers was completed, making the loans free of rent for 10 of the 20 years and giving a special premium of 300 crs. if the size of the dwelling unit was increased from the stipulated minimum of two rooms and a kitchen to three rooms and a kitchen and the same premium if water, drainage, and central heating were installed.

The provisions about family-owned homes went into force in 1938. During the first two years about 2,000 applications were granted, and a rapid increase seems to be in prospect.

COMPETITION BETWEEN THE YOUNG AND THE OLD

For a definite population policy it is clear that families with fewer than three children and families with incomes above the present limits for eligibility must also be given relief with regard to housing costs. The road for continuation of the program thus opens up. The start had to be made, however, with those suffering most and at the same time least able to help themselves in their housing plight: the families with several children. That scheme, having been sanctioned by law and public enthusiasm and given time to show that it works, is laying the foundation for expanding the social housing system toward complete responsibility for the sector left unprovided by private housing.

To this sector of public housing there belong also some unfavored groups besides families with children. The whole question of differentiating housing accommodations according to typical needs, e.g., service for infirm people and more cooperative housekeeping for working wives, has been singularly overlooked by private building interests and thus forces itself upon public initiative. The Population Commission in Sweden focused special attention on the plight of the incomplete families, which were trying to maintain their homes. Widowers and divorced men with children experience housekeeping difficulties of other than economic origin. Widows and divorcees with one or two children may be quite as badly off as complete families with three children or more. Unmarried mothers are often forced to separate from their children in order to obtain work. For all these groups the material possibility of founding homes and of living with their children, even if separated from them for working hours, would ideally lend itself to the family houses, where these are equipped with nurseries. To create such possibilities for the incomplete family to participate in the favored family housing was repeatedly stated as desirable by the Population Commission, e.g., in the Report on Day Nurseries. [15] Even if it was never directly shown how the regulations about income limit and rent deductions should be formulated for these cases, some inclusion in a sliding scale was considered feasible. These problems where children are involved may be solved in one effort, sometimes even in the same houses.

The problem of the infirm and the old is fundamentally different. Not only ought they for their own and others' convenience be kept separate from the boisterous family houses, but the argument for public building, increasing the supply of large-sized apartments equipped with special child supervision and play facilities, does not apply and makes it doubtful whether on the whole they should have claims to new houses. Build new houses for the families with children and there will be plenty of small second-class dwellings for old people.

There arises an explosive problem in this connection. At the same time that Sweden was formulating the objectives of social housing as a family policy, another discussion was bringing the interests of the old into the limelight. This interesting conflict gives a presentiment of the war between young and old that is bound to come. It became imminent when the Population Commission voiced the demands of the young of the country, whereas other public agencies had just reached the point of realizing the dreams of more complete security for the aged. Competition for public funds does arise. With the coming increase in number, importance, power, and maintenance needs that is going to fall to the old in all Western countries on account of the pending age distribution, nothing is gained by evading this problem.

The clash became evident in the housing field. In the discussion about the National Pensions Act it was said that cheap rents would be necessary in some regions in order to supplement the pensions. The Bureau of Building Loans was asked to give a preliminary report on such a scheme of housing for the aged. When that agency proposed (in 1937) the building of subsidized small dwelling units for old people, the Population Commission demanded a rational weighing of how much of the public resources to be made available for social purposes should be allotted to different age groups. It further asked for rational coordination of the schemes for support to be given in cash or in kind [6] and finally consideration of the desirability of encouraging only building of larger dwellings.

The last was the crucial point. The whole idea of the new housing program, since it had become a family policy, was that public building activities should be made to affect advantageously the composition of the total stock of dwellings. That the community itself should, when the market within some 10 or 20 years would be flooded by small-sized apartments, contribute to this excessive building was considered highly irrational. To do so when the one type lacking was the cheap large-sized dwelling units for families was considered doubly so, as these families now had to live packed in just the small units that would be suitable for the old people. Nothing but a planned transfer of these families to new houses and a reconditioning of the old

[6] If old people are not infirm, there are not the same strong reasons for the principle of support in kind that there are for children. There would thus be no need for building new housing but perhaps need for increasing cash pensions.

houses for the old people could be defensible if social housing was to be developed in a planned way. There might be local variations, making such reconditioning impracticable. In rural districts and small towns there might be particular difficulties in finding any houses suitable for reconditioning; but these instances ought to be seen as exceptions. New houses for the new citizens and old houses for the old would be a rational compromise. It would also in a general way be psychologically motivated, as the old people are already conditioned to the old type of housing.

Criticism of this kind, mainly exerted by the Population Commission, stopped the first proposal to start building for the old. A second investigation was ordered. In 1938 the new committee proposed both the erection and reconditioning of houses for pensioners with the practical proposals showing a considerable predilection for new houses. [34] In 1939 the Riksdag granted a provisional sum of one million crs. as a grant to communities for the starting of such building activities. If it has been difficult for state authorities to avoid building new houses for old people, it will be far more true in the local municipalities where personal considerations play an important role. It must not be overlooked that aged persons have votes, but children have not. And it must not be overlooked that building small dwelling units for old people is a more inexpensive way of satisfying the social conscience than building large ones for families. A combination of narrow-minded fiscal economy and the natural sentimentality about the aged will appeal to many communities. The children will suffer. And the future, reckoned both in human beings and in the composition of the nation's housing capital, will be cheated.

SUMMARY

In appraising the total structure of the new Swedish housing program as presented here in its varied details, some generalizations appear to be appropriate. One important feature is the stress on the necessity of an integrated plan (for the country as a whole as well as for every individual community) based on demographic, economic, technical, and hygienic data and norms. The tearing down of old houses should be slowed up somewhat for the next 10 to 20 years when the family curve reaches a peak and slum clearance be kept as a labor reserve for the slackening off of the housing demand to be expected in the period thereafter. The plan should be kept flexible so as to provide for shrinking or expansion from year to year of building activities as the desire to influence business conditions dictates. The ultimate goal, however, is the satisfaction of studied social needs, and the danger in this respect would be that business optimism might overrule social dissatisfaction.

As a matter of fact the building program has not been greatly rushed. One of the reasons is that Sweden has enjoyed a boom since the formulation of its long-range housing plan, and so public investment has not had to resort to housing in any such degree as had been foreseen as an antidepression measure. What will happen in coming lean years depends on whether unemployment will be the dominant feature, making building as expedient as calculated.

In stimulating the development of more new dwellings and more appropriate dwellings the various measures should be coordinated. Active educational propaganda and a gradually tightened enforcement through housing inspection should encourage families with children who can afford it by their own means to come into the market with an increased demand for larger and better equipped dwellings. Thereby the private building industry would get an impetus in the right direction. A democratic country cannot have two laws, however, one for the rich and another for the poor. A prerequisite for such an enforcement of housing laws is, therefore, that families with children who cannot meet the new standards by their own means are given assistance from the state and municipalities. Thus the housing legislation has been corrected partly in order to put pressure on municipalities to build family houses. The interplay between housing legislation and housing inspection, on the one hand, and public housing assistance, on the other, between forcing economically capable families out of undersized dwelling units and providing the economically incapable families with apartments in the new family houses, cannot be said to have as yet reached any final harmony. This should not be surprising as authorities have to step lightly in such delicate regions of municipal economy and private housing patterns, but the road is clear and progress is being steadily made.

A rational delimitation is drawn between private and public housing activity. Public enterprise should not compete with private enterprise but only take as its responsibility the satisfaction of those human needs which an economy dependent on profits could make no claims to covering: the extra housing needs of children in a family. From the point of view of the private real estate and rental market the new supply created by the public building activity consists in reality only of the old small dwellings from which these families move to the new family houses. This can only discourage private business from building the undesired dwelling units but does not at all discourage building activity in the right direction. At the same time private housing has been given the services of a prognosis of the development of housing demands, which strongly points out that such a redirection is very much in the interest of private real estate. Add to this that only the ownership and operation of the new family houses, produced by public assistance, should be kept in public or quasi-public control as nonprofit projects, while their actual construction would regularly be contracted in the ordinary way, and it becomes understandable why enlightened representatives for private business actually do not feel the new radical housing policy to be much of an encroachment upon their domain.

Various interests can thus only be favored by a concentration of both public and private building activity on the large-sized family dwellings. In other ways the reforms have been planned so as to evade criticism for social waste and neglect of individual responsibility. Some such adverse criticism, usually following social housing, is rooted in a fear that some people and often not the most worthy ones get advantages ahead of others. In this special scheme of socialized housing such criticism can be met most successfully. Children are the most overcrowded. Children, and hence the population of the future, are subject to the most damaging effects of poor housing. Children increase family costs so much in other directions than housing as not to leave a family, even when enjoying housing aid, in a favored position compared with others of the same social strata or doing the same work. This kind of subsidy can thus never be a premium for being of no account. Finally, the population situation is such that if the community does not remove some of the costs for children from the parents, the parents will prefer a birth strike.

CHAPTER XV

FEEDING A NATION

I N its main outlines the problem of feeding the nation parallels the problem
of housing the nation. What can be done to align housing policies in a
long-range plan can be done also in the field of nutrition. Housing and
food both present problems of production as well as of consumption. Both
represent particularly large items in national incomes and in individual
family budgets. They are similar with regard to the tremendous social gains
in the avoidance of waste which can result from coordinated plans. They
are similar, too, in that social concern was first devoted to production problems only. Programs of subsidized building and subsidized agriculture were
undertaken as temporary depression measures, while the corresponding needs
of a housing policy and of a nutritional policy were overlooked. Thus in
both fields policies were extemporized without programs, and this is true not
only in Sweden but elsewhere. They are similar, furthermore, in that for
both housing and nutrition policy the family viewpoint offers an integrating
point for the rationalization of production and consumption. In both there
stands out as a social objective the closing of the gap between children's
present underconsumption and an acceptable minimum standard. In both
cases this problem cannot be solved without the whole nation shouldering
responsibility for the children.

The problems of housing and nutrition are also different, however, and the
treatment of a social nutrition policy cannot therefore be fundamentally a
repetition of the discussion of social housing. The problems are different
first because in food the producers are more numerous, more scattered, and
less well organized. The farmers themselves constitute a social responsibility
in modern times, while the contractors and landlords do not. The situation
with regard to production is dissimilar in the two fields also because the community has never considered competing with the private entrepreneurs in
operating farms. The intervention eventually necessary will have to take
place at a greater distance from production proper than with regard to
housing, where the state may institute building activities. The two fields

differ in consumption too. National nutrition is keeping more nearly abreast of economic progress than is national housing. Food needs can never be so drastically neglected as can the need for shelter. Food items are the most essential and the least flexible in any budget. This is duly mirrored in the fact that the percentage of the family income spent for food is the best single measure of poverty. However poor, the family will first satisfy its hunger, no matter how large a portion of its resources that may take. Because of this primacy of food consumption the standard of nutrition has not lagged as far behind the general development of wages and level of living as the standard of housing.

A further difference between the two fields concerns the amount and degree of individual choice that has to be left in social intervention. In housing the community could dictate how houses should be built; it could even produce them. The family first chooses whether it wants to move into a house. After that the personal element shows itself in furnishing and using the place. In regard to food, however, a choice is made several times a day, a peculiarly personal choice. Interference by providing the family with food is thus a much more delicate matter than procuring a home for it. Public measures must respect this difference as to individualization of consumption and therefore in the realm of food policy allow a much greater distance between the subsidy and the final consumption. There is finally the difference between housing and nutrition that in regard to both consumption and production regulatory measures in nutrition may be of short duration, while in housing they take on a much more inflexible long-range investment character. The state can afford to experiment in food policy. It can create several schemes which interchange or interlock. It can change subvention schemes according to varying conditions in production, export, and so forth. The freer range of action is, however, counterbalanced by the greater necessity socially of taking care of the producers in farming than of the producers in housing.

For all these reasons, and in particular because the nutrition standard of the consumers is not so endangered while the plight of the producers, the farmers, has attained the status of a national problem, food policy must give more consideration to production problems than a housing policy would. Within the framework of such a production policy, however, a rational plan can be devised for letting the underconsumers, the children, meet the overproducers, the farmers. A nation with children hungry and at the same time with surplus food is not prepared to talk much about either democracy or common sense.

National Diet Improved

As poor people have to allocate a relatively larger share of their resources to the essential item of just keeping alive than do the well-to-do, the percentage spent for food will give some general indications of the level of living. For Sweden it is easy to illustrate how this percentage has declined during the last few decades. The major part of this new expansion of the family budget has been taken up by larger proportions spent for housing, for taxes, and for various items associated with greater cultural or civic participation: organization dues, gifts, travel, and related items. The family, generally speaking, now moves within a wider economic range than before.

Studies made in 1914, 1923, and 1933 of working-class and lower middle-class urban households, having employment and consisting of a man, wife, and some minor children, but otherwise selected so as to be fairly representative, illustrate the changes occurring. Through the Social Board, account books were furnished to households. For a whole year detailed entries were to be made, the family being paid for the completion of the book, with extra premiums for particularly careful accounts. This method, of course, implies a further selection as to households, inasmuch as only relatively superior families would be interested or able to meet the requirements. But in Sweden with its relatively high standard of education, this does not mean as much as it does in countries where there is still illiteracy. In the 1933 study (published in 1938) 87.7 per cent of the account books were completed. The number of urban households included in the final report was 1,245. Data from a simultaneous but still incomplete study of 653 rural households will also be cited.[1]

These studies, together with other information about economic conditions, indicate a substantial improvement in nutritional conditions, particularly among the urban population. The real annual wage income for fully employed industrial workers increased 40 per cent between 1914 and 1933. The corresponding gains were smaller for most other population groups, but all social and occupational classes registered an additional improvement on account of the decrease in family size.

The proportion of the income used for food declined to a considerable extent. The average for the families sampled in the 1914 study was 46 per cent while the corresponding proportion for 1933 was 35 per cent. These two figures are not strictly comparable, but they are nevertheless suggestive of the change which occurred. The absolute amount of money spent on food

---

[1] The calculations based on this material to be used frequently in this and subsequent chapters were related to three income classes — incomes of less than 3,000 crs., between 3,000 and 5,000 crs., and 5,000 crs. or more — and to three social classes — industrial workers, clerical workers and officials of lesser rank, and finally middle-class families. In the published presentation, however, the social division only is used in general data, the income division only when the material is analyzed by family type. When data concerning family type are given, tables relate to actual family size while in the general data the tables relate to a theoretical household of 3.3 consumption units, sometimes called a "normal household."

increased, even taking into account the change in value of money. The increase was still greater when computed per food requirement unit. Most of the increase accounted for was due to increased consumption of expensive meats, whole milk, butter, cheese, eggs, sugar, vegetables, wine and other alcoholic beverages. There was, on the other hand, a decrease in the consumption of certain inexpensive foodstuffs which met nutritional requirements.

CHILDREN, THE UNDERCONSUMERS

In spite of the general improvement in nutritional status, children did not participate fully in the progress attained. It is difficult to understand why statistics have so rarely touched upon the relation of children to nutritional status. Even in the multitude of studies referred to by the League of Nations Committee on Nutrition, [*146* and *147*] there are few in which the findings are analyzed so as to show the differentials in families of varying size. When the population discussion started in Sweden, only one or two older studies bore directly on this question, and their significance was not appreciated. Only at the direct request of the Population Commission were the findings of the last of the budget studies analyzed by family size. A similar request procured the help of the National Council of Nutrition for analyzing and evaluating dietary standards in different types of families. What was thus drawn from official sources became strong ammunition indeed for social reforms. When one sees how consumption is distributed between families with or without children, it is quite clear that there was truth in the slogan used during the campaign years in Sweden: "The childless drink the cream and the children get the skimmed milk." The commodities which have to be given up when the family grows are those especially needed in childhood.

The figures in Table 27 relate to total consumption within the family without regard to number of persons. Hence they do not reveal the whole picture as 45 quarts of cream a year for two childless adults is abundant, while 20 quarts divided among at least six persons in the same economic class when children are present may represent hardship. To demonstrate more exactly the reduction in food quantities as size of family increases, another tabulation may be included, showing how much is available per consumption unit, i.e., per full-grown man, in families of different size (Table 28).[2] This shows not only the effect of children on the diet of parents but also how appallingly low is the annual consumption of such articles as butter in large families. The crucial question is whether this means undernourishment.

The Population Commission asked the Nutrition Council, working with

---

[2] Consumption units are calculated according to the scale indicated in Table 28 despite the fact that it underestimates the needs of younger children.

TABLE 27. — ANNUAL CONSUMPTION OF SELECTED DAIRY PRODUCTS
IN URBAN FAMILIES IN SWEDEN, BY INCOME AND FAMILY SIZE, 1933

INCOME AND FAMILY SIZE	TOTAL CONSUMPTION PER FAMILY			
	Cream (liters)	Skimmed milk (liters)	Butter (kg.)	Margarine (kg.)
Income less than 3,000 crs.				
Families without children . . . . ⁄	17.9	40.9	28.9	20.4
Families with 2–3 children under 7 years . . .	16.9	11.7	23.9	35.3
Families with 4 children or more under 15 years	13.1	77.2	24.6	71.3
Income of 3,000–4,999 crs.				
Families without children	22.6	13.6	31.6	16.9
Families with 2–3 children under 7 years . . .	15.3	12.3	36.3	25.2
Families with 4 children or more under 15 years	20.1	31.6	41.7	55.0
Income of 5,000 crs. or more				
Families without children	45.2	5.8	38.7	16.1
Families with 2–3 children under 7 years . . .	20.3	20.3	49.4	30.0
Families with 4 children or more under 15 years	19.7	25.4	59.1	63.4
All income groups				
Families without children	25.5	20.4	32.1	17.8
Families with one child under 7 years	22.5	3.8	33.5	24.9
Families with one child 15 years and over . .	20.4	8.3	42.3	25.0
Families with 2–3 children under 7 years . . .	17.3	14.6	37.0	29.4
Families with 2–3 children under 15 years . .	24.2	19.3	40.2	37.4
Families with 4 children or more under 15 years	18.4	39.4	44.0	61.5
Families with 4 children or more, the oldest being 15 years and over	18.1	98.2	47.6	76.2

Source: Cost of Living Study, 1933 (*Levnadsvillkor och hushållsvanor i städer och industri-orter omkring år 1933*).

the General Board of Health, to investigate the problem of the extent of underconsumption. The nutrition expert, Dr. E. Abramson, made the calculations which are published partly in the Commission's Report on Nutrition [*10*] and partly in the Cost of Living Study of 1933. [*82*]

The supply of calories shows greater variability by size of family than by income (Table 29).[3] The underconsumption of iron and of vitamins is particularly marked (Tables 30 and 31). A persistent downward trend with the presence of children is proof enough that here is a law governing the welfare of families.

[3] This result may, however, best be explained in part by the fact that almost no families with incomes under 2,000 crs. were included in the study. Families with very high incomes were also underrepresented. In other words, the income range was covered less completely than the family-size range.

TABLE 28. — ANNUAL FOOD CONSUMPTION PER CONSUMPTION UNIT IN SWEDEN, BY SOCIAL GROUP[a] AND HOUSEHOLD TYPE[b]

SOCIAL GROUP AND HOUSEHOLD TYPE	TOTAL CONSUMPTION PER FAMILY									
	Meat (kg.)	Milk and cream (liters)	Butter (kg.)	Margarine (kg.)	Eggs (no.)	Flour (kg.)	Bread (kg.)	Potatoes (kg.)	Fresh vegetables (kg.)	Fruit (kg.)
Farm and Forestry Workers										
Small households . .	49.1	333.9	15.8	8.7	191	148.1	19.1	193.1	12.2	38.9
Middle-sized households . . .										
Without children .	48.6	390.8	13.6	7.0	195	155.6	6.5	156.4	7.7	25.6
With children . .	41.3	375.6	9.4	10.4	177	135.7	11.4	167.9	6.0	24.2
Large households With 0–2 children .	38.1	336.4	8.7	8.0	117	126.0	15.5	161.3	3.7	17.3
Large households With 3 children or more	36.2	313.9	5.9	9.9	114	134.8	8.5	162.2	4.3	17.6
Farmers										
Small households . .	54.1	419.9	16.9	3.2	231	159.0	6.6	193.0	8.4	49.2
Middle-sized households										
Without children .	43.5	399.1	12.9	2.0	204	165.9	3.2	190.1	11.3	45.1
With children . .	45.7	409.9	15.5	2.3	205	154.7	4.1	182.4	9.1	34.8
Large households With 0–2 children .	41.6	360.8	12.0	2.7	177	144.8	4.9	164.1	10.6	34.5
Large households With 3 children or more	38.6	374.4	11.7	3.3	150	145.7	6.2	162.9	7.8	25.0
Urban Household										
Small households . .	58.5	257.5	16.9	9.4	309	45.3	47.9	109.0	21.2	52.9
Middle-sized households										
Without children .	53.8	246.5	13.9	9.3	255	52.3	45.5	105.1	17.8	39.9
With children . .	50.7	267.3	13.6	10.2	267	48.0	46.4	107.4	17.0	44.5
Large households With 0–2 children .	45.0	234.8	11.5	10.5	231	57.8	40.8	98.6	13.5	37.2
Large households With 3 children or more	41.3	250.7	9.4	12.5	208	59.1	40.6	98.5	12.3	34.4

[a] A person under 16 years of age is considered a child. Middle-sized households consist of 3–4 persons. Consumption of large families is overestimated since the consumption scale used represents an underestimation of the relative food requirements of children. Children under 4 years of age were counted as .15 consumption units, 4–6 years as .40 units, 7–10 years as .75 units, and 11–14 years as .90 units. Examples on modern consumption scales in which a greater relative weight is attributed to the nutritional needs of children are given in *Diets of Families of Employed Wage Earners and Clerical Workers in Cities* by Hazel K. Stiebeling and Esther F. Phipard, Circular No. 507, U. S. Department of Agriculture, Washington, D. C., 1939.
[b] For definitions of household types see Table 21.

Source: Population Commission, Report on Nutrition (*Betänkande i näringsfrågan*).

EDUCATIONAL PROPAGANDA AND ECONOMIC AID

The regularity in all these series is alarming. This will certainly not result in the best possible physical quality for the next generation. Some remedies must be scrutinized. That the evils arise from both economic strain and lack of wisdom can be seen from the underconsumption of calories

TABLE 29. — UNDERCONSUMPTION* IN REGARD TO CALORY VALUE OF FOOD IN URBAN FAMILIES IN SWEDEN, BY FAMILY SIZE AND INCOME

	PER CENT OF FAMILIES WITH SUBNORMAL CONSUMPTION AMONG				
FAMILY SIZE	All families	Industrial and clerical workers with incomes			Middle-class families
		Less than 3,000 crs.	3,000–4,999 crs.	5,000 crs. or more	
All families	22	25	23	19	24
Families with no children	10	—	13	—	10
Families with one child	15	13	16	—	29
Families with 2 children	22	26	21	—	24
Families with 3 children	29	27	25	23	17
Families with 4 children or more	38	49	39	32	—

a Optimal consumption per consumption unit was regarded as 3,000 calories daily. A slightly corrected scale for determining consumption units when evaluating calories, protein, vitamins, calcium, etc., was used rather than the one used in the 1933 urban study previously referred to.

Source: Population Commission, Report on Nutrition (*Betänkande i näringsfrågan*).

TABLE 30. — DAILY CONSUMPTION OF PROTEIN AND MINERALS PER CONSUMPTION UNIT IN URBAN FAMILIES IN SWEDEN, BY FAMILY SIZE

FAMILY SIZE	PROTEIN (g.) *a*	ANIMAL PROTEIN (g.) *a*	CALCIUM (g.) *b*	PHOSPHORUS (g.) *c*	IRON (mg.) *d*
All families	93.3	56.4	1.14	1.77	16.3
Families with no children	99.6	63.9	1.19	1.84	17.8
Families with one child	96.5	60.2	1.17	1.78	17.0
Families with 2 children	93.9	57.1	1.18	1.79	16.3
Families with 3 children	93.9	55.2	1.16	1.79	16.2
Families with 4 children or more	87.2	48.2	1.08	1.68	15.0

a Standard: 70 grams.
b Standard: 0.68 grams.
c Standard: 1.32 grams.
d Standard: 15 milligrams.

Source: Population Commission, Report on Nutrition (*Betänkande i näringsfrågan*).

TABLE 31. — DAILY CONSUMPTION OF VITAMINS PER CONSUMPTION UNIT IN URBAN FAMILIES IN SWEDEN, BY INCOME AND FAMILY SIZE

INCOME AND FAMILY SIZE	VITAMIN[a] A	VITAMIN[b] B₁	VITAMIN[c] B₂	VITAMIN[d] C
Income less than 3,000 crs.				
Families without children	4,874	360	755	71
Families with 2–3 children under 7 years . . .	4,077	347	725	60
Families with 4 children or more under 15 years	2,731	301	568	48
Income of 3,000–4,999 crs.				
Families without children	5,560	337	720	72
Families with 2–3 children under 7 years . . .	4,562	336	728	62
Families with 4 children or more under 15 years	3,383	274	580	46
Income of 5,000 crs. or more				
Families without children	5,789	315	655	75
Families with 2–3 children under 7 years . . .	5,402	342	742	72
Families with 4 children or more under 15 years	4,125	306	674	57
All income groups				
Families without children	5,399	340	719	72
Families with one child under 7 years	5,152	337	715	70
Families with one child 15 years and over . .	4,978	340	694	66
Families with 2–3 children under 7 years . . .	4,687	341	732	65
Families with 2–3 children under 15 years . .	4,306	316	666	60
Families with 4 children or more under 15 years	3,512	292	612	50
Families with 4 children or more, the oldest being 15 years and over	3,426	292	602	51

[a] International units (standard 4,000 units per person over 10 years of age).
[b] International units (standard 300 units).
[c] Sherman-Bourquin units (standard 50 units).
[d] Milligram ascorbic acid (standard 50 units).

Source: Population Commission, Report on Nutrition (*Betänkande i näringsfrågan*).

(Table 29). Underconsumption existed even in the middle-class families without children. So decidedly was the deficiency increased with economic pressure, however, that a main responsibility has, as in all other fields, to be placed on the unfair competition of children's many needs with other items in the family budget. Economic support and educational inducement to change are both needed.

Education of housewives in the choice and preparation of wholesome food was strongly urged by the Population Commission. It was recommended that courses for housewives emphasize the importance of food values as well as the art of cooking. A general course in homemaking, including wise food selection even if eating in restaurants, was recommended for both boys and girls through the public schools. It was suggested that more information concerning nutrition be included in vocational training for domestic workers, teachers, doctors, dentists, and other groups. Most important of all was the proposed reform in the training of home economics teachers. "A home economics teacher must primarily be trained to give instruction in how families of different composition in different economic groups under different social conditions, in different work conditions, etc., should be able to utilize available economic resources for obtaining a diet as nutritious as possible." [10]

To spread simple propaganda it was suggested that the state pay for pamphlets in large numbers, together with posters for schools, offices of social agencies, and similar places. All these methods had been used before, but it was believed that the time had come for an organized campaign for enlightenment on a large scale. Radio was to play an important part in a much more purposive way than hitherto. Even subsidizing short films was proposed. It was recommended that false recommendation of food products in advertising be legally prohibited. In short, an effective campaign was needed in order thoroughly to condition the Swedish people with regard to improved food habits without making them unduly health conscious and finicky. That results could be achieved had been proved by the experience of the consumers' cooperatives in increasing the consumption of citrus fruits. "The aim is gradually to teach people to regard the use of faulty foods in the same way that they already regard certain hygienically unpleasant habits."

But education will never be enough. Economic conditions fix the limits of what can be achieved by intellectual appeals. It must follow that when consciousness about what is the right food increases, consciousness of what is happening to one's own children sharpens also. Prudence will lead parents not to have children rather than to expose them to a dietary standard that the whole nation knows leads to malnutrition. This is exactly what has happened. The result may be read in the birth records of some of the most conscientious groups in Sweden. Food costs work in the same direction as other costs. They are particularly effective as food costs are so large an item in a family budget and so relatively inflexible. For the same reasons the nutritional policy must be of particular importance in population policy.

Economic reforms have to be coupled with educational reforms in order to make them human. Economic reforms to support the nutritional standard of children are the more called for as the food producers in Sweden as in many countries have been subsidized at the expense of society. The reform which must still be accomplished in this field is the transformation of the farming subsidy so as to fit the interests of children. In so far as such an integration is successful no new real costs for nutritional reforms need be involved.

AGRICULTURAL POLICY

The system of support for agriculture in Sweden, introduced early in the depression of the thirties, has been expensive. Deplorably enough, it has been working nearly contrary to the interests which have been here described as supreme, as it has made foodstuffs expensive for families with children. Low-income groups have been held indemnified for increased prices through a rise in wages. That is true, but it is also true that the rise in income could have gone much farther had not part of it been eaten up by the state support for agriculture. From the farmers' point of view it looked different. They would say that prior to that "correction" of prices, the underpaid farmers were helping to support other classes by giving them cheap agricultural products. Even the farmers, however, have no interest in a system according to which an abnormal part of the cost of the agricultural policy has been carried as an indirect tax burden by the poorest and by the children of the nation. The advantages, besides going to the farmers in Sweden as producers, have been going to the consumers, or dealers, in England.

The agricultural crisis finally came in Sweden in 1930 and obviously came to stay. In the beginning this was not generally perceived, and the political situation was such that only provisional measures could be agreed upon in the haste made necessary by the catastrophic price fall. In 1932 the number of farmers going bankrupt reached a maximum. In that year, also, farm operators gave notice of a change in the collective agreement. They wanted, because of their own distress, to reduce the already low wages for farm labor. What gave Sweden an agricultural policy in 1933 was in itself an alliance of historic importance: a deal between the labor party and the farmers. Workers and farmers have since then been the solid foundation of all governmental activity. The workers sacrificed their own immediate interests and promised to help the farmers get higher prices on agricultural products, while the farmers promised to support the Labor party in its quest for an expansion of the system of public works to cure unemployment.

The Swedish system of support for agriculture has existed since that time. As Swedish agriculture was about meeting the demand for vegetables and had only a manageable surplus in animal products, it was not necessary to attempt any direct limitation of production. The home market has through import restrictions of various kinds, however, been reserved for the Swedish producers at the same time that a system of export bounties has been applied to relieve the domestic market of animal products to such a degree that prices could be kept up within the country. The prices maintained have generally been the averages of 1925–1929. These export bounties were financed partly by certain levies on farm products and partly by a very heavy tax on margarine, the poorer classes' butter. This latter tax was aimed also at restricting the consumption of margarine in favor of butter.

The social effects of this agricultural policy are clearly visible. [*144* and *179*] A large-scale income redistribution was effected. Some 300 million crs. per year were transferred to the farmers. This *per se* was defensible as farmers as a class were working under great economic difficulties. The incidence on the various income groups and family types of the burden for supporting the farmers was socially undesirable, however, and not at all in line with population policy. The system actually amounted to a high and steeply regressive indirect tax on foodstuffs. Not only bread but particularly milk, eggs, meat, butter, and even margarine were made more expensive. There is no wonder that as a result there arose a growing feeling of political tension. The farmers were still poor in spite of the heavy burdens carried by the consumers and pressed for still higher prices on farm products, while the consumers increasingly felt the hardships and injustices inherent in the distribution of this burden. At the same time there was an accumulating economic tension in the very basis of this whole system of agricultural support, threatening to explode it. The sharp and steady upward production trend endangered it, as a defense of the domestic price level effected by dumping is naturally feasible only when the amounts to be exported are relatively small proportions of the total production. The total amount of the export bounties could for a time be kept reasonably low only because of two causal factors, both of obviously temporary character: the rapid increase in national consumption from the bottom of the depression to the top of the boom period and the general rise of international prices during the same period. In the years just before the new war it was apparent to the independent economists of the country and became gradually realized also by the politicians that this extemporized agricultural policy without a program had to be radically changed. [*173*]

This analysis also gives the clue to a rational solution. "What our children do not eat in sufficient quantities is high-grade animal foodstuffs, butter, milk, meat, bacon, and eggs. These are at the same time, without comparison, the most important of the market products of agriculture." [*173*] The solution, then, seems to involve letting the community buy these products for its children. Why not let taxpayers pay for them and at the same time pay for the support of agriculture in direct proportion to their ability rather than let the poor consumers pay for it in inverse proportion to their economic resources? Why not let the children in Sweden eat enough rather than pay for feeding England or Germany?

The psychological and political soil was prepared. What had seemed only an irresponsible suggestion of experts and reformers in 1934 became the vigorous proposal of the Population Commission in 1938 and a political

program in 1939. Had it not been for the outbreak of the war the new social
integration of nutritional and agricultural policy in Sweden should probably
by now have been on the way to realization. It was backed not only by
ideals and plans but also by hard political and economic necessities. As the
war is probably not going to change the fundamental facts, i.e., the production trends and the consumption demands, this part of the population program more surely than any other will have its victorious comeback.

The Population Commission, when analyzing the nutrition problem,
went deep into the whole complex of problems concerning agricultural trends
and the farmers' plight. The nutritional measures should be integrated into
the production policy. They should be given the character of internal dumping to be effected in a threefold way: through a free school meal to all
children, through the furnishing of free health food to mothers and children
on doctors' prescriptions, and through trying a two-price system for agricultural surplus commodities.

THE NATIONAL SCHOOL MEAL

The reports of district health officers portray the underconsumption of
children and especially the monotonous and meager fare of school children
much more vividly than the data presented above. The "coffee abuse" and
the long way to schools combine to cause many children not to get any cooked
food until late in the afternoon. Sometimes the deficiencies are caused by
too strict regionalism, as in the case of the milk-and-meal diet in Norrland.
The sending of fruits to these districts by charity, sometimes organized on a
large scale, and the freight reduction granted by the government had not
done much more than bring the existence of the dietary need to the attention of the citizens.

As a first remedy the Population Commission proposed a free school meal
every day to every child in the country. Such a measure would be sound, as
it would take care of quite an important part of the agricultural surplus.
Regardless of deficiencies in the diets of children it would transfer some of
the cost of supporting children from the budget of individual parents to that
of the nation, a change desired in itself and advocated as a practical measure
of population policy.

School meals are, of course, not unknown in Sweden. During the school
year 1935–1936, 6 per cent of all public school children received some school
meal. Such benefits were open to only a selected few, however, who were
mostly stigmatized as destitute. The recipients were chiefly located in cities
while the Commission showed that the need was greatest in the country on
account of lower average incomes and greater distances to school. Also, the
school meals were not organized so as to give the most desirable supplement
of healthful foods.

The proposal was gradually to make such a school meal available to all. In order to overcome technical difficulties only a fifth of all school districts were to start in the first year. Thereafter the number would gradually increase. The question of school meals in secondary schools would finally have to be faced also. Any school which offered school meals at all would have to offer them to all pupils in order to be eligible for state grants, and meals would have to be given free of cost.

These principles fundamentally derive from the population policy. They are also intended to remove all class distinction from the most innocent of all, namely, the children, in regard to such a life essential as food. Schooling, as such, is free to everyone. Why not extend the functions of the school according to the same principles? As about 40 per cent of all children belong to the families with three or more children, on whom charges ought not to be levied, there would remain so few well-to-do families from whom to derive any income for the project that it would not seem worth the trouble to fix different dues. The well-to-do parents may of course dispense with public bounties if they want to. They need never feel that they are accepting a dole as they will certainly pay for these luncheons in their tax bills. The school meal for children should, on the whole, be regarded neither as a commodity for which to pay nor as a charitable gift for which to thank. It should be regarded as common cooperative householding on the part of all citizens.

The food to be served was designed as the main meal of the day for the children. Only through providing a substantial meal is there any chance of effectively making up for the frequent quantitative and qualitative deficiencies in the diet which children receive in their homes, whether on account of poverty or of ignorance. In order to make this meal a truly protective one it was decreed that, while it need not give more than about 800 to 1,000 calories, it should contain at least half the protective food values required per day for an adequate diet and almost completely satisfy the need for vitamin C and for vitamin A. It was further required that during the cold seasons some part of the meal be served hot. A list of model school menus was published in the report of the Commission. [*10*] This school meal was designed, too, to be integrated as much as possible in the educational process, thus reducing costs and at the same time increasing the opportunities for progressive self-activity within the school. In this way also the best channel would be opened to dietary reforms in the parental homes of the children and in their own prospective homes.

Some costs in addition to those for purchasing the foodstuffs would have to be foreseen. In order to induce municipalities to save on these, they were to be borne by the local communes, while the state was generally to carry the cost of the food at a specified amount per child per day in order not to encourage greed in that respect. Provisions for space were to be made whenever necessary, and the school districts should be subsidized for this purpose according to existing rules for state aid for school buildings.

This school meal was calculated to cost about 34 million crs. annually, exclusive of building costs of which 25 million would be provided by state subsidies. With the exception of citrus fruits, which were to be supplied even though they had to be imported, most of this money would go to products which the Swedish farmers were already producing in abundance. Some shift toward truck farming instead of grain production would probably be stimulated by the school meal program.

At an early stage of the investigation an arrangement was made by the Population Commission and the Cabinet which resulted in the experimental organization of school meals in certain districts. Since 1937 state grants have been available for such school meals. These grants amounted to 500,000 crs. in 1939 and 400,000 crs. in 1940. The program was started first in Norrland and in certain distressed areas with residual unemployment. The regulation that such meals should be free to all children in any school enjoying state grants has been enforced. A report from Norrland to the Population Commission testifies: "The provision of school meals has had a good effect on all the children. All teachers have emphasized their great value and have without exception stated that they have seen the children become vigorous and full of energy because of this feeding."

PROTECTIVE FOOD FOR MOTHERS AND BABIES

The children below school age would obtain no advantages from this scheme. In a later report on day nurseries by the Population Commission [15] it was proposed that the same state grants be made accessible for meals for children in publicly controlled day nurseries, kindergartens, vacation camps, and so forth. By such a measure the cost of upkeep of these institutions could be reduced and the quality of their fare improved.

The main problem left unsolved by the plan was that of the children in the home. For those who really suffered from deficient diet due to economic straits, free food to be given on doctors' prescriptions was proposed. In order to attain more complete protection of the children, the same advantages have to be available to their mothers. Consequently the proposal included pregnant and nursing women. [10]

What is here suggested is not free commodities available to all. Individual need has to be proved, but the need is only a dietary one, no income limits being fixed. The only doctors having the right to prescribe protective food to be obtained free of charge are those who are at the health stations described above. Regular attendance at such a clinic is thus a prerequisite. Without the stipulation of any economic limits, it is evident that selection would be made according to the doctors' discretion, who would take into account the social and economic conditions that might in part be the cause of the malnutrition.

The food prescriptions would carry no relief stigma. A notification of the food needed should be sent to the local Child Welfare Board, which, in turn, would issue coupons for the necessary foodstuffs to be bought from specified dealers. The Child Welfare Board would pay the dealer and the state in turn would remunerate the Welfare Board up to 80 or even 100 per cent in tax-ridden communities. The cost to the state if such a system were completely put into effect would amount to approximately 5 million crs. annually, chiefly for increased consumption of milk, butter, cheese, and other foods rich in vitamin C. This program is still far from realization. More has been done in regard to a similar program for free distribution of protective medicines (Chapter 16).

A TWO-PRICE SYSTEM ON FOODSTUFFS

These two measures of school meals and free protective foods will not, however, take care of all the agricultural surplus or provide a substitute for export subsidies. The millions for the latter are donated to British and other foreign consumers by the Swedish state and financed by indirect taxation on many of its poorest citizens and the children. This precipitates the question of replacement of foreign dumping with a domestic program. When differences between prices in the home market and in export markets can be made up by the state, why not pay similar price differences between two markets within the country? Such a proposal of a two-price system was presented by the Population Commission. It was stubbornly maintained from the very beginning, in fact from the first discussion of such price differentiation in 1934, however, that the occasion must not be utilized for an artificial creation of two price levels according to different income groups, i.e., price reduction for persons on relief and full price for others. The problem of low incomes generally has to be attacked in some truly constructive, but for the economic system probably quite radical, way. No panaceas here and there, wherever an occasion offered itself, were to be sanctioned, at least as long as there existed one disfavored group discernible without any means test, namely, children.

The proposed Swedish two-price system thus is a system for children, being a measure not of relief but of family policy. It is built up as a rational plan for expanding consumption exactly where the statistics quoted above show it to be most needed. It is only in that sense that the two-price system may be called new. Giving food as relief has been utilized since time immemorial, the very symbol of private charity being the lady with the soup bowl. Also, the idea of distributing surplus products free or at reduced costs is not new. In Denmark a law has since 1933 provided for distribution of food to needy people through a state subvention for meat, and lately also for bacon and milk. In the United States, Great Britain, and other countries similar schemes have been adopted. In Sweden itself flour was distributed in this way in 1933, and later butter, fish, and fruits. The distribution has, however, had the character of relief, the foodstuffs being given free or at low cost to needy districts or needy people after applications from a municipality, the Salvation Army, or other agencies. No two-price levels had been fixed, no rights for eligibility legally defined, no plan for the integration of such consumption in the nation's housekeeping constructed.

The original suggestion in the Report on Nutrition by the Population Commission [10] provided for coupons to be issued to all families with three or more children and to all broken or otherwise handicapped families with one or two children. No income limit would restrict the eligibility of the families.

The foodstuffs to be reduced in price for the children were obviously those for which there was a farm surplus. In order to effect a real increase in consumption not only the desired expansion of consumption of a commodity should be subsidized but also the total amount consumed. Otherwise the purchase at reduced price might come to substitute for instead of supplement what would otherwise have been bought. The unpleasant necessity of close control would in the same way be decreased. A general approximation of what the total annual consumption of a commodity ought to be and then reduction of the price for that total would be the only logical measure in order to increase consumption for the good of children as well as of farmers. To please the farmers butter was singled out for experiment, as it would give the most perceptible results. The consumption of margarine could be reduced for the families with children and the trade would be fairly easy to control.

Only the broad outlines of such a two-piece system were presented by the Population Commission. Its proposal was for further investigation, which was also swiftly expedited as the Agricultural Commission, appointed in 1938, was given a mandate to take up the problem for further consideration in connection with general reform of the whole agricultural policy.

The war intervened, stopping imports of fodder and fertilizers as well as of the raw materials for the margarine industry and also in other ways fundamentally changing the whole structure of supply and demand. The crop in 1940 was poor, increasing the difficulties of farmers. Rationing was established for some food items, sometimes in order to limit consumption of imported goods like coffee, tea, and cocoa, the supply of which could not be replenished because of the curtailment of trade to the west, sometimes only in order to prevent hoarding and speculation as with domestic products like sugar, flour, and bread. The sale of margarine was temporarily prohibited, partly to economize on the stock of raw materials, partly to maintain the demand for butter. Prices on all agricultural products were raised forcibly, endangering the welfare of the children.

In this situation the suggestion from the Population Commission of price reductions on foodstuffs for families was tried out in a restricted way. Rebates on butter were introduced for certain social categories, namely, all children if the assessed income of parents did not exceed 1,500 crs. (which means an actual income considerably higher, particularly if there are several children) and also the parents if such income did not exceed 500 crs., all pensioners, and some other limited categories. On application other persons or families might obtain butter rebates. As a matter of fact every sixth person in Stockholm and every third person in Gothenburg became beneficiaries of this new form of public support to agriculture. For children and pensioners two kilograms (not quite four and one-half pounds) of butter could be bought every 5 weeks, the price being fixed at 1.30 crs. per kilogram below the actual price quotation on butter, a reduction of about one-third of the ordinary cost. For other adults the quantities for price reduction were somewhat smaller. This project was war-born. It was partly a relief policy, partly a measure of agricultural policy. It was somewhat affected by the preceding population discussion, but it does not faithfully follow a courageous population pattern.

In the summer of 1940 the problems of how to safeguard the nutritional standards of children, and generally how to defend the level of living of families with children had not as yet been attacked in any broad and constructive way in Sweden. Experts were pointing out that the rising costs of living, the increased indirect taxation, and the towering unemployment were as always falling with a particularly heavy incidence on families with children. But the voice of the humanitarians is a weak political force in time of national danger. Under the impact of this danger with the attendant widespread maladjustments and uncertainties within the whole economic structure, the politicians are not likely to be greatly concerned with children's rights.

CHAPTER XVI

HEALTH FOR THE NATION

S OME of the most painful adjustments that contemporary society has to make have to do with the simple human needs of health. Waste and carelessness with human lives have certainly characterized not only nature and warfaring herds; they are still found to an incredible degree in the mode of living of peaceful modern civilizations. Only the socially most disastrous diseases, plague, and contagion have been fully recognized as responsibilities of the community. The other needs of health work have barely become organized: in some countries as public health measures, in others as private medicine; for some purposes as philanthropic organizations and for others as cooperative group medicine. Sometimes the needs are just neglected. The demarcation of the various forms of medical services has been neither planned nor systematic. The dilemma is that the disorder is stabilized. To some degree it represents vested interests. It also represents sets of attitudes, values, and prestige considerations that are just as difficult to change. In many cases agencies for medical care have been created by such great personal sacrifices for humanitarian reasons that it seems ungrateful to declare the very system obsolete. Yet such is the judgment that will be passed by everyone who can look at health needs not only with human sympathy but also with cold objectivity.

Nowhere does health occupy the same paramount position on social programs as education. It is a curious historical accident that a public school system is taken for granted while a national health system is something to fight about. Probably the reason that the democratic right to education is more generally recognized than the right to health is that the democratic creeds were formulated during the era of enlightenment. Our ideals in modern democracy stem from the eighteenth and early nineteenth centuries, which with their preoccupation with and appreciation of intellectual values preceded the biologically minded period. If declarations of social demands were rewritten today, there is no doubt that the one fundamental human right of vital concern for the whole people would be proclaimed to be the right to health, especially the children's right to health.

For society as a whole illness causes an enormous waste. In no country are there adequate statistics on the waste of poor health. It is known that men and women, some of them trained at great expense to society, work only intermittently and, when they do, often inefficiently because of poor health. The productive apparatus is wasteful and investment in human capital is depreciated. At the same time illness itself is to a large degree social in its effects. Not even the wealthiest citizen can consider his health and his illness as purely private matters. There is no other successful method of dealing with sick neighbors except curing them. The elementary demand for equality may furnish the constitutional principle for a new order in the field of medical care. Cooperative administration is the only rational cure.

But to many, even if admitting the logic of the idea, any complete socialization of health may seem abhorrent. It may indeed call for a reorganization of that system of medical care which, as it has grown, has nevertheless given immense service. There could be little practicality in erasing all that is and erecting a new structure of health care overnight. Just because this extreme of socialization has to be avoided, it will pay to look around for a sector where present-day services are least institutionalized and least perfected, where the damage done to health is most catastrophic, where the ability to pay privately for medical care will most seldom exist, and where, consequently, the vested interests also are of least importance. That is the case with regard to children. Pediatrics is a new specialty and in its private form an exclusive one, reaching only a few and those chiefly in large cities. The damage done to children's health is directly a sabotage of the nation's own tomorrow. A family's ability to pay for medical care will always be in inverse relationship to the number of children. By narrowing the claim for socialized medicine to a demand for nationalization or perhaps just democratization of medical care for children, the ideal becomes practical.

MEDICAL COSTS IN FAMILIES

A truly cooperative responsibility for health does not exist in any society. Sweden has no claims to perfection. For some needs all social strata have excellent medical care; for some others a wide difference will be found between the clientele of the private doctor and that of the clinics. Some age groups of children receive satisfactory health inspection; other groups are neglected. There may be studied in Sweden, however, the development over a long period of a reasonably adequate and coherent public system of medical care. A framework has been created within which large portions of the population and large sectors of medical services are already included and into which the rest could be brought without severe disturbance. This system of public medical care is further characterized by the fact that it is not the brain child of social experimenters but has developed from within through centuries. It has therefore one important advantage, worthy of study, in that there are relatively few vested interests, organizations, or habits of thinking that would need to be broken down in order to achieve a harmonious expansion into a national system of medical services. The main fields of health control, of medical and dental care, of distribution of medicines and hospitalization are organized in such a way that they can easily be integrated. A mapping of that system and an evaluation of its present working will be attempted here from the point of view of the needs of the individual family and of the public support it can count upon for preserving the health of its children.

When as in Sweden the costs of medical care are to a large extent redistributed through the public budget, the worst class differences and individual hazards are eliminated. But as long as medical care costs anything at all a kind of class difference remains, based not so much on income as on size of family and reaching high up into the middle-class groups. Private means to pay for part of medical care will stretch relatively far for single persons and will allow little for the large family. In the course of the population discussion Sweden was due to realize this. In a general way the fact that children were underprivileged with regard to health care was also realized.

No separate health survey has been made in Sweden. Some glimpses of how health costs differ between large and small families may, however, be seen in the general studies of cost of living, the most recent of which deals with conditions in 1933. [82] This material consists, as has been stated in regard to food expenditures, of household account books carefully and systematically kept for a whole year (Chapter 15). The fact that the material is narrow in scope and not fully representative makes the figures less significant but still does not seem seriously to affect the relationships between expenditures of different family types and income classes.

Only the private expenditures for medical care can, of course, be obtained from budget statistics. It must be borne in mind that the public budgets of state, provinces, and communes furnish supplementary health care. Should this not have been the case, i.e., should the comparison be made in any country where health continues to be an ordinary purchasable commodity according to the strength of the private purse, it would stand out in still greater clarity that the health of children is the most neglected.

Of considerable social interest is a comparison of costs for medical care for families in different income groups having different numbers of children. When actual medical costs are studied, it is evident that the possibility of receiving adequate medical care declines with increasing family size (Table 32).

TABLE 32.—EXPENDITURES FOR MEDICAL CARE IN URBAN FAMILIES IN SWEDEN, BY INCOME AND FAMILY SIZE, 1933

INCOME AND FAMILY SIZE	TOTAL EXPENDITURE PER FAMILY FOR				
	All medical care (crs.)	Fees to doctors (crs.)	Dental care (crs.)	Medicine (crs.)	Hospital care and miscellaneous (crs.)
Income less than 3,000 crs.					
Families without children	48.8	18.6	12.3	9.8	8.1
Families with 2–3 children under 7 years	42.3	20.6	5.9	9.7	6.1
Families with 4 children or more under 15 years	39.6	20.8	5.1	10.8	2.9
Income of 3,000–4,999 crs.					
Families without children	84.2	23.4	26.3	19.0	15.5
Families with 2–3 children under 7 years	73.7	27.0	14.4	16.2	16.1
Families with 4 children or more under 15 years	69.1	23.7	10.0	19.6	15.8
Income of 5,000 crs. or more					
Families without children	104.6	37.1	23.6	22.3	21.6
Families with 2–3 children under 7 years	101.9	22.1	34.7	26.1	19.0
Families with 4 children or more under 15 years	138.5	22.0	59.5	21.5	35.5
All income groups					
Families without children	77.4	24.6	21.6	16.8	14.4
Families with one child under 7 years	76.4	25.4	21.1	17.7	12.2
Families with one child 15 years and over	98.3	24.7	39.3	14.0	20.3
Families with 2–3 children under 7 years	73.9	23.8	18.3	17.5	14.3
Families with 2–3 children under 15 years	85.1	29.0	23.6	18.5	14.0
Families with 4 children or more under 15 years	86.8	22.5	26.1	18.3	19.9
Families with 4 children or more, the oldest being 15 years and over	96.9	33.3	30.1	21.2	12.3

Source: Cost of Living Study, 1933 (*Levnadsvillkor och hushållsvanor i städer och industriorter omkring år 1933*).

Comparisons of the medical care that money buys clearly reveal the systematic neglect of children. What is spent for medical purposes seems to be a fairly constant part of the total income of any one group without regard to the number of family members whose health must be cared for. This rigidity in the family budget is worth close attention, as more children in a family evidently does not mean more patients for doctors, or, if more patients, it means less frequent visits. Expenses for dental care even show a tendency to decrease with increasing number of children except in the highest income group.

Since doctors' and dentists' fees remain unchanged or even decrease when more members are added to a family, obviously the medical profession would gain rather than lose if children's medical care is socialized. The practical conclusion about the desiderata for society is no less clear cut. If the under-privileged group is the children, the health reforms have to center on the children.

COMPARING FAMILY AND COMMUNITY COSTS

If the average of 2 per cent of income found to be spent in all the groups studied for medical care was representative for the whole people, it would indicate private expenditures of above 100 million crs. annually, or about 16 crs. per person. In actuality there is, of course, an uneven distribution of costs. The budget studies refer to a certain selection of families, excluding the poorest and the wealthiest. The former are many more than the latter; they may not spend even 2 per cent of their meager incomes. But as there is no other estimate at hand and as the purpose is only to arrive at a broad generalization, the estimate may stand. It is a curious coincidence that the public costs for medical care also come to about 16 crs. per person, or 100 million crs. annually. For the fiscal year 1932–1933, the medical costs borne by society amounted to around 100 million crs. of which 33,300,000 crs. came from the national budget, 32,500,000 crs. from the provincial governments' budgets (1932), and 34,700,000 crs. from the communes' budgets (1932). Since then public expenditures have been increased but so probably have private expenditures also.

Stated broadly, the medical care of the Swedish people is about half socialized. That is true, however, only if the criterion is that part of the payment is made in the form of cash by the citizens themselves. Other criteria may be used, yielding different results. Judging by the distribution of doctors, the private sector would seem to account for only about one-third of the total. Part of the earnings of doctors in public service is, however, derived from private practice. The nurses and midwives are nearly all in public service. The dentists are private practitioners to a larger extent. It must also be remembered that some of the money paid by the patients goes to hospitals, doctors, and dental clinics which are publicly organized. Another part, in fact the whole item for medicine, goes to pharmacies, which are state-controlled institutions. Finally, a considerable part of the private expenditures is provided from the health insurance funds, accident insurance, invalid pensions, etc. Any final decision as to what should be considered public medicine is a matter of definition. Summarizing the generalizations it would seem, judging from whether private citizens or official agencies are distributing the expenditures, that the medical field in Sweden is about half socialized; judging from the personnel side, that it is about two-thirds socialized; judging from who is in the final instance carrying the cost burden, that it is considerably more socialized; and judging finally from the degree of control, that it is almost completely under public responsibility. It must be remembered, however, that in practically all instances the patients have to defray part of the costs. Public health care does not mean altogether free health care.

Public health as it is related to sanitation, i.e., water control, food control, housing inspection, and similar activities, is well regulated and reasonably effective in Sweden. Provision for health inspection is authorized for infants and mothers. A complete system is proposed for school children, but as yet it is only partly instituted. Public provisions for health control of preschool children aged one to seven is entirely lacking. District medical services, instituted long ago for the poor and for certain endemic diseases, are now broadened as to social groups and improved through increased personnel. The sale of medicines and sickroom supplies has been under state control for centuries. The latest development is to give mothers and children certain medical supplies free of charge. The most completely socialized of all the medical services is hospitalization. Supported mainly by taxes, it provides everyone with excellent care in general wards with all services included in low fees. Semiprivate care subject to public regulations is also available at slightly higher fees. On the whole the curative care of illness is better provided for than the preventive care of health.

In order not to convey an idealized picture, it should be stated at the outset that conditions are not perfect. The deficiencies will be discussed; they have all followed the general trend of penalizing the family. As, however, the medical care of children is only a part, integrated in a fairly complex system of public medical services, this very system must be described as a background. The point of departure for new reforms in Sweden is to take full responsibility for health care of children.

PUBLIC HEALTH

What the family can reasonably expect from general public health measures it probably already receives in Sweden. It is guaranteed that the water is pure, the sewer functioning, the streets cleaned, the garbage quickly and securely disposed of, and the electrical fixtures carefully insulated, because all these necessities are furnished by public utility companies, owned by the people themselves through the state or local governments. The citizens further feel assured that houses are safely built and food is marketed according to sanitary rules as there is compulsory inspection by community authorities. They know that the schoolhouses in the whole country are sanitary, that the teachers are healthy, and that the factories are up to the standards of industrial hygiene, because all these are under a unified system of inspection with the same rules applying to the whole country, even if the rules may often represent minimum rather than optimum standards. The family may further rest assured, if it lives in a town, that its apartment is not a menace to health as housing inspection is compulsory in all cities and a number of other districts.

These and many similar safeguards are hedged about the family, sometimes effected through specialized inspectors and always under the responsibility of the chief district medical officer. The outstanding deficiencies are that housing inspection in rural areas is not thorough enough, that the district nurses are not obliged to make regular visits, and that specialized agencies for larger areas are not available. The new statute of sanitation (1936) will be insufficient if it only states the regulations about housing quality and overcrowding but fails to provide for the enforcement of these regulations. The organizational deficiency is probably that the immediate responsibility for this inspection and the enforcement of regulations is in the hands of local authorities in the multitude of small communities. It is easy to understand that the members of the local health board are not eager to enforce the regulations, as the violators may include themselves and their neighbors. Safe standards will not be achieved until the authority for maintenance of health standards is depersonalized by applying it to larger areas. This holds true not only for housing inspection, where violations become glaring, but also for the public health organization as a whole in rural districts. The health district ought to be larger than the local community.

When doctors were first employed in the field of general public health, this function was not their only one. It may be said that the Swedish system of socialized medicine started because sanitation was not a large enough assignment for medical men at the early date of 1750 when the government first provided them. Each province, of which there were and are 24, has a medical officer, engaged and paid by the authorities. This district medical officer has always had a double responsibility: general public health and the care of the sick. The original 24 health officers are now chief, or provincial, medical officers with a number of district doctors under them. In about 200 rural districts and the 200 urban districts,[1] the medical officers still have this twofold

---

[1] The administrative system is somewhat complicated. Each of the 24 chief medical officers and each of their 24 assistants as well as each of the 346 district medical officers in rural districts is paid by the state (with the exception of some assistants), while each of the 202 medical officers in urban districts is paid by the city. Several motions have been made in the Riksdag to transfer them to the state system and at the same time increase their number. It may be of interest to get a complete picture of the status of Swedish doctors as of 1938: 866 are engaged in general hospitals, 161 in mental hospitals, 122 in tuberculosis hospitals, 360 in institutions (railroad, state medical schools, etc.). Adding these and the district medical officers gives a total of over 2,100 public posts. Since some persons hold more than one position, the number of doctors in public service is somewhat smaller (1,859). The number of private practitioners is 1,028, while 174 licensed doctors are not engaged in practice. The total number of 3,061 qualified doctors gives about 48 doctors per 100,000 population as against 128 in the United States, the distribution, however, being different. The great portion of doctors in public service means a particularly high degree of utilization of their services. The excellently trained district nurses and midwives are, under proper control of doctors, given great responsibility.

function: public health and medical care. Since the former function in recent times has grown enormously with vaccination and other checks on contagious diseases, control of venereal disease, babies' and mothers' health centers, and other developments, the future policy has become uncertain. It will be necessary either to separate the functions of public health and medical care or to divide the districts into smaller units. The first solution would allow greater specialization but the second would allow closer contact with the public as patients. Both developments are actually taking place. The complete division of health and sick care has the support of certain experts. With the growing number of specialists connected with hospitals and clinics it may be said to be coming about. This is being further accelerated by dividing the functions of the medical officers into several specialized posts in the larger cities. But the second solution has been easier to achieve in rural districts and is well under way. The number of districts is growing year by year, and the Medical Board favors a general plan which would add 10 new districts annually.

In that realm of public health which lies between preventive and curative services are to be found the national campaigns against tuberculosis and venereal disease, both delegated to the district physician in so far as they do not demand hospitalization. His has been the job of catering to the dispensary clinics, set up all over the country around the turn of the century. Free clinical visits were available to all who believed themselves threatened with tuberculosis, which was at the time christened "the national disease." For the sick, hospital care was arranged, but the more than 200 dispensaries had to carry out disinfection work, to follow up the patient's family, to propagate preventive sanitary rules, and to perform other services. The results of this campaign can be seen from statistics on tuberculosis mortality, which declined from 1.94 per 1,000 population in 1911–1915 to 1.08 in 1931–1935 and to 0.81 in 1938. So successful has this campaign been that in 1935 the Medical Board could propose a reorganization of tuberculosis treatment, discontinuing the special dispensary clinics with their own dispensary nurses and reintegrating that treatment into the general system of the district physicians' and the district nurses' routine work.

At another time venereal diseases were selected for a special intensive campaign and again the main responsibility was placed upon the district medical officer. The results of the synchronized campaign by law, doctors, and public authorities can be seen in the dramatic statistical curves. Syphilis has in two decades been practically eradicated (Table 33). Of the few hundred new cases every year, one-third have been infected in foreign countries.[2] Here is the story of how it was done. In 1918 a Venereal Disease Act was passed.

[2] Gonorrhea has not been similarly brought under control. The average annual number of cases registered in 1916–1920 was 15,422; in 1931–1939, 11,851; and in 1939, 12,072.

Since then regulations have been enforced according to what is commonly called the Nordic System, under which infecting another person is a criminal offense. The patient is not prosecuted. He is only asked to go for treatment and is given that treatment privately and free of charge. On the other hand, anybody who, knowing he is infected with a venereal disease, has sexual intercourse is liable to punishment. The minimum penalty is a fine

TABLE 33. — NEW CASES OF SYPHILIS ANNUALLY IN SWEDEN, 1915–1939

YEAR	NUMBER OF NEW CASES	YEAR	NUMBER OF NEW CASES
1915	2,681	1928	1,162
1916	2,741	1929	1,000
1917	2,925	1930	1,116
1918	4,256	1931	1,189
1919	6,303	1932	811
1920	3,560	1933	543
1921	2,479	1934	447
1922	1,480	1935	421
1923	1,087	1936	381
1924	853	1937	297
1925	698	1938	343
1926	937	1939	378
1927	1,212		

Sources: Annual Medical Statistics (*Allmän hälso — och sjukvård*) and Annual Yearbook of Sweden : 1940 (*Statistisk Årsbok*).

of 50 crs. and the maximum a sentence of two years at hard labor. The doctor has to try to ascertain the name of the person having infected his patient and then notify the health board in the district of the source of infection. In turn the health board must make that person undergo treatment. If any of those known to be infected are recalcitrant they may, with the aid of police, be placed in hospitals. This Swedish legislation, with its compulsory follow-up of treatment, has been copied by other countries. The cost to the state has amounted to approximately one-half million crs. annually. The family has been given a bulwark against one of its worst dangers.

The range of services rendered by the district medical officer is wide. Lately a number of functions for health inspection of mothers and children have been added to his work. Indicating as they do a new comprehensive approach to medical reforms, they will be discussed in a separate section as they concern the special domain of socialized medicine for children. Here it suffices to round out the general background picture by stressing that the district doctor is not only a public health officer but also a general practitioner. He is the one to provide the minimum safeguards for medical care in his area. He is available for both office calls and home visits. This applies no longer only to poor people. Anybody has the right to call the district physician or to visit him in his office. Everybody has then the right to his cheap services, and the doctor has the duty to comply with given regulations as to fees. These charges provide the medical officer with a flexible income in addition to his salary, which is paid by the state or the community. The fixed schedule of fees varies between 1 and 3 crs. per consultation in order to allow scaling according to the economic status of patients. If the patient contributes to a sickness insurance fund, that fund will reimburse him for two-thirds of the doctor's fee. This holds true even if the doctor is a private practitioner and not a state official. If the patient is indigent, he will secure a statement to that effect from the poor relief authorities, present it to the district doctor, and receive free care. The doctor will later be reimbursed for that service by the relief administration, thus having no inducement to discriminate against the poorer patients. This is neither a system of open, free, anonymous clinics, so dreaded in the name of socialized medicine, nor a panel system, which as in England and Germany puts the doctors at the mercy of the insurance funds.

Home visits also are paid for according to a special schedule. Rural patients at long distances from the central offices are at a disadvantage. In order to compensate them a law of 1926, revised in 1939, furnishes state subsidies for the total cost of doctor's travel above 3 crs. per visit and one half of his fee above 7 crs.

Medical care could, of course, never be actually described by focusing only on the doctors and forgetting the nurses. The district nurses also have a double role, serving both in a supervisory capacity and in a nursing capacity. District nurses will, however, give free attendance only to bed patients of very low incomes. In some places they may find time to nurse paying patients also. Their main function is to serve as assistants to the district doctors in their health clinics.

In the case of nurses also there is the problem of whether the increase in their services should lead to increasing specialization among nurses or increasing the number of general nurses. At a time just previous to the present reform era the tendency was for greatly specializing their supervisory functions. Some nurses or social workers were engaged as housing inspectors, some nurses were engaged solely for dispensary work, some only as school nurses in a community. Visualizing a time when some 10 nurses or social workers might have to visit a family on their specialized missions, the tendency has recently been reversed. A general district nurse is preferred but smaller districts are demanded. Simultaneously the nation is adding new functions to those of the district nurse, who is becoming school nurse, clinic assistant, health instructor in the baby and mother's health centers, and so forth.

As this organization of district nurses was only integrated into a state system with state subsidies in 1920, having previously been totally dependent on the local community, and only in 1935 reorganized with the aim of greater completeness, the whole setup will only gradually be achieved.

HOSPITALIZATION

A case of illness demanding hospital care is the very focus of a public system of medicine. If a poll were taken in Sweden, it would probably be agreed that the Swedish hospital system comes nearer to perfection than any other of the nation's public services in the field of medicine. Hospitalized illness is not a financial nightmare to any citizen. First-rate care by the most prominent surgeons and specialists on the staff is available to all social groups.

The fees of private doctors would rarely appear prohibitive for casual illness, demanding single home or office visits. The situation is decidedly different for hospital visits. The cost calls much more directly for cooperative organization. This has been realized, so that only a narrow margin is left to private organization, which amounts to about 3 per cent of all general hospital beds and less than ½ of 1 per cent of the beds in mental hospitals.

This situation is not of recent date. It originated far back in the eighteenth century when a royal decree of 1772 ordered a public hospital to be erected in every province. That development has been continued. The country has never had any discussion about the principles of private versus public hospital care, and it probably never will. The country is free from drives for hospital funds as from most other drives for charitable purposes. It has been taken for granted that fundamental human needs should be taken care of by sure, community methods. Public sentiment may be aroused both to pity about illness and to pride in its institutions, but this responsibility may be expressed through taxation. Though it would be too much to say that the Swedish public feels a joy in giving when paying taxes, most people feel them to be reasonable in a businesslike way. Citizens realize that administrators of private funds have no monopoly on skill, honesty, and efficiency. Nor have they wanted to forsake their own power of democratic control. There has, in short, never been any argument as to the competitive value of public and private hospitals.

Although hospitals are public, it does not follow that there is one country-wide agency administering them. All have local boards for practical details of management and, at the same time, central supervision by the Medical Board. In their financing and general directing, which most clearly determine their character as private or public, they may belong to different authorities. The state assumes immediate responsibility for institutions for mental diseases and the provincial authorities for general and isolation hospitals. Special hospitals, which are not the direct responsibilities of any of these authorities and which in different forms are being built in great numbers for various purposes, are coordinated into a state-wide program that takes advantage of such previously existing facilities even when they are provided by universities, special funds, and other sources. They may be ordered to take special cases or to treat a certain number of patients according to fixed regulations about fees.

First to be considered are the isolation hospitals because of their association with the dreaded childhood diseases. Not only is care in these hospitals free for certain contagious diseases but also, according to the Epidemic Diseases Act of 1919, hospitalization is compulsory for scarlet fever, diphtheria, acute infantile paralysis, cholera, smallpox, typhoid fever, dysentery, and sleeping sickness. There is no compulsory isolation, however, for whooping cough and measles. These are treated at the ordinary fixed rate, generally 2 crs. daily. The total number of beds in isolation hospitals was 6,501 in 1938 or somewhat more than one bed per 1,000 inhabitants.

General hospitals are run mainly by the provincial authorities or by large cities. Central hospitals in the cities had control of 18,187 beds in 1938, while in small districts cottage hospitals, each under the supervision of a single doctor, contained 1,624 beds. In every general hospital a patient has upon admittance by the institution's doctor the right to full treatment at a fixed daily fee, generally 2 crs. for residents and 6 crs. for nonresidents. Children's hospitals (2,060 beds) are run according to the same principle and so are maternity hospitals (1,682 beds), where delivery and care for 10 days are free. Some 1,604 additional beds are publicly administered in other social institutions, besides 4,823 beds in homes for incurables and 989 beds for various specialized treatments. Together these hospitals offer about 5 beds per 1,000 population. Tuberculosis, sometimes treated in the general hospitals, accounts for an additional 8,894 beds in the special sanitaria alone, or about 1½ beds per 1,000 population or 1½ beds per annual death from tuberculosis. Mental hospitals contain 23,569 beds, or nearly 4 per 1,000 population. Private general hospitals contain only 1,239 beds and private mental hospitals only 94 beds.

All hospitals must meet fixed requirements of a high standard, subject as they are to the control of the General Medical Board which applies the same minimum requirements in all regions of the country. The charges are not only low everywhere, but they are also inclusive of all costs: nursing, supplies, laboratory and other examinations, anesthetics, medicine, and doctor's fees. They are further fixed according to certain schedules and can thus always be calculated in advance. The doctors in the hospitals, on the other hand, receive fixed salaries and, after their period of internship and assistant service, hold life tenure and receive pensions. They enjoy remarkable social prestige, ranking generally above private practitioners as they are professionally highly selected. Patients are normally well satisfied with the services of their own hospitals, and no loss of social prestige is attached to their utilization.

There is still a margin provided for private or semiprivate care within this system of public hospitals. The chief of a hospital or, in the largest institutions, the chief of a department is permitted a private office and also a small private ward. For hospitalization in the latter the charges are again moderate and fixed, ranging on the average from 6 c̄rs. for a bed in a double room to 18 crs. for the most expensive private rooms.

These charges are inclusive, the doctors receiving a certain percentage as a private profit. Separate payments for operations are not demanded and cannot be collected even from these patients. That fees will be given voluntarily for many of the services which are rendered to the higher income groups is, however, realized, and the General Medical Board has published an advisory schedule for surgical fees that has to be made known to any such patient, giving some main categories of operations and the range of fees considered appropriate within different income groups. The total range is 150–600 crs. Thus the private and public interests continue to be interrelated instead of to clash.

EVALUATION

The whole Swedish health system is based on a few broad assumptions. The first is that medical consultation should be available to all at a low fixed fee and that such medical services should by state guarantee be first rate. The second is that, even if costs are low, they ought not to be done away with. What is being avoided is a system whereby one section of the population would be thrown upon charity and another would be dependent upon private medicine. The main group does not belong to either category. No question is generally raised about the income of the patient, an open-door policy being the goal. It is true that a small group will be unable to pay. In such cases the relief authorities pay, and the amount is debited to the general relief account of the client. But the overhead costs for all medical care are paid by the citizens through taxation according to economic ability. Neither does it change the social character of the system that some well-to-do people disregard the fact that they have already paid through taxation for their own medical care and prefer to pay a private doctor's bill. The significant feature is democratic equality.

What, then, is the situation with regard to the controversy concerning free choice of doctor? To tell the truth, this choice is considerably limited and still the problem has never disturbed the Swedish public. If somebody wants help from a district doctor at the standard rate, there is little choice of doctor, as there is most often only one medical officer in the district. Still the medical officer may more often than not be called a family doctor, being called in whenever sickness falls upon a family. The patient, however, is also free to consult the staff of the nearest central hospital. Finally, for those who can afford to pay for completely free choice, there are always private doctors available. In the hospitals there is a greater number of doctors. It is, however, not the patient's choice but the nature of his illness or the consideration of expediency in the institution that determines the selection of doctors. No complaint has ever been raised against this system. As taxpayers the patients would hardly be unreasonable enough to recommend a surplus of salaried physicians just for the whimsical desire to be allowed to choose among them. Rational as the people on the whole are, they would never cherish the illusion that the private patient knows best how to judge between different doctors.

Two things must perhaps be repeated to make this situation understandable. First, the professional standards for the doctors in public service are unusually high. Their position represents the peak of the medical career. Second, no patient enters any contract with a physician. Not even the patients carrying sickness insurance are referred to only one official or a panel of doctors but are free to choose any doctor who will meet certain requirements. Thus the Swedish people are hardly aware of the problem of free choice of a doctor so much discussed in some other countries. They are just as personally grateful and emotionally attached to their doctors as are patients anywhere else. It would thus seem as if the problem itself were a somewhat unreal one.

The limitations of the health program must also be considered. There remains one chief sector of medical care that has not yet been covered by any complete public program, namely, consultation by specialists. The hospital clinic does to a certain extent furnish it, the same low range of fees generally being applied as with the district physician although not fixed by law but mostly by instructions from the hospital board. More generally, however, perfect democracy fails in just this portion of the medical field. To the same extent private physicians have had their greatest domain here.

Some city and university hospitals maintain clinics for specialized cases. These clinics are advertised as open at low fees (2 crs. per first visit and 1 crn. per consecutive visit) to people of limited means. No means test is applied, however, and there is only a gentlemen's agreement that patients with means should not avail themselves of these services. These clinics are admittedly too rushed to be able to give the individualized care that all other forms of public medicine are able to furnish. The worst feature is that the services are regarded as given "on the assembly line." Here one will hear the first outcries of no choice of doctor and rightly so as the patient cannot even be sure that the same doctor will be assigned to treat him on consecutive visits. Evidently, here is some deficiency in the organization and some economizing that gives doubtful results. It should not be inferred, however, that these clinics are medically substandard. Here it has only been indicated that they are socially substandard.

The whole matter of specialist consultation and specialist care outside the resources of the local hospital is being gradually but unsystematically attacked. Certain illnesses, e.g., cancer, rheumatism, and disabling nervous disorders, are being attacked on a centralized basis, with patients from the whole country allowed to enter central hospitals and clinics. For quite a number of specifically listed ailments also a reimbursement for the extra expense of such travel is made out of state appropriations. This is, however, only a beginning.

Another limitation may undoubtedly be found in the lack of coordination between the district medical officer, who is a general practitioner, and the hospital doctors, who are more often specialists. The hospital doctors make too few home calls. The district doctors must find that it hinders their campaigns for preventive medicine to have too frequently to break away for separate home calls. There is, however, no systematic difficulty. There is only some inertia involved in bringing about a change toward greater rationality, efficiency, and more complete democracy through an integration of their services.

NEED OF MORE CHILDREN'S HOSPITALS

The building of specialized children's hospitals has lagged behind in the era of development of hospitalization. The isolation hospitals do take care of a number of the typical childhood diseases. Beds are of course also available for children in the general hospitals. Some excellent specialized hospitals for children exist in the larger cities. In general it still holds true, however, that too many children's illnesses are inexpertly cared for in the homes.

In 1939 a proposition by the government was voted in the Riksdag, aiming at providing two beds for children per 10,000 inhabitants in connection with the public general hospitals. It should be remembered that most other hospitals are paid for by the provincial governments. Only in the case of mothers and children has the responsibility so truly been felt as one and the same for the whole nation that the state directly shoulders it.

FREE PRENATAL CARE

Curative medicine having reached that stage where future improvements will appear practically automatically, the reform goal can now be concentrated on preventive activity. That, from the community's point of view, is the same as building up the health of children. The studies of costs for medical care have demonstrated the family's point of view. Privately bought health care does not expand when children are born. Both cost considerations and general health considerations must strongly favor a huge expansion of public medical services for children. A children's medical program was advocated from the very beginning in the population discussion. Its recommendation may also be inferred from numerous passages in the reports of the Population Commission, and the materialization of this social program is well under way. There will certainly be no other fields where future social missionaries will find it easier to arouse public enthusiasm.

This responsibility has to start with the children even before birth. That is to say, it has to start with the mothers. Their need of prenatal and postnatal care has to be met on account of the children. Also its administrative setup can most profitably be linked with infant health through common consultation centers.

During the past half century medical science has made rapid progress in controlling maternal health through prenatal supervision. In Sweden this scientific knowledge on the part of the medical profession has long been on a high general level. Private practitioners early made this theoretical knowledge available for the economically secure social classes in the form of prenatal services. Somewhat slower in starting, in the large cities just after the turn of the century, a few outpatient clinics for economically less favored groups were opened in connection with maternity hospitals or maternity departments in general hospitals. Progress was thus being made, encouraging enough to those concerned, and probably a matter of pride when Sweden compared herself with most other countries. The idea, however, of regular, repeated, routine examinations for all prospective mothers was completely accepted neither by the public nor by the local authorities.

Concerted effort to invest in prenatal care for the good of the whole people began first about 1930. Clinics for pre- and postnatal care were planned in connection with baby centers, as the mothers should cultivate the habit of turning to one agency in all matters concerning maternity and infant health. The experimental services recommended by the General Medical Board were instituted from 1931 to 1933 and carried on with these double purposes.

At this stage of long-range planning the population discussion arose. The prospective network of infant and maternity centers had hitherto been envisioned by medical technicians to be realized in installments over a long period of time. Now, suddenly, the ground was cleared for immediate action as both public opinion and political powers became ready to make the necessary investments by one far-reaching appropriation.

The Population Commission swiftly took advantage of all this new enthusiasm for family welfare, as did the General Medical Board. The latter agency renewed pressure for its program in a report of April, 1935, in which it was directly stated that "The rapidly falling birth rate makes it a matter of greatest importance that the care of children's health and their upbringing be well organized and that the state and other authorities institute purposive measures to aid their citizens and families in this respect."

The Population Commission combined the different plans which had been initiated by other authorities and matured by practical experiments in its general scheme for safeguarding both medically and economically the welfare of mothers and infants. In one of its first reports late in 1935 on maternity care, [2] this problem was brought to the foreground. At the same time the Population Commission added some important viewpoints and somewhat changed the administrative details.

The Commission is certain that correctly planned maternity care easily accessible to all women would spare many lives which otherwise would be lost — this applying to the mother as well as to the fetus — and would prevent illness and poor health conditions on the part of the mother which may have a permanent effect upon her health.

Apart from the significance of the proposed service as a means of preserving life, promoting health, and preventing sickness, its importance from an economic point of view may also be emphasized. Experience proves that an advisory service for infant care means lower hospital expenses and, generally speaking, fewer doctors' bills for these children, so that the costs of such a service may properly be considered as canceled through this effect alone.

According to the general principle that costs for the next generation should, wherever possible, be transferred from the individual family to the community as a whole, the demand was made by the Commission that all these services should be made available free of charge to everyone without discrimination. Health and a reasonable degree of medical comfort should not be guaranteed only to the mother of means. But neither should the community restrict its tax-paid protection to mothers so poor that they would otherwise be wholly unprotected. Health services should be offered to all mothers and all infants as a regular part of society's cooperative care of its next generation. This stand by the Population Commission was supported by the General Medical Board, which may here be quoted although the statement represents less radical and less systematic thinking on these problems than was later possible.

There are arguments both for and against the introduction of fees. One might first of all argue that it would be unwarranted for the community to take on the burden of expenses which the individual may well afford to assume. It might be pointed out in this connection, however, that the number of those in a better economic situation, who will avail themselves of this care, will probably be relatively small and that the majority will fall within the low-income group or be without means. Under these circumstances it will probably not be of any importance whether or not the better situated are compelled to pay a fee. The difficulty of drawing a line between those who should pay and those who should not pay is an additional and even stronger argument against the fixing of fees. If the limit is fixed so low that it would be possible to assume a considerable reduction in the burden on the public treasury, such a measure would tend to act as a check and materially reduce the number of applicants. It must not be overlooked that there is no question here of sick care and, therefore, of cases in which the person in charge of the child feels obliged to seek aid at the earliest moment. The measure is aimed at ordinary children, especially in good health, and it is natural to assume that the expenses for such care would be considered to be of a kind that could be avoided without risk or inconvenience. The same is true of maternal care. For these reasons the Board wishes to advise against the introduction of obligatory fees. . . .

The proposals materialized in a plan by the Population Commission whereby all local districts should be supported with substantial government appropriations when instituting centers for maternal health supervision. The centers should be organized according to three different types, depending on the size of the community and the availability of specialists.

1. *Mother and baby health clinics* should be established in larger cities as separate units, headed by specially trained gynecologists, obstetricians, and pediatricians. In this type of clinic the medical care of babies and mothers should be separated by having different specialized doctors as directors. The maternal health clinic should be headed by a specialist who is chief of a public hospital or has a corresponding position. The baby health clinic should be headed by a pediatrician and might be established in combination with a children's hospital. Both types of clinics should serve the immediate area and also be central clinics to which patients from the less specialized centers could be referred.

2. *Mother and baby health centers* should be established in other cities and industrial districts. Specialist training might not be available; both maternal and infant care should be given in the same center. The size of the area to be covered should be determined so as to fill the working day of a

nurse. Branches of the center could be set up, making use of the services of the same doctor.

3. *Mother and baby health stations* should be located in the offices of the medical officer in the rural districts. Two clinics a month should be held. The district nurse, or the district midwife, should render assistant service. The nurse should also, in addition to clinic visits, take on responsibilities for field services.

Home visits by the nurses should be made an important part of the scheme, particularly in the rural districts. In sparsely populated districts these should constitute the main service with only occasional visits by the mothers to the health station. Educational propaganda should be a feature of the work in all centers. In order to cover the country a network of such centers should be set up. Thus 115 centers of the first two types and 250 of the third have been planned.

This outline was followed when the proposal successfully went through the Riksdag and was adopted in 1937. Local initiative was made responsible for the planning of such health centers, state grants were made available but only to such centers as offered services free of charge to all social classes without income limitations. The grants consist partly of one lump sum up to half the total cost of the establishment and equipment of the health center with a maximum of 1,000 crs. and partly of an annual subsidy toward the salary and traveling expenses of physicians, nurses, and midwives, based on number of cases of both mothers and babies.

The scheme is completed. The money is voted. Now it is only a question of local initiative as to whether maternity and infant health centers are being created. It may be too early to pass judgment on what is being achieved, since the laws have been in operation only since January, 1938. Too rapid progress could not be expected, as the development is in the hands of the provincial governments and they are faced with the claim, sound and profitable in the long run, that every province must present a complete plan for its centers before the General Medical Board can endorse them and the state grant be paid. This plan may, however, call for completion within a given period of time, even 5 or 10 years. Such planning necessitates some elaborate work: studies of local needs; negotiations with semiprivate clinics, especially for the combination with already existing baby health centers; reorganization of philanthropic enterprises like the old "Milk Drops" (milk stations, *gouttes de lait*), and so on.

After 2½ years of operation (July, 1940) all provinces but three had been able so to organize their work that they could be included in the national system and obtain the government subsidies. A total of 260 mother and baby health stations with 50 branches are to be found in the country, 34 mother and baby health centers, and in cities 21 baby health

clinics and 13 maternity health clinics. Support is, however, guaranteed
for complete coverage of the nation.

Prenatal care must be supplemented with some extra care at the time
of actual childbearing in order to become effective. Prospective mothers
will have to be taught to desire the former, but they are themselves already
eagerly seeking the latter. The delivery care that Swedish society provides
will be more fully treated in the following chapter, which gives a picture
of the economic support of childbearing proper.

It is somewhat discouraging to realize that a catastrophe in the population
situation was necessary to bring about these reforms. Fully sufficient reasons
of another order would seem to have been present long before. When
infants die although medical knowledge knows how to prevent it, the
technical development of a civilization has most cruelly outdistanced its
humanitarian development. That has long been allowed to happen. The
advocates of family reform created the slogan "3,000 children die unnecessarily every year in Sweden." That argument aroused the public conscience.
It rested on statistics concerning infant mortality in high- and low-income
groups in Stockholm. The material available refers to children born
from 1918 to 1922 (Table 34). The difference in infant mortality of 4.89

TABLE 34. — INFANT MORTALITY IN RELATION TO INCOME CLASS
IN STOCKHOLM, 1918–1922

	INFANT DEATHS PER 1,000 BIRTHS				
ITEM	All income groups	When father's income was			
		Less than 4,000 crs.	4,000– 5,999 crs.	6,000– 9,999 crs.	10,000 crs. or more
Deaths during					
1st year	36.7	48.9	38.3	31.9	14.3
Deaths during first month	18.0	24.0	15.1	19.7	11.4
Deaths during 2–12 months	18.7	24.9	23.2	12.2	2.9
Stillbirths per 1,000					
live births	15.1	17.5	15.8	13.0	8.0

Source: Rietz, E., *Sterblichkeit und Todesursachen in den Kinderjahren*, Stockholm, 1930.

per cent and 1.43 per cent in the two income groups at extreme ends of the
scale is a grave accusation in a society that believes itself to be a democracy.
There can be read in such figures what uneven income distribution does
to those who have nothing to do with its causes but all to do with the
future of the country. Differences in family income mean differences in
food, housing, and medical care. A program of population policy becomes
a program of humanitarian justice when it tries to equalize these very

differences. What has been attempted in the fields of housing and nutrition has already been described. In regard to medical care as much will have to be accomplished. The objective of the new reforms is, quantitatively stated, to bring all infant mortality down to the level of that for the well-to-do classes in Stockholm. It can be done.

FREE HEALTH SERVICES FOR CHILDREN

The next important step in planning health reforms for children is regular, repeated, and intensive health inspections. Health centers are organized; babies are examined free; district nurses and district midwives are instructed to teach child care; but what happens when the babies grow? It would be only expedient if the same centers took care of the preschool children also, following them right to the school door where the school doctor and the school nurse take them over. Both the General Medical Board and the Population Commission have expressed their approval of such an arrangement:

The Commission agrees with the unanimous expert opinion in declaring that it is in accordance with this whole line of reform that maternal and child welfare centers will not only soon expand geographically to include the whole country but will also keep on serving their child clientele past the infant stage until school medical care begins. [2]

Such is as yet not the case. Health centers are including children up to a maximum of two years of age only. More than a consideration of costs has prevented immediate expansion. A limitation of the center's program has been necessitated also by a lack of trained personnel. The fact that first prenatal care and thereafter infant care could be emphasized in the development of health work had some connection with the circumstance that well-trained and still partly unemployed midwives were available. Ten years or more will pass before there will be a sufficient number of district nurses for even the child welfare centers now planned. It will take still longer to develop adequate services for children of the forgotten preschool years if nothing extraordinary is done to accelerate the progress. Here, then, is a sizable gap requiring a special program of action.

Particularly difficult, but for that reason all the more challenging to those who draw up the social programs, is the problem of maintaining mental health in these age groups. However difficult, psychological advice is not less important than that concerned with physical health. To give general advice on child guidance in these health clinics will at some future date have to be included in the scope of the country-wide health centers. As yet it is hard to see when this can be perfected. The training of physicians does not include any firsthand study of child psychology. The possibility of instituting traveling child psychology consultation bureaus has not been discussed in Sweden. Neither has a study been made of the possible coordination of clinics for guidance work with the public nursery schools, the heads of which are the only ones trained in preschool child psychology.

Safeguarding children's health during all years will for the later age groups have to utilize some form of school medical services. In Sweden they are not unknown, but they must be developed in order to provide a complete child health program. They were started during the 1860's. Dependent on local initiative, they have only slowly reached a degree of effectiveness. According to a recent (1935) study, there were municipally engaged doctors in elementary schools in 62 per cent of the urban communities and in 28 per cent of the rural communities. Only in certain northern districts has the state taken over the responsibility for this activity. On the other hand, the state has contributed to the salaries of school doctors in the secondary schools and in normal schools since 1892. A program has been worked out by the Medical Board for a state-supported program of complete medical services in the public schools of the whole country. As in so many other instances, it has been found that only national responsibility can make all regions equally fit to present their share of the future population in top form. Rural substandards particularly leave no other hope for equality.

The 1935 report cited mentions that activities of school doctors exist in a certain number of places. It does not pretend to evaluate the effectiveness. This touches on one of the moot points of the whole problem. Development has certainly been retarded because it has not been clearly stated what the limits of the responsibility of the school doctor should be. Contrasted with the ideal of any social rationalist that all medical care of school children except for special treatment should be completely in his hands, there is the actual situation with mass examinations now and then, and an interval of years between them, giving sometimes little more than the appearance of real medical service. Parents have consequently sometimes been tempted not to seek medical advice for children until it has been too late.

All responsible persons in the field must realize that school doctors should definitely be either only school hygienists, responsible for the school's sanitary facilities, the healthfulness of the accommodations and the school schedule, the preparation of wholesome school luncheons, and related activities, or they must be real doctors, responsible with the assistance of the school nurse for making the school the control station for the health of the children. In the new Swedish proposal the functions of the school medical officer are defined and their scope expanded according to the wider alternative. Most of the diagnostic and advisory work should be left to the school doctor. When treatment is necessary, the school doctor in the larger communities should refer children to the family doctor or to a special clinic. In smaller districts, where routine work for the school physician is less heavy and the availability of other medical consultation less likely, it has been considered proper, or at least not impossible, for him also to make recommendations and prescriptions when he can do so in his ordinary school office hours.

The main objective is not to set up some perfect system in some locality to show off but to develop a system in every district and not tolerate any backward regions. As in many other instances, what is here described is the national minimum program. That is the concern of the state. There is no limit as to what the individual municipality may add, but as a minimum school children should be examined at these times: when they enter school, in the third and last grades of the primary school, and in continuation school. In addition, problems should be investigated as they appear. The municipalities would be responsible for the preparation of a special reception room in the larger schools and even for paying for other necessary equipment. The state should furnish the doctor and the nurse. It would cost the public annually about 1,300,000 crs., of which the state and the municipality would each contribute half.

As yet it has been generally overlooked that at the point in life when the pupil leaves his books and is turned loose on the labor market his health status ought to be interpreted in vocational guidance terms. It has been proposed, not by official authorities but by women's organizations, that before a pupil's graduation the school doctor should undertake vocational guidance, not only advising each pupil what occupations his physical make-up and state of health make unsuitable but also pointing out deficiencies to be corrected in order to be physically fit for a chosen vocation. At that time pupils ought also be given a partial transcript of the health card that should be kept for each individual from birth until the end of the school period.

FREE DENTAL CARE FOR CHILDREN

In the general description of medical costs it was apparent that the costs of dental care were most directly responsive to economic pressure. For a long time there has been a widespread desire in Sweden to make children's dental health independent of their parents' economic status. Already at the beginning of the century some school dental clinics had been established, but such undertakings were only sporadic. As they were dependent upon local initiative, urban municipalities only shouldered the responsibility. In rural districts the Red Cross has been active for the same purpose. Since 1913 the authorities have through repeated statements indicated an awareness of the necessity of organizing a far-reaching reform program. In 1929 an experimental plan was organized. The Red Cross and the General Medical Board were given grants for trying out dental hygiene programs in different districts, using various methods with permanent or traveling clinics. Several committees both before and after that time had made proposals. Several plans had been rejected by one or the other of the parties involved, including the organized dentists.

At the time of the revival of awareness of nation-wide responsibility for child welfare, however, a new proposal by a Committee on National Dental Care was presented and successfully developed. [39] Thus, in 1938 an act was passed in the Riksdag providing for national dental care, with special emphasis on the nationalization of dental care for children, beginning January 1, 1939. The program was to be developed over a 10-year period.

According to this plan, 500 dental districts plus 100 traveling dental clinics with 800 salaried dentists and the same number of district dental nurses are to be established. About 40 of these dentists started to operate during the first year. In each province a specially equipped central clinic is to be provided. Thus the rate of progress is dependent upon local initiative. The state will refund half the cost of the first clinical equipment up to a maximum of 3,000 crs. and further contribute 3,000 crs. annually to the dentist and 1,000 crs. to the dental nurse. The total annual cost to the state has been calculated as 5,500,000 crs. and to the provincial councils as nearly 2,000,000 crs. The sum of 600,000 crs. has been nationally appropriated for the budget year 1940–1941. For continuous and full care of the children's teeth the parents without regard to income will pay 5 crs. annually for the first child, 3 crs. for the second, 2 crs. for the third, and nothing for additional children. The municipalities will have to pay for all who cannot pay their own fees, and they also possess the right not to make any charge at all. In this case they are to reimburse the provincial government for the patients. The dentist's salary is to be fixed in two ways. It may be either a flat salary of 7,800 crs. plus three age increments of 500 crs. after three years' service or a smaller fixed salary of 7,200 crs. plus a share of the fees paid, amounting to not less than 10 per cent of these.

This mainly tax-supported dental care is open to children from the age of three years with an annual examination and treatment compulsory for every child once registered. The first group to be completely examined and followed through the years, however, will be the school beginners. Thus the dental sanitation of the people will widen gradually. Already adults are permitted to use the public dental clinics to the extent that time and resources permit. Since "children first" is the rule, adults are less cared for so far. Their problems will be different when national dental health control has been in effect since early childhood.

Thus, still one more item in the budget, significant for the general health but often neglected when the family expenditures increase, has been made the common responsibility of all.

Free Protective Medicine for Children

Among medical costs that of medicines needs to be considered next. To remove these costs from dependence on individual family income would be only logical. Social organization in this field is not foreign to the Swedish people. It must also be admitted that already through the centuries-old system of publicly controlled pharmacies, the cost of medicine has been reduced in Sweden. Control of the market is effected by the state authorities in two ways, through the selection of pharmacists and through fixing prices of all medical goods. When a pharmacy becomes vacant, a government concession is granted to the applicant who is most competent as for any other civil service post. About 450 such pharmacies handle every pill and bottle of medicine sold in the country. In addition, some few firms have been given concessions for the manufacturing and wholesale distribution of pharmaceutical goods. A movement has recently been initiated for completely socializing this whole trade.

But publicly controlled pharmacies, even if they are operated at low cost, cannot provide a sufficient safeguard for children. The large quantities of preventive medicines consumed by children in families of good economic status are generally unavailable to their poorer playmates. The Population Commission has, therefore, proposed that the state shall take over the costs for such medicines. [10] Cod-liver oil, various preparations of vitamins, calcium, phosphorus, iron, and iodine would, on a doctor's prescription, be free to those visiting the health centers with both children and pregnant mothers eligible. No income limit is set. No stigma would attach to receiving these commodities free. Compared with the free protective food proposed to be furnished in the same way, the providing of free medicine would have a much wider spread. It has been calculated that if half of those bearing children each year take advantage of this privilege for themselves and their children, especially those children under one year of age, about 40,000 would be benefited at an annual cost of almost 1,000,000 crs. This is a small cost to the people but not a small gain for spreading to all the health prophylaxis that medical science can give but that is now enjoyed only by the few.

A law to this effect was passed by the Riksdag in 1939, coming into force on January 1, 1940. It started with a semiannual provision of 150,000 crs. and of 300,000 crs. for the fiscal year 1940–1941. All the details of the proposal as given above apply to the law, but it must be stressed that the law applies only to defined preventive medicines. For families living at a distance from doctors' offices, the district midwife or district nurse may requisition necessary medicines. The Population Commission had further proposed that free medicine be given to school children. This proposal, with that for the school meal, has yet to be developed. No reasons exist for discontinuing this reform movement until all children get all necessary medicines free. The risk of frivolous overconsumption and waste is so little; the gain in social fairness and common sense is so great.

*   *
*

To this whole picture of social medical care there must be attached one warning of interpretation. The Swedish people would hardly recognize it under the name of socialized medicine. Steps were taken in that direction long before any unfortunate connotation was invented for the term "social." The program is to be considered as nothing more than management based on the principles of cooperation and good neighborliness which cheaply and securely build a health foundation that no family could achieve unaided.

CHAPTER XVII

PROVISIONS FOR CHILDBEARING

O F ALL the events in the life of a family none is more poignantly accompanied by worries and costs than the advent of a child. The
practical problems are often overwhelming; the subjective problems accentuate the practical. Pregnancy itself quite normally causes not only
bodily discomfort but also mental disturbances of varying degree and
character. The bearing of a child is an experience filled with rich emotions,
but there is instability in the situation. The knowledge of being carried by a
physiological process to some unavoidable and final event also brews a
feeling of suspense that may turn into more than dramatic tension. As
social conditions have developed, other difficulties have been added with the
result that far too often anxiety, and sometimes despair, has come to accompany the prospect of childbearing. Abortion might under those physical,
mental, and social circumstances become a more tempting solution because
of the momentary pressure than it need be under a long-range view of the
same problems. Getting rid of the child should not be regarded as the way
out that society should sanction. The actual problems involved in childbearing must be scrutinized in order to find out where society can give
sensible support.

The first problem to be faced in all families awaiting a child, regardless
of status or income, concerns the health of the mother, her chance of carrying the pregnancy to a happy end, her nausea or other troubles, her fear
of the labor pains, and her duty to take such preventive care of herself as
will ensure the best prognosis both for herself and for the child. Translated
into social policy, this calls for a program of prenatal and obstetrical care of
the best medical quality. The former of these services has already been
described in the previous chapter. When such prenatal service is also concerned with the discomforts and worries of pregnant mothers, there will be
less fear of childbearing and less reluctance to have more children. The next
problem is concerned with the arrangement for delivery itself and the extra

costs accompanying it. This also is common to all women in both high and low social groups. Provisions organized by community cooperation in this sphere will not only aid the family but also serve at the same time to improve health conditions in society. A nationally guaranteed organization for delivery care, with subsidies for the incidental costs at childbirth, will in general terms become the next item on the social program for families.

In some cases these "normal" worries and costs are not all. The drama of childbearing often takes on a tragic tinge. Economic resources may be depleted by more than the actual costs of delivery. The income of the mother may cease if she has been working. Unemployment may threaten her, or she may have nowhere to hide herself and no means of paying her expenses during the last most critical months if she is unmarried. It is this latter situation which has so often led to abortion or even suicide. Some form of emergency maternity aid must be added to the social program just as emergency means are provided for the unemployed. Finally, the mothers without husbands face not only a temporary but a lifelong crisis. Laws must protect the incomplete family of mother and child and exact of the father his part for the support of the child. Some social devices must also be found by which, when the father remains deficient in his duties, the community protects the interests of the child. The economic shock should be received by somebody stronger than the single mother and her child. Laws about paternity, guardianship, right to inheritance, and family name must be complemented with some community budgeting of the sums due children without fathers (Chapter 18).

When some scheme materializes to integrate into the social system efforts to meet cooperatively these needs relating to childbirth, women may be said to be safeguarded against the graver physical, psychological, and social hazards of bearing children. Sweden has chosen to let the nation rather than the individuals carry the responsibility. In the following survey of the legal and economic aspects of such services, it will be seen how far she has succeeded.

Free Delivery Care

Since ancient times maternity cases in Sweden have mainly been cared for by midwives, who are by no means to be considered as quacks. Since the eighteenth century they have been licensed persons with excellent medical education. Practically all childbirths in all social classes and in or outside hospitals are even at the present time taken care of primarily by the midwives. The competency of the midwife working outside maternity hospitals has been further ensured by requiring her to return every 10 years for a repetition course at the training hospital.

The earliest state responsibility for childbirth was to provide training for midwives in a few endorsed hospitals before licensing them for practice. Later midwives were included in a national system providing for their being employed by municipalities and also incorporated into the increasing provisions for hospitalized delivery care. This country-wide system was finally stabilized in 1920 when the country was divided into a number of districts with one midwife for each district and one or more reserve midwives for each province. The state has since then been paying part of the salaries and fixing regulations about fees for services. The extent of this organized midwife practice as it functioned before the reforms to be described below may be judged from the figures for 1936, showing 1,627 district and reserve midwives, 97 midwives additionally engaged by certain communities, and 121 midwives in attendance at hospitals, as compared with only 440 midwives in private practice. Such a centrally controlled system, rooted in tradition, has had apparent advantages. Delivery in the home, if the patient had one, has never been exorbitantly expensive. The collaboration between doctors and midwives has been excellent. The delivery care has been combined with a time-consuming personalized nursing service for both mother and baby, generally providing also instruction in, and demonstration of, elementary child care and hygiene. For nursing, bathing the baby, and other care, the midwife has returned regularly over a period of weeks.

Also, the results of such expert care for a large proportion of the population are seen in the decline in death rates. In 1934 maternity mortality in Sweden was 2.5 per 1,000. It was 1.8 for patients delivered in their homes by midwives or in exceptional cases by midwife and doctor and 3.2 for the hospitalized cases which evidently included many of the graver cases transferred from the former category. On the whole, the Swedish figures for maternity mortality are better than for any other country except New Zealand, Norway, and Holland, despite the fact that Sweden, with its low birth rate, must have a comparatively greater proportion of women bearing first children and thus incurring greater risks. The advantages cannot, however, be measured in statistics alone. The comfort provided by the midwife-nurses is unmeasured but not unappreciated. The Swedish mothers have been favored by having somebody helping with their deliveries who at the same time was professionally reliable and could take time to "hold hands." When the whole system came in for revision, there was no question of abandoning the midwife services. It had proved to be a system far superior to that in many other countries where doctors monopolize the care even of normal cases but are unable to devote the time necessary for passive waiting and so must often precipitate surgical delivery, while another large proportion of the population is likely to be left without adequate care at all.

The habit of hospitalization for delivery gradually increased as the technical developments within the science and art of obstetrics and the prevalence of small dwellings made home delivery less adequate or desirable, but the midwife followed the cases to the hospital. She assumed the continuous responsibility, while the attending doctors made more perfunctory appearances. Hospitalization was particularly favored over home delivery since only doctors were supposed to give anesthetics and since in hospitals hygienic conditions were better, there was more quiet, and other conditions were more satisfactory. Whatever the medical, psychological, or social reason may be, hospitalization has recently become as common as delivery in the patient's home. In 1937 only 41 per cent of all babies were born in private homes with midwives and doctors in attendance. The unattended cases were so few that they are statistically insignificant.

A continued increase in the hospital facilities for delivery care had to be foreseen. The Committee on Medical Care [40] proposed a vast scheme, and the opinions of experts, organizations, and interested lay persons were heard. The Population Commission could take advantage of this evidence when it formulated its proposal for a national scheme for free delivery care for all mothers. [2] The oustanding characteristic of the plan is that both the hospital and the home care of delivery cases be organized on equally favorable terms. It was not considered appropriate to force the development in either of these directions. Instead the midwives in field service were given new tasks in connection with hospital care and also in health centers for mothers and infants.

The Population Commission does not consider it to be in the interest of the community that it should contrive in creating such regulations or conditions that all maternity care be institutionalized, i.e., be removed from the expectant mother's home to an institution designed for this purpose. Childbirth cannot under ordinary conditions be compared with sickness but is a psychological act which, as experience shows, can take place in her own home without risk to the mother, provided the home satisfies reasonable demands for space and cleanliness and provided that a well-trained midwife be available at the time of delivery. The circumstance that in spite of the expansion of institutional care the death rate in connection with childbirth has not been materially lowered during recent decades scarcely gives support for the belief that institutional care for all expectant mothers would contribute essentially to a reduction of the risk in question.

When, however, the removal of the expectant mother to an institution is justifiable for medical and social reasons, as for instance overcrowding in the home, etc., it would seem to be the duty of the community to make satisfactory provisions for care in such instances. Furthermore, attention must be paid to a personal desire, often expressed by the women themselves, to have the opportunity at the time of childbirth to seek care in an institution designed for that purpose. This desire can be explained by, among other factors, the feeling of greater security which such care must bring as well as by the likelihood that the experiences of delivery will be easier. From several points of view, therefore, the Commission finds it desirable that the government cooperate to the end that institutional maternity care, at a cheap rate, be made available to every woman who wishes to avail herself of such care. [2]

Of primary importance to the working out of this system was the inclusion of all maternity hospital care in a state system providing such care out of general funds, a maximum cost to the patient of only 1 crn. a day for food being all that was permitted. This daily charge per bed included both mother and child and the subsidized care was made available in all institutions. The next step was to be the inclusion of the country-wide district midwife system in a state organization, midwives being paid by the state and all care in the home of the patient being rendered free of charge. In order to avoid competition and waste between the two systems, cooperation between in- and outpatient maternity care was to be instituted. The district midwife might be given temporary work in an institution when she was not occupied with work in her district or she might be engaged on suitable occasions in maternity institutions, subject to call in the outpatient service.

These proposals, which in their technical details utilized most of the suggestions made by the previous Committee on Medical Care, were speedily carried by the government to the Riksdag, which voted the reforms in 1937. The decision resulted in a law of June 4, 1937, concerning the district midwife system, and a royal order of July 21, 1937, on institutionalized maternity care. Both were in substantial agreement with the proposal. Delivery cases might be hospitalized either in separate maternity hospitals or in maternity wards in general hospitals or in the small cottage hospitals. Facilities were to be created for some maternity rooms in connection with midwife stations. Two midwives were to be engaged in a larger district rather than one each in two smaller districts, thus ensuring more continuity in services both for the patients in such maternity rooms and patients in their homes.

The number of beds to be added to the already available specially earmarked maternity beds, 1,750 in 1936, was 400. For the erection of new maternity hospitals or maternity wards in general hospitals state grants were made available to an amount of 2,000 crs. per bed. Simultaneously annual subsidies were voted, to be fixed in law, paying to both new and old institutions 3 crs. per day for 10 days. The provincial governments have to meet the rest of the costs. State grants should be available only if the hospital restricted its charge to the patient to 1 crn. per day. The delivery care as such, including operations, dressings, etc., is totally free. A further expansion of the program in its institutional aspects is the support of waiting homes for expectant mothers from distant localities. A state subsidy of 2 crs. per day was made available for patients and the cost of establishing such homes subsidized in the same way. In order further to relieve the cases of mothers in the remote regions, the state was to pay the mothers personally 1 crn. per day for 15 days in order to keep domestic help at home while the housewife spends the time in the waiting home.

Despite all efforts to improve and cheapen hospital maternity care, the midwives working outside hospitals are not being discarded. Their services are still more firmly built into a national system. The districts are made larger, one or more midwife-nurses being engaged for them. The direct administration is in the hands of the provincial government through its Board of Midwifery, but the state pays the minimum salary to the midwives. The provinces still furnish them with an apartment, necessary instruments, supplies, telephone, and other equipment and may also raise the salary above the minimum. To the annual salary is added special remuneration from the state for more than 25 deliveries yearly. Travel costs may be paid either by the patient or by the province. In no case may the midwife claim any fee from the patient either for delivery care proper or for care and consultations before and after childbirth. She may also be required by the Board of Midwifery to serve in a maternity hospital.

As the personnel and partly also the organization rendering service in delivery cases was already at hand, the state could practically carry through all these reforms in one day, January 1, 1938. Although some expansion has been planned for the near future, the size of the expected annual state contributions may be judged from the sum of 2,139,500 crs. which was appropriated in the budget of 1939–1940.

It is of interest to distribute these costs over the number of babies born in order to determine the average costs of a baby to the community. About 25 crs. come from the state for every child. It must be remembered, however, that the above-mentioned grants do not cover all running expenses in the institutions, as some are continually being borne by the provincial and municipal authorities. Cost of training doctors and other attendants is only partly included.

The typical cost of a baby to the individual family is much easier to ascertain, but it differs according to type of maternity care chosen. A baby born in its own home with a midwife attending will cost nothing. If the medical officer is called in, his fee varies according to distance traveled but is always low. A baby born in a ward in a maternity hospital, which in many institutions is quite small and homelike, costs 1 crn. a day for the first 10 days of the lying-in period and thereafter the general hospital cost of approximately 2 crs. per day. As the average period of delivery care has been found to be 11 days, the total cost would be 12 crs. There is no pressure, however, to stop the private care that some mothers in the upper income groups may want to enjoy. The general procedure is to ask for a bed in a double or single room in the chief doctor's private ward in a public hospital. The costs would then be the same as for any hospitalized illness. The standard fees for the best care and food in a single room, with the best specialists attending, in the big cities or university towns is 200–275 crs. including doctors' fees.

Delivery costs can no longer be an obstacle for childbearing in Sweden. Thus the extra burden on the family budget is alleviated in one fundamental respect. At the same time a country-wide, state-controlled system gives excellent opportunities to combat influences detrimental to the health of mothers and babies. What women fear when they face childbirth is, however, not only death or ill-health and costs, but pain as well. It has been repeatedly demanded, therefore, that anesthetics at childbirth should also be made an equal right for all women, irrespective of their economic means. Only for one reason has some hesitancy on this point caused delay. Anesthetics cannot be given by midwives and so the allegedly fair competition between hospitalized and nonhospitalized delivery care is in fact greatly influenced in favor of hospitalization. A new hope now presents itself. As the Swedish portable Aga-apparatus for the patient's self-administration of nitrous oxide analgesia in intermittent doses lately has been widely tested and approved, the General Board of Health has suggested that the midwives also be given permission to utilize it. The time may have come for making anesthetics at childbirth free for everybody. When this is realized, the feeling of security for a woman nearing childbirth will have been greatly enhanced.

MATERNITY BONUS

Even when the birth of a child is made considerably more secure by the state's protective measures as the free right of every woman, there remain other expenses to consider. Some of these are of such a nature that up to a certain minimum they are identical for everybody. They are inevitable in all economic classes. They can be calculated in advance and therefore can easily be transferred to community budgets. They include certain minimum expenses for a layette, bedding for the child, clothes, travel to the hospital or sending for a nurse, and, finally, household help in the home. Consequently, these must be considered expenses eligible for public grants under a new policy aimed at relieving the individual families of the extra costs of children.

There may, however, in some cases be a more thorough disturbance of the family budget on the occasion of childbirth. A loss of wages may be involved. In earlier legislation this outstanding economic loss, caused by pregnancy and childbearing, was the only one considered for social remuneration. According to a Workers' Protective Law of 1900 mothers in industry were compelled to abstain from work for six weeks after childbirth. Women's organizations were anxious that this negative rule should be recompensed by some social bonus. In Sweden some compensation was provided through the sickness insurance funds. Since 1913 state subsidies have been paid to such funds for benefits to woman members.

In 1931, the needs of destitute mothers generally came to be regarded as a public responsibility, and 28 crs. were voted as a bonus available to every mother below a very low income limit. This bonus was paid out of state funds although handled by the sickness insurance funds. Complementary to these two government schemes, the same insurance associations on their own account offered a possibility of higher allowances by a scheme of voluntary contributions. The administrative combination of state subsidies with the sickness insurance system was intended to encourage increased membership.

These earlier efforts to solve what is in itself a social problem were brought together and magnified under one heading by the Population Commission:

> The last reminder of the Commission concerns the principle upon which our system of maternity aid is built, with voluntary insurance on the one hand, and on the other financial aid, according to a means test. Women are thereby divided into two separate categories, one of which — those who are insured — receives a maternity subsidy from the state without proving need, whereas the other category — those not insured — enjoys the same privilege to a smaller degree only after they have proved need, even if such proof is made summary. This division into categories is especially unsatisfactory in view of the fact that it is just those who are the worst situated economically who are subjected to the lower conditions, while those in more favorable economic circumstances can demand the right to state aid by merely joining a recognized sick benefit organization. [5]

A new law was drafted, creating a unified system instead of the old double one. A maternity bonus was proposed for every woman without any income limit. The Population Commission then went on to consider what expenses these benefits were actually to cover.

> Since compulsory maternity insurance would not furnish a satisfactory solution as long as sickness insurance is only voluntary, the Commission has gone no further than to recommend an arrangement whereby childbearers would receive aid in defraying the expenses connected with confinement directly from state funds similar to the procedure in the present maternity aid system. It is here proposed that this be called a "maternity bonus.". . .

After this the Commission wants to consider how much the proposed maternity bonus should amount to. For this purpose the Commission has attempted to estimate the extra expenses connected with childbirth. The Commission desires to detail the steps in this calculation, but feels it necessary to remark that, in the nature of things, any such estimate can to a large extent be only approximate. The Commission concludes that the expenses can be estimated at 100 crs. in round numbers. The Commission has included the following items of expenditure:

Traveling expenses, either for the childbearer to and from place of confinement or for the midwife to and from the childbearer.

Home assistance, including full-time help during the time the childbearer is absent from home or confined in bed at home — as a rule 10 days — and temporary help with heavier household duties two weeks prior to and two weeks after parturition.

Equipment for childbearer, such as proper maternity girdle and dress near the end of pregnancy as well as bedding and layette for the infant. The expenses for bedding and layette for the infant are necessarily higher for a first child than for subsequent children, but this is probably counterbalanced by the fact that help in the home in this case can be arranged at smaller cost. [5]

The final outcome was, however, not a proposal for 100 crs. but for a bonus of 75 crs. This bonus was not to be considered as assistance for those on the margin of poverty but was to be extended to all women without regard to income.

The Commission is of the opinion that the maternity bonus should in principle be given to all women as an expression of the public appreciation of motherhood.

There are, evidently, some women in such favorable economic circumstances that the maternity subsidy would be no special advantage. But, if the people in the higher income groups are excluded, the diminution of public costs would be so insignificant that such a gain would not counterbalance the loss incurred in the surrender of the principle. A rough estimate leads to the probable conclusion that at present only about 1 per cent of all births would occur in families with a taxable income in excess of 10,000 crs. . . . It may be expected that childbearers within the highest income groups and prosperous classes will anyway not demand the maternity bonus. [5]

Revolutionary as it may seem to shift over from private to public budgeting of such a personal cost item and to carry it not only for the poor but as an honored gift to all mothers, the scheme met with approval. The government proposed a bill and in 1937 the Riksdag endorsed it. Only one change was made in the original program, slight in effect but important enough in principle. The complete coverage of all mothers was subject to an income limit. This limit, however, was placed above the middle-class group, being fixed at a taxable annual income of 3,000 crs., which often amounts to a net income of 5,000 crs. Not quite 10 per cent of the mothers can by this rule be excluded from the new bonus. No means test is involved, the decision about income limit being of a strictly formal character. It goes without saying that the bonus is being paid to married and unmarried mothers alike. The law went into effect January 1, 1938.

The change in the reform plan represented by the income restriction is characteristic of a lag in the development of political opinion. The population motivation for the new scheme could not wholly overcome the older philosophy of relief. The fundamental principle of the previous period in social planning was "help to help oneself." Community help should be used only to fill certain gaps in individual incomes. The new outlook contains a much wider recognition of the community as collectively responsible for certain costs of living for the citizens. In actual parliamentary politics these fundamental differences were hard to make clear. The lapse in public generosity was due both to the conservatives arguing that not "everybody ought to be made a reliefer" and to the laboring class's lack of understanding "why rich people should get a bonus." The old clichés have a pernicious longevity. Thus are illustrated some psychological difficulties in making the transition from curative to prophylactic social policy.

Aid to Destitute Mothers

A maternity bonus for every confined woman, coming as a present from the government at the birth of a child, cannot and should not, of course, give the illusion of covering all costs that may be involved, even when actual delivery care is free. The distress for some women may be considerably more accentuated. Despair may grip them. Suicide and suicidal plans are by no means rare testimony of the terrible pressure to which pregnancy may lead. Abortions are a still more frequent testimony. Any society contemplating its abortion laws must have an honest appreciation of these individual tragedies. There can be only two ways out of the dilemma, either legalizing abortion on social and economic grounds or removing those grounds by radical social measures.

Sweden has taken the latter road. Abortion laws have been made more liberal in respect to humanitarian and eugenic considerations, but economic and social causes for abortions are not recognized. The country could hardly as a democracy make the public confession that the advent of a child would be such a misfortune that the nation could find no other way out than by permitting the destruction of the fetus. Instead, an inventory was taken of all social resources available to the pregnant woman. Where the results showed deficiencies, these had to be filled. It could not be accepted that the bearing of a child should mean economic distress to anybody in a country that is not poor and that wants children. A special fund was proposed to give what help may be needed in individual cases, thus assuring greater flexibility than state funds usually allow. [5] The emergency character of such an appropriation was repeatedly stressed. Here it was a question of saving lives of future citizens and of saving women from destruction in bearing future citizens.

Both married and unmarried mothers were entitled to aid. The maximum amount of such aid was to be 300 crs., supposedly covering the bare necessities of life for a period of 15 weeks. As most women, particularly the married ones, would not need help for living expenses during such a long period, the amount of financial aid could be reduced correspondingly. Specific needs may in each instance determine the limit and the form of maternity aid. Direct aid was supposed to be the principal form, although loans could be utilized when there was reason for them, thus including in this form of aid persons not ordinarily poor but temporarily in difficulties. With reference to the purpose of maternal aid in order to combat abortions, this is of special significance since the women seeking abortions can probably be found in no small degree within that category. It is only through the existence of help in the form of loans that there is a chance to help also those women who wish never to accept any aid from the community even though it does not have the characteristics of poor relief.

Maternal aid became popular from the time it was first presented. The Riksdag adopted a law at the 1937 session which was put into operation as of January 1, 1938. Few social schemes have aroused as much interest as this centralized chest for the welfare of mothers. The first surprise came in the financial field. For the first period of activity, namely, the remainder of the budget year 1937–1938, an appropriation had been voted of one million crs. That had been intended to suffice for six months, but after four months 1,750,000 crs. had been spent. For the budget year July, 1939, through June, 1940, 5.8 million crs. were appropriated as grants and 150,000 crs. as loans. For 1940–1941 the allocations were increased to 6.5 million crs. and 120,000 crs., respectively. Behind the first overdrawing of financial resources, in itself a rare thing in Sweden where social blueprinting functions within a structure most parts of which are well controlled, there is the bitter revelation of a vast amount of semipoverty that had not before been publicly acknowledged.

The special maternity aid boards that have been appointed in the various provinces were called upon to deal with applications in a far more personal form than any of the insurance schemes of recent times. Examination of the figures for the first half of 1939 reveals that 25,612 applications were granted, constituting 92 per cent of all applications occurring during the same period. The average amount was 194 crs. Most interesting of all, no less than 47 per cent of all women becoming mothers during the period enjoyed this benefit. The scope of this activity means that board members have seen the inner life of a majority of families, otherwise unknown to social workers, since they have never requested public assistance. The drab poverty above relief groups has become known. As a matter of fact, the majority of the people have been found to live on such a narrow margin that an extra demand upsets the equilibrium of their budgets. The maternity grant has in many instances given these mothers what they could never otherwise accumulate, namely, a capital in hand, small in itself but still large enough to permit some expenses which would otherwise constitute debt. It has been used, as it was intended, for specific needs. The money may go to looking after the pregnant woman's teeth, may equip the family with new bedding, or may — and that is for the married mother the foremost help — pay for a temporary improvement needed in the nutritional standard of the family. In the case of the unmarried mother the grant is of most value when it takes her to a quiet boarding home for the couple of months when she cannot work and when she wants to be hidden from the world, those months which have been a specter for so many.

The maternity aid is an interesting form of state philanthropy. In comparison with most of the other schemes within the population program, it can be expected to become outmoded when economic conditions generally and women's wages particularly become more ample. As long as society remains only in the anteroom of Utopia, however, this transfer of the best characteristics of private philanthropy to a state program should prove gratifying to all.

CHAPTER XVIII

THE INCOMPLETE FAMILY

THE population program of Sweden aimed to strengthen the family, to alleviate its worst trials and tribulations, and to make possible harmonious living. It was not believed that such a goal could be furthered by disqualifying those children who are born and reared outside the complete family. They, too, are citizens of tomorrow and it is just as urgent to provide the best opportunities for growth for them as for children in complete families.

The simplest case is the widow's family. It has become a common ideal in Western countries that the death of the main supporter shall be cushioned by some kind of social assistance. This ideal has been transmitted into reality in varying degrees and forms. In Sweden it was argued that when the bottom was falling out of the family economy through the death of the supporter or his permanent disability, which is economically much the same in its effect, the ordinary family reforms would not be enough. The income must be supplemented by regular cash payments. A system of state pensions for the children of widows and invalids was demanded.

Similar problems of support, when the basic family income dries up, may occur temporarily with other forms of disability of the supporter, such as illness and unemployment. What society is prepared to do in order to help the families temporarily in distress will be discussed in the following chapter.

Fathers sometimes have a tendency to disappear also when there is no problem of disability. In so far as the main family income is supplied by that parent who moves away from the common household, any family security program will again have to find means for safeguarding the family interests. That leads logically to a demand for some state guarantee of payments for children in divorced families.

Some children not only lose a father but also never had a legal one. The one-sidedness with which parental responsibilities are recognized when children are born out of wedlock necessitates social intervention for the protection of children. Legal provisions must operate to coerce the father who does not assume his responsibilities. Paternity regulations and social guarantees for economic support become the two minimum essentials in any program that would utilize society's means for defending children.

What Sweden has recently tried to do in order to improve the status of children in incomplete families is described here. Fortunately enough, a whole program for their security did not have to be improvised at once. The legislative activity of the last two decades had already provided for considerable protection. That activity has been illustrative of practical Scandinavianism. Some of the new laws have been drafted simultaneously in the different countries in order to assure consistency. Others have been explicitly copied from one Scandinavian country to another. Denmark has particularly served as a model to encourage Sweden and Norway.

Note should be taken also of the existence of Child Welfare Boards in Swedish communities. Since 1915 all practical activities for the welfare of children have been centralized in local agencies, which coordinate the tasks that might otherwise have been dispersed in all directions as private philanthropy, state regulations, and court procedures. Now the responsibility for all of those phases of child life from dependency to delinquency is vested in one welfare board. There is a regulation that the board's members, who may number not less than three but sometimes may reach 10, should include a woman.

The Widow's Family

Inheritance laws may not be of vital interest to the majority of people, as few have anything substantial to inherit. In spite of the fact that the number of accounts in savings banks is almost twice as high as the total number of households and that the majority of the agricultural workers are independent owners or members of their families it can be taken for granted that real security in the form of capital is rare for most families. As far as civil laws regulate how people may dispose of such possessions as they do have, it becomes vital to any family policy to safeguard the family interests. According to the Swedish marriage law in force since 1921, the relative status of man and wife is defined as equal. Up to that time the husband was the economic trustee of the family and also of the wife. The modern law states that both partners have equal rights and also equal responsibilities. Thus half of the duty to support the family falls upon the wife. It is expressly stated, however, that this economic duty may be fulfilled "through payments in cash, work in own home, or otherwise." Economically all possessions are jointly owned and administered and partners have the right when separating to half of all property, whether owned by either of them at time of marriage or acquired later. Through special legal agreements (marriage settlements, wills, etc.) property may, however, be reserved for individual ownership. It is expressly stated that one mate cannot sell, present, pawn, or bequest real property without the consent of the other.

These regulations make it obvious that on the death of one marriage partner the other does not literally inherit but rather takes possession of his half of the property. The rest is inherited by the children as direct descendants if there is no will. If there is a will, it cannot encroach upon more than half of the children's share. It is thus evident that a man with wife and children cannot ordinarily dispose of more than a quarter of the family's posessions in the form of a bequest, since one-half belongs to the wife and one-quarter is the legal minimum inheritance for the children. The same holds true of the wife. In order not to have to break up the home and family economy on the death of one of the parents, it is fairly common practice to make a joint will, prescribing that the estate shall remain undivided until the death of the second spouse. Thus, if there is property in a family, there is security for the widow and children. In most cases, however, there is no property. Security has been provided by the current income. Some substitute for that income must be found.

Good beginnings for implementing the social responsibility for keeping homes together under extraordinary economic stress can be found in various countries. The Swedish Labor party had repeatedly proposed state pensions for widows and children to the Riksdag. Some royal committees have also expressed their interest but failed to give the measure vigorous support.

In 1934 a new committee was called upon to consider the whole complex problem of children's pensions. The point of departure was definitely determined by the social insurance structure then being built up in Sweden. Thus it happened that no discussion of the principles concerning the limits of family support for children or cash versus kind subsidies was even attempted by that committee. The immense scope and complex interrelationships of the problems of the economy and of children were not recognized until a year later. The Committee on Children's Pensions waived all debate on principles and went to work on a practical basis. It found that the idea of cash pensions to all children was impossible to realize and so ended by formulating proposals for certain forms of state subsidies in the absence of the supporter, i.e., of the father. So restricted to practical considerations were the proposals that they failed to discuss even theoretically the parallel case of distress when the mother dies or disappears, or the situation when the mother is the supporter, or the desirability of facilitating women's reentry into the labor market. By thus failing to recognize the equality of the father and mother's duty of support, the committee worked somewhat

330 NATION AND FAMILY

contrary to the spirit of the marriage law; but despite the theoretical discrepancies the practical achievements should not be forgotten.

A first report proposed regular monthly pensions for orphan children and children of invalid or deceased fathers. [23] The proposal was carried on the wave of public enthusiasm for child welfare at the parliamentary session in 1937, and the law has been in force since January 1, 1938. Beneficiaries are orphan children and the children of widows and of such fathers as are invalids, i.e., incapable of work according to the definition in the National Pensions Act. The benefits for orphans are fixed at 300, 360, and 420 crs. per child annually in the three main cost of living regions. For children of invalids and widows the amounts are smaller, and they are also reduced for brothers and sisters following the first child. The sums obtainable follow the scale given in Table 35.

Children under two years of age receive an additional 60 crs. annually. These sums are all decreased according to general rules in relation to family income. If a widow has an income above 600, 800, or 1,000 crs., respectively,

TABLE 35. — CHILDREN'S PENSIONS IN SWEDEN, BY NUMBER OF CHILDREN AND COST OF LIVING REGION

NUMBER OF CHILDREN	REGION I (crs.)	REGION II (crs.)	REGION III (crs.)
One child	240	300	360
Two children	420	525	630
Three children	600	750	900
Each subsequent child	120	150	180

Source: Act on Assistance to Children of June 18, 1937. Registration Number S.F. 1937 : 382.

in the three regions or an invalid together with his wife has an income over 900, 1,125, or 1,350 crs., the total amount of pensions to children will be diminshed by seven-tenths of the additional income. The amounts have been determined so as to correspond roughly to the usual cost of boarding out a child. It thus marks the plan as one of reasonable substitution by paying the mother for keeping the children rather than paying strangers after separating them from their homes. As will be noted, the mother herself receives no benefit.

The costs for the pensions are carried chiefly on the national budget but also to a certain degree by the local communities according to the same rules that regulate the national pensions generally (Chapter 19). Children's pensions are also administered through the Pensions Board, thus showing their close relationship with the schemes for providing a subsistence basis for all groups incapable of earning their own support through productive labor. Parliament voted 16.4 million crs. for the pensions in 1938, 14 million crs. in 1939, and 12 million crs. in 1940. This amount actually means that some 70,000 children under 16 years of age or about 5 per cent of all children are given assistance. All other reforms planned for children under the population program are intended to be enjoyed over and above these cash amounts, which are to fill in the basic gap when the main support fails.

PROBLEMS

The scheme of children's pensions was set up before the general discussion concerning the family policy of the state, and some inconsistencies and conflicts of doctrine developed. A theoretical economic solution has been found for widows with children, but the scheme is not generally applicable as the cost would be almost prohibitive. Because of the low income scales of Swedish workers and farmers, a large number of families have to support children on incomes lower than those paid by the community to the widows' families.

The Population Commission, although praising the children's pensions, had to tackle this inequality. While the Commission had stated in gener-alities that income deficiencies for children should mainly be corrected through a giant program of free services in kind, the comparison with the children's pensions tempted them to extend the cash principle to provide an economic minimum for all families, even if a much lower one than for widows' children. The result of this compromise thinking was a proposal in the Report on Clothing [11] for state subsidies for all families with three or more children who were on poor relief and in other extremely low income categories. This proposal has not been carried out. It was planned as a temporary measure until the social services were developed to such an extent that they would considerably decrease the cost of support for children and until a broad general survey could be made of cash pensions according to social security ideals to children of widows, of social services as planned in a national family policy, of the possibility of guaranteeing minimum income in families with children, and of some coordinated scheme of assistance. Such a survey is to be made by a committee appointed in 1937 for the purpose of harmonizing the various social reforms of old and recent dates.

The specific problem for the widower may be not only an economic one. The organization of his household and the care of his children become the outstanding problems on the death of a mother. If the income is low, the hiring of a paid and competent housekeeper will often seem impossible. The problem has obtained some social recognition in that poor relief authorities sometimes have granted economic aid to provide a housekeeper in such cases. More often the practical solution has been that the man must look for something cheaper than a housekeeper and so remarries. Looking upon that from the children's point of view, it is obvious that the women who are willing to become wives in poor homes with children often cannot be the best selection and so a particular stepmother problem is created. The present neglect of the problems of widowers has popularly been criticized as both discrimination against the man himself and disrespect for the value of a mother and housewife.

Another open problem in connection with children's pensions concerns the widow and her relation to the labor market. Nothing has been stated in the law as to whether she should first seek work. The prerequisites for the pension have to do only with whether or not she has an income. The effects of the law in this respect have not been studied. Does the pension by being fixed too low force the mother into wage earning or does it, by being fairly ample, curb her ambitions to perform remunerative work? These questions cannot be answered generally, as the desires of the mother, her suitability for home or wage work, the number of her children, her age, and many other factors must enter into consideration. Only two general questions can be raised. First, will the general effect of the pension be such as to keep the mothers in the home or not and is that effect desirable? Second, as pensions are paid only while the children are minors, what will happen to the mother's chances of earning a living afterwards when her connection with the labor market has long been broken?

These and other questions are expected to be answered by the new Committee on Social Care, whose main task is to coordinate the different forms of social aid according to one basic and coherent social philosophy. In the meantime the children's pensions are continuing to do good to thousands of individuals and to demonstrate to society that it can afford to provide for children without a supporter.

THE DIVORCED FAMILY

The divorced woman and her children are naturally often in the same situation as the widow and her children. The practical difference is that the man is living in the one case and that his duty for supporting his family supposedly can be enforced.

The Swedish divorce law of 1915, revised in 1920, was drawn in close collaboration with Denmark and Norway. The most common way of obtaining a divorce is first to ask for a legal separation by mutual agreement. After a year of such separation, divorce is granted by a court on application. If no separation papers have been taken out, the divorce will ordinarily be granted only after three years of actual separation. Besides those two types, which are by far the more general (together averaging

87 per cent of all divorces in 1917–1933), there also exists the possibility of obtaining an immediate divorce by a court in cases of bigamy, adultery, and exposure to venereal infection. A curious situation has recently arisen as adultery has ceased to be a criminal offense,[1] while it still remains a cause for immediate divorce. Finally, there exists the possibility of obtaining a divorce when the other partner has been sentenced to a long term of imprisonment, is convicted of alcoholism, or has been insane for three years.

With regard to the partition of the estate, divorce carries practically the same consequences as death. Children would, however, be permanently supported through amounts fixed by the court and paid by the parent who does not have them in custody. Also, the husband or wife may under certain circumstances be awarded alimony or damages. According to the spirit of the law, this would not ordinarily be the case but would, for instance, cover the situation in which the wife has lost her earning capacity on account of marriage.

Practically, divorce most often raises the question of the economic security of the woman. The average age of the divorced woman in Sweden is nearly 39 years (1931–1935), and the average duration of the marriage terminated by divorce is more than 12 years. If the woman has not continued her wage-earning work, the possibilities of obtaining such work are obviously slight. If she has children, and 68 per cent of the divorced women have children (averaging 1.5 children), the demand to start supporting herself will rarely be made. Just as clearly as in the case of widows, the laws have not encouraged a social philosophy under which a woman should be able to claim lifelong support just because she has once been married. Her enjoyment and sacrifices in a marriage ought to have approximated those of the husband. Duties toward children, however, inject another factor.

With regard to state-advanced support, the argument was presented that in a case where the father did not pay the amounts for the support of his children fixed by the court in the divorce suit, the children should be indemnified to a certain minimum extent. A legal provision was thus enacted, allowing on application the advance of such amounts out of state funds. They were to be recovered by the state from the father.

The Illegitimate Family

Most provisions in Western society concerning child welfare are made on the supposition that the family is the normal institution for the bearing and rearing of children. Still, a great number of children fall outside this framework. In Sweden that is particularly true, approximately one-seventh of all babies born are technically classified as illegitimate. The last decades

[1] Adultery was rarely charged even earlier as the clause in the law was considered obsolete and few people would expose such private deviations in behavior before the court.

have shown a steady rise in humanitarian attitudes toward unmarried mothers. This may not be interpreted as merely another sign of general cultural progress. It may rather be interpreted as a reminder that in the traditional society children and mothers were protected by their families and by the local mores, one of the most important of which in Sweden was the habit of marriage after a child was conceived. In that stable society a reasonable harmony was achieved between practical conditions and social patterns, but rapid industrialization has both destroyed this old-time factual safeguard and at the same time fortified official morals and intensified the condemnation of unmarried mothers and their children. The so-called humanitarian laws of our century are thus only efforts to legislate with regard to a lag that has proved disastrous.

This new attitude was first applied to the children themselves. In order that they should not suffer unduly because of the lack of wisdom of their parents, a protective law for children born out of wedlock was passed in 1917. Since then neither fatherhood nor motherhood can be anonymous. Legally foundlings cannot exist. All children are entered in the continuous national register with both a mother and a father. All laws and social advantages pertaining to children apply to those born outside as well as within marriage. As far as legal prescriptions and official institutions are concerned, there is no discrimination against illegitimate children, whether in regard to welfare, schooling, stipends, civil service positions, church ceremonies, or similar privileges.

Fathers of illegitimate children are, however, not as socially evident as mothers. Their willingness to assume their paternal responsibilities will have to be strengthened by some legal sanctions. According to Swedish procedure, the father is first encouraged to enter into a contract with the mother, admitting his fatherhood and assuming the responsibility for paying a definite amount for the support of the child. In case no such voluntary contract can be procured, the mother arraigns the father in court to have paternity legally established. According to Swedish law, any man having had sexual intercourse with the mother at such a time that the conception could have occurred may be designated as the father. If statements by the two partners are conflicting as to such intercourse, the testimony of the one who is considered by the court to be the more reliable is accepted. Blood tests may be asked by the man in order to prove that he cannot be the father; otherwise evidence of the sexual relation is sufficient. In the case of a woman having had relations with more than one man, there is no legal possibiliy of discharging the arraigned man on that account. Neither does there exist any collective paternity similar to the much-discussed regulation in Norway and Denmark. It is the belief in Sweden that the child should have at least the illusion of a real father, even if he is somewhat arbitrarily chosen. Both parents are, according to the law, responsible for the support of the child, the one caring for him, however, being allowed to count that as maintenance in kind. In addition, the father may be called on to pay for the mother's maintenance six weeks before and six weeks after delivery.

Since the weak position of a child which has only one effective parent is recognized, a public guardian to serve with the mother must be appointed for any child born out of wedlock. The local Child Welfare Board takes appropriate steps as soon as it receives notification of the birth of a child. A pregnant woman is asked to give such notification three months before the expected birth. If she fails to do so, notification will come after the birth, as all births are reported by the assisting midwife or by the official in charge of the delivery ward to the national register of the population. Socially interested private citizens are selected as guardians or in some cities professional social workers so serve. No charge for this service is levied on either parent. The guardian will generally protect the child's interests until he or she is 16 years old and particularly help the mother to see through court the paternity and maintenance suits or otherwise help her with contracts, collecting the maintenance allowances, and so forth. In many cases the guardian will try to persuade the parents to marry. Particularly in some permanent relations where the marriage ceremony was not previously thought necessary, it is now often concluded in order to get rid of the interference of the guardian.

In addition to this formal protection, economic difficulties might remain. Public opinion came to consider it absurd that the children should suffer from irregularity of support when such support was once promised. At the same time it could no longer be expected in the urbanized society with its greater isolation between the generations that the maternal grandparents, as often had previously been the case, should take care of the children without compensation. The special committee which in 1934 had been called upon to investigate the economic principles of child maintenance and which had proposed the children's pensions also proposed that the state should advance support for children born out of wedlock and afterwards collect the money from the fathers. [24] Children of divorced parents were included in the same proposal. Thus, in case the father is economically unable to pay the fixed support, the one to suffer the loss is the community and not the child.

The committee argued as follows:

What primarily differentiates these categories of children from others is the fact that there exists someone who, although under obligation to provide for the children, fails to do his duty. As a consequence the children may suffer want which, at the present time, is being remedied by the poor relief authorities. As a means of supporting children, poor relief, however, has its serious drawbacks. These drawbacks reveal themselves strikingly in the cases of those children who, because of the discordant home environment in which they have been reared, are handicapped, as compared with children who have enjoyed the proper care at home. Furthermore, it may well be that mothers who have not been obliged to seek poor relief on their own account may hesitate to seek it for their children, with the result that the children may be in danger of suffering serious want. To this must be added that these children have, as a rule, either by court decision or by agreement, been formally granted the right of receiving regularly paid allowances for maintenance from their fathers. [24]

These proposals were carried in the Riksdag on the huge wave of public interest in population measures that made the session of 1937 epochal. A law was passed for the state to advance payments for the support of certain children of unmarried or divorced mothers. The sum to be advanced should equal the one agreed upon in the contract or fixed by the court. To avoid misuse, however, a maximum amount is fixed, being made fairly low but parallel to the pensions paid by the state to children who have lost their main supporter as related above. These amounts are graded according to cost of living areas, varying between 240 and 360 crs. a year. Mothers' incomes will also cause gradual reductions of these payments. An application for such advanced funds is made by the mother after one payment by the father is in default. As soon as the state has made a decision concerning support, a decision which generally covers one year at a time, it takes over the child's economic claims against the father and seeks reimbursement from him. Thus the state has taken on the role of bursar for the children, not allowing them to suffer the hazards of negligent fathers.

The amounts paid are covered by an appropriation from the state for three-fourths of total costs, one-fourth being paid by the local communes. In 1938–1939 the state grant was 2.5 million crs.; in 1939–1940, 4.8 million crs.; and in 1940–1941, 4.5 million crs. The increase is due not only to an increase in number of children enjoying this aid but also to the realization that a smaller percentage will be recovered from the fathers than was at first calculated. This may seem to be poor business for the state, but it only means that the bursar activity is being superseded by real support. Knowing the previous economic fate of these children, no one is willing to raise any objections to the order now established.

One group of children is exempt from this right to state-advanced support, the group whose paternity has not been legally established. This is evidently a necessary consequence of the connection of this aid with the legal contract for support. The group arises from two contingencies. One is when the mother is not able to give any clue at all as to which man is the father.

This group of negligent mothers has thus, although for technical and not moral reasons, become ineligible to a share in this social protection. There evidently remains a question whether the children should really be made to suffer because not only one but both parents fail to do their duty. In most cases those children will, however, be taken care of directly by society in one of its institutions or in foster homes. The other contingency arises, for the same technical reasons of lack of formal contracts about support, in those cases where the mothers do not wish to give the names of the fathers. This group will, however, diminish as the new law makes it to the real interest of the woman to reveal the name of the father.

Open Problems

Reforms concerning the illegitimate family which await future legislative action involve the right to name and inheritance from the father. Such proposals, which would finally extinguish the legal differences between legitimate and illegitimate children, have caused much heated discussion. Some of the more conservative have argued that such a right would cause damage, and perhaps scandals, to an eventual legitimate family by the same man. In the present legislation the legitimate family has the first claim also on income as support for extramarital children cannot be garnished from the father's salary or otherwise exacted if it would leave too narrow a margin for his legitimate family. Others have retorted that a realization of real obligations could only be developed if first-born children were always considered as first obligation; that the man had better not create a new family before he has taken care of the previous one, whether legitimate or not; and that joint parenthood should be considered as a *de facto* marriage as far as certain legal effects for the child are concerned. In Norway the reforms have been carried out without the expected scandals. In Sweden the Population Commission has strongly endorsed the reforms, but it could not work out final proposals because of the lack of interest on the part of the then acting minister of law, who was an elderly bachelor professor belonging to the Farmers' party and very much out of touch with modern family reforms.

The map of security for the incomplete family is nearing completion. Some questions have been raised, chiefly by foreign commentators, as to whether this social protection, particularly in regard to unmarried mothers, would not encourage illegitimacy. The answer is an emphatic "No." The position of the unmarried mother, even with all the protection provided, cannot be better than if she were married or if she had never had a child. The basic philosophy of the population program with regard to this point is that illegitimacy should be prevented but that the woman should not be punished when the child is born. The child in particular should not be punished.

The whole educative program of early sex education and continuous education to respect family values is a preventive program. The availability of contraceptive information is another step in the same direction and should certainly be supported by anyone who is interested in obliterating the social evil of illegitimacy. If there should be an element of punishment, it ought rather to be directed toward the father, who is presumably the one least faithful to his duties. It could then take no more adequate form than exacting the suggested duties from him even to the extent of having to give name and inheritance to his child. This would be the kind of legal reform that might have some deterrent effect and the only type which could be accepted for the purpose, as it would not harm the children. That is the main criterion for evaluating any laws that deal with children's lives.

CHAPTER XIX

SOCIAL SECURITY AND SOCIAL CARE OF THE HANDICAPPED

THE economic organization in modern industrial society is unable consistently to support man under all conditions. It leaves a number of vacuums in periods of stress, such as unemployment and illness. The individual is often not able to bridge these periods of vanishing incomes and/ or extraordinary expenditures, even assuming a maximum of ambition and foresight on his own part. There is, furthermore, a limit to the foresight and savings which can reasonably be demanded of an ordinary man when income is low and consumption perhaps lower than the hygienic and cultural standards demand. Finally there are definite economic advantages in socializing those risks. With this general motivation a system of social security has been erected in Sweden as in other countries. The point to be emphasized here is that practically all measures of family security directed toward relieving the differential costs of children would not be effective if the economic order were left free to ruin people as before. A population and family policy demands as its very basis general social security. This is true in an objective and technical sense, as every expert will agree. It is even more true politically and psychologically. Indeed, a population program would never succeed politically if it had to force through on its own such an enormous change in the whole economic system as is implied in letting all carry some ultimate responsibility for all.

Laying a solid foundation of security was the first step in Sweden. Remedial social policy, alleviating the worst of temporary ills, was early attended to. Next a basic organization of social insurance was developed, covering the risks to income. Only then had the time come for a constructive and preventive social policy centering its activity in the children. It is not a matter for surprise that during such a growth of the social reform structure with social philosophies sometimes conflicting and sometimes overlapping the parts become ill-matched. In this book such misfits have often been noted. In order to make them more understandable it becomes necessary briefly to sketch how the more general security system works. It can then be judged whether, taking old and new reforms together, the family has won a genuine basic security.

Illness, unemployment, accidents, and old age were all covered in earlier times as part of the function of protection that the larger three-generation family bestowed on all its members. This family responsibility was further strengthened and also supported by the neighborhood, the parish, and particularly the church. After the Reformation, during which the Catholic Church lost most of its huge worldly possessions, poverty gradually became recognized as an affair of the secular local community. In the new social order the responsibility for all these economic irregularities is in process of being transferred to the only organization which is large enough to carry the risks accumulated in our modern way of life, the large community. Likewise a number of other protective tasks which earlier had been provided for within the family are now transferred to more expert public bodies. Families are no longer held responsible for idiots and inebriates; they are relieved of the burden for crippled and deliquent children; they have at their command not only a whole series of institutions but also an interlocking system of social assistance and social control.

Old age and childhood show the closest parallels in this transition from familial to social protection. They both belong to the normal life expectancy of all individuals. They were both in earlier times cared for side by side in a family that normally encompassed three generations. They show, however, a discrepancy in their social roles just now in that old age has been openly recognized as an occasion for socially arranged security, while children fall into the vacuum created by the lag when they lose their place in the economically determined framework of the individual family and have not yet been allowed one in that larger society which the Swedish people like to call "The National Home" (folkhemmet). This lack of parallelism between social responsibility for young and old does more than create tension. It causes real competition both emotionally and economically.

DIRECT RELIEF

Before embarking upon a discussion of the more modern forms of social security in Sweden it seems appropriate to call attention to the traditional system of locally administered and financed direct relief. The Swedish system of direct relief (in Sweden called poor relief or care of the poor) has its historical roots far back in medieval times. When the obligation on the part of every local community to care for its indigent citizens finally was legally established during the latter part of the eighteenth century, it meant not much more than formal recognition of what had been a general pattern for a long time.

Modern poor relief includes both institutional care and home relief in cash or in kind. The annual number of recipients during the 1930's was around half a million persons, constituting 7 to 9 per cent of the total population. This figure includes temporary relief cases as well as all children in families on direct relief. Only recently have the recipients of old-age pensions become more numerous than the direct relief group.

Since the incidence of general relief increases with the number of children in the family, it is easy to understand why approximately one-third of the recipients of direct relief in 1937 as compared with one-fifth to one-fourth of the total population were children under 16 years of age. In spite of the fact that they receive old-age benefits and old-age assistance, the aged also have a high general relief incidence. Almost every fourth person over 75 years of age and about every seventh person between 67 and 75 years of age was on direct relief in 1935. It is probable, however, that the latest reforms in the old-age pension system have somewhat reduced this proportion.

There are those who see certain advantages in the direct relief system and even those who express themselves, as if in the interest of economy, in favor of a transfer of all relief back to the local communities. (This is, incidentally, not the only example of how the arguments concerning public welfare policies run along similar lines in different countries.) It is argued that public assistance, so far as possible, should be given only after a thorough checkup of each individual case and that only local authorities know the people in the particular communities well enough for the purpose. It is claimed, furthermore, that those authorities will be the more eager to keep out those not in need if the communes carry the full financial responsibility for the relief system. Arguments of a somewhat more humanitarian type are sometimes presented also. The fact that genuine need itself represents the sole basis for eligibility should make possible a more complete coverage of all families and persons in severe distress than could be expected from a rather mechanical state-administrated social security program, which is organized on a categorical basis but not yet in such a way that all groups of needy persons are included in the system.

Regardless of what the merits of such arguments may be, the system has some obvious disadvantages. Although direct relief technically does not constitute a grant but rather a loan, which in many instances actually is repaid, it is regarded as extremely humiliating. This is because indigent people do not generally have a right to receive it on certain mechanically ascertainable grounds. The fact that public assistance in this form often is given to families who are in need mainly because of the number of their children may, therefore, influence the attitude toward childbearing in a number of cases. Most people want security not only against starvation but also against "getting on poor relief." There is, as the Population Commission has emphasized, far too little preventive effort in the relief system except possibly in some of the richer and larger communities. [11] Even from a merely ameliorative standpoint relief amounts are in many cases inadequate. The average monthly grant for permanently supported cases (families or individuals) was 36 crs. in 1937. A special study for 1934 made by the Population Commission showed that the average annual value of direct relief given to 17,000 families with 3 or more children under 16 years of age was 365 crs. [11] Even if this figure also includes families which were on relief only part of the year or had some means of their own, it is doubtful that many of the households enjoyed even a fair level of living. General averages do not tell much, however, since the local differences are enormous. The mean amount for relief households in Stockholm was 738 crs., while it was only 183 crs. in agricultural communities located in a southwestern region of the country. Communes which give obviously inadequate amounts are usually those which suffer most from the financial burdens that direct relief represents.

That this unevenness in financial loads and relief standards really represents a serious problem is most easily understood in view of the fact that Sweden has more than 2,500 communes, many of them with less than 1,000 population and virtually all of them wholly responsible for local poor relief. One of the dilemmas, most difficult to escape, which is caused by such local discrepancies is whether indigent people should get the full benefit of the comparatively high standards in certain communities even if they have gone there for this very purpose or whether residence requirements should be strictly enforced although everyone knows that they may seriously endanger the freedom of mobility. This problem has not been adequately solved. Indigent migrants may have particular difficulties in getting on the relief rolls. In some instances they may be induced to go back to their home communities. The regular procedure, in most cases, is to give them relief but charge it to the communes from which they have come. This causes much ill-feeling among the communes, however, and even frequent legal proceedings. Sometimes such proceedings reveal rather objectionable practices in relief administration. The increase in migration undoubtedly represents one of the most serious challenges to the whole poor relief system.

One of the strongest arguments for the more recent forms of public assistance which are administrated or at least substantially supported by the state is that they help to make relief standards and relief burdens more uniform throughout the country. The fact that local direct relief is rather extensive in Sweden and that the administrative problems which characterize it, therefore, make themselves severely felt has, in other words, contributed to the eagerness to develop other social security programs. The trend has, at any rate, been in the direction of the state taking over more and more of the responsibility for cases in which need is influenced by some factor which is comparatively easy to ascertain (old age, widowhood, disability, unemployment, etc.). In other words, it has been the intention that local direct relief should be gradually liquidated by the removal of one group after another. Not until the late 1930's, however, did the relief group show any tendency to decline. This has been due to many factors. Aid given under other programs was not always considered sufficient. The increase in unemployment during the early twenties and early thirties increased the needy group. A gradual change occurred in the attitudes of the local relief agencies which, particularly after the World War, became far less restrictive than formerly. The Swedish system of health insurance should also be taken into account. Although otherwise substantial enough it is organized on a voluntary basis and particularly fails to reach some of the most needy groups. A large part of the direct relief group consists simply of people who are sick. It is significant that around 15 to 20 per cent of the persons aided are cared for in hospitals. This fact, however, does not indicate the full extent to which need of direct relief is caused by poor health. Some experts even go so far as to say that half the recipients of general relief suffer from poor health.

Whatever the merits or shortcomings of the Swedish direct relief system may be, it functions as a tolerably good last line of defense which takes care of a great number of cases otherwise not at all or only inadequately provided for. The existence of this rather substantial reserve institution should be kept in mind in the final evaluation of Swedish public welfare policies.

OLD-AGE SECURITY

Society has gradually taken over from the family the responsibility for support of the aged. This has been necessitated by the forces of industrialization and is already recognized as a national duty in most countries. When the present population trend is duly considered, a new motive for this security measure becomes apparent as it is important to free the young family in its homemaking and childbearing period from the burden of supporting the older generation. In the individual family duties toward the older generation sometimes place heavy obstacles in the way of marriage for the young and still more in the way of having children. These hindrances would, of course, be insuperable if the younger generations had not acquired a certain harshness of attitude. Division of responsibility tends to become the pattern. Daughters are generally more heavily burdened with the support and care of the older generations while the sons are freer to support new families.

Costs for old age have increased just as have costs of children, even if not proportionally, because no cost of preventive measures and of personal investment need be included for the old. At the same time the costs for the aged will become increasingly burdensome because there will be fewer children in the future to share the cost of the support of the parental generation. The present population of childbearing age has not paid for its own future old-age support by carrying the costs of a new generation. But this involves the more general problem of population and social policy. The rapidly changing age distribution makes it necessary to consider two steps simultaneously. The one is to change the demographic development quickly before the stock of possible parents, now reaching a peak, has shrunk too much in order to restore as much as possible the balance in the age pyramid, filling in with children at the bottom where the pyramid is now narrowing. The other is to solve the problem of old-age security as quickly as possible, though on a low subsistence level, before the stupendous sums soon to be required as the proportion of aged increases paralyze the political body into inaction. As the political power of old people also grows, however, the real danger may be not for them but for the children. It may therefore be more appropriate to say that it is necessary to develop a complete scheme for maintenance of old people before the new era in social policy can start focusing on children and family.

Different countries have tried different roads to the commonly acclaimed goal of social security for the aged. In principle the systems are regarded as falling under two typical patterns. The choice is most often made between a contributory insurance system and a tax-supported system. Both methods may of course be developed simultaneously. Such is the case in the United States where old-age benefits are based on an insurance scheme whereas old-age assistance is tax-supported aid to the needy. Sweden, too, has a combination of both methods. There is a great difference, however, in that the two systems are unified and integrated in Sweden whereas in the United States they are more or less unrelated to each other. The Swedish system is chiefly tax-supported, only a small percentage of the cost being covered by individual contributions. Even that part of the pension which to some extent corresponds to the American old-age assistance has the character of a right and is not considered as relief. Every aged or disabled person who on the basis of objectively ascertainable facts is considered to be in need is legally entitled to a specified amount of supplementary pension in addition to his old-age benefit or basic pension.

Even that part of the Swedish system which rests on individual contributions differs from other schemes in that it is free from any connection, administrative or financial, with the labor market. It is a national pension for all aged and contributed to by all. The universal efforts to create a counterbalance for the economic disturbances brought about by industrialization cannot in the long run be confined only to those people who have worked as wage earners. The employer-employee relationship is not the only one that is incapable of fulfilling its functions in a socially satisfactory way. Those who obtain their living from other sources than a payroll are also to be taken into account. It is an outstanding achievement of Swedish democracy that at the very time when the working classes have come into power and gained control over public affairs, they have not restricted the political gains of social security to their own social group but have, on the contrary, forcefully demanded the expansion of social protection to include all citizens.

This general principle of complete coverage was recognized from the very beginning. In 1913 the original law on old-age security for all citizens was passed. It did not make such a revolutionary break as to become economically sufficient, however, and the rise in prices during the World War made its appropriations still more inadequate. It is easy enough to sum up the chief imperfections of that earlier system. First, the amounts were too small or, as it was said, they were "just enough to let one neither live nor die on." In cases where both the annuity accruing from contributions and a state pension were received, the average amounts at the close of 1932 were 13.17 crs. plus 169.72 crs. for men and 5.33 crs. plus 156.07 crs. for women. It is thus apparent as a second criticism that women were in an unfavorable position. Women generally received lower percentages of their contributions in annuities and lower pensions allotted out of state funds. Furthermore, as a form of taxation the contributory system was steeply regressive in relation to income and thus pressed most heavily upon the poorer income groups. Finally, the piling up of a huge fund, amounting to 607 million crs. in 1933 and continuing to grow, was financially hazardous and served no particular purposes.

This old-age pension law, in force since 1914, has been a main issue in political struggles. The Labor party consistently advocated a considerable increase in the annuities. Several minor changes were enacted but not until the parliamentary session of 1935, when the Labor party had been in power for three years, was a fundamental reform carried through. The new law went into effect on January 1, 1937. [34] Even then the more conservative parties would not allow a differentiation of the annuities according to the cost of living in different regions. The Labor government as a protest left office in the summer of 1936 when such a proposal of theirs failed to win the approval of the Riksdag. After having been a dominant issue in the election campaign of the summer and after the Labor party regained power in September, 1936, the amendments to the pension law were accepted at the meeting of the Riksdag in 1937, and became effective on January 1, 1938. [35]

The general aim of the new law was specified by the Minister of Social Affairs when introducing the bill:[1]

A system of people's pensions should at least aim to spare decent citizens with no income or with insignificant income the humiliation of having to apply for poor relief in their old age or to become dependent on the aid of relatives for their support. The people's pension introduced in 1913 and improved in 1921 has not been able to fulfill this main task. A large number of those who now receive such a pension have been compelled also to seek poor relief for their maintenance. The pension benefits are such meager amounts that, except in rare instances, not even the most extreme thrift would suffice to secure the bare necessities of life.

The new law on people's pensions continues to combine security for old age with security for invalidism, with a view later to making health insurance compulsory for all people. Thus, incapacity for earning an income is the general prerequisite for claiming an annuity, but the definition of such incapacity is made quite formal in the case of age by setting a definite age limit of 67 years. Otherwise, invalidism is thus defined in the law: "Permanent disability shall be considered as established when a person on account of old age, physical or mental disease, incapacity or defect is unable to support himself through labor befitting his strength and skill." No mention is made of the economic situation of the invalid.

Every citizen between 18 and 65 years of age has to pay pension contributions. This annual contribution is combined with the income tax both as a method of calculation and as an actual payment. There is a minimum and a maximum charge, 6 crs. being the minimum. One per cent of the annual taxable income is to be paid, with a maximum, however, of 20 crs. per person and of 40 crs. for a married couple. This maximum is set so as to give each contributor at least the actuarial value of his contributions. The annual income to the state, which was 45.3 million crs. in 1938, averages about 50 million crs.

The pensions paid out, however, amounted in 1939 to about 127 million crs. by the state and about 31 million crs. by the primary municipalities with a prospective rise in the national contribution to 225 million crs. in 1950. The fund is not altogether abolished but its rate of growth is definitely limited. It may not exceed 1,000 million crs. In comparison with the expenditures and income just quoted it is thus far from self-sustaining. Even its capital is only sufficient for about four years' payments of pensions. As it is now arranged, the fund is chiefly to be regarded as an equalization fund,

[1] Parliamentary proceedings, 1937.

out of which the extra amounts required by changes in size of age groups may be met.

In calculating the benefit the two constituent parts are definitely separated. The one is derived from contributions (basic pension) and the other from general taxation (supplementary pension). The system becomes further complicated in that the basic pension is regulated to consist annually of one fixed and one variable part: a fixed sum of 70 crs. and an amount which varies with the size of total paid contributions and consists of one-tenth of such contributions.

In addition to this basic pension, a supplementary pension is paid as a social right to everybody who has a basic pension and whose income does not exceed a certain maximum limit. The following amounts per annum are paid, less seven-tenths of the annual income of the pensioner in excess of 100 crs. In many cases, as specified below, this income limit is higher.

In lowest cost of living region, Group I	250 crs.
In next lowest cost of living region, Group II	350 crs.
In most expensive cost of living region, Group III	450 crs.

The classification of localities by cost of living is made by the General Social Board in accordance with rules laid down by the government. This threefold division of regions is utilized in many of the social support schemes in Sweden, as has been noted, for instance, in regard to children's pensions.

Not only do amount of benefit and local financial contribution vary according to this regional system but also the income limits for eligibility to supplementary pensions.

It was previously indicated that these income limits are raised in certain cases. In addition to the 100 crs. of general exemption, there is an extra exemption in the case of so-called privileged incomes. This regulation is intended to favor and not exclude concomitant schemes for old-age assistance. Included in these privileged incomes are all pensions or assistance from gifts or from inheritance and pensions or assistance from former employment. In addition benefits from voluntary insurance, e.g., sickness or life insurance, and, as perhaps the psychologically most important exemption, economic support given by relatives are exempt. It is specifically stated that if aged parents live with their children and get their sustenance from them, no deduction of the pension allotted to them shall be made.

All these extra exemptions are, however, limited to a low maximum of 300, 350, and 400 crs., respectively, in the different cost of living regions. The pension decreases in proportion to the amount of the remainder. As the income decreases below these limits, the supplementary pension will fill in gaps in such a way that the sum total of the pension and income becomes somewhat greater as income increases. That means simply that it is desired to reward and not to punish economic foresight or attempts to earn an income even in old age. Finally, this pension scheme includes facilities for cheap voluntary insurance, where the national pension fund directly competes with private insurance companies (law of 1913, revised 1935).

The scope of the national pension system is enormous. Some 440,000 people were receiving supplementary pensions at the end of 1939, of whom 147,000 were on relief before the age of 67 because of invalidism and 293,-000 were receiving old-age pensions. The latter constituted from 55 to 60 per cent of all people 67 years of age and over. When the system is working completely, all persons 67 years of age and over will have the benefit of the basic pension.

<h3 style="text-align:center">EVALUATION</h3>

It is proper to try to evaluate these pensions in terms of the preponderant question of whether they are sufficient to live on. Do they liberate old people from poor relief? Or are they to be regarded only as state subsidies to the communities as part coverage of their somewhat greater cost of maintaining poor and old people?

There has been much discussion on these points. It should be realized that the merits of the system as a social device should not be judged by the economic effects only. Here a double problem faces all countries, an economic problem and an administrative and technical problem. It is the consensus in Sweden that the legal scheme for old-age security as such has been carried near to perfection. There is a division of opinion, however, as to its economic adequacy.

There will also always be differences of opinion as to what is enough to live on and still more on what is a desirable standard for the aged. Experts for grouping communities into cost of living regions have estimated that a bare subsistence for two old persons would be respectively 700, 900, and 1,100 crs. in the three types of communities. The pensions in the same regions include the fixed part of 70 crs. from the contributory scheme, and the state supplementary pension fixed at 500, 700, and 900 crs. for individuals or 640, 840, and 1,040 crs. for a married couple. To this should in all cases be added the increments of 10 per cent on total contributions. Without any reduction in the pension there may be private incomes of 100 crs., or 200 crs. for married people, and extra exemptions for married people, if both have such incomes, of 600, 700, and 800 crs. In a most favorable case of private incomes in the districts of highest cost of living a married couple may thus have 800 crs. extra exemptions, plus 200 crs. basic income, plus 140 crs. basic pension, plus 900 crs. supplementary pension, plus per cent increments, or above 2,040 crs. As private income increases, the pension is not quite correspondingly decreased.

The best situated families are those in which both man and wife are pensioners. Of all people 67 years of age and over about 55 per cent of the men and 37 per cent of the women are living with their mates. As calculations go, these decisions on size of income for an old couple seem to be as close as any fixed rules may come to human needs, notwithstanding that the latter are always more variable than any averages can indicate. The case of the single man or woman is, of course, much less favorable, although a larger proportion of the aged single people have to be cared for in institutions.

If pensions are compared with average incomes earlier in life, the inadequacy may at first seem glaring. It must be remembered, however, that a family has to be supported on the wage but not on the pension.[2]

Thus only with utmost caution may pensions be compared with average incomes. According to the census of 1935–1936, the average incomes in the groups where pensions would be most frequent were 2,070 crs. for male industrial workers, about 1,640 crs. for farmers, and 1,530 crs. for farm laborers. These figures are based on income tax returns, which are generally to be corrected as too low, particularly for farmers. The statistics as to wages only, given by the Social Board, are higher, e.g., in 1937 male industrial workers averaged 2,974 crs.; sales clerks, 2,425 crs.; two types of farm laborers, 1,221 crs. and 1,526 crs. Women's wages are about two-thirds of these totals. Counting income risks through unemployment and other factors and remembering that many must have lower than these average incomes, it is safe to say that large numbers of the population do not by their labor earn incomes commensurate with the pensions. In this light the pensions do not seem excessively small.

A further indication that pensions are not just substituting for poor relief is found in the fact that many persons who were never labeled needy and hence did not receive public assistance are now beneficiaries not only of basic pensions but also of supplementary pensions. This is far from defending the national pensions as generous. It is only stressed that if a particular value is placed on having fixed pensions, these must be kept low in comparison with other incomes. The value of having pensions legally fixed as to both eligibility and amount is not questioned in Sweden. The ensuing rigidity and even the possibility of obtaining a pension which is lower because it has to be fixed as an equalized legal right is far preferred to any more flexible pension system involving consideration of individual needs.

Conflicts, however, are likely to arise between municipal direct relief and national pensions. There has no doubt been a temptation on the part of local authorities to withdraw public assistance when a pension was being received by a relief client. Even if municipal avarice is difficult to over-

---

[2] Minors with invalid fathers are carrying pensions of their own.

come, the pension system in itself, from the very outset, included provisions for resolving the conflict. The first buffer was a rule that only if a person's standard of living on the state pension became quite satisfactory should public assistance money be withdrawn. For people who have been wholly dependent on poor relief the pensions could rarely suffice for total cost of living. In 1940 about 30 per cent of the beneficiaries of supplementary pensions also received poor relief. The pensions were intended for more normal cases, constituting a foundation income but encouraging both some savings during earlier years and the retaining of supplementary sources of income of different kinds, such as small savings, life insurance, voluntary people's pensions, subsidies from children, cheap housing, and so forth. Still, the Pension Board has been asked to make an investigation of the need and possibility of raising the pensions.

In order further to make it possible to remove the stigma of poor law assistance in those residual cases where the pensions would not be adequate, a law (1918, revised 1936) has been enacted enabling those municipalities which find it necessary to continue the payment of relief to pensioners to do so in the form of additional municipal pensions. Also, municipal increments scaled for the cost of living regions may be stipulated. The main object in regulating a certain part of municipal aid through these specific pensions is to release them from the legal and psychological implications of poor relief. It was necessary that the state pensions, equal all over the country's three regions, be minimum sums. Here was an opportunity of creating in a similar way contractual rights to a cash pension for the locally necessary subsistence amounts on top of the state pension, following objective income rules and not requiring the beneficiaries to submit to any means test. As the state was relieving the local municipalities of immense responsibilities through the pension scheme, this would be economically feasible and would help to perfect the system of national pensions. Only a few communities have as yet taken advantage of this possibility for freeing their old people from dependency. The general trend, however, is such that insurance of all types is diminishing the domain of direct relief.

Institutionalization and Housing for the Aged

The previous section dealt with old-age security on a cash basis. It remains to be seen how far this has to be supplemented by some care in kind. For several reasons this care will have to take the form chiefly of housing programs or institutionalization.

As this study endeavors to present the Swedish reforms as constituents of a rational plan, or of a plan capable of being adjusted so as to become rational, it ought to be stressed that different sections of the aged population can be cared for in different ways. One section of the old population, particularly the relatively healthy and preferably married old people in rural districts, should be able to live on a cash benefit provided by the state, fixed as to amount and claimed as a contractual right. Quite often they will have a little cottage or be given some dwelling at no rent or low rent. Another section, especially the relatively healthy and preferably married old people in urban districts, ought to be able to live on the cash benefit if provided with cheap housing facilities, the most common complaint being that the pension is insufficient to cover the rent. A last section, especially the infirm and many single persons, would fare best by being taken care of in institutions. Even these institutions could, however, be planned and administered more on a hotel basis or, for the weaker individuals, on a hospital basis, as the pensioners will have some money with which to pay for their own support.

Differentiation of the housing market is under way, as has been described in Chapter 14, making available cheap housing facilities with state subsidies for beneficiaries of national pensions. This is intended to supplement the margin between the cash pensions and the actual cost of living in some places through an additional benefit. As it is given directly in kind and is not convertible into cash, it should allow a close adjustment to individual needs.

On the borderline between private apartments and institutions for the aged, there have, of course, existed a number of projects, both philanthropic and municipal, where old people could have cheap homes and some care. Only one development may be worthy of special mention, as it represents an attempt to convert some social waste to the benefit of the old, the so-called flower courts. This privately administered welfare enterprise is financed through what used to be the excess of flowers sent to funerals. [119] In 1921 a movement was started to create a new habit, not for mourners in the family but for more distant relatives, to pay tribute to the deceased person by sending the flower money to a fund and a token from that fund to the house of mourning. In Stockholm some 30 organizations are affiliates of the fund. In the provinces some 150 organizations work in a corresponding way. Each flower fund is local, as no national organization exists. In Stockholm the annual income of this direct exchange for flowers amounts to about 30,000 crs. with an additional 48,000 crs. from larger gifts. With the help of the sums thus collected eight large apartment houses have been financed, housing about 1,000 families consisting of aged persons in apartments of from one room to 2½ rooms and kitchen. Not only is housing made cheaper but also housekeeping is facilitated by having a low-priced restaurant in the house, and the transition to more dependent care when infirmity sets in is facilitated by a nurse always being on duty. Even hospitalization is available.

In considering the institutional care of the aged, nothing much has to be said about Sweden that would not be true of other countries. The accomplishments in this field have a long history even if the most important activity for the moment is to change these very traditions. Without trying to trace the institutions back to the Middle Ages, it might be stated as a generalization that so far as the occupants in the old-fashioned poorhouses, intended both for incapable poor and for old people, are concerned, the poor people tend to be increasingly taken care of outside of institutions and the care of old people is being more and more institutionalized. At the same time the mental defectives and other handicapped categories have been provided specialized care. The poor are being divided up into groups according to specific needs. Poverty is being remedied by curing the sick, putting the unemployed to work, placing the vagabonds in workhouses and, above all, giving public assistance in cash to everybody who is merely poor and able to take care of himself. On the other hand, the old parents and relatives are less frequently cared for in the homes of their descendants than formerly.

As part of their direct relief system most communes in Sweden have their own homes for old people, developed from the almshouses, but about 30 years ago rechristened "Old Folks' Homes." The theory back of these numerous small institutions has been that the aged should not be uprooted but should be allowed to stay in their own neighborhoods and near their own people. Laws about legal domicile as ground for the right to enjoy this care have also strengthened the adherence to this principle.

So recent is the campaign for separating the various groups of the poor and the old and remaking the relief institutions into just homes for aged that difficulty exists in getting exact information as to the number of inmates belonging to each category. The total number of inmates living in those institutions in 1937 was 42,646, two-thirds of whom were 67 years of age and over. The average annual cost per person is about 750 crs. Higher standards and psychologically more understanding and tender care of our old generation in those homes are common goals toward which the whole development aims. Provisions have been made for inspection. Together with the development of professional pride among the personnel, unionized in a strong association, there has been a rapid improvement in standards. Some of these homes, built in pavilions and with housekeeping facilities for old couples, are regarded as model institutions.

There would be few questions of principles involved in future progress if it were not for the competition between different means of social security, chiefly between old people's homes, old-age benefits, and home relief. These difficulties have, in fact, been of considerable practical importance, although by themselves they ought not to be insurmountable. In old people's homes the cost for the boarders may be paid either from their own income, by relatives, by pension incomes, or by public assistance of the community. The last is a poor law administration with the stigma remaining, even though methods and regulations are much humanized. Means test will in that case be involved, repayment claimed, perhaps by recovery out of the estate, and franchise is lost if total maintenance is paid by the community. If a person is permanently taken into custody by the poor relief administration, he loses his pension right. This administration has the right to cash the pension benefit for inmates in its own specified institutions, but the pensioner has by general practice the right to a certain small share of the pension for private use.

HEALTH SECURITY

In Sweden security against sickness is in the main accomplished by having public medical care available at low cost to everybody and by extending the sphere of public health control (Chapter 16). So successfully has this worked that there has not been the same need in Sweden for that other type of pooling health risks which is dominated by the insurance principle. Any social insurance scheme is nothing more than a financial system of sharing burdens, built on top of an essentially private organization of consumption. The organization of services remains the same; the costs remain the same; only the distribution is shifted. The radical step for transforming the system of medical care is thus never taken by health insurance or cooperative group medicine but only by a thorough democratization of the services themselves.

There still remains a field, though relatively small, for health insurance. [*38*] Its predominant function is not to cover health costs but to indemnify against income loss during illness. The pooling of medical costs may be added; but its importance is secondary to that of social responsibility for medical care proper. This has to be clearly borne in mind for an understanding of Swedish health insurance. Many of the criticisms raised against sick benefit funds in other countries, particularly in Germany, do not apply in Sweden.

Health insurance is not compulsory in Sweden. Still it covers nearly one-third of the population 15 years of age and over (in 1940, it covered 1,510,000 persons). The voluntary principle is one distinguishing mark. Public grants is the second one. Its availability to every person in the nation is the third. It can thus truly be called social insurance.

This cooperative organization for meeting health risks originated in the medical funds of the old guilds. In the 1870's, however, an era of more purposive growth began. In 1891 the first law sanctioned the existence of mutual sick benefit funds and provided a small grant for administrative costs. In 1910 more rigid regulation was effected and more generous grants were made available. In 1931 the provisions now in force were embodied in a law and became effective on January 1, 1932. Proposals had in the mean-time been advanced to make this insurance compulsory but many reasons, not the least of which was financial, made such a step seem too hazardous. There is no doubt, however, that such an enlargement to a nation-wide compulsory system parallel with the national pension system is high on the social agenda in Sweden.

At present all sickness insurance funds have to be registered if they have 50 members or more. The ones eligible for state grants must have 100 members and are chosen on application, one for every local district. Anybody between 15 and 40 years of age is eligible for participation provided he is in good health. No income limits are fixed and no restriction to any social group, as for example to industrial workers, is made. However, persons who have no wage-procuring job can be members only for the medical benefit part. To this group belong married women who are just housewives. On the other hand, persons with taxable incomes, after exemptions, of 8,000 crs. may not be members for medical benefits but only for the recovery of lost income. The fees are also scaled to take care of such differences. Thus the annual dues are determined solely with reference to those advantages for which members want to purchase insurance.

The benefits earned through this mutual venture, which has the general characteristics of a folk movement with prestige attaching to service on boards, are twofold: medical benefits and day benefits. The medical benefits constitute simply an insurance system for part of all costs directly involved in medical care. Home visits, office calls, and hospital care are included. For hospital care all costs, equivalent to the fee in a general ward in the nearest hospital, are paid. For physician's services the rule is that two-thirds of the cost of consultation is borne by the fund and one-third by the patient himself. This division of liability is the most interesting feature. It never makes the patient totally uninterested in the fees, which might tempt him to run up high costs. But the interests of the medical profession also have to be safeguarded. No panel of doctors is thus prescribed. There is no limit to the choice of doctor. There is not even any regulation of fee. It is only provided that the recipient be indemnified for two-thirds of the cost as prescribed in a model scale of fees. If he pays more, it is up to himself. Socially this system works satisfactorily with perhaps some minor defects. The size of the daily benefit to be received during incapacity for work is fixed according to the dues the member pays. He insures himself for a daily income of 1, 2, 3, 4, 5, or 6 crs. The payments of such a benefit for one illness end after two years with some specific exceptions.

The rules for preventing misuse of the medical benefit include the stand-ardization of fees and the restriction of benefits to two-thirds of the cost. In order not to foster idling at the expense of the insurance fund, it is prescribed that daily benefits cannot be paid for the first three days of any illness, that a doctor's certificate is necessary, and that the fund engages visitors to check on the patient. As the fund takes somewhat into account the economic situation of the member when deciding the benefit he is entitled to insure himself for, these benefits will rarely exceed earnings and thus in themselves are not too great a temptation for simulation of illness.

This whole system of insurance is three-fourths self-liquidating. State and municipal grants cover the remainder. The state grant is calculated in the form of a fixed annual contribution of 3 crs. per member, plus half the actual cost of the medical benefit and 0.50 crn. for every day's benefit. It has been estimated that the cost to the state in 1940–1941 will amount to 17.6 million crs.

An evaluation of this insurance scheme may be difficult. The weakness of the voluntary system is that the poorest classes find insurance too expensive and stay out. A compulsory system would for the same reason necessarily mean state responsibility for a greater proportion of the total cost. But at least half the costs for direct relief could probably be converted from public charity to an insurance right. At the same time a local responsibility would then become a national responsibility.

EMPLOYMENT SECURITY

Income risks have come to be a constituent part of present-day society. It must be duly stressed that the risk that the family may suddenly lose all its economic support exists in all social groups. It is part and parcel of our whole economic structure, and we must face the fact that the family is by and large uninsurable against this fundamental risk. In most occupational groups not even a subsistence minimum can be guaranteed the income earners. In business and in farming the risks have of late become especially serious. Only in one social situation has something seemed possible in the way of reassuring the earner, namely, in case he is employed by somebody else and particularly if he is a manual worker. Unemployment insurance is practically the only field of social insurance in Sweden where the aid has been restricted to the wage earners.

This introduction to a treatment of unemployment policy and insurance is not made in order to point out that industrial workers are a favored group. It is rather presented in order to indicate why the Swedish democracy, otherwise socially advanced, has not made unemployment insurance one of its main issues. It has instead proceeded to erect a more general preventive structure against that and other income risks.

Stabilizing economic cycles and creating permanent maximum utilization of all the country's human and material resources must from that broader point of view be the most important unemployment cure. The general economic policy of the country aimed at accomplishing this result can here neither be described nor discussed. Integrated in it are the agricultural policy, referred to in an earlier chapter, the labor market policy founded on the principle of independent collective bargaining, the monetary and credit policy, and the fiscal policy allowing the state to balance business fluctuations by running a counter cycle of its own. This whole system of flexible and coordinated efforts to raise and stabilize production and employment is ultimately designed also to create family security and particularly to decrease the unemployment risk.

The trade unions, started in the 1880's, have achieved a complete victory in their fight for collective bargaining. As of July 1, 1940, the Swedish Confederation of Trade Unions had about 963,000 paying members. Some other groups are unionized although not affiliated with the central organization. Among them is a group of about 30,000 syndicalists. The membership of the unions thus constitutes nearly one-fourth of the total population 15 years of age and over and embraces practically all male industrial workers with women workers, farm laborers, and some other groups less intensively unionized. The main organizational principle is that of industrial unions among all workers in a shop instead of unionization according to crafts. Two large groups of white-collar employees are likewise unionized. They are the Central Organization of Civil Servants (about 10,000 members) and the Central Organization of Salaried Employees (about 55,000 members).

Unions would have remained only a form of organization for strikes if there had not been an employers' organization to meet at the conference table. Several such organizations were started in 1902 after a general strike. Now the Swedish Employers' Federation confederates most of them, having a membership as of July 1, 1940, of 6,139 employers, employing about 426,-000 workers. Farmers, newspaper, railway and shipping firm operators form other associations, loosely tied with the main organization in order not to have to collaborate in all actions. The Swedish cities, finally, have a special organization for obtaining collective agreements with municipal workers.

Negotiation has gradually come to take the place of violence and exploitation in the Swedish labor market. Few are those who now doubt the value of unionization. The attitudes have shifted interestingly within this century from the time when workers were brutes and employers exploiters to the summer of 1939, when their two leaders, photographed together, issued a joint statement to be presented at the World's Fair in New York. That reflects the attitudes crystallized chiefly in the so-called Principal Agreement of Saltsjöbaden (1939), which is a code of behavior for the two parties in the labor market by which to avoid violence and damage to the public. It binds them to settle all disputes by their own system of negotiations. The act has been called the signing of the labor peace in Sweden. It is the final victory of the members of trade unions who started out as martyrs and missionaries.

Strikes and lockouts were once harsh; they are now orderly. Wages were low and arbitrary; they are now fairly high and not determined without consent of the powerful workers themselves. Employment was irregular and uncertain under the arbitrariness of bosses; it is now regulated and planned to reduce fluctuations. The workers have achieved these successes by themselves. Employers and employees have been equally opposed to the state directly interfering in the labor market. They have particularly wanted to keep wages for their own struggles and settlements. The state has, however, confirmed the right of both parties to federate and their duty to enter into negotiations demanded by the other party, the last in a law of 1936. A system of state conciliation in labor disputes has also been established. The first law was enacted in 1906 and a new one in 1920. Such conciliation is only advisory, presenting terms for agreements but without power to enforce them. Through a law of 1935 it is further provided that when work is to be stopped according to a decision by either party, the other party and the state conciliator — there are seven such in different districts — should be notified a week in advance. This orderly way of conducting even strikes and lockouts could, of course, be introduced in a labor market only with a mature organization. Finally, a Labor Court has been established for settling disputes about interpretation of agreements. Outside that formal sphere it has, however, no competence.

Thus one aspect of employment security has been fairly well assured, that which derives from control of warring interests on the labor market. Similarly, the more technical difficulty of obtaining employment has been partially solved by public employment agencies, first provided in 1906 (private ones being state controlled since 1844) and since 1940 administered under direct state control. Private employment bureaus are not permitted, although some traditional licenses continue to be granted. State grants are also available for paying traveling expenses of persons applying for jobs.

The last and most unyielding difficulty is that of managing economic shifts which entail ups and downs in employment. Here also the Swedish nation has of late become rather confident of its ability to cushion the worst economic impacts. Creating opportunity for employment rather than alleviating the consequences of unemployment was regarded as the main task for a state program. There was no question that unsatisfied consumption needs still existed. To meet them by a state work program became more and more possible as the resistance to state intervention in the sphere of business gradually yielded. The economic depression of 1931–1934 became the test. The program was first looked upon purely as providing opportunity for getting men to work instead of paying doles. In the intermediary stage it was considered more of a spending device and, finally, it was seen as an integrated scheme of purposive and planned stabilization of production.

Prior to 1933 the unemployment policy consisted of a scheme for public works at low emergency wages, so-called relief work (corresponding to the works program in the United States although less differentiated) and then cash doles for the remainder. No one was eligible for a dole who refused to take any labor opportunity offered. With the new economic policy inaugurated at the parliamentary session of 1933, these regulations were changed. The state would no longer be confined to a passive role in economic life. The old system was not altogether abolished, but it was largely superseded by a new one comprising three main avenues for the cure of unemployment: retraining in schools and camps for younger persons in an overcrowded or obsolete trade; unemployment insurance increasingly substituted for the cash dole in cases of short-time unemployment; and public works financed by credit expansion as the direct means to counteract the economic recession resulting in unemployment. Under this scheme public works should be useful although not urgent projects (thus sometimes called "emergency projects," although they may better be translated as "planning but precipitated projects"), and they should pay wages according to the level in the local open labor market with workers not certified as in need but hired on the open market. Building of hospitals, schools, and homes and the construction of bridges and similar projects were chosen for the purpose. Aside from such work, directly employing a number of persons, subsidies for orders of materials to private industries were provided on a large scale. Only a shrinking proportion of public works managed under a modification of the old scheme and directly under the Unemployment Commission was allowed to pay wages below the established scales.

The final stage and thus the most important in this connection is not what happened in the depression already over but what was planned for the next one. The expansionist philosophy is a main foundation, but the application involves less diffuse, and more directed, spending. Projects are blueprinted in advance to be put into effect when needed. An inventory has been made of work considered necessary within the next 10 years. From this a list of projects with different degrees of urgency has been drawn up for eventual use. A preparational budget is also voted every year to be used if the government finds that a depression is imminent. Moreover, a rational budgeting system has been constructed, combining a maximum degree of fiscal flexibility from year to year with guarantees for fiscal soundness in the long run.

With this main line in Swedish unemployment policy endorsed by the citizens and proved effective during the last depression, it is only natural that the problems of unemployment insurance have become secondary.

Not distributing and alleviating unemployment but creating employment has been the keynote of the active economic policy in Sweden. There is still another reason for this apparent lack of interest in one of the creeds of social security. The trade-union system of the industrial workers in Sweden being as strong as it is, its funds had of old been able to give support to members both in unemployment periods and in labor dispute periods. Through fairly expensive dues paid weekly by the workers, a kind of self-insurance had been organized. To discard this democratic "help to self-help" by superimposing a system of compulsory unemployment insurance was not deemed desirable. Therefore the new Swedish system of unemployment insurance (1934) is voluntary. [26] Whenever a fund created by the employed themselves is operated in accordance with certain rules and is submitted to control by the Social Board, it will become state-approved and get state subsidies paid out of general taxes. These subsidies are higher in those fields where wages are low and unemployment frequent. On the average 50 to 60 per cent of the benefits paid are to be derived from state subsidies, but the administration is in the hands of the workers themselves.

Not only may trade unions create unemployment insurance funds but also independent funds may be approved. Any worker may belong to only one such fund and in order to claim benefits he must have paid at least 52 weekly contributions, of which 26 should be during the last year before becoming unemployed. On losing his job he must further apply for work at a state Employment Service Office, the only recognized employment agency. The benefit generally varies between 2 and 6 crs. daily for a maximum of 156 days each year. This period is generally shortened by the fund's own regulations to 120 days. The worker's contributions vary according to the benefit desired, according to income, and according to unemployment risk in his line of work. They range between 0.20 and 0.45 crn. weekly for a daily benefit of 2 crs. and between 0.45–1.40 crs. for a benefit of 4 crs.

The employers do not participate in these funds. Neither the Swedish workers nor the public authorities have been concerned about getting the divisional system of contributions from employer, employee, and state in operation in any of the insurance schemes. The workers know that at the conference table, when checking economic data for determining their wage scale, they are in a position to see to it that portions adequate to maintain the unemployment insurance are included in the reward for their labor. They might be just as successful in keeping up wages while letting the employer in reality carry the unemployment cost. They do not want, however, to relinquish an administration which is traditionally theirs, and they are capitalistically minded enough to want to be able to purchase different benefits.

This insurance for incomes lost on account of unemployment is obviously not intended to be any cure for unemployment. It is designed only as an emergency measure to carry over short periods of unemployment, in which it would be wasteful to organize public works or to move the employee to another district where jobs are more numerous. Such an insurance scheme may provide a cushion for the small irregularities in employment. The larger irregularities have to be met in other ways.

ACCIDENT INSURANCE AND PHYSICAL HANDICAPS

In the inventory of risks occupational diseases and accidents have to be particularly noted. A scheme of compulsory workmen's compensation was provided for by a law of 1901. It is now substantially changed and administered in accordance with the Industrial Accident Insurance Act of 1916 and 1929. Every employed person and every apprenticed person is insured for all accidents when working or on the way to the place of work. If desired, a private insurance fund, with unlimited mutual liabilities, may be set up by employers. If this is not done, insurance must be provided through the State Insurance Institution (*Riksförsäkringsanstalten*). Not only industrial workers have to be so insured but also all domestic servants by their employers, the pupils in the trade schools by their school board, and so on. The entire cost of this insurance is levied on the employer, being, in fact, only a forced pooling of risks for covering his liabilities.

The benefits include *for accident and occupational sickness* the cost of all medical treatment and all supplies and a daily benefit if the illness lasts more than three days, calculated on the worker's annual earnings to a maximum of 3,000 crs. to increase progressively with income and amounting to two-thirds of that income, with a maximum of 5.50 crs. per day; *for remaining invalidism* an annuity equaling two-thirds of the annual earnings or, if partially injured, a lower sum and, if needing special treatment, a higher one although not surpassing previous income; and *in case of death* a funeral benefit with a minimum of 100 crs., an annuity to the widow or widower corresponding to one-fourth of the annual earnings and to each child under 16 years of age one-sixth of the earnings. In some cases parents are also entitled to annuities. The accumulated annuities should, however, not exceed two-thirds of the earnings of the deceased. Administrative costs are partly paid by the state.

Over 1.2 million employed (1,204,000 in 1937) are insured in the State Accident Insurance Institution while 619,000 workers are insured privately by their employers. In 1939, 13.7 million crs. were paid out in life annuities and nearly 18.4 million crs. for medical care, daily benefits, and so forth. A rigid factory inspection (since 1890) guards against employers charging accidents to their running expenses and, also independent of any insurance, works toward high standards of security all over the country.

If a person is permanently disabled for work, there can be no need for him to undergo repeated means tests and decisions as to how to obtain his living. In Sweden such cases have been thought typically fitted to receive pensions from the community, determined in proportion to their own income. For the family this is of practical importance both as to security for its breadwinner and so that the young will not have to carry insuperable burdens.

The pensions for invalids are exactly parallel to the national pensions earlier described. They may be enjoyed by anybody from the age of 16 who is not able to work for his own support. The technical limit for such disability becomes set as "inability to earn more than a third of what normal people in the same vocation and same locality can get." Control is fairly rigid with the applicant liable to an observation period in a public hospital in doubtful cases.

Similar cash pensions are paid to the blind from the age of 16. According to the law enacted in 1934 and in force since 1935 anyone whose "vision is so impaired that he is unable without assistance to make his way along a street or in a locality with which he is unacquainted" has the right to an annual amount of 500 crs. Those taken care of in a school or institution at the expense of the state and those with good private resources are not eligible. In 1940–1941, 3,420 cases were eligible for compensation for the blind, and the cost to the state was 1.65 million crs. In the census of 1930 the number of blind people was estimated at 6,000.

Crippled and blind persons are, however, not exactly well equipped to utilize a cash pension. Before the community acquiesces in hopelessness and pays for their minimum maintenance, moreover, much could often be done to rehabilitate those unfortunates and help them make some adjustment. This would operate particularly for the benefit of parents of handicapped children. They may look forward to some financial assistance when the child reaches 16 years of age, and they may before that time find helpful resources for his education and sometimes even complete care. Most interest has attached to the schooling of blind children. Such school attendance was made compulsory in 1896 and every parish was compelled to pay for such education. Primary schools with four grades for blind children give ordinary instruction, while blind children in the age groups above 10 years are in the Special Institute for the Blind at Tomteboda, Stockholm, where instruction is given for six years. All costs — including board, lodging, clothes, traveling — for these children are defrayed by the state and the provincial councils. The schooling is both general and vocational. For those afflicted with blindness at a later age two schools give special instruction. Many philanthropic agencies help the blind, but the state cooperates in such things as establishing depots for work material and exempting all such material from transportation charges.

The deaf and deaf-mutes have been similarly taken care of. Compulsory school attendance of the latter group covers eight years. The country is divided into seven districts for this with one such school in each district. The cost is borne by the local district and the state. Ninety per cent of the pupils are actually made to learn to speak and to read lips. Only the mentally backward have to rely on writing and gestures. The total number of deaf-mutes reported in the census of 1930 was 5,537. There were 672 in schools for the children in 1939.

Crippled children and persons becoming crippled as a result of infantile paralysis or other causes are given similar combined schooling and institutional care. This is partly achieved through the activity of the National Pension Board which has quite a wide program of health care, medical treatment, and vocational rehabilitation for its invalids and for persons threatened with invalidism. In this field, however, strong private organizations had early started to guard the interests of the cripples. The best means for state support therefore were judged to consist of generous grants to these institutions. Schools, clinics, trade schools, and homes for institutional cases are provided for about 1,200 cripples. Numbers of others are helped to get artificial limbs, work materials, marketing of their products, scholarships, and other aids.

In this whole world of the physically handicapped it is extremely difficult to judge whether what is done is adequate. Through state and community activities originating in many different forms, however, a family should have such provisions that it need not be reduced to hopelessness by the prospect of having such an onerous responsibility as a severely handicapped child.

Social Care of the Deficient and Delinquent

There remain several other classifications of the handicapped for whom protective measures are taken. The institutional care of the mentally diseased has grown considerably in recent years.

In earlier times most of the mild cases of mental disease went around as the village simpletons, living at home or being farmed out. Or they might be "sent on the round" like some of the poor cases. This refers to the old custom by which poor people had certain "days free" in succession among all the village households. It was a sort of cooperative organization of poor relief. The unmanageable, on the other hand, were locked up somewhere, in the almshouse or wherever they were safe. With rising humanitarian standards and medical understanding hospitals have come to be provided for ever-increasing numbers. No inference should be made that mental disease is increasing. It is certain only that organized care of the mentally diseased is increasing.

Mental hospitals are a state responsibility. They have been briefly discussed in an earlier context. Here it suffices to say that in addition a number of specialized institutions also exist, e.g., institutions for epileptic children.

Special classes in the public schools take care of large numbers of mentally backward children in ungraded groups. For the imbeciles who have capacity for learning some practical chores, boarding schools have been erected with care paid for by provincial councils. There are some 1,700 pupils in such schools. A number of these must have continued institutional protection and for them occupational homes, housing about 1,500 cases, have now been erected with the help of state subsidies. Asocial mental defectives are segregated in special institutions; approximately a thousand are so cared for. There are, finally, the institutions for the lowest category of mental defectives, the idiots. Institutions of different kinds are state-aided for a total of about 3,200 persons, while for idiots needing medical treatment the state itself administers two institutions with a capacity of about 750 patients.

This picture indicates lack of coordination. Socially minded experts in the field have long been demanding a more comprehensive program and one that will allow more special diagnosis and control than is often possible in the unconnected local institutions. Provisions for rural children of only slightly impaired mental ability are also lacking as ungraded classes are difficult to obtain in isolated districts. And, as everywhere, there is room for improvement in fitting defectives into the occupational structure. Finally, legislation is needed to make care of the mental defectives by a family or agency compulsory.

The same lack of legal system, although public funds are available, applies to all the physically and mentally handicapped mentioned. The families are nevertheless saved from having to carry alone the burden of children ill-fitted for the world. They can rest fairly well assured that their burden of caring for the incapable is being relieved, but they cannot be fully assured that the form of care is the best that science can prescribe. As, however, this is still less the case in regard to even normal children, it may not be the proper time to stress more reforms.

One of the worst family plights is to have an inebriate as one of its members. Particularly when the person is the father, the supporter and head of the family, the consequences are disastrous. Cruelty and beating may not even be reported to police for fear of revenge. In Sweden there was a time about 100 years ago when these unhappy conditions were extraordinarily oppressive. Drunkenness was widespread, but the missionary spirit was also strong. The temperance movement was one of the strongest forces in Swedish society during the nineteenth century. Indeed, it was this folk movement that laid the foundation of cooperative action for social betterment.

The struggles and successes of this movement shall not be related here. Only the present administrative setup may be briefly indicated. The chief means of restricting alcoholic consumption in Sweden is the state monopoly of the liquor trade. There is a system of rationing. The obtaining of a ration book is subject to rigid control and the maximum ration is limited to four liters of strong liquor a month. The chief guardian of temperance is the local Temperance Board to be found in every community. If none is specially appointed, the Poor Relief Board functions as a Temperance Board. By an act of 1913, in force since 1916 and revised in 1931, such a board may take action to remove a person who is intemperate in the use of alcohol to State Homes for Inebriates with a view to retraining for temperance. There are twelve such homes, two of which are for women. This internment of dangerous inebriates is, however, only the last of a number of preventive measures by the Temperance Board, which first gets in contact with the inebriate, warns him, and may withdraw the liquor book with which the drinker buys liquor from the only retailer, the state monopoly. Thus again is illustrated the close interlocking of the Swedish system of social rights and responsibilities, ideals and practical regulations which alone can make social intervention successful.

The number and role of prisons need not be treated here. The chief, and as yet unfulfilled, demand on the prison system from the family point of view is that imprisonment ought not to brand a whole family. At least divorce is made easy for persons married to those of long imprisonment. No provision is made for special indemnification for the family's loss of income.

Juvenile delinquency is a family problem of a different order. In that respect also Sweden has a different practice from most countries. Sweden does not legally admit that such a thing as criminality exists among children. The country therefore has no children's courts. The local Child Welfare Boards handle all complaints about juvenile delinquency just as they look to the welfare of children generally. They do not pass judgment, but they investigate cases and then proceed in an ascending scale of severity. First, they may warn the parents and the child. Second, they may admonish the child to visit certain community institutions aiding home education: a kindergarten, an afternoon club, a trade school, and so on. Third, they may transfer the child to the state home for protective education. These used, of course, to be just reform schools. In 1936 thoroughgoing investigations and public disapproval of their rigid methods led to a reorganization. The homes were transferred to state ownership, special courses were instituted for retraining of their personnel, and their very names were changed. At the end of 1939, 600 boys and 446 girls were in these institutions. If ideal conditions are not yet attained, there is at least concerted action to make these institutions truly reeducative and it must be remembered that there is a definite leveling of all institutions up to the standard of the best ones.

*   *

*

Better integration of the system of social insurance and social care is constantly going on in Sweden. A "mopping up" of imperfections is still needed, but by and large the Swedish social security as a system has advanced as far as it can without entangling the citizens in a net in which security hampers productivity. This is not a conservative view. The most radical social leaders now state that what is wanted is not more security but more constructive social policy: more work and housing possibilities for women supporters of families; more training and work for invalids and second-rate workers, e.g., the chronically diseased; more work and social planning against unemployment. We have visualized the end of the current era of social security in Sweden. The new things done and needing to be done belong to a period operating under another set of ideals. Before those ideals could be developed, however, this foundation had to be laid.

CHAPTER XX

OPPORTUNITIES FOR EDUCATION

E QUAL educational opportunities for all the youth of a country has come to be one of the most valued aspects of the creed of democracy. Education for their children is one of Swedish parents' most cherished ambitions. What they most want to gain by reducing the number of children to one or two perhaps is the possibility of "giving them a good education."

In the present stage of social development education is the main factor in social mobility. Even if the Swedish class structure is not rigid, the chances for the vocationally fixed to enter other groups are relatively limited. This holds true not only for what we may call horizontal mobility but also for vertical mobility within most occupations as they are organized in terms of competence. A person's basic education and first choice of vocation are actually becoming more and more decisive for life.

The expansive period of industrialization during the last century, with its golden times for the self-made man, has passed. During that period many roads were suddenly thrown open; a few people could have specific training; the bright and courageous had their chance. That was the time when the errand boy could hope to become chief of a world trust or the peasant boy a captain among contractors. Now such opportunities are becoming more and more rare. They may still exist on the fringes of the business world but in the bulk of the vocations and professions another order now prevails. Entrance into the occupational world is mainly attained through some form of training. It may be the academic type of training; or training in a practical school for commerce, trades, homemaking, or agriculture; or an apprenticeship in a craft or trade. Once working in the vocation, the pigeonhole is determined, often for life. Chance moving around into different lines of work is at present nearly unknown in Sweden. The Swedish occupational structure necessitated by the modern demands on specific training and perhaps strengthened by the typically Swedish predilection for skill and orderliness has had to sacrifice flexibility for security. Chances of "getting ahead" remain, however, even if promotion has to be achieved within one's own field and is often restricted by the vocational equipment first acquired. It should also be noted that the rich activities in civic organizations and in the broadly democratic politics in Sweden offer new avenues for personal ambitions. For all kinds of success, however, some schooling has come to be more important than ever.

If social mobility is made possible chiefly through education, it is understandable that parents early in their children's lives determine that they "are not going to stop where I had to." Educating the children to give them a starting point above the parents on the social ladder is thus characteristic of such a society as the Swedish, and it becomes a major problem of social engineering to readjust the national school system for its new task as the almost exclusive channel for regular social mobility between the generations.

Survey of School Facilities

A survey of how well the social system meets the ambitions of parents is thus indispensable for constructing a program of family policy. Such a comprehensive survey was not made by the Population Commission, as the whole Swedish educational system had been radically reformed in 1927. Only suggestions as to relatively minor reforms and adjustments were made by the Commission in order to supplement the nominal equalization of opportunities achieved in 1927 with a real equalization of the economic possibilities for utilizing the opportunities.

A brief survey of the Swedish school system is given here, partly in order to correct the conceptions about that system in foreign countries, which often lead to undue enthusiasm. Even in Sweden itself the accounts of how early compulsory education was started and of how completely illiteracy is eradicated have led to a tendency to overlook certain deficiencies obvious in any comparison with other countries.

The merits of the educational system may be listed first. Public school education has been compulsory for all Swedish children since 1842, the compulsion being recognized not only as the duty of the children to attend school but also as the duty of the community to provide educational facilities. Illiteracy has declined to such an extent that this classification now includes only the uneducable (idiots, individuals handicapped through blindness, etc.). According to the 1930 census only 0.11 per cent of all persons between 15 and 70 years of age and 0.31 per cent of all persons 70 years of age and over were unable to read or write, while an additional 0.09 and 4.5 per cent, respectively, in these different age groups knew only how to read and not how to write.

A system of trade schools and a high degree of integration between the primary and secondary schools has been an aid to educational progress in Sweden. The endeavor is further to equalize the standards of the grade schools all over the country. The state pays teachers' salaries for a seven-grade school in all districts, while the local community supports any additional grades. There is also but one standard of training for the teachers in the grade schools: a three-year course after high school for teachers in the two primary grades and a four-year course for teachers on the higher level. All the teacher-training institutions are state schools. No regional differences are tolerated. The teachers may move all over the country, thus increasing the uniformity of the system. Wherever they are, from primary grades through the university, they have permanent tenure.

The importance of this independence cannot be overestimated. The teachers are traditionally a highly esteemed group. Without this prestige of the teacher it is difficult to see how children could acquire respect for education. And without the teachers' independence of local pressure, it is difficult to see how children could acquire the respect for, and the habit of, free discussion and exchange of opinions that fundamentally are democracy. The Swedish teachers even take a vital part in politics, particularly in municipal affairs, and definitely affiliate with various political parties. There has been no vsible harm from this so long as three conditions exist: first, that the nation has a fairly high democratic culture; second, that there is no spoils system, positions and gratuities not being earned by party loyalty; third, and that is more or less both cause and effect of the second, that the parties are chiefly bearers of different sets of ideals and attitudes.

The primary school is the school for all social classes. Secondary schools are established so as to take over the children after the fourth or sixth school year. Up to puberty the school is for all pupils, being truly what it is called in Sweden the people's school (folkskola). Private preparatory schools for children from the higher income strata earlier played some role but they have not held out in the competition with the public schools.

To turn to the deficiencies of the grade schools, it must be said that the public school course is of too short duration. Since 1936 the compulsory school period has comprised seven school years of eight or nine months' duration. After that there is a continuation school of 180 hours minimum after 7 years of grade school and 360 hours after 6 years of grade school. This is compulsory for all who do not attend other schools. The great majority of Swedish children thus cease full-day schooling at the age of 14. Further opportunities exist, but they are not compulsory.

There are other respects in which the system falls short of the goal set for itself. In 1936, 5.8 per cent of all pupils attended school only half time. This condition has been permitted to continue in some rural districts with sparse population. Another deficiency is being attacked through consolidation of scattered schools. Still 4.3 per cent of the pupils in 1936 attended schools in which all grades were taught by one teacher, who had had training only for the primary grades. Otherwise, for the children who attend full-time schools, there is no difference in the quality of teachers so far as required training is concerned. As the rural districts offer teachers comparatively higher social status than the urban districts do and as they provide particularly good opportunities for civic activities and neighborhood leadership, those choosing to teach in rural schools are in no way inferior to the teachers in urban schools.

After the grade schools opportunities for both practical and academic work branch out. The trade school system offers training in industrial, commercial, domestic, agricultural, and handicraft vocations, often combined with part-time work in shops. From the trade schools pupils may graduate to higher technical, commercial, and agricultural colleges, for which entrance qualifications can also be acquired through academic secondary schools (*tekniska gymnasier,* etc.). Thus the academic and nonacademic pupils converge at several levels. The main criticism to be made of the trade schools is that, having been extended to the whole country only since 1918, they do not yet answer all the country's needs.

The most creditable feature of the secondary schools is that they are cheap. Practically all secondary schools are public, and it is a matter of suspicion if somebody "has to" go to a private school. The standards for secondary school teachers are high. University degrees obtained at about the age of 25 or 30 are required (M.A. in lower secondary schools, Ph.D. in higher). The status of these teachers too is correspondingly high, although perhaps not relatively so outstanding on their level of education and in relation to their pupils as the grade school teachers' prestige on their level.

The system is schematically as follows. After 6 years of grade school the pupil attends either a 4-year municipal high school or a state lower secondary school (*realskola*), or after 4 years of grade school he attends a 5-year state lower secondary school. These forms may end with an intermediate examination (*realskola-examen*). Thereafter many opportunities are open for positions in various practical and clerical occupations, for attending technical and commercial schools, for entrance into some civil service grades, for entering training schools for nurses and public school teachers, and so forth. Continuing higher studies of a more academic type means three or four additional years at a gymnasium. While the gymnasiums allow considerable specialization, they mainly concentrate on classics or on science. The final examination is the "student-examen." At the age of 19 or 20 the Swedish student thus has his university entrance qualification, which is required for many jobs and for entrance to professional schools.

Professional schools, which are practically all state schools, require 4 to

5 years of study at a university for a secondary school teacher, 10 years for a teacher in a gymnasium, 4 years for civil and naval engineers, 4 to 7 years for architects, 8 to 10 years for physicians, 3 to 4 years for dentists, and 5 years for lawyers and for theologians who are to enter the Swedish state church. The universities thus are designed solely for professional training and research. They are inheritors of the ideal of cultivation of learning and are not intended to give dashes of general culture. The idea of spending some time at a university in order to be polished off and obtain useful or pleasurable contacts is wholly foreign to Swedish thought. On the other hand, the appreciation of erudition and research may be said to be typical. The academic profession is traditionally awarded a social status higher than in any other country and is matched only by that of the occupants of the highest positions in the Swedish civil service.

The universities are self-governing, i.e., administered by the professors themselves. Even schools of lesser rank have a large degree of independence. The final control over this whole educational edifice is vested in state authorities, which are, however, strictly bound by laws and regulations guarding the rights of the teachers. For the students education is practically free. Small fees occur here and there. Laboratory supplies have to be paid for in some courses. Commercial training requires considerable expenditures because the professional schools in that field have been founded through private endowments, etc. By and large, however, cost is not a deterrent to higher education.

Looking at the secondary schools and institutions of higher learning from the point of view of shortcomings, it may be hazarded that they hide a weakness in their lack of adjustment to modern conditions of life. The lower secondary schools are, on the whole, the least progressive units in the whole Swedish edifice of schools. There also used to be a discrepancy, difficult for young students to adjust to, between the secondary schools, which up to the age of 18 to 20 kept the young under a rigid school routine that outlined the work for every hour of the day, and the universities which maintained the medieval ideals of free studies, in which the student plans his own work and takes his examination when he feels ready for it. On both sides some attempts have recently been made to remedy this disharmony without giving up the fundamental distinction between them.

The completion of the democratic educational system was the result of the reforms in 1927. At that time girls obtained the same rights as boys to secondary education totally financed from community funds. At the same time private schools were practically abolished, as they were then denied the state support they had had earlier. In private schools now will be found chiefly pupils who have to go there for some special reasons. The public institutions have the prestige.

To what extent do the young Swedes take advantage of these different educational opportunities? What is their educational level generally? Facts may be given first, and their implications analyzed later. The vast majority stop with the elementary school. The following percentages refer to the population 15 years of age and over, according to the census of 1930: elementary school only, 85.6 per cent; vocational school training, 5.1 per cent; special training or high school without university entrance requirements, 6.7 per cent; university entrance requirements and further academic studies, 2.5 per cent. In the younger age groups the proportions of those with more education are for obvious reasons somewhat higher.

There can be no doubt that a wider dissemination of vocational training and also of general academic work at the lower secondary level would be desirable, but there is no particular desire for larger numbers at the higher educational levels. Typical of the Swedish idea of democracy, the desire is to build from the bottom, to raise the minimum standards of education, and to enforce them over the entire country. This predilection, proper to a democracy of vigilant voters, makes all educational reforms expensive in Sweden. There can be no appropriation which is not aimed to lift the standard of all districts, to extent improved educational facilities to economically disadvantaged regions and groups.

ADJUSTING THE NATIONAL AND FAMILY COSTS OF SCHOOLING

The community carries most of the educational costs. So successfully has education been socialized that the public school system has become the prototype for organizing other needs of children on a more cooperative basis. Part of that success is explained by the economy inherent in a large state organization. Despite the fact that excessively large classes rarely exist, classes with more than 40 students being practically unknown in any type of school, the combined costs for the community, state, and municipality average approximately 240 crs. for pupils in the grade schools and 665 crs. for those in the secondary schools, exclusive of depreciation and interest on building costs. The averages conceal some regional variations, but even in Stockholm, the most expensive city, the cost per grade school pupil is not double the average. Although the public carries the main part of the educational costs some expenses remain for the parents, and these will always be subject to the general rule of increased pressure as the number of children grows.

In the cost of living studies earlier referred to (see chiefly Chapter 15), the private costs for educating children have been found to average 21, 51, and 135 crs. annually among industrial workers, clerical workers, and middle-class families, respectively. These chiefly reflect the utilization by the middle class of schools with higher tuition costs. In itself, this cost for education does not seem to be heavy. Compared with other countries, it really is trifling. It is still apparent when families of different size are compared (Table 36), however, that in the less well-to-do families it is the only child who will get the full benefit of this education. Educational costs seem to follow the general rule for all consumption that brother is brother's worst enemy. The competition among children's needs is once more illustrated.

TABLE 36. — EXPENDITURES FOR CHILDREN'S EDUCATION IN URBAN FAMILIES IN SWEDEN, BY FAMILY SIZE AND INCOME, 1933

FAMILY SIZE	TOTAL EXPENDITURES PER FAMILY WITH SPECIFIED INCOME			
	All income groups	Less than 3,000 crs.	3,000– 4,999 crs.	5,000 crs. or more
Families without children	—	—	—	—
Families with one child under 7 years	0.7	0.5	0.6	1.0
Families with one child 15 years and over . .	79.7	14.2	43.4	222.7
Families with 2–3 children under 7 years . . .	2.3	1.1	2.0	3.8
Families with 2–3 children under 15 years . .	55.3	8.8	35.1	131.9
Families with 4 children or more under 15 years	68.0	8.2	30.0	152.8
Families with 4 children or more, the oldest being 15 years and over	79.8	11.5	43.1	148.4

Source: Cost of Living Study, 1933 (*Levnadsvillkor och hushållsvanor i städer och industriorter omkring år 1933*).

The practical conclusion of an analysis of the data is that education could be more fully equalized through abolishing the remaining school fees and through provision of free school materials. These two suggestions were made by the Population Commission and since then other agencies have had them under investigation.

Through the school reforms of 1927 fees were in the main reduced to only "fuel-and-light" in state secondary schools. The cost of secondary education for girls, earlier expensive as girls were not allowed to attend the state secondary schools and gymnasiums, was considerably reduced as a result of this reform. The proposal to eliminate all school fees has nearly been realized since the Board of Education made a report in 1938 concerning the increased state subsidies which would be necessary.

The question of free school materials had previously been attacked by some local communes, about one-tenth of them, particularly the large ones, having already provided such material. In this respect the Population Commission found it appropriate to suggest that all school material be given free to all pupils in the compulsory grade school. Poor children, who have sometimes been helped by being allowed to borrow textbooks from a school stock or library, would be the ones to profit most by having a shelf of fundamental books on different subjects when leaving school. A special committee was asked to prepare such a proposal for the government. This resulted in a report in 1939. Since the principle of free school materials has already been realized in the other Scandinavian countries, the same step will in all probability be quickly taken in Sweden. The cost to the state would amount to 5.2 million crs. annually, of which 3.1 million crs. have previously been paid by local communes.

Incidental costs, such as fees and materials, are, however, not the chief element that makes education available to some and prohibitive to others. Any reduced or even free tuition can never be truly democratic as long as the economic maintenance of pupils during the period of study is overlooked. Economic hardships are still connected with lower secondary and vocational education when parents do not live in a locality with the desired type of school and with higher training in all cases where it is a problem of whether the young man or woman can afford to postpone earning his own living.

Rural children and children in small towns are especially handicapped by living at a distance from schools. A survey of localities from which the students came to the universities showed that for each 100,000 of population living in cities, 247 students came to the university; from smaller cities without secondary schools, 137; and from the country, only 47.

Many of the measures already treated in other chapters as forming part of the population program are more favorable for densely populated areas than for rural areas. For that reason it is doubly necessary to compensate rural youth by making possible the attainment of some of its desired opportunities. Foremost among these are educational opportunities. A movement in that direction has been started by consolidating grade schools, aided by the utilization of buses. At the next stage of trade schools and lower secondary schools it will, however, be impossible to collect all children every day, even by school buses and other means of travel. The Population Commission therefore suggested state stipends for board and lodging of rural children. The Board of Education has made a report on the problem, presenting a definite proposal in July, 1939.

A similar problem exists for higher learning or professional training. Most young people need to work for their own support in the years between 16 and 20. Very few can finance studies almost up to their thirties. The selection of students for higher education has thus remained chiefly on an economic basis despite efforts at democratization. Also the credit system long used for financing studies in Sweden is most available to young people who can offer adequate security.

The Swedish people have always cherished the illusion that higher learning is democratically available. A study in 1936 [*213*] on the economic and social position of students might have brought a rather unpleasant revelation (Tables 37 and 38). The comparison made in Table 38 was, however, not presented. An investigation with such results would soon have to be followed by a proposal for an improved state of affairs. In this particular case the Minister of Education, Mr. Arthur Engberg, took a personal interest and developed the plan for an "open house and open table" for superior students. A proposal for free board and lodging was drafted by a special committee in 1937.

Scholarships have existed since the founding of the universities with donations increasing annually in number and amounts. These scholarships have been a great aid but have rarely been large enough to assure students of their living. Nearer the ideal have been the state study loans, free of interest during the period of study for both university students and other pupils without economic resources. These constitute a compromise, however. They are not just gifts, since they must be repaid, but yet they are not large enough and the number is far too small. Only from 12 to 15 per cent of the applicants obtain loans. The average loan has declined to about 1,000 crs. At least double that sum would have to be available for students who have no other economic assets.

In order fully to understand the economic situation of a Swedish university student it should be realized that rarely is he able to earn money and work his way through as is so customary in the United States. The explanation for this difference is without doubt found partly in the more aristocratic traditions of Swedish university life. But in modern time the studies are also so organized that they hardly give him enough free time, and in addition the labor market is so organized that irregular work is practically excluded. The Swedish student has, however, had much easier access to regular credit than in any other country. Besides the state loans mentioned above, saving banks and the ordinary commercial banks have traditionally been prepared to make loans to a student, if substantial persons in his locality would underwrite it. Many poor youth have been able to finance their studies in this way. As the statistics show, however, the economic hindrances still result in a biased selection from the social, and presumably also intellectual, point of view. Hence, the committee proposed that the state should give a number of stipends to bright but poor students to be used for board and lodging.[1] Its main arguments were the public interest in a fairer selection of students according to intelligence and ability and not economic means, resulting in greater social mobility and higher professional standards. As a start such stipends should be available only for students attending the two state universities in Upsala and Lund and the state medical school in

---

[1] Swedish university students never live in dormitories.

TABLE 37. — UNIVERSITY STUDENTS IN SWEDEN [a] FROM DIFFERENT OCCUPATIONAL CLASSES

OCCUPATION OF FATHER	PER CENT OF STUDENTS SPECIALIZING IN			
	Theology	Law	Medicine	Science
Total	100.0	100.0	100.0	100.0
Professional men, teachers, and civil servants with university training	19.5	37.9	33.9	30.4
Civil service	5.8	14.1	10.6	8.3
Teachers in grade schools	8.5	3.3	4.8	7.8
Industrialists and businessmen	2.9	15.4	13.7	6.9
Retailers	9.8	10.4	12.7	9.9
Clerical workers and low grade officials . . .	12.8	6.1	7.2	10.5
Farmers	17.9	7.0	8.8	13.0
Workers	22.2	5.6	7.9	12.5
Unknown	0.6	0.2	0.4	0.7

[a] Based on a survey of a limited number of schools.

Source: Wicksell, Sven, and Larsson, Tage, *Utredning rörande de Svenska universitets — och högskolestudenternas sociala och ekonomiska förhållanden*, Lund, 1936.

TABLE 38. — INCOME OF FATHERS OF UNIVERSITY STUDENTS AND OF ALL MALES 40 YEARS OF AGE AND OVER IN SWEDEN

INCOME (Crs.)	PER CENT OF UNIVERSITY STUDENTS WITH FATHERS IN SPECIFIED INCOME CLASS	PER CENT OF MEN 40 YEARS OF AGE AND OVER IN TOTAL POPULATION IN SPECIFIED INCOME CLASS
Total	100.0	100
Less than 1,500	9.8	39
1,500–2,499	7.9	20
2,500–4,499	18.6	19
4,500–7,499	18.0	6
7,500–9,499	7.9	1
9,500 or more	33.5	3
Unknown [a]	4.3	12

[a] Unknown income ordinarily means an income under the tax limit of 600 crs.

Source: Calculations by E. von Hofsten based on data from Sven Wicksell and Tage Larsson and on the 1930 Swedish Census.

Stockholm. In the 1939 session of the Riksdag a grant of 220,700 crs. was voted for the first year. In 1940, 194,700 crs. were granted. Cash loans from the fund mentioned above are also available to the beneficiaries of the special stipends.

More schools want the same opportunities for their pupils. The United Student Corporations have strongly expressed the opinion that such stipends ought to be granted to all student groups. They would be a sound investment in terms of higher quality among the professional elite. At the same time, one of the most severely felt inequalities in Swedish society would be removed.

Behind all this public responsibility for the democratization of higher education, there is no romantic notion that such education ought to be made much more common. Not the quantity but the quality of the students has to be raised. Not increased opportunities but a more equitable distribution of opportunity is demanded. There exists no expectation or desire in Sweden to make higher education available to larger and larger masses as the foundation of general culture. It is instead fully realized that increasing the number of students can only lead to reducing quality. Higher education is thus to be kept for the few in order to be truly adequate for the higher degrees of intelligence. But this small group should be selected more democratically among the people and the overrepresentation of the ones who have economic well-being as their chief asset should be reduced. This process, however, is not to be achieved by prohibitive measures but only through increasing the competition by an influx of fresh new intelligence from the broad masses. A democracy is particularly dependent for successful operation upon whether it has a fair representation of the people in its administrative and governing posts. A democracy in which the laboring classes had the political power but only the sons of the capitalists executed power would suffer from dangerous tensions.

ADULT EDUCATION

This reluctance to enlarge the institutions of higher education must be seen against the background of other cultural possibilities. The high degree of civic activity and political participation in Sweden today is certainly desirable and should be increased. It is, however, in the main not attributable to the system of formal schooling but to the never-ceasing adult education. True culture cannot be spoon-fed. It comes only as a result of individual activities and thus emanates chiefly from the educative process that goes on outside of schools. Adult education thus becomes a foundation stone for the whole structure of democratic education. It does not raise new claims on major reforms in order to achieve justice or present greater advantages to families with children. It is nevertheless of tremendous importance in a population policy. Adult education is the one vehicle which truly and without a hint of coercion can disseminate new knowledge and implant new attitudes toward the family among the people. It is the medium best adapted for country-wide enlightenment in sex hygiene and birth control and the one which can also best integrate family education and practical knowledge about home conditions so that these will be a respected part of the citizen's life and not a fad taught in schools and put away with the textbooks. Finally, it is the medium which has made the great majority of the adult population so civic conscious that they can debate social issues, such as the population program, coherently and intelligently. They thus are the most solid help both for voting for the adoption of that program and for seeing it materialize in specific reforms.

This expansion of the educational media beyond formal schools has been realized or, in order not to make Swedish society seem suprarational, it has just happened to be the trend in Sweden. Adult education has had a tremendous expansion. Starting with libraries and popular lectures, it acquired its first stronghold in the folk high school (*folkhögskola*), patterned originally after the famous Danish ones. Sixty of these have courses for young men and women around 20 years of age running from October to May and continuing for two years if wanted. Many of the schools are conducting extra summer courses mostly for young women. Chiefly rural youth, but lately also industrial workers, have their own folk high schools. These schools are free from examinations and formalism and are built upon informal instruction and discussion among students living together. About 5,000 to 6,000 young people attend these schools annually, deriving from them no direct training for careers but a solid foundation for practical life, for intellectualizing everyday activities, for tempering political and economic issues with common sense. State stipends are paid to the young people for attending these schools. State grants are available to the schools, and the provincial governments have taken over most of their upkeep.

Most important of all, however, adult education means the genuinely Swedish institution of study circles. Some operate with an expert leader and some just involve meetings based around a book, a radio series, a study plan from the central office, or a more experienced fellow worker. Studies are always in the form of discussion. The most valuable educational result is the stable but critical and yet positive outlook that the Swedish worker possesses. True democratic education is possible only in such schools without a teacher, where there is no pressure to agree with the instructor.

Two features should be noted concerning the Swedish adult education movement which help to explain why it is a force in a democracy and why it does not need any fundamental reform. First, it is education not only for the people but by the people. It is created by the members of the great

popular (folk) movements themselves: trade-unions, consumers' cooperatives, women's organizations, lodges, farm youth, church members. It has
never been started by educational authorities or philanthropic individuals.
The state support of 41,500 crs. granted in 1940 is only for organizational
costs. An additional small sum has generally been granted for university
circles for which university instructors are employed. The main support is
obtained indirectly through the state grants to libraries (1.6 million crs. in
1940). The subsidy for each local library is computed according to the number of study groups served.

Second, adult education serves no one purpose. It is neither meant for
helping individual careers nor is it carried on as labor-tinged propaganda.
A glance at the selection of subjects will show that. The list is headed by
organization technique and problems, that is, for serving in the chosen movement of politics and ideals. Next come languages, chiefly English in later
years. This self-study is amazingly efficient in comparison with prolonged
school exercises with unwilling pupils. Third are political science and local
government, studied objectively with attention to current problems. Next
are singing and music. In this the nonutilitarian character of this educational
movement is obvious. Trade-unionism and arithmetic follow. If any criticism is to be made, it is that individual and political interests have received
more attention than family problems. This is both a cause and an effect
of the smaller participation of women than of men. Ten years ago only
16 per cent of the participants were women. Now, however, they constitute
30 per cent of the total. Particularly the population problem and the ensuing
mass of new social legislation have aroused the interest of women. As a
reciprocal effect also a favored place has been gained for these subjects. They
were chosen as the central subjects for 1939–1940.

When it is said that the different adult education movements do not prepare for careers, this should be taken as true both of their aims and also of
the interests which bring the students in. On the other hand, a civic and political career may open up for those having educated themselves. This in
turn makes a new form of social mobility possible outside the formal school
channel but still with education as one of its foremost vehicles. It is often
these ardent students with their practical but critical turn of mind, intrin-
sically loyal to the great folk movements of which they are a part, from
whom the administrators of municipal affairs are recruited. Through the
special form of Swedish democracy, with its many small, honorary but laborious posts on councils, boards, and so forth, an outlet is created for all
of this self-trained political intelligence. Also in labor unions, cooperative
councils, and other organizations, the officers are largely drawn from this
same group. Their advancement to the Riksdag, which mostly consists of
farmers and workers, and even to the Cabinet has been noteworthy in the

last two decades of Swedish political life. These careers in local and national politics and administration are a national continuation of adult education. It could also be said that the wide political participation of a large proportion of the people not only as voters at elections but also as representatives and functionaries is itself active adult education.

This means that both cultural participation and a career of advancement and importance outside the purely vocational sphere are sensed as attainable by practically everybody. These are also the reasons why the exclusive belief in formal schools as educational agencies does not exist in Sweden. It has rather been feared that school training for too many years would saturate youth and make them close their minds to further education, training, and reading instead of preparing them for education as a never-ceasing process. The program, then, as interpreted from tendencies and attitudes in Sweden would result in widening educational opportunities for occupational purposes, whether through academic or vocational training, and in reducing their cost. This leaves educational opportunities for democratic participation and culture to be molded by the adult citizens themselves.

CHAPTER XXI

RECREATION AND THE FAMILY

M AN does not live by bread alone. A family policy that merely provides food, shelter, and economic security is not sufficient. The need of enjoyment is also important. In a word, there are times in the life of an individual when a victrola means as much to him as vitamins. The poor, even when fed and housed, have human desires. They want leisure, and in their leisure they want some recreation. And this no less than food is an economic problem. In it, too, the cardinal question is the number of children in the family, for the more children there are, the less there is to spend on recreation.

That is where public authorities have always sinned. From degrading poor relief to dignified social security the one common characteristic has been the deadly boredom to which the beneficiaries have been condemned. What representatives of the old ways of thinking have greatest difficulty in tolerating is the festivity and pleasure that now sometimes become part of some public institutions, schools first of all. Here is a fundamental dilemma in all social aid. As long as our social thinking was concerned with repairing the worst ills of poverty, recreational needs could not be recognized. A somewhat revengeful attitude was natural, letting the poor suffer as a stimulus for them to try to attain a richer life.

The population viewpoint in social policy necessitates a change in attitude in this respect. Children should only be born as a matter of joy; whatever kills that joy misses its effect. That is one reason why all means tests are so inappropriate in regard to a social policy in favor of families. General considerations about the necessity of safeguarding the element of joy in the lives of families have to be kept in mind in the formation of practically all of the programs discussed above, which advocate a generosity that would not be necessary if the goal was only to help people already born just to survive.

An intelligently conceived family policy must also directly safeguard facilities for inexpensive recreation. It must, furthermore, contrive to release the parents, the mothers especially, for participation in extrafamilial activities.

It must also encourage such forms of recreation as can be enjoyed by the whole family.

FAMILY DEPRIVATION OF RECREATION AND CULTURE

The most cursory consideration of family finance shows that there is sharp competition between having children and enjoying recreation. The more children the less recreation is the general rule.

The Swedish study of cost of living in 1933 revealed some such conflicts in its figures on expenditures for books and culture. The data in Table 39 must be read in the light of the fact that they are for urban households. The same relationship is to be found in the figures showing expenditures for participation in civic activities, trade unions, adult education programs, and

TABLE 39. — EXPENDITURES FOR CULTURE IN URBAN FAMILIES IN SWEDEN, BY INCOME AND FAMILY SIZE, 1933

INCOME AND FAMILY SIZE	TOTAL EXPENDITURES PER FAMILY			
	All cultural costs (crs.)	Books (crs.)	Newspapers (crs.)	Stationery, telephone, etc. (crs.)
Income less than 3,000 crs.				
Families without children	62.4	17.5	26.0	18.9
Families with 2–3 children under 7 years . . .	49.3	12.1	30.2	7.0
Families with 4 children or more under 15 years	39.0	6.2	25.0	7.8
Income of 3,000–4,999 crs.				
Families without children	118.2	35.1	42.9	40.2
Families with 2–3 children under 7 years . . .	81.1	20.6	37.7	22.8
Families with 4 children or more under 15 years	69.8	13.9	32.4	23.5
Income of 5,000 crs. or more				
Families without children	191.5	61.6	44.9	85.0
Families with 2–3 children under 7 years . . .	151.2	56.5	39.2	55.5
Families with 4 children or more under 15 years	189.0	54.3	46.5	88.2
All income groups				
Families without children	115.4	34.9	38.2	42.3
Families with one child under 7 years	105.6	30.7	36.4	38.5
Families with one child 15 years and over . .	99.6	26.1	39.9	33.6
Families with 2–3 children under 7 years . . .	94.1	29.4	36.1	28.6
Families with 2–3 children under 15 years . .	99.6	23.0	38.5	38.1
Families with 4 children or more under 15 years	104.5	26.2	35.7	42.6
Families with 4 children or more, the oldest being 15 years and over	92.3	20.7	36.7	34.9

Source: Cost of Living Study, 1933 (*Levnadsvillkor och hushållsvanor i städer och industriorter omkring år 1933*).

similar activities, which play so large a part in Swedish democracy. The sacrificial costs for labor solidarity may also be traced in Table 40.

Gifts play an important role in social life in Sweden. For all kinds of personal occasions, weddings, birthdays, silver weddings, and other anniversaries, there are collections for gifts. They may also to a certain degree be regarded as entrance tickets to, or their lack at least as excluding from, some types of social contacts.

TABLE 40. — EXPENDITURES FOR SOCIAL CONTACTS IN URBAN FAMILIES IN SWEDEN, BY INCOME AND FAMILY SIZE, 1933

INCOME AND FAMILY SIZE	TOTAL EXPENDITURES PER FAMILY			
	All social costs (crs.)	Dues to occupational organizations[a] (crs.)	Dues to political and social clubs[b] (crs.)	Gifts[c] (crs.)
Income less than 3,000 crs.				
Families without children	145.7	55.7	4.7	85.3
Families with 2–3 children under 7 years . . .	98.8	57.3	4.2	37.3
Families with 4 children or more under 15 years	95.2	53.7	3.9	37.6
Income of 3,000–4,999 crs.				
Families without children	155.4	26.4	9.2	119.8
Families with 2–3 children under 7 years . . .	146.3	42.5	7.4	96.4
Families with 4 children or more under 15 years	105.1	35.4	2.4	67.3
Income of 5,000 crs. or more				
Families without children	133.1	33.0	13.6	186.5
Families with 2–3 children under 7 years . . .	210.1	29.6	13.3	177.2
Families with 4 children or more under 15 years	219.3	28.2	30.9	160.2
All income groups				
Families without children	167.3	36.5	8.7	122.1
Families with one child under 7 years	162.8	39.8	11.5	111.5
Families with one child 15 years and over . .	146.2	41.7	9.2	95.3
Families with 2–3 children under 7 years . . .	156.2	42.5	8.4	105.3
Families with 2–3 children under 15 years . .	151.9	41.3	10.2	100.4
Families with 4 children or more under 15 years	142.7	36.9	12.6	93.2
Families with 4 children or more, the oldest being 15 years and over	131.3	45.6	8.6	77.1

[a] Trade unions, teachers' organizations, etc.
[b] Temperance lodges, churches other than the state church, adult education, etc.
[c] Does not include gifts to members of the household or used clothing but does include periodical allowances.

Source: Cost of Living Study, 1933 (*Levnadsvillkor och hushållsvanor i städer och industriorter omkring år 1933*).

Expenditures for travel, including not only pleasure trips but also commuting, are likewise related to family size (Table 41). The cutting down of these expenses to a lower total the more family members there are is thus interesting. In some degree this must offset the natural tendency for the

TABLE 41. — EXPENDITURES FOR AMUSEMENTS AND TRAVEL IN URBAN FAMILIES IN SWEDEN, BY INCOME AND FAMILY SIZE, 1933

INCOME AND FAMILY SIZE	TOTAL EXPENDITURES PER FAMILY					
	All recreational costs (crs.)	Amusements [a] (crs.)	Sport materials (crs.)	Toys, etc.[b] (crs.)	Travel [c] (crs.)	Own vehicles [d] (crs.)
Income less than 3,000 crs.						
Families without children	103.3	25.7	0.8	7.1	57.1	12.6
Families with 2–3 children under 7 years .	96.4	20.4	1.8	9.1	47.5	17.6
Families with 4 children or more under 15 years	46.3	12.6	3.5	6.8	14.8	8.6
Income of 3,000–4,999 crs.						
Families without children	213.8	37.0	7.7	12.9	120.3	35.9
Families with 2–3 children under 7 years .	177.1	26.2	2.8	15.5	86.5	28.1
Families with 4 children or more under 15 years	144.7	27.2	4.9	11.7	72.9	28.0
Income of 5,000 crs. or more						
Families without children	610.1	87.0	4.2	29.6	184.1	305.2
Families with 2–3 children under 7 years .	345.2	47.4	19.9	44.9	164.9	68.1
Families with 4 children or more under 15 years	297.2	39.2	10.6	30.5	127.7	89.2
All income groups						
Families without children	255.8	43.1	5.0	14.3	113.3	80.1
Families with one child under 7 years . .	210.8	39.2	4.8	20.8	113.4	32.6
Families with one child 15 years and over .	193.8	47.5	2.9	13.6	90.0	39.8
Families with 2–3 children under 7 years .	199.5	31.1	7.8	22.9	100.1	37.6
Families with 2–3 children under 15 years .	116.9	38.7	8.8	18.7	102.2	48.5
Families with 4 children or more under 15 years	176.4	28.2	6.5	17.2	79.4	45.1
Families with 4 children or more, the oldest being 15 years and over	197.5	49.7	8.3	12.8	91.2	35.5

[a] Entrance fees to theaters, circus, etc., radio license, dues to sport clubs and other purely social clubs, and children's allowances.
[b] Camera, films, radio, smaller musical instruments, and losses in hazard playing.
[c] Tickets and costs for baggage but not for food and hotels.
[d] Bicycles, boat, automobile plus all costs for same (fuel, insurance, taxes, etc.).

Source: Cost of Living Study, 1933 (*Levnadsvillkor och hushållsvanor i städer och industriorter omkring år 1933*).

larger families to move to the more countrylike atmosphere on the outskirts of towns.

Finally, a series of comparisons may be given which show consumption on the borderline between necessities and luxuries (Table 42). That cost for bodily care should be smaller totally in a large family than in a childless one is important as indicative of the cultural and aesthetic decline following child-bearing. From the items on help in the house it may be judged how much leisure the mother may be able to have. Not only labor but also social isolation is reflected in the figures for household help in the families with chil-

TABLE 42. — EXPENDITURES FOR COMFORT IN URBAN FAMILIES IN SWEDEN, BY INCOME AND FAMILY SIZE, 1933

INCOME AND FAMILY SIZE	TOTAL EXPENDITURES PER FAMILY		
	Bodily care[a] (crs.)	Servants[b] (crs.)	Temporary help in home[c] (crs.)
Income less than 3,000 crs.			
Families without children	27.1	—	2.5
Families with 2–3 children under 7 years . . .	25.0	7.6	1.4
Families with 4 children or more under 15 years .	19.9	—	2.1
Income of 3,000–4,999 crs.			
Families without children	52.7	0.8	10.6
Families with 2–3 children under 7 years . . .	35.2	9.1	6.1
Families with 4 children or more under 15 years .	25.8	5.8	8.0
Income of 5,000 crs. or more			
Families without children	68.5	52.7	11.9
Families with 2–3 children under 7 years . . .	69.4	152.9	26.3
Families with 4 children or more under 15 years .	53.5	191.3	22.9
All income groups			
Families without children	48.0	10.5	8.4
Families with one child under 7 years	48.7	36.3	11.7
Families with one child 15 years and over . . .	43.3	16.2	8.5
Families with 2–3 children under 7 years . . .	43.0	52.9	11.1
Families with 2–3 children under 15 years . . .	42.7	33.3	11.1
Families with 4 children or more under 15 years .	34.2	69.1	11.9
Families with 4 children or more, the oldest being 15 years and over	36.4	15.1	10.0

[a] Soaps, beauty preparations, hairdresser, toothbrushes, etc.
[b] Cash payments to permanent servants but not value of board and lodging.
[c] Cash payments to temporary help, fees to day nursery, etc.

Source: Cost of Living Study, 1933 (*Levnadsvillkor och hushållsvanor i städer och indus-triorter omkring år 1933*).

dren. A low average for cost of servants denotes, of course, that some few families have domestic servants while the majority have none or at the most employ a laundress.

From all the figures for culture and recreation two practical suggestions can be drawn. One is that the costs of rearing children should be subsidized to such an extent that something may be left of the family income to allow for more than the most drab and boring thriftiness. The second is that more abundant recreational facilities must be developed for larger families and for the individual members of such families, the mothers first of all.

PROVIDING RECREATIONAL FACILITIES FOR FAMILIES

Demands for extended recreational facilities for families, and especially for children and housewives, must be appraised in relation to the recent legislation which makes holidays with pay a legal right for all workers. The 1938 session of the Swedish Riksdag created by law what has been called the people's vacation, [43] following the recommendation in 1936 of the International Labour Office. All persons employed in private or public service who have worked at least six months during the year have the right to a continuous vacation with full pay of one day for every month they have worked in the previous year. When this law gave the formal right to a paid vacation, both the state and the large civic organizations at once became conscious of the responsibility for providing the means to enjoy it.

One committee presented a proposal restricting the right of private persons to monopolize nature — woods, shores, and mountains — as private property. [44] A vehement discussion has been carried on concerning the proposal to reserve seashores as public grounds and to forbid the erection of private houses on them unless special permission is granted. These attempts build on an old tradition. According to Swedish law, a property owner is generally not allowed to keep people away from his land but only from the lot where he has his house, his "yard." Picking berries in the forests has always been an unrestricted common right for anybody, while hunting and fishing require a license.

Other suggestions have dealt with facilities for constructing summer homes and particularly vacation villages where cottages could be rented. The Cooperative Housing Society has already in the last 10 years carried out this idea of a cooperatively owned seaside resort with permanent homes, cottages for rent, a restaurant, and a separate camp for children (*Årsta Havsbad* near Stockholm). To prevent the development of a profit interest in this field, such cooperative organizations and the Workers' Travel Association have sponsored similar projects and state subsidies for the purpose have even been discussed. Such projects naturally increase the opportunities for joint family vacations. The Swedish Tourist Association with its membership of over 180,000 dues-paying members at the end of 1939 has for decades provided information about and cheap access to enjoyable nature. It has dotted the country with tourist cottages, youth hostels, mountain huts, ski tracks, and, in short, made into a vast folk movement what in many other countries is provided or not provided according to private profit interests.

At the beginning of the population discussion the State Railway, which now controls practically all lines in Sweden, began to issue family tickets for travel by large families. Any family group without regard to economic resources can, when traveling together, pay for two adult tickets and thereafter pay one-fourth price for the tickets of any additional family members under 21 years of age. In order further to facilitate vacation travel for a family as a family unit it has been proposed by the Committee on Recreation that round-trip family tickets at reduced prices be issued for extended periods. It has also been proposed that greater reductions should be made for families at periods slightly out of season in resort districts, such as the seaside and mountains. These social advantages are easily put on a sound business basis when a country has, as does Sweden, a largely socialized system of railroads.

Vacations have thus first been provided for the employed. Distinct efforts are also being made to make possible recreation on a family basis. But what about the mothers "employed" in their own homes with no employer against whom to assert their right to a vacation and no one to substitute for them during their absence?

The unique position of the homemaker is worthy of closer scrutiny. First it must be stated, however, that only a minority of the homemakers are what may be called active mothers. A calculation in the Swedish extra census of 1935–1936 demonstrated that no less than 45.8 per cent of all families with both husband and wife living had no children under 15 years of age living at home and that 24.0 per cent had no children whatsoever in the house. Only about one-eighth of all married women (12.0 per cent) had to function in active motherhood with 3 or more children under 15 at home.[1] Such statistical realism first reduces all problems of mothers' recreation to a problem of limited dimensions. If women without children are not able to safeguard their own recreation, they certainly have no claim on public favors. Also mothers in families with both children and a servant should be excluded from public pity. Still, the residual problem for the minority of active mothers carries its direct population importance because they are the ones to care for the children and because their situation serves as an example to others, thus motivating more family limitation.

In comparison with other groups in society the homemaking mother still

[1] This does not coincide with data presented in Table 14, which were tabulated on a somewhat different basis.

retains more personal freedom as to how she spends her daily time and arranges her work within the home. But what about leisure if on account of children she is not free to leave the house or in possession of any independent means to do anything with her free time? And what about the isolation, the incessant servitude which is fatiguing just because it has no definite limits, and, in many cases, the actual exhaustion?

The Population Commission may be quoted on the subject of helping these mothers, which sometimes has been thought too commonplace a matter to deserve treatment in the serious setting of a public report.

Under the industrial conditions at present prevailing, a mother is becoming more and more tied down. It is a nervous strain for her to give a child the almost 24-hour attention it needs during its first years. Even if this aspect of child care does not loom too large with the advent of the first child, it may be a motive for further limitation of children. The mother wants to be free and regain leisure again. This desire for greater leisure should not be condemned on moral grounds as a lack of responsibility. It is better to understand its psychological implications. It must be compared with the great deal of personal mobility that the young women have enjoyed before marriage, with the husband's and wife's social and recreational life together before the advent of children, with the continuation of the husband's life outside of the home, filled with recreational and social interests, and with the richer social life which on the whole characterizes all population groups in our day. . . .

Just as the added expenses of children serve to lower the economic standard of the family, so is this confinement an extra burden on the mobility of the parents, changing too much their mode of life before and after the birth of children. Just as it is assumed that relief from certain extra expenses connected with children would have a positive influence from a population aspect, so it is similarly assumed that if there could be some relaxation from the confinement during the earliest years of children, the influence would be the same. The question, however, should not be considered from the point of view of population policy alone but also from the viewpoint of the mothers' demands for happiness and spiritual growth. [15]

Being on duty 24 hours a day and 12 months a year, as most mothers of young children are, their problem is a twofold one, both of getting an annual vacation and of getting some daily, or at least weekly, leisure time. Both problems can be fairly easily solved for the classes that have private servants. Servants, like most other luxuries, however, have a pronounced tendency to appear in the families without children. They do so first for personal reasons. Having a choice, which is a consequence of their scarcity, the domestic servants prefer families where they are not tied down and irritated by children. They do so still more for economic reasons, as the families with children are those which can spend least on servants' wages.

It has been calculated that in Sweden less than 100,000 of the 700,000 homes with children have domestic servants, although the number of servants exceeds 200,000. While the professional group find servants a normal solution of their child supervision problems, it is not normal in the sense that it is available for the average mother. Nor is it conceivable that anyone would recommend that social measures should be taken to subsidize from public funds the employment of private servants, even for homes with children. The continuous services of more than one female person per household could not be provided for in a national economy with limited means and a normal sex ratio. A future has rather to be foreseen in which a still smaller proportion of families will have at their command private servants as a prerequisite for mothers' recreation. Other ways of solving that problem have to be investigated.

Special measures have been experimented with in regard to an annual vacation for housewives. In 1938 the idea was tried out of giving a number of housewives, who had long been in need of a vacation, a holiday with state pay. Special stipends were provided for their visit to take courses arranged at the folk high school at Gripsholm. In 1939 this experimental activity was continued and extended. Weeks of rest, discussions, excursions, and lectures in varying combinations and proportions for various groups have been tried.

The great majority of mothers and housewives must, however, seek their vacations together with, or at least in the same form as, other groups of the population. Plans and programs especially for mothers are in the main unnecessary. But there will always be the question of how to procure a substitute for a mother if she does have the opportunity to go away. The time-honored custom of having relatives or neighbors take on an extra duty for the household at such times has been passing as a natural consequence of the splitting up of family and neighborhood groups. Quite recently the Housewives' National Organization in Sweden has attempted through its clubs to reinstitute such neighborhood services among the members, one member taking care of the children for a time in exchange for the same service at another time. In some degree this attempt will probably continue to succeed, thus giving an interesting illustration of how old primary social formations are expanded into purposively organized groups with a community of interests as the basis. Thus the very conception of neighborhood becomes a dynamic and selective force rather than the community of blood relationship or habitation as of old.

Organization of exchange services for temporary supervision in each other's households or even lodging of each other's children is one of the avenues opened up anew. Another service, which has been sponsored by some of the voluntary, civic organizations, is the labor service by young girls, chiefly college students and others. This idea, which is also only tentatively being tried out since 1938, obviously owes something to the influence

---

of the German labor camps. The girls are housed in a camp or more often in a large house on some estate. They are under the control of some person chosen by the organization and they give part of their time to some home in which the mother wants to go away on a vacation. As a method for passing summer vacations for young girls otherwise not compelled to work, this is probably excellent. As few housewives would, however, leave their homes in the inexperienced hands of these young girls, their services may in the long run mean less for facilitating housewives' vacations and more for alleviating overfatiguing work for housewives staying at home as supervisors. They will also undoubtedly have certain consequences in substituting but underbidding for domestic and agricultural servants. If the movement takes on greater proportions, it will have to be judged chiefly by its effect on labor conditions. As yet it is mainly a harmless experiment in giving domestic training to young girls.

A further possibility is the most important one, namely, the utilization of professional labor to substitute for the housewives in their absence. That problem has first had to be faced for more urgent causes of absence, i.e., illness. In a large number of communities so-called home-helpers have been engaged by the municipality, the local Red Cross, the Housewives' Club, a child welfare bureau, and other agencies for service of a few days in different homes when the mother has to be absent. Since the state pays for help in the homes of pregnant women while they are awaiting parturition and since the Maternity Aid Boards have widely utilized this form of help, there is a scarcity of women eligible for such work.

The same home-helpers might be utilized for facilitating vacations. Their number would have to be increased and their tasks freed from the emergency or charity connotation they now have. This is partly to be explained by the fact that the home-helpers have been trained in special schools with a religious atmosphere, in which the work is presented as a special calling. There is, however, no reason why the home-helpers should not just be responsible persons with good professional standing as housekeepers.

A still more ordinary and businesslike combination for part-time domestic service or child supervision may be instituted. Until lately temporary work in homes has been chiefly organized for charwomen and somewhat for cooking and serving at elaborate dinners. Recently a sort of part-time labor exchange for other purposes, spending a night with the children, relieving the mother of a week's work, etc., was organized by one of the large civic organizations often referred to, namely, the Consumers' Cooperative in Stockholm. What was new was not the possibility of getting such services in themselves but of their being provided through an agency which guaranteed their quality and responsibility and which had given the personnel a short but specific period of training. It is significant that the organization launching this idea worked with the definite social goal of offering part-time employment opportunities for many women, mostly married and childless, who are partly unemployed within their own homes. Many other organizations in many other communities have of late taken up the idea, and the public employment exchanges have also become interested.

The provision of such part-time helpers does not *per se* solve any economic problem for the families. The organizations have generally not charged for administration costs, but the services rendered have had to be fully remunerated. The aid consists chiefly in the organization of a clearinghouse for services and in the guarantee of the quality of the services, which is most important for a mother who wants not only to be free but to be free with a feeling of security and with an easy conscience about her home.

The short-time domestic services have largely been provided in urban districts. What seems to be most needed for rural mothers is a full-time annual vacation. They can better integrate daily leisure in their work. Their children do not require constant close supervision, and there are often other persons in or around the homes. In a farm home the father himself shares some of the educational responsibilities. Some weeks' vacation for a rural mother with a home-helper or a neighbor taking over her charges ought, if economy allows or state stipends are available, not to meet unsurmountable organizational difficulties.

In urban districts the mothers will feel the desire rather to have some daily or weekly time off. They are more isolated in the homes on account of their children, and recreational facilities are temptingly close at hand. For an urban housewife it is also easier to arrange short-time substitutes, and so she will probably have to sacrifice some of the community measures for long vacations because of her greater opportunities for frequent recreation. The best summer vacation for her would probably often be not to get away from the family but rather to get away with the family from the city and live a more simple life close to nature. The very desire for new experience will require different types of vacations for the two groups. Some exchange of urban for rural homes for vacations and vice versa has been tried out.

For both groups, urban and rural, the realization is far from the idealized scheme, which has been indicated here. As in all questions of home organization, a wall of traditions has to be broken through before it is acknowledged that "it works." With regard to housewives' vacation, not the least difficulty has been their own inertia, their belief that the house would not stand and that the family could not survive their absence.

COLLECTIVE CHILD CARE

The ultimate reason why it does not seem possible that the community should pay somebody to work in private homes in order that the mothers may sometimes leave is that it is such an impracticable and expensive and therefore wasteful arrangement. If the recreation of grown women should be indissolubly bound up with such an arrangement, there would either never be any considerable recreation for them or there would not be many children born. Looking into the future, one sees that in densely populated communities cooperative arrangements for the care of small children must be developed. The cooperative employment of one woman to look after the children in 10 apartments would be an immense step forward over the present practice whereby 10 women are so engaged. If individual families want on account of their attachment to individualistic values to organize their homes in a labor-wasting way, it may be left to their free choice. When the question arises, however, whether the community should help in that organization and pay for it, wholly or partly, laborsaving and cost-reducing devices have to be sought.

Such a problem has arisen. Many mothers in urban households have long since been unable either to stay with their children all the time or to pay a substitute during their absence. When the community felt the responsibility of offering something better than locking up children in the apartment or letting them run loose in the streets, the day nursery was resorted to. The same problem now faces ever-increasing groups of women. It faces them not only during absence for wage earning but also as a means of providing in some much more generally applicable way for relief from their work in the home. This need on the part of the mothers and the inclination to organize cooperative nursery care for such purposes could not obtain the sanction of society if it were contrary to the welfare of the children themselves.

In a population program such an aspect has its obvious place, and in 1938 the whole double-sided complex of that problem, answering the needs of recreation for mothers and of enriched education for children, was the subject of a report by the Population Commission. Attention may thus be turned to the whole field of preschool educational activity, including both the recreational aspect and the problem of healthier family organization in general.

The oldest institutions for daily care of children in the preschool age groups have a century-old history in Sweden, having been founded as early as 1836 under the name of infant schools. These were under the direct influence of the reform movement which Robert Owen had started in England. Their program had a social as well as a pedagogical purpose. The ones to be taken care of were poor children, but they were cared for only part of the day and they were scheduled to have a certain amount of educational instruction. Since 1854 similar institutions have taken the form of day nurseries. These institutions were in turn motivated by a desire to be helpful to gainfully employed mothers or to homes where special circumstances, such as a large number of children, made care of the home difficult. Supervision and bodily care were provided, but there was little constructive education. Since 1896 the kindergarten movement, deriving its formulas from Froebel's work in Germany, has geen gaining ground. It has rested exclusively on pedagogical considerations. A number of expensive private kindergartens were first provided, but since 1904 the so-called public kindergartens (*folkkindergarten*) have also been available. A desire to widen the activities to include preschool children or broader social groups led to arranging kindergarten hours fitted into the daily schedule of the day nurseries and welcoming a larger number of neighborhood children. In 1929 the last new development started as play schools or nursery schools within the larger cooperative building developments. The children's parents have organized to care for some aspects of child welfare which could not be undertaken by private families in a large city. The character of the cooperative nursery is neither philanthropic nor exclusive. It caters to all categories of children and has a variety of activities, including both infants' wards, all-day nursery groups, shorter school days with nursery school or kindergarten programs, and afternoon clubs. Altogether these institutions house only about 10,000 children, however (Table 43).

On this foundation something had to be built. The Population Commission clearly saw the need for both expanding and subsidizing these activities. In a report prepared by the present author in collaboration with a medical expert the Population Commission expressed the belief that making available

TABLE 43. — UTILIZATION OF PRESCHOOL INSTITUTIONS IN SWEDEN

ITEM	TOTAL	DAY NURS-ERIES	KINDER-GAR-TENS	NURS-ERY SCHOOLS	AFTER-NOON WORK-SHOPS	MIXED FORMS (COOP-ERATIVE NURS-ERIES)
Number of children included in investigation	9,572	3,729	1,978	948	805	2,112
Both parents living together . . .	7,525	2,447	1,817	819	629	1,813
Mother gainfully employed . . .	3,319	2,045	222	194	138	720
Father a widower	65	19	10	8	16	12
Mother a widow	259	108	40	27	34	50
Gainfully employed	196	94	27	15	16	44
Mother divorced	361	191	33	26	31	80
Gainfully employed	299	167	18	21	24	69
Mother unmarried	742	524	38	40	44	96
Gainfully employed	681	504	35	30	30	82
Others	591	425	36	26	49	55

Source: Population Commission, Report on Day Nurseries (*Betänkande angående barnkrubbor och sommarkolonier m. m.*)

more preschool education would certainly serve the qualitative population goal by building up a better generation for tomorrow and that it might possibly also serve a quantitative population goal by making more children seem possible for more mothers.

A survey of typical needs was made by the Population Commission in order to show that preschool institutions should not be thought of as something exceptional but rather as a normal supplement to an industrialized and urbanized way of living.

Obvious deficiences in the children's home environment indicate need for joint care of small children. Children living in overcrowded homes belong first of all in that category. In cities and towns a beneficial change in the children's environment can be arranged by admitting them to a nursery for a few hours every day. [*15*]

Increasing recreational space and play possibilities are desirable even in situations which cannot technically be defined as overcrowded, but the number of such situations is not small. It may be recalled from the housing reports that not less than 58 per cent of the children under 15 years of age in urban districts were overcrowded according to the norm of more than 1½ persons per room.

Whatever may be said about the health risks of such congested living, it is obvious that as "upbringing space" it is not sufficient.

Overcrowding distorts all education. Besides the fatigue, disturbance, and irritability which are commonly present, overcrowding makes it impossible to carry directly into effect rational methods of upbringing. The only punishment approved by modern experts, namely "social disapproval by isolation," i.e., leaving the child alone, becomes impossible where there is simply no extra room. The developmental danger of manifold prohibitions becomes absolutely unavoidable in the interests of the many others living under the same roof. Hetzer found that among the parents who visited a Parents' Bureau in Vienna seeking advice on child care, 80 per cent of the less well-to-do admitted that they could not follow the recommendations given on account of overcrowding. This is mentioned here merely to point out that it has not been until these small everyday difficulties were investigated scientifically that they have been given any official attention. Children living under overcrowded conditions ought to be given the chance to rest in a favorable environment at least during part of the day. They must be given room for physical activities. Even the play materials which in our industrialized civilization replace free experimentation in a country environment could only be available to these children if commonly owned and commonly used. Cooperation here is the same as rationalization. [*192*]

The next category to be declared eligible for the part-time cooperative nursery care was the only children. It was recommended that they be given an opportunity to enjoy social life with those of their own age in order to receive valuable training in group life and a more appropriate evaluation of self in comparison with others.

Also children who are not only children but who have a psychologically pressing situation within a family (a foster child or stepchild) or among the sisters and brothers, such as the youngest or the only one of the sex or otherwise "unequal" status, may need a change in environment.

Problem children were mentioned as the next category. Their stay in a nursery school may be limited or extended according to individual demands, preferably on a doctor's recommendation.

In the field of mental hygiene it is becoming more and more evident that a wrongly educated or a maladjusted child can regain mental health through early reeducation and readjustment. To a large extent this mental hygiene process can be carried on in the friendly atmosphere of the play school with its group environment and under the direction of a trained and understanding personnel. Doctors at child guidance clinics express a desire for more and more of such cooperation with a carefully planned educational environment for part of the day and are more and more inclined to believe in its favorable effects. It is, however, not the intention that the play school in general should carry out any real therapy in difficult cases of neurotic children, but without inconvenience to the other children it ought sometimes to be able to eliminate minor environmental traumata and minor character defects. [15]

Special day institutions for observation and treatment of more serious cases may also be encouraged, as doctors otherwise far too often recommend a change of environment for observation and constructive reeducation in institutions and foster homes, which separates the children completely from their parents. Special needs of special children may thus be cited in order to make an inventory of the demands for nursery schools, but the Population Commission considered this educational institution in a much broader aspect, finding it favorable for most children.

There is at present pretty general agreement that contacts with other children are of real value for a large number of children — even though parents in general come to possess a better informational basis for their job than is at present the case and even if they come to have emotionally more harmonious relations with their children than they now often do. Children both in the cities and in the country ought to be accustomed to adjusting to more than one environment or one set of relations. Modern society with its mobility and rapid changes in occupations and living quarters and interests puts these demands on people quite generally. If the children of our country are to be given the training best fitted to make them cope with the world and become optimal citizens, education should rest not only on their own homes where they will always be most firmly and securely rooted and where they will get the personal satisfaction of sympathy and affection, but they should also be made able to adjust to a changing environment. Contact with other children as equals is especially valuable in developing the ability to adjust to the changing demands which men and women have to face in modern life, not least in their working conditions. Those families are few indeed which can on their own satisfy all these needs of children. [*15*]

Having thus taken stock of the children's need, the Commission made a similar inventory of demands created by the various situations of mothers. There appeared first, of course, the gainfully employed mothers who are on the increase, totaling about 10 per cent of married women according to the Swedish census of 1930 and considerably more in the cities. The proportion is now higher (Chapter 22). Without deciding that such mothers should seek nursery care for their children, society has to take into account that an increasing number of mothers, and no longer only the underpaid beneficiaries of the charitable day nurseries, prefer some kind of cooperative care and supervision for their children.

Here enters the problem also of the employed unmarried mothers to whom the Commission gave special attention. Their separation from their children is artificially caused by society through the lack of housing facilities with nursery care.

The relative frequency of boarding the child with the maternal grandparents is also decreasing more and more under the social circumstances of the modern family. The system of boarding out children in foster homes will probably become more and more common. The community has undertaken responsibility for finding and controlling such foster homes as well as for care of children in orphanages when other care cannot be provided. But when doing this, the community has simultaneously cut off some other possibilities of keeping parents and children together in the same home. It should be strongly emphasized that the community has not given its foster child organization such an external form as would best promote the creation of real homes for those children who are not parts of a complete family. [*15*]

The building of homes in which cooperative child care is available will unfortunately not take care of all unmarried mothers. For example, this will not help the large proportion of domestic servants with children who live in the homes of their employers. Neither will housing projects and nursery schools help individual mothers in rural areas where population is sparse. But what can be done for others should also be done for these exceptions.

The investigation ended by proposing a state subsidy for all preschool institutions of approved quality. The activities should be expanded, the number of institutions increased, and the standards of quality improved.

To the extent that the general usefulness of these institutions is acknowledged, it becomes a social responsibility to give them a firmer and more secure foundation. In the future they cannot be left as before to find their way, depending upon insufficient or temporary financing. [*15*]

In connection with this practical proposal the Commission suggests state aid in support of such institutions but does not undertake any classification or internal evaluation of the many different and changing forms of activity. It does not attempt to say whether day nurseries are more worth while than kindergartens. As a compromise it proposes that the state authorities recognize as their interest that part of all activities within the different institutions which is of a general character. Such an activity is the part-time educational session that includes bodily care, educational activities, and contact with other children for a few hours daily. Wherever qualitatively approved care is given, a subsidy should be available for the half-day sessions whether those cover the complete or only partial program of an institution.

Thus the motivation for state support is based on the assumption that as far as children over three years of age are concerned, cooperative education for part of the day is useful for all children in all social classes. Further needs, demanding full-time nursery care of children, are recognized but, according to the opinion of the Commission, such special needs in some families and in some localities cannot be legitimate reasons for obtaining larger subsidies. To organize such care and to pay for it should be left, as has been done hitherto, primarily to parents under a cooperative plan. It should not be supposed that wage-earning mothers need permanently be so ill paid that they together with their husbands cannot carry some of the costs for their children. In the cases where this is not economically possible, institutions and communes should be called upon to carry the cost on their social budgets for the hours extending beyond the state-supported service. The quality demanded should make all day nurseries over into nursery schools.

It was proposed that the state subsidy to preschool institutions cover half the expenses for activities during a four-hour period but with a maximum of 0.50 crn. per child per day. In order to be eligible, such institutions could not charge fees higher than 5 crs. per month. Inspection, control, and technical advice were to be made available through officials in a new bureau under the Social Board. This proposal has been released to secure the opinions of those involved and is at present being elaborated. Details may be changed but it appears that only financial considerations can long retard the realization of a state-controlled and state-subsidized system of preschool care.

Not only preschool institutions proper were made part of this proposal. Also, older children have sometimes been taken care of in afternoon play groups. The Commission wanted to solve the problem of children's recreation simultaneously and so widened the proposal to include all kinds of clubs and institutions for afternoon care of school children, all on the condition that they maintained a minimum standard and engaged educational personnel. Thus it definitely was the responsibility of the local communities to arrange for recreation grounds, such as playgrounds in the parks, fields for games, sport fields, and beaches. When costs were increased through the employment of personnel, state grants should be available.

Including the children's right to recreation in the advantages to be provided socially meant much in one specific respect, namely, with regard to the summer vacation of city children. Summer camps and colonies have been erected all over the country, subsidized by provincial governments and local municipalities, by schools, by the Red Cross, by the National Association against Tuberculosis, and by many other civic organizations. It was estimated that in 1936, 16,000 such places were open for children, mostly free of charge, as only 6 per cent of the incomes of the camps came from parents.

Many other forms of recreational activity for children, which according to the Population Commission could be subsidized, have gained impetus in recent years. The larger cities compete in providing daily bathing buses for children who are taken out to the seaside or a lake to bathe and play under supervision and are served a meal, all free of cost. Also, supervised play in the city parks belongs largely to a development that has taken place at an accelerated rate of speed since the days when Sweden became more child conscious and turned toward more generous provision not only of the bare necessities for children but also of some joy and gaiety in their lives. The pride of any municipal board member, when he can show the sun-tanned city children returning from a municipal bathing excursion, is a sign of a change in the fundamental attitudes as to whether spending for children can be a joy or only a burden both to individuals and to the nation.

CHAPTER XXII

ONE SEX A SOCIAL PROBLEM

CAN there be national planning with regard to population without encroaching on individual freedom? Does such planning necessarily carry with it connotations of totalitarian methods? A test of the Swedish experiment in democratic population policy lies in the position taken with regard to women's problems and women's strivings for emancipation.

In Sweden as elsewhere popular attitudes toward women's problems are still chaotic in most groups. Traditional thinking is enmeshed in an accumulation of vague interests, confused emotions, and pure nonsense, involving the whole question of women's status. They are inherited from the epoch of early industrialism and focused in the doctrine that women's place is in the home and not on the labor market. At bottom there lies a set of real and harassing problems. How is women's scheme of life to be determined by their function as childbearers? In how far should young women's work and life plans be geared to the future eventuality of marriage and motherhood? How are the relations within the triangle of work-support-marriage to be organized in order to avoid an unreasonable degree of economic and personal waste? A final answer to these questions has not been worked out in any modern country.

Meanwhile women are in the peculiar situation that work and economic support, otherwise depending upon productive contributions in an economic market and regulated by impersonal contracts, are also offered by the choice of marriage. This involves a very personal type of contract. Remuneration is only slightly related to efficiency of work and is largely determined by the good will and capability of the husband. Woman's work in the home has acquired a high value and traditionally involves social status. The value, however, is not determined by the quantity and quality of her own labor but is derived from the status the husband has acquired in his field. The highest esteem is, therefore, most often the reward of the housewife who presides over a home in which there is practically no work at all for her to do.

In upper-class groups, particularly in cities, a pattern was developed long ago according to which men attended to all outside activities while women stayed at home, regardless of whether for ornamentation or for work. Women could always be counted as occupied with part-time supervisory functions and part-time service-consuming leisure. In the course of industrialization this design of living was democratized, and it still forms the goal for millions of women. Farther back in time and more particularly in an agrarian society it had never been prescribed that men should be the earners and women the houseworkers or that men should be the workers and women nonworkers. The division of labor between the two sexes had been of a much simpler, noneconomic kind. Men took on the tasks farther away from home and women the tasks nearer home, whether or not the tasks were laborious and income producing. This division of labor in turn will have to be regarded as determined by the distinguishing biological fact that women were bearing the children and, therefore, most naturally charged with rearing them. The crucial question even today is to what extent and with what consequences that fact must determine the division of labor between the sexes and how in a modern money and market economy various forms of economic support within and outside homes can be made congruous with it.

LOOKING BACKWARD

Housework is becoming less labor consuming. For every 100 men and women who were entrepreneurs or otherwise engaged in remunerative work outside the home in Sweden in 1880, there were 102 adult females — wives, relatives, and servants. The comparable number in 1930 was only 56. In this calculation it was assumed that wives, registered as without profession, as well as female relatives and servants were mainly engaged in housework. If male and female relatives and servants are excluded from the calculation, there were, in 1880, 93 wives classified as without gainful work for every 100 men and women who were entrepreneurs or remuneratively employed, while the corresponding figure for 1930 was only 44. The same change may also be expressed in another way. While in 1880 only 4 per cent of all adult women were working outside homes (their own or others'), 21 per cent were so engaged in 1930.

In manufacturing and mechanical industries the relative increase of women workers has not been rapid. Uncertain as early statistical data are, it seems as if women, both married and unmarried, constituted a fairly high proportion of industrial workers even in the seventeenth and eighteenth centuries. Between 1805 and 1850 women constituted from 7 to 10 per cent of all workers in manufacturing and mechanical industries. The proportion increased to 16.1 per cent in 1900, 17.8 per cent in 1910, 22.8 per cent in 1920, and 23.4 per cent in 1930. In commerce their relative growth is more outstanding, from 12.4 per cent in 1880 to 23.0 per cent in 1900 and 39.0 per cent in 1930. Similarly in those free professions which can be followed through the census years women have increased from 0.3 per cent of the membership in 1860, 1.6 per cent in 1880, and 1.8 per cent in 1900 to 32.6 per cent in 1930. In civil service the same trend is discernible. In 1930 about two-fifths of all women working outside homes were engaged in industry, two-fifths in commerce, and one-fifth in public service and professions. Women's attempts to enter the higher qualified and better paid vocations outside of homes have been even more successful than appears in these aggregate figures, as within every one of the larger subgroups they have been moving upward.

Looking closer at what really has happened, a dramatic story is revealed. Back of it all is the progressive industrialization, diminishing the relative importance of agriculture in the national economy. Much of the routine work in all homes, rural and urban, has been gradually absorbed by industry, leaving housework increasingly in the position of involving merely preparation of finished or semifinished products instead of their manufacture. For understanding the movement for the emancipation of women as it actually developed it should be noted also that the growth of commerce and the professions was eliminating housework. Women had in their old-time housework possessed much of the responsibility and acquired much of the training for trading, for producing merchandise, for writing, for teaching, for curing ills, and so forth, but these jobs were gradually structuralized. They became specialized and their lawful pursuit was guarded by rules about qualifications. Their profitable organization was dependent on capital. In the earlier period women were neither allowed the free mobility nor the access to professional education necessary for pursuing professional interests nor were they trusted with rights over money. It is thus only logical that the movement for women's emancipation, which is to be seen mainly as a thrust not for conquering new territory but rather for regaining their part of an old one, had as its first goals the attainment of professional education and legal rights in personal and economic matters. In 1859 women were allowed to enter the normal schools, in 1870 to take university entrance examinations and study medicine, and in 1873 to carry on most other university studies. Only in 1863 were legal rights (at the age of 25 years) made unconditional for an unmarried woman, the father or another male relative previously being her guardian. Only in 1920 did married women gain full legal status. The husband previously had been her lawful guardian. (In 1864, however, certain rights over private property were established.) Legal restrictions of rights to trade and manufacture followed a parallel road to abrogation. Not until 1920 were women finally awarded full political suffrage.

In the past the energy of the women's movement was for the most part geared to fighting for these legal rights. It should be understood that this century-long fight for emancipation did not cause the underlying changes in social structure but accompanied them, symbolizing adjustment difficulties along with the general process of democratization. The right to inherit, the right to education, the right to have a vocation, the right to enter economic contracts, and the right to vote all had to be exacted by political appeal and won in the Riksdag. It is thus also understandable that when the last issue, that of work versus marriage, was finally raised it was carried on by the feminists as a fight for preserving a human right, the married woman's right to work. No important legal barriers existed any more although there were many institutional ones, and the adversaries of women's rights were demanding that even legal barriers again be erected. Society at large was slow in attaining a wholehearted understanding of this right of married women to work outside their homes.

The family as it was, and is, actually functioning was trying to erect a fundamental chasm between old inherited values and new techniques. It derived its prestige from the family having been the basis for familial production where the contribution of the wife, even excluding the bearing of offspring, was not only enough to pay for her support but often directly profitable. She had been part of the assets of the farm and had been as necessary in its economics as the farmer himself, the land, the livestock, and the equipment. What happened to families in the transition period of industrialization went rather unanalyzed. A family ideology was developing that it was the duty of the husband to support the family. The duty of the wife was to stay at home. So dim were people's historical recollections that this ideology took on the prestige of old family ideals. In reality the idea that the wife should be supported and that she should be freed from productive work was new indeed.

This family ideology of the transition period acquires strength both from the necessity felt by housewives, and their men, to defend their actual pattern of life in moral terms and from fear of increased competition in the labor market from new masses of women released from homework as the labor market is increasingly brought under the influence of specialization and industrialization. The opinions with regard to feminine questions and particularly the problems of wage-earning married women are thus especially sensitive to downward economic swings, increasing unemployment, and intensified competition for jobs in the labor market. Married women constitute a minority in the labor market and as such are stamped by social visibility. It is fairly easy in periods of large-scale unemployment to arouse a strong reaction against their appearance as job seekers on the argument that they are supported by husbands and should stay at home instead of taking jobs from others.

There are also some interesting class differences to be observed. The farm population is on the whole still rather outside the whole question. In so far as they have to voice any opinion, however, they usually side with the transitional family ideology as it refers to an old family type near and dear to them. The working class, whose married women have been compelled by economic necessity to work outside their own families in other people's households and to some extent in factories, has in a particularly strong degree identified its ambitions with the transitional family ideology. This class has, in fact, taken out a considerable portion of the raised standard of living in the release of their women from the plight of working for other people. As, however, the principles of the Labor party are particularly strong in the matter of women's equal rights and as, furthermore, the two sexes are largely noncompeting groups in the industrial field at least in the short run, the reactions against married women's work in periods of unemployment are not particularly articulate in the working class. In the white-collar and professional classes, on the other hand, the urge on the part of married women to earn an income for themselves is strong. At the same time there is also more actual competition between the two sexes. As instances in which family incomes would remain fairly high even if the wife stayed at home are more prevalent in this group, it is but natural that the problem would be most vociferously raised among them.

On these bases of divergent interests and attitudes in the various strata of the population the ideological fight over the married woman's right to work had been carried on for decades in Sweden as in other countries. On one side were the women's organizations, fighting for the liberty of women to decide about their own lives, i.e., fighting for the married woman's work as a human right. On the other side were most of the members of the Conservative party as well as substantial proportions in all other political parties. Their principal argument was centered on preservation of the family institution. Their auxiliary reason was that married women, who should rightly be supported by their husbands, should cede their supposed rights "to double positions" instead of competing with unemployed family supporters. Those attacks increased in Sweden during the depression of the early thirties until in 1934 at least nine motions were presented in the Riksdag demanding restrictions on married women's right to work. Parliament demanded an investigation. Women were thus definitely placed on the defensive after a long period of steady progress.

The situation became more explosive when the population crisis focused attention on married women as deficient propagators. To understand fully how dangerous this constellation was it is only necessary to recall that the population and family argument had for several decades been effectively utilized against job-seeking married women. The principal reason why their work was considered unwholesome for society was that it was supposed to break up the family and particularly to prevent the bearing and rearing of children. In this situation anything could have happened. The remarkable thing is that in this crucial moment the population argument was wrenched out of the hands of the antifeminists and instead used as a new and formidable weapon for the emancipation ideals. The old debate on married women's right to work was turned into a fight for the working woman's right to marry and have children. The change in public opinion concerning women's problems brought about by this reformulation of the issue was tremendous. It should be noted that in the beginning the feminists themselves were merely bewildered, as their past experiences had made them suspicious of the very term "population policy." The gain was purely a gift to them. Only gradually did they come to appreciate their new strategic situation.

In the chaos out of which the new family ideology was created much of the success undoubtedly depended on seizing the initiative. Another initiation of the population debate might have made all the difference, but the turn of the issue was not the result of any trick or accident. Otherwise the far-reaching effect would not be explainable in this fairly rational political milieu. The economic irrationality from a national point of view of not utilizing the productive resources available, often invested with costly training, was first pointed out. Also, it was shown that remunerative work for the wife, sometimes only for a few stabilizing years in the beginning of marriage, must be thought of as a precondition for marriage in many cases, particularly among young people. The fertility of working wives might be low but nobody should think that these wives would bear more children if they were compelled to stay at home and the families were deprived of part of their incomes. From a population point of view the demand should rather be greater security for working women against dismissal because of marriage or childbirth and in addition organizational devices which would make it easier for them to bear and rear children.

The victory on the ideological plane was quick and complete. The attacks on the married woman's right to work were defeated. In fact this right was set forth in legal statutes against willful employers. For the first time the women's movement got a quiet frontier on the legal border and could indulge in constructive long-range planning. The wider societal reforms necessary for materializing the working women's asserted right to have children are still for the most part in the discussion stage. It may well be that the social engineering involved in the new family policy is up against its real test of effectiveness.

PETTY REFORMS

The new alignment in Sweden with regard to women's problems was given authoritative interpretation by two royal commissions, the Population Commission and the Committee on Women's Work. [22] The latter had the whole issue of women's work under study and proposed a number of general reforms for women workers. The former was chiefly concerned with proposals to protect marriage and childbirth for working women. Both commissions took the position that not only the rights of women but also the welfare of the families demand possibilities of work for married women.

Without ambitions for solving the feminist question, the Committee on Women's Work expressed itself in favor of greater labor mobility of women and a closer approximation to equality between men and women in the labor market. Only a small sector of the problem can, however, be reformed directly through legislation, as the most important barriers to women's work are not inscribed in laws and public regulations. Particularly in the trades and in private business they operate chiefly through selective assignments and a traditionally narrow limitation to definite lines of work, whereby women are often put in positions which make further training or promotion impossible. No committee can do much more than analyze the effects and make recommendations regarding the situation. Something in addition could be attempted with regard to the schools for the country's youth, as they sometimes arbitrarily exclude one sex from certain careers.

In Sweden, where girls acquired the same right as boys to state-supported secondary education only in 1927, it would not be surprising if some remnants of discrimination against girls were found in other corners of the public educational edifice. Therefore the Committee first proposed fair chances for the girls in occupational schools and also stated as a general desideratum that "all training institutions in so far as they prepare for occupations, open to both sexes, ought to be coeducational. There is otherwise a certain probability that the lack of fraternal contact with vocational colleagues of the opposite sex during the training period will render cooperation difficult in the future and also contribute to the persistence of certain obsolete and emotionally conditioned misconceptions about the opposite sex."

The petty remnants of legal barriers against women's work are found in one constitutional law (*Regeringsformen*) and one supplementary law (the so-called Law of Competency of 1925), making merit the only consideration for appointments to most civil service posts but still containing a list of exceptions for women. The first of these and the first to be tackled by the Committee on Women's Work is the function of minister in the Lutheran state church. Because of the reasons given above and because of changing social conditions, "The Committee considers it urgent that the problem of women's entry into the clerical professions should be solved as soon as possible." A second exemption has been concerned with the possibility of women being engaged in certain capacities in prisons, reformatories, homes for inebriates, and mental hospitals for men. The Committee pointed out that social work in general has come to include more elements of personal care and education and less of surveillance and proposed that women be allowed to compete for all posts in prisons, reformatories, and hospitals for men. A similar belief that women are unsuited for dealing with cases of violence has operated to exclude women from certain positions in the regular civil service. Because the police force is connected with the provincial governments, women cannot become provincial governors or mayors in small towns without a separate chief of police. What is most odd is that there is only one post in the Swedish Cabinet a woman is not allowed to hold and that is Minister of Social Affairs, as he is also the head of the police administration. It was proposed that this exemption be removed. Women are further not allowed to teach gymnastics to male pupils on the secondary level. The Committee proposed a change. Its argument might be quoted as it typifies its attitudes:

Primarily it should be stressed that in so far as such a rule is in general pedagogically valid, it should also exclude men from similar work with girls, particularly in view of the fact that male gymnastic methods might harm young girls more than vice versa. The Committee is of the opinion that, having a law that states that only the best qualified shall get a position, it is superfluous to safeguard men's superiority by still another one; and so the regulation that women should not be qualified as gymnastic teachers of young males should be dropped. [22]

Before the government had had time to formulate any proposals or even to take a stand on these questions, the Riksdag of 1939 was ready to ask the government for a general revision of the laws concerning women's eligibility for positions in the civil service, thus giving hope of victory for the issues presented.

Married Women in the Labor Market

The dilemma between gainful work and motherhood makes itself felt in many ways throughout all of women's lives even before their marriage and, in fact, even if they never marry. Public opinion has been too concentrated upon the single phenomenon of the increase of married women in the labor market. The problems of women's less purposive training, their restriction to certain fields of work, their low wages, and their failure to become mothers on account of external circumstances have seemingly been forgotten.

In consequence of the development noted in the beginning of this chapter there are an ever-growing number of women who combine marriage with remunerative work. As with many new developments the shock of the phenomenon is greater than the phenomenon itself. In Sweden only about 10 per cent of all married women (8.2 per cent if "retired," "capitalists," and some other uncertain categories are excluded) were engaged in gainful employment according to the 1930 census and 14.1 per cent according to the extra census of 1935–1936. These figures are, however, somewhat unrealistic as both the wives working in agriculture and the wives working as their husbands' partners in shops and handicrafts are not included unless they are taxed separately. The increase has been sharp, however. In 1920 the proportion was only about 5 per cent. In Stockholm the proportion of married women with remunerative employment increased from 15 per cent in 1920 to 25 per cent in 1930. The total effect on the labor market was not great, however, as between the same two censuses gainful employment among all adult women increased only from 36 per cent to 38 per cent.

A considerable increase would be expected regardless of whether the women were married. The increase is accounted for not only by the additional number of married women but also by the trend whereby fewer and fewer unmarried women stay at home. Yet they still do so to an extent that would not be expected. As compared with only 11 per cent of all unmarried men between 15 and 50 years of age in 1930 (10 per cent in 1920), 23 per cent of all unmarried women in the same age group in 1930 (24 per cent in 1920) were not independent workers or work seekers. This larger proportion of women at home could not be explained by more women students but only by the tradition of remaining "home daughters." A decrease in their number is due to occur, as they constitute a most important labor reserve. During the period under discussion, however, the increase in women who married and retained their positions explains the greater part of the increase of working women. It is well to notice that not only is retention of a job after marriage a growing custom but also marriage itself is becoming more frequent (Chapter 3). It may well be that the increase in the number of women retaining their work is caused by that category who can marry because they continue to work, i.e., who would otherwise remain in the unmarried group.

The findings of the Committee on Women's Work regarding married women and the labor situation thus definitely disproved any claims that married women could be regarded as an intruding group on the labor market. The next question to be tackled was the more intricate one of how this same phenomenon looks from the angle of the family. In that respect the sheer numbers of women who work in a particular census year is less significant than some other data. When do they work? How long? How uninterruptedly? How does the life cycle of a marriage look with an earning wife? Anybody will guess offhand that in the total percentage given above a large proportion will be made up of young women prolonging their employment some few years after marriage, thus consolidating the basis for the family economy. A longitudinal study of the employment of wives rather than these cross-sectional figures should, therefore, be revealing.

An opportunity to make such a study offered itself in connection with the population discussion. That discussion was responsible for the extra census in 1935–1936, and the Committee on Women's Work was allowed to include questions as to how long a period during marriage had been spent in gainful employment. The questions were asked of a 20 per cent representative sample of all marriages, in which man and wife had been married after the year 1900 and were living together at the census date. In 82 per cent of these marriages the wife had been solely concerned with homemaking from the beginning of the marriage. In nearly 6 per cent of the cases she had had full-time work during the whole or greater part of the marriage. In nearly 4 per cent she had had part-time work during a corresponding period, and in nearly 9 per cent she had had some employment for a shorter time or at irregular intervals. This gives a somewhat better picture than cross-sectional averages as to how the family meets the arrangement of working wives. A still more realistic picture is obtained if different patterns in different age groups are taken into consideration, showing not only that younger people are more likely to follow the design of combined marriage and employment but also that in a large proportion of marriages women work only in the beginning. This is illustrated by the fact that 10.6 per cent of those married less than 5 years reported themselves as having been fully employed during the period of marriage, while the same was true of only 5.6 per cent of those married 5–9 years, and the proportion rapidly decreased in the older marriages (to 3.3 per cent and 2.2 per cent in the two next 5-year groups and to 1.0 per cent among those having been married 20–35 years). These figures are highly suggestive even if they may have been influenced to some extent by the fact that the new generation of married women is more likely to stay on the labor market than were their predecessors.

The most decisive external factor in the wife's retaining gainful work should be the income level of the husband. Data from the 1930 census are revealing in this regard.[1] Moreover, the special census of 1935–1936 demon-

	INCOME OF HUSBAND (crs.)					
	Less than 2,000	2,000– 2,999	3,000– 3,999	4,000– 5,999	6,000– 9,999	10,000 or more
Per cent of families in which the wife had gainful work	32.8	33.3	28.6	21.7	17.6	14.6

strated generally how much better off families with working wives are than those in which the wife does not work.

The economy is partially responsible for the combination of marriage and work on the part of wives. Different social patterns and different amounts of satisfaction from work may provide the residual explanation. Society has little right to interfere or even to comment on how two people choose to make their living as long as the methods are not definitely antisocial. One problem which can legitimatize society's curiosity is the question as to what happens to the children. One relationship is obvious from the data, namely, that wage-earning wives have fewer children than those who remain at home.

Total childlessness appeared, according to the data from the census of 1935–1936, about three times as frequently among wives who had been fully employed for the whole duration of their marriages as among wives who had never had outside work (59.7 per cent as against 17.7 per cent) and on the average they had not quite a third as many children (0.69 as against 2.42). Such a comparison is crude, however. Among those fully employed are included the great number of young women who have recently married and not yet started their childbearing. Standardizing the data by age and duration of marriage, it is found that the differences in extent of total childlessness and in the average number of children in families having children according to the employment status of the wife remain substantial.[2]

Some circumstances influencing these statistics should, however, be noted in order to prevent a too hasty conclusion. First, it is impossible to judge what is cause and what is effect, particularly with regard to the high frequency of total childlessness in marriages with fully employed wives. Many sterile married women and many women whose husbands are sterile must as a consequence of their childlessness find it opportune to continue an occupation or to take one up anew, even if they should have been perfectly willing to give up their work for children. Furthermore, among these working wives there must be a relatively large number of women who would not want to have children even if they worked only at home. Finally, there must be a

2

EMPLOYMENT STATUS OF WIFE	PER CENT OF FAMILIES WITHOUT CHILDREN	AVERAGE NUMBER OF CHILDREN IN FAMILIES WITH CHILDREN
Fully employed during whole period of marriage . .	39.4	2.06
Fully employed during more than half of period of marriage	30.7	2.10
Partly employed during whole period of marriage .	26.7	2.75
Some employment during married life	22.5	2.68
No employment during married life	18.3	2.92

number of women who would perhaps want children if they could stay at home and have the same family income as if they worked but who would not be willing to bear children on the husband's income alone. Nobody knows either how large these groups are or whether this selective factor furnishes a complete explanation of the difference in total sterility between working wives and wives staying at home. It should be added that the same selective factor works, *mutatis mutandis,* in relation to the smaller number of children among employed than unemployed wives. A second warning is necessary. When a working woman has a child she may quite often give up her work temporarily. If she is having more children, she might prefer giving up outside work for good. So childbearing itself operates as a selective factor, tending to transfer those women who bear children into the category classified as "employed for shorter periods" or "in the beginning of the marriage." The comparison between groups of employed and nonemployed wives thus rarely becomes clear cut or even statistically fair. The high degree of childlessness among employed wives is to a certain extent a delusion. It may also be added that even the lower proportion of childlessness among wives staying at home, 18.3 per cent, is high enough to warrant some comment. When the number of children in the family is taken into consideration the same cautions in interpretation should be exercised. It may, however, seem easier to explain why employed wives do not have as large a number of children as wives who are not working. One or two children give them the chance to experience the joy of motherhood, whereas the obstacle to employment that additional children would constitute must be taken more and more into account.

An interesting side light as to how different types of employment may be adaptable to childbearing functions may also be obtained from the Swedish statistics. Wives who work only part time, especially those who have had such partial employment during a large part but not all their married lives, are quite near those never employed as far as the number of children in fertile marriages is concerned. This must presumably be at least partially explained by the fact that the work is largely of such a character that it is especially adaptable to individual circumstances. This is clear from the fact that in this category are included women who cooperate with their husbands, e.g., in business, skilled trades, and other occupations. It again becomes evident that it is not the work itself but the organization of work that hinders motherhood most. Also in this category, however, the reversal of causes works. Women with children have a reason for seeking part-time work while childless women may prefer full-time employment.

Married women in rural areas have more children than urban women, even when employed. Here is an interesting indication that the attitudes and the organization of living which are significant for fertility not only are dependent upon the single factor of gainful employment among wives but also are determined by other circumstances. The factor of environment is, obviously, influential in creating family attitudes somewhat independently of economic organization.

The most important knowledge that can be gained from the recent Swedish findings relates to the connection between family size and income. The similarity of the curves in Figures IX and X is striking. Whether the wife is employed or not, the typical patterns are irregular but relatively high fertility in the lowest income groups, definite decreases in number of children and increases in sterility in the middle-class income groups, and slight increases in number of children in the highest income groups.

Competition between gainful employment and motherhood definitely exists. Still, the Swedish Committee on Women's Work did not feel assured that employment in itself need be a reason for extreme family limitation. The present social setting of such employment ought rather to be changed in order to establish more harmony between the desire for motherhood and the desire for work. Until recently proposals had mostly been punitive measures to get the women out of the work situations. These negative methods for solving the dilemma were definitely not successful. The Committee went to considerable trouble in listing and analyzing all the proposed panaceas and then letting representatives of employers and employees in different fields state their views. These conferences with vitally interested persons made the foundation of the Committee's final conclusions much more solid than any program of experts alone could have been.

The first generalization was as follows:

The Committee decidedly opposes any and every effort to prevent married women by law from keeping or seeking gainful employment outside the home.

Such a prohibition would be contrary to the legal regulations which prescribe that the wife as well as the husband should, each according to capacity, assist in maintaining the family. The partners are duty bound to support each other and the children. It would, furthermore, be contrary to the public interest which requires that every individual should be utilized to the best of his capacity. Society cannot afford to lose a large part of its productive labor. Restrictions would furthermore react unfavorably on the general utilization of women's work and their training. Women in general would run the risk of having their training become superfluous, and the money spent for it regarded as wasted. It is finally contrary to the social requirement that human beings should preferably arrange their sex relationships within the socially approved form of matrimony. If married women are forbidden to work, they might prefer to omit sanctioning their sex relations by the marriage ceremony.

Some proposals have been made of a bonus or marriage loan for women who leave work to be married. The Committee declared these proposals to be entirely without justification.

It cannot be considered reasonable that the community which has often defrayed the costs of occupational training should also pay more in order not to have this training utilized.

A similar conclusion was stated with regard to suggestions that money paid into pension funds should be refunded when women leave their work for marriage.

It could not be considered right that a sum of money saved for a specific purpose, e.g., old age or survivors, should be utilized for a different purpose, e.g., establishing a household. In the second place, ordinary rules applying to giving up employment should be applicable also to leaving for marriage. In the third place, it would be unwise seemingly to encourage young people to omit long-run economic planning by promising them the immediate prospect of receiving a certain amount of ready money.

The next problem, that of part-time work, has often been treated with emotionalism, as it has long been a stand of ardent feminists that such work might easily become full-time work with part-time pay, thus tending generally to lower the wage level of women. The Committee first examined the practical possibilities of such work, knowing it to be a godsend to many married women.

In certain branches of industry there could well be a division of work into shorter periods. In certain occupations it would also be more advantageous to have a larger number of part-time workers than a smaller number of full-time workers. It is also to be expected that the quality of work would be better in shorter work periods and that this would be especially true of married women. They would find this work a welcome change. At the same time, when the work period is not too long, anxiety about things at home would not have a chance to replace joy in working.

As part-time work in civil service is not so sensitive as the private labor market to the effects of irregularities, it was recommended that as far as circumstances permitted and the employees themselves desired, half-day jobs ought to be arranged in the civil service.

Few advantages were found in reserve service and temporary substitutions. Because of its uncertain character this kind of service is of much less value to married women.

Through substitute work they can, to be sure, get a chance to maintain their skills, and in many cases they may be anxious to get the extra income from such emergency work. In the majority of cases, however, just because it cannot be definitely counted on in advance, it will upset the organization on which the woman's work at home is based. It has been proved from experience that it is,

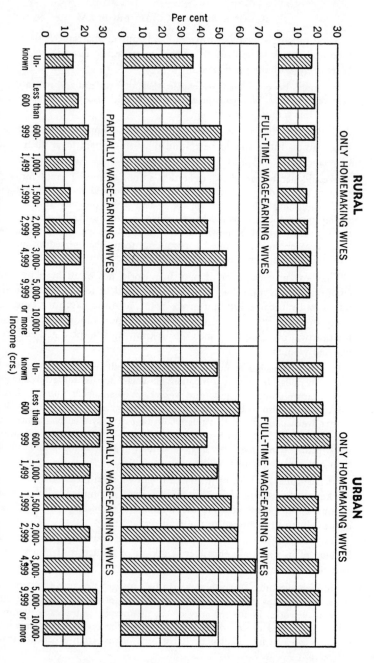

Fig. IX. — Total Childlessness in Different Income Groups, by Employment of Wife

Source: Committee on Women's Work (*Betänkande angående gift kvinnas förvärvsarbete m.m.*, 1938:47)

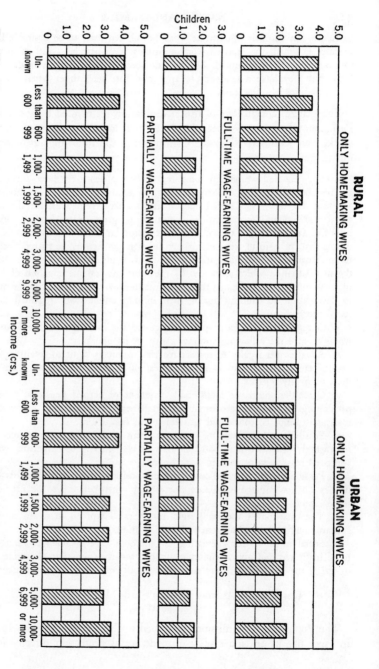

FIG. X.—Number of Children in Families with Children in Different Income Groups, by Employment of Wife

Source: Committee on Women's Work (*Betänkande angående gift kvinnas förvärvsarbete m.m., 1938:47*)

therefore, less valuable. Substitute work has shown itself to be desirable largely in cases in which the married woman employs domestic help and is, therefore, to a large extent not occupied. Not only do such job opportunities appear irregularly, but they have a tendency to appear at just such times when the home responsibilities also increase.

The general conclusions of this investigation, demanded by the Swedish Parliament because of repeated private bills to restrict women's right to work, were summarized by the Committee in the following uncompromising terms:

Even if married women in some regards are a relatively new phenomenon on the labor market, our investigation has not found any support for the hypothesis that this factor should fall outside the ordinary framework for the present social and economic organization of cultural progress. After having gone into intensive factual studies of the matter, it seems far more evident to this Committee that the gainful work of married women can neither be spared nor ought to be restricted. The organization of society will instead have to adjust itself to the new situation which is caused by the more general participation of women in work outside the home. At the same time, however, the possibility for mothers to devote time to children during their infancy ought to be regained through social reorganization.

With regard to various proposals suggested for investigation the Committee wants to give the following summarization of its opinions:

1. All attempts legally to restrict married women's right to retain or obtain gainful employment, just as all other restrictive measures against such work, must be firmly rejected.

2. Gratuities, marriage loans, bulk payment of earned pensions, premature pensioning and similar economic encouragements for voluntary retirement on marriage cannot be considered as serving any social aim.

3. Possibilities for obtaining part-time work and temporary positions ought increasingly to be provided both for married women and other persons who for approved reasons want shorter work hours.

4. Possibilities for married couples to get positions in the same locality ought, if they do not damage legitimate interests of other persons, to be provided to some extent.

5. The question of the legal right for married women to retain their own surname ought to be given renewed consideration.

6. Social measures for alleviating the mother's care of small children ought to be instituted and given economic support, but they ought to the same extent to satisfy the needs of mothers engaged both in employment and in homework.

Defense of Married Women's and Mothers' Right to Retain Work

The Population Commission subscribed to the above proposals. In order to carry out its specific task to provide social protection directly for the family, this authority, however, took a more advanced stand on certain questions than did the other committee. It could not be content with only averting the attacks which had so recently been directed against married women's rights. It sent the legislative boomerang back, attacking instead the employer's right to dismiss people on such grounds as marriage and childbearing.

Although the employers in Sweden who discriminated against married women employees were relatively few, their influence on public opinion was intensified by their persistency. In order to locate them, the two committees had already cooperated in 1935 in sending out a questionnaire to a number of private and semipublic employers. Those answering included 648 employers of industrial workers and 1,534 employers of clerical workers, with a total of 190,624 employees of which 85,016 were women. Confirmation was obtained on what was already partly known, that the practice of dismissal was much more ruthless in the case of office workers than in the case of factory workers. The homes of the former were protected by dismissing female employees who married in the case of 18.4 per cent of the employers in business as against only 4.8 per cent of the employers of factory workers. Most persistent in their practice of such dismissal were banks, insurance companies, and offices which employed large numbers of white-collar workers.

The first step taken by the Population Commission was to address severe admonitions to the employers in some of its early reports against this social misuse of their power. It was even suggested that if they did not change their rules within a reasonable time, punitive legislation might have to be introduced. Under the pressure of public opinion, chiefly emanating from the women's organizations but supported by the Population Commission, some employers actually did change their policy. Without doubt some hints about a selective boycott of discriminating firms, although never sanctioned by any organization, contributed to bringing about this change. No decisive victory had, however, been won during the four years of vehement discussion, so that the Population Commission lost patience in 1938 and was responsible for proposing a law providing that "employed persons may not be severed from a position on account of marriage, pregnancy or childbearing." [12] Unmarried mothers were included in the protection. The proposed law was aimed at protecting the independence of civil status and motherhood generally. It should apply to employers who regularly had more than four persons employed, thus making exemptions for reasons of convenience in the case of the small employer, particularly in retailing and domestic service. Employment must have started a year before the marriage or the childbirth. The penalty imposed was the payment of damages, generally wages for three months.

This proposal gained the support of both Cabinet and Riksdag and a law to this effect has been in force since July 1, 1939. The government, however, sharpened the stipulation so as to cover all employees in enterprises with more than two persons employed and also to cover betrothals. On the other hand, the required period of service was extended to two years. The law now states that an employer must not give notice to leave on account of engagement, marriage, pregnancy, or childbearing, nor on such accounts decrease the salary and other advantages attached to the position. In certain lines of work, however, an employee may be debarred from employment during the period when pregnancy is noticeable and may be temporarily deprived of her salary. Finally, any woman employee may at the time of childbearing have the right voluntarily to abstain from work for 12 weeks without being subject to dismissal on that account. Conflicts should be settled by the labor court with regard to all employers having collective agreements and otherwise should be settled by the general court.

The law does not give economic advantages to the married woman who works. Only in the civil service where employees always enjoy more security than in private business could such absences for childbearing be compensated by any economic remuneration for lost wages. In its very first report the Population Commission proposed that a major part of civil service salaries should be retained during a 3 months' leave of absence for childbearing, and the Riksdag enacted such a law. This advantage, like practically all laws with a population motivation, referred to unmarried and married women alike, thus making it an actual possibility in Sweden for a woman to bear an illegitimate child and retain civil service status and state pay.

For obvious reasons the same regulations could not be forced upon a private employer. It certainly cannot be considered the responsibility of the employer to pay the social costs for the children. The Population Commission had proposed that the loss of income from work on account of childbearing be carried on the nation's cost account for children by provision for a daily benefit of 3 crs. out of national funds. Public opinion did not support this last proposal. The stumbling block was the differential treatment for gainfully employed mothers as against mothers engaged in housework. If the former, ordinarily having incomes of their own to budget on, should need such considerable extra support, it was not seen how the latter would be able to manage at all. This problem remains unsettled.

The new law protecting the working woman's right to marry or have children as she pleased was nearly more than women had asked for. The Commission on Women's Work had not expressly called for it, and several women's organizations expressed their misgivings lest the new protection should become a boomerang, hurting women's interest on the labor market more than serving it. Their argument was that some employers might avoid difficulties by not engaging women at all. As a matter of fact, some such results were recognized during the very first months as was also the employers' expression of irritation by withdrawing certain benefits earlier paid to women leaving positions on account of marriage. These difficulties seem, however, to have been of a transitional character. The benefits may be lost; they were in any case not widespread. And in so far as they were solace for dismissal, women can obviously not continue to count on them when dismissal no longer threatens. Utilization of female labor could by and large not be forsaken on account of an issue of such comparatively slight economic importance to the employer. Any eventual curtailment of opportunities for women by some few employers will probably be more than offset by the prevailing tendency on the part of women to join unions and thus attain direct power in labor negotiations. It is even possible that this solidarity and urge to organize will become psychologically fortified if women face the fact that employers are endeavoring to curb such fundamental human rights as marrying and bearing children.

The victories for Swedish women have been won on that one ideological alignment which alone can make the position of the working mother accepted by all as a matter of course, that her marrying and her childbearing are to be encouraged and not discouraged by society. So expressed, her rights coincide with the interests of society. In other words, what is protected is women's right to have those very children that society also wants. That more children can be expected from working wives when they feel free to follow their own desires has been demonstrated in the degree to which these rights have been vindicated and also in some factual experience among the group of women in civil service who already in 1936 had their family rights better safeguarded.

The right of working women to comply with sanctioned social rules and enter marriage when in love is protected. Earlier, the attitudes on the part of the employers had so directly encouraged premarital sex relations that they were more and more excused and justified. Even some clergymen of the state church had found themselves compelled by their consciences to sanction such liaisons. There were also some attempts to legitimatize the practice whereby a couple notified the world of betrothal or even had the banns for marriage published and then openly lived together, sacrificing nothing but the marriage ceremony (and the children). Such a makeshift might have been fairly easily brought about in Sweden with its sex attitudes looking more to hearts than to formalities. But it is difficult to see how such a development could have been preferred by those who caused it, as it was inconsistent with their rationalizations about protecting the family. It is nevertheless a fact that extramarital sex relations, illegitimacy, and abortions had followed the efforts to enforce celibacy rules on the "modern nuns" in offices and banks. Thus, radical as may have appeared the Population Commission's desire to give freedom to work to married women, it ultimately served the truly conservative goals of protecting the formal marriage rites and of facilitating childbearing for a growing group of women.

There were never any attempts to exclude unmarried mothers from the protection. The Population Commission expressed the opinion that unmarried women, who did not seek the easy way out through abortion, were to be honored and not dishonored. It further pointed out that they needed protection even more than married mothers. Even if the new regulations were contrary to the feelings in many quarters, nobody dared to voice any opposition.

Open Problems

Although the ideological battle has been fought and won, many practical difficulties remain to be overcome before the dilemma of the working mother is solved. Legally the dilemma is now abolished in Sweden. Also the condemning attitudes are being gradually vanquished. But this does not conjure away the very real troubles of an economic, institutional, and psychological nature standing in the working mother's way. The difficulties here touched upon go deep down to the fundamental problems of modern marriage itself; they concern women's fate as such, the purposiveness of their lives, and the inherent doubt as to how to plan them. It would be futile even to try to specify a practical solution of these basic problems in any truly realistic terms. The only thing that can be attempted is a sort of check list of still open problems.

Has the wage-earning mother found any sensible solution to her home organization problem? Has she found some satisfactory adjustment to the traditonal demands upon her time by husband and children? Have women on the whole found some means of harmonizing investment in training and vocational ambitions with the incidence of marriage? Does marriage serve as a break in their life plans or are the life plans even of the spinsters arranged mainly with marriage in view, or is a rational balance possible?

The feminine sex is a social problem. Whether a woman is young or old, whether she is married or not, whether a wife works or not, she is likely to be a problem. This problem is largely economic in origin as marriage and family are as yet poorly adjusted to the new economic order. This is of vital importance to the individual and society as the family is the essential societal relationship.

The Economic Dilemma

Looking first upon women as competitors in the labor market, there certainly has been some reason to fear them. By their closer affiliation with the family economy the incomes of both unmarried and married women have often had the character of being supplementary as against the fundamental importance in ordinary cases of men's incomes for support of selves and others. Thus, women have been tempted not to sustain the wage demands of their fellow workers but rather to undercut them. Such competition has helped to depress the wage level. The complaints will probably not stop and can not rightly stop before women take their participation in the labor market in full sincerity. The uncertainty of women, tending as they do to keep up two possible future bases for support, will have to end. Still in this balancing of accounts it should be remembered that the inimical effect on the labor market is not one of women working but rather one of marriage itself as incessantly threatening to redetermine women's lives. From the family aspect nothing but good in an economic sense could presumably come from the fact that the wife is a wage earner. The few cases where a completely incorrect economic calculation about costs and gains to the household induces her to work outside the home may be disregarded.

A problem of quite different importance is created by the fact that the very existence of income-earning wives puts nonearning wives in a questionable position. It cannot be denied that the economic situation of housewives appears in a most unfavorable light when marriages are divided into two types, those with two supporters and those with only a man supporter. The inherent dilemma of the housewives is derived from the fact that what is even now the customary family type, namely, the average man-supported family, has in reality never been "normal" but is a transitional phenomenon. The family of old could rightly be called the mutually supported family. All family members, without calculation as to exact shares, took part in both production and consumption. The nature and the degree of dependency were relatively similar for all. Only in the transition stage, when the male heads of households had surrendered to industrialism but that process had not yet markedly changed the functions of women, did the special dilemma of wives appear. Their status in the family has declined in comparison with that of the preindustrial period of familial economic organization. The wives have become dependent, i.e., they have no free and interchangeable basis of support. However much they perfect their housework to become truly professional, they do not receive remuneration in direct relation to their activities. They cannot even submit their work to the test of competition. They do not enter into labor contracts. In other words, they fall outside the economic order. Their incomes are never directly related to their toil but only to the level of the husbands' incomes. The most exquisite talent or the most laborious solicitude may be rewarded with starvation wages, while expensive leisure, even demanding attendance of others in the smallest personal affairs, may cost far more than the women enjoying it could ever have earned themselves.

This complete dissolution within the home between work and remuneration, tasks and security, is illuminated by the very presence of income-earning wives. It does not always remain a latent dilemma of housewives but often comes to the surface on the occasion of death or separation. Widowhood occurs less frequently than formerly, divorce much more frequently. And women have a longer average life to plan for. Sweden has attempted to alleviate this particular type of insecurity through the system of pensions to widows' children during their minority and the advance of support to children involved in divorces. Complete security, however, for the married women themselves has been neither achieved nor even attempted. Society has not considered it proper to provide for the discontinuity in women's lives and their risks in marriage by assuming social responsibility for their support. If marriage is no longer an economically profitable status, some fundamental rearrangements in marriage itself and in its connection with work and support have to be demanded. To find any practical solution at all for individuals there seems to be no better advice than that women should try to retain some occupational skill as a final resource if the security slips or the marriage fails.

THE VOCATIONAL DILEMMA

This disharmony in the relation between marriage and gainful employment is at the bottom of many of women's problems. How shall life be planned so as to reconcile these two factors? Knowing that in Sweden only about three-fourths of the women 40 years of age have married and knowing that at least 10 per cent of those also have gainful employment outside the home, knowing further that the duration of women's marriages does not wholly coincide with their adult lives, and that the tasks of caring for minor children occupy a still smaller period, it seems incredible that the life of a whole sex could long continue to be planned only for motherhood, even supposing that the fate and the security of the mothers were fully satisfactory. Knowing, on the other hand, that so many women really do give up gainful work for their homes, it would be equally irrational to disregard the reasons for such a rupture in the world of work and support for women.

One practical conclusion must concern young women at their first decisive crossroad. Their vocational choice must probably take one of two main directions: either toward occupations which could be given up with all interests directed toward home or toward occupations which mean a more serious devotion for life. Young women ought to be able to decide with a certain degree of firmness whether they mainly desire eventually to desert wage earning for making a home of their own or whether they would rather think in terms of keeping up their vocational activities even after marriage. In our day young girls with their ability to analyze their own inclinations and aptitudes could certainly make this choice consciously. Thereafter the more detailed choice of vocation could fall under these two categories. In the one case, the young woman would choose as any young man chooses and devote all her energy to training and work. In the other case, she would choose work or training which would be of service to the home later to be set up but which would also offer an eventual career so related to housework that opportunities and skills would not be altogether lost even after years of household work. Thus the discontinuity of tasks now marring a woman's life would be applicable only to the woman deliberately choosing it and, even so, would be somewhat neutralized by her preparation for a career auxiliary to the tasks she performs within the family.

This is a plea for rationality. Regardless of whether it is possible of realization or not, it remains the only arrangement that could change what is now the most profound curse on every woman's life, the uncertainty of her life plan. As her life now evolves, on the average, it contains first some vocational preparation, although often shortsighted, and then some years of work, professional or otherwise, with a low independent income. Thereafter one of two things happens. Either that kind of life is prolonged, most often without the training and the zest sufficient for much of a career, with an ever-growing disillusion as the expectation of exchanging the job for a good marriage does not materialize. Or, for some other women, marriages do take place and then there normally follows a score of years occupied with housework, for which training has rarely prepared them. When the busy years are over and the children are grown, there are only empty decades ahead for the mother with neither sufficient work in her home nor much chance to be reinstated in the earlier vocational life. To make it worse, in these middle years the affective and the sexual bases for the marriage are often wavering. In an age far too early for death the feeling of justification of life and of security in economic support won through marriage start to give way even for those who do not experience the loss of the husband through divorce or death.

There are only questions for this problem. What ought to be the proper relation between work and marriage? How should work in the home be defined and how should it be economically provided for so as to fit within the framework of modern economic life? How should the marriage contract be combined with the home labor contract? How should training be chosen so as neither to handicap the married women in the home nor to handicap all women at large?

The Home Organization Dilemma

The home organization of the wife who works outside the home also constitutes a problem. It is true that in many cases the woman's own wages enable her to pay a servant to substitute for her in the home. A testimony in that direction is the common experience that the best domestic servants flock to the homes of professional women. So profitable may such division of labor be, utilizing the best fitted for the household tasks, that the net burden of housework under such circumstances becomes much smaller for the married woman than for the unmarried one. In a comprehensive survey of women teachers the Swedish Committee on Women's Work found that the unmarried teachers were far more subjected to household chores than the married ones. While 37 per cent of the unmarried teachers in the higher grades and 69 per cent of those in the primary grades managed their households singlehanded, this was the case in only 11 per cent and 25 per cent of the corresponding married groups. This left the married teachers more time for recreation, for study, or for that extra burden which is children.

To solve working mothers' home problems or any family problems by servants will, however, be possible only for a small group and not at all possible for that majority which takes employment when the husband's income is too low. Also, this solution is becoming increasingly impracticable as servants become more expensive and less accessible, and as, on account of their legitimtae demands for regularity in amount of work and of leisure, they become less and less fitted for that flexibility which is considered the very charm of having a household of one's own. The old-fashioned virtue of liberal and irregular hospitality is being just as efficiently drained out of the modern homes which are dependent upon servants as it was once made possible by those very servants. In that respect, unimportant as it is in comparison with the larger issues under discussion, it will become important to gain flexibility by attaching one's own need of services to an enterprise on a larger scale than the small private unit of one family's home.

Pooling of household work would appeal even more to the working woman with regard to her children. She knows that optimum care for her children is much more difficult to buy than expert care for her material needs. She is particularly aware that the person engaged for the one series of these tasks will seldom be the right one also for the other series. But the types of service are only possible in another organizational structure than that of ordinary private households. Translated into the world of reality, this means simply cooperation among many households. Urban housing for those families which contain working wives could easily be transformed into more rational family houses with cooperative service. More differentiation on the housing market is needed for serving that large proportion of families who do not have a full-time person assigned to home duty.

The younger families in Sweden have been looking for some kind of household organization with more cooperation for the work but just as much, or really more, of the family privacy retained. Neither the private servant nor the public day nursery quite fits their needs. Instead of the private servant for the individual family, there is a tendency to organize household work and child supervision cooperatively for several families through some sort of collective or cooperative apartment house with a nursery for the children. Particularly as the whole trend as to occupations for women is to increase the middle-class groups — lighter work in industry, decreased work in agriculture, increased employment in clerical work, social service, and professions — some such intermediary step between private luxury and public charity becomes a crying need.

This new form of housing organization has not only been advocated in Sweden, but it has already been developing. A number of the housing projects belonging to the Cooperative Housing Society have in varying degrees met the needs through cooperative nurseries, through shops for ready-to-serve or half-prepared food, and other services. A privately organized cooperative society built the first collective house in 1934 with one large kitchen serving meals both in a restaurant and through food elevators directly in the private apartments, with floor maids to be engaged by the hour, with a common nursery, and with other cooperative devices. Lately the business and professional women in Stockholm have built a novel family house according to a similar scheme. Because of the joint nursery, the workshop for fathers, and other homelike details, but above all because of the cooperative administration, these houses have a distinctly different character from apartment hotels.

This is arguing from a new angle for the same scheme which has been treated at length in the previous chapter as providing mothers with opportunity for relaxation or time for work and providing the children in small families and restricted environments with educative facilities for enriching their lives. There is no doubt that a functional setup could be established which would be far more adequate for the modern type of family than the present vain attempt at urban imitation of the closed family unit on a country estate.

The Psychological Dilemma

To rectify the organizational forms of housekeeping to take cognizance of the fact that for some women the tie between marriage and homework is dissolved will take both decades and tremendous courage and open-mindedness.

The relations between husband and wife when both are engaged in gainful work will probably take still longer to settle harmoniously. Looking at it practically, however, an improvement in this psychological adjustment could really be effected through reforms in verbalisms concerning the family, in the deeply propagandistic advertisements and comics, and in the teachings of home, school, and church about the natural superiority of men and their duty of being sole supporters. As it now is, few are educated or mentally prepared for the new mode of family living.

Within the homes the change to be expected is a mutually helpful division of the laborious family tasks which cannot be farmed out to paid persons. This is already taking place, although no country in the Old World can yet compete with the New World in the domestic helpfulness of its men. The proposals in Sweden, by both the Population Commission and the Committee on Women's Work, that boys be given courses in home economics and family relations is one important step in that direction. These proposals are being indefatigably pushed by the powerful organizations of housewives, of women teachers, and of professional women. Such instruction will be valuable not only for the practical help in the home but even more for changing popular attitudes concerning sex and marriage and the role of women.

The psychological relation of the working mother to her children, finally, is not necessarily a difficult one. But as a certain tension is observable, it may be that some subtle changes in public opinion are needed, so that real companionship and not only number of hours spent in common shall become most highly valued in the relation between parents and children.

The most disquieting questions as to psychological satisfaction are not those concerning the working mothers. Given time, a practical will to reform less important details in life and some adaptation to the new partnership marriages will probably result in the emergence of a fairly stable organization for family life. What is more puzzling to the young woman considering her future married life is her status if a homemaker. What was called the economic dilemma of the homemaker also has a psychological aspect. When the homemaker chooses the lot of dependence, she chooses dependence on some one individual. How will that dependence work out in terms of mental tensions and satisfactions? How long is a woman going to accept the fact that when young so much of her life is organized just to "catch" a man and become married? Could her life be rearranged so as to give her a more clearly definable status? Could marriage be made to require real "man-sized" tasks of women? How are women to endure the lack of a schematic network of daily work routine, such as characterizes other strata of life? How are they going to stand that time distribution which scatters much of their work when the rest of the world is at leisure and gives them leisure at odd hours when nobody else has it? How are they going to adjust to the fact that they have the hardest job and the least freedom of movement when young and when they are so close to the period when they were freely playing around? How are they going to get help in their job of caring for the children when small? And how are they going to get some tasks to put meaning into their lives when the children are gone? How are they going to avoid aging too early, when their life-chosen tasks of marriage and child-bearing so often end in their early forties or fifties? How can security be gained and equality reached if only the man is going to be incorporated in the complex economic world? Can that sort of life still be made truly personal and filled with primary satisfactions or will it have to decline into a life secondary in character, thus breeding secret dissatisfaction?

These problems may seem willfully exaggerated, but they are already at work in the subconscious of wives and of all women. They play an indubitable, even if indefinable, role in attitudes with regard to childbearing among women today. As they have been listed here, they give hints of a complicated pattern of brooding over riddles, never solved and rarely even openly expressed. Introducing a new form of marriage where most of the determinants causing troubles and questions are done away with will by comparison expose the problems of the more old-fashioned family. Reviewing all discussions on the problem, "Should married women work?" this seems to be the fundamental dilemma: that *the very existence of one type of marriage begs the question as to the other type.* This criticism works both ways, making both kinds of wives unduly uncertain of themselves. The irritation noticeable in all the discussion about the working mother may in the last instance be attributable to that very threat which men and women feel against the marriage type so long taken for granted.

That such uncertainty exists with regard to the whole field of married women's status is of tremendous importance for the population problem itself. This was the implication drawn by some women members of the Population Commission who published as a separate appendix an analysis and an accusation called "The Crisis of Women." If it is true, and it seems to be from the wealth of discussion in fiction, magazines, and books on the subject, that mothers are in danger of becoming a mentally malcontent group, no population program can remain indifferent. It might then happen that, despite all income equalization for children, despite all of society's solicitude for mothers and children, the whole population program might fail because women are fundamentally dissatisfied with the status defined for them. There is in the end the danger that it might be one day said of the Swedish Population Commission that it failed to tackle the very problems of marriage itself.

Summarizing what may be expected from these women themselves in regard to the future of Swedish population, it is believed that the reforms called into being in Sweden will help them better to combine motherhood and remunerative work. The practical difficulties are so numerous, however, that there will probably be a long transitional period when women will either have to shun too heavy maternal responsibilities or give up their gainful work. The risk is great that society will proceed so slowly in solving these problems of women's existence that new and even more desperate crises may invade the whole field of women, family, and population.

SELECTED BIBLIOGRAPHY

Public Reports and Investigations
S.O.U. = *Sveriges officiella utredningar.*
S.O.S. = *Sveriges officiella statistik.*
Signed appendices are listed under the names of their authors. Laws and decrees may be found in a series *Svensk författningssamling.*
Decisions by the Riksdag may be found completely in a series *Riksdagens protokoll,* summarized in a series *Lagtima riksdagen år . . .*

Population Commission
1. Unpublished report on Married Women in Civil Service, 1935.
2. Report on Maternity Care. *Betänkande angående förlossningsvården och barnmorskeväsendet samt förebyggande mödra- och barnavård.* S.O.U. 1936: 12.
3. Report on Family Taxation. *Betänkande angående familjebeskattningen.* S.O.U. 1936:13.
4. Report on Planned Saving and Homemaking Loans. *Betänkande angående dels planmässigt sparande och dels statliga bosättningslån.* S.O.U. 1936:14.
5. Report on Maternity Bonus and Maternity Aid. *Betänkande angående moderskapspenning och mödrahjälp.* S.O.U. 1936:15.
6. Report on Sterilization. *Betänkande angående sterilisering.* S.O.U. 1936:46.
7. Report on Repeal of the Anticontraceptive Law. *Yttrande angående revision av 18 kap. 13 § Strafflagen m.m.* S.O.U. 1936:51.
8. Report on the Sexual Question. *Betänkande i sexualfrågan.* S.O.U. 1936:59.
9. Report on Abortion. *Yttrande i abortfrågan.* S.O.U. 1937:6.
10. Report on Nutrition. *Betänkande i näringsfrågan.* S.O.U. 1938:6.
11. Report on Clothing, etc. *Betänkande angående barnbeklädnadsbidrag m.m.* S.O.U. 1938:7.
12. Report on Married Women. *Betänkande angående förvärvsarbetande kvinnors rättsliga ställning vid äktenskap och barnsbörd.* S.O.U. 1938:13.
13. Report on Rural Depopulation. *Betänkande angående "landsbygdens avfolkning."* S.O.U. 1938:15.
14. Report on the Ethical Aspect of the Population Question. *Yttrande med etiska synpunkter på befolkningsfrågan.* S.O.U. 1938:19.
15. Report on Day Nurseries, etc. *Betänkande angående barnkrubbor och sommarkolonier m.m.* S.O.U. 1938:20.

428   SELECTED BIBLIOGRAPHY

16. Report on Demographic Investigations. *Betänkande med vissa demografiska utredningar.* S.O.U. 1938:24.
17. Final Report. *Slutbetänkande.* S.O.U. 1938:57.

Committee on Social Housing
18. *Betänkande med förslag rörande lån och årliga bidrag av statsmedel för främjande av bostadsförsörjning för mindre bemedlade barnrika familjer.* S.O.U. 1935:2.
19. *Betänkande med förslag rörande ändringar i vissa delar av hälsovårdsstadgan samt anordnande av förbättrad bostadsinspektion i städer och stadsliknande samhällen.* S.O.U. 1935:49.
20. *Betänkande med förslag rörande lån och bidrag av statsmedel till främjande av bostadsförsörjning för mindre bemedlade barnrika familjer i egnahem m.m.* S.O.U. 1937:43.
21. *Promemoria rörande bostadsbyggnadsverksamheten.* S.O.U. 1939:50.

Committee on Women's Work
22. *Betänkande angående gift kvinnas förvärvsarbete m.m.* S.O.U. 1938:47.

Committee on Children's Pensions
23. *Utredning med förslag rörande bidrag åt barn till änkor och vissa invalider samt föräldralösa barn.* S.O.U. 1936:6.
24. *Utredning med förslag rörande förskottering av underhållsbidrag till barn utom äktenskap m.m.* S.O.U. 1936:47.

Committee on Rural Housing
25. *Betänkande med förslag rörande ändringar i vissa delar av hälsovårdsstadgan, anordnande av bostadsinspektion på landsbygden m.m.* S.O.U. 1933:57.

Committee on Unemployment Insurance
26. *P.M. rörande frivillig arbetslöshetsförsäkring m.m.* Stockholm, 1933.

Committees on Unemployment
27. *Arbetslöshetens omfattning, karaktär och orsaker.* S.O.U. 1931:20.
28. *Utredning angående bekämpande av ungdomsarbetslösheten.* S.O.U. 1934:11.
29. *Allmänna arbeten för arbetslöshetens bekämpande i Sverige 1929–1934.* S.O.U. 1934:44.
30. *Åtgärder mot arbetslöshet.* S.O.U. 1935:6.

Committees on Old Age Pensions, etc.
31. *Statistiska undersökningar och kostnadsberäkningar.* Vol. I. S.O.U. 1930:15.
32. *Ibid.,* Vol. II. S.O.U. 1932:36.
33. *Undersökningar angående det sociala hjälpklientelet.* S.O.U. 1934:14.
34. *Betänkande med förslag rörande revision av den allmänna pensionsförsäkringen.* S.O.U. 1934:18.

SELECTED BIBLIOGRAPHY 429

35. *Utredning med förslag rörande dyrortsgrupperade folkpensioner.* S.O.U. 1935:62.
36. *Betänkande angående pensionsstyrelsens invaliditetsförebyggande verksamhet.* S.O.U. 1937:23.
37. *Betänkande med utredning och förslag rörande statsbidrag till anordnande av bostäder åt åldringar och änkor i s.k. pensionärshem.* S.O.U. 1938:40.

Committee on Health Insurance
38. *Betänkande angående en reformerad sjukförsäkring m.m.* S.O.U. 1929:24.

Committee on Dental Care
39. *Folktandvård.* S.O.U. 1937:47.

Committee on Medical Care
40. *Betänkande angående den slutna kroppssjukvården i riket.* S.O.U. 1934:22.

Committee on Organization of Teacher Training
41. *Betänkande med utredning och förslag angående folk- och småskoleseminariernas organisation m.m.* S.O.U. 1935:44.

Committee on Reforms for Small Farms
42. *Betänkande med förslag till underlättande av arbetet i de mindre lanthemmen.* S.O.U. 1939:15.

Committees on Recreation
43. *Betänkande med förslag till lag om semester.* S.O.U. 1937:49.
44. *Betänkande med förslag angående reglering av strandbebyggelsen m.m.* S.O.U. 1938:45.

Official Statistics
Annual:
45. Statistical Yearbook. *Statistisk Årsbok.*
46. Population Changes. *Befolkningsrörelsen.*
47. Mortality Causes. *Dödsorsaker.*
48. Health. *Allmän hälso- och sjukvård.*
49. Child Care. *Samhällets barnavård.*
50. Poor Relief. *Fattigvärd.*
51. Wages. *Lönestatistisk årsbok.*
52. Accident Insurance. { *Olycksfall i arbetet.*
53. { *Riksförsäkringsanstalten.*
54. Old Age Security. *Folkpensioneringen.*
55. Crime. { *Brottsligheten.*
56. { *Fångvården.*
57. Local Municipalities. { *Årsbok för Sveriges kommuner.*
58. { *Kommunernas finanser.*
59. Cooperation. *Kooperativ verksamhet i Sverige.*

430 SELECTED BIBLIOGRAPHY

Census Years:
Folkräkningen 1930.
60. Population and Districts. Part I. *Areal, folkmängd och hushåll inom särskilda förvaltningsområden m.m. Befolkningsagglomerationer.* S.O.S. 1935.
61. Age, Sex and Civil Status. Internal Migration. Part II. *Bygdeindelning. Folkmängden efter ålder, kön och civilstånd. Den inrikes omflyttningen.* S.O.S. 1936.
62. Occupation and Income. Part III. *Folkmängden efter yrke, inkomst och förmögenhet,* Vol. I. S.O.S. 1936.
63. Foreigners. Invalidity. Part IV. *Utrikes födda. Utländska undersåtar. Lyten. Arbetsoförmåga.* S.O.S. 1936.
64. Religion. Language Minorities. Part V. *Trosbekännelse. Främmande stam. Främmande språk m.m.* S.O.S. 1937.
65. Education. Vocational Change, etc. Part VI. *Hushåll. Skolbildning. Yrkesväxling. Biyrke m.m.* S.O.S. 1937.
66. Occupation and Income. Part VII. *Folkmängden efter yrke, inkomst och förmögenhet.* Vol. II. S.O.S. 1937.
67. Occupation and Income. Part VIII. *Folkmängden efter yrke, inkomst och förmögenhet.* Vol. III. S.O.S. 1938.
68. Family and Children. Part IX. *Äktenskap och barnantal.* S.O.S. 1939.

Särskilda folkräkningen 1935/36.
69. Population by Governmental Units, Sex, Marital Status, Broad Age Groups, etc. Part I. *Folkmängden kommunvis efter kön. Civilstånd och större åldersgrupper. Befolkningsagglomerationer. Obefintliga.* S.O.S. 1937.
70. Population by One- and Five-Year Age Groups, Sex, and Marital Status. Part II. *Folkmängden i ettårs- och femårsklasser efter kön och civilstånd.* S.O.S. 1937.
71. Rural Housing. Part III. *Specialundersökning av bostadsförhållandena i 100 landskommuner.* S.O.S. 1938.
72. Organization of Census, Representativeness, etc. Part IV. *Allmänna folkräkningen den 31 December 1935. Granskning av resultatet. Partiellafolkräkningen den 1 Mars 1936: Organisation. Folkmängd. Representativitet m.m.* S.O.S. 1938.
73. Disability for Work and Unemployment. Part V. *Arbetsoförmåga och arbetslöshet.* S.O.S. 1939.
74. Number of Children in Normal Families. Part VI. *Barnantal och döda barn i äktenskapen.* S.O.S. 1939.
75. Families, Households, Dwellings. Part VII. *Matlagshushåll. Bostadshushåll och bostäder.* S.O.S. 1940.
76. Vocation, Education, Income. Part VIII. *Yrke. Yrkesväxling. Skol- och yrkesutbildning. Inkomst och förmögenhet.* S.O.S. 1940.

Cost of Living Studies
77. *Levnadskostnaderna 1913–14.* 3 Vols. S.O.S. 1919–1921.
78. *Livsmedelsförbrukningen inom mindre bemedlade hushåll åren 1914 och 1916.* S.O.S. 1917.

79. *Livsmedelsförbrukningen inom mindre bemedlade hushåll under krisåren 1914–1918.* S.O.S. 1922.
80. *Levnadskostnaderna på landsbygden vid år 1920.* S.O.S. 1923.
81. *Levnadskostnaderna i städer och industriorter omkring år 1923.* S.O.S. 1929.
82. *Levnadsvillkor och hushållsvanor i städer och industriorter omkring år 1933.* S.O.S. 1938.

Housing Studies
83. *1912–14 års allmänna bostadsräkningar.* S.O.S. 1920.
84. *Allmänna bostadsräkningen år 1920.* S.O.S. 1924.
85. *Undersökningar rörande de mindre bemedlades bostadsförhållanden i vissa svenska städer.* 3 Vols. S.O.S. 1916–1918.
86. *Allmänna bostadsräkningen år 1933.* S.O.S. 1936.

Other Publications
87. ANDREEN-SVEDBERG, ANDREA: "Preventivmedel." Appendix X, Population Commission, Report on the Sexual Question. [8].
88. ———: "Vissa problem vid sexualundervisningen i skolan." Appendix XVI, Population Commission, Report on the Sexual Question. [8]
89. ASKELÖF, T., and STRAHL, IVAR: *Lagen om folkpensionering.* Stockholm, 1938.
90. BERGMAN, ROLF, HÖJER, J. A., LILLIESTIERNA, HJALMAR, and MYRDAL, ALVA: "Om bostadens inflytande på de boendes hälsa." Appendix VI, Report by Committee on Social Housing. [18]
91. BONOW, MAURITZ: *Staten och jordbrukskrisen.* Stockholm, 1935.
92. ———: *Sveriges livsmedelsförsörjning.* Stockholm, 1940.
93. BRAATOY, BJARNE: *The New Sweden; A Vindication of Democracy.* New York, 1939.
94. BURGDÖRFER, FRIEDRICH: *Bevölkerungsentwicklung im Dritten Reich.* Heidelberg–Berlin, 1935.
95. ———: *Volk ohne Jugend.* Berlin, 1934.
96. CHARLES, ENID: *The Menace of Under-Population.* London, 1936.
97. CHILDS, MARQUIS W.: *Sweden, The Middle Way* (rev. and enl. ed.). Yale University Press, New Haven, 1938.
98. ———: *Sweden, Where Capitalism Is Controlled.* New York, 1934. (John Day Pamphlets, No. 39.)
99. ———: *This Is Democracy; Collective Bargaining in Scandinavia.* Yale University Press, New Haven, 1938.
100. COLE, MARGARET, and SMITH, CHARLES (editors): *Democratic Sweden; A Volume of Studies Prepared by Members of the New Fabian Research Bureau.* London, 1938.
101. CRAMÉR, HARALD: "Om innebörden av prognoser för befolkningsutvecklingen," *Nordisk Försäkringstidskrift,* April, 1936.
102. DAHLBERG, GUNNAR: "Die Fruchtbarkeit der Geisteskranken," in *Zeitschrift für die gesamte Neurologie und Psychiatrie.* Berlin, 1933.
103. EDIN, KARL ARVID, and HUTCHINSON, EDWARD P.: *Studies of Differential Fertility in Sweden.* London, 1935. (Stockholm Economic Studies, No. 4. Institute for Social Sciences, University of Stockholm.)

432   SELECTED BIBLIOGRAPHY

104. ELMGREN, AXEL, and SKÖLD, PER EDVIN: *Den offentliga fattigvården.* Stockholm, 1937.
105. ERIKSSON, BERNHARD: *De nya lagarna om folkpensionering och barnbidrag.* Fjärde reviderade upplagan. Stockholm, 1937.
106. ———: *Sjukkassereformen. Förordning om erkända sjukkassor.* Andra omarbetade upplagan. Stockholm, 1933.
107. ERIXON, SIGURD: *Svenskt folkliv.* Stockholm, 1939.
108. *Familj och moral, sammandrag av Befolkningskommissionens betänkande i sexualfrågan.* Stockholm, 1937.
109. FISCHER, E. M., and RATCLIFF, R. U.: *European Housing, Policy and Practice.* Federal Housing Administration, Washington, 1936.
110. *Form. Svenska slöjdföreningens tidskrift* (monthly publication).
111. GLASS, D. V.: "Population Policies in Scandinavia." *Eugenics Review,* July, 1938.
112. ———: *The Struggle for Population.* Oxford, 1936.
113. GOODSELL, W.: "Housing and the Birthrate in Sweden," *American Sociological Review,* December, 1937.
114. GRAHAM, JOHN: *Housing in Scandinavia.* The University of North Carolina Press, Chapel Hill, 1940.
115. GÅRDLUND, TORSTEN: "Förefintliga rådfrågningskliniker för sexualupplysning i Sverige." Appendix XII, Population Commission, Report on the Sexual Question. [8]
116. ———: "Historisk redogörelse för förslag och offentliga utredningar om sexualundervisning och sexualupplysning." Appendix XV, Population Commission, Report on the Sexual Question. [8]
117. ———: "Historisk redogörelse över preventivlagens tillkomst." Appendix I, Population Commission, Report on Repeal of the Anticontraceptive Law. [7]
118. ———: "Vissa uppgifter om preventivteknikens utbredning." Appendix XI, Population Commission, Report on the Sexual Question. [8]
119. HEDIN, ALMA: "Funerals Without Flowers," *Forum,* May, 1935.
120. HERLITZ, NILS: "The Civil Service of Sweden," in L. D. WHITE, *The Civil Service in the Modern State.* University of Chicago Press, Chicago, 1930.
121. ———: *Sweden: A Modern Democracy on Ancient Foundations.* University of Minnesota Press, Minneapolis, 1939.
122. HOFSTEN, ERLAND VON: *Hur den svenska landsbygden avfolkas.* Stockholm, 1940.
123. HOFSTEN, NILS VON: "Steriliseringar i Danmark enligt nu gällande lagar." Appendix II, Population Commission, Report on Sterilization. [6]
124. ———: "Steriliseringar i Sverige 1935-1939," in *Nordisk Medicin.* August, 1940.
125. ———: "Steriliseringar i Sverige under år 1935 och första halvåret 1936." Appendix I, Population Commission, Report on Sterilization. [6]
126. ———: "Till medicinalstyrelsen anmälda aborter under tiden 1/7 1935-31/12 1936." Appendix, Population Commission, Report on Abortion. [9]
127. HOGBEN, LANCELOT: *Political Arithmetic.* A Symposium of Population Studies. London, 1938.

128. HOHMAN, HELEN FISHER: *Old Age in Sweden.* Social Security Board, Washington, 1940.

129. HÖIJER, ERNST: "The Organization of Official Statistics in Sweden," *Baltic and Scandinavian Countries,* September, 1937.

130. International Labour Office: *An International Enquiry into Costs of Living.* Geneva, 1931.

131. ———: *International Survey of Legal Decisions on Labour Law 1936–37.* Geneva, 1938.

132. ———: *Labour Courts. An International Survey of Judicial Systems for the Settlements of Disputes.* Geneva, 1938.

133. ———: *International Survey of Social Services, 1933.* 2 Vols. Geneva, 1936.

134. ———: *The Law and Women's Work.* Geneva, 1939.

135. ———: *Worker's Nutrition and Social Policy.* Geneva, 1936.

136. ———: *The Worker's Standard of Living.* Geneva, 1938.

137. JERNEMAN, TOR: *Handbok rörande folkpensioner, barnbidrag, bidragsförskott och mödrahjälp.* Andra upplagan. Stockholm, 1938.

138. JOHANSSON, ALF: *Bostadslagstiftning och bostadspolitik.* Arbetarnas Bildningsförbund. Stockholm, 1939.

139. ———: "De demografiska betingelserna för bostadsmarknadens och bostadsstandardens utveckling." Appendix IV, Report by Committee on Social Housing. [18]

140. JONSSON, J. H.: "Sweden Leads in Old-Age Pensions," *Savings Bank Journal,* July, 1937.

141. KUCZYNSKI, ROBERT R.: *The Balance of Births and Deaths.* New York, 1928.

142. ———: *The Measurement of Population Growth; Methods and Results.* New York, 1936.

143. ———: *Population Movements.* Oxford, 1936.

144. LANGE, GUNNAR: "Den svenska jordbruksproduktionens omfattning och utvecklingsmöjligheter." Appendix III, Population Commission, Report on Nutrition. [10]

145. League of Nations: *Child Welfare Committee.* Child Welfare Councils (Denmark, Norway, Sweden). Geneva, 1937.

146. ———: *Nutrition.* Final report of the mixed committee of the League of Nations on the relation of nutrition to health, agriculture, and economic policy. Geneva, 1937.

147. ———: *The Problem of Nutrition.* 4 Vols. Geneva, 1936.

148. ———: *Statistical Yearbook.*

149. ———: *Survey of National Nutritional Policies, 1937/38.* Geneva, 1938.

150. ———: *Urban and Rural Housing.* Geneva, 1939.

151. "Legosängsavgifter vid lasarett och sjukstugor år 1939," in *Årsbok för Sveriges Landsting.* Stockholm, 1939.

152. LINDAHL, ERIK, DAHLGREN, EINAR, and KOCK, KARIN: *National Income in Sweden, 1861–1930.* 2 Vols. London, 1933. (*Wages, Cost of Living and National Income in Sweden, 1860–1930.* Vol. III. Stockholm Economic Studies, Nos. 5a, 5b. Institute for Social Sciences, University of Stockholm.)

153. LINDSTEDT, G.: *Öfversikt af den svenska fattigvårdens historia intill 1871.* Stockholm, 1915.

434 SELECTED BIBLIOGRAPHY

154. LORIMER, FRANK, and OSBORN, FREDERICK: *Dynamics of Population*. New York, 1934.
155. MAUNSBACH, A. B.: "Om folktandvårdsförfattningarnas tillämpning under år 1939," in *Tidskrift för fattigvård och annan hjälpverksamhet*, 1940.
156. MONTGOMERY, ARTHUR: *Svensk socialpolitik under 1800-talet*. Stockholm, 1934.
157. MONTGOMERY, G. A.: *The Rise of Modern Industry in Sweden*. London, 1939.
158. MYRDAL, ALVA: "Barnantalets familjepsykologiska betydelse." Appendix V, Population Commission, Report on the Sexual Question. [8]
159. ——: "Bostäder och barn," in *Socialt. Arbeid*, Oslo, 1936.
160. ——: "Can Sweden Evolve a Population Policy?" *American-Scandinavian Review*, June, 1937.
161. ——: "Education for Democracy in Sweden," in *Democracy and Education*. New York, 1939.
162. ——: "Familj och lön," in *Fackföreningsrörelsen*, 1937.
163. ——: "A Programme for Family Security in Sweden," *International Labour Review*, June, 1939.
164. ——: "Befolkningskommissionens arbete 1935–1938," in *Social Årsbok 1939*. Stockholm, 1939.
165. ——: "Föräldrafostrans socialpedagogiska uppgifter och organisation." Appendix XVII. Population Commission, Report on the Sexual Question. [8]
166. ——: *Stadsbarn*. Stockholm, 1935.
167. ——: "Sweden's Population Policy," *Journal of Heredity*, 1939.
168. MYRDAL, ALVA, and MYRDAL, GUNNAR: *Kris i befolkningsfrågan*. Stockholm, 1934. People's edition, 1935.
169. MYRDAL, ALVA, and Others: in *Women in the Community*, ed. by K. Gloerfelt-Tarp. Oxford University Press, 1939.
170. MYRDAL, GUNNAR: *Das politische Element in der nationalökonomischen Doktrinbildung*. Berlin, 1932.
171. ——: "Das Zweck-Mittel-Denken in der Nationalökonomie," in *Zeitschrift für Nationalökonomie*. 1937.
172. ——: "Industrialization and Population," in *Economic Essays in Honour of Gustav Cassel*. London, 1933.
173. ——: *Jordbrukspolitiken under omläggning*. Stockholm, 1938.
174. ——: "Kontant eller in natura i socialpolitiken," in *Nationalökonomisk Tidskrift*. Copenhagen, 1938.
175. ——: "Några metodiska anmärkningar rörande befolkningsfrågans innebörd och vetenskapliga behandling." Appendix I, Population Commission, Report on the Sexual Question. [8]
176. ——: *Population, A Problem for Democracy*. The Godkin Lectures, 1938. Harvard University Press, Cambridge, Mass., 1940.
177. ——: *Vetenskap och politik i nationalekonomien*. Stockholm, 1930.
178. ——: "With Dictators as Neighbors," *Survey Graphic*, May, 1939.

179. ———: "Översiktlig analys av det jordbrukspolitiska problemet i Sverige på något längre sikt." Appendix II, Population Commission, Report on Nutrition. [10]

180. MYRDAL, GUNNAR, and BOUVIN, SVEN: *The Cost of Living in Sweden, 1830–1930.* London, 1933. (*Wages, Cost of Living and National Income in Sweden, 1860–1930,* Vol. I. Stockholm Economic Studies, No. 2. Institute for Social Sciences, University of Stockholm.)

181. MYRDAL, GUNNAR, and WICKSELL, SVEN: "Utsikterna i fråga om den framtida befolkningsutvecklingen i Sverige och de ekonomiska verkningarna av olika alternativt möjliga befolkningsutvecklingar." Appendix VIII, Population Commission, Report on the Sexual Question. [8]

182. MYRDAL, GUNNAR, and ÅHRÉN, UNO: *Bostadsfrågan som socialt planläggningsproblem.* Stockholm, 1933. Also published as official report 1933:14.

183. NYSTROM, BERTIL: "Åtgärder till förbättring av de mindre bemedlades bostadsförhållanden i vissa städer." Appendix I, Report by Committee on Social Housing. [8]

184. OHLIN, BERTIL: "Economic Recovery and Labour Market Problems in Sweden," *International Labour Review,* April–May, 1935.

185. PEEL, ROY V.: "Lessons from Scandinavian Cities," *Public Management,* April, 1936.

186. RIETZ, E.: *Sterblichkeit und Todesursachen in den Kinderjahren.* Stockholm, 1930.

187. QUENSEL, C.–E.: "Det erforderliga barnantalet inom äktenskapen i en stationär befolkning." Appendix IX, Population Commission, Report on the Sexual Question. [8]

188. ———: "Skilsmässofrekvensen med särskild hänsyn till barnantalet." Appendix VI, Population Commission, Report on the Sexual Question. [8]

189. The Royal Social Board: *Social Work and Legislation in Sweden.* (Also Swedish and French editions.) Stockholm, 1938.

190. SCHMIDT, C. C.: "The Organization and Functions of the Swedish Royal Social Board," *American Journal of Sociology,* September, 1931.

191. SIMON, SIR E. D.: *The Smaller Democracies.* London, 1939.

192. *Småbarnsfostran.* Report from Conference on Preschool Education. Papers by E. Köhler, A. Lichtenstein, E. Moberg, and Alva Myrdal. Stockholm, 1937.

193. *Social Årsbok 1939.* Utgiven av Centralförbundet för Socialt Arbete. Stockholm, 1939.

194. STERNER, RICHARD: "Levnadsstandarden i svenska familjer." Appendix VII, Population Commission, Report on the Sexual Question. [8]

195. ———: "Svenska folkets näringsförhållanden." Appendix I, Population Commission, Report on Nutrition. [10]

196. STERNER, RICHARD, and JANSSON, GUNNAR: "Bostadssociala förhållanden inom vissa städer och stadsliknande samhällen." Appendix II, Report by Committee on Social Housing. [18]

197. *Stockholms Sanitära Statistik.* (Weekly publication by the City of Stockholm.)

198. Stockholms Stads Statistik. 5. Byggnader och bostäder. *Allmänna bostadsräkningen i Stockholm 13/12 1935.* Stockholm, 1937.

199. Svenska Fattigvårds- och Barnavårdsförbundet. *Svenska Fattigvårds och Barnavårdsförbundets Kalender, 1934.* Stockholm, 1934.

200. *Swedish Arts and Crafts.* Swedish Modern — A Movement toward Sanity in Design. Published by the Royal Swedish Commission, New York World's Fair, 1939. Stockholm, 1939.

201. "Social Problems and Policies in Sweden," *Annals of the American Academy of Political and Social Science,* May, 1938.

202. THOMAS, BRINLEY: *Monetary Policy and Crises.* London, 1936.

203. THOMAS, DOROTHY S.: "Analysis of Internal Migration in the Swedish Census of 1930," *Journal of the American Statistical Association,* March, 1937.

204. ———: "Internal Migrations in Sweden," *American Journal of Sociology,* November, 1936.

205. ———: "The Swedish Census of 1935–1936," *Journal of the American Statistical Association,* September, 1936.

206. WAHLUND, STEN: "De partiellt arbetsföras sysselsättningsproblem," in *Social Årsbok 1939.* Stockholm, 1939.

207. WESTMAN, AXEL: "Den ofrivilliga steriliteten." Appendix II, Population Commission, Report on the Sexual Question. [8]

208. WETTERDAL, PER: "Den spontana aborten." Appendix III, Population Commission, Report on the Sexual Question. [8]

209. WICKSELL, KNUT: *Lectures on Political Economy.* 2 Vols. London, 1935.

210. ———: *Lären om befolkningen.* Stockholm, 1910.

211. ———: *Några ord om samhällsolyckornas viktigaste orsak och botemedel.* Upsala, 1880.

212. WICKSELL, SVEN: *Ur befolkningsläran.* Stockholm, 1931.

213. WICKSELL, SVEN, and LARSSON, TAGE: *Utredning rörande de svenska universitets- och högskolestudenternas sociala och ekonomiska förhållanden.* Lund, 1936. (Official reports 1936:34.)

214. WIKMAN, K. ROB. V.: *Die Einleitung der Ehe.* Eine vergleichend ethnosoziologische Untersuchung über die Vorstufe der Ehe in den Sitten des schwedischen Volkstums. In *Acta Academiae Aboensis.* XI. Åbo, 1937.

215. WILLIAMS, FAITH M., and ZIMMERMAN, CARLE C.: *Studies of Family Living in the United States and Other Countries; An Analysis of Material and Method.* U. S. Department of Agriculture, Washington, 1935.

216. WOHLIN, NILS: "Den jordbruksidkande befolkningen i Sverige." Vol. IX, *Emigrationsutredningen,* 1909.

217. ———: *Den svenska jordstyckningspolitiken i de 18. och 19. århundradena.* Stockholm, 1912.

218. ———: *Den äktenskapliga fruktsamhetens tillbakagång på Gotland.* Stockholm, 1915.

219. ———: *Torpare-, backstugu- och inhysesklasserna.* Vol. XI, *Emigrationsutredningen,* 1908.

INDEX

Abortion, 116, 165, 175, 182, 185, 197, 205–12, 315–16, 324–25, 417–18

Abramson, Dr. E., 276

Adoption, 118

Age groups, 77, 81, 87–89, 92, 98, 169, 258–59, 340. *See also* Children; Pensions

Agricultural Commission, 287

Agricultural factors, 17–20, 29–30, 59, 69 *n.*, 85, 90, 91, 218–21, 399–400; modernization, 223; policy, 272, 281–83, 356. *See also* Farmers

Åhrén and Myrdal, *The Housing Question* . . . , 239

Årsta Havsbad, 385

Arts and Crafts Society, 230–31

Austria, 26, 81

Belgium, 137, 262

Bergman, Dr. Rolf, 248–50

Birth control, 2–3, 5–9, 24, 26, 37, 44, 50, 83, 94, 98–99, 170–74; education, 115, 179, 181, 185, 199–205, 377; income factor, 61–76, 96; motives, 51–76, 102–103, 120, 190–92, 244; principles, 109–12; propaganda, 196–97; public opinion, 170–71; and sex, 170–71, 188–96; techniques, 51, 85, 110, 173, 189–91, 199–205. *See also* Abortion; Clinics; Eugenics; Fertility; Illigitimacy; Legislation; Sterilization

Birth rate, 7, 23, 26, 38, 77–78, 259; other countries, 7–10, 26. *See also* Population

Blind, Special Institute for the, 361

Bonus, *see* Subsidies

Budget, family, 142–44, 219–31. *See also* Child costs; Consumption

Building industry, 237–38, 240, 255, 260, 270. *See also* Housing

Building Loans, Bureau of, 268

Business factors, 88, 91, 138

Cabinet, the, 163, 166, 182, 216, 285, 378, 405, 416

Capital punishment, 11

Capitalism, state, 86

Cash allowances, *see* Subsidies

Castration, 214

Catholic Church, 136, 340

Census, 68–73, 79, 88, 138, 163, 165, 234, 239, 241–42, 386, 395, 407–408

Charity: organized, 283; private, 152, 286

Child costs, 126–31, 159, 320–21. *See also* Budget; Subsidies

Child welfare, 97, 138–39, 248–50, 256–57, 286, 328–31; boards, 215, 286, 328, 335, 364, 389. *See also* Medical care

Childbearing, 145, 304–309, 315–26, 335, 402–404, 408–18. *See also* Parenthood; Women

Children, *see* Legislation; Mortality; Nurseries; Parenthood

City planning, 237

Civic activities, 58, 88, 376–77

Civil service, 88, 136, 138, 219, 221, 223, 369–70, 400, 405, 411, 416; Central Organization, 356

Class differences, 126, 146–49, 173, 366, 398–99, 402. *See also* Social factors

Clinics, and health centers, 117, 129, 164, 200–204, 285, 290, 293, 302–14; dental, 292–93, 311–13; psychological, 309–10, 394. *See also* Medical care

Clothing, 67 *n.*, 127, 132, 150, 166, 331. *See also* Subsidies

Coal industry, 135

Collective paternity law, 334

Collectivist activities, 5, 20, 91, 103, 137, 231, 356. *See also* Cooperative enterprises

Communism, 103

Conservative party, 157–58, 163, 166–67, 345, 402

Consumers' cooperatives, 231, 280, 389

Consumption, 87–89, 151–53. *See also* Clothing; Food; Housing; Recreation

Continence, 51, 189–90, 193, 200. *See also* Birth control, techniques

Contraceptives, *see* Birth control, techniques

437